MW01631053

# CREDIT RISK MODELLING

The Cutting-edge Collection

# CREDIT RISK MODELLING

## The Cutting-edge Collection

Technical Papers published in Risk 1999–2003

Edited by Michael B. Gordy

Published by Risk Books, a division of the Risk Waters Group.
Haymarket House
28–29 Haymarket
London SW1Y 4RX
Tel: +44 (0)20 7484 9700
Fax: +44 (0)20 7484 9758
E-mail: books@riskwaters.com
Sites: www.riskbooks.com
www.riskwaters.com



ISBN 1 904339 08 5

British Library Cataloguing in Publication Data
A catalogue record for this book is available from the British Library

Managing Editor: Sarah Jenkins
Assistant Editor: Kathryn Roberts
Assistant Technical Editor: Konstantinos Ntounas

Typeset by Mizpah Publishing Services, Chennai, India

Printed and bound in Great Britain by Bookcraft (Bath) Ltd, Somerset

# Contents

CONTENTS

## IV. VALUE-AT-RISK FOR CREDIT PORTFOLIOS



## V. BASEL II



## VI. ASYMPTOTIC METHODS IN VAR



## VII. PRICING MULTI-NAME DEFAULT RISK



## VIII. VALUE-AT-RISK FOR ASSET SECURITISATIONS

# Authors

**Angelo Arvanitis** is head of the risk department at Egnatia Bank and board member of the bank's portfolio management subsidiary. Prior to that, Angelo headed the quantitative credit, insurance and risk research at BNP Paribas. Previously, he was a vice president at Lehman Brothers in New York. He has also spent time in structured products at BZW in London. He has had various papers published, his main subject being the management of credit and insurance risks. Angelo gained a BA in physics at the University of Athens. He continued his studies at the University of California, the London School of Economics and the doctoral programme in finance at the University of Chicago. He co-authored *Credit: The Complete Guide to Pricing, Hedging and Risk Management*, (London: Risk Books), which has become a bestseller.

**Marco Avellaneda** is professor and director of the division of financial mathematics at New York University's Courant Institute of Mathematical Sciences, where he teaches and conducts research. He specialises in options, derivative securities and quantitative trading strategies. His ideas in the area of derivatives, which include the uncertain volatility model and maximum entropy algorithms for model calibration, have been widely used in Wall Street. He has acted as PhD advisor to many of the current generation of traders and quantitative researchers in Wall Street. Aside from his academic position at NYU, he was vice president at Morgan Stanley from 1996 to 1998 and consultant at Banque Indosuez, BNP Paribas and Royal Bank of Canada. He is currently associated with Gargoyle Strategic Investments, a fund that specialises in volatility trading strategies.

**Reza Bahar** is a managing director at HVB Risk Management Products, Inc., heading the dynamic capital structures group. He was formerly a managing director in Standard & Poor's Risk Solutions department. As head of product/analytic solutions and research for Risk Solutions, he was responsible for managing analytical and data products including Credit Pro, CreditModel, the loss and recovery database and Credit Index. He was also responsible for research and modelling, and other analytic product development. Before joining Risk Solutions, he was a managing director at Standard & Poor's Structured Finance Department. As head of derivative ratings, he was responsible for managing the ratings and surveillance of derivative product companies, structured investment vehicles, and structures based on credit default swaps. He also oversaw S&P's rating transition and default research. Prior to joining Standard & Poor's, he taught at Pace University and Lehman College. He was also a consultant on econometric modelling and evaluation of survey research. Reza holds an MSc in statistics and a BSc(Econ) from the London School of Economics.

**Anil Bangia** is vice president of the credit derivatives research group at JP Morgan Chase Bank based in New York. He first joined JP Morgan in 2000 and was responsible for developing and supporting analytical models for risk management and economic capital calculations for all retained credit risks of the bank's credit portfolio. In his current role, he is responsible for enhancing the pricing and risk management analytics for counterparty credit risks in derivative transactions as well as for traditional credit products such as loans and commitments. Prior to joining JP Morgan, he spent three years at Oliver, Wyman and Company, a management-consulting firm, in their risk management practice. He holds a PhD in engineering from Princeton University, and is a CFA charterholder.

**Hans Boscher** is a vice president of research at Deutsche Bank in Frankfurt concentrating on credit derivatives, credit hybrids and convertibles. Prior to that he was trading exotic options and CPI-linked products at Deutsche Australia Ltd. in Sydney. He holds a PhD in statistics from the University of Dortmund.

**Bruce Broder** has been working at JP Morgan since 1995, with the last six years in the Derivatives Research group. After a number of years developing credit analytics on the trading desk, he later managed the development of credit analytics libraries and their delivery to risk management systems and desktop applications. Dr Broder now leads a cross-asset team within the Derivatives Research group that is responsible for developing strategic approaches to analytics delivery in a multi-asset and global setting. This work includes interface standardisation, analytics architecture componentisation and distributed computing.
Dr Broder received his PhD in electrical engineering from Princeton University in 1990.

**Christopher Browne** is currently at DrKW overseeing the development and application of a sophisticated portfolio analysis and optimisation system. This system covers both equity and fixed-income, including structured credit, product classes in a consistent framework. The system is applied to internal proprietary trading and to external client portfolio and balance sheet analysis. Before joining DrKW, Chris was recruited into CSFB to spearhead their credit portfolio advisory business for clients. Previously, he worked for BNP Paribas on capital allocation and quantitative models for the credit, insurance and risk businesses. Chris's primary interests are managing portfolios of residual or unhedgable risks. He has both a master's degree and a PhD from Imperial College, London in electronic engineering.

**Peter Bürgisser** is professor of mathematics at Paderborn University (Germany). During the period 1999–2000, he was a credit risk analyst at UBS AG at the level of associate director. His research interests include algebraic complexity theory, computer algebra and mathematical finance, and he is the author of several research papers and two research monographs. In 1986, Peter received his diploma in mathematics from Zurich University. He received a PhD in mathematics from Konstanz University in 1990 and his habilitation in mathematics from Zurich University in 2000. He has also done postdoctoral studies at Berkeley (USA), Bonn (Germany) and Hong Kong.

**Umberto Cherubini** is an associate professor in mathematical finance at the University of Bologna, faculty of statistics, and founder of Polyhedron Computational Finance, a consulting firm in financial mathematical modelling. He teaches graduate courses in finance in Masters programmes at University of Bologna, the Catholique University in Milan and Hitotsubashi University in Tokyo. He is also a fellow of the Financial Econometrics Research Center (FERC) of the City University Business School in London, a fellow of the Bank of Italy research institution "Ente Einaudi", as well as a member of the scientific committee of Abiformazione (the education branch of ABI, the Italian Banking Association). Before joining academia, he worked in the economic research department of Banca Commerciale Italiana in Milan, where he headed the forecasting methods and risk management unit. He holds degrees from the University of Florence and New York University.

**Ashish Dev** is executive vice president and head of enterprise-wide risk solutions at KeyCorp. Six groups report to him: economic capital; data warehousing and Basel II preparation; risk grading models/scorecard models; product pricing & RAROC for all products; operational risk; and new product development. Some of Ashish's models have directly influenced international regulatory capital adequacy rules. He has been the prime mover in creating a new credit portfolio management function in the bank. Prior to joining KeyCorp in 1999, Ashish was head of quantitative research and analysis at Bank One. Ashish has a MS in applied mathematics and a PhD in economics from State University of New York at Stony Brook. He also holds the CFA professional designation.

**D. Wilson Ervin** is a managing director of Credit Suisse First Boston (CSFB) and head of strategic risk management (SRM). SRM is responsible for assessing the overall risk profile of CSFB on a global basis and for recommending corrective action where appropriate.
Mr Ervin chairs CSFB's overall

risk committee (CARMC) and also serves on other oversight bodies. He is based in New York. Previously, Mr Ervin worked at Credit Suisse Financial Products (CSFP), the former derivatives subsidiary of CSFB, where he was responsible for new product structuring in the Americas and US corporate marketing. Mr Ervin joined CSFP at its founding in 1990. Prior to 1990, he held various responsibilities in CSFB, including positions in fixed-income and equity capital markets, Australian investment banking, and in the mergers and acquisitions group. He joined CSFB in 1982. Mr Ervin received his AB, *summa cum laude*, in economics from Princeton University.

**Vladimir Finkelstein** is head of modelling and risk management in the credit derivatives strategies group at Goldman Sachs. Prior to joining Goldman Sachs in 2000, for nine years Vladimir was at JP Morgan, where he first was responsible for interest rate derivatives research in New York, and later for global credit derivatives research. Vladimir holds a PhD in physics from NYU and MS degree from Moscow Institute of Physics and Technology.

**Rüdiger Frey** is professor of financial mathematics at the University of Leipzig, Germany. Prior to joining the university, he held positions as assistant professor of finance at the University of Zurich and as a UBS research fellow in financial mathematics at the Federal Institute of Technology (ETH) in Zurich. He holds a diploma in mathematics from the Univeristy of Bonn, where he received his PhD in financial economics in 1996. His main research fields are quantitative risk management and the pricing and hedging of derivatives under incompleteness and market frictions. Rüdiger has published research papers in leading journals and has given seminars at a number of important international conferences and institutions. He has also been involved in consulting projects for Swiss insurance companies and banks.

**Jon Frye** is senior economist in the capital group at the Federal Reserve Bank of Chicago. His main responsibilities are to perform research in portfolio credit risk models and to assess the quality of bank economic capital models. Prior to joining the Federal Reserve, Mr Frye developed market risk and counterparty credit exposure models at large US banks. He holds a PhD in economics from Northwestern University. Over the years, Mr Frye has published many articles in *Risk* magazine, beginning with "Greek Alphabet Soup" in Volume 1(4), continuing through to today.

**Thomas Garside** is managing director of finance and risk management at Oliver, Wyman & Company, where he specialises in applying and implementing risk concepts to retail, commercial and investment banking, asset managers and insurance companies. Thomas' areas of special interest include assisting clients in their preparation for the anticipated changes to the Basel Accord, the development and implementation of risk-based capital approaches for insurance businesses, the strategic impact of future regulatory regimes (such as Basel II and EU/FSA directives), effective approaches to enable more active credit portfolio management and the evolving roles of the risk and finance functions. Thomas has authored many articles on risk, and is a frequent conference speaker in both the US and Europe. Thomas graduated from St. Catherine's College, University of Oxford in 1989 with a first class BA(Hons) degree in engineering science; and in 1993 received a DPhil in experimental and computational fluid dynamics.

**Dariusz Gatarek** is a manager in the capital markets group of Deloitte & Touche, based in Warsaw. Where he advises clients on how to manage financial risks, evaluating risk management strategies and setting hedging objectives. He is also a specialist in the pricing of financial derivatives. Prior to joining Deloitte & Touche, Dariusz spent six years with BRE Bank during which he created equity warrants in the Polish market and was responsible for implementing modern risk measurement methods, such as value-at-risk. Before joining BRE Bank, Dariusz served in the faculty of mathematics at University of New South Wales and in the Polish Academy of Science, where he still is associate professor. Dariusz has published a number of papers on financial models, of which perhaps his work with Alan Brace and Marek Musiela on Brace–Gatarek–Musiela (BGM) models of interest rates dynamics is the most well-known. This model is used by leading investment banks worldwide and is becoming a benchmark model of interest rate derivatives. He also contributed to analytical methods for credit risk. He holds a PhD and DSc in applied mathematics from the Polish Academy of Sciences.

**Michael B. Gordy** is a senior economist in the research and statistics division of the Federal Reserve Board. His current research focuses on the design, calibration, computation and validation of models of portfolio credit risk, and on the adaptation of these models to setting regulatory capital requirements. He serves as an associate editor of the *Journal of Banking and Finance*. Michael received his PhD in economics from MIT in 1994 and a BA in mathematics and philosophy from Yale University in 1985.

**Lane Hughston** holds the professorial chair in financial mathematics at King's College London. He received his DPhil in mathematics from the University of Oxford, where he was a Rhodes Scholar. Before joining King's College he was director of derivative product risk management at Merrill Lynch, where he was responsible for managing the development of pricing and hedging models for interest rate and foreign exchange derivatives. Before working at Merrill Lynch, he headed a research team at Robert Fleming Securities specialising in Japanese equity warrants and convertible bonds. Prior to that, he was fellow and tutor in applied mathematics at Lincoln College, Oxford. His research interests include a wide range of topics in mathematical finance and its applications in an investment banking context, and he is the author of numerous publications in this area. He is the editor of several well-known books on risk, including *Vasicek and Beyond: Approaches to Building and Applying Interest Rate Models* (1996), *Options: Classic Approaches to Pricing and Modelling* (1999), and *The New Interest Rate Models: Recent Developments in the Theory and Application of Yield Curve Dynamics* (2000).

**David Jones,** as senior advisor to the Federal Reserve Board, carries out and supervises research and policy analysis in the areas of securitisation, bank capital adequacy, credit risk modelling, and economic capital systems. His current responsibilities focus on international efforts to reform the Basel Capital Accord where he has helped design Basel II provisions relating to securitisation, credit risk mitigation, and the internal ratings-based (IRB) approach to credit risk capital. Mr Jones holds a PhD in economics from Harvard University, and served on the faculty of Northwestern University's department of economics before joining the Federal Reserve in 1981.

**Michael Kalkbrener** is vice president in the risk analytics and instruments department of Deutsche Bank and specialises in developing risk measurement and capital allocation methodologies. His current responsibilities include credit portfolio modelling and the development of a quantitative model for operational risk. Prior to joining Deutsche Bank in 1997, he worked at Cornell University and the Swiss Federal Institute of Technology where he received the *venia legendi* for mathematics. Michael holds a PhD in mathematics from the Johannes Kepler University, Linz. He has published a number of research articles in computer algebra and mathematical finance and serves on the editorial board of the *Journal of Symbolic Computation*.

**Sean Keenan** is currently a vice president in Citigroup's risk architecture group. He is involved in the development of quantitative tools and methodologies for assessing credit risk including debt rating models for C&I lending, default prediction and early warning systems for large corporate obligors and risk assessment methodologies for a variety of asset-backed and structured loan products. Prior to joining Citigroup, Sean was with Moody's Risk Management Services, where was involved in the development and validation of quantitative credit scoring and default prediction and default-rate forecasting models, and was the primary author of several Moody's annual corporate bond default studies. Sean holds a PhD in economics from New York University.

**Philippe Khuong-Huu** joined Goldman Sachs in 2001 as a managing director in the position of global head of interest rate products. Prior to joining Goldman Sachs, he occupied various positions at JP Morgan from 1991. He has held the following positions at the Bank: head of equity derivatives trading in Tokyo (1991–1993); head of fixed-income options trading in New York (1993–1995); head of fixed-income options trading in London (1995–1996) and head of global fixed-income options trading in New York (1996–2000). He was also named global head of credit derivatives trading in 1999. In 2000, he joined the newly created e-finance unit LabMorgan as head of market development. Prior to working at JP Morgan, he worked in the equity derivatives index arbitrage group at Société Générale in their Paris and Tokyo offices. Philippe received a degree in mathematics and physics from École Polytechnique, Paris in 1986 and a degree in economics and statistics from ENSAE (École Nationale des Statistiques et de l'Administration Économique) Paris in 1988.

**H. Ugur Koyluoglu** is a director of Oliver, Wyman & Company's Finance & Risk Practice, where his responsibilities include developing and implementing quantitative and qualitative tools for better management of credit, market, insurance and operating risks, capital and value. He has worked with banks, insurers and regulators in North America, Europe, Latin America, Middle East and Southeast Asia. Prior to joining Oliver, Wyman & Company, Dr Koyluoglu taught applied mathematics and engineering at Princeton University and Koc University in Turkey. He has published more than 40 papers in archival journals and conference proceedings in the areas of credit risk, insurance risk, risk and capital, random vibrations and structural damage due to earthquakes. Dr Koyluoglu holds a PhD in civil engineering and operations research from Princeton University, and BS in civil engineering from Bogazici University.

**Alexandre Kurth** is director of credit risk control at UBS AG, Zurich, where he is responsible for development and parameter estimation of credit risk measures. Previously, Alexandre worked for the Swiss Bank Corporation, Corporate Center Portfolio Management and was a research/teaching post-doctoral fellow at the University of British Columbia in Vancouver. Alexandre's research interests include credit portfolio modelling and algebraic transformation groups (for former academics). Alexandre has had various articles on credit risk and algebra published in scientific and business-related journals and has made presentations at various credit risk-related conferences. Alexandre received his Diploma in mathematics from the University of Basel in 1990 and his PhD in mathematics (Switzerland and Canada) in 1996.

**Jean-Paul Laurent** is a professor at ISFA Actuarial School within the University of Lyon. He is also part-time professor at École Polytechnique in the economics department and a scientific consultant to BNP Paribas. He has previously been research professor at CREST, an academic institution in Paris and head of quantitative research teams within BNP Paribas. His current research interests are credit risk modelling and the assessment of risk. He has published over 20 articles in academic and professional journals. Jean-Paul holds a PhD from Paris I University.

**Elisa Luciano** is full professor of mathematical methods for economics and finance at the University of Turin, Italy, school of economics. She is fellow of ICER, Turin, and associate fellow of FERC, City University, London. She has been distinguished visiting scholar at the Johnson Graduate School of Management, Cornell University, and at the Wharton School of the University of Pennsylvania. She teaches also at the École Supérieure en Sciences Informatiques, Université de Nice-Sophia Antipolis, and at the École Nationale Supérieure de Cachan, Paris, France. Her main research interest is quantitative finance, with special emphasis on portfolio selection and risk measurement. She has published extensively in academic journals, including the *Journal of Finance and Applied Mathematical Finance*.

**Robert Maksymiuk** currently works in the Polish branch of Ernst & Young in their financial and commodity risk service as risk manager. His responsibilities include advisory on quantitative methods of risk measurement and derivatives pricing, and capital adequacy requirements as well as selection and implementation of financial risk measurement software. Previously, he was employed in BRE Bank SA in the risk management department. His responsibilities included the development of financial instruments pricing methods and implementation of risk measurement software. He worked with Dr Dariusz Gatarek, which give him a opportunity to be involved in an enhanced study on interest rate derivatives pricing, including HJM and BGM frameworks and credit risk modelling. Robert graduated from Warsaw University with MSc degree in financial mathematics ("Gaussian HJM model"). He is also a co-author of two books (in Polish) on derivatives pricing and risk management and of a technical paper published in *Risk* magazine.

**Richard Martin** is in charge of the fixed-income capital management team at BNP Paribas, London. The group analyses risk, reward and economic capital in the fixed-income business and is actively involved in many aspects of applied quantitative research. Richard's most recent contribution is the application of the saddlepoint method as a portfolio management tool, and this is the subject of a recent series of papers in *Risk* magazine, for which he was awarded Quant of the Year 2002 (by *Risk*). Previous to joining BNP Paribas, he worked at GEC's Hirst Research Centre in London for several years and also studied for a PhD at University College London on time-series analysis, completed in 1998. He maintains a broad interest in mathematics and science and has written journal papers on a wide variety of subjects.

**Roy Mashal** is an associate with the quantitative credit research group at Lehman Brothers Inc, New York. His main research interests are the pricing and risk management of multi-name credit products such as CDOs, credit default baskets, and the modelling of counterparty exposure. Roy is an expert in specification and estimation of copula-based financial models. He holds a BSc and an MSc from Tel Aviv University and is a PhD candidate at the Columbia Business School.

**Alexander McNeil** is professor of mathematics at the Swiss Federal Institute of Technology (ETH) in Zurich. Since joining ETH in 1996, he has concentrated on developing statistical methodology for integrated financial risk management. His particular interests include extreme value theory (EVT), risk theory, financial time-series analysis and the modelling of correlated risks. He has published papers in leading statistics, econometrics, finance and insurance mathematics journals and is a regular speaker at international risk management conferences. Alexander has a BSc in mathematics from Imperial College, London and a PhD in mathematical statistics from Cambridge University, which he completed in 1993.

**Sandro Merino** is head of quantitative analysis at UBS Wealth Management and Business Banking, where he is responsible for methodologies in credit pricing, credit portfolio management, and structured finance. Prior to joining UBS, Sandro was head of credit risk control for the Winterthur Group. He also held research positions at the Heriot-Watt University of Edinburgh, at Strathclyde University of Glasgow and the Oxford Centre for Industrial and Applied Mathematics (OCIAM). Sandro has been invited to speak on mathematics at many conferences and has been an invited lecturer on finance several times. He also has his works published frequently in mathematical journals, risk management magazines, and co-authored the book *Mathematical Finance and Probability: A Discrete Introduction*, 2002 (Basel: Birkhauser Verlag).

**Krishan Nagpal** is a director at HypoVereinsbank (HVB), where he is involved in the structuring and modelling of various credit-related transactions and products. Prior to joining HVB, he worked at CDC Capital markets and Standard & Poor's (S&P). At S&P he was responsible for quantitative analysis of various derivative product companies, structured investment vehicles and other credit derivative transactions. Before working in the financial sector, he had held research and teaching appointments at the Universities of California, Michigan and Northeastern. He has worked in the areas of systems and control, estimation theory and system identification for dynamical systems. He received a PhD in electrical engineering, a Masters in chemical engineering, applied mathematics and electrical engineering from West Virginia University.

**Marco Naldi** is senior vice president of quantitative credit research at Lehman Brothers. He is responsible for the development of the new Lehman Brothers Risk Model, a tool for the risk management of benchmarked portfolios. His current research focuses on portfolio default risk, counterparty risk, capital structure arbitrage, and on empirical issues related to the valuation of multi-name credit derivatives such as basket default swaps and CDOs. Prior to joining Lehman Brothers in 1998, Marco received his PhD in finance from Columbia Business School, where he also taught as an adjunct professor.

He had previously earned a PhD in economics from the University of Bologna (Italy). His academic interests focused on market microstructure, corporate finance and empirical asset pricing.

**Mark Nyfeler** has worked for UBS Warburg since 2002, but has been affiliated with the company in its various forms (UBS Warburg Dillon Read and UBS AG, Wealth Management and Business Banking) since 1997, in Switzerland and in the US. He is currently responsible for credit portfolio modelling and stress testing. Mark has been an invited speaker at several risk management conferences and has co-authored several published articles. He is currently a referee for *Risk* magazine. Mark received his diploma in mathematics from ETH Zurich in 2000.

**Ludger Overbeck** is the head of the research and development team in the risk analytics and instrument department of Deutsche Bank's credit risk management. His main responsibilities are the credit portfolio model for the group-wide RAROC process, the risk assessment of credit derivatives, ABS and other securitisation products, integration of risk types, and operational risk modelling. Before joining Deutsche Bank in 1997, Ludger worked with the Deutsche Bundesbank in the supervision department examining internal market risk models. He gives regular lectures at the mathematics department of the University in Bonn and in the business and economics department at the University in Frankfurt. He is also a regular speaker at academic and practitioner conferences. His work has been published in several journals, magazines and practitioners handbooks. His contribution to the literature on risk modelling includes the book *Introduction to Credit Risk Modeling,* (with C. Bluhm and C. Wagner), 2002, (CRC Press/Chapman & Hall), and he contributed to *Credit Ratings: Methodologies, Rationale and Default Risk* (London: Risk Books). Ludger obtained a PhD in probability theory from the University of Bonn. After two post-doc years in Paris and Berkeley, Ludger finished his habilitation in applied mathematics during his affiliation with the Bundesbank. In 2001, he received a habilitation in business and economics in Frankfurt.

**George Pan** is director in integrated credit trading at Deutsche Bank, where he has worked since July 2002. Before joining Deutsche Bank, he was a vice-president in credit derivatives research at JP Morgan, where he was in charge of the development and implementation of the debt-equity arbitrage model. He joined JP Morgan in 1995 and was with the interest rate swap derivatives and emerging market credit derivatives trading desks between 1995 and 1999. He received his PhD in physics from the University of Maryland, College Park in 1993.

**Michael Pykhtin** is an assistant vice president at the capital allocation & quantitative analysis department of KeyCorp. His main responsibility is developing portfolio risk models for capital allocation purposes. His research interests also include pricing credit and weather derivatives. Michael has published his work in *Risk* magazine and presented his research at Risk conferences. Prior to joining KeyCorp in 2000, Michael was a researcher in theoretical physics, studying vibrational dynamics at surfaces and interfaces of materials. He holds a PhD degree in physics from the University of Pennsylvania.

**Wolfgang Schmidt** is currently professor for quantitative methods at the Hochschule für Bankwirtschaft (Business School for Banking and Finance) in Frankfurt. From 1992 to 2002 he was director and head of research and analytics at Deutsche Bank AG in Frankfurt. Prior to joining Deutsche Bank, he held teaching and research positions at the University of Jena, Berlin, Moscow and Tbilissi. He graduated in mathematics from Dresden University of Technology and holds a PhD and habilitation in the field of probability theory from the University of Jena. Professor Schmidt is author of numerous research papers in the fields of probability theory, stochastic processes and mathematical finance. His current research interests include mathematical finance, risk management, credit default modelling and term structure modelling.

**Jorge Sobehart** is a vice president/senior analyst at Citigroup Risk Architecture. He is currently involved in the probabilistic assessment of credit risk for portfolio risk management. Previously, he was a member of Moody's Standing Committee on Quantitative Tools and vice president/senior analyst in Moody's Risk Management

Services, where he developed and validated two credit risk models: RiskCalc for public firms and RiskScore. During his career, he has worked and acted as a scientific consultant for several prestigious companies and institutions, and also acted as a referee for professional journals. He has contributed to conferences in addition to publishing technical reports in many different fields. Dr Sobehart has advanced degrees in physics and has postdoctoral experience at the Los Alamos National Laboratory.

**Kevin Thompson** is senior quantitative analyst at BNP Paribas. Prior to joining the credit derivatives team in 1999, he worked on statistical and quantum field theory, mathematical biology and partial differential equations theory. He developed the now widely used "optimisation approach" to strip probabilities of default from default swap prices. At BNP Paribas, Dr Thompson, together with colleagues Abrar Hanid-Awan, Richard Martin and Christopher Browne formed the fixed income capital management team. Kevin and Richard jointly produced groundbreaking research into analytic methods (including the saddlepoint method) to analyse the loss distribution of credit portfolios. His current research interests include the application of statistical physics to credit portfolio modelling, understanding higher order default dependence and analysis of non-homogeneous portfolios. Dr Thompson holds BScs in both mathematics and dynamical systems, and a doctorate in theoretical physics.

**Stuart M. Turnbull** is senior vice president, head of quantitative credit research, Lehman Brothers, New York. Prior to joining Lehman Brothers, he was in risk management at the Canadian Imperial Bank of Commerce. When Stuart was an academic, he was the Bank of Montreal professor of banking and finance, Queen's University (Canada), and a research fellow, Institute for Policy Analysis (Toronto). He is a graduate of the Imperial College of Science and Technology (London) and the University of British Columbia. He is the author of *Option Valuation*, and (with Robert A. Jarrow) *Derivative Securities*. He has published over 40 articles in major finance and economic journals, and in law and economics journals, as well as many articles in practitioner journals. He is co-author with Robert Jarrow of the J-T model of pricing credit derivatives, which is widely used by financial institutions. He has been a consultant to many financial institutions. He is an associate editor of *Mathematical Finance*, the *Journal of Derivatives*, the *International Journal of Theoretical and Applied Finance*, and has served as an associate editor for the *Journal of Finance*.

**Oldrich Vasicek** is a founding partner of KMV Corporation (now Moody's KMV), where he is involved in the theory of credit risk measurement and management. In his early career, he was a vice president in the management science department of Wells Fargo Bank in San Francisco. He has taught graduate finance at the University of Rochester, University of California at Berkeley, and at ESSEC (École Supérieure des Sciences Économiques et Commerciales) in France. He holds a PhD in probability theory from Charles University in Prague. He has published over 30 articles in financial and mathematical journals and has received a number of honours, including the Graham and Dodd Award, the Roger F. Murray Prize, the Award of the Institute for Quantitative Research in Finance and the *Risk* Magazine Lifetime Achievement Award. He has been inducted into the Derivatives Strategy Hall of Fame, the Fixed Income Analysts Society (FIASI) Hall of Fame and the Risk Magazine Hall of Fame.

**Armin Wagner** is director of credit risk control at UBS AG, Zurich, where he is responsible for the implementation of Basel II and the overall consistency of the credit risk framework. Previously, Armin worked for the Swiss Bank Corporation, Market Risk Model Audit and held a research position at CERN, Geneva. Armin's research interests include Basel II, credit portfolio models and parameter estimation. Armin has had various articles on credit risk published in scientific and business-related journals and has made presentations at various credit risk-related conferences. Armin holds a PhD in physics from his studies in Germany and Switzerland.

**Ian Ward** is analyst in over-the-counter (OTC) derivatives research for Deutsche Bank, where he has been since 1997. Prior to moving to Deutsche Bank, Ian was a business analyst of OTC derivatives IT at Morgan Grenfell. Ian has a BSc in mathematics from the University of Bath and an MSc mathematical modelling and numerical analysis from Oxford University.

**Tom Wilde** is a director in the risk management department of Credit Suisse First Boston. He is responsible for development and implementation of credit risk portfolio and economic capital models and internal and external liaison on the Basel II reforms of regulatory capital. Mr Wilde is the technical architect of CreditRisk+, the credit risk portfolio model published by CSFB. Mr Wilde has been involved in the Basel II reforms since inception in 1998. He has worked extensively on the proposals with ISDA, including chairing ISDA's work in 2001 on counterparty risk, and working with industry groups and regulators on various aspects of the reforms. Mr Wilde was named "Risk Manager of the Year for 1999" by the Global Association of Risk Professionals (GARP), in recognition of his work in credit risk modelling. Mr Wilde received his PhD in pure mathematics from Warwick University and BA in mathematics from Cambridge University. He qualified as a chartered accountant with KPMG in Birmingham, UK before joining CSFB in September 1995.

**Michael Wolf** is executive director for credit risk control of UBS AG, Zurich, where he is responsible for the credit risk framework. Previously, Michael was a research fellow in the project "Verwaltung im Wandel" of "Deutsche Forschungsgesellschaft" and was head of the "knowledge-based systems group" at SYSTOR AG. He was also chairman of SGAICO (the Swiss Group of Artificial Intelligence and Cognitive Science). Michael has had various articles published in the domains of artificial intelligence, decision support systems for corporate financial analysis and knowledge management.
He received his diploma in psychology (mathematical and organisational psychology) in 1984 and his PhD in information sciences in 1998, both from the University of Konstanz (Germany).

**Jingyi Zhu** is associate professor of mathematics at the University of Utah, where he engages in teaching and research in mathematical finance and computational fluid dynamics. His main research interests in finance include interest rate modelling and credit risk analysis, and in particular their computational aspects. He joined Fixed Income Derivative Research at Salomon Brothers in 1997 and later worked as vice president in the same group that became part of Salomon Smith Barney, in charge of MUNI derivative research and trading desk support. Jingyi Zhu has published in other areas such as computational fluid dynamics, combustion and material sciences. He received his PhD in mathematics from the Courant Institute of Mathematical Sciences of New York University in 1989.

# Introduction*

**Michael B. Gordy**

Once a wallflower, credit risk emerged in the late 1990s as the belle of the ball. Credit risk has traditionally been crudely priced and managed only through lending limits. To an increasing extent, it can now be priced using well-grounded contingent claims models and managed dynamically. The opacity associated with the traditional banker–borrower relationship is slowly giving way, at least for the largest borrowers, to the transparency needed for arms-length market transactions. The emergence of new ways to trade credit has stimulated refinement of models and improvement in the quantity and quality of credit-related data. In a virtuous cycle, the new models and data sources have in turn helped to increase the liquidity and variety of traded instruments.

This blossoming has been chronicled in the pages of *Risk* magazine. *Risk* has been an indispensable source on the development of new credit derivatives and securitisation structures, on the evolution of contract designs, and on the state of liquidity and infrastructure for trading in these instruments. Of even greater impact, perhaps, has been the exposition of theoretical models, numerical techniques, and empirical results in *Risk*'s technical articles. These articles have served not only to educate practitioners on the state-of-the-art in theory, but also to bridge the considerable gap between elegant abstraction and robust application. What was once a trickle of articles in this area has grown into a rather steady stream. By 2001, five out of six issues of *Risk* offered a technical article on credit risk. This volume, which collects together the best of those articles, is one beneficiary of the prolific flow.

Intertwined with these developments has been the effort to reform the 1988 Basel Accord. In its time, the 1988 Accord was an enormous success. It halted and reversed the downward spiral in capital levels at the largest internationally active banks, and represented a milestone in international cooperation among regulators. By setting different capital charges for different classes of lending (eg, corporate vs residential mortgage vs OECD sovereign), it established the idea that capital charges should be in some sense proportional to risk. The degree of risk-sensitivity is, of course, quite primitive by today's standards, as the capital charge on commercial loans is a uniform 8% of loan face value, regardless of the financial strength of the borrower or the quality of collateral. In the late 1980s, however, to be "about right on average" was perhaps good enough.

In financial markets, opportunity is the mother of invention. The failure to distinguish between commercial loans of very different degrees of credit risk provides an incentive to transfer the risk associated with high-quality borrowers off-balance-sheet and retain direct exposure only to relatively low-quality instruments. By the mid-1990s, Merton (1995), among others, observed that repackaging of low-risk loans via securitisation could permit banks to obtain much more favourable capital treatment on the same underlying risk. By the late 1990s, as documented by Jones (2000), the arbitrage of regulatory capital had become routine, and eventually led to current efforts towards reform.[1]

Much of the limelight fell on innovation in the design of securitisations and credit derivatives. However, the new instruments provide only the infrastructure for risk transfer. Portfolio managers still must decide which risks to transfer and at what price. Circumvention of the 1988 Basel Accord requires the ability to identify those instruments for which regulatory capital requirements were excessive. Though obvious enough for loans to top-rated corporate borrowers, the bulk of lending by large banks straddles the border between the agencies' investment and speculative grades. In this range, the benefits to freeing capital must be weighed against the costs of structuring the risk-transfer. Moreover, as regulatory requirements become a less binding constraint, the need increases for a well-founded economic capital measure to guide

**The opinions expressed here are those of the author, and do not reflect the views of the Board of Governors of the Federal Reserve Board or its staff.*

internal capital allocation and to benchmark performance by line-of-business. KMV Portfolio-Manager was the first of the new generation of rigorous portfolio value-at-risk (VAR) models. A milestone year in this field was 1997, which introduced JP Morgan's CreditMetrics, Credit Suisse First Boston's CreditRisk+, and McKinsey's CreditPortfolioView.[2] The open publication of the details of these models made them highly influential among practitioners, academics and policy makers. (*Risk* played its part here as well, through the publication of Wilson's (1997a, 1997b) methodology for CreditPortfolioView.) Not long after came comparative studies such as Koyluoglu and Hickman (1998) and Gordy (2000). These showed how the models could be represented in a common mathematical framework, and in so doing clarified their underlying similarities and differences. Finally, the new risk-measurement tools called for imposing hard numbers upon what previously had been qualitative indicators of the default risk and collateral strength of a debt instrument. Analyses of historical ratings performance, conducted mainly by the rating agencies themselves, and of recoveries following default provide ready-made calibration for most model parameters.

The mid-1990s also witnessed the arrival of a new generation of pricing models. The earlier generation of structural models offer economic insight into how defaults arise and allow equity and debt to be priced in a mutually consistent framework. In practice, however, they have had only limited success. For these models to remain tractable, the firm's capital structure has to be quite simple. Moreover, the empirical performance of the models is uneven. For borrowers of high credit quality or for short maturity instruments, the default threshold is too remote to explain observed market spreads. Though Longstaff and Schwartz (1995), Zhou (2001) and others provide important extensions to the basic Merton framework, a new "reduced-form" approach circumvents the limitations of the structural approach. Models such as Jarrow and Turnbull (1995), Duffie and Singleton (1999) and Lando (1998) are simple to implement and are effective at fitting observed credit spreads across the term-structure. Pricing of single-name credit derivatives follows naturally. Hughston and Turnbull (Chapter 1) offer an especially elegant and intuitive introduction to these models. By introducing a dependence structure for the default intensities of obligors in a portfolio, the reduced-form framework can be extended naturally to price basket default swaps (Li, 1999) and securitisation tranches (Duffie and Garleanu, 2001).

To the extent that innovations in securitisation and credit derivatives were motivated by regulatory arbitrage, one might argue that the limitations in the 1988 Basel Accord helped stimulate the developments of the 1990s. As the decade drew to a close, the new tools for measuring and pricing credit risk in turn gave shape to regulatory reform efforts. The Basel Committee on Banking Supervision (1999) undertook a detailed study of how banks' internal models might be used for setting regulatory capital. The Committee acknowledged that a carefully specified and calibrated model could deliver a more accurate measure of portfolio credit risk than any rule-based system, but found that the present state of model development could not ensure an acceptable degree of comparability across institutions and that data constraints would prevent validation of key model parameters and assumptions.[3] It seems unlikely, therefore, that regulators will be prepared in the near- to medium-term to accept the use of internal models for setting regulatory capital. Nonetheless, regulators and industry practitioners appear to be in broad agreement that a revised Accord should permit evolution towards an internal models approach as models and data improve.

Fairly early in the Basel II process, it became clear that the revised Accord would feature ratings-based assignment of capital charges. To minimise incentives and opportunities for regulatory arbitrage, it was recognised that the risk-weight function would need to be calibrated to be broadly consistent with the results of economic capital models. In general, however, the amount of capital allocated to an instrument by these models depends on the portfolio in which the instrument is held. A ratings-based approach, by contrast, requires portfolio-invariant capital charges. In Gordy (forthcoming), I demonstrate that a broad class of credit risk models yield portfolio-invariant capital charges if it is assumed (a) that the credit portfolio is infinitely fine-grained in the sense that any single obligor represents a negligible share of the portfolio's total exposure, and (b) that a single, common systematic risk factor drives all dependence across credit losses. An asymptotic, single-factor version of CreditMetrics underpins the risk-weight function in the Internal Ratings-Based (IRB) approach of Basel's second consultative paper (Basel Committee on Banking Supervision, 2001). Though much less obvious, industry pricing models also play a role in Basel proposals. For example, the IRB maturity adjustment in the forthcoming third consultative paper is calibrated to spreads produced by the pricing algorithm in KMV PortfolioManager.[4]

Throughout the Basel II process, *Risk* has provided a valuable forum for regulators and practitioners. Some of the articles collected here, especially Wilde (Chapter 21), were instrumental in explaining Basel II proposals to practitioners. Even more interesting, many of the articles were written to influence the course of Basel deliberations. Kalkbrenner and Overbeck (Chapter 23) demonstrate the need to recalibrate the maturity adjustment to be consistent with an unrelated decision to change the VAR target solvency probability. They also make clear the potential sensitivity of the maturity adjustment to assumptions on market spreads. Frye's (Chapters 16 and 17) work on the implications of systematic risk in recoveries points to a missing element in the current generation of credit VAR models. In my view, Frye's recommendation that the capital rule should be tied to an instrument's expected loss would do more harm than good. The default event and loss-given-default play distinct roles in all leading models of credit risk, and so a mandated shift to expected loss as a summary statistic might degrade bank internal systems. Nonetheless, his warnings have stimulated academic studies (eg, Altman, Brady, Resti and Sironi, 2002) and have been especially influential in thinking about the treatment of commercial real estate, for which risk in collateral value is almost inseparable from the default event. The models of Pykhtin and Dev (Chapter 32 and 33) and Gordy and Jones (Chapter 34) both figure directly in the treatment of securitisation tranches in the forthcoming third consultative paper. Ervin and Wilde's article on pro-cyclicality in Basel II (Chapter 22) is, to my knowledge, the earliest published analysis of this now-contentious issue. Their appraisal of the advantages and drawbacks of different ways to ameliorate pro-cyclicality remains the most sophisticated to date.

Taking a bird's eye view of the articles collected for this volume, I see four unifying themes. First, data limitations prohibit a one-size-fits-all approach to credit risk. While this is nothing new (and, indeed, is much less the case than it was a decade ago), we now have a variety of markets or other data sources to which prices and risk models may be calibrated. For many obligors, the credit default swap market is now more liquid than the market for the underlying debt obligations. Martin, Thompson and Browne (Chapter 4) offer a flexible method for calibrating the term structure of the default-intensity to CDS prices. Liquidity tends to be concentrated at only a few maturities in this market, so an important aspect of their methodology is that it allows users to weight observations in accordance with their perceived reliability. For many obligors in bank portfolios, CDS spreads are unavailable but equity markets are liquid. In this case, structural models have a natural advantage. Pan (Chapter 6) extends the Merton framework to allow for stochastic default barriers. This gives rise to non-zero probabilities of instantaneous default, and thus to significant short-term credit spreads, which improves the empirical performance of the structural model. The additional source of uncertainty is identified with uncertainty in the recovery value of senior unsecured debt, so can be calibrated quite easily. The model is in the "imperfect accounting information" spirit of Duffie and Lando (2001), but is built squarely around the practical need for parsimony. Avellaneda and Zhu (Chapter 5) also propose a structural model with stochastic default barriers. Their approach, following Hull and White (2001), seeks to marry the flexibility of the reduced-form approach in fitting the term structure of default probabilites with the economic foundation of a structural model. This approach assumes the availability of credit spread data, rather than equity market and leverage data, so might be applied most naturally to aggregate data on bond spreads by credit rating grade.

Striking a more cautionary note, a second theme concerns the difficulty of backtesting default prediction models. Part II of this book pulls together a lively debate on the relative predictive power of ratings, KMV EDFs, and a hybrid measure developed at Moody's. The power curves, entropy measures and non-parametric rank-order tests employed in these chapters form a toolbox that can be applied to internal bank rating systems as well. My own reading of the debate suggests that it remains inconclusive. The omnibus tests used in these chapters pit rating systems against one another on the performance sample as a whole. The outcomes of these tests are dominated by performance on the lowest grades, which supply the greatest number of defaults, and therefore may not reveal much about relative performance on higher quality obligors. More generally, it seems that it is less instructive to ask which rating system is better than it might be to ask which system is better suited for particular circumstances or borrowers. For example, one might wonder whether the informativeness of equity-based indicators relative to agency ratings is higher or lower during periods of market turbulence. The power curves in Sobehart and Keenan (Chapter 11, Figure 2) all show a crossing point. Could this indicate that the judgement of agency analysts is most valuable in sorting among the weakest firms, while the collective wisdom of the equity market is most informative for firms at some distance from the default point? One might also wonder whether the equity-based methods are as powerful for firms with complex capital structures and opaque assets (such as banks) as for firms with simple capital structures and transparent assets.

The third theme concerns the application of asymptotic methods in credit risk modelling. As noted above, the IRB approach implicitly assumes that the bank portfolio is perfectly fine-grained, so the asymptotic behaviour of credit VAR naturally arises in Wilde's exposition of Basel II (Chapter 21). The models of economic capital for securitisation tranches (Part VIII) were designed with Basel II in mind, so the assumption of an asymptotic portfolio appears here as well (note, though, that the collateral pool itself is not required to be infinitely fine-grained). The potential applications for asymptotic methods extend well beyond the regulatory sphere because these methods can dramatically simplify model solution. To see why this is the case, consider a generic risk-factor model framework. Let $i = 1,\ldots, m$ index the positions in a portfolio. Let $U_i$ denote the loss on instrument $i$, and let $\nu_i$ denote the exposure size. Let $W$ denote the vector of systematic risk factors, and assume that, conditional on $W$, the $U_i$ are mutually independent. Finally, let $L_m$ denote the credit loss on the portfolio of $m$ positions as a percentage of total exposure, that is,

$$L_m = \frac{\sum_{i=1}^{m} U_i \nu_i}{\sum_{i=1}^{m} \nu_i}$$

Under mild regularity conditions, Gordy (forthcoming) shows that as $m \to \infty$, $|L_m - E[L_m|W]| \to 0$ almost surely. The intuition is straightforward: as $m$ goes to infinity, the idiosyncratic risks associated with the individual positions are diversified away, so portfolio loss $L_m$ becomes indistinguishable from $E[L_m|W]$, which represents the systematic component of portfolio loss. This limiting behaviour holds whether "loss" is defined on a book- or market-value basis.

In many circumstances, it is much easier to work with $E[L_m|W]$ than with $L_m$. In particular, if $W$ is univariate (ie, there is only a single systematic risk factor) and if $E[L_m|w]$ is monotonic in $w$, then quantiles of $E[L_m|W]$ correspond one-to-one with quantiles of $W$. VAR for target solvency probability $\alpha$ is simply $E[L_m|W_\alpha]$, where $W_\alpha$ is the $\alpha$th quantile of the distribution of $W$. Thus, we have an analytical expression (and typically a very simple one) for VAR. Moreover, portfolio capital can be allocated to the individual positions by setting a capital charge of $\nu_i E[U_i|W_\alpha]$ for position $i$. As observed by Vasicek (Chapter 24), application of asymptotic methods to KMV PortfolioManager date back at least to 1991.

While the assumption of a single systematic risk factor may be implausible, many users of credit VAR models impose strictly stronger assumptions in practice. For example, imposing a constant asset-value correlation across obligors in CreditMetrics or KMV PortfolioManager is equivalent to assuming a single systematic factor *and* assuming that every obligor has the same sensitivity to this factor. In Basel's forthcoming third consultative paper, the "factor loading" on the systematic factor varies by credit rating and by borrower type (ie, corporate vs retail vs commercial real estate), and so is more flexible than some calibrations of internal models used today.

To see the power of the asymptotic methods in practice, consider the example used by Merino and Nyfeler (Chapter 20) to demonstrate the accuracy of their Fourier transform methodology. The test portfolio has 15,000 obligors of varied exposure size and credit quality, which might be representative of large middle market portfolios. A single risk factor is assumed. I rescale Merino and Nyfeler's results to express loss as a percentage of total exposure. The first two columns in Table 1 present the rescaled reported standard

**Table 1. Statistics of the Loss Distribution***

| | Monte Carlo | Fourier method | Asymptotic |
|---|---|---|---|
| Std Dev (%) | 0.807 | 0.804 | 0.800 |
| Skewness | 1.607 | 1.589 | 1.600 |
| $VAR_{80\%}$ (%) | 1.546 | 1.553 | 1.540 |
| $VAR_{90\%}$ (%) | 2.076 | 2.070 | 2.063 |
| $VAR_{95\%}$ (%) | 2.580 | 2.576 | 2.570 |

*Monte Carlo and Fourier method results are as reported in Chapter 21 (Table 2), rescaled by estimated total exposure.

deviation and VAR as well as skewness, which is scale-invariant. In the third column, I present the corresponding asymptotic quantities. As shown in the Appendix below, loss in this example is asymptotically gamma-distributed, so calculation of the numbers in the third column is trivial.

The Fourier method produces very accurate results. While the mathematics is not trivial, the computational challenge is minor by comparison to full Monte Carlo. Nonetheless, the asymptotic method produces a similarly accurate approximation, and is far simpler to understand and implement. Clearly, the gain to solving the full model, whether by Monte Carlo or some other approximation method, is very small. This is not to deny Merino and Nyfeler's contribution. To the contrary, I believe their technique could be of great benefit on portfolios of more modest size or when the risk-factor structure is richer. My point is merely that idiosyncratic risk cannot play much of a role in the performance of a portfolio of 15,000 loans. The benefits to assuming it away may vastly outweigh any costs to accuracy.

Modest violations of the asymptotic assumption can easily be addressed. The idea of a "granularity adjustment," first suggested by Gordy (forthcoming), is that the contribution of idiosyncratic risk to VAR can be well-approximated by a term proportional to $1/m$. Although the regulatory use of the granularity adjustment proposed in the second consultative paper has since been dropped in Basel negotiations, the methodology generated significant interest among practitioners.[5] Wilde (Chapter 25) discovered a simple analytical solution for the granularity adjustment, and Martin and Wilde (Chapter 27) are responsible for putting the method on a rigorous mathematical footing. Pykhtin and Dev (Chapter 26) compare the adjustments implied by different modelling assumptions. Incidentally, Wilde (Chapter 25) provides an explicit and simple solution to the granularity adjustment for the test model used by Merino and Nyfeler (Chapter 20). Thus, the small gap between the full Monte Carlo results and the asymptotic results in Table 1 could easily be narrowed.

The challenge in modelling dependence is the fourth main theme. If credit portfolios are typically large enough so that portfolio risk is overwhelmingly dominated by its systematic component, then VAR will be driven by (a) our distributional assumptions on the systematic factors $W$, and (b) how we calibrate the sensitivity of obligor performance to the systematic factors. The latter issue is explored by Koyluoglu, Bangia and Garside (Chapter 12). They take as their starting point the oft-quoted finding of Koyluoglu and Hickman (1998) and Gordy (2000) that the well-known credit VAR models, despite their differences, can give similar results if calibrated in a harmonised manner. They then ask whether such harmony is likely to be observed in practice. The models are designed to take advantage of different sorts of data in the calibration process (for example, equity market data for CreditMetrics and lending book non-performance data for CreditRisk+). While this diversity is indeed an important reason to have a variety of models at hand, Koyluoglu, Bangia and Garside show that the different calibration techniques can be expected to lead to rather different results. The same issue is approached in a different manner by Martin, Thompson and Browne (Chapter 14). They ask what it means to assume a constant "correlation" in a Merton model. The typical way is to assume a constant asset-value correlation. An equally defensible alternative is to assume that, for any two obligors $i$ and $j$, a constant value of the rescaled joint default probability given by $\Pr(D_i \cap D_j)/(\Pr(D_i) \cdot \Pr(D_j))$, where $D_i$ is a default indicator (equal to one in the event of default, zero otherwise). This latter measure could arise naturally in calibration of CreditRisk+ and is also used by Nagpal and Bahar (Chapter 13) for modelling dependence. Martin, Thompson and Browne show that the relative capital charges across rating grades depends strongly on the choice of correlation measure. Frye's contributions (Chapters 16 and 17) also are relevant here, as he is asking whether it is realistic to assume zero dependence of recoveries on the systematic factors.

As shown in Gordy (2000), VAR is highly sensitive to distributional assumptions. By tweaking the distribution for W, one can change VAR dramatically without changing either the mean or variance of the loss distribution. The opportunities for "gaming the system" under an internal models approach to regulatory capital are obvious. Frey, McNeil and Nyfeler (Chapter 15) show how copula techniques offer a powerful and rigorous way to hone in on this issue. They caution, in particular, that the normal copula that is embedded in the standard portfolio Merton approach (as in CreditMetrics and KMV PortfolioManager) has the awkward property of zero tail dependence, which effectively implies zero correlation across obligors conditional on a systematic stress event. Copula techniques are also directly relevant to specification of dependence in pricing models for wrong-way derivative exposures, basket default swaps, and CDOs. These applications are demonstrated in Part VII.

## Appendix: Asymptotic loss distribution in Merino–Nyfeler example

Merino and Nyfeler (Chapter 20) employ a simple version of CreditRisk+ to demonstrate their methodology. This is a default-mode model, so loss per dollar of exposure for loan i is $U_i = (1 - R_i)D_i$, where $D_i$ is a default indicator and $R_i$ is the recovery rate. Recovery is assumed to be non-stochastic, so acts merely as a scaling factor on exposure $\nu_i$. We can assume zero recovery without loss of generality.

Dependence across obligors is generated by assuming a single systematic factor W that is distributed gamma with mean 1 and standard deviation 0.8. Conditional on W, obligor i has probability of default $\bar{q}_i W$. The $\nu_i$ in this exercise are drawn by multiplying variates from a beta(1.2, 5) distribution by 100. The obligors are allocated evenly across three credit rating grades with $\bar{q}$ of 0.5%, 1.0% and 1.5%, respectively. Merino and Nyfeler do not report the realised sample of exposures, so results cannot be replicated precisely. However, the noise due to "sampling variation" in Merino and Nyfeler's sample can be minimised through rescaling by total portfolio exposure.[6] The reported mean loss is 2,923, and as expected loss in this experiment equals total exposure times the average default probability of 0.01, we can estimate total exposure as 292,300. The standard deviation of loss and VARs reported in the first two columns of Table 1 above are the corresponding quantities reported in Chapter 21 (Table 2, "fMC" and "NM" columns) divided by this estimated total exposure.

The conditional expected loss rate is given by

$$E\left[L|W\right] = \frac{\sum_{i=1}^{m} \nu_i \bar{q}_i W}{\sum_{i=1}^{m} \nu_i}$$

The equal distribution of exposure across the three credit rating grades implies that $\Sigma_{i=1}^{m} \nu_i \bar{q}_i / \Sigma_{i=1}^{m} \nu_i$ equals the average of the $\bar{q}_i$, which is 1%. Therefore,

$$E[L|W] = 0.01W$$

Consequently, the standard deviation of $E[L|W]$ is simply 0.01 times the standard deviation of W, and the αth quantile of $E[L|W]$ is simply 0.01 times the αth quantile of W. The coefficient of skewness of $E[L|W]$ equals that of W.

1 *A conference hosted by the Bank of England in September 1998 proved a watershed event for many participants in this process. See the coverage by Nicholas Dunbar in "The Accord is dead - long live the Accord," Risk, October 1998.*

2 *CreditMetrics is now property of the RiskMetrics Group.*

3 *In an industry practitioner response, GARP (1999) acknowledges the obstacles to immediate adoption of an internal models regulatory regime, but argues that the challenges can be met through an evolutionary, piecemeal approach to regulatory certification of model components.*

4 *Of course, the robustness of the maturity adjustment to other sources of spread data was studied in detail.*

5 *See especially Chapter 8 in "The Internal Ratings-Based Approach: Supporting Document to the New Basel Capital Accord", Basel Committee on Banking Supervision (2001).*

6 *The sampling variation is not eliminated by the Monte Carlo procedure because the drawn sample of exposures is held fixed throughout the simulation. The mean and standard deviation of total exposure is 290, 322 and 1803, respectively, so there remains significant uncertainty even in the estimate of expected total loss.*

**BIBLIOGRAPHY**

**Altman, E. I., B. Brady, A. Resti and A. Sironi,** 2002, *The Link between Default and Recovery Rates: Implications for Credit Risk Models and Procyclicality*, NYU Stern School of Business Working Paper FIN-02-049, July.

**Basel Committee on Banking Supervision,** 1999, *Credit Risk Modelling: Current Practices and Applications*, Bank for International Settlements, April.

**Basel Committee on Banking Supervision,** 2001, *The New Basel Capital Accord*, Bank for International Settlements, January.

**Credit Suisse Financial Products,** 1997, *CreditRisk+: A Credit Risk Management Framework* (London: Credit Suisse Financial Products).

**Duffie, D., and N. Garleanu,** 2001, "Risk and Valuation of Collateralized Debt Obligations", *Financial Analysts Journal*, January–February, 57(1), pp. 41–59.

**Duffie, D., and D. Lando,** 2001, "Term Structures of Credit Spreads with Incomplete Accounting Information", *Econometrica*, 69, pp. 633–64.

**Duffie, D., and K. J. Singleton,** 1999, "Modeling Term Structures of Defaultable Bonds", *Review of Financial Studies*, 12, pp. 687–720.

**GARP Committee on Regulation and Supervision,** 1999, Response to Basle's *Credit RiskModelling: Current Practices and Applications*, Global Association of Risk Professionals, September.

**Gordy, M. B.,** 2000, "A Comparative Anatomy of Credit Risk Models", *Journal of Banking and Finance*, 24(1–2), January, pp. 119–49.

**Gordy, M. B.,** "A Risk-Factor Model Foundation for Ratings-Based Bank Capital Rules", *Journal of Financial Intermediation*, Forthcoming.

**Gupton, G. M., C. C. Finger and M. Bhatia,** 1997, *CreditMetrics - Technical Document*, JP Morgan & Co, April.

**Hull, J., and A. White,** 2001, "Valuing Credit Default Swaps II: Modeling Default Correlations", *Journal of Derivatives*, Spring, 8(3), pp. 12–21.

**Jarrow, R., and S. Turnbull,** 1995, "Pricing Derivatives on Financial Securities Subject to Credit Risk", *Journal of Finance*, March, 50(1), pp. 53–86.

**Jones, D.,** 2000, "Emerging Problems with the Basel Capital Accord: Regulatory Capital Arbitrage and Related Issues", *Journal of Banking and Finance*, January, 24(1–2), pp. 35–58.

**Koyluoglu, H. U., and A. Hickman,** 1998, "Reconcilable Differences", *Risk*, October, 11(10), pp. 56–62.

**Lando, D.,** 1998, "Cox Processes and Credit-Risky Securities", *Review of Derivatives Research*, 2, pp. 99–120.

**Li, D. X.,** 1999, "The Valuation of Basket Credit Derivatives", *CreditMetrics Monitor*, April, pp. 34–50.

**Longstaff, F. A. and E. S. Schwartz,** 1995, "A Simple Approach to Valuing Risky Fixed and Floating Rate Debt", *Journal of Finance*, July, 50(3), pp. 789–819.

**Merton, R. C.,** 1995, "Financial Innovation and the Management and Regulation of Financial Institutions", *Journal of Banking and Finance*, June, 19(3–4), pp. 461–81.

**Wilson, T.,** 1997a, "Portfolio Credit Risk (I)", *Risk*, September, 10(9), pp. 111–17.

**Wilson, T.,** 1997b, "Portfolio Credit Risk (II)," *Risk*, October, 10(10), pp. 56–61.

**Zhou, C.,** 2001, "The Term Structure of Credit Spreads with Jump Risk", *Journal of Banking and Finance*, 25, pp. 2015–40.

# I

# PRICING CREDIT RISK

1

# Credit Derivatives Made Simple

**Lane Hughston and Stuart M. Turnbull**
King's College London; Lehman Brothers

*Using some elementary results in probability theory, Lane Hughston and Stuart M. Turnbull revisit some useful formulas for pricing credit derivatives.*

The so-called "reduced-form" approach to credit modelling, introduced by Jarrow and Turnbull (1992, 1995), takes the term structure of interest rates for the appropriate credit class as a given input. If a firm has a sufficient number of different traded bonds of the same seniority outstanding, then it is possible to construct a firm-specific term structure of interest rates. Otherwise, firms are allocated to credit risk classes. Default is modelled as a point process in this approach. Let $t = 0$ denote the present. Over the small interval $(t, t + \Delta t]$ in the future, the probability of default, conditional on no default prior to time $t$, is assumed to be given by an expression of the form $h_t \Delta t$, where $h_t$ is referred to as the intensity or hazard rate process. Using the term structure of credit spreads for each credit class, Jarrow and Turnbull infer the expected loss over the interval $(t, t + \Delta t]$, in the risk-neutral measure; this is given by the product of the conditional probability of default in that measure, and the loss rate (one minus the recovery rate). In the numerical examples given by Jarrow and Turnbull (1995, 2000), random changes in the credit spread occur only in the event of a default.

To model the ever-present volatility of credit spreads, a more detailed specification is required for the intensity process and/or the recovery rate. Das and Tufano (1996), for example, keep the intensity function deterministic and assume that the recovery rate depends both on the state of the economy at the time of default and an idiosyncratic component. The spot interest rate for default-free discount bonds is used as a proxy for the dependence of the recovery rate on the state of the economy.

The formulation in Jarrow and Turnbull (1995), on the other hand, is quite general, and allows for the intensity function to be an arbitrary random process. Lando (1994, 1998) uses the Jarrow and Turnbull framework, and assumes that the intensity depends on a set of state variables. In the theory of point processes, the idea that the hazard function might depend on a set of state variables was introduced by Cox (1972). Roughly speaking, a Cox process, when conditioned on the state variables, behaves like a Poisson process. Lando shows that the value $Q_{ab}$ at time $a$ of a credit-risky (ie, defaultable) discount bond that promises to pay one unit of currency at time $b \geq a$ if default does not occur, and nothing if default does occur, is given by:

$$Q_{ab} = I(\Gamma > a) E_a \left[ \exp\left( -\int_a^b (r_s + h_s) ds \right) \right] \quad (1)$$

Here $I(x)$ denotes the indicator function for the event $x$, and $\Gamma$ denotes the time of default. Thus $I(\Gamma > a) = 1$ if default occurs at some time after $a$, and is zero if default occurs no later than time $a$. We write $E_t$ for expectation in the risk-neutral measure, conditional on information given up to time $t$, and $r_t$ denotes the default-free spot interest rate. Duffie and Singleton (1997) assume that in default the value of a bond is proportional to its value just prior to default (also see, for example, Duffie and Huang 1994; Duffie, Schroder and

*The authors are grateful to S. Babbs, P. Balland, and J. Turetsky for their helpful comments. The views expressed in this chapter are those of the authors and do not necessarily represent those of Lehman Brothers.*

Skiadas 1994; Duffie and Singleton, 1995). This assumption leads to a natural extension of Lando's work, and gives rise to a useful and intuitively natural representation for the value of a credit-risky discount bond. For example, the value at time a of a discount bond that promises to pay one dollar at time b is given by:

$$Q_{ab} = I(\Gamma > a)E_a\left[\exp\left(-\int_a^b (r_s + h_s L_s)ds\right)\right] \quad (2)$$

where the loss process $L_t$ is given by $L_t = 1 - R_t$, where $R_t$ is the recovery process. The interpretation of $R_t$ is that if the bond is worth some designated amount $Q_{ab}^-$ just before default at time t, then upon default the bond is only worth the original amount $Q_{ab}^-$ times $R_t$, and this is paid off immediately to the creditors. In that sense, $R_t$ measures the percentage of value recovered after the default. It should be noted that there is no loss of generality in assuming the existence of such a "proportional" drop process if we assume that $R_s$ varies according to the maturity of the bond under consideration.

In this chapter, which is largely of a pedagogical nature, we show how to derive Equations 1 and 2, and some related results, using simple results from probability theory. Most of what we have to say here may already be familiar to experienced credit derivatives practitioners, but we hope that there may be some merit and novelty in the particular manner of exposition employed. Section 2 reviews the main probabilistic ideas that we shall need. In Section 3 we derive an expression for the valuation of a discount bond, assuming that in the event of default the value of the bond is zero, and in Sections 4 and 5 we examine two related types of credit derivatives. In Section 6 we consider the pricing of securities that are affected by counterparty risk, and we derive a formula due to Jarrow and Yu (1999). Finally, in Section 7 we present a derivation of the Duffie–Singleton formula for risky discount bonds with a proportional recovery function.

## 2. Some well-known probabilistic results

We begin with a few basic results concerning the modelling of the default event. Let $\Gamma$ denote the time of default. The conditional probability of default over the small interval $(t, t + \Delta t]$, given survival up to time t is:

$$\Pr\left[t < \Gamma \le t + \Delta t \middle| \Gamma > t\right] = h_t \Delta t \quad (3)$$

Suppose for the moment that the intensity function is a deterministic function of time. In that case, given that default has not occurred by time zero, the survival probability is:

$$\Pr[\Gamma > t] = \exp\left(-\int_0^t h_s ds\right) \quad (4)$$

This is the probability that default has not occurred by time t. As a consequence we see that the *unconditional* probability of default occurring in the small interval $(t, t + \Delta t]$ is given by:

$$\Pr[t < \Gamma \le t + \Delta t] = \Pr\left[t < \Gamma \le t + \Delta t \middle| \Gamma > t\right]\Pr[\Gamma > t] \quad (5)$$

Then if we write:

$$\Pr[t < \Gamma \le t + \Delta t] = \rho_t \Delta t \quad (6)$$

it follows that the density function $\rho_t$ for the default event occurring during the small interval $(t, t + \Delta t]$ is given by:

$$\rho_t = h_t \exp\left(-\int_0^t h_s ds\right) \quad (7)$$

The probability of surviving until time t, given survival up to time $s \le t$, is given according to the usual rules of conditional probability by:

$$\Pr\left[\Gamma > t \middle| \Gamma > s\right] = \frac{\Pr[\Gamma > t]}{\Pr[\Gamma > s]} \quad (8)$$

from which it follows from Equation 4 that:

$$\Pr\left[\Gamma > t \middle| \Gamma > s\right] = \exp\left(-\int_s^t h_u du\right) \quad (9)$$

We deduce therefore from Equations 3 and 9 that the conditional density function for the default time occurring in the small interval $(t < \Gamma \le t + \Delta t]$, conditional on no default up to time s, is given by the formula:

$$\Pr\left[t < \Gamma \le t + \Delta t \middle| \Gamma > s\right] = h_t \exp\left(-\int_s^t h_u du\right)\Delta t \quad (10)$$

Now suppose we consider the case when the intensity $h_t$ is a random process. For example, it may be dependent in some way on the history of a multi-dimensional Brownian motion up to time t. In particular, the dependence could be through a vector of macro-economic and firm-specific variables that affect the hazard function. This is typical of the situation we have in mind in the analysis of credit derivatives, in which case the multi-dimensional

Brownian motion is also responsible for driving the term structure of a set of default-free discount bonds within the scope of a standard Heath–Jarrow–Morton (1992) interest rate framework. Now conditional on the relevant information set, eg, on a given trajectory or path for the Brownian motion up to time t, the survival probability for time t is given by the right side of Equation 4, and the associated density function for default in the interval $(t, t + \Delta t]$ is given by Equation 7.

To determine the unconditional survival probability, we must consider all possible such Brownian trajectories, and take an appropriate weighted average. As a consequence of this intuitive argument we see that:

$$\Pr[\Gamma > t] = E\left[\exp\left(-\int_0^t h_s ds\right)\right] \tag{11}$$

where the expectation is taken over all possible paths of the Brownian motion.

Let us denote by $G_t$ the information set or *filtration* associated with the events on which the trajectory of $h_t$ depends up to time t. In our example above, $G_t$ would contain the information of the history of the Brownian motion up to time t. Then the probability, based on information known at time a, of surviving until time b, given survival up to time a, is the following conditional expectation:

$$\Pr\left[\Gamma > b \middle| \Gamma > a\right] = E\left[\exp\left(-\int_a^b h_s ds\right)\middle| G_a\right] \tag{12}$$

Note that the probability at time a of survival until time b, given survival until time a, is a random variable, since in particular it depends on the information set $G_a$. Thus as we vary a, for a fixed value of b, we obtain a random process, adapted to the filtration $G_a$, which we shall denote $\pi_{ab}$.

To illustrate the idea, we consider a simple example. Let us suppose a person is born today at time zero; then $\pi_{ab}$ can be taken to represent the probability once the person has reached age a, that death will occur later than age b. From the point of view of today, the probability $\pi_{ab}$ is unknown, it is random, since it depends on a variety of factors not yet fully determined, relating to health and lifestyle, which indeed may change unexpectedly between now and time a. A downturn in quality of health, for example, would result in an increase in the hazard rate. It is interesting to observe that there is a striking analogy between the process for such a system of survival probabilities, and the process for the system of discount bonds in the HJM theory.

## 3. No recovery in the event of default

In the case of no recovery in the event of a default, the payoff to a discount bond is unity if default does not occur, and zero otherwise. Let $B_t$ denote the value of a unit initialised money market account. By definition we have:

$$B_t = \exp\left(\int_0^t r_s ds\right) \tag{13}$$

which represents the value of continuously investing, without default risk, at the short-term interest rate.

According to the standard risk-neutral pricing methodology in a complete market (see, for example, Bensoussan, 1984), the value $Q_{ab}$ at time a of a credit-risky discount bond that matures at time b is:

$$Q_{ab} = B_a E_a\left[\frac{I(\Gamma > b)}{B_b}\right] \tag{14}$$

Here, and in what follows, the operator $E_a$ denotes conditional expectation, in the risk-neutral measure, given the full information set $F_a$ up to time a. Intuitively speaking, the "full" information set consists of the Brownian filtration $G_a$ together with the information as to whether a default has taken place by time a, and if so at what time the default occurred.

We note that if default occurs by time a, then $I(\Gamma > a) = 0$, and *a fortiori* we have $I(\Gamma > b) = 0$, from which it follows that $Q_{ab} = 0$. To value $Q_{ab}$ in the general situation, it will be helpful if we introduce some more notation. Again letting $\Gamma$ denote the random time of default, we introduce the "survival indicator" process:

$$\Gamma_t = I(\Gamma > t) \tag{15}$$

Thus $\Gamma_t$ is unity if default has not yet occurred by time t, but drops to zero on default. Additionally, we introduce the information set $I_t$, which tells us whether the jump has taken place by time t, and if so at what time the jump occurred. In other words $I_t$ is the history of $\Gamma_t$ up to the designated time.

The full information set $F_t$ contains information about the Brownian motion history and the default history. We represent this by the relation:

$$F_t = G_t \vee I_t \tag{16}$$

Now consider the conditional expectation:

$$E_a(\Gamma_b) = E\left(\Gamma_b \middle| F_a\right) \tag{17}$$

To evaluate this expression, we condition on a trajectory of the Brownian motion and then take the expectation across all trajectories. We represent these steps as follows. We have:

$$E(\Gamma_b|F_a) = E\left[\Gamma_b|(G_a \vee I_a)\right] \quad (18)$$

and thus:

$$E(\Gamma_b|F_a) = E\left[E\left[\Gamma_b|(G_b \vee I_a)\right]|F_a\right] \quad (19)$$

since $F_a = G_a \vee I_a \subset (G_b \vee I_a)$. But if we are given the Brownian information set up to time b, and the default information set up to time a, then by use of Equation 9 we have:

$$E\left[\Gamma_b|(G_b \vee I_a)\right] = \Gamma_a \exp\left(-\int_a^b h_s ds\right) \quad (20)$$

from which it follows that:

$$E(\Gamma_b|F_a) = \Gamma_a E\left[\exp\left(-\int_a^b h_s ds\right)|F_a\right] \quad (21)$$

or equivalently:

$$E_a(\Gamma_b) = \Gamma_a E_a\left[\exp\left(-\int_a^b h_s ds\right)\right] \quad (22)$$

since $E_a$ denotes conditional expectation, in the risk neutral measure, given the information set $F_a$. We shall use this conditional expectation argument in deriving some of the results that follow.

The value of the risky discount bond $Q_{ab}$ is given by:

$$Q_{ab} = B_a E_a\left[\frac{\Gamma_b}{B_b}\right] \quad (23)$$

To evaluate this expression, we condition on the information set $G_b$. Note that this information set contains the information about the trajectory of the spot interest rate. The argument then proceeds as follows:

$$\begin{aligned} E_a\left[\frac{\Gamma_b}{B_b}\right] &= E\left[\frac{\Gamma_b}{B_b}|F_a\right] \\ &= E\left[\frac{\Gamma_b}{B_b}|(G_a \vee I_a)\right] \\ &= E\left[E\left[\frac{\Gamma_b}{B_b}|(G_b \vee I_a)\right]|F_a\right] \\ &= E\left[\frac{1}{B_b}E\left[\Gamma_b|(G_b \vee I_a)\right]|F_a\right] \quad (24) \end{aligned}$$

Inserting Equation 20 into Equation 24, we get:

$$Q_{ab} = \Gamma_a B_a E_a\left[\frac{1}{B_b}\exp\left(-\int_a^b h_s ds\right)\right] \quad (25)$$

for the risky discount bond price. By use of Equation 13 we then obtain:

$$Q_{ab} = \Gamma_a E_a\left[\exp\left(-\int_a^b (r_s + h_s) ds\right)\right] \quad (26)$$

which is Equation 1. This remarkable result was derived by Lando (1994), and shows how the risky discount bond prices can be obtained by a procedure according to which the risk-free spot interest rate is augmented by the default hazard rate in the risk-neutral measure.

## 4. Valuation of a credit-risky interest-paying instrument

An immediate application of the result of the previous section is the valuation of an instrument that pays interest $Y_s$ on a continuous basis until time b, provided that default has not occurred. If default occurs, the payments stop. The value $V_a$ of this instrument at time a is:

$$V_a = \Gamma_a B_a E_a\left[\int_a^b B_s^{-1} Y_s \Gamma_s ds\right] \quad (27)$$

Conditioning as in the example in Section 3, we get:

$$\begin{aligned} E_a\left[\int_a^b B_s^{-1} Y_s \Gamma_s ds\right] &= E_a\left[\int_a^b E\left[B_s^{-1} Y_s \Gamma_s|(G_b \vee I_a)\right] ds\right] \\ &= E_a\left[\int_a^b B_s^{-1} Y_s E\left[\Gamma_s|(G_b \vee I_a)\right] ds\right] \\ &= E_a\left[\int_a^b B_s^{-1} Y_s \exp\left(-\int_a^s h_u du\right) ds\right] \quad (28) \end{aligned}$$

from which it follows that:

$$V_a = \Gamma_a E_a\left[\int_a^b Y_s \exp\left(-\int_a^s (r_u + h_u) du\right) ds\right] \quad (29)$$

This result was derived by Lando (1994).

## 5. Valuation of an instrument that pays in the event of a default

Here we consider an instrument that pays $Z_t$ at time t if default occurs. The contract matures at time b. If default does not occur over the lifetime of the contract, the payoff is zero. Let $V_a$ denote the value of this instrument. Default occurs at the random stopping time G. The value at time a is:

$$\begin{aligned} V_a &= \Gamma_a B_a E_a\left[B_\Gamma^{-1} Z_\Gamma\right] \\ &= \Gamma_a B_a E_a\left[E\left[B_\Gamma^{-1} Z_\Gamma \middle| (G_b \vee I_a)\right]\right] \\ &= \Gamma_a B_a E_a\left[\int_a^b B_s^{-1} Z_s h_s \exp\left(-\int_a^s h_u du\right) ds\right] \end{aligned} \quad (30)$$

where here we have inserted the density function for default during the small interval $s < \Gamma \le s + \Delta s$, given no default up to time a, using Equation 10. Gathering terms together we thus obtain:

$$V_a = \Gamma_a E_a\left[\int_a^b Z_s h_s \exp\left(-\int_a^s (r_u + h_u) du\right) ds\right] \quad (31)$$

This result was derived by Lando (1994). It is worth noting that Equation 31 can be obtained in an intuitively appealing way from Equation 29, by substituting the product of the hazard rate and the randomly timed "one-off" payment made on the default appearing in Equation 31 for the continuous cashflow appearing in Equation 29.

The key results embodied in Equations 26, 29 and 31 provide the basic building blocks for the valuation of credit-risky instruments.

## 6. Default events and counterparty risk

Events in the economy can affect the probability of default for particular debtors. For example, the Russian treasury default in 1998 had a negative effect on a number of western financial institutions that had exposures to Russian debtors.

If we are considering the likelihood of default by a particular debtor, the event of default by another debtor may have a direct effect. For example, default by an industry competitor may have a positive or negative effect depending on the nature of the industry and the cause of default. For a financial institution A holding an obligation from an institution B, the event of default by institution B may have an adverse effect on institution A. In pricing obligations issued by institution A we need to consider its dependence on institution B. See Jarrow and Turnbull (2000, Chapter 18) for a general discussion of credit counterparty risk.

Let us consider, for example, the case of a discount bond issued by institution A. For simplicity we shall assume that if A defaults, no payment will be made to bond holders. We assume, moreover, that the intensity process $h_t^A$ for institution A can be written in the following form:

$$h_t^A = \Gamma_t^B \alpha_t + \left(1 - \Gamma_t^B\right)\beta_t \quad (32)$$

Here $\Gamma_t^B$ is the survival indicator process for institution B. In other words, $\Gamma_t^B = 1$ up until B defaults, after which $\Gamma_t^B$ vanishes. Thus Equation 32 means that the intensity process for institution A is given by $a_t$ until institution B defaults, at which point institution A becomes stressed as a consequence and its default intensity shifts to a new process, given by $\beta_t$. In reality, one envisages a network of such interlocking dependencies involving perhaps many different kinds of institutions.

The value of the risky bond issued by institution A is given, assuming no recovery in the event of A defaulting, by Equation 26, with Equation 32 inserted for the intensity process. Thus we have:

$$Q_{ab} = \Gamma_a^A E_a\left[\exp\left(-\int_a^b \left(r_s + \Gamma_s^B \alpha_s + \left(1 - \Gamma_s^B\right)\beta_s\right) ds\right)\right] \quad (33)$$

Now by use of Equation 10 we see that the density function for the default time of institution B, given no default up to time a, and given the economic information set $G_b$, is given by the expression:

$$\rho_s^B = h_s^B \exp\left(-\int_a^s h_u^B du\right) \quad (34)$$

for $a \le s \le b$, where $h_s^B$ is the intensity process for institution B. Thus if we take the expectation of the default time, conditioning on the Brownian information space, it follows that the risky bond prices are given by:

$$\begin{aligned} Q_{ab} = \Gamma_a^A E_a\Bigg[&\exp\left(-\int_{t=a}^b r_t dt\right) \int_{s=a}^b h_s^B \exp\left(-\int_{u=a}^s h_u^B du\right) \\ &\times \exp\left(-\int_{x=a}^s \alpha_x dx - \int_{x=s}^b \beta_x dx\right)\Bigg] \end{aligned} \quad (35)$$

This expression is due to Jarrow and Yu (1999).

## 7. Partial recovery on default

Let us now consider the case where if default occurs, the value of the instrument drops to a fraction $R_a$ of its value immediately prior to the default. We call $R_a$ the recovery process, which here will be allowed to be random and adapted to the same economic information set that drives the intensity. Thus upon default, at time s, we have:

$$Q_{sb} = R_s Q_{sb}^{-} \quad (36)$$

where $Q_{sb}^{-}$ denotes the value of the bond just before the default at time s, and $0 \le R_s \le 1$. Now clearly we can regard the credit-risky discount bond in this case as a contingent claim with a payoff that is a kind of hybrid of the cases considered in Sections 3 and 5. For instance, if no default occurs during the life of the bond, the payoff at maturity is unity; whereas if default occurs at some intermediate time s with $a \le s \le b$, then we have an immediate payoff $Z_s = R_s \bar{Q}_{sb}$ at that time.

The value of the bond can therefore be expressed as a sum of two terms: the first term is of the form in Equation 26, representing the value of the terminal payout in the event of no default; the second term is of the form in Equation 31, representing the amount recoverable in the event of a default. Putting these expressions together we get:

$$Q_{ab} = \Gamma_a E_a \left[ \exp\left( -\int_a^b (r_s + h_s) ds \right) + \int_a^b Z_s h_s \exp\left( -\int_a^s (r_u + h_u) du \right) ds \right] \quad (37)$$

For $\bar{Q}_{ab}$ therefore we consider the value of $Q_{ab}$ assuming no default has yet occurred, and we set $Z_s = R_s \bar{Q}_{sb}$ to obtain the following "recursive" formula for $\bar{Q}_{ab}$:

$$\bar{Q}_{ab} = E_a \left[ \exp\left( -\int_a^b (r_s + h_s) ds \right) + \int_a^b R_s h_s \bar{Q}_{sb} \exp\left( -\int_a^s (r_u + h_u) du \right) ds \right] \quad (38)$$

Our problem now is to boil this formula down to a manageable expression for the discount bond price that avoids the recursion. We proceed as follows. Let us first introduce a new process $S_{ab}$ defined (for fixed maturity b) according to the formula:

$$S_{ab} = \bar{Q}_{ab} \exp\left( -\int_0^a (r_s + h_s) ds \right) \quad (39)$$

Since $\bar{Q}_{bb} = 1$, corresponding to the fact that in the event of no default the payoff is unity, we have:

$$S_{bb} = \exp\left( -\int_0^b (r_s + h_s) ds \right) \quad (40)$$

Therefore, multiplying Equation 38 by the augmented discount factor appearing in Equation 39 we get:

$$S_{ab} = E_a \left[ \exp\left( -\int_0^b (r_s + h_s) ds \right) + \int_a^b h_s R_s \bar{Q}_{sb} \exp\left( -\int_0^s (r_u + h_u) du \right) ds \right] \quad (41)$$

and hence:

$$S_{ab} = E_a \left[ S_{bb} + \int_a^b h_s R_s S_{sb} ds \right] \quad (42)$$

Breaking the integral into two parts, we can rewrite the expression above in the form

$$S_{ab} = E_a \left[ S_{bb} + \int_a^b h_s R_s S_{sb} ds - \int_0^a h_s R_s S_{sb} ds \right] \quad (43)$$

Since the third term inside the brackets is known at time a, it can be removed from the conditional expectation, and we have:

$$S_{ab} + \int_0^a h_s R_s S_{sb} ds = E_a \left[ S_{bb} + \int_0^b h_s R_s S_{sb} ds \right] \quad (44)$$

The term now appearing on the right is a martingale $m_{ab}$ over the interval $[0, b]$, and thus by taking a stochastic differential we get:

$$dS_{ab} + h_a R_a S_{ab} da = dm_{ab} \quad (45)$$

By introduction of an integrating factor, we can write the expression above in the form:

$$d\left( S_{ab} \exp\left( \int_0^a h_s R_s ds \right) \right) = \exp\left( \int_0^a h_s R_s ds \right) dm_{ab} \quad (46)$$

from which we can deduce by integration that for each value of the maturity date b the process:

$$M_{ab} = S_{ab} \exp\left( \int_0^a h_s R_s ds \right) \quad (47)$$

is also a martingale. We need to check that $E[|M_{ab}|] < \infty$ for all a in the interval $[0, b]$. In fact we have $|M_{ab}| \le 1$, which follows immediately from Equations 39 and 47, providing we bear in mind the following inequalities: $|\bar{Q}_{ab}| \le 1$, $0 \le R_a \le 1$, $r_a > 0$, and $h_a > 0$. By use of the martingale relation $M_{ab} = E_a[M_{bb}]$, we thereby deduce that:

$$S_{ab} \exp\left( \int_0^a h_s R_s ds \right) = E_a \left[ S_{bb} \exp\left( \int_0^b h_s R_s ds \right) \right] \quad (48)$$

It follows then from Equations 39 and 40 after some elementary rearrangement that:

$$Q_{ab} = \Gamma_a E_a \left[ \exp\left( -\int_a^b (r_s + h_s L_s) ds \right) \right] \quad (49)$$

where $L_s = 1 - R_s$ is the loss process. This result, which is due to Duffie and Singleton (1997), is Equation 2.

We note that throughout the discussion in this section we have kept the maturity date b fixed, so in principle the recovery process itself can depend on b, and indeed on other indexes, eg, the degree of seniority. This is natural, because bonds of varying maturity and seniority may have different recovery processes associated with them even if they all default simultaneously.

## BIBLIOGRAPHY

**Bensoussan, A.,** 1984, "On the Theory of Option Pricing", *Acta Applicandae Mathematicae*, 2, pp. 139–58; reprinted in L. P. Hughston (ed), *Vasicek and Beyond*, 1996 (Risk Publications).

**Cox, D.,** 1972, "The Statistical Analysis of Dependencies in Point Processes", in P. Lewis (ed), *Symposium on Point Processes* (New York: John Wiley & Sons).

**Das, S., and P. Tufano,** 1996, "Pricing Credit Sensitive Debt When Interest Rates, Credit Ratings, and Credit Spreads are Stochastic", *Journal of Financial Engineering*, 5(2), pp. 161–98.

**Duffie, D., and M. Huang,** 1994, *Swap Rates and Credit Quality*, Stanford Working Paper.

**Duffie, D., M. Schroder and C. Skiadas,** 1994, *Recursive Valuation of Defaultable Securities and the Timing of Resolution of Uncertainty*, Stanford and Northwestern Working Paper.

**Duffie, D., and K. Singleton,** 1995, *Econometric Modelling of the Term Structures of Defaultable Bonds*, Stanford University, Working Paper.

**Duffie, D., and K. Singleton,** 1997, "An Econometric Model of the Term Structure of Interest Rate Swap Yields", *Journal of Finance*, 52, pp. 1287–321.

**Heath, D., R. Jarrow and A. Morton,** 1992, "Bond Pricing and the Term Structure of Interest Rates: A New Methodology for Contingent Claims Valuation", *Econometrica*, 60(1), pp. 77–105.

**Jarrow, R., and S. Turnbull,** 1992, "Drawing the Analogy", *Risk*, October, pp. 63–70; reprinted in *Derivative Credit Risk: Advances in Measurement and Management*, 1995 (London: Risk Publications).

**Jarrow, R., and S. Turnbull,** 1995, "The Pricing and Hedging of Options on Financial Securities Subject to Credit Risk", *Journal of Finance*, 50(1), pp. 53–85.

**Jarrow, R., and S. Turnbull,** 2000, *Derivative Securities*, Second Edition (South-Western Publishing Company).

**Jarrow, R., and F. Yu,** 1999, *Counterparty Risk and the Pricing of Defaultable Securities*, Working Paper, Johnson Graduate School of Business, Cornell University.

**Lando, D.,** 1994, *Three Essays on Contingent Claim Pricing*, Cornell University.

**Lando, D.,** 1998, "On Cox Processes and Credit Risky Securities", *Review of Derivatives Research*, 2(3), pp. 99–120.

2

# Applying HJM to Credit Risk


**Robert Maksymiuk and Dariusz Gatarek**

Ernst & Young; Deloitte & Touche



*Pricing credit risk remains a topic of intense debate among practitioners. One popular approach is extended here by Robert Maksymiuk and Dariusz Gatarek, who show that, by substituting hazard rates for interest rates, default options can be priced in a Heath-Jarrow-Morton framework.*


This article aims to show that the Heath-Jarrow-Morton (1992) approach to the term structure of interest rates can also be applied to the problem of arbitrage-free pricing of credit derivatives. We extend the concepts of Jarrow and Turnbull (1995) and Jarrow, Lando and Turnbull (1997) to the general framework given by Heath, Jarrow and Morton.

Our general theorem is as follows. Let $Y(t)$ and $\lambda(t,T)$ be stochastic processes. Define:

$$\lambda(t) = \lambda(t,t)$$

$$A(t,T) = \exp\left\{-\int_t^T \lambda(t,s)ds\right\}$$

$$X(t,T) = Y(t)A(t,T)$$

$$M(t) = Y(t) + \int_0^t \lambda(s)Y(s)ds$$

Assume that Y has bounded variation and $\lambda(\cdot,T)$ is an Itô process, ie:

$$d\lambda(t,T) = a(t,T)dt + \sigma^*(t,T)dW(t) \qquad (1)$$

where W is a d-dimensional Wiener process, a and $\sigma$ are stochastic processes and $\sigma^*$ denotes the transpose of $\sigma$.

## Theorem

If M and $X(\cdot,T)$ are martingales for any $T > 0$, then:

$$a(t,T) = \sigma^*(t,T)\int_t^T \sigma(t,s)ds$$

for any $0 \le t \le T < \infty$.

The proof of this is shown by Itô's lemma (Metivier, 1982):

$$dX(t,T) = Y(t)dA(t,T) + A(t,T)dY(t) + d\langle Y,A\rangle(t)$$

The variation of M is bounded. Therefore, $\langle M,W\rangle = \langle Y,A\rangle = 0$ and:

$$dX(t,T) = Y(t)dA(t,T) + A(t,T)dY(t)$$

Hence:

$$dX(t,T) = A(t,T)dM(t) + X(t,T)\{\lambda(t) - \lambda(t)\}dt$$

$$+X(t,T)\left\{\frac{1}{2}\left|\int_t^T \sigma^*(t,s)ds\right|^2 dt - \int_t^T a(t,s)dsdt\right.$$

$$\left.-\int_t^T \sigma^*(t,s)dsdW(t)\right\}$$

Since both M and $X(\cdot,T)$ are martingales for any $0 \le t \le T$:

$$\frac{1}{2}\left|\int_t^T \sigma^*(t,s)ds\right|^2 = \int_t^T a(t,s)ds$$

and therefore:

$$a(t,T) = \sigma^*(t,T)\int_t^T \sigma(t,s)ds$$

The theorem will be applied for both the term structure of interest rates and credit risk.

## Term structure of interest rates

Let $B(t,T)$ be the price at time t of a zero-coupon bond with maturity T and $r(t,T)$ be the continuously compounded forward rate prevailing at time t over the interval $[T, T + dT]$. By definition:

$$B(t,T) = \exp\left\{-\int_t^T r(t,s)ds\right\}$$

Given the initial investment of one at time zero, the amount generated at time t by continuously reinvesting in the spot rate is equal to:

$$\beta(t) = \exp\left\{\int_0^t r(s,s)ds\right\}$$

Let:

$$Z(t,T) = \frac{B(t,T)}{\beta(t)}$$

As there should not be an arbitrage opportunity between the zero-coupon bonds and the saving account, $Z(t,T)$ should be a martingale. Let:

$$Y(t) = Z(t,t) = \frac{1}{\beta(t)} = \exp\left\{-\int_0^t r(s,s)ds\right\}$$

The process $Y(t)$ has finite variation. Obviously:

$$Y(t) + \int_0^t r(s,s)Y(s)ds = 1$$

Constant is a martingale. Assume that $r(t,T)$ is an Itô process (Assumption 1):

$$dr(t,T) = a(t,T)dt + \sigma^*(t,T)dW(t)$$

Then, by our theorem:

$$a(t,T) = \sigma^*(t,T)\int_t^T \sigma(t,s)ds$$

which is the Heath-Jarrow-Morton condition.

## Credit risk

Let $\tau$ be the time when firm XYZ goes bankrupt. The following point process is connected with this time:

$$N(t) = I_{\{\tau>t\}}$$

Let $P(t,T)$ be the price of a risky zero-coupon bond issued by XYZ. Assume that the recovery rate is equal to zero. By Baxter and Rennie (1997):

$$P(t,T) = B(t,T)E\left(N(T)\middle|F_t\right)$$

where $B(t,T)$ is the price of a risk-free zero-coupon bond and the reference measure $E$ is the forward measure (Baxter and Rennie, 1997). If interest rates and default are driven by independent processes (which is usually assumed), the same equality holds if $E$ is the spot arbitrage-free measure. Define for any $0 \le t \le T < \infty$ the conditional expectation:

$$X(t,T) = E\left(N(T)\middle|F_t\right)$$

By definition, $X(t,T)$ is a martingale. If $N(t) = 0$ then $X(t,T) = 0$ also, hence $X(t,T) = N(t)A(t,T)$, where $A(t,T)$ is non-increasing with respect to $T$. Assume that $A(t,T)$ is positive and differentiable with respect to $T$. Define:

$$\lambda(t,T) = -\frac{\partial \log A(t,T)}{\partial T}$$

Obviously:

$$X(t,T) = N(t)\exp\left\{-\int_t^T \lambda(t,s)ds\right\}$$

Since $\lambda(t) = \lambda(t,t)$ is the intensity of $N(t)$, the process:

$$N(t) + \int_0^t \lambda(s)N(s)ds$$

is a martingale. Assume that $\lambda(t,T)$ satisfies Assumption 1:

$$d\lambda(t,T) = b(t,T)dt + \gamma^*(t,T)dW(t)$$

By our theorem:

$$b(t,T) = \gamma^*(t,T)\int_t^T \gamma(t,s)ds$$

which is, again, the Heath-Jarrow-Morton condition. Hence, the Heath-Jarrow-Morton model works also in the case of credit risk.

The initial spread term structure depends on the initial term structure of $\lambda$. If the recovery rate is zero, they are equal to each other. So the main benefit of using Heath-Jarrow-Morton is preserved – the model is fully specified by the initial term structure of $\lambda$ and its volatility structure. If the recovery rate is not equal to zero and it may be represented as:

$$\delta(\tau) = \delta B(\tau,T)$$

where $\tau$ is the default time and $\delta$ is the deterministic constant between zero and one, the risky bond may be treated as a portfolio containing risk-free bonds and risky bonds with recovery rate equal to zero. If the recovery rate is random, it is impossible to hedge against its changes and the market become incomplete unless the recovery rate itself is tradeable.

We note that default probability per unit time $\lambda$ is not prevented from being negative in this model. While it is possible to imagine negative interest rates, there is no reasonable interpretation for negative probability. Therefore, the use of the Gaussian Heath-Jarrow-Morton credit risk model becomes more controversial than that of the Gaussian Heath–Jarrow–Morton interest rates model. All questions dealing with interest rate models (such as the Markov representation) remain unanswered in the case of credit risk.

BIBLIOGRAPHY

**Baxter, M., and A. Rennie,** 1997, *Financial Calculus*, (Cambridge University Press).

**Duffie, D., and K. Singleton,** 1999, "Modeling Term Structures of Defaultable Bonds", *The Review of Financial Studies*, 12(4), pp. 687–720.

**Heath, D., R. Jarrow and A. Morton,** 1992, "Bond Pricing and the Term Structure of Interest Rates: A New Methodology", *Econometrica*, 61, pp. 77–105.

**Jarrow, R., and S. Turnbull,** 1995, "Pricing derivatives on financial securities subject to credit risk", *Journal of Finance*, 50, March, pp. 53–85.

**Jarrow, R., D. Lando and S. Turnbull,** 1997, "A Markov Model for the Term Structure of Credit Risk Spreads", *Review of Financial Studies*, 10, Summer, pp. 481–523.

**Metivier, M.,** 1982, *Semimartingales*, (Berlin: De Gruyter).

**Schönbucher, P. J.,** 1998, "The Term Structure of Defaultable Bond Prices", *The Review of Derivatives Research*, 2(2/3), Fall, pp. 161–92.

3

# The Price of Credit

**Vladimir Finkelstein, Bruce Broder and Philippe Khuong-Huu**
Goldman Sachs; JP Morgan; Goldman Sachs

Generating a zero-coupon curve is the first step in pricing any derivative structure, as any practitioner of interest rate derivatives knows. To generate the curve, one needs to calibrate it to the market prices of benchmark instruments, eg, par interest rate swaps. Although there is no unique way to do this, the term structure of par swap coupons is "dense" enough to leave very little uncertainty about discount factors, as well as the zero-coupon and forward rates.[1]

In the rapidly growing business of credit derivatives, participants face a similar but more challenging problem. Consistent pricing and risk management needs to be based on robust estimates of the term structure of default probabilities implied by the market. However, the market prices of liquid instruments exposed to default risk, such as corporate or sovereign bonds, and par spreads of asset swaps and credit default swaps (CDSs), do not provide this information directly. In addition to default probabilities, these prices depend on the level of default-free interest rates and recovery value, which will be paid to investors on default. As a result, to generate the term structure of default probabilities for a specific obligor from the market prices of risky and risk-free instruments one needs to make several assumptions.[2]

The most important of these is concerned with the recovery value of the traded risky security. This amount can be represented as $R*DC_t$, where $DC_t$ is the investor's claim submitted upon default at time t and R is the recovery fraction ($0 \le R \le 1$). The recovery fraction, R, is a parameter with much uncertainty. One can estimate the expected value of R using historical data and make assumptions about its distribution, but even this is little more than an educated guess.

The value of the investor's claim upon default of a traded risky bond has been the subject of much discussion (see, eg, Jarrow and Turnbull, 1995; Duffie and Singleton, 1999; Duffie, 1998; Madan and Unal, 1999; and Jarrow, Lando and Turnbull, 1997). Jarrow and Turnbull (1995) define the claim as the present value at the time of default of a risk-free bond with an identical cashflow structure to the original bond (risk-free claim). In contrast, Duffie and Singleton (1999) define the claim as the market price of the risky bond immediately before the default event occurs (risky claim). The two definitions are quite different. In particular, the former default claim is always larger than the latter. However, in both cases the risky bond is "strippable", in that it can be represented as the sum of discounted risky cashflows, each with the same type of default claim as the security itself. Thus, under both definitions the risky zero-coupon bond $Z_R(0, t)$ with an embedded recovery value is the building block for all bond analytics, just like the risk-free zero-coupon bond in conventional interest rate calculations. The price of a risky bond of maturity M paying coupons $C_i$ at times $t_i$, $i = 1,\ldots, N$, where $t_N = M$, can be represented as:

$$B_M(t=0) = \sum_{i=1}^{N} \Delta_i \hat{C}_i Z_R(0,t_i) + Z_R(0,M) \qquad (1)$$

where $\hat{C}_i$ is the forward expected value of coupon payments and $\Delta_i$ is the coupon day count fraction. The price of the risky zero-coupon bond, $Z_R(0, t)$, can be expressed in terms of the price of a risk-free zero-coupon bond, $D(0, t)$, via:

$$Z_R(0,t) = \frac{D(0,t)}{(1+S_q(0,t))^t} \qquad (2)$$

where $S_q(0, t)$ is the annualised quoted credit spread, commonly used by market participants.

Apart from some computational problems associated with the risk-free and risky claims (which we will not discuss here), these definitions are inconsistent with market practice. Analysis of legal documentation shows that

*This chapter was a Masterclass paper with JP Morgan in* Risk *Magazine. JP Morgan is a member of the London Stock Exchange and is regulated by the Securities and Futures Authority.*

the investor's claim upon default for a traded coupon bond with no guaranties, be it corporate or sovereign with a fixed or floating coupon, is given by the outstanding principal amount plus the accrued interest on the last coupon.[3] As a result, for a unit notional the default claim is always close to par. This depends only slightly on the actual coupon and does not depend at all on the bond maturity. Following Duffie (1998), we call this type of claim a "par claim".[4] We believe this is the only type of default claim for publicly traded bonds that should be used to calculate default probabilities (over-the-counter deals may have all kinds of tailored default arrangements). Below, we show that with this default claim definition, generation of the default probability term structure is straightforward and the results may have important consequences for relative value analysis. We also estimate the impact of correlation between credit spreads and risk-free interest rates on the pricing of CDSs and risky bonds.

The currency of the OTC deal is often different from the one in which credit default spreads are well defined and hedging instruments are available. As a result, to ensure consistent pricing and risk management one needs to analyse the relationship between default spreads of the same obligor in two currencies. We show that the correlation between the credit spread and the forward foreign exchange rate has a significant effect on this relationship.

## Calibrating default probabilities

We consider the problem within a standard risk-neutral framework with instantaneous default-free (risk-free) rate $r_t$. We set the value date as $t = 0$. Then, in the risk-neutral measure Q, the price of a default-free (risk-free) zero-coupon bond, $D(0, t)$, is given by the expectation:

$$D(0,t) = E_0^Q\left[\exp\left(-\int_0^t r_\tau d\tau\right)\right]$$

The instantaneous risk-free forward rate $\hat{r}_t$ is defined by:

$$\hat{r}_t = \frac{-d\ln D(0,t)}{dt}$$

The market gives the term structure of these rates.

To describe a default event, we introduce a time-dependent (and possibly stochastic) variable $s_\tau$, which gives the "risk-neutral" probability of default $s_\tau d\tau$ between time $\tau$ and $\tau + d\tau$ conditional on no default before time $\tau$. This default probability per unit time, $s_\tau$, does not generally coincide with the real probability of default. The expected value of this probability is estimated from the market prices of risky instruments. Writing $Z(0, t)$ for the price of a risky zero-coupon bond that pays US$1 at time t if there is no default between 0 and t, and otherwise pays zero, one has:

$$\begin{aligned} Z(0,t) &= E_0^Q\left[z_s(0,t)\right] \\ z_s(0,t) &= \exp\left(-\int_0^t (r_\tau + s_\tau)d\tau\right) \end{aligned} \tag{3}$$

(Lando, 1997). We call $Z(0, t)$ the clean risky discounting factor, to emphasise the zero recovery value. The default probability per unit time, $s_\tau$, can therefore be interpreted as an instantaneous clean credit spread. The additional discount factor $p(0, t)$, given by:

$$\begin{aligned} p(0,t) &= \frac{Z(0,t)}{D(0,t)} \\ &= \exp\left(-\int_0^t \hat{s}_\tau d\tau\right) \le 1 \end{aligned} \tag{4}$$

can be viewed as the probability of no default between time 0 and t, and the clean forward instantaneous credit spread, $\hat{s}_t$, as the forward probability of default per unit time.

The present value of a payout $A(t)$ made at time t under no default conditions can be expressed as:

$$\begin{aligned} PV_{ND}(A) &= E_0^Q\left[A(t)z_s(0,t)\right] \\ &= \hat{A}_{ND}(t)Z(0,t) \end{aligned} \tag{5}$$

where $\hat{A}_{ND}(t)$ is the forward value of the payout conditional on no default. If there is a non-zero correlation between clean credit spreads and risk-free interest rates, $\hat{A}_{ND}(t)$ can differ from the unconditional forward price even for a payout with no default exposure, such as the payout on a risk-free floating rate.

For a security paying $A_D(t)$ if default occurs between time $t - dt$ and t one has:

$$PV_D(A_D) = E_0^Q\left[A_D(t)z_s(0,t)s_t dt\right]$$

Pricing any defaultable financial instrument, whether for market-making purposes, relative value analysis or marking-to-market of existing deals, involves two steps. First, using market prices of risk-free zero-coupon (discount) bonds, generate a clean risky discounting curve. This involves choosing a set of risky benchmark instruments for a given obligor and making assumptions concerning the recovery value. Second, for the given structure under consideration, specify a recovery value in default and calculate the price by adding up the discounted cashflows contingent on default and no default scenarios.

Consider again the pricing of a risky bond described in Equation 1, this time using the "par claim" definition:

$$DC_t = 1 + C_i(t - t_{i-1}) \tag{6}$$

where $t_{i-1} \le t \le t_i$. Assuming that the recovery fraction R has an expected value of $\bar{R}$ and is not correlated with interest rates and credit spreads, one has:

$$B_M(t=0) = \sum_{i=1}^{N} \Delta_i \hat{C}_{i,ND} Z(0,t_i) + Z(0,M) + \sum_{i=1}^{N} \bar{R} E_0^Q \left[ \int_{t_{i-1}}^{t_i} (1 + C_i(t - t_{i-1} + \delta_{i1})) s_t z_s(0,t) dt \right] \tag{7}$$

where the value date corresponds to $t_0 = 0$, and the day count adjustment is non-zero only for $i = 1$ and accounts for the claim on accrued interest from the last coupon date until the value date. The first and second sums in Equation 7 represent the payments conditional on no default and default respectively.

Consider, for example, the price of a risky bond paying a floating coupon $(L_{i-1} + S_B)$ with frequency $\Delta_i = \Delta$, where $L_{i-1}$ is a money market default-free rate and $S_B$ is a constant spread, just after a coupon date (that is, $\delta_{11} = 0$). After some minor simplifications that introduce only slight inaccuracy, one can get a useful approximation in the form:

$$\begin{aligned} B_M(t=0) &\approx \Delta \sum_{i=1}^{N} \left( S_B + (1 - \bar{R}_S) \hat{L}_{i-1,ND} \right) Z(0,t_i) + (1 - \bar{R}_S) Z(0,M) + \bar{R}_S \\ &= \Delta \sum_{i=1}^{N} \left[ \left( S_B + (1 - \bar{R}_S) \hat{L}_{i-1,ND} \right) Z(0,t_i) + \bar{R}_S \hat{L}_{i-1} D(0,t_i) \right] \\ &\quad + (1 - \bar{R}_S) Z(0,M) + \bar{R}_S D(0,M) \end{aligned} \tag{8}$$

where $\bar{R}_S = \bar{R}(1 + 0.5 S_B \Delta)$, $\hat{L}_{i-1}$ and $\hat{L}_{i-1,ND}$ are respectively unconditional and conditional on no default forward rates. From Equation 8, one can see that the coupon and principal cashflows are treated very differently in default. The claim on a payment of principal is given by the face value at maturity, just like for the risk-free claim. However, the claim on a risky coupon payment is equal to $L_{i-1}$ at the coupon date regardless of the actual level of the coupon. Thus, unlike the risk-free and risky claims, with a par claim there is no such thing as a "generic" risky zero-coupon bond, $Z_R(0,t)$, with an embedded recovery value. In this case, the clean risky discounting factors, $Z(0,t)$, should be used as building blocks for risky bond analytics. To price any credit derivative instrument, including risky zero-coupon bonds with non-zero recovery, one needs to specify clearly the structure of the default claim and use the clean risky curve to calculate the value.

It is often assumed that the quoted credit spread, $S_q(0,t)$, provides an accurate measure of default risk and so bonds traded at the same quoted credit spread are equally risky. Both risk-free and risky claim definitions confirm this conclusion. However, if a bond defaults according to the par claim, this is not correct. For the same recovery fraction, $\bar{R}$, and clean risky zero-coupon curve, $Z(0,t)$, and thus the same default probabilities, a bond with a higher coupon should trade on a higher quoted spread than a bond with a lower coupon. It is easy to understand why. At default, both bonds collapse to almost the same recovery value. As a result, holding a bond with a high coupon places more money at risk than investing in a lower-coupon bond and so demands a higher return in a no-default situation. The example shown in Table 1 corresponds to a risk-free flat curve of 6% and a flat par credit spread curve of 10% (not unusual in emerging markets). The bonds of all maturities paying an annual 16% coupon are traded at par (US$100), and the quoted credit spread is 9.43%. For all three claim definitions, we calibrate default probabilities to this market, and price two fixed-coupon bonds of 10-year maturity, paying respectively 7% and 21% coupons, with a recovery fraction of 0.2. For

**Table 1. Effect of default claim type on prices and spreads**

| | Price for risk-free/ risky claim | Quoted spread for risk-free/ risky claim | Price for par claim | Quoted spread for par claim |
|---|---|---|---|---|
| Bond with 7% coupon | 56.50 | 9.43% | 60.26 | 8.38% |
| Bond with 21% coupon | 124.16 | 9.43% | 122.08 | 9.78% |

both risk-free and risky claims, the quoted credit spread of these bonds is still 9.43%. However, for the par claim, the prices and quoted spreads of discount and premium bonds differ from those calculated using the other two claim definitions.

In reality, using bonds for calibration of the clean risky curve is often difficult. Usually, there are not many bonds available for a given obligor that one can use, they can differ in funding costs and liquidity, and can be affected by supply/demand biases. However, rapid development of a CDS market allows one to use par spreads of different maturities (running cost of default protection for a particular obligor) to estimate $Z(0, t)$. In a credit default swap of maturity M, the protection buyer pays a fee $F_M$ to the protection seller as long as default does not occur. If default takes place, the protection seller pays the swap notional to the buyer and receives the recovery value of the reference risky bond plus the accrued fee from the last coupon payment date. A standard CDS has a pool of deliverable reference bonds with a cheapest-to-deliver provision. As a result, it is safe to assume that, for a given obligor, all CDSs should be characterised by the same recovery value, independent of CDS maturity and the fee being paid.

For a par CDS with coupon $F_M^{par}$, the present values of the two contingent swap legs (no default and default) should be equal, leading to the equation:

$$F_M^{par}\sum_{i=1}^{N}\Delta_i Z(0,t_i) = \sum_{i=1}^{N}\int_{t_{i-1}}^{t_i}\left[1-\hat{R}_t - F_M^{par}(t-t_{i-1})\right]\hat{s}_{t,ND}Z(0,t)dt \quad (9)$$

where $\hat{R}_t = \bar{R} * DC_t$ is the recovery value of the reference bond, $DC_t$ is the par default claim given by Equation 6 and $\hat{s}_{t,ND}$ is the clean forward credit spread conditional on no default. To generate the clean risky discount curve using Equation 9 one needs to determine the expected values on the right-hand side of the equation. If there is no correlation between risk-free interest rates and clean credit spreads, the conditional and unconditional forward clean spreads are equal, $\hat{s}_{t,ND} = \hat{s}_t$, and the solution is straightforward. For a given term structure of par spreads (fees) $F_M^{par}$ and prices of risk-free zero-coupon bonds $D(0, t)$, utilising the standard "boot-strapping" method in Equation 9 and taking into account Equation 4, one can determine the term structure of forward default probabilities $\hat{s}_t$ and prices of clean risky zero-coupon bonds $Z(0, t)$.

**1. Adjustment to forward spreads due to correlation**

Adjustment for a forward clean spread increases for higher correlation $\rho$ between credit spreads and interest rates. All curves are flat

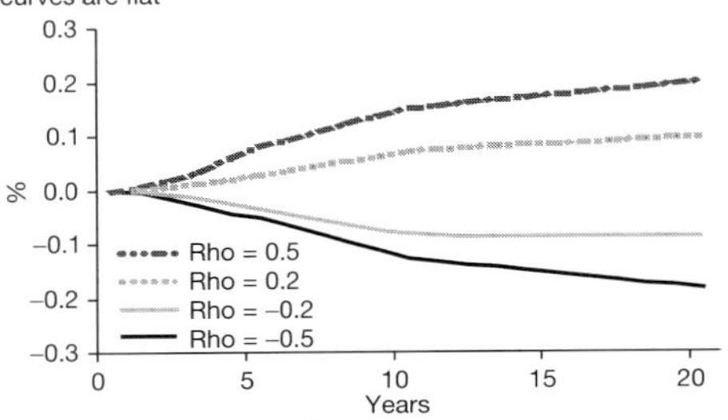


Other parameters: $\hat{r} = 5\%$, $\hat{s} = 5\%$, interest rate volatility $\sigma_r = 15\%$ and mean reversion speed $\beta_r = 0.1$, credit spread volatility $\sigma_s = 80\%$ and mean reversion speed $\beta_s = 0.4$.

For a non-zero correlation between risk-free rates and clean credit spreads, calculating the correlation adjustment $(\hat{s}_{t,ND} - \hat{s}_t)$ should be part of each step of the "boot-strapping". The adjustment obtained using Monte Carlo simulations is shown in Figure 1 for lognormal mean-reverting risk-free interest rates and clean credit spreads.[5] The adjustment increases with increasing correlation, volatility, rate level and spread level. It is larger for longer maturity, and decreases with increasing mean reversion. In particular, for positive correlation, $\hat{s}_{t,ND}$ is higher than $\hat{s}_t$. As a result, for a given term structure of par spreads $F_M^{par}$, the forward default probabilities, $\hat{s}_t$, calibrated using Equation 9, would decrease.

The price of a risky bond would be affected differently by rate/spread correlation. Forward values of risk-free interest rates, $\hat{r}_{t,ND}$, conditional on no default are given by $\hat{r}_{t,ND}, = \hat{r}_t + \hat{s}_t - \hat{s}_{t,ND}$ as:

$$\hat{r}_{t,ND} + \hat{s}_{t,ND} = \frac{E_0^Q\left[(r_t + s_t)z_s(0,t)\right]}{Z(0,t)} = -\frac{dZ(0,t)/dt}{Z(0,t)} = \hat{r}_t + \hat{s}_t \quad (10)$$

In particular, for positive correlation, $\hat{r}_{t,ND}$, is lower than $\hat{r}_t$, and thus $\hat{L}_{i,ND}, < \hat{L}_i$. For a given clean credit spread curve, one can see from Equation 7 that the price of a fixed-coupon risky bond increases with rising correlation as the contribution of the recovery value to the bond price goes up. However, for a risky floater paying the money market risk-free rate plus spread, the effect is reversed. The decrease in the value of floating coupons conditional on no default is more important than the increase of the recovery value contribution, and the price of the floater goes down with increasing correlation.

## Different currencies

It is often important to know the relation between the clean risky discount curve of the same obligor in two currencies. For example, a market-maker may need to sell default protection on a particular company in Japanese yen (foreign currency), while, owing to good liquidity, the CDS par spread for this name may be much better defined in US dollars (domestic currency). One would be tempted to price a CDS or a synthetic note in Japanese yen using the US dollar forward clean credit spreads, $\hat{s}_t$, and risk-free rates corresponding to a new currency (eg, Japanese yen risk-free rates). However, as a clean risky zero-coupon bond pays only in the case of no default, one needs to use the no-default forex forward rate rather than the unconditional one in pricing a synthetic clean risky zero-coupon note $Z_\Phi(0,t)$ in foreign currency. If correlation exists between the forex rate and interest rates in both currencies on one side and the credit spread on the other, there should be a correlation adjustment to the credit spread curve in the foreign currency. This adjustment has the same origin as the well-known "quanto adjustment" for currency protected structures. There are two types of contribution to this adjustment.

The first is brought about by a possible jump in the exchange rate in the case of default. For example, let the foreign currency depreciate by a fraction $\alpha(\alpha < 1)$ if the obligor defaults. The probability of this event is given by the clean spread $s_t$. To satisfy the unconditional forward forex rate $\hat{X}(t, t + dt)$ (the number of units of foreign currency per US dollar at time t), the forward forex rate conditional on no default, $\hat{X}_{ND}(t, t + dt)$, should be lower than $\hat{X}(t, t + dt)$ by $\exp(-\alpha s_\tau d\tau)$ times. As a result, the no-default forex rate can be represented as:

$$X_{ND}(t) = X(t)\exp\left(-\alpha\int_0^t s_\tau d\tau\right) \tag{11}$$

where $X(t)$ has the same drift given by the interest rate differential as the unconditional forex rate at time t, and the forward forex rate, $\hat{X}(0,t)$, is given by:

$$\hat{X}(0,t)^{-1} = \frac{E_0^Q\left[X(t)^{-1}\exp\left(-\int_0^t r_\tau d\tau\right)\right]}{D(0,t)} \tag{12}$$

The second exposure arises from correlated movements of the exchange rate and credit spread under no default conditions. Dynamic hedging of the synthetic note $Z_\Phi(0,t)$ with the dollar-denominated one, $Z(0,t)$, would result in a second-order (gamma) effect on the hedger's profit and loss. For example, for a short position in $Z_\Phi(0,t)$, as the dollar strengthens one would need to sell part of the hedge in $Z(0,t)$. If the credit spread is positively correlated with the dollar, it would widen with the dollar getting stronger, the hedger's profit and loss would suffer, and this additional expense would need to be passed to the buyer of $Z_\Phi(0,t)$ in the form of a negative credit spread adjustment.

To calculate the adjustment, assume that the credit spreads are generated in dollars and we wish to price a synthetic note in currency Φ. Consider a risky payment in currency Φ with maturity t and zero recovery value. For clean forward spreads, standard no-arbitrage considerations lead to:

$$\exp\left(-\int_0^t \hat{s}_{\Phi,\tau} d\tau\right) = \frac{Z_\Phi(0,t)}{D_\Phi(0,t)} = E_0^Q\left[X(t)^{-1}\exp\left(-\int_0^t ((1-\alpha)s_\tau + r_\tau)d\tau\right)\right]\frac{X(0)}{D_\Phi(0,t)} \tag{13}$$

where $D_\Phi(0,t)$ is a risk-free zero-coupon bond in currency Φ.

We calculate the adjustment to a clean credit spread numerically using Monte Carlo simulation for lognormal forex rates, lognormal and mean-reverting credit spreads, and risk-free interest rates in both currencies. Figure 2 shows the effect of mean reversion on the size of the spread adjustment. The devaluation parameter $\alpha = 0.2$ leads to a contribution of –60 basis points (bp) even for short maturities. The rest of the adjustment depends on the correlation between the forward forex rate and clean credit spreads, and grows

**2. Effect of mean reversion on lognormal spread adjustment**

Spread adjustment decreases with increasing mean reversion of credit spreads

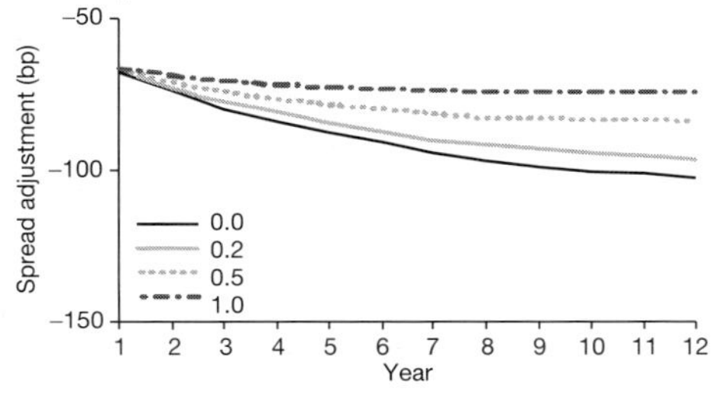


Other parameters: $\alpha = 0.2$, $\hat{r}_\$ = 5\%$, $\hat{r}_\Phi = 4\%$, $\hat{s} = 3\%$, interest rate volatility $\sigma_\$ = 12.5\%$, $\sigma_\Phi = 15\%$ and mean reversion spread $\beta_\$ = \beta_\Phi = 0.1$, forex volatility $\sigma_x = 20\%$, credit spread volatility $\sigma_s = 80\%$ and correlation parameters $\rho_{\$S} = \rho_{\Phi S} = 0.05$, $\rho_{xs} = 0.4$.

gradually with increasing maturity. Even for moderate volatility levels, this contribution can reach –40 bp for longer maturities and low-spread mean reversion. The adjustment gradually decreases for increasing mean reversion, similar to the adjustment discussed at the end of the previous section.

It is often convenient to have a closed-form solution for the adjustment to speed up the calculations. To obtain this, one may assume the spot exchange rate $X(t)$ to be lognormally distributed with volatility $\sigma_X$, and interest rates in both currencies and the credit spread to be normal stochastic variables characterised by forward spot volatilities and mean-reversion coefficients. Again, the normal model for credit spreads does not seem reasonable.[5] However, in some important cases the closed-form solution provides a reasonably accurate approximation to the simulation results, which used a more realistic spread distribution. The discount clean credit spread:

$$S_{\Phi}^{cl}(0,t) = t^{-1}\int_0^t \hat{s}_{\Phi,\tau}d\tau \tag{14}$$

is given by:

$$S_{\Phi}^{cl}(0,t) = S^{cl}(0,t) + \delta S(0,t)$$

where:

$$S^{cl}(0,t) = t^{-1}\int_0^t \hat{s}_{\tau}d\tau$$

is the discount clean credit spread in dollars and the spread adjustment has the form:

$$\begin{aligned}\delta S(0,t) = {} & -\alpha S^{cl}(0,t) + \frac{(1-\alpha)\alpha}{2t}\int_0^t \sigma_s^2\left(\frac{1-e^{-\beta_s(t-\tau)}}{\beta_s}\right)^2 d\tau \\ & + \frac{1-\alpha}{t}\int_0^t \sigma_s \frac{1-e^{-\beta_s(t-\tau)}}{\beta_s} \\ & \times\left[\sigma_s\rho_{\$s}\left(\frac{1-e^{-\beta_\$(t-\tau)}}{\beta_\$}\right) - \sigma_\Phi\rho_{\Phi s}\left(\frac{1-e^{\beta_\Phi(t-\tau)}}{\beta_\Phi}\right) - \sigma_X\rho_{Xs}\right]d\tau\end{aligned} \tag{15}$$

where $\sigma_s$ is the default spread basis-point volatility, $\sigma_\$$ and $\sigma_\Phi$ are the basis-point spot volatilities for the interest rates in the two currencies, $\sigma_X$ is the spot forex rate volatility, $\rho_{\$_S}$ and $\rho_{\Phi_S}$ are the correlation between the interest rates in the two currencies and the credit spread, $\rho_{X_S}$ is the correlation between the spot forex rate and the credit spread, and $\beta_S$, $\beta_\$$ and $\beta_\Phi$ are the mean-reversion coefficients for credit spread and interest rates.

Analysing Equation 15, one can see that significant devaluation in the case of default may result in a very substantial spread adjustment even for short maturities. Another important feature is the role of mean reversion. As the spot volatility of the credit spread may be very high (above 100% in percentage terms), one should expect mean reversion to be strong. Without it, in a few years the credit spread might easily reach extremely high or low levels. This, in particular, might result in an unrealistically large spread adjustment.

Comparing the closed-form solution seen in Equation 15 with the simulation results, one finds that for small correlation parameters and values of $\alpha$ as well as low volatility levels, the adjustment is small and the difference is not very significant. However, if the risky synthetic note is issued in a currency strongly correlated with credit spreads, for example a Mexican peso note with Mexican default exposure, the adjustment can be substantial for reasonable spread and volatility levels, as can the differences between the two adjustment calculations.

The difference in the spread is largest for zero mean reversion, and the closed-form adjustment in this case can be inaccurate. However, for higher mean reversion, the difference is reduced substantially and the closed-form approximation can be applicable.

1 *One can get two-way reliable quotes for maturities up to 30 years with one-year increments.*

2 *Risk here is just associated with a possibility of default of the obligor.*

3 *See, for example, the* Offering Circular for the Russian Federation 10% Bonds due 2007, *October 28, 1997, page 11, or the* Prospectus Supplement for Tyco International 6.125% Notes due 2009 and 6.875% Notes due 2029, *January 7, 1999, page 16.*

4 *In Duffie (1998), the claim on the accrued interest was not taken into account.*

5 *Under the assumption of normal interest rates and clean credit spreads, the correlation adjustment can be calculated in a closed form. Although this assumption does not seem reasonable (clean credit spreads cannot be negative as they determine the probability of default, and thus cannot be normally distributed), for strong mean reversion of spreads the closed-form approximation may be of adequate accuracy.*

**BIBLIOGRAPHY**

**Duffie, D.,** 1998, "Defaultable Term Structure Models with Fractional Recovery Value of Par", Working Paper, Graduate School of Business, Stanford University.

**Duffie, D., and K. Singleton,** 1999, "Modeling Term Structures of Defaultable Bonds", *Review of Financial Studies*, 12, pp. 687–720.

**Jarrow, R., and S. Turnbull,** 1995, "Pricing Options on Financial Securities Subject to Default Risk", *Journal of Finance*, 50, pp. 53–85.

**Jarrow, R., D. Lando and S. Turnbull,** 1997, "A Markov Model for the Term Structure of Credit Risk Spreads", *Review of Financial Studies*, 10, pp. 481–523.

**Lando, D.,** 1997, "Modelling Bonds and Derivatives with Default Risk", in M. Dempster and S. Pliska (eds), *Mathematics of Derivative Securities*, pp. 369–93 (Cambridge University Press).

**Madan, D., and H. Unal,** 1999, "A Two-Factor Hazard-Rate Model for Pricing Risky Debt and the Term Structure of Credit Spreads", Working Paper, RH Smith School of Business, University of Maryland.

4

# Price and Probability

**Richard Martin, Kevin Thompson and Christopher Browne**

BNP Paribas; DrKW

*The extraction of implied forward default probabilities from default swap prices presents many theoretical and practical difficulties. Here, Richard Martin, Kevin Thompson and Christopher Browne develop an innovative optimisation method using the conditional probability of default over a period to address the problem. The approach gives significantly better results than the traditional bootstrap method.*

The term structure of credit risk is a fundamental parameter in marking-to-market credit-risky instruments such as insurance products, structured deals (eg, collateralised loan obligations) and credit derivatives, and also in marking-to-market counterparty risk on standard derivatives contracts. How to obtain the term structure from prices of traded instruments is an important issue that is still an active area of research. In this chapter, we present a new method by which the term structure of credit risk can be extracted from the prices of credit default swaps, which are an ideal financial instrument for the purpose.

In a standard T-year credit default swap, a protection buyer pays a fixed periodic premium, $X_T$, to a protection seller, in return for a guaranteed payment if the reference entity defaults. The contingent payout is generally equivalent to the non-recoverable fraction of the reference asset's value at the time of default. For the sake of simplicity, suppose that the payout upon default is $(1 - \delta)N$, for some assumed recovery rate $\delta$ and notional amount N. Let us also ignore any accrued premiums that may be outstanding at the time of default. The premium $X_T$ is dictated by the market view of the likelihood of default before the maturity date. When a number of such instruments are traded, on the same reference but with different maturities, it is possible to derive a set of market-implied default probabilities by equating the present value of the premium and payout legs.

The instantaneous forward rate of default (or forward hazard rate) at date $t + T$, as viewed from date t, is defined as:

$$\lambda_t(T) \equiv -\frac{\partial}{\partial T}\ln\left(1 - Q_t(T)\right)$$

where $Q_t(T)$ is the cumulative probability of default in the interval $[t, t + T]$ viewed from date t. Let $\lambda(T) \equiv \lambda_0(T)$ be the instantaneous forward rate of default as viewed from today (time 0). Then the probability of default occurring by time T is:

$$Q(T) \equiv Q_0(T) = 1 - \exp\left(-\int_0^T \lambda(u)du\right)$$

and the instantaneous probability of default at time $\tau$, given survival to that date, is:

$$\lambda(\tau)\exp\left(-\int_0^\tau \lambda(u)du\right)$$

Supposing that the default swap premium payments are to be made at times $T_1, \ldots, T_F$, the following equation relates the premium paid and market-implied instantaneous forward rate of default:

$$\sum_{i=1}^{F}\exp\left(-\int_0^{T_i}\lambda(u)du\right)D(T_i)X_T = (1-\delta)\int_0^T \lambda(\tau)\exp\left(-\int_0^\tau \lambda(u)du\right)D(\tau)d\tau \qquad (1)$$

Here we have divided through by the notional so that $X_T$ denotes the default swap rate (the fraction of the notional to be paid as premiums). $D(T)$ denotes the discount factor for maturity $T$.

## Bootstrap method

The usual way of calculating the market implied default probabilities is as follows. If default swaps of maturities $T^{(1)} < T^{(2)} < \cdots < T^{(M)}$ are traded in the market at rates $X_{T^{(1)}}, X_{T^{(2)}}, \ldots, X_{T^{(M)}}$, then there is a version of Equation 1 corresponding to each maturity. The usual procedure is to approximate the integral on the right-hand side of each of these equations by discretising over maturity dates and using piecewise constants or some spline approximation to $\lambda(t)$ on each interval $[T^{(j)}, T^{(j+1)}]$. The resulting system of equations is then solved sequentially to extract values $\lambda_j \equiv \lambda(T^{(j)})$ at each maturity date. The expression:

$$X_T = \frac{(1-\delta)\int_0^T \lambda(\tau)\exp\left(-\int_0^\tau \lambda(u)du\right)D(\tau)\,d\tau}{\sum_{i=1}^{F}\exp\left(-\int_0^{T_i}\lambda(u)du\right)D(T_i)} \quad (2)$$

can then be used to estimate the premium charged for a default swap of any maturity $T$, where $F$ is the number of payments made up to time $T$.

There are three significant problems with the bootstrap method:

- It is iterative: each $\lambda_{j+1}$ is a function of $\lambda_1, \ldots, \lambda_j$. Consequently, a single unreliable quote $X_{T^{(j)}}$ will give an unreliable estimate not only for $\lambda_j$ but also for all the subsequent rates.
- Interpolation methods such as linear splines can give rise to problematic "negative forward default rates", $\lambda_j$, for certain sets of market quotes.
- One can determine only as many $\lambda_j$ as there are quotes. The implied default swap rate curve (Equation 2 as a function of $T$) will exactly reproduce market quotes using these values, but relies on the spline interpolation of the forward probabilities to predict the price of non-traded maturities. Different interpolation schemes can give very different results.

## Proposed method

Suppose we replace the $\tau$-integral in the numerator of Equation 2 with a sum of $P$ integrals over the intervals $(t_i, t_{i+1})$, each interval being of length $\Delta$, in such a way that all cashflows occur at times that are integer multiples of $\Delta$ (with $t_0 = 0$ and $t_P = T$). Next, approximate the discount factor on each period by an average $D(t) \approx \frac{1}{2}(D(t_i) + D(t_{i+1}))$. This gives the following approximation to Equation 2:

$$X_T \approx \frac{(1-\delta)\sum_{i=0}^{P-1}\frac{1}{2}(D(t_i)+D(t_{i+1}))\int_{t_i}^{t_{i+1}}\lambda(\tau)\exp\left(-\int_0^\tau\lambda(u)du\right)d\tau}{\sum_{i=1}^{F}\exp\left(-\int_0^{T_i}\lambda(t)dt\right)D(T_i)} \quad (3)$$

Here the sum in the denominator is over premium payment dates, but that in the numerator is over the discretisation just described. Note that Equation 2 is regained as $\Delta \to 0$.

At this stage let us introduce the forward conditional probability of default in the period $(t_i, t_{i+1}]$:

$$q_i = 1 - \exp\left(-\int_{t_i}^{t_{i+1}}\lambda(t)dt\right) \qquad (0 \le i \le P-1)$$

The cumulative probability of default by time $t_i$ is:

$$Q(t_i) = 1 - \exp\left(-\int_0^{t_i}\lambda(t)dt\right)$$

which may be obtained from the forward probabilities $q_i$ via the recursion:

$$Q(t_{i+1}) = Q(t_i) + (1 - Q(t_i))q_i$$
$$Q(0) = 0$$

The integral in the numerator of Equation 3 is simply the difference between the cumulative probabilities of default at times $t_i$ and $t_{i+1}$. Therefore, Equation 3 can be rewritten as:

$$X_{T^{(j)}} \approx \frac{(1-\delta)\sum_{i=0}^{(T^{(j)}/\Delta)-1}\frac{1}{2}(D(t_i)+D(t_{i+1}))(1-Q(t_i))q_i}{\sum_{i=1}^{F^{(j)}}(1-Q(T_i))D(T_i)} \equiv R^{(j)}(q_0, \ldots, q_{P-1}) \quad (4)$$

Equation 4 suggests that it is easier, and more natural, to focus on $q_i$, the probability of default in the interval $(t_i, t_{i+1}]$, rather than on $\lambda(t)$, the instantaneous forward rate of default. This approach is analogous to that taken in the Brace-Gatarek-Musiela model (1997) for interest rates, where emphasis is on the directly observable $\Delta$-period forward Libor rate, rather than on the instantaneous forward rate used in the Heath-Jarrow-Morton (1992) approach.

The objective is then to find the q's such that the modelled quotes $R^{(j)}(q_0, \ldots, q_{P-1})$ agree with the observed market quotes $X_{T^{(j)}}$, or at least are acceptably close to them (for $j = 1, \ldots, M$). If we assume that $X_{T^{(j)}}$ is subject to a Gaussian error of variance $\sigma_j^2$ then an appropriate function to minimise is:

$$\frac{1}{2}\sum_{j=1}^{M}\left(\frac{X_{T^{(j)}} - R^{(j)}(q_0,\ldots,q_{P-1})}{\sigma_j}\right)^2 \qquad (5)$$

Unfortunately, the objective function in Equation 5 has M terms, which is insufficient to determine a complete set of P parameters when P > M. This is a problem when the desired discretisation of Equation 3 is fine or when there are only a few quotes to hand. More information is required if the objective function is to have a unique minimum. There is, however, an additional assumption that can be used, for it is intuitively reasonable to require that consecutive values of $q_i$ be close. We may state this more precisely by requiring that the set of $q_i$ should minimise:

$$G(q_0,\ldots,q_{P-1}) = v\sum_{i=0}^{P-1} d(q_{i+1};q_i)^2 + \frac{1}{2}\sum_{j=1}^{M}\left(\frac{X_{T^{(j)}} - R^{(j)}(q_0,\ldots,q_{P-1})}{\sigma_j}\right)^2 \qquad (6)$$

where we adopt the following measure of distance between two probabilities q′ and q:

$$d(q';q) = \sqrt{(q'-q)\ln\frac{q'}{q} + (q-q')\ln\left(\frac{1-q'}{1-q}\right)}$$

This is shown in Figure 1. Note that $d(q';q)$ is non-negative, with $d(q';q) = 0$ if and only if $q' = q$. For fixed q′, the distance measure tends to infinity as q tends to zero or one (and vice versa). This imposes an infinite penalty against negative probabilities (unlike the absolute difference measure $d(q';q) = |q' - q|$).[1] Therefore, unlike the bootstrap method, our procedure cannot give negative probabilities. The first term in Equation 6 will be large if consecutive $q_i$'s differ significantly, which provides a penalty against having a forward curve that is too rapidly varying; the second term is a penalty against not fitting the data well enough.[2] Thus minimisation of Equation 6 should give a sensible set of conditional forward probabilities while still fitting to market data. The parameter v controls the balance between the two terms.

## Numerical example

Table 1 contains a typical set of default swap quotes for maturities of one to 10 years, where the recovery rate for the reference in question was 30%. The table shows the actual versus modelled quotes for v equal to 10, 500 and 10,000 (having fixed $\sigma_j = 10^{-4}$ and assuming semi-annual premium payment dates). As expected, the lower the value of v, the better the fit to market data. For v = 10, the error between modelled and market quotes is less than 1/100th of a basis point for each maturity. The fit remains good even for v = 10,000, although this value will correspond to a much smoother set of forward conditional probabilities. Figure 2 displays the values of the $q_i$ for the cases v = 10 and v = 10,000 (taking a discretisation Δ = six months). v = 10 gives a very good fit of the market data. v = 10,000 corresponds to a less accurate fit, with the emphasis being on obtaining a smoother curve.

Figure 3 displays the "instantaneous" forward rates obtained from the same market quotes using the bootstrap approach with linear splines (where linear interpolation of quotes was used for years six, eight and nine). The method gives rise to negative rates that clearly cannot be interpreted

**1. The distance function of $d(q';q)^2$**

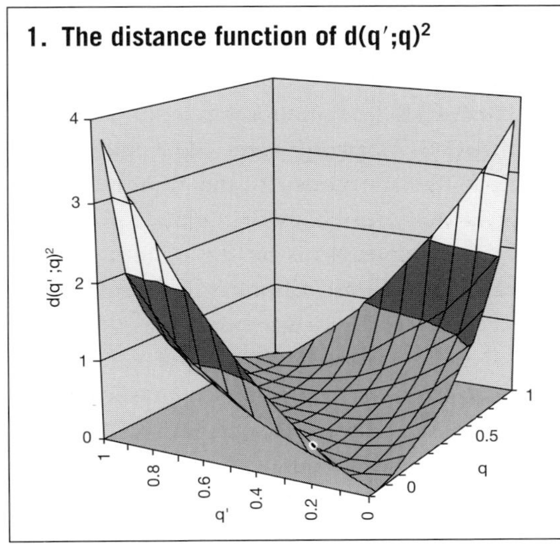


**Table 1. Default swap quotes**

| Maturity (years) | Discount factor | Market quote (bp) | Modelled quotes (bp) | | |
|---|---|---|---|---|---|
| | | | v = 10 | v = 500 | v = 10,000 |
| 1 | 0.931820 | 45 | 45.000 | 45.02 | 45.5 |
| 2 | 0.866762 | 55 | 55.001 | 55.04 | 54.8 |
| 3 | 0.806772 | 65 | 64.993 | 64.69 | 63.8 |
| 4 | 0.750876 | 70 | 70.013 | 70.60 | 74.3 |
| 5 | 0.699114 | 95 | 94.990 | 94.54 | 91.2 |
| 6 | 0.650255 | – | 102.980 | 102.74 | 100.6 |
| 7 | 0.604807 | 105 | 105.004 | 105.16 | 105.7 |
| 8 | 0.562855 | – | 108.005 | 108.25 | 109.5 |
| 9 | 0.523594 | – | 111.604 | 111.74 | 112.5 |
| 10 | 0.487314 | 115 | 114.999 | 114.97 | 115.0 |

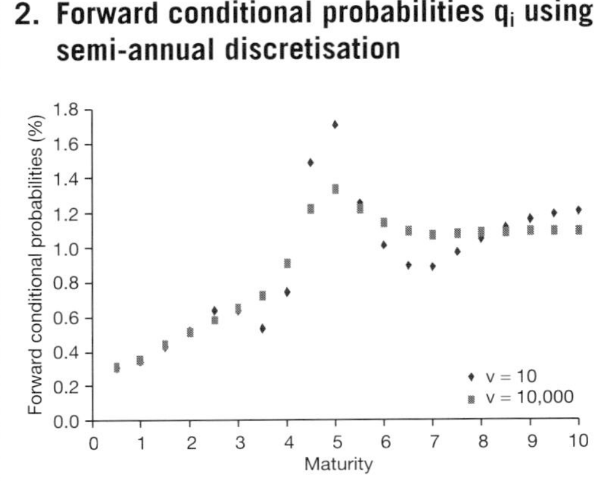


**2. Forward conditional probabilities $q_i$ using semi-annual discretisation**

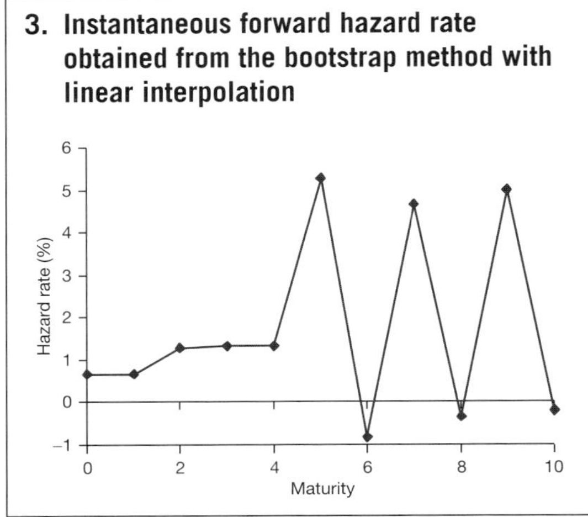


**3. Instantaneous forward hazard rate obtained from the bootstrap method with linear interpolation**

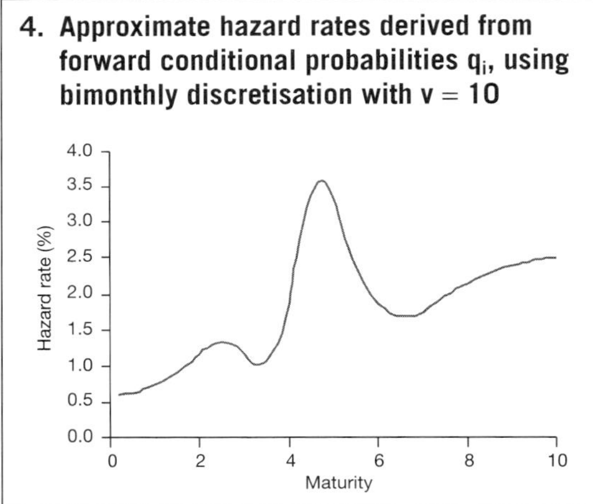


**4. Approximate hazard rates derived from forward conditional probabilities $q_i$, using bimonthly discretisation with v = 10**

as probabilities. This graph should be compared with the "rates" obtained from the new model by scaling the forward conditional probabilities by the time discretisation used. (Figure 4 shows the result using a discretisation of $\Delta$ = two months for the case v = 10.) It is apparent that, in the continuum limit $\Delta \rightarrow 0$, we have $q(t_i)/\Delta \sim \lambda(t_i)$. The continuum limit of this method could in principle be adopted as a method of fitting the continuous hazard rate function $\lambda(t)$. The results are clearly much more sensible than those achieved via the bootstrap method.

The maximum maturity considered in this example is 10 years, and time-discretisations of $\Delta$ = six months and $\Delta$ = two months were used for the results shown in Figures 2 and 4. This required the minimisation of the objective function depending on 20 and 60 parameters $q_i$, respectively. This might at first appear an extremely cumbersome computational task. Remarkably, though, in all the examples we have considered the method has proved to be fast and we have not encountered problems with multiple minima. (The minimisation for 20 parameters takes less than a second, and for 60 parameters about six seconds, on a Pentium machine; but no attempt has been made to optimise the minimisation algorithm.) The speed can be attributed to the ease of computation and presumed convexity of the objective function.

## Discussion

We have presented a new method by which the term structure of credit risk can be extracted from the prices of credit default swaps (though risky bonds could also be used). The method consists of choosing a time discretisation $\Delta$ and then finding a set of $\Delta$-period forward conditional default probabilities that give a smooth forward rate curve while also fitting the given prices. One has the option of giving equal weighting to all market quotes or giving lower weighting to those quotes believed to be unreliable. This is in contrast to current bootstrap algorithms where the bootstrapped instantaneous forward rate corresponding to an unreliable quote has an adverse effect on all remaining rates. Our method also obviates the problems associated with using splines to interpolate the bootstrapped rates. It also works well in situations where there is a limited amount of market data, and is robust in the presence of bad data (showing a tendency to be able to identify quotes that are underpriced or overpriced).

Further opportunities for research include the generalisation of this technique to include credit migration, in which ratings transitions as well as default events are modelled (Jarrow, Lando and Turnbull, 1997). The objective would be to obtain a set of forward transition matrices that allow a set of observed quotes to be fitted exactly, subject again to a constraint that successive matrices be "close".

1 *A related observation is that, for small probabilities, it is the ratio, as well as the absolute difference between* $q'$ *and* $q$ *that is important.*

2 *Minimisation of* $G$*, as given in Equation 6, can also be thought of as obtaining the maximum a posteriori estimate of* $(q_0,\ldots,q_{P-1})$*, if the prior density is:*

$$\mathrm{pr}(q_0,\ldots,q_{P-1}) \propto \prod_{i=0}^{P-2}\left(\frac{q_i}{1-q_i}\Big/\frac{q_{i+1}}{1-q_{i+1}}\right)^{v(q_{i+1}-q_i)}$$

**BIBLIOGRAPHY**

**Brace, A., D. Gatarek and M. Musiela,** 1997, "The Market Model of Interest Rate Dynamics", *Mathematical Finance*, 7(2), pp. 127-55.

**Heath, D., R. Jarrow and A. Morton,** 1992, "Bond Pricing and the Term Structure of Interest Rates: A New Methodology for Contingent Claims Valuation", *Econometrica*, 60, pp. 77-105.

**Jarrow, R., D. Lando and S. Turnbull,** 1997, "A Markov Model for the Term Structure of Credit Risk Spreads", *Review of Financial Studies*, 10(2), pp. 481-523.

5

# Distance to Default

**Marco Avellaneda and Jingyi Zhu**

Courant Institute of New York University; University of Utah

*So-called default barrier models were devised to enforce consistency between credit spread or ratings-based and firm value-based estimates of default probability, an important concern for the credit derivatives market. Here, Marco Avellaneda and Jingyi Zhu use a continuous time framework to recast this methodology as a control problem, which is then implemented numerically*

Credit derivatives provide synthetic protection against bond and loan defaults. A simple example of a credit derivative is the credit default swap, in which one counterparty makes periodic payments to another in exchange for the right to be paid a notional amount if a credit event happens. Recently, we have seen the emergence of "wholesale" credit protection in the form of first-to-default swaps written on a basket of underlying credits. Pricing credit derivatives requires quantifying the likelihood of default of the reference entity. Default probabilities can be estimated from the spreads of the bond issued by the reference entity.[1]

Two kinds of mathematical frameworks for pricing credit derivatives have been proposed: the structural models, introduced by Merton (1974) and others (Black and Cox, 1976, Brennan and Schwartz, 1980, Titman and Totous, 1989, Kim, Ramaswamy and Sundaresan, 1993, Shimko, Tejima and van Deventer, 1993, and Geske, 1977), and the reduced-form models of Duffie and Singleton (1999). Here, we are concerned with the structural approach, and in particular the "default barrier" methodology recently introduced by Hull and White (2001). This chapter draws from Hull and White (2001) and extends it in several directions.

First, we consider a continuous-time version of the Hull–White model in which the default index follows a general diffusion process. We show that, in this general framework, calibration of the default barrier leads to a new free boundary problem for the associated Fokker–Planck partial differential equation.

Second, based on these results, we propose a new interpretation of the default barrier model in terms of a risk-neutral distance-to-default process for the firm (or risk-neutral debt-to-value ratio, etc). We show that finding a default boundary that is calibrated to a set of default probabilities is equivalent to specifying an appropriate "excess drift" for the distance-to-default process. This excess drift can be interpreted as a market price of risk for the value of the firm, *à la* Merton (1974), which renders the process consistent with observed credit spreads.

Finally, we discuss the numerical implementation of the model, using a finite difference scheme for the Fokker–Planck equation, coupled with a Newton–Raphson scheme for determining the excess drift at each successive time step. The theory is applied to calculating the default boundaries and drifts for AAA and BAA1 credits under different assumptions about default probabilities and volatility functions.

## The barrier diffusion model

Following Hull and White (2001), we define the function $P(t)$ to be the probability that the firm has defaulted by time $t$.[2] The default probability density is given by $P'(t)$. In particular, $P'(t)\Delta t$ represents the probability of default between times $t$ and $t + \Delta t$, as seen at time zero. Just as in Hull and White (2001), we consider a "default index" associated with the firm, represented by an Itô process $\{X(t),\ X(0) = X_0\}$:

$$dX(t) = a(X(t),t)dt + \sigma(X(t),t)dW(t) \qquad (1)$$

where $W(t)$ is the standard Wiener process. The firm defaults at time $t$ if:

$$X(t) = b(t) \quad \text{and} \quad X(s) > b(s),\ s < t \qquad (2)$$

where $b(t)$ describes a barrier function. A financial-economic interpretation of this barrier function will be given below. The default time is, by definition, the first time that X(t) hits this barrier, ie:

$$\tau = \inf\{t \geq 0 : X(t) \leq b(t)\} \tag{3}$$

Let f(x, t) be the survival probability density function of X(t), given by:

$$f(x,t)dx = \text{Prob}[x < X(t) < x + dx, \tau \geq t] \tag{4}$$

for $x \geq b(t)$.

From standard results in probability theory, the function f(x, t) satisfies the forward Fokker–Planck equation:

$$f_t = \frac{1}{2}(\sigma^2(x,t)f)_{xx} - (a(x,t)f)_x, \quad t > 0, \quad x > b(t) \tag{5}$$

with initial and boundary conditions:

$$f(x,t)_{|t=0} = \delta(x - X_0) \tag{6}$$

$$f(x,t)_{|x=b(t)} = 0 \tag{7}$$

We note that the integral:

$$\int_{b(t)}^{\infty} f(x,t)dx \tag{8}$$

represents the survival probability up to time t, 1 – P(t). Therefore, the default probability P(t) is related to the survival probability density f(x, t) and the barrier b(t) by the equation:

$$P(t) = 1 - \int_{b(t)}^{\infty} f(x,t)dx \tag{9}$$

We see from this equation that the barrier function b(t) must be chosen appropriately so that the pair {f(x, t), b(t)} is consistent with the given default probabilities $\{P(t); t > 0\}$. To see this in a more explicit way, we differentiate the default probability with respect to time in Equation 9, and use the equations satisfied by f, whence:

$$\begin{aligned} P'(t) &= -\int_{b(t)}^{\infty} \frac{\partial f}{\partial t} dx + f(b(t),t)b'(t) \\ &= -\frac{1}{2}\int_{b(t)}^{\infty} (\sigma^2 f)_{xx} dx + \int_{b(t)}^{\infty} (af)_x dx \\ &= \frac{1}{2}\frac{\partial}{\partial x}(\sigma^2 f)_{|x=b(t)} \end{aligned} \tag{10}$$

Thus, aside from Equation 7, the survival density function must satisfy this additional boundary condition at the barrier x = b(t). This gives rise to a free boundary problem for the forward Fokker–Planck equation, since the boundary b(t) is unknown and must be determined consistently with the two boundary conditions in Equations 7 and 10.

## Similarity transformation

We observe that the model is invariant under a scaling, or similarity, transformation. Let $\sigma_0$ be a positive number, and consider the transformation:

$$\tilde{x} = \frac{x}{\sigma_0}, \ \tilde{b}(t) = \frac{b(t)}{\sigma_0}, \ \tilde{\sigma}(\tilde{x},t) = \frac{\sigma(x,t)}{\sigma_0}, \ \tilde{a}(\tilde{x},t) = \frac{a(x,t)}{\sigma_0} \tag{11}$$

It follows immediately that the new function $\tilde{f}(\tilde{x}, t)$ given by:

$$\tilde{f}(\tilde{x},t) = \sigma_0 f(x,t) \tag{12}$$

also satisfies Equations 5–7 and 10. In particular, if σ(x, t) is a constant, we can "scale out" the volatility parameter – solutions with arbitrary constant volatility σ can be derived from the solution with σ = 1. The latter case is, in essence, the Hull and White (2001) model, in which the default index is taken to be a standard Brownian motion.

If σ is not a constant, the proposed diffusion model allows us to incorporate volatility functions that depend on the index value as well as time. This observation can be useful if one expects the volatility of the credit default index to increase as the firm approaches default, for example.

## Distance-to-default

We propose the following definition: let P(t) denote the market-implied default probability of the firm. A risk-neutral distance-to-default process (RNDD) is a diffusion process satisfying:

$$dY(t) = \tilde{a}(Y,t)dt + \tilde{\sigma}(Y,t)dW(t) \tag{13}$$

such that $Y(0) > 0$ and $\text{Prob}[\inf_{s<t} Y(s) \leq 0] = P(t)$.

This definition is consistent with the notion that a firm defaults when the value of its assets falls below the value of the debt.[3]

We notice that if we set:

$$Y(t) = X(t) - b(t) \tag{14}$$

where X(t) is the default index process discussed in the previous section, then Y(t) is a RNDD process with $\tilde{a}(Y,t) = a(X,t) - b'(t)$ and $\tilde{\sigma}(Y,t) = \sigma(X,t)$. Furthermore, we have:

$$dY(t) = dX(t) - b'(t)dt \tag{15}$$

Therefore, the problem of finding the barrier in the continuous-time analogue of the Hull–White model is equivalent to the problem of finding the excess drift in the distance-to-default process that makes the latter "risk-neutral" (calibrated to data on default probabilities).

The RNDD survival density $u(y, t)$ is related to the default index survival density $f(x, t)$ by:

$$u(y,t) = f(y + b(t),t) \quad (16)$$

It follows that the Fokker-Planck equation for the survival probability of the RNDD process is given by:

$$u_t = b' u_y - (au)_y + \frac{1}{2}(\sigma^2 u)_{yy}, \quad y > 0, \quad t > 0 \quad (17)$$

$$u|_{t=0} = \delta(y - Y_0) \quad (18)$$

$$u|_{y=0} = 0, \quad t > 0 \quad (19)$$

$$\frac{1}{2}\left[\frac{\partial}{\partial y}(\sigma^2 u)\right]_{|y=0} = P'(t), \quad t > 0 \quad (20)$$

Here, $b'$ must be chosen adaptively in such a way that the second boundary condition shown in Equation 20 is satisfied at all times. We conclude that the free boundary problem for the default index is transformed into a control problem for the RNDD. In this reformulation, $b'(t)/\sigma$ can be viewed as a "market price of risk" associated with the firm's perceived creditworthiness, consistently with Merton (1974).

## Initial layer and matching of solutions

We first consider the special case where the coefficients $\sigma$ and a are constants and $b(t)$ is an affine function. Without any loss of generality we set $a = 0$.[4] This special case will be used later to construct the general solution.

Assume accordingly that the default barrier is given by the equation:

$$\bar{b}(t) = -\alpha - \beta t, \quad \alpha > 0, \quad 0 < t < t_0 \quad (21)$$

In this case, it can be shown that the corresponding default probability is given by:

$$\bar{P}(t) = 1 - \int_{\bar{b}(t)}^{\infty} f(x,t)dx$$
$$= N\left(\frac{-\alpha - \beta t - X_0}{\sigma\sqrt{t}}\right) + e^{\frac{-2(\alpha+X_0)\beta}{\sigma^2}} N\left(\frac{-\alpha + \beta t - X_0}{\sigma\sqrt{t}}\right) \quad (22)$$

where $N(x)$ is the standard cumulative normal distribution and the density is:

$$\bar{P}'(t) = \frac{\alpha + X_0}{t\sqrt{2\pi t}\sigma} e^{-\frac{(\alpha+\beta t+X_0)^2}{2\sigma^2 t}} \quad (23)$$

This follows from standard properties of Brownian motions. Under the same assumptions, the survival probability density is given by:

$$f_{\alpha,\beta}(x,t) = \frac{1}{\sigma\sqrt{2\pi t}} e^{-\frac{(x-X_0)^2}{2\sigma^2 t}} \left[1 - e^{-\frac{2(\alpha+X_0)}{\sigma^2 t}(x+\alpha+\beta t)}\right] \quad (24)$$

for $-\alpha - \beta t \leq x \leq \infty$.

The RNDD probability density is given by:

$$u_{\alpha,\beta}(y,t) = f_{\alpha,\beta}(y - \alpha - \beta t, t)$$
$$= \frac{1}{\sigma\sqrt{2\pi t}} e^{-\frac{(y-\beta t-Y_0)^2}{2\sigma^2 t}} \left[1 - e^{-\frac{2Y_0}{\sigma^2 t}y}\right] \quad (25)$$

for $y \geq 0$, where $Y_0 = X_0 + \alpha > 0$ is the initial distance-to-default.

In Figure 1, the default probability $\bar{P}(t)$ and the default probability density $\bar{P}'(t)$ as functions of t are shown for several sets of positive $\alpha$ and $\beta$ values. In all these cases, we take $X(t)$ to be a standard Brownian motion with drift zero, $\sigma = 1$ and $X_0 = 0$. In this case, $\alpha > 0$ is the initial distance-to-default. We observe that $\bar{P}'$ is unimodal and drops to zero exponentially after reaching its maximum. The reason is that the barrier, which is linear in time, outgrows the square root scaling in time of the Brownian motion. Therefore, as time increases and passes over a certain level, the default probability density will decrease towards zero.

We now consider the solution of the model for arbitrary data $P(t)$. The idea is to use the straight line model for a finite but small time $t_0$, and then to match this solution to a numerically computed $b(t)$. The need for an "initial layer" arises from the fact that the $\delta$-function initial data vanishes to all orders for $t = 0$ and must be regularised

**1. Default probability density for some $\alpha$ and $\beta$ values**

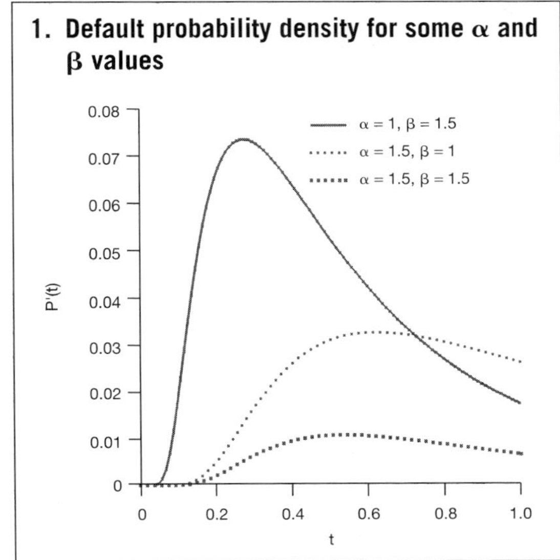

**2. Survival distribution at t = 0.5**

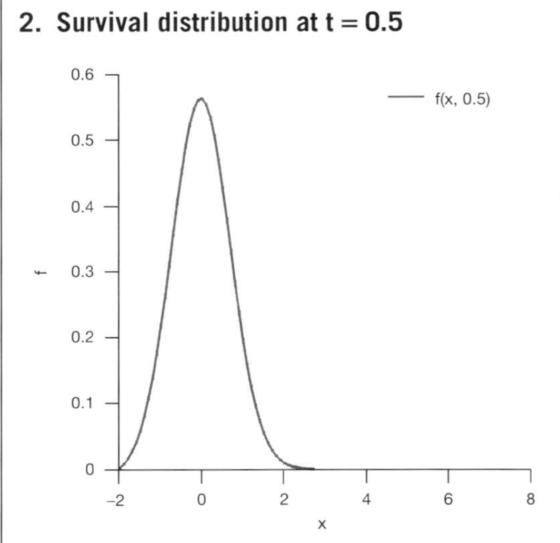


consistently with the boundary conditions that we want to impose for small values of t. For a given default probability data P(t), let us choose the parameters $\alpha$ and $\beta$ in such a way that:

$$\bar{P}(t_0) = P(t_0) \tag{26}$$

$$\bar{P}'(t_0) = P'(t_0) \tag{27}$$

where $P(t_0)$ and $P'(t_0)$ are estimated from the market data. A simple Newton–Raphson solver can lead to a solution of $\alpha$ and $\beta$ for small values of $P(t_0)$ and $P'(t_0)$. In Figure 2, we consider an example where $t_0 = 0.5$ is chosen, and $P(0.5) = 0.01$ and $P'(0.5) = 0.02$, which lead to $\alpha = 1.044$ and $\beta = 1.949$. The survival distribution at $t = 0.5$ is plotted in the figure.

Once the initial survival distribution at $t = t_0$ has been determined, we use it as an initial condition for the partial differential equation (PDE) problem in Equations 17–20. Since this distribution is derived from the default probability conditions in Equations 26 and 27, the compatibility condition seen in Equation 20 is automatically satisfied at $t = t_0$. A second-order finite difference algorithm is described below to solve the PDE for time beyond $t_0$.

## Numerical algorithm for general default probabilities

The numerics are based on the "RNDD formulation", ie, on solving a control problem for the unknown drift coefficient $b'(t)$. For simplicity, we write down the scheme for the case $\sigma = 1$ and $a = 0$. The extension of the algorithm to variable coefficients is obvious.

We start from $t = t_0$ with the initial condition from the initial layer solution, that is:

$$u(y, t_0) = u_{\alpha,\beta}(y, t_0), \quad y \geq 0 \tag{28}$$

A second-order finite difference algorithm for Equations 17–19 can be constructed as follows. Define $y_j = (j - 1/2)h$ and $t^n = n\Delta t$, and let $u_j^n$ represent the numerical approximation to $u(y_j, t^n)$. We consider a Crank–Nicholson scheme:

$$\begin{aligned} \frac{u_j^{n+1} - u_j^n}{\Delta t} = \lambda^{n+\frac{1}{2}} \frac{u_{j+\frac{1}{2}}^{n+\frac{1}{2}} - u_{j-\frac{1}{2}}^{n+\frac{1}{2}}}{h} + \frac{u_{j+1}^n - 2u_j^n + u_{j-1}^n}{4h^2} \\ + \frac{u_{j+1}^{n+1} - 2u_j^{n+1} + u_{j-1}^{n+1}}{4h^2} \end{aligned} \tag{29}$$

with boundary condition $u_0^n = 0, \ n \geq 0$, where $\lambda^{n+1/2}$ is an undetermined drift that depends on the time-step n and will be determined inductively. Here $u_{j+1/2}^{n+1/2}$ is calculated from a predictor step, which involves Taylor extrapolations in space and time with an upwind scheme approximation for the spatial derivative.[5]

For each value of $\lambda^{n+1/2}$, the resulting tridiagonal system is solved using a standard linear algebra package. The value of $\lambda^{n+1/2}$ that matches the extra boundary condition in Equation 20, $\lambda_*^{n+1/2}$, is found by using the Newton–Raphson iteration method. Finally, we equate the calculated $\lambda_*^{n+1/2}$ with the drift, ie:

$$b'(t^{n+\frac{1}{2}}) = \lambda_*^{n+\frac{1}{2}} \tag{30}$$

and extend the barrier in one time step:

$$b(t^{n+1}) = b(t^n) + \lambda_*^{n+\frac{1}{2}} \Delta t \tag{31}$$

The numerical stability of the algorithm, ie, the continuous dependence of the function $b'(t)$ on the probability density $P'(t)$, is an important consideration, given the fact that credit default data is discrete and that, consequently, the probability density needs to be constructed by interpolation. We mention here without proof that the free-boundary problem and the algorithm admit a unique, stable solution on any interval where the probability density $P'(t)$ is positive. Further comments on stability and the issue of interpolation of probabilities are made in the study of concrete examples in the next section.

## Examples

For the numerical example, we introduce a finite domain $(0 \leq x \leq 20)$, which is large enough to cover the dynamics of the solutions studied in this section. Also, we use an initial layer with $t_0 = 0.5$.

**Table 1. Default probability for banks**

| Year | AAA | | | BAA1 |
|---|---|---|---|---|
| | Expected recovery rate | | | |
| | 30% | 50% | 70% | 50% |
| 1 | 0.0052 | 0.0073 | 0.0122 | 0.0222 |
| 2 | 0.0097 | 0.0136 | 0.0227 | 0.0285 |
| 3 | 0.0119 | 0.0166 | 0.0277 | 0.0315 |
| 4 | 0.0135 | 0.0190 | 0.0316 | 0.0339 |
| 5 | 0.0150 | 0.0210 | 0.0351 | 0.0360 |
| 6 | 0.0164 | 0.0229 | 0.0382 | 0.0380 |
| 7 | 0.0176 | 0.0246 | 0.0410 | 0.0396 |
| 8 | 0.0188 | 0.0264 | 0.0439 | 0.0415 |
| 9 | 0.0203 | 0.0284 | 0.0473 | 0.0437 |
| 10 | 0.0220 | 0.0307 | 0.0512 | 0.0466 |

**3. Default boundaries for AAA and BAA1 companies**

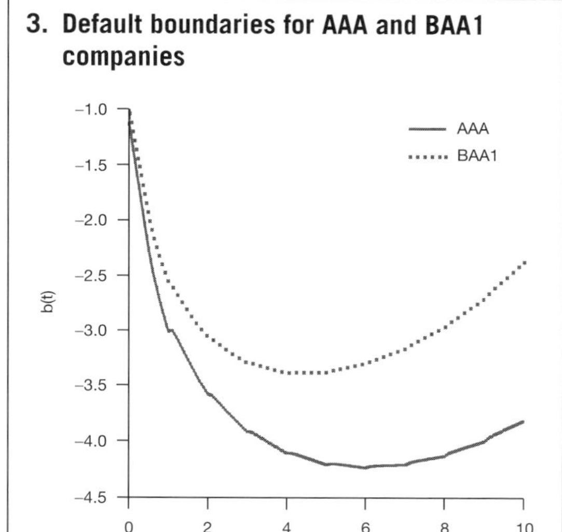


**4. Barriers from different volatility structures**

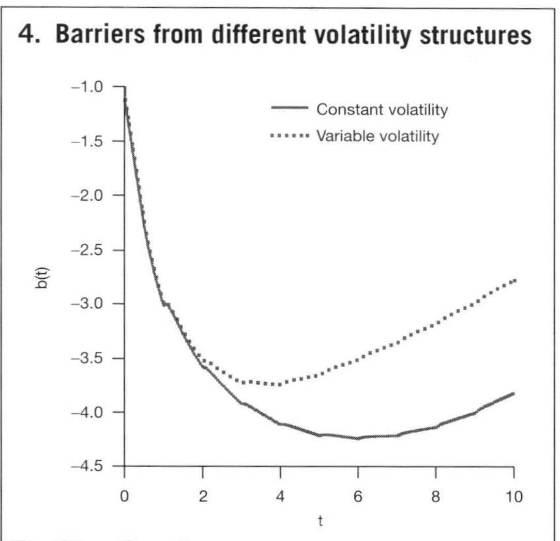


Unless explicitly noted, a constant volatility $\sigma = 1$ is assumed. In the finite difference calculations, we use 400 points in the x direction and choose $\Delta t = 0.05$.

In the first example, we consider default probabilities for the bank industry with Standard & Poor's AAA and BAA1 ratings.[6] The default probabilities for several recovery rates are shown in Table 1, where a bank's default probabilities in each of the next 10 years are listed. For instance, 0.0073 means that an AAA-rated bank would have a 0.73% probability of defaulting within the next year and, likewise, 0.0136 means that it would have a 1.36% probability of defaulting within the second year. These default probabilities were estimated based on an expected recovery rate of 30%, 50% and 70%.

As discussed in Hull and White (2000), different expected recovery rates cause very different default probability estimates. As a consequence, our default barriers will exhibit a strong dependence on the expected recovery rate assumed. In our calculations, the data from Table 1 is expanded to generate a piecewise constant function of time $P'(t)$. In Figure 3, default barriers for AAA and BAA1 banks from our model are plotted for $0 \le t \le 10$, based on data sets in Table 1 with a 50% expected recovery rate. The shapes of the curves for these two ratings are quite similar, since they both belong to the same industry and therefore bear similar characteristics as to when the firm is more likely to default in the future. The barrier for the lower rating (BAA1) is always above the barrier with the higher rating (AAA), indicating that it is much more likely for the firm with a lower rating to default.

One of the advantages of the generalised model presented here is the ability to incorporate general volatility structures. Here, we consider an example where the volatility is increased to a higher level once the Brownian path gets near to the default boundary, and compare the result to the result with a constant volatility ($\sigma = 1$). In particular, we choose:

$$\sigma(x) = \begin{cases} 1 & 0 \le x \le 2 \\ 1 - \frac{1}{4}(x-2) & 2 < x \le 4 \\ \frac{1}{2} & x > 4 \end{cases} \tag{32}$$

In Figure 4, default barriers from our model are plotted for $0 \le t \le 10$, based on the data set with expected recovery rate 0.5 in Table 1. Two barrier curves represent the cases with the constant volatility and the variable volatility, respectively. We find that the barrier with variable volatility lies

5. Comparison with Hull–White model

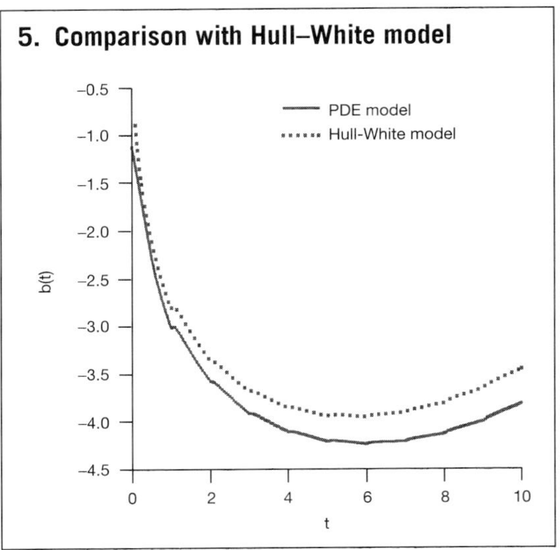


6. Default boundaries for different recovery rates

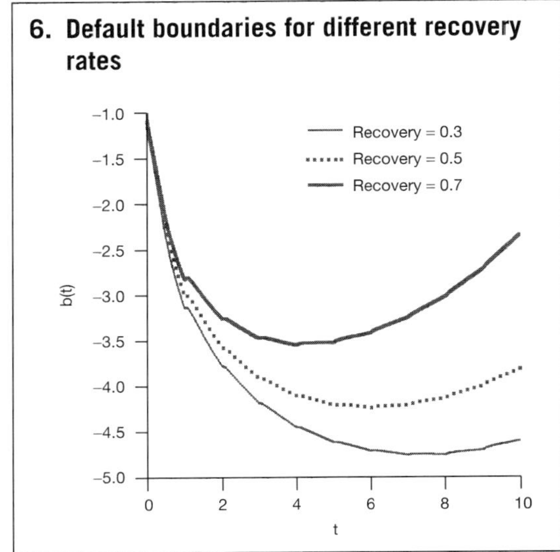


above the barrier with constant volatility. This is because the average volatility in the variable case is lower than the constant volatility level chosen for the problem. To achieve the same exit probability, the barrier has to move up to accommodate a lower volatility.

Next, we compare this PDE model with the original Hull–White model in this application. We implemented the Hull–White model (2001) with the same discretisation and numerical parameters. The results are shown in Figure 5, where default probabilities assuming an expected recovery rate of 50% are used. With regard to the shape and location of the barriers, the main difference between the models is that in Hull–White paths are allowed to exit from the barrier only at discrete times, whereas the paths can exit any time in the PDE model. This explains the fact that the barrier from the PDE model lies slightly below the Hull–White barrier.

Barriers for default probabilities with other expected recovery rates can also be calculated. In Figure 6, barriers corresponding to default probabilities for AAA banks listed in Table 1 for recovery rates of 30%, 50% and 70% are plotted. As expected, since default probabilities for a lower recovery rate are smaller than the corresponding default probabilities for a higher recovery rate, the barrier for this low recovery rate will lie below a barrier with a higher recovery rate.

In General, default probability data is discrete, as shown in Table 1. Since the PDE method requires interpolation of the probabilities, it is important to verify that different interpolation methods for the default probability density function do not produce significant changes in the barriers generated by the model. In all the above

7. Different interpolation methods for default probs

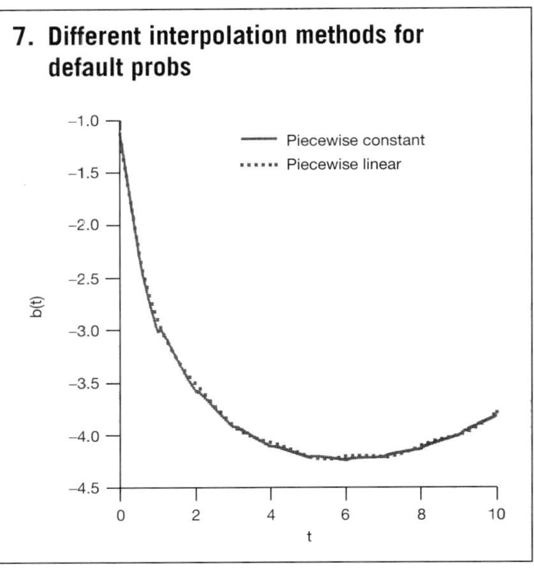


calculations, we used a piecewise constant default probability density $P'(t)$ calculated in a straightforward way from cumulative default probability data. To study the sensitivity to different interpolation schemes, we considered a piecewise linear interpolation scheme for $P'(t)$, requiring that the $P(t)$ generated be consistent with the data at the original data points. In Figure 7, we plot the barriers that result from these two default probability densities. The numerical results indicate that the scheme is stable with respect to small perturbations of the probability density function representing the data.

In Figure 8, we display the default probability density (input) and the drift function $b'(t)$ (output) for the case of AAA-rated banks. This figure shows qualitatively the way in which the drift "responds" to the default probability density data: an increase in the default probability will certainly lead to an

**8. Default probability and corresponding drift**

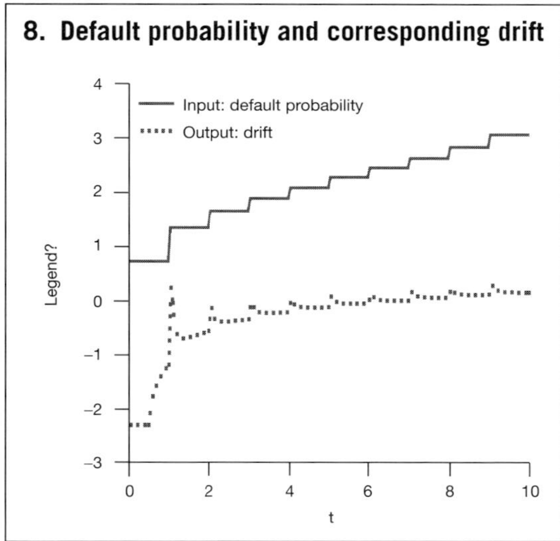


**9. Blow up of default boundary**

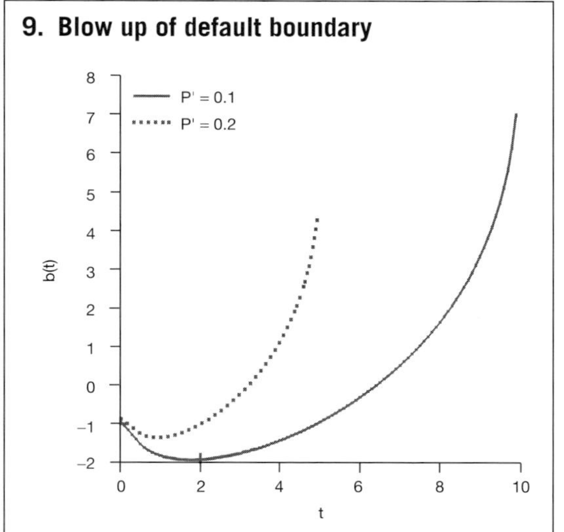


**Table 2. Forward default probabilities**

| Year | AAA | BAA1 |
|---|---|---|
| 1 | 0.244002 | 0.301495 |
| 2 | 0.165700 | 0.182113 |
| 3 | 0.096906 | 0.103299 |
| 4 | 0.068161 | 0.071312 |
| 5 | 0.053285 | 0.055123 |

increase in the drift, which moves the barrier up, making the paths more likely to exit the barrier.

Once the default barrier for a firm has been calculated for a period ($0 \le t \le T$), it is also possible to calculate forward default probabilities at a certain future time $T_0 > 0$ using this model. In fact, we just need to solve the PDE starting from $T_0$ with the default barrier fixed, and start the survival density from $T_0$:

$$u(x, T_0) = \delta(x - X_0) \tag{33}$$

so the initial distance-to-default at $T_0$ is the same as today. We discussed the equivalence between the drift $a(t)$ and the default boundary $b(t)$ in the "Distance-to-default" and "Initial layer and matching of solutions" sections above, but here they will have different roles to play. If there is enough information available, it is possible to fit the drift to a forward default probability structure. In Table 2, we present the five-year forward default probabilities from the results in Figure 3.

Intuitively speaking, these are the default probabilities for the next six to 10 years, given that the firm has survived the first five years and the default probability for the next instant is the same as today. It is observed that the forward default probabilities are much larger than the spot probabilities, because the shape of our barrier function is concave upward.

Finally, as a verification of the numerical scheme, it is mathematically interesting to study the case where the default probability reaches a level where a default is certain to happen by certain time T, as predicted by the input default probability. This should be reflected in the fact that the default boundary will be exited before this particular time T by virtually all Brownian paths $X(t)$, which can only happen when $b'(t)$ blows up at this time and the curve $b(t)$ becomes "vertical" as t approaches T. To verify this, we choose a uniform default probability density $P'(t) = 0.1$. In this case, the cumulative default probability $P(10) = 1$, which means that the firm will necessarily default before $T = 10$ with probability one. In Figure 9, we see that the barrier function $b(t)$ indeed becomes vertical as t approaches 10. The same figure also shows the result of another experiment where the default probability density is increased to 0.2, where the blow-up time is pushed to approximately $T = 5$, as predicted from the fact that $P(t)$ reaches one as t approaches five.

## Conclusions

Generalising the Hull–White model (2001) to continuous-time default index models, we propose a general framework for modelling default indexes as diffusions and default events as first-passages across barriers that generalise the Hull–White discrete model based on a discrete random walk. We show that the calibration of such continuous-time default index models to default probability data leads to a free-boundary problem for the corresponding Fokker–Planck equation. We also established an isomorphism between the default index formulation of Hull and White and the concept of a RNDD index. This isomorphism allows us to reinterpret the derivative of the Hull–White default boundary as a "market price of risk" that has to be added to the distance-to-default process of the firm to make it consistent with observed default probabilities extracted from bond spreads or credit ratings.

We proposed a simple numerical algorithm for finding the unknown drift, based on a discretisation of a control problem. Several examples and tests were presented, indicating that the algorithm produces reasonable results and is stable with respect to small perturbations of the input probability densities.

Finally, we point out that it is also possible to construct "non-parametric" models that implement the concepts of risk-neutral default index and RNDD. These models would be based on fitting the first-passage times of random paths across a barrier to given default probabilities. For example, a Monte Carlo simulation of different scenarios for the distance-to-default of a firm can be generated using econometric data on the volatility of the firm. In a second step, the probabilities of the different scenarios can be appropriately recalibrated to reflect contemporaneous data on cumulative default probabilities, as in the weighted Monte Carlo method (Avellaneda *et al.*, 2000).

1 *A more difficult problem, which often occurs in practice, is to estimate the default probabilities for a firm that has not issued any publicly traded debt.*

2 *We assume henceforth that this probability has been determined from bond spreads or another procedure (Hull and White, 2000).*

3 *The* RNDD Y(t) *can be interpreted as the difference between the value of the assets and the debt, or the log of the debt-to-equity ratio, etc, seen in a "risk-neutral" world.*

4 *The case of Brownian motion with drift is analogous, with the only difference being that the slope of the line defining the barrier must be modified.*

5 *We note that this numerical scheme is second-order accurate in both space and time, and all our calculations are unconditionally stable with respect to the choices of* $h$, $\Delta t$ *and* $\lambda^{n+1/2}$.

6 *Data and sources are available from the authors upon request.*


**BIBLIOGRAPHY**

**Avellaneda, M., R. Buff, C. Friedman, N. Grandchamp, L. Kruk and J. Newman,** 2000, "Weighted Monte Carlo: A New Technique for Calibrating Asset-Pricing Models", *International Journal of Theoretical and Applied Finance*, 4(1), pp. 91–119.

**Black, F., and J. Cox,** 1976, "Valuing Corporate Securities: Some Effects of Bond Indenture Provisions", *Journal of Finance*, 31, pp. 351–67.

**Brennan, M., and E. Schwartz,** 1980, "Analyzing Convertible Bonds", *Journal of Financial and Quantitative Analysis*, 15, pp. 907–29.

**Duffie, D., and K. Singleton,** 1999, "Modeling Term Structure Models of Defaultable Bonds", *Review of Financial Studies*, 12, pp. 687–720.

**Geske, R.,** 1977, "The Valuation of Corporate Liabilities as Compound Options", *Journal of Financial and Quantitative Analysis*, 12, pp. 541–52.

**Hull, J., and A. White,** 2000, "Valuing Credit Default Swaps I: No Counterparty Default Risk", *Journal of Derivatives*, 8(1).

**Hull, J., and A. White,** 2001, "Valuing Credit Default Swaps II: Modeling Default Correlations", *Journal of Derivatives*, 8(3).

**Kim, J., K. Ramaswamy and S. Sundaresan,** 1993, "Does Default Risk in Coupons Affect the Valuation of Corporate Bonds?", *Financial Management*, Autumn, pp. 117–31.

**Merton, R.,** 1974, "On the Pricing of Corporate Debt: the Risk Structure of Interest Rates", *Journal of Finance*, 2, pp. 449–70.

**Shimko, D., N. Tejima and D. van Deventer,** 1993, "The Pricing of Risky Debt When Interest Rates are Stochastic", *Journal of Fixed Income*, 3, pp. 58–65.

**Titman, S., and W. Totous,** 1989, "Valuing Commercial Mortgages: An Empirical Investigation of the Contingent Claims Approach to Pricing Risky Debt", *Journal of Finance*, 44, pp. 345–73.

6

# Equity to Credit Pricing

**George Pan**
Deutsche Bank

*The rapid growth of credit derivatives markets has highlighted the distinction between reduced-form and firm-value models of default. Here, George Pan presents a new, practitioner-tested version of the latter type, providing a closed-form formula linking default probability and equity market data.*

In recent years, there has been much interest in linking credit risk with equity market data. This idea was originally presented by Merton (1974), and was already suggested in the Black and Scholes (1973) article on option pricing. The simple link between credit spreads and stock prices has been used by many practitioners over the years. But the summer 1998 crisis, which saw a sharp increase in both credit spreads and equity volatility, accentuated the need to treat equity volatility as a crucial component of credit. In light of this, many financial institutions have started to complement the traditional credit analysis and ratings with equity-based models that are now offered by several risk management companies (KMV, Moody's Investors Service, etc). Regulators have also been encouraging the development and use of internal credit models to calculate bank economic capital.

We have also witnessed the exponential growth of credit derivatives in recent years. Initially driven by sovereign markets and balance-sheet management of bank portfolios, they have since evolved in investment-grade and high-yield corporate markets as the instrument needed to bridge the gap among various cash securities (bonds, loans, convertible bonds, etc) as well as between market participants (bank portfolio managers, insurance companies, money managers, collateralised debt obligation managers, hedge funds, etc). This chapter presents a simple formula that was designed by market practitioners and quantitative researchers at JP Morgan Chase. The use of an approximation for the asset volatility term, as well as for the drift term, leads to a generic closed-form solution that can approximate any sophisticated model relying on similar fundamental assumptions. In addition, we identify the standard deviation of recovery value as a parameter playing an important role in the calculation of the probability of default and its term structure. The closed-form formula presented here uses only observable market data and financial data and parameters supported by many statistical sources and studies (stock price and volatility, debt-per-share, and mean and standard deviation of recovery value of debt).

*The author would like to thank Jean-Pierre Lardy, Lionnel Pradier and Vladimir Finkelstein for their contribution to this work and for helpful discussions in writing this chapter.*

## Model description

The starting point for the model is the approach originally presented by Black and Cox (1976), Leland (1994), and Longstaff and Schwartz (1995). According to this approach (called "asset model" below), an event of default occurs when the asset value of the firm crosses a predetermined barrier (recovery value of the firm's debt).

Based on the asset model, we derive the closed-form formula for the probability of no default for any given time horizon $t$. The basic assumptions of our model are shown in Figure 1. We introduce a random variable $V$, which we call asset value, although it does not necessarily coincide with the actual asset value of the firm. We then define the default event as the first crossing of the barrier $L \cdot D$ by the variable $V$, where $D$ is a given debt-per-share. $L$ is the global recovery on the debt as a whole and is itself a random variable.

**1. Merton framework with a down-and-out random barrier**

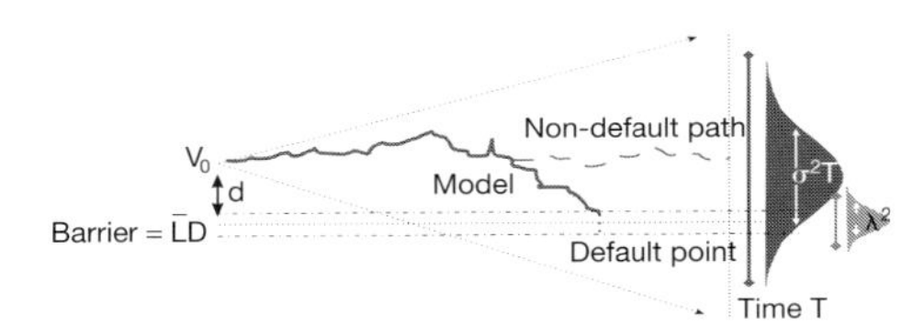


We consider that the asset V behaves as a lognormal variable with zero drift:

$$\frac{dV_t}{V_t} = \sigma dW_t \qquad (1)$$

where $W_t$ is a standard Brownian motion and $\sigma$ is the asset volatility.

We account for uncertainty of the recovery L by assuming it has a lognormal distribution with mean $\bar{L}$, and a percentage standard deviation $\lambda(\lambda \geq 0)$. Specifically:

$$\bar{L} = E[L],\ \lambda = \text{Stdev}(\ln(L)) \text{ and}$$
$$LD = \bar{L}D\exp\left(\lambda Z - \frac{\lambda^2}{2}\right) \qquad (2)$$

where Z is a standard normal random variable that is independent of $W_t$. The introduction of $\lambda$ is based on extensive empirical studies of recovery rates upon default (see Portfolio Management Data/Standard & Poor's loss/recovery database). One prevalent finding of these studies is the extreme variance of the distribution of recoveries. In addition to some industrial sector dependence, the recovery rate can be greatly affected by factors such as whether default is triggered by financial or operational difficulties and whether the company will be restructured or liquidated. This finding necessitates the inclusion of $\lambda$ as an important parameter in pricing credit risk.

For an initial value $V_0$ of V at time t = 0, default is thus defined to occur when:

$$V_0\exp\left(\sigma W_t - \frac{\sigma^2}{2}t\right) < \bar{L}D\exp\left(\lambda Z - \frac{\lambda^2}{2}\right) \qquad (3)$$

Define a process:

$$X_t = \sigma W_t - \lambda Z - \frac{\sigma^2}{2}t - \frac{\lambda^2}{2}$$

so that $X_t \sim N(-1/2\,A_t^2, A_t^2)$ where $A_t^2 = \sigma^2 t + \lambda^2$. Then default may be expressed as:

$$X_t < \ln\left(\frac{\bar{L}D}{V_0}\right) - \lambda^2 \qquad (4)$$

We approximate the process $X_t$ with the Itô process $Y_t$ where $Y_t \sim N(\mu t, \theta^2 t)$ with variance $\theta^2 t = A_t^2 = \sigma^2 t + \lambda^2$ and drift $\mu t = -1/2\,A_t^2$. We now make use of the distributions for first hitting time of Brownian motion. In particular, we have (Musiela, Marek and Rutkowski, 1998):

$$P(Y_s > y, \forall s < t) = N\left(\frac{\mu t - y}{\theta\sqrt{t}}\right) - \exp\left(\frac{2\mu y}{\theta^2}\right)N\left(\frac{\mu + y}{\theta\sqrt{t}}\right) \qquad (5)$$

By substituting $\theta$ and $\mu$ as above, and setting $y = \ln(\bar{L}D/V_0) - \lambda^2$ we obtain the closed-form formula for the probability of no default P(t) between time 0 and t:

$$P(t) = N\left[-\frac{A_t}{2} + \frac{\ln(d)}{A_t}\right] - dN\left[-\frac{A_t}{2} - \frac{\ln(d)}{A_t}\right] \qquad (6)$$

where $d = V_0 e^{\lambda^2}/\bar{L}D$ and $N[\cdot]$ is the cumulative standard normal distribution.[1] Note that Equation 6 implies a non-zero probability of default at t = 0 for $\lambda > 0$. Thus the introduction of a time-independent distribution of the barrier results in a non-zero probability of instantaneous default at time 0. This property contrasts with previous asset-based models in that they do not allow for non-zero initial default probabilities and therefore produce short-term spreads that are too low.

It is intuitive that the closer to the barrier (the smaller $V_0/\bar{L}D$) and/or the higher the asset volatility, the higher is the probability of default. In the short end (small t), the main driver of default probability is the uncertainty, represented by $\lambda$, surrounding the actual level of the barrier. The higher $\lambda$ corresponds to a higher probability of default. Moreover, $\lambda$ becomes an even more important parameter as one moves higher up the credit spectrum.

The par credit spread $S_P$, which is the fee of a credit default swap whose value is zero, can be found by applying an asset-specific recovery rate R:

$$S_P(t) = (1-R)\frac{-\int_0^t Z_{rf}(\tau)dP(\tau) + 1 - P(0)}{\int_0^t Z_{rf}(\tau)P(\tau)d\tau} \qquad (7a)$$

where $Z_{rf}(\tau)$ is the risk-free discount factor.[2] It is important to distinguish the asset-specific recovery R from the global recovery L. While L is the average recovery on the company's overall outstanding debt, which is a parameter in determining the default probability, R is the recovery for a

## PANEL 1. UNCERTAINTY OF DEFAULT BARRIER

Traditional asset-based models generally produce short-end spreads that are too low, as one cannot reach the barrier by pure diffusion in a short period. Hull and White (2001) proposed to overcome this problem by using a time-dependent default barrier that is calibrated to the market. An alternative approach is to incorporate a jump process. Here, we simply introduce explicitly the uncertainty of the default barrier, as shown by extensive empirical studies of recovery rates in the event of default. The short end of the term structure of default probabilities is primarily driven by λ, as illustrated in the figure.

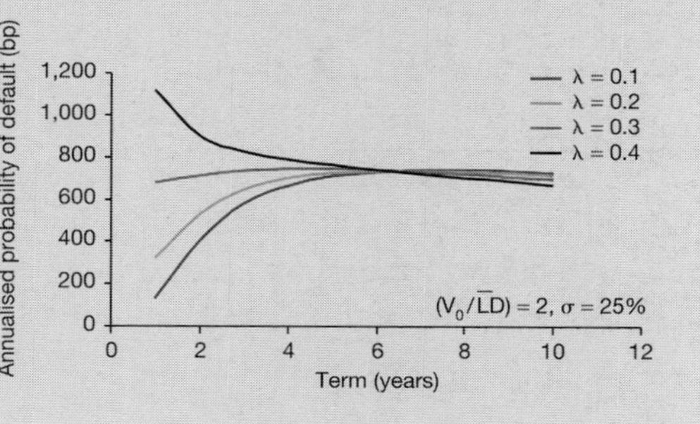


specific debt of the company, which is a parameter in the valuation of the credit spread for this particular bond or loan. The asset-specific recovery R for an unsecured debt is usually lower than $\bar{L}$ as the secured debt will have higher recovery. Define $p(t) = -1/t \ln(P(t))$ as the annualised probability of default. A simple approximate expression for the par credit spread $S_P$ can be obtained from Equation 7a by assuming a constant $p(t) \cong p$, and $P(0) \cong 1$ such that:

$$S_P(t) \cong (1-R)p = -(1-R)\ln(P(t))/t \tag{7b}$$

We have yet to link the initial asset value $V_0$ and the asset volatility $\sigma$ to market observables in order to use Equation 6 to calculate the probability of no default. We accomplish this by examining the boundary conditions. In particular, we focus on the long end (large t), since the short end (small t) is mainly driven by λ. Let S be the stock price and $\sigma_S$ be the stock volatility. For large t, the two regimes that become more and more probable with time, especially for high-yield names, are away from the barrier (S >> LD) and near default (S → 0). Consider:

$$\eta = \frac{1}{\sigma}\ln\left(\frac{V}{LD}\right) = \frac{V}{\sigma_S S}\frac{\partial S}{\partial V}\ln\left(\frac{V}{LD}\right) \tag{8}$$

which represents the distance (in a lognormal space) between the asset value and the default barrier in terms of standard deviation. Clearly η plays an important role in determining probability of no default (Equation 6). We want to establish the boundary condition for η. Near default (S → 0), we have:

$$V \cong V_{(S=0)} + \frac{\partial V}{\partial S}S + O(S^2) = LD + \frac{1}{\alpha}S + O(S^2) \tag{9}$$

where $\alpha = \partial S/\partial V$ and $V_{(S=0)} = LD$. Substituting V into Equation 8, up to the first-order approximation of S, we have:

$$\eta \cong \frac{1}{\sigma_S} \tag{10}$$

for the regime S → 0. Away from the barrier (S >> LD), we assume S/V → 1 as a boundary condition for V. Therefore:

$$\eta \cong \frac{1}{\sigma_S}\ln\left(\frac{S}{LD}\right) \tag{11}$$

for the regime S >> LD. The simplest expression for η that simultaneously satisfies the boundary conditions (Equations 10 and 11) is:

$$\eta = \frac{S+LD}{\sigma_S S}\ln\left(\frac{S+LD}{LD}\right) \tag{12}$$

Comparing Equations 12 and 8, we have V = S + LD. Thus:

$$V_0 = S_0 + \bar{L}D \tag{13}$$

for the initial value $V_0$ of V at time t = 0 where $S_0$ is the current stock price, and:

$$\sigma = \sigma_S^* \frac{S^*}{S^* + \bar{L}D} \tag{14}$$

for the asset volatility using some given share price $S^*$ and implied share price volatility $\sigma_S^*$. Here, we limit ourselves to an assessment of the share price volatility $\sigma_S^*$, obtained from either historical or implied data, which is representative for a given stock price $S^*$. With Equations 13 and 14, the closed-form formula involves only market observable parameters.[3]

Another assumption that has been made is that the asset has zero drift ($\mu_V = 0$), which again can be validated at the boundary where S → 0, and S >> LD. Keep in mind that for pricing credit, it is not the asset drift itself, but rather the drift of the asset relative to the default boundary that is relevant. Near the default barrier, we have:

$$\mu_V dt = \frac{dV}{V} = \frac{S}{\alpha V}\frac{dS}{S} = (r - p)\frac{S}{\alpha V}dt$$

where r is the stock financing rate and p is the dividend yield, respectively. Thus $\mu_V \cong 0$ for $S \to 0$. On the other hand, $\mu_D = 0$ since the debt notional should be steady when the company is near default. Away from the barrier, it is reasonable to assume that the company would issue more debt as the equity value grows, or pay a dividend to keep the leverage level, D/V, steady. Thus, $dV/V = dD/D$, ie, $\mu_V = \mu_D$. Therefore, the drift of the assets relative to the default barrier would in fact become zero.

The debt-per-share D is determined based on financial data from consolidated statements as follows. One first calculates all the liabilities that participate in the financial leverage of the firm. These include the principal value of all financial debts, short-term and long-term borrowings, convertible bonds, as well as quasi-financial debts such as capital leases, or underfunded pension liabilities or preferred shares depending on their financial burden to the firm. Non-financial liabilities such as account payables, deferred taxes, reserves, etc, are not included. Debt-per-share is then calculated by dividing the value of the liabilities by the equivalent number of shares. This includes the number of common shares outstanding as well as any equivalent number of shares necessary to account for other classes of shares or other instruments of the firm's equity capital. The financial data used in the debt-per-share calculation must be adjusted for recent past events or future predictable events that are already priced in by the market.

## Empirical data

The mean ($\bar{L}$) and the percentage standard deviation ($\lambda$) of the global recovery L have been estimated using the Portfolio Management Data/Standard & Poor's database. The database contains actual recovery data for about 300 non-financial US companies that defaulted from 1987 to 1997. Defaulted instruments include bonds and bank loans. Based on the study of this historical data, $\bar{L}$ and $\lambda$ are estimated to be 0.5 and 0.3, respectively. A lower $\lambda$ is expected for the financial sector due to the sector-specific government regulations. In the empirical studies below, we assume $\bar{L} = 0.5$ and $\lambda = 0.3$, and we exclude banks, brokerages and other financial firms.

We now examine statistically how well the model works for a portfolio of names. We took a snapshot of the JP Morgan Chase closing par spreads of three-year (the shortest tenor that is liquid) credit default swaps (CDS) as of July 2, 2001 for 298 names, which represents all the JP Morgan Chase North America actively traded credit derivatives, of both investment grade and high yield, excluding banks, brokerages and other financial companies as well as companies without public equity. We then calculated the CDS implied stock volatilities and plotted those against the 360-day (the longest horizon available from Bloomberg) historical stock volatilities (see Figure 2). The CDS implied stock volatility is found by solving Equation 7a to match the CDS market spread for a given stock price and debt-per-share of the company. Note that the data points are scattered fairly evenly across the 45° line. This holds even within the same industrial sector and across different credit ratings.

We have compared time series of model spreads with those of market spreads. Figure 3 shows two examples that compare the five-year

**2. Historical v. credit implied stock volatility for 298 investment-grade and high-yield corporates**

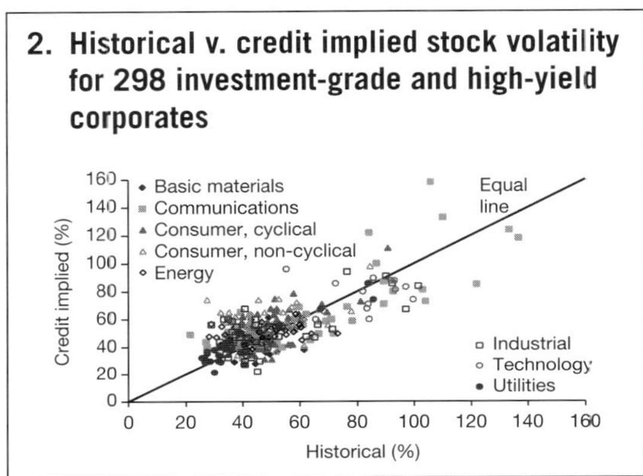


**3. Comparison of the five-year CDS market par spreads with the model par spreads**

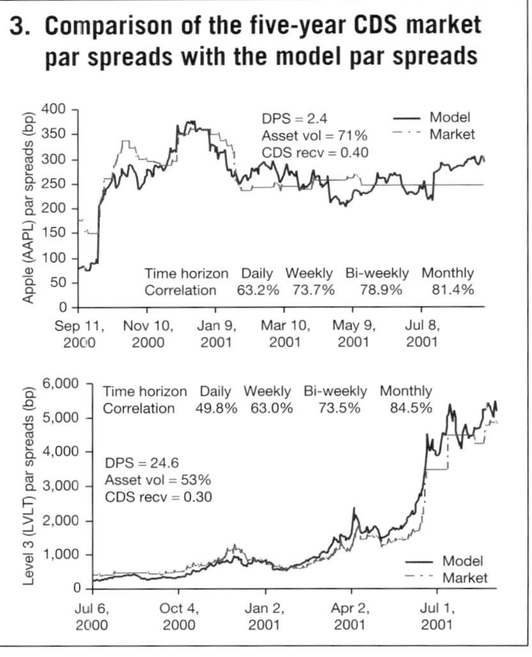

CDS market par spreads (JP Morgan Chase closing CDS spreads) against the model par spreads, as calculated using Equation 7a. We calculate time correlation between variation of the model spreads and that of the market spreads over different time intervals, namely, $\rho(u_i, v_i)$, where $u_i = \ln(C^{mod}_{i+\Delta i}/C^{mod}_i)$, $v_i = \ln(C^{mkt}_{i+\Delta i}/C^{mkt}_i)$ and $C^{mod}_i$ and $C^{mkt}_i$ are the model par spread and the market par spread, respectively, with $\Delta i$ = one day, one week, two weeks and one month. The figure clearly shows that, even though the variations may be poorly correlated on a daily basis, they tend to catch up with each other over a period of two weeks to a month. Note that the model par spreads in Figure 3 are calculated using daily closing stock prices. However, a fixed asset volatility for the whole period is used because of the lack of historical implied volatility. Adjusting the asset volatility along the path according to Equation 14, as one would do in practice as the market moves, should result in higher time correlation.

Figure 4 compares, for 39 high-yield names from various industry sectors, the maximum and minimum model spreads against those of the CDS market (JP Morgan Chase closing CDS spreads) from March to November 2000. The figure also shows the comparison of the average spreads for November. The model spreads are calculated using a fixed volatility for the whole period. Note again that the data points are located evenly across the 45° line, indicating that the difference between the model spreads and the market spreads goes in both directions for a diversified portfolio of names. The model demonstrates robust capabilities in difficult market conditions and over time.

**4. Maximum, minimum and average model spreads v. those of market spreads for 39 high-yield names**

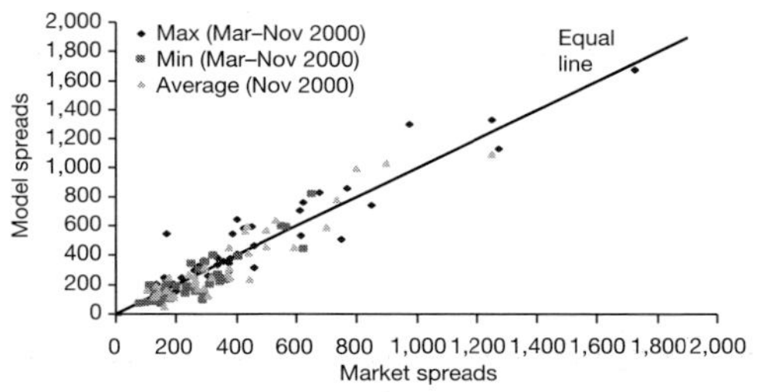

Define $\varepsilon^i = (C^{mod} - C^{mkt})/C^{mkt}$ as the basis for reference name i. The results of Figures 3 and 4 suggest that for a diversified portfolio of names, $\varepsilon$ is fairly evenly distributed around zero. We have examined the pair-wise correlation of the variation of basis, ie, $\rho(\Delta\varepsilon^i, \Delta\varepsilon^j)$, where $\Delta\varepsilon^i_k = \varepsilon^i_{k+1} - \varepsilon^i_k$ from July 6, 2000 to February 8, 2001 between any two names in a diversified portfolio of 15 companies from different industry sectors, including technology, energy, cable, airline, healthcare, chemical, auto parts and retail. The basis varies partly because the credit market does not always react in the same way and to the same degree as the equity market would react to any given piece of information. Not surprisingly, companies from the same or similar industry sector tend to have higher correlation for basis variations due to the fact that, from time to time, the securities of these companies are driven by sector-specific news. Nevertheless, the average correlation for the diversified portfolio is reasonably low, at about 5%, with a standard deviation of 10%. Thus, the basis risk is diversifiable.

## Conclusion

We have presented a simple closed-form formula that provides a robust relationship between

## PANEL 2. PROBABILITY OF NO DEFAULT

The probability of no default formula (Lardy, Finkelstein, Khuong-Huu and Yang, 2000):

$$P(t) = N\left[-\frac{A_t}{2} + \frac{\ln(d)}{A_t}\right] - dN\left[-\frac{A_t}{2} - \frac{\ln(d)}{A_t}\right]$$

is expressed as a function of market observable parameters:

$$A_t^2 = \left(\sigma_S^* \frac{S^*}{S^* + \bar{L}D}\right)^2 t + \lambda^2 \qquad d = \frac{S_0 + \bar{L}D}{\bar{L}D} e^{\lambda^2}$$

where $S_0$ is the initial stock price; $S^*$ is the reference stock price; $\sigma_S^*$ is the reference stock volatility; D is the debt per share; $\bar{L}$ is the global debt recovery; $\lambda$ is the percentage standard deviation of the default barrier; and $N[\cdot]$ is the cumulative standard normal distribution function.

default probability, equity price and volatility. The formula involves only market observable parameters and is capable of producing various shapes for the term structure of default probability. Back testing using historical market data suggests that the model is not biased, that it tracks the trends of the spread movements in a robust manner and that the basis risk is diversifiable.

This approach allows the use of equity derivatives to hedge credit risks on a name-by-name basis in a diversified portfolio of exposures. It can be applied as a price discovery tool to determine a fair market price of the credit risk for illiquid credits that have public equity, or as an arbitrage tool to build a proprietary portfolio of relative value of debt, equities and equity derivatives. The closed-form formula of default probability can be used as a credit rating tool that feeds from observable parameters, and more frequently updated market data such as stock prices. In addition, the simplicity and transparency of the closed-form solution makes it an ideal candidate to perform risk management and analysis of large portfolios of credit exposures. The computational efficiency of such a closed-form formula would allow a large portfolio to be recalculated daily, or even more frequently during the day on a real-time basis, and allow the computation of economic capital, value-at-risk and stress tests.

1 *In deriving Equation 6, the Itô process* $Y_t$ *can be viewed as a process that, for* $\lambda \neq 0$*, begins in the past at* $-\Delta t = -\lambda^2/\sigma^2$ *with a constant drift* $-\sigma^2/2$ *and a constant variance rate* $\sigma^2$*. The probability of no default thus obtained (Equation 6) implicitly includes the possibility of* $Y_t$ *crossing the barrier in the period* $[-\Delta t, 0]$*. An alternative to this approximation is to integrate over the barrier distribution. We can then obtain a closed-form solution using the cumulative bivariate normal distribution. The numerical differences between the two approaches are marginal for practical cases. We would like to thank an anonymous referee for pointing out this alternative approach.*

2 *In the case of a constant risk-free rate, we can obtain a closed-form formula for the par spread:*

$$S_P(t) = r(1-R)\frac{1-P(0)+e^{r\xi}(G(t+\xi)-G(\xi))}{P(0)-P(t)e^{-rt}-e^{r\xi}(G(t+\xi)-G(\xi))}$$

*where* $r$ *is the continuous compounded risk-free rate,* $\xi = \lambda^2/\sigma^2$*, and the function* $G(u)$ *is given by Rubinstein and Reiner (1991):*

$$G(u) = d^{\frac{1}{2}+z}N\left(-\frac{\ln(d)}{\sigma\sqrt{u}} - z\sigma\sqrt{u}\right) + d^{\frac{1}{2}-z}N\left(-\frac{\ln(d)}{\sigma\sqrt{u}} + z\sigma\sqrt{u}\right)$$

*where:*

$$z = \sqrt{\frac{1}{4}+\frac{2r}{\sigma^2}}$$

3 *Note* $V_0$ *does not necessarily correspond to the real initial asset value, nor does* $\sigma$ *necessarily correspond to the real asset volatility of the firm. Nevertheless, these simple expressions are able to approximate the distance to default* $\eta$ *in Equation 12.*

**BIBLIOGRAPHY**

**Black, F., and J. Cox,** 1976, "Valuing Corporate Securities: Some Effects of Bond Indenture Provisions", *Journal of Finance* 31, pp. 351–67.

**Black, F., and M. Scholes,** 1973, "The Pricing of Options and Corporate Liabilities", *Journal of Political Economy* 81, pp. 637–59.

**Hull, J., and A. White,** 2001, "Valuing Credit Default Swap II: Modeling Default Correlations", *Journal of Derivatives* 8(3), Spring, pp. 12–21.

**Lardy, J-P., V. Finkelstein, P. Khuong-Huu and N. Yang,** 2000, *Method and System for Determining a Company's Probability of No Default*, JP Morgan internal document.

**Leland, H.,** 1994, "Corporate Debt Value, Bond Covenants, and Optimal Capital Structure", *Journal of Finance* 49, pp. 1213–52.

**Longstaff, F., and E. Schwartz,** 1995, "A Simple Approach to Valuing Risky Fixed and Floating Rate Debt", *Journal of Finance* 50, pp. 789–819.

**Merton, R.,** 1974, "On the Pricing of Corporate Debt: The Risk Structure of Interest Rates", *Journal of Finance* 29, pp. 449–70.

**Musiela, M., and M. Rutkowski,** 1998, *Martingale Methods in Financial Modelling*, Second Edition, pp. 468–70 (Berlin: Springer-Verlag).

**Portfolio Management Data and Standard & Poor's,** *Loss/Recovery Database*, Available at www.pmdzone.com.

**Rubinstein, M., and E. Reiner,** 1991, "Breaking Down the Barriers", *Risk* April, pp. 28–35.

# 7

# Getting the Pricing Right

**Angelo Arvanitis**
Egnatia Bank

*As the liquidity of the credit derivatives market grows, the credit risk in over-the-counter interest rate derivatives can now be priced consistently with this market. Here, Angelo Arvanitis shows how to use default swaps to hedge the default and spread risk implicit in these instruments.*

This chapter describes a general procedure for pricing and managing counterparty risk in interest rate derivatives. The method takes into account variable exposures and random default times. We consider pricing of contracts on a stand-alone and on a portfolio basis.[1] In the latter case, existing deals within a master agreement are taken into account for pricing new transactions, as they are netted in the event of default. Previous theoretical studies include Jarrow and Turnbull (1995) and Hull and White (1995).

Since we will always consider potential defaults until the maturity of the contract or portfolio in question, it is not necessary for pricing to consider changes in the credit spread over the life of the contract. If we were considering shorter periods then credit spread changes should be included in the analysis, since the portfolio value (PV) at the end of the period of interest depends on the credit spread and should therefore be marked-to-market (for example, see Arvanitis, Gregory and Laurent, 1999).

We focus on standard derivatives, ie, interest rate and cross-currency swaps, caps, floors and swaptions. This analysis can be extended to exotic products, but the calculations can become complex and we do not present this work here. We demonstrate how standard default swaps can be used to hedge default and credit spread risk in these contracts.

## The model

Consider a bank that enters into an interest rate swap with a risky counterparty ABC. The bank bears the risk that ABC will default and therefore it should be compensated by receiving a credit spread $x$ above Libor, as shown in Figure 1.

The spread $x$ is determined by the probability that ABC will default and the loss to the bank under this scenario. It will be shown below that the determining factors are the shape of the risk-free yield curve, the volatility of the interest rates, the swap maturity and ABC's default probability. The last of these is derived from the ABC default swap premiums. Here, we will assume that only ABC can default, but the theory can be extended to the general case where both counterparties are risky (for example, Duffie and Huang, 1996). If there is bilateral default risk, then the spread should be reduced to compensate ABC for the fact that the bank is not risk-free.

The value of $x$ should be fixed such that at inception the swap has zero PV (when counterparty risk has been properly taken into account). We assume that, in the event of default of ABC when the bank is owed money, it will receive $\delta$ times the risk-free PV, where $0 \leq \delta \leq 1$ is a fixed recovery rate. If the bank owes ABC money, then it will have to pay the total PV to ABC. These two scenarios are shown in Figure 2, where PV denotes the risk-free PV. This is the loss suffered relative to the risk-free swap and it should not be confused with what is presented in the hedging section.

**1. Interest rate swap with risky counterparty ABC**

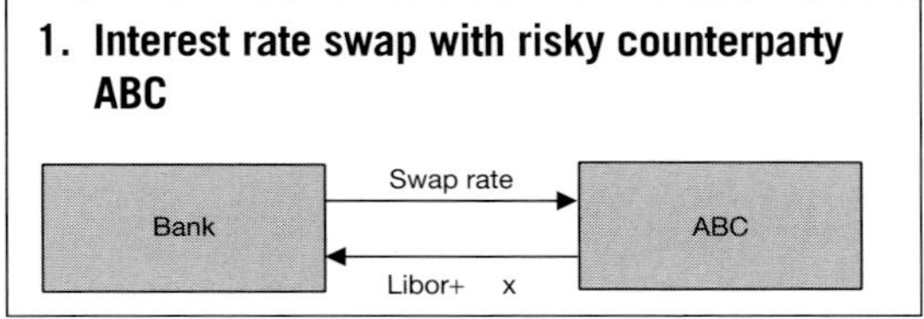


*Angelo Arvanitis would like to thank Jon Gregory for helpful comments and discussions.*

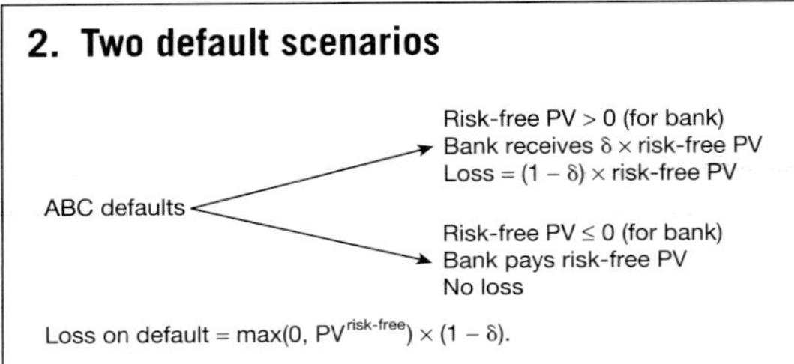


The expected loss (EL) is defined as the expected value today of all possible losses from default during the lifetime of the deal. An equivalent way of expressing this is that the expected loss is the difference between the risky and the risk-free PV, hence:

$$EL(swap) = PV^{risk\text{-}free}(swap) - PV^{risky}(swap) \quad (1)$$

Note that this is actually a general expression for any deal or portfolio of deals. The key point in the analysis is always the calculation of the expected loss, either on a stand-alone or on a portfolio basis. For the swap we are considering, we require the spread to compensate for the expected loss, ie:

$$PV^{risky}(swap + x) = PV^{risk\text{-}free}(swap) \quad (2)$$

Using the above expression for the expected loss and since the risk-free PV is sub-additive, this can be simplified to give:

$$PV^{risk\text{-}free}(x) = EL(swap + x) \quad (3)$$

which shows clearly that the spread $x$ is compensation for the expected loss. Note that the above equation is non-linear and must therefore be solved iteratively.

If we let $h_s$ represent the hazard rate of default (the default probability within a very short time period between $s$ and $s + ds$) and denote the time of default by $\tau$, the default density is given by:

$$\frac{dP(\tau < s)}{ds} = \exp\left(-\int_0^s h_u du\right) h_s \quad (4)$$

It can now be shown that the expected loss is given by:

$$EL = (1-\delta)E\left[\int_0^T \exp\left(-\int_0^s h_u du\right) h_s Df_s \max(PV_s, 0) ds\right] \quad (5)$$

where $Df_s$ is the (risk-free) discount factor. To simplify matters, we assume that the default probability is independent of the risk-free interest rate. Next consider a contract with maturity $T$. We discretise the interval $[0, T]$ into $N$ smaller subintervals. A suitable discretisation interval could be the period between swap payment dates (eg, three months), which is accurate, while allowing the calculations to be done quickly. Under the independence assumption between market parameters and default events we get a simple expression for the EL:

$$EL = (1-\delta)\sum_{i=1}^{N} E\left[\max(0, PV_{t_i}) \times Df(t_i)\right] \times p(t_i) \quad (6)$$

where $p(t_i)$ is the risk-neutral marginal default probability of ABC in the interval $[t_{i-1}, t_i]$. If $A(t)$ is the ABC survival probability at time $t$, then $p(t_i) = A(t_{i-1}) - A(t_i)$. The expected loss for a swap is thus equivalent to a weighted sum of European-style swaptions having maturities ranging through the life of the underlying swap. This leads to an analytical expression for a single swap. Similar closed-form formulas can be derived for caps/floors and swaptions, which make pricing very fast. More complex products, such as cross-currency swaps and portfolios of deals, can be priced via Monte Carlo simulation.

## Expected loss vs economic capital

Later, we will show how it is possible to hedge dynamically the credit risk of an interest rate derivative, if there is a sufficiently liquid market in the underlying default swaps. If this is the case then, by arbitrage arguments, the spread $x$ for the deal should represent the cost of the hedging strategy (ie, the cost to transform the risky deal into a risk-free deal). The expected loss on the contract equals the expected cost of the hedge. As will be shown in the last section, the hedge has to be dynamically rebalanced and therefore, because of stochastic default swap premiums, its cost is not fixed *a priori*. Under this scenario, historical default probabilities are not relevant.

However, if the market for default swaps is not sufficiently liquid, then the bank must take on the additional credit risk. Economic capital needs to be held against a credit portfolio to cushion against possible adverse credit events, such as multiple defaults. A certain percentile of the credit loss distribution, eg, 99.9% (depending on the bank's policy) defines the economic capital. One way to calculate $x$ is to require that it covers the marginal increase in economic capital (the additional capital required to support the new deal). In this case, we do not use risk-neutral parameters, since capital is calculated using historical parameters. The actual deficit probability of ABC is the appropriate parameter to use in such a case and may (for example) be estimated according to its rating. Since a typical credit loss distribution

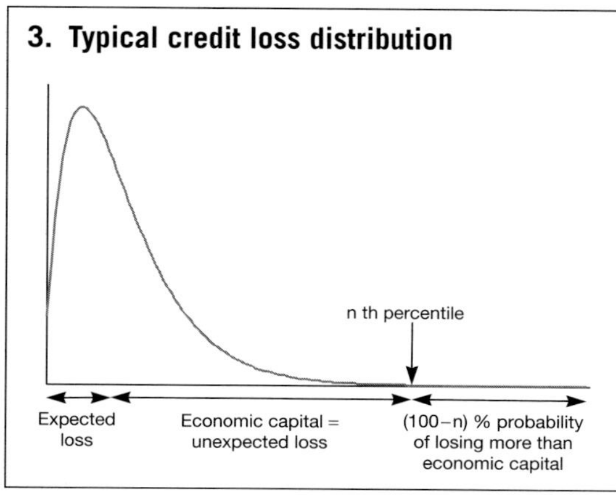


3. Typical credit loss distribution

(see Figure 3) is highly skewed, the economic capital could be higher than the expected loss, even though we cannot be conclusive. In general it is not possible to conclude which method will give a higher x. The relative magnitude of the two prices will depend on the relationship between the risk-neutral and the historical default probabilities, which is driven by the risk premiums. On one hand, real default probabilities tend to be smaller than the risk-neutral ones, particularly for good credits. On the other hand, for the same inputs, because the credit loss distribution is highly skewed, the economic capital is much higher than the expected loss. These two factors have opposite effects. For Aaa rated assets, the risk-neutral default probabilities tend to be substantially higher than the historical ones. In this case, it would be expected that the risk-neutral price be higher than the capital-based price.

For the purposes of this chapter, we will assume that a reasonably liquid market for default swaps does exist and that we can price using risk-neutral expectations without any need to consider capital.

## Portfolio effect

Under a master agreement, it is possible to net deals in the event of default. To calculate the spread of a new deal with a counterparty for which there is at least one master agreement, existing deals should be taken into account since the risks will cancel out to some degree. This means that the spread will be less than or equal to the spread for the stand-alone deal. The total risky PV should be the same as if a risk-free deal without the spread had been added to the portfolio:

$$PV^{risky}(portfolio + deal + x) = PV^{risk\text{-}free}(deal) + PV^{risky}(portfolio) \quad (7)$$

As with the stand-alone case (Equation 3), it can be shown that this leads to:

$$PV^{risk\text{-}free}(x) = EL(portfolio + deal + x) - EL(portfolio) \quad (8)$$

The interpretation of the above equation is that the spread is compensation for the marginal increase in the expected loss, which will be almost always less than the stand-alone expected loss. Therefore, taking into account the other deals will almost always reduce the spread. The expected loss on a portfolio basis will be equal to the stand-alone expected loss only when the new deal is perfectly correlated with the existing portfolio. This will almost never be the case in practice. To account for the portfolio effect, we need to simulate all the underlying parameters (various interest and forex rates) and to price every existing deal under all these scenarios, in order to correctly quantify the effect of adding the new deal to the portfolio.

## Interest rate swap

Consider entering into a five-year dollar interest rate swap. Throughout the examples in the chapter, it is assumed that the default swap curve is flat at 250 basis points across maturities and that the recovery rate is constant at 30%. We show in Figure 4 the exposure profiles for the payer (the bank pays fixed) and the receiver swaps with quarterly payments. The exposure profile is defined as the one standard deviation over the forward exposure.

In this example, the exposure of the payer swap is always above that of the receiver. The yield curve is upward sloping and the swap rate is therefore higher than the spot interest rate. This makes the forward value of the payer swap positive and that of the receiver swap negative.

4. Exposure profiles for five-year dollar payer and receiver interest rate swaps with quarterly payments

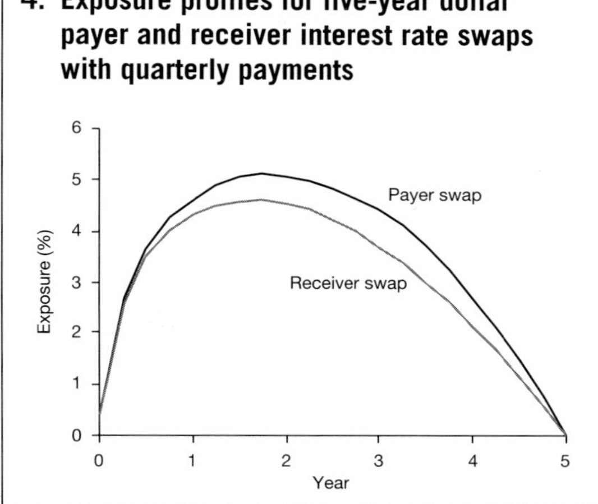

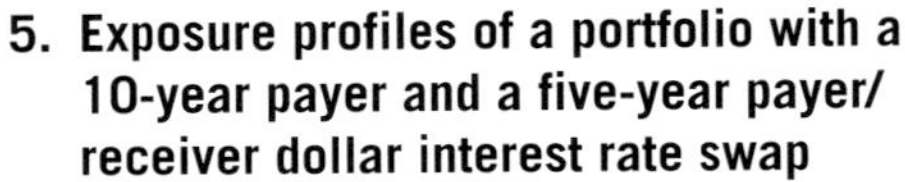

**5. Exposure profiles of a portfolio with a 10-year payer and a five-year payer/receiver dollar interest rate swap**

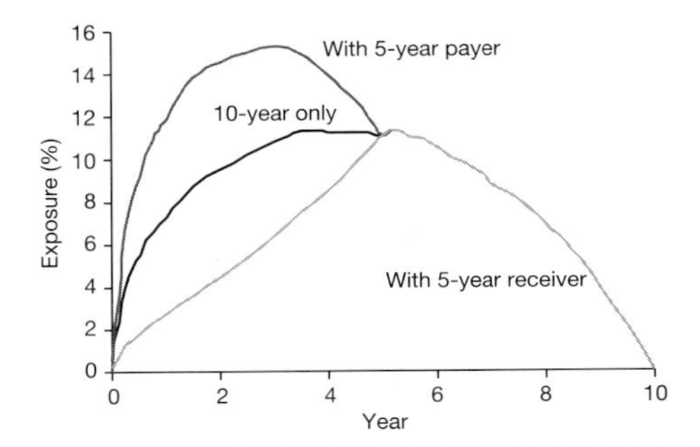


For a downward-sloping yield curve the reverse is true, while for a humped yield curve this effect can be either way.

We now show the importance of considering the impact of existing deals with ABC when pricing a new deal (assuming all deals are covered by a single master agreement). To demonstrate this, we consider that the bank has one existing 10-year payer (pay fixed) interest rate swap with ABC. We then consider the effect of adding a new five-year interest rate swap of the same notional. In Figure 5, we show the effect on the portfolio exposure depending on whether this is a payer or a receiver swap.

From Figure 5, it is clearly seen that adding the payer swap increases the exposure up to five years, while adding the receiver swap reduces it. In Table 1, we show the marginal increase in the expected loss of the portfolio and the corresponding credit spread for the new five-year swap. The spread of the payer swap is hardly reduced in the portfolio relative to the stand-alone case, since its exposure is almost perfectly correlated with that of the 10-year swap (they are not perfectly correlated since the swap rates differ). For the receiver swap, the spread is reduced dramatically, since it offsets much of the exposure of the existing 10-year swap. The bank should be willing to enter into the five-year receiver swap at a spread below the stand-alone market rate, which can be very competitive. This is a direct consequence of the fact that this new trade is well diversified with the existing portfolio of the bank.

## Cross-currency swap

For cross-currency swaps, the most important risk is the forex risk on exchange of notional at the maturity of the deal. This effect is even more pronounced if the forward forex rate is far from the spot rate. If the bank pays the currency with the higher interest rates (the discount currency) and it receives the currency with lower rates (the premium currency), there will be a large exposure caused by the exchange of principal, and the spread can be much larger than in the reverse swap.

Consider undertaking a US$/¥ fixed/fixed cross-currency swap of five-year maturity. The volatility of the US$/¥ forex rate is 15%. We show in Figure 6 the exposure profiles for the payer (the bank pays fixed dollar) and receiver swaps with quarterly payments.

The exposure for the dollar payer cross-currency swap is much higher than that for the interest rate swaps. This is due to the additional forex risk at maturity. This is reflected in the pricing, shown in Table 2.

**6. Exposure profiles for five-year US$/¥ payer and receiver cross-currency swaps with quarterly payments**

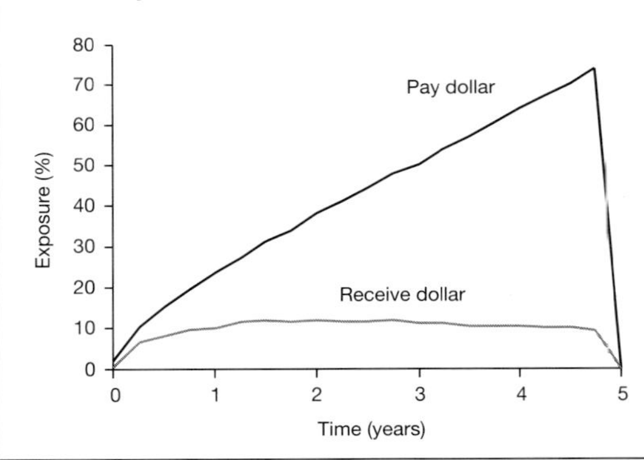


**Table 1. Expected loss and spread (x) for payer and receiver interest rate swaps (bp)**

| | Payer swap | | Receiver swap | |
|---|---|---|---|---|
| | Exp. loss | x | Exp. loss | x |
| Stand-alone | 13.3 | 3.2 | 10.1 | 2.4 |
| Portfolio basis | 13.1 | 3.1 | –10.0 | –2.4 |

**Table 2. Expected loss and spread (x) for US$/¥ cross-currency payer and receiver swaps (bp)**

| | Dollar payer swap | | Dollar receiver swap | |
|---|---|---|---|---|
| | Exp. loss | x | Exp. loss | x |
| Cross-curr. swap | 181.4 | 38.0 | 31.3 | 6.4 |

When we consider the impact of adding a cross-currency swap in an existing portfolio, the most important factor is the exchange of notional. For example, if there is another cross-currency swap that has an opposite exchange at close future dates, then the risk can be dramatically reduced.

There are many other factors that can determine the additional risk of a new deal. For example, the risk of high interest rates for a receiver swap will be reduced if there is a short cap position in the portfolio, whereas a receiver swap and a long cap position create a large credit exposure due to a potential interest rate rise. There can also be some subtleties. Consider being long a payer and a receiver swaption. If only one is exercised then the overall credit risk is increased, rather than if both or neither is. Credit risk plays a role in the exercise decision, which should therefore be based on the overall risky PV of the portfolio.

## Caps and floors

For caps and floors, the premium is normally paid upfront, which means there is only credit risk on a long position. The calculation of the expected loss here is easier since the PV can only be positive and all that needs to be calculated is the forward value of the contract in question. This allows analytical expressions to be derived. Table 3 shows the expected loss for caps and floors as a function of the strike. We do not show a spread since there are no periodic payments.

## Swaptions

In cash-settled swaptions, as in caps and floors, the PV is always positive. For physical-delivery (swap-settled) swaptions, there is an additional risk, since upon exercise the bank enters into a risky swap, rather than receiving the risk-free value as in the cash-settled case. It is still possible to derive an analytical expression for a physical-delivered swaption (for certain one-factor interest rate models). This involves a two-dimensional integral that represents the joint probability of exercise of the swaption and at the same time the swap exposure being positive. In Table 4, we give examples of the expected loss for different swaptions. An alternative way to structure a physical-delivery swaption would be to have a conditional charge (either upfront at the exercise date or as a spread on the swap). For example, for a physical-delivery swaption with strike 6%, the upfront credit charge for the swaption only is 21.7bp. Conditional upon exercise of the swaption, there should be a spread of 10.6bp on the swap.

**Table 3. Expected loss and spreads for dollar-denominated caps and floors for five years (bp)**

| | Cap exp. loss | Floor exp. loss |
|---|---|---|
| Strike = 6% | 37.2 | 7.5 |
| Strike = 7% | 21.1 | 15.8 |
| Strike = 8% | 11.6 | 30.7 |

**Table 4. Expected loss and spreads for dollar-denominated two-year swaption on a five-year payer swap (bp)**

| | Cash-settled | Physical delivery | |
|---|---|---|---|
| | Exp. loss | Exp. loss | X |
| Strike = 6% | 21.7 | 51.1 | 10.6* |
| Strike = 7% | 9.7 | 26.1 | 7.8* |
| Strike = 8% | 3.0 | 10.6 | 5.8* |

*Spread on swap, conditional on exercise of swaption.

## Collateral

Common practice for reducing the credit exposure is to take collateral, which can be liquidated in the event of default. Commonly, there will be a threshold exposure below which collateral is not required. Above this threshold, the collateral will be called in blocks and therefore the minimum margin call amount is also important. We give an example in Figure 7 showing the exposure to be almost capped by the threshold with some additional risk caused by the minimum margin call amount.

The above analysis is only a simplified treatment. We should also consider the correlation

**7. Effect of collateral on the exposure profile of an interest rate swap**

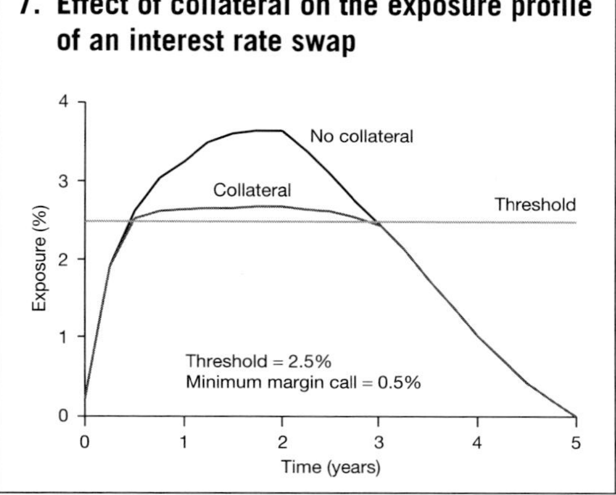

between the exposure and the collateral value. If it is positive, then the credit risk will be further decreased, since the value of the collateral is likely to increase with the exposure. For example, if the collateral for a cross-currency swap position is denominated in the currency the bank receives, then the bank is better protected against increased exposure, which is caused by the strengthening of that currency.

## Wrong-way exposure

A so-called "wrong-way" exposure arises when there is an unfavourable correlation between the value of a derivative and the default probability of the counterparty. This correlation means that the expected exposure conditional on default is considerably larger than the unconditional expected exposure. Wrong-way exposure can apply to all types of deals but it is best illustrated using a cross-currency swap. For example, suppose that we believe that conditional on default, the expected value of an forex rate $FX_t^d$ will be given by a factor $\eta$ times the unconditional forward forex rate $FX_t$:

$$E\left[FX_t^d \middle| \text{default}\right] = \eta FX_t$$

Such an effect is easy to incorporate into this model. Consider a 10-year cross-currency swap with counterparty ABC where the bank receives floating dollars and it pays floating Thai baht. We show in Table 5 that the expected loss and the spread on the swap increase substantially as $\eta$ decreases. The reason for this is that if the bank pays Thai baht then at default the exposure on the swap will be large and positive when $\eta < 1$ (the baht has depreciated against the dollar).

The above analysis is a simple and tractable way in which to incorporate correlation between the exposure and default probability. JP Morgan (1999) gives a more comprehensive discussion of wrong-way exposure.

**Table 5. Impact of "wrong-way" exposure on the credit risk for a cross-currency swap (bp)**

| | Expected loss | Spread |
|---|---|---|
| $\eta = 1.0$ | 142.3 | 21.4 |
| $\eta = 0.9$ | 239.3 | 36.0 |
| $\eta = 0.8$ | 366.5 | 55.4 |
| $\eta = 0.7$ | 509.3 | 76.8 |

## Hedging default risk

We propose a general strategy for hedging credit spread and default risk. We demonstrate these techniques by applying them to an interest rate swap. The analysis can be applied to all the other products discussed including portfolios. Arvanitis and Laurent (1999) discuss similar ideas relating to hedging credit derivatives.

Before default the value of the contract for the bank is $PV^{risky}$. After default, its value becomes:

$$\delta \max(0, PV^{risk\text{-}free}) + \min(0, PV^{risk\text{-}free})$$

Therefore, the loss at default time is given by:

$$Ld = \delta \max(0, PV^{risk\text{-}free}) + \min(0, PV^{risk\text{-}free}) - PV^{risky}$$

To hedge the default risk, the bank has to trade DS standard default swaps on ABC (which can be of any maturity). DS is determined such that there is no gain or loss in the hedged portfolio if default occurs. Since the payment made by a default swap is $(1 - \delta_{ds})$, where $\delta_{ds}$ is the recovery rate, it is required that:

$$Ld + (1 - \delta_{ds})DS = 0$$

Therefore:

$$DS = \frac{PV^{risky} - \delta \max(0, PV^{risk\text{-}free}) - \min(0, PV^{risk\text{-}free})}{(1 - \delta_{ds})}$$

We can distinguish two cases:

*Case 1*

$$PV^{risk\text{-}free} > 0, \quad DS = \frac{PV^{risky} - \delta PV^{risk\text{-}free}}{(1 - \delta_{ds})}$$

In this case, DS will most likely be positive, ie, the bank needs to buy protection. The protection should equal the risky PV less the recovery amount. It is possible for DS to be negative if $PV^{risky} < \delta PV^{risk\text{-}free}$, which occurs in a small region, where $PV^{risky}$ is close to zero (it can also occur if the recovery rate is close to one but this is unlikely). In this case, the bank should hold a short position that offsets the gain of $\delta PV^{risk\text{-}free} - PV^{risky}$ made at default.

*Case 2*

$$PV^{risk\text{-}free} \le 0, \quad DS = \frac{-PV^{risk\text{-}free} + PV^{risky}}{(1 - \delta_{ds})}$$

In this case, the bank should take a short position in default swaps to hedge the positive jump in the profit and loss in the event of default. This occurs because the bank marks the deal at the risky PV, but it only pays the risk-free PV in the event of default. For example, for a swap the impact is biggest when it is close to breakeven, since in this case the difference between the risk-free and the risky PV is close to the EL.

## Hedging credit spread risk

Using the above strategy, there is still an exposure to changes in the credit spread. For example, if the credit spread widens, then the profit and loss on the swap will be negative (since the risky PV will decrease), while the PV of the long default swap position will increase. However, it is only by chance that these terms will cancel. One way these can be made to cancel is in the choice of the default swap maturity. More formally, we delta-hedge the swap position with respect to changes in the credit spread, ie:

$$\Delta_{ds}(t_{ds})DS = \Delta_{swap}$$

This means that we choose the maturity of the default swap $t_{ds}$, so that the bank is hedged against small changes in the credit spread, while still being protected in the event of a default as described above. However, this could still leave the bank exposed to large changes in the credit spread that could arise, for example, from a rating change. We can therefore hedge the gamma as well as the delta of the swap position. This will require one more default swap in order to have enough free parameters. We require that:

$$DS = DS_1 + DS_2$$
$$\Delta_{ds1}(t_{ds1})DS_1 + \Delta_{ds2}(t_{ds2})DS_2 = \Delta_{swap}$$
$$\gamma_{ds1}(t_{ds1})DS_1 + \gamma_{ds2}(t_{ds2})DS_2 = \gamma_{swap}$$

We have four parameters and three equations to satisfy so we could, for example, fix the maturity of one of the default swaps. We illustrate the delta and delta-gamma hedging strategies in Figure 8. The

**8. Delta and delta-gamma hedging strategies**

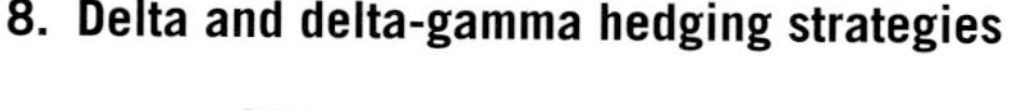

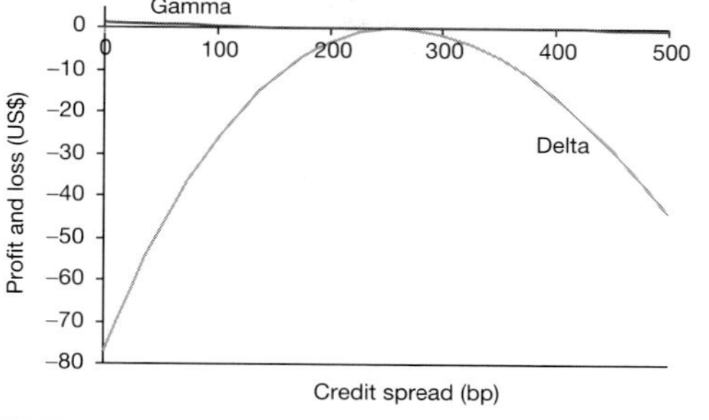


delta hedge is sufficient for reasonably small changes in the spread. For large jumps in the credit spread, the delta-gamma strategy works well.

## Conclusion

In this chapter, we have made a first attempt towards developing an integrated approach to the management of credit exposure across capital markets. The traditional approach in derivatives has been to consider credit as a non-traded risk that can only be managed using traditional tools, such as credit lines and collateral. This approach, even though valuable and intuitive, can lead to divergence from the pricing of credit derivatives, where credit is actually traded. In the method presented, credit is treated as just another source of risk (along with interest rates, forex, etc). Although more illiquid than the other sources of risk, the proposed method still allows credit to be actively managed.

It has been shown that "portfolio" pricing can lead to better risk management and at the same time it can provide more aggressive pricing to the marketers. We believe that it is feasible to develop such a pricing system at a reasonable cost. What we presented is only an application of the diversification principle on credit. It is definitely possible, and perhaps desirable to develop similar "portfolio" pricing techniques for interest rates, forex or equities.

1 *Note that we use portfolio here to mean all deals with a single counterparty.*

**BIBLIOGRAPHY**

**Arvanitis, A., J. Gregory and J-P. Laurent,** 1999, "Building Models for Credit Spreads", *Journal of Derivatives,* Spring, pp. 27-43.

**Arvanitis, A., and J-P. Laurent,** 1999, "On the Edge of Completeness", *Risk,* October, pp. 61-5.

**Duffie, D., and M. Huang,** 1996, "Swap Rates and Credit Quality", *Journal of Finance,* 51, pp. 921-50.

**Hull, J., and A. White,** 1995, "The Impact of Default Risk on the Prices of Options and Other Derivative Securities", *Journal of Banking & Finance,* 19, pp. 299-322.

**Jarrow, R., and S. Turnbull,** 1995, "Pricing Derivatives on Financial Securities Subject to Credit Risk", *Journal of Finance,* March, pp. 53-85.

**JP Morgan,** 1999, "Wrong-Way Exposure", *Risk,* July, pp. 52-5.

# 8

# On the Edge of Completeness

**Angelo Arvanitis and Jean-Paul Laurent**

Egnatia Bank; ISFA Actuarial School, University of Lyon

*The profit and loss of a book of credit contingent contracts should be hedged both against defaults and the volatility of the default swap premiums. Angelo Arvanitis and Jean-Paul Laurent present a hedging strategy where the main emphasis is placed on reducing the possibility of big losses at default time. The hedge is not perfect, but it allows a substantial reduction of risk*

Our aim is to provide a comprehensive framework for hedging credit contingent contracts, such as quanto default swaps, cancellable derivative contracts and first- and second-to-default swaps. Insurance against counterparty default risk in standard over-the-counter derivatives also falls into this category. Our hedging strategy relies on dynamically trading a portfolio of "standard default swaps" in such a way that the credit contingent contract is fully hedged at default time. We subsequently show that most of the risks involved in these credit contingent contracts can be hedged. Standard default swaps and risky floating-rate notes (FRNs) are closely related financial instruments (Duffie, 1999). We do not consider hedging one against the other, but rather the hedging of exotic credit contracts with simpler ones. Since trading risky FRNs involves managing repo margins and short-sell constraints, and for the sake of simplifying the presentation, we will use standard default swaps when presenting hedging strategies. The value of standard default swaps and thus of credit contingent contracts depends on the risk-free yield curve. Since our hedging strategy provides a significant reduction of the future net cashflows of the hedged portfolio, both at default time and prior to default, interest rate risk is hedged as well.

As an introduction to the hedging principle, we consider the most simple case, of rolling over short-term default swaps against a long-term default swap position. We then introduce credit contingent contracts on single and multiple underlyings and elaborate the proposed hedging strategy. We show how it is embedded in risk-neutral valuation. First, we concentrate on hedging at default time and, to ease the exposition, we focus on the use of short-term default swaps. Then we assess other risks of practical importance, such as imperfect hedge at default time and the volatility of net premiums prior to default. The former can unfortunately only be estimated, while the latter is mainly related to changes in the default swap premiums. A proper use of financial instruments and choice of maturity of underlying default swaps allows a substantial reduction of risk.

*The authors thank Stefano Galluccio, Jean-Michel Lasry and Baudouin Miroux for helpful comments and discussions.*

## Hedging long-term default swaps

The basis of our hedging approach will be to trade a series of default swaps against the position in the credit contingent contract. In a standard default swap contract on a risky floating-rate note, the holder of the swap pays a periodic premium to the protection seller up to the maturity date of the default swap or the default date, whichever occurs first. In return, in case of default, the protection buyer receives a payment equal to the lost fraction of the notional of the note. Let us consider the following dynamic strategy:

- We sell a standard default swap with maturity T, on an underlying risky floating-rate note trading at par. We receive a periodic premium $p_T$ in order to be insured against default of the bond.

- We buy a short-term three-month default swap on the same risky floating-rate note; then we roll over this short-term position quarterly until time T. We pay a time-varying quarterly premium that reflects the varying short-term risk of the firm issuing the underlying note.

If default occurs at any time $\tau$ before T, the cashflows offset each other and the first-order risk (losing the principal) is perfectly hedged. The remaining cashflows are the differences between the fixed long-term default swap premium and the short-term default swap premiums. Let us consider the special case where the premiums of the short-term default swaps are constant across time; to avoid a straightforward arbitrage opportunity, these premiums have to be equal to the periodic premium of the long-term default swap. In this case, we get a perfect hedge.

## Contract definitions

SINGLE UNDERLYING CONTRACTS

A T-maturity credit contingent contract promises to pay a cashflow $C(\tau)$ if a given issuer defaults at time $\tau$, for $\tau \leq T$, against a periodic premium $p_T(C)$. The cashflow paid in case of default may depend on multiple variables, such as recovery rates, exchange rates, bond and derivative prices, energy prices or the average temperature in a certain region. This class of products is very broad and provides a natural vehicle for market participants to transfer credit risk to the dealers. We consider below some practical examples.

*Counterparty risk on standard derivatives*

An important application of credit contingent contracts is hedging default risk on derivatives. The buyer of the hedging contract, when his/her counterparty defaults, will receive the risk-free mark-to-market on the underlying derivative times one minus the recovery rate, provided that this value is positive. This results in full credit protection. These insurance contracts can be used either on individual underlyings or to hedge the aggregate credit exposure of a book, in order to take advantage of netting and reduce the cost.

*Cancellable contracts*

In a cancellable contract, periodic premiums are exchanged between two counterparties up to the default time of a third party. Then, the contract terminates without any further payments. For example, the holder of a cancellable swaption receives a standard swaption payout if, and only if, the third party does not default. If the seller of the cancellable swaption is default-free, the cancellable swaption is equivalent to a swaption sold by the third party, with no recovery. However, a cancellable swap is different from a risky swap. Indeed, the buyer of a risky swap has a negative exposure in case of default, when the present value of the swap is negative, which is not the case for the cancellable swap. The holder of a risky fixed-rate bond can enter into the corresponding cancellable swap in order to create a synthetic risky floating-rate bond. If he/she enters into a standard swap instead, he/she is exposed to the uncertainty of the mark-to-market on the swap at default time.

*Quanto default swaps*

In a quanto default swap, either the premium payments or the cashflows in case of default are not in the same currency as the underlying bond. Consider a multinational that has issued a dollar-denominated bond. The premium of the quanto default swap is payable in euros and in case of default, the payment equals the recovery rate on the US dollar bond payable in euros. Expressed in dollars, the payment equals $\delta e(\tau)$, where $e(\tau)$ is the US$/€exchange rate at time $\tau$ and $\delta$ is the recovery rate. If a euro-denominated bond of the same issuer was trading, under the assumption that the recovery rate does not depend on the currency, the quanto default swap would have turned into a plain vanilla default swap on the euro bond. If such a bond is not available or illiquid, the static arbitrage between the risky floating-rate note, the default swap and the risk-free floating-rate note does not hold anymore. A quanto default swap is designed to provide protection to the holder of illiquid foreign currency bonds or non-traded loans.

MULTIPLE UNDERLYING CONTRACTS

We extend our hedging framework to multiple underlying contracts, in particular first- and second-to-default swaps.

*Consider a basket of bonds or loans*

The buyer of a first-to-default swap pays a periodic premium until the first security in the basket defaults. He/she is insured against this first default, ie, he/she receives the unrecovered part of the first defaulted bond or loan. In a second-to-default swap, the buyer pays a periodic premium in order to be insured against the second default in the pool. When the first default occurs, the periodic premium has still to be paid. After the first default, the second-to-default swap coincides with the first-to-default on the remaining bonds.

## Rolling over the hedge

SINGLE UNDERLYING CONTRACTS

When a standard long-term default swap is hedged by rolling over a series of short-term default swaps, the cashflows in case of default exactly offset each other. This leads to a natural hedge ratio of one short-term against one long-term default swap. For a general credit contingent contract, the natural hedge ratio is the relative magnitude of the two payouts in case of default. For the sake of simplicity, we consider that we can deal in short-term digital default swaps; a digital default swap pays one unit of notional in case of default. The hedging strategy consists of holding $C(t)$ short-term (digital) default swaps at any time t, where $t \leq \min(\tau, T)$. This is a perfect hedge in case of default. The cash outflows associated with the hedging portfolio are $C(t)\lambda(t)dt$, where $\lambda(t)dt$ is the short-term digital default swap premium at time t.

MULTIPLE UNDERLYING CONTRACTS

In the first-to-default swap, we can consider buying a portfolio of short-term default swaps on the underlying bonds and rolling over the position until the first default occurs. The outflows on the hedging portfolio are the sum of the short-term default swap premiums. To hedge a second-to-default swap, the dealer should only hedge in a similar way after the first default occurs. In both cases, we get a perfect hedge in case of default.

## The average cost of the hedge

Duffie (1999), among others, has extended the standard risk-neutral valuation framework to the pricing of credit contingent contracts. Our hedging strategy provides a simple interpretation of risk-neutral pricing formulas.

The first step in modelling credit contingent contracts is the specification of the process for the default event arrival date(s), $\tau$. In probabilistic terminology, this process is referred to as a point process. This framework has become standard in credit risk modelling (both in retail and corporate markets), in life and non-life insurance, in reliability theory and quality control. A basic tool in the analysis of these contracts is the hazard rate function or (risk) intensity of the process $\lambda(t)$. $\lambda(t)dt$ is the (risk-neutral) probability of the default event occurring during the time interval $[t, t + dt]$. In hazard rate-based models, the probability of the event occurring during any infinitesimal time interval is proportional to $dt$. The risk intensity also has key financial interpretations. Putting aside formal rigour, the insurance premium that has to be paid at time t for a short-term digital default swap contract with maturity $t + dt$ is equal to $\lambda(t)dt$; the premium of a standard short-term default swap is equal to $\lambda(t)(1 - \delta)dt$, where $\delta$ is the recovery rate, ie, the probability $\lambda(t)dt$ of getting a payment times the payout $1 - \delta$. In particular, constant short-term default swap premiums and constant credit spreads are obtained when the arrival of the default time is modelled through a Poisson process (ie, constant risk intensity). Various stochastic models have been proposed for $\lambda(t)$ and the corresponding dynamics of short-term default swap premiums. (See Arvanitis, Gregory and Laurent, 1999, for a presentation of models and inference techniques.)

In risk-neutral pricing, the continuously paid periodic premium $p_T$ on a T-maturity credit contingent contract is determined as follows:

$$E\left[\int_0^T \left(\exp - \int_0^t (r + \lambda)(u)du\right) p_T dt\right] = E\left[\int_0^T \left(\exp - \int_0^t (r + \lambda)(u)du\right) C(t)\lambda(t)dt\right] \quad (1)$$

where $r(u)$ denotes the short-term risk-free rate at time u and E denotes the risk-neutral expectation. The left-hand side of Equation 1 corresponds to the present value of the premiums $p_T dt$ received by the dealer, when selling the T-maturity credit contingent contract. The right-hand side represents the present value of the cash outflows associated with rolling over $C(t)$ short-term digital default swaps. The corresponding premiums are $C(t)\lambda(t)dt$.

The exponential terms:

$$\exp - \int_0^t (r(u) + \lambda(u))du \quad (2)$$

are simply discount factors, corrected for the probability of not receiving the scheduled cashflow, if default occurs. Clearly, the rollover hedging strategy is embedded in the risk-neutral pricing formula.

If we consider a first-to-default swap with two counterparties, assuming for simplicity a zero-recovery rate for both counterparties, no simultaneous defaults and one unit of notional, the continuously paid periodic premium $p_T$ of a first-to-default swap is determined by (Duffie, 1998):

$$E\left[\int_0^T \left(\exp - \int_0^t (r + \lambda_1 + \lambda_2)(u)du\right) p_T dt\right] =$$

$$E\left[\int_0^T \left(\exp - \int_0^t (r + \lambda_1 + \lambda_2)(u)du\right) (\lambda_1 + \lambda_2)(t)dt\right] \quad (3)$$

The hedging portfolio corresponds to buying one unit of each underlying default swap. The term $(\lambda_1(t) + \lambda_2(t))dt$ simply corresponds to the premiums paid to hold the hedging portfolio. Thus, the pricing equation states that the expected value of the aggregate premiums received by the dealer (when selling the contract) $p_T dt$ equals the expected value of the aggregate premiums paid on the hedging portfolio, constructed by rolling over the two short-term default swaps.

## Can we hedge at default time?

While our hedging principle is quite simple, in some cases it is almost impossible to get a perfect hedge at default time. However, it is possible to assess these risks.

### ILLIQUID HEDGING UNDERLYINGS

To implement the hedge, we must be able to trade default swaps. Difficulties in trading these may prevent us from adjusting the hedge ratios or rolling over the hedging portfolio (Krakovsky, 1999).

### UNCERTAIN HEDGE RATIO

When the ratio of the promised payout to the payout of the underlying hedging default swap contract is predetermined at default time, it is straightforward to calculate the hedge ratio. However, this is not always the case. For example, if we hedge a credit contingent contract whose payout is not proportional to the recovery rate, with standard default swaps we are exposed to significant recovery rate risk.

In a quanto default swap, the default of a major local issuer could destabilise the economy and trigger currency devaluation. In implementing the hedging strategy, we must take into account the jump in the exchange rate $e(t)$ at default time. More precisely, we should have $e(\tau^+)$ short-term default swaps in our portfolio, where $e(\tau^+)$ is the exchange rate after default. Since this is, in general, unknown, we can only hope to be correct on average, and the accuracy of the hedge deteriorates. The dealer will have to construct a hedge using local currency default swaps, which is different from the one constructed under the assumption that default does not affect the foreign exchange rate.

### SIMULTANEOUS DEFAULT EVENTS

In the case of a stock market crash, several brokerage firms may simultaneously default. The case of systemic risk is similar. The failure of a major bank may cause a disruption in the payment system. In the extreme case where the two default events occur together, we need only one of the two underlying default swaps to hedge the first-to-default swap. In the intermediate case where there is both a common default event and some specific issuer default event, it is not possible to get a perfect hedge at default time since we do not know in advance if default is due to systematic or specific risk. The joint distribution of default times is degenerate and the holding of two default swaps is now a super-replicating hedge at default time.

## Managing the residual premiums

Net premiums paid prior to default are also volatile, mainly due to the variability of the default swap premiums. Let us turn back to the simplest case of hedging a plain vanilla long-term default swap by rolling over short-term default swaps. If the premiums of short-term default swaps vary through time, reflecting changes in credit quality, the hedged portfolio has a negative exposure to an increase in these premiums. Indeed, the rollover strategy is the analogue of short-term funding of fixed-rate long-term bonds. However, the risks involved in an increase of short-term credit spreads are usually substantially lower than the risk of losing the principal. When considering credit contingent contracts, the risks involved in the variability of default swap premiums can be dealt with by a suitable choice of financial hedging instruments and maturity of underlying default swaps, while protecting the profit and loss at default time.

### MATURITY OF UNDERLYING DEFAULT SWAPS

To simplify the exposition, we have primarily considered hedging with short-term default swaps. If we consider the case of constant default swap premiums, it can easily be seen that the use of longer maturity default swaps provides exactly the same cashflows. In the practical case of time-varying default swap premiums, a substantial reduction in the volatility of net premiums can be achieved by a suitable choice of the underlying default swaps. For instance, let us consider a T-maturity credit contingent contract such that $C(t)$, while random, remains close to $C(0)$. If the short-term default swap premiums $\lambda(t)$ are highly volatile, then the variance of the net premiums will be dramatically reduced if the dealer uses T-maturity default swaps, instead of short-term default swaps. In particular, the dealer is protected against an increase in short-term premiums. Let us turn back to the hedging of a short position in the first-to-default swap. We have seen that positive correlation of short-term default swap premiums increases the residual risks. Instead of rolling over the two short-term default swaps, we can consider buying two long-term plain default swaps. The premium outflow is no more volatile. On the other hand, in case of default, the value of the remaining default swap at the first default time is uncertain. Though it may become negative, it will usually be positive. Indeed, default is likely to be associated with an increase of the credit spreads of the two counterparties. The portfolio consisting of the two long-term default swaps is a conservative hedge of the first-to-default swap. Thus, a proper choice of underlying default swaps improves the effectiveness of the hedge substantially. It provides better protection against the volatility of credit spreads. However, even in some simple cases, the uncertainty on net premiums is not eliminated. Let us consider the simple example of a quanto default swap and constant short-term default swap premium, $\lambda dt$. We denote by $p_T(e)dt$ the premium received by the seller of the quanto default swap. To be hedged at default, we need to hold, at time t, a total amount of $e(t)$ standard default swaps, whatever the maturity of the underlying default swaps. Moreover, since default swap premiums are constant, there are no capital gains or losses in holding long-term standard default swaps. The net premium payment is $(p_T(e) - \lambda \times e(t))dt$. Unless the exchange rate is constant, it cannot be set to zero by any choice of underlying default swap.

### CORRELATION BETWEEN HEDGING CASHFLOWS AND FINANCIAL VARIABLES

As discussed already, $C(t)\lambda(t)dt$ are the premium outflows associated with the hedging strategy of a credit contingent contract. The first issue is the correlation between the cashflows $C(t)$ and the short-term premiums $\lambda(t)$. This effect is illustrated through the cancellable swap contract. If the third party has issued large amounts of debt to be serviced by floating payments, a substantial increase in the level of the interest rates could trigger default. This is what happened in the syndicated Eurodollar loan market in Mexico and Brazil in the early 1980s, when dollar interest rates soared. Default risk intensity becomes positively correlated with interest rates. Regarding hedging, the fixed-rate payer will have to pay on average more to buy a short-term default swap when the required notional increases. Conversely, negative correlation between the cashflows $C(t)$ and the short-term premiums $\lambda(t)dt$ will tend to stabilise the total payments and reduce residual hedging risks. Similarly, with multiple underlying default swaps, the short-term default swap premiums $\lambda_1(t)dt$ and $\lambda_2(t)dt$ tend to be positively correlated, due to common underlying risk factors, such as business cycles or country risk. The premium outflows associated with the hedging strategy are equal to $(\lambda_1(t) + \lambda_2(t))dt$ and the variance of residual cashflows increases.

Whenever the premium cashflows depend upon financial variables, such as interest rates or stock prices, we can reduce their magnitude. As an example, let us turn back to the hedging of a T-maturity long-term default swap, ie, $C(t) = 1$, with a quarterly rollover of three-month default swaps. Let us assume that the associated premiums are linear functions of three-month Libor, $a + b$ Libor with $b > 0$ (Lando, 1998). Then, we have negative exposure to an increase in Libor rates. We may consider buying a T-maturity cap with nominal equal to b and strike $c = (p_T - a)/b$. It can easily be shown that the aggregate premium plus the cap cashflow remain positive until maturity T. This is a super-replicating strategy, and thus an upper bound for the hedging cost. To lower the cost, we may consider higher strikes to protect the profit and loss against large upward movements in Libor.

### LINES OF CREDIT

As can be seen from credit contingent contracts and first-to-default swaps, the outflows $C(t)\lambda(t)dt$ and $(\lambda_1(t) + \lambda_2(t))dt$ are usually negatively related to an increase in the default swap premiums. A simple protection consists of holding lines of credit. As an example, consider the hedging of a credit contingent contract with bounded nominal $C_{max}$. Consider a line of credit, with ceiling $C_{max}$, maturity equal to the maturity of the credit contingent contract and periodic fee equal to $\alpha dt$. If the credit spread $\lambda(t)$ goes above some pre-specified spread $\beta$, the line of credit provides a payment equal to $C_{max} \times (\lambda(t) - \beta)dt$. Let us note that the seller of the previous credit guarantee, which may be a commercial bank, incurs exactly the same loss on a standard line of credit subscribed by an issuer of risky debt. Thus, using a standard credit product, we are able to cap the outflows at the level $C_{max} \times (\alpha + \beta)dt$.

MANAGEMENT OF THE CARRY

Let us turn back to the simplest case of hedging long-term default swaps against rolling over short-term default swaps. To ease the exposition, we assume in this example that short-term default swap premiums $\lambda(t)dt$ are deterministic and increasing with time. Then, our hedging strategy has a positive carry at the inception of the hedge, ie, conditional on no default, the net premiums $(p_T - \lambda(t))dt$ start from positive and become negative later. The pattern of the net premiums depends on default time and the premiums accrued on the short-term and long-term positions will, in general, be different. It is worth emphasising that, in our example, short-term premiums are deterministic, and there is no risk of unexpected change in the credit spread curve. Indeed, it can be shown that the positive net premium $(p_T - \lambda(t))dt$ is exactly compensated by a capital loss of the same magnitude on the long-term default swap. Thus, the value of the position at time $dt$, conditional on no default, remains equal to zero. However, if default arises at time $dt$, and the long-term credit swap has not been sold out, the potential loss in the long-term default swap vanishes and we are left only with the positive cashflow $(p_T - \lambda(t))dt$.

To illustrate these issues further, let us consider a dealer who has sold a 10-year credit contingent contract with $C(t) = 2$ over the first five years and $C(t) = 1$ over the five remaining years. He/she will receive a premium $p$ until default time or maturity. Such a contract may be used for credit protection of amortising loans. Consider the hedging portfolio built with a unit five-year default swap and a unit 10-year default swap. This clearly hedges the credit contingent contract at default. Let us now consider the structure of the premiums. In an arbitrage-free market, it can be shown that $p > p_{10Y}$ (otherwise, buying the credit contingent contract and selling the two simple default swaps would be an arbitrage opportunity). Similarly, it must be $P < p_{5Y} + p_{10Y}$. Thus, the net premium for the dealer is negative during the first five years and positive thereafter. As above, the length of the premium payment leg is randomly distributed due to uncertain default times.

First- and second-to-default swaps provide another example of such effects. Let us consider two bonds of the same notional and a zero-recovery rate. An investor who is long the first- and second-to-default swaps and short the two plain vanilla default swaps is perfectly hedged at default. If the premium of the second-to-default swap is smaller than any of the single default swaps, then the net premium received after the first default is always positive. To compensate for this effect, the net premium received before the first default must be negative. In an arbitrage-free market, the premium of the second-to-default swap is indeed smaller than any of the two single default swap premiums. To prove this, let us consider the following strategy: we buy one of the two default swaps (say default swap one) and we sell the second-to-default swap. We denote by $p_{1,T}$ and $p_{S,T}$ the corresponding premiums and $\tau_1$ and $\tau_S = \max(\tau_1, \tau_2)$ the default times. Until the first default, the net premium is $p_{S,T} - p_{1,T}$.

- If counterparty two defaults first, then the second-to-default swap becomes a default swap on counterparty one, and we fully hedge the second default by the long position in default swap one. The net premium remains $p_{S,T} - p_{1,T}$.
- If counterparty one defaults first, then we receive the notional of the first bond at time $\tau_1$. This can be invested in a money market account to provide protection against the second default. The net premium becomes $p_{S,T}$.

If $p_{S,T}$ were greater than $p_{1,T}$, we would have constructed an arbitrage opportunity. Similarly, in an arbitrage-free market, we must have $p_{S,T} < p_{2,T}$.

FINITE MATURITY AND DISCRETE PREMIUMS

Instantaneous default swaps are not available in the market. Discrete payment dates affect the effectiveness of the hedge, in particular when the nominal amount at risk $C(t)$ varies substantially between two payment dates. When considering a first-to-default swap, we must also consider the periodicity of the premium payments. If premiums are discretely paid, say quarterly, then when the first counterparty defaults, there remains short-term insurance on the second counterparty that still has economic value. Thus, the hedging strategy is super-replicating and it is only with continuously paid premiums that we may obtain perfect replication at default time.

## Conclusion

This chapter is intended to be a step towards a better understanding of the hedging of exotic credit derivatives and a bridge between risk-neutral valuation of these contracts and the cost of the hedge approach. These products lie between insurance and finance. Like insurance contracts, they give rise to payments conditional on the occurrence of an event. Like financial contracts, they can be dynamically hedged. Our hedging approach is intended to protect the profit and loss at default time. We have also considered residual risks, ie, net premiums paid prior to default, associated with the hedged portfolio. Rather than going through model-dependent calculations, we have tried to provide economic insights regarding the management of these residual net premiums through appropriate financial tools and trading strategies.

**BIBLIOGRAPHY**

**Arvanitis, A., J. Gregory and J-P. Laurent,** 1999, "Building Models for Credit Spreads", *Journal of Derivatives,* 6(3), pp. 27–43.

**Duffie, D.,** 1998, *First-to-default Valuation*, Graduate School of Business, Stanford University.

**Duffie, D.,** 1999, "Credit Swap Valuation", *Financial Analysts Journal*, January–February, pp. 73–87.

**Krakovsky, A.,** 1999, "Gap Risk in Credit Trading", *Risk*, March 1999, pp. 65–7.

**Lando, D.,** 1998, *On Cox Processes and Credit-risky Securities,* Working Paper, University of Copenhagen.

# II

# MEASURING DEFAULT RISK

9

# Measuring Default Accurately

**Jorge Sobehart and Sean Keenan**

Citigroup

*Jorge Sobehart and Sean Keenan measure the cumulative accuracy of default risk models and see what improvements can be made.*

Credit risk can be defined as the potential that a borrower or counterparty will fail to meet their obligations in accordance with the terms of a loan agreement or contract indenture. For most individual and institutional investors, bonds and other tradable debt instruments are the main source of credit risk. In contrast, for banking institutions, loans are often the primary source of credit risk.

Because loans to middle-market, unrated firms are generally an important portion of most banking institutions' portfolios, banks often require ongoing credit assessments for these assets. However, since institutions' individual exposures to such firms are often relatively small, it is typically uneconomical for them to devote extensive resources to the analysis of each individual borrower. Not surprisingly, these economic factors have caused banking institutions to be among the earliest adopters of quantitative credit risk models. The use of reliable models can offer a cost-effective means of expediting the credit approval process, provide monitoring functions over different divisions within an institution and help in the implementation of portfolio-wide credit risk management systems.

As banks become more familiar with credit modelling technology, their focus is widening to include model validation and benchmarking. In its recent reports on credit risk modelling, the Basel Committee on Banking Supervision (1999, 2000) stressed that the area of model validation will prove to be a key challenge for banking institutions in the foreseeable future. Coinciding with the Basel reports, several model validation studies[1] using statistically significant samples of borrowers have been reported for the US market, where Moody's Investors Service has been in operation long enough to create sizeable and reliable samples for both public and private firms. Similar studies exist for European and emerging markets.

Institutions that retain borrowers' credit histories, including default or credit loss information, are in a position to conduct similar validation tests and make objective determinations as to the relative performance of different credit risk models. However, the highly infrequent nature of default events and the averaging effect (over multiple credit cycles) present challenges in assessing the accuracy and reliability of credit risk models for most institutions. Many standard statistical tests of model accuracy are not sensitive enough to adequately distinguish between models. The objective of this chapter is to provide some guidance on testing and benchmarking default risk models, using simple, yet powerful performance measures based on the cumulative accuracy of the models. More precisely, we will elaborate on the meaning of receiver operating characteristics (ROC) curves and their summary statistics.

Measures of cumulative accuracy have become increasingly popular because they can be used to compare the performance of different types of default risk models. The data requirements for using these performance measures consist of multiple risk measures for a cross-sectional or panel data set of borrowers,[2] and associated default or loss information that provides the criterion of accuracy. Here, we focus on default prediction accuracy as opposed to loss prediction, so the

*The analysis and conclusions set forth are those of the authors only.*

data requirement would be a set of dated default flags.

## Cumulative accuracy measures

Although accuracy in predicting defaults is only one dimension of model quality, it is often the most prominent one in discussions of credit risk models. Because credit risk models are often used to generate opinions of credit quality, on which investment decisions are taken, it is important to understand each model's strengths and weaknesses in the context of default prediction.

In some contexts, such as portfolio monitoring, an ordinal ranking of default risk is all that is needed. In other contexts, such as commercial lending, a classification model is required. Potential obligors may need to be classified into "acceptable risk" and "unacceptable risk" groups. This places additional burdens on the model, as not only must it produce an accurate ordinal ranking, it must also produce scores that are stable in absolute terms, relative to the pre-specified cut-off value.

Such classification models can err in one of two ways. First, the model can indicate low risk when, in fact, the risk is high. Typically referred to as a Type I error, this corresponds to highly rated borrowers who nevertheless default on their obligations. Secondly, the model can indicate high risk when, in fact, the risk is low. Typically referred to as a Type II error, this corresponds to low-rated firms that should, in fact, be rated higher.

We begin our description[3] of model performance by assuming two models being tested on a population of borrowers. It is the task of the models to distinguish defaulters (right distribution) from non-defaulting borrowers (left distribution), as shown in Figure 1.[4] In practice, defaulters are a small fraction of the borrowers and the two populations overlap considerably for risky borrowers. Figure 1a shows a hypothetical decision axis that represents one situation in our example. This axis is conceptualised as the output of model 1 that represents the borrower's credit quality. In Figure 1a, it is assumed that the criterion $C_1$ (cut-off point) adopted by a user for classifying a borrower as a defaulter has been established at a fairly high value along the model decision axis. In this example, the selected cut-off point $C_1$ is in compliance with the decision to be lax in judging the credit quality of a borrower. Borrowers whose risk scores are above $C_1$ should

**1. Relationship between cut-off and separation**

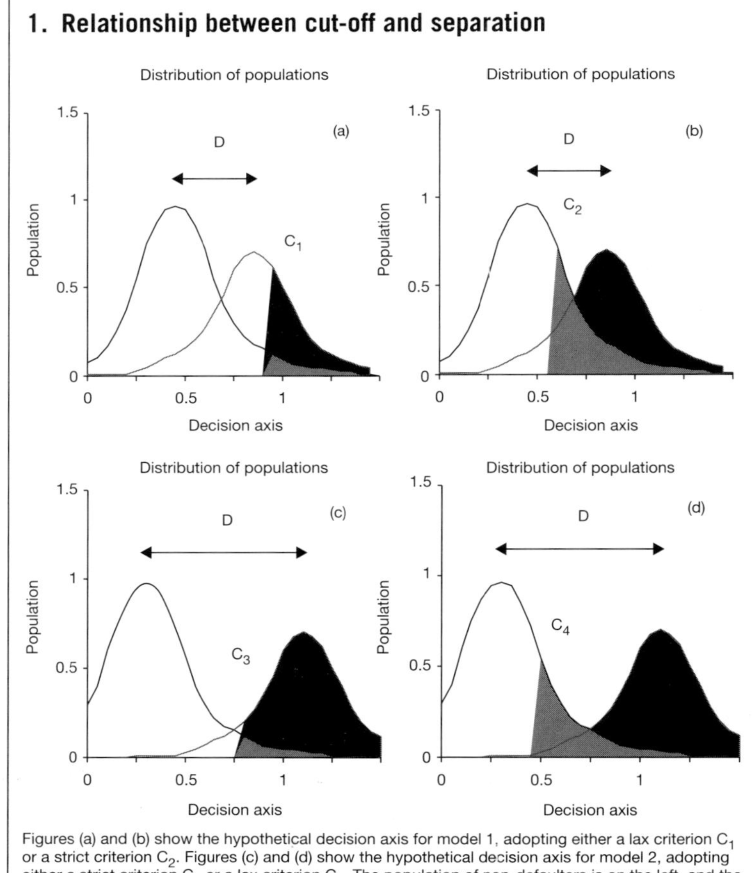


Figures (a) and (b) show the hypothetical decision axis for model 1, adopting either a lax criterion $C_1$ or a strict criterion $C_2$. Figures (c) and (d) show the hypothetical decision axis for model 2, adopting either a strict criterion $C_3$ or a lax criterion $C_4$. The population of non-defaulters is on the left, and the population of defaulters, exaggerated for illustrative purposes, is on the right be classified as likely defaulters. This criterion results in a small fraction of defaulters to be classified correctly (Type I error). In Figure 1b, the user is shown to have adopted a lower cut-off value $C_2$, in accordance with instructions to assume a strict criterion in judging the borrower's credit quality. This criterion results in a large fraction of non-defaulters to be classified incorrectly (Type II error). In Figures 1c and 1d, the user of model 2 is seen to have adopted somewhat different, but corresponding criteria, $C_3$ and $C_4$, under these same guidelines.

For each borrower, there are four possible outcomes in the identification of defaulters.

1. *Hit:* the model correctly classifies the borrower as a defaulter.
2. *Miss:* the model assigns low risk to a defaulter.
3. *False alarm:* a low-risk borrower is classified as a defaulter.
4. *Correct rejection:* the model assigns low risk to a high quality borrower.

The proportions of these possible outcomes depend on two aspects of the decision-making situation: the cut-off C, which the user uses to classify borrowers; and the separation D of the population of defaulters and non-defaulters along the decision axis, which depends on the model's ability to differentiate the populations.

Figure 1 indicates how the cut-off C and the separation D contribute to the proportion of behaviours occurring in each possible contingency. In Figures 1a and 1b, D is fairly small as the populations of defaulters and non-defaulters overlap along the decision axis. In Figures 1c and 1d, the populations are separated by a greater amount. This indicates that model 2 can differentiate risky borrowers better than model 1.

In each panel of Figure 1, the shaded area under the population of defaulters represents the proportion of hits attained. The shaded area represents the proportion of false alarms generated by the model in response to the risk characteristics of the borrower. The unshaded area under the population of defaulters represents misses occurring when the model assigns a low risk to a defaulter. Finally, the unshaded area under the non-defaulter population represents correct rejections.

A key question about model performance is how effectively a model separates the two populations for different decision cut-offs. The separation of populations is related to both the selected cut-off C and the distance D. This relation is easily represented in the ROC curves[5] and the closely related cumulative accuracy profiles (CAP).[6]

The ordinate of the ROC curve is scaled as the hit rate (proportion of hits attained for all borrowers). The abscissa is scaled as the false alarm rate (proportion of false alarm responses for all borrowers). In contrast, the abscissa of a CAP curve is scaled as the fraction of all borrowers ordered by model output. Because defaulters usually represent a small fraction of the population of borrowers, ROC and CAP curves will look similar. However, ROC curves for an ideal model that produces perfect predictions are not well-defined, while CAP curves are steep but well-behaved. We focus on ROC curves because they are more familiar to most readers. A similar analysis will apply to CAP curves.

The formula for the hit rate (HR) is:

$$HR(C) = \frac{H(C)}{H(C) + M(C)} \quad (1)$$

Here H(C) is the number of hits and M(C) is the number of misses for a cut-off C. Note that H + M is the total number of defaulters.

The formula for the false alarm rate (FAR) is:

$$FAR(C) = \frac{F(C)}{F(C) + R(C)} \quad (2)$$

Here F(C) is the number of false alarms and R(C) is the number of correct rejection for a cut-off C. Note that F + R is the total number of non-defaulter obligors. Using HR(C) and FAR(C), we can construct the ROC curves shown in Figure 2. Notice that the main problem of model comparison is the fact that different models produce

**2. ROC curves**

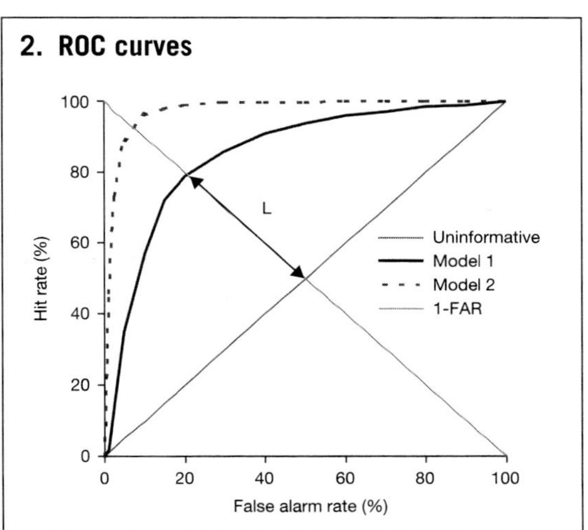


ROC curves for models 1 and 2 based on the hypothetical decision axes and criteria of Figure 1. The area under the ROC curve defines a global summary statistic of model performance. The distance L between the model's ROC curve and the uninformative (random) ROC defines a local (less powerful) measure of the separation between the population of defaulters and healthy firms different score scales, so the value of cut-off criteria may differ. To compare different models, one needs a framework independent of the absolute value of the model scores and cut-off. The ROC curves eliminate the dependence on the absolute value of the cut-off by plotting hit rate $HR(C)$ versus false alarm rate $FAR(C)$.

The departure of a model's ROC curve from a chance performance line (diagonal $HR = FAR$) is a measure of the model's ability to separate the two populations. The curves in Figure 2 show that model 2 is more sensitive at identifying defaulters than model 1 for the same level of false alarms. It is clear from Figures 1 and 2 that minimising one type of error usually comes at the expense of increasing the other type. That is, the probability of making a Type II error increases as the probability of a Type I error is reduced. Although it is possible for some credit risk models to commit less of one type of error than another, investors and financial institutions usually seek to keep the probability of making either type of error as small as possible. In practice the trade-off between Type I and Type II errors depends on the cost to the organisation. For example, the cost of Type I errors can be the loss of principal and interest that was promised, or a loss in the market value of the obligation. In contrast, losses resulting from Type II error can include the loss of return and origination fees when loans are either turned down or lost through non-competitive bidding.

While ROC curves are a convenient way to visualise the model's performance, it is often convenient to summarise the predictive accuracy into a summary statistic. There are a variety of such summary statistics, obtained by comparing the ROC curve of any set of model outputs with the ideal ROC for a perfectly predictive model; the closer the ROC is to its ideal, the better the model performs. In contrast, the closer the model's ROC is to the uninformative ROC (diagonal), the worse the model performs.

One such summary statistic, which is global, focuses on the area that lies above the uninformative ROC and below the model ROC. The more area there is below the model ROC and above the uninformative ROC, the better the model is doing overall (Hanley and McNeil, 1982). The maximum area that can be enclosed above the uninformative ROC curve is identified by the ideal ROC and its value is 1/2. Therefore, the ratio of the area between a model's ROC and the uninformative ROC to the area between the ideal ROC and the uninformative ROC summarises the predictive power over the entire range of possible risk values. We refer to this measure as the ROC accuracy ratio (RAR):

$$RAR = 2\int_0^1 HR(FAR)\,d(FAR) - 1 \qquad (3)$$

RAR is a fraction between 0 and 1. Risk measures with RARs close to 0 display little advantage over a random assignment of risk scores, while those with RARs near 1 display almost perfect predictive power. RARs are global performance statistics similar to the CAP accuracy ratios (AR) described in Keenan and Sobehart (1999).

Since the upward-sloped diagonal $HR = FAR$ represents the case where the population of defaulters and healthy firms overlap completely (non-informative case), one may wonder if the downward-sloped diagonal $HR = 1 - FAR$ also provides information on the separation of the populations. In fact, the distance along this diagonal is an insightful - but less powerful - measure based on the local properties of the ROC curve. Let $C^*$ define the cut-off value for which the ROC curve (the hit rate $HR(C)$) intersects the diagonal $1 - FAR(C)$, as shown in Figure 2. Using Figure 1 as a guiding tool, the cut-off $C^*$ represents the point where the shaded area under the normalised population of defaulters equals the unshaded area under the normalised population of non-defaulters. The distance between the model's ROC curve and the uninformative ROC, measured along this diagonal, defines a natural local statistic:

$$L = \sqrt{\left(HR(C^*) - \frac{1}{2}\right)^2 + \left(FAR(C^*) - \frac{1}{2}\right)^2} \qquad (4)$$

Distance $L$ is composed of two contributions. The first term is the difference between the median of the population of defaulters and the cumulative fraction of defaulters correctly classified by the model at cut-off $C^*$ (the shaded area in Figure 1). The second term is the difference between the median of the non-defaulter population and the cumulative fraction of false alarms at cut-off $C^*$ (the cross-hatched area in Figure 1). Predictive models will be able to separate the two populations and, therefore, will have $HR(C^*)$ close to 1 and $FAR(C^*)$ near 0. Poorly performing models will confuse the two populations and, therefore, will have both $HR(C^*)$ and $FAR(C^*)$ near 0.5. Thus risk measures with $L$ close to 0 display little advantage over a random assignment of risk scores, while those with $L$ near $1/\sqrt{2}$ indicate a good separation of the populations of defaulters and healthy firms.

Importantly, because L is only a local measure as opposed to a global cumulative measure such as RAR, it does not provide an unambiguous absolute ranking of model performance when ROC curves have irregular shapes or cross each other. Given that L is measured at only one point along the curve, a higher L does not necessarily indicate a greater ability to distinguish between defaulters and healthy firms for the entire range of credit scores.

Finally, it is important to realise that, because of the sparseness of defaults in most credit data, accuracy statistics may sometimes yield spurious model performance differences based only on data anomalies. To avoid these problems, we suggest the use of the above performance measures combined with resampling techniques to leverage the available data and reduce the dependency on the particular sample at hand. A typical resampling technique proceeds as follows. From the initial sample of borrowers, a sub-sample is selected at random. The selected performance statistic is calculated for this sub-sample and recorded. Another random sub-sample is then drawn, and the process is repeated until a distribution of the performance statistic is established and error bounds can be calculated.

1 *For details see Herrity, Keenan, Sobehart, Carty and Falkenstein (1999), Keenan and Sobehart (1999), Sobehart, Keenan and Stein (2000), Sobehart, Stein, Mikityanskaya and Li (2000), and Falkenstein, Boral and Carty (2000).*

2 *A cross sectional data set contains one observation on many individuals, while a panel data set contains observations over time on many individuals.*

3 *Our presentation follows closely that of Burton (1972).*

4 *The population of defaulters has been exaggerated (the shaded area in Figure 1).*

5 *These curves are also known as dubbed curves and power curves. See Burton (1972), Swets (1988), Provost and Fawcett (1997), Hoadley and Oliver (1998).*

6 *Keenan and Sobehart (1999).*

**BIBLIOGRAPHY**

**Basel,** 1999, *Credit Risk Modeling Practices and Applications*, Basel Committee on Banking Supervision, April.

**Basel,** 2000, *Supervisory Risk Assessment and Early Warning Systems*, Basel Committee on Banking and Supervision (4), December.

**Burton, G. A.,** 1972, *Experimental Psychology*, pp. 137–44 (John Wiley).

**Falkenstein, E., A. Boral and L. V. Carty,** 2000, *RiskCalc Private Model: Moody's Default Model for Private Firms*, Moody's Investors Service Special Comment, May.

**Herrity, J., S. C. Keenan, J. R. Sobehart, L. V. Carty and E. Falkenstein,** 1999, *Measuring Private Firm Default Risk*, Moody's Investors Service Special Comment, June.

**Hanley, A., and B. McNeil,** 1982, "The Meaning and Use of the Area Under a Receiver Operating Characteristics (ROC) Curve", *Diagnostic Radiology*, 143(1), pp. 29–36.

**Hoadley, B., and R. M. Oliver,** 1998, "Business Measures of Scorecard Benefit", *IMI Journal of Mathematics Applied in Business & Industry*, 9, pp. 55–64.

**Keenan, S. C., and J. R. Sobehart,** 1999, *Performance Measures for Credit Risk Models*, Moody's Risk Management Services, Research Report, also: "Would You Credit It?", *Risk*, 13(7).

**Provost, F., and T. Fawcett,** 1997, *Analysis and Visualization of Classifier Performance: Comparison Under Imprecise Class and Cost Distributions*, proceedings from Third International Conference on Knowledge Discovery and Data Mining, Newport Beach, California, August 14–17.

**Sobehart, J. R., S. C. Keenan and R. Stein,** 2000, "Validation Methodologies for Default Risk Models", *Credit*, 1(4), pp. 51–6.

**Sobehart, J. R., S. C. Keenan and R. Stein,** 2000, *Benchmarking Quantitative Default Risk Models: A Validation Methodology*, Moody's Rating Methodology, March.

**Sobehart, J. R., R. M. Stein, V. Mikityanskaya and L. Li,** 2000, *Moody's Public Firm Risk Model: A Hybrid Approach to Modeling Default Risk*, Moody's Investors Service Rating Methodology, February.

**Swets, J. A.,** 1988, "Measuring the Accuracy of Diagnostic Systems", *Science*, 240, pp. 1285–93.

10

# A Credit Risk Catwalk

**Sean Keenan and Jorge Sobehart**

Citigroup

*Today's credit portfolio manager is spoilt for choice when it comes to credit risk models. Whether traditional credit ratings, firm-value models as used by KMV Corporation, or the latest neural network systems, all have their defenders and detractors. But can they be objectively compared? Here, Sean Keenan and Jorge Sobehart show how.*

The aim of this chapter is to provide guidance for testing and benchmarking credit risk models. Transparency in model validation and benchmarking is extremely important, since reliable models can provide a cost-effective means of expediting the credit approval process, and can provide a consistency check on credit assessment and monitoring functions. Poorly performing models could have serious consequences for credit risk management practices. We focus on default prediction models, although the techniques described can easily be adapted for models predicting loss, or other types of credit events.

Many financial institutions find that multiple risk measures are available for each borrower or potential borrower. These may include internal risk grades, model-generated risk scores and credit opinions from rating agencies expressed as symbolic ratings. Some commercially available credit risk models make extraordinary claims of predictive accuracy, which are usually backed up by anecdotal comparisons instead of well-documented evidence of superior performance (see, for example, Kealhofer, Kwok and Weng, 1998). In such cases, it is beneficial to compare the relative performance of the different measures of credit quality using an objective and rigorous methodology. Institutions that have borrowers' credit histories, including default or credit loss information, are in a position to conduct validation tests and make objective determinations as to the relative performance of different credit risk measures.

In this chapter, we describe four simple, yet powerful, techniques for comparing the performance of credit risk models and analysing information redundancy:

1. cumulative accuracy profile;
2. accuracy ratio;
3. conditional information entropy ratio; and
4. mutual information entropy.

These techniques are quite general, and can be used to compare different types of models even when the model outputs differ and are difficult to compare directly. Specifically, discrete risk ratings can be compared with continuous numerical outputs. Even categorical outputs such as letter and alphanumeric symbols used by rating agencies can be evaluated side by side with numerical credit scores. The requirements for implementing these tests are data consisting of multiple risk measures for a cross-sectional or panel data set, and associated default or loss information that provides the criterion of accuracy. Here, we will focus on default prediction accuracy as opposed to loss prediction, so the data requirement is a set of dated default flags.

## Basis for inter-model comparison

Comparing the performance of different credit risk models is difficult because the models themselves may be measuring different aspects of credit risk, and may be expressing the outputs in different ways. For example, some models explicitly estimate a probability of default, or expected default frequency (EDF; see Kealhofer, Kwok and Weng, 1998), which is therefore a number between zero and one. Others, such as internal bank scores, rank risk on some ordinal scale, say

1–10 or 1–100. Rating agencies rank along a relatively coarse 21-bin alphanumeric scale, while other models such as Z-scores produce scores reported to several decimal places.

Model forms also vary widely – credit risk models have developed using every available type of linear and non-linear statistical technique. Because of this variety, internal model diagnostics are not helpful for comparisons.

Many validation tests found in the literature (see Caouette, Altman and Narayanan, 1998) are of limited scope for practical model comparisons. Commonly cited diagnostics such as the F-statistic or Akaike information criteria may be helpful for comparing the internal performance of simple regression models. However, similar tests are not available for expert systems, neural networks and other default prediction models, let alone risk scores assigned by analysts. Moreover, even in the linear regression case, the assumptions that underlie these diagnostics are frequently violated in practice (such as independence of samples or the Gaussian distribution of errors). Although it is usually not difficult to determine to what extent these assumptions are violated in each case, it is difficult to determine how to correct the t-statistics or other statistics that authors cite to demonstrate they have a "good" model. The techniques discussed below are useful not only because of their power and robustness, but also because they can easily be applied to any type of model output, including analyst-assigned risk ratings.

Inter-model comparison is essentially a comparison of model errors produced on data sets used for model training and validation. Because default events are rare, it is often impractical to create a model using one data set, and then test it on a separate "hold-out" data set containing out-of-sample and out-of-time observations. Such tests would be the best way to compare different models' performance. However, there is rarely enough default information to support these tests. Too many defaulters omitted from the training set will impair the model estimation, while too many defaulters omitted from the hold-out sample will reduce the power of the validation tests. The model builder's task is more often one of "rationalising" the default experience of a sample, which contains both defaulters and non-defaulters. The modeller seeks to determine those characteristics that distinguish defaulters from non-defaulters, so that defaulters can be consistently identified when confronted with a new and different sample of obligors.

Whether expressed as probabilities of default, discrete orderings or continuous risk scores, model outputs are "opinions" of credit quality representing different degrees of belief of default-like characteristics. Default prediction models can err in one of two ways. First, the model can indicate low risk when, in fact, the risk is high. Typically referred to as "type I error", this corresponds to highly rated issuers who nevertheless default on financial obligations. An example would be a firm that defaulted on publicly held long-term bonds while holding an A rating from an agency. Second, the model can indicate high risk when, in fact, the risk is low. Typically referred to as "type II error", this corresponds to low-rated firms that should, in fact, be rated higher. A model that identifies a start-up fashion retailer as a low-risk borrower relative to Ford Motor Company would be committing a type II error.

It is possible for some risk measures to be better at (ie, commit less of) one type of error than another. However, success at minimising one type of error necessarily comes at the expense of increasing the other type of error. A claim such as "model X assigned very high probability of default to 90% of the defaulters in the sample" provides an incomplete picture, since we do not know how often the model assigned a high probability of default to a creditworthy borrower who did not default. This is particularly true for models that have been constructed with a proportion of defaulters to non-defaulters that is not representative of the true population of borrowers (see Caouette, Altman and Narayanan, 1998, pp. 112–22).

Unfortunately, this type of misleading argument is frequently used to reinforce the credibility of some models. It is not unusual to see anecdotal comparisons of the output of quantitative models (eg, an EDF) against the historical default rate of an agency rating, and incorrect conclusions drawn as to the performance of the model based solely on a higher value of the model output. Good models balance both types of error by effectively differentiating the relative credit risk across the entire spectrum of borrowers' credit quality, and do this consistently over time.

To demonstrate the usefulness of the methodology we introduce here, we compare several univariate and multivariate models on a validation data set extracted from about 9,000 public firms for the period 1989–99. The total number of firm-year observations is about 54,000, including more than 530 default events. It should be stressed that the purpose of the comparison is not to show which of the selected models is better, but to show how performance measures differentiate the models.

To illustrate the performance measures, we compare outputs from the following models:

- a univariate model based on return on assets (ROA) only;
- a Z-score model (a widely used benchmark);[1]
- a hazard model of bankruptcy (see Shumway, 1998);
- a variant of the Merton (1974) model based on concept of distance to default:

$$\text{Distance to default} = \frac{(\text{MVA} - \text{default point})}{\text{MVA } \sigma}$$

  where MVA is the market value of the firm's assets and $\sigma$ its volatility, and the default point is approximately equal to current liabilities plus 50% of long-term liabilities; and
- a non-linear regression model (see Sobehart *et al.*, 2000) based on both market and financial information.

These models represent a wide range of modelling approaches varying from simple univariate and multivariate analysis to implementations of contingent claims analysis and adaptive computation. We also consider Moody's long-term debt ratings, both as a benchmark, and to illustrate the flexibility of the performance measures, even though the stated goal of Moody's ratings is not short-term default prediction *per se* (see Keenan, Shtogrin and Sobehart, 1999). The results for agency ratings are not included in the performance tests described here because most of the obligors in the data set are unrated companies.

## Accuracy accounting

Credit risk model outputs can be interpreted as a ranking of obligors according to the extent to which they exhibit defaulter-like characteristics. One set of performance comparison measures is based on getting an accurate account of how the model performs over an entire data set when ranked from riskiest to safest. These measures are superior to anecdotal comparisons because they compare models' ability to predict many default events as well as many non-default events. This section describes methods for directly comparing credit quality discrimination over an entire data set comprised of both defaulters and non-defaulters.

### CUMULATIVE ACCURACY PROFILES (CAPs)

A common feature to all models and agency ratings is the exponential-like curve displayed by the default rate as a function of credit quality or risk score. The better the model, the steeper the curve relative to the distribution of underlying scores. However, a simple analysis of the curvature of the default rate would provide an incomplete picture of the discriminatory power of a model.

A more refined method is the use of CAPs, which help to visualise local features across the spectrum of credit quality, and give a graphical representation of each risk measure's ability to distinguish defaulters from non-defaulters.

CAP curves belong to the class of performance measures generically known as dubbed curves, lift curves or power curves. These curves are widely used in many fields to visualise the overall performance of a model to separate two populations. To plot a CAP curve, companies are ordered by risk score from riskiest to safest. For a given fraction x% of the total number of companies ordered by risk score, a type I CAP curve is constructed by calculating the percentage $y(x)$ of the defaulters whose risk score is equal to or lower than the one for fraction x. A type II CAP curve is constructed similarly using the function $z(x)$ of non-defaulters. Technically, the CAP curve for type I errors represents the cumulative fraction of default events for different percentiles of the risk score scale, and the CAP curve for type II errors represents its complement.

A good model concentrates the defaulters at the riskiest scores and so the percentage of all defaulters identified (the y variable above) increases quickly as one moves up the sorted sample (along the x-axis). If the model were totally uninformative – if, for example, it assigned risk scores randomly – we would expect to capture a proportional fraction of defaulters with each increment of the sorted sample. That is, x% of the defaulters would be contained in the first x% of the observations, generating a straight line CAP.

A good model also concentrates the non-defaulters at the lowest riskiness. Therefore, the percentage of all non-defaulters (the z variable) should increase slowly at first. One of the most useful properties of CAPs is that they reveal information about the predictive accuracy of the model over its entire range of risk scores for a particular time horizon. Hypothetical type I CAPs for ideal, intermediate and uninformative (random) risk models are presented in Figure 1. Similar curves are shown for type II CAP plots. The vertical dashed line represents the fraction of defaulters in the total population. In Figure 1, the fraction of defaulters has been exaggerated to a hypothetical

**1. Hypothetical cumulative accuracy profiles**

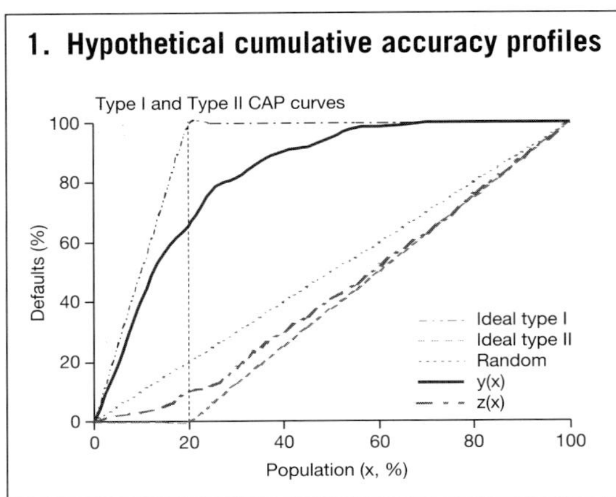


**2. Selected cumulative accuracy profiles**

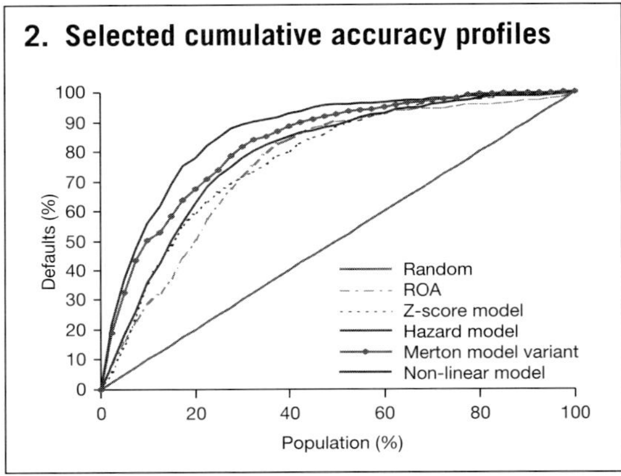


**Table 1. Selected accuracy ratios**

| Model | Accuracy ratio |
|---|---|
| ROA only | 0.53 |
| Z-score model | 0.56 |
| Hazard model | 0.59 |
| Merton model variant | 0.67 |
| Non-linear model | 0.73 |

20% for illustration purposes. In practice, the fraction of defaulters is much lower (in our validation sample, around 1%). Figure 2 shows the results for the benchmark models.

### ACCURACY RATIOS (ARs)

It is convenient to have a single summary measure that ranks the predictive accuracy of each risk measure for both type I and type II errors. We obtain such a measure by comparing the CAP of any risk measure with both the ideal and random CAPs. The closer the CAP is to its ideal, the more area there is between it and the random CAP. The largest amount of area that can possibly be enclosed is identified by the ideal CAP. The ratio of the area between a model's CAP and the random CAP to the area between the ideal CAP and the random CAP is the AR. Differences in the proportion of defaulters/non-defaulters in the data sets used to test each model affect the relative performance of each model. Thus, the AR measures are directly comparable for any and all models as long as they are applied to the same data set.

Here, we derive an AR that provides the same performance measure for type I and type II errors. The definition of AR is based on the sample frequencies for defaults/non-defaults. Technically, the AR value is defined as:

$$\mathrm{AR} = \frac{1}{1-f}\left(2\int_0^1 y(x)dx - 1\right) = \frac{1}{f}\left(1 - 2\int_0^1 z(x)dx\right) \quad (1)$$

Here $y(x)$ and $z(x)$ are the type I and type II CAP curves for a population $x$ of ordered risk scores, and $f = D/(N + D)$ is the fraction of defaults, where D is the total number of defaulting obligors and N is the total number of non-defaulting obligors. A geometrical interpretation of Equation 1 can be obtained by examining Figure 1 in detail and noticing that the vertical dashed line is located at $x = f$.

The AR measures the proportion of defaulters in a sample that can be identified per increment of the risk score that is being evaluated. It is a fraction between zero and one. Risk measures with ARs close to zero display little advantage over a random assignment of risk scores while those with ARs near one display almost perfect foresight. Most of the models we tested had ARs in the range of 50–75% for the selected sample of public firms. To reduce the sensitivity of the AR to outliers and the rare-event nature of defaults (small samples) we perform sensitivity tests using random resampling (see Herrity *et al.*, 1999). Table 1 shows AR values for the tested models.

## Entropy-based performance measures

### INFORMATION ENTROPY (IE)

IE is a summary measure of the "uncertainty" that a probability distribution represents. This concept originates in the fields of statistical mechanics and communication theory (see Shannon and Weaver, 1949, Jaynes, 1957, and Pierce, 1970). Intuitively, the information entropy measures the overall "amount of uncertainty" represented by a probability distribution.

We define information entropy as follows. Assume the existence of an event with only two possible outcomes: (A) issuer defaults with probability p and (B) issuer does not default with probability $1 - p$. The amount of additional information an investor requires to determine which outcome actually occurred is defined as:

$$\text{Information} = -\log_2(p) \qquad (2)$$

where $\log_2(p)$ is the logarithm of p in base two.

If only the first outcome is possible, then $p = 1$ and the information required is $-\log_2(p) = 0$. In this case, there is no uncertainty about the outcome and, therefore, there is no relevant information that was not previously known. If the two events are equally likely for the investor (uninformative case), then $p = 1/2$ and the amount of information required reaches a maximum value of $-\log_2(p) = 1$ (bit). Exactly one bit of information (the equivalent to a yes/no type of answer) is the information required by the investor to know which of the two equally likely possibilities have occurred.

The use of two as the logarithmic base has certain advantages for this example but any base can be used. Usually, the natural logarithms are used for convenience. Note, however, that the amount of information depends upon what logarithmic base is used, which determines the unit of measure of information.

The information entropy of the event is defined as:

$$H_0 = p\log(p) + (1-p)\log(1-p) \qquad (3)$$

Figure 3 shows the information entropy as a function of p, and reaches its maximum when the probability is $p = 1/2$. This is a state of absolute ignorance because both possibilities are equally likely for the investor. If the assigned probability of an event is lower than 1/2, one outcome is more likely to occur than the other. That is, the investor has less uncertainty on the possible outcomes. The reduction in the uncertainty of the outcomes is reflected in the reduction of entropy.

**3. Information entropy as a function of p**

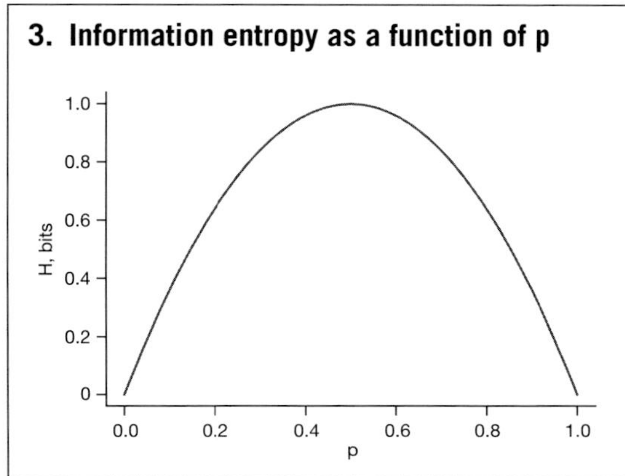


Consider again the two mutually exclusive outcomes of an event: (A) issuer defaults and (B) issuer does not default, one of which must be true. Given a set of risk scores $S = \{R_1, \ldots, R_n\}$ produced by a model, the conditional entropy that measures the information about the propositions for a specific risk score $R_j$ is:

$$h(R_j) = -\left(P\left(A\middle|R_j\right)\log P\left(A\middle|R_j\right) + P\left(B\middle|R_j\right)\log P\left(B\middle|R_j\right)\right) \qquad (4)$$

where $P(A|R_j)$ is the probability that the issuer defaults given that the risk score is $R_j$ and $P(B|R_j) = 1 - P(A|R_j)$. This value quantifies the average information gained from observing which of the two events A and B actually occurred.

The average over all possible risk scores is the conditional information entropy:

$$H_1(s,\delta) = H_1(R_1,\ldots,R_n,\delta) = \sum_{k=1}^{n} h(R_k)P(R_k) \qquad (5)$$

For models with continuous outputs, the most straightforward way to estimate the quantities defined in Equations 4 and 5 is to use a bin-counting approach. The range of the model output is divided into a number of bins of size $\delta$, related to the accuracy of the output. Because Equation 4 requires estimating the conditional distributions of defaults and non-defaults, the bins of size $\delta$ have to be bigger than the precision of some of the model outputs to provide meaningful statistics. For illustration, we use $\delta = 5\%$ of the model output range for each model.[2] Thus, the IE defines an absolute measure of the amount of uncertainty contained in the models as long as all the models' outputs describe the same data set.

The properties that make the information entropy so appealing are: if the risk score set S contains more information about the two outcomes than another set S′, then $H(S) < H(S')$; and acquisition of new information can never increase the value of H.

## CONDITIONAL INFORMATION ENTROPY RATIO (CIER)

In the same way we reduced the CAP to a single AR statistic in order to have a measure that lends itself to comparison across models, we can use IE to produce another summary statistic for how well a given model can predict defaults. This is done via the CIER. The CIER compares the amount of "uncertainty" there is about default in the case where we have no model (a state of more uncertainty about the possible outcomes) to the amount of "uncertainty" left over after we have

**Table 2. Selected information entropy ratios**

| Model | CIER |
|---|---|
| ROA only | 0.06 |
| Z-score model | 0.09 |
| Hazard model | 0.11 |
| Merton model variant | 0.14 |
| Non-linear model | 0.19 |

**Table 3. Selected mutual entropy ratios**

| Model | ROA | Z-score model | Hazard model | Merton model variant | Non-linear model |
|---|---|---|---|---|---|
| ROA only | 0.94 | 0.98 | 0.97 | 0.97 | 0.97 |
| Z-score model | | 0.91 | 0.96 | 0.96 | 0 95 |
| Hazard model | | | 0.89 | 0.95 | 0 93 |
| Merton model variant | | | | 0.86 | 0.87 |
| Non-linear model | | | | | 0.81 |

introduced a model (presumably, a state of less ignorance).

To calculate the CIER, we first calculate the IE $H_0(p)$, where p is the default rate of the sample. That is, without attempting to control for any knowledge that we might have about credit quality, we measure the uncertainty associated with the event of default. This entropy reflects knowledge common to all models – that is, the likelihood of the event given by the probability of default. We then calculate the IE $H_1(S_1, \delta)$ after having taken into account the predictive power of the model. The CIER is one minus the ratio of the latter to the former, that is:

$$\mathrm{CIER}(S_1, \delta) = \frac{H_0 - H_1(S_1, \delta)}{H_0} \qquad (6)$$

If the model held no predictive power, the CIER would be zero. In this case, the model provides no additional information on the likelihood of the outcomes that is not already known. If it were perfectly predictive, the information entropy ratio would be one. In this case, there would be no uncertainty about the outcomes and, therefore, perfect default prediction.

Because CIER measures the relative reduction of uncertainty when the model is introduced, a higher CIER indicates a better model. Table 2 shows the results for the tested models. Using the resampling technique described above, the typical deviation is 0.02.

MUTUAL INFORMATION ENTROPY (MIE)

The information-based measures introduced above are not the only tools available for characterising credit risk models. Many information-based statistics can be expressed in terms of the information entropy. To quantify the dependence between two models, 1 and 2, we use a modified version of the MIE (also called information redundancy).[3] Let $S_1 = \{r_1, \ldots, r_n\}$ and $S_2 = \{R_1, \ldots, R_m\}$ be the risk scores associated with models 1 and 2 for a given set of obligors. The mutual information entropy is defined as:

$$\mathrm{MIE}(S_1, S_2, \delta) = \frac{1}{H_0}\left(H_1(S_1, \delta) + H_1(S_2, \delta) - H_2(S_1, S_2, \delta)\right) \qquad (7)$$

Here $H_0$ is the entropy of the sample, and:

$$H_2 = -\sum_{j=1}^{n}\sum_{k=1}^{m} P(r_j, R_k) \times \left(P\left(A \middle| r_j, R_k\right)\log P\left(A \middle| r_j, R_k\right) + P\left(B \middle| r_j, R_k\right)\log P\left(B \middle| r_j, R_k\right)\right) \qquad (8)$$

The conditional entropy $H_2$ is also implemented with a bin counting approach. A partition size $\delta$ is chosen and the outputs of the models are discretised into integers $j = 1, \ldots, n$, $k = 1, \ldots, m$ depending on what bin of size $\delta$ they fall into.

The mutual information entropy is a measure of how much uncertainty about default events is introduced by model 2 given the output of model 1 with accuracy $\delta$. The last two terms in Equation 6 represent the marginal contribution to the overall uncertainty introduced by model 2. If model 2 is completely dependent on model 1 then $\mathrm{MIE}(S_1, S_2, \delta) = 1 - \mathrm{CIER}(S_1)$, ie, the uncertainty introduced by the two models reduces to the uncertainty of one model only. Because the MIE is calculated with the joint conditional distribution of the risk scores $S_1$ and $S_2$, this measure requires many defaults to be accurate.

Table 3 shows the results for selected pairs of the tested models. In contrast to the CIER, a higher MIE value reveals an increase of the overall uncertainty. Note that the diagonal elements of Table 3 are related to the values of Table 2 through the equality $\mathrm{MIE}(S_1, S_1, \delta) = 1 - \mathrm{CIER}(S_1)$.

## Model precision

A key issue in model comparison is to determine whether a higher degree of refinement in the scale of a given model's output reflects greater precision and hence a more powerful model, or whether small increments in estimated risk do not add statistically significant value to the assessment of credit risk. That is, we must determine whether model outputs can be aggregated in coarse grades with no significant loss of information.

Importantly, this limitation does not apply only to agency ratings or other discrete score outputs. Due to data limitations and statistical significance, most models will exhibit a granularity of their outputs. For example, EDFs are provided with granularity of 1/1,000 in steps of 2 basis points, although the true precision and statistical significance are unknown (see McQuown, 1993). If the resolution for very low EDFs (high-quality credit) is statistically significant, it could indicate that at least a few defaults occurred for what the model considers high-quality obligors. In that case, the model is not distinguishing these defaulters from the true population of high-quality obligors. In contrast, if there are no defaulters among the population of high-quality obligors, the EDF value is only determined by the statistical method used to create the distribution of low EDFs (for example, kernel estimation, spectral methods or simple histograms). In this situation, the precision of the model for the high credit quality tail might not be supported by the default data directly but could be simply an artefact of the algorithm used to process the data.

These two situations would be reflected on the performance measures described above, such as CAP curves or AR. That is, the model precision can be defined in terms of its impact on a performance measure. The analysis is done by quantifying the average information gained with each refinement of the model output, ie, by generating an ensemble of surrogate data sets of model outputs, each of which reproduces the basic properties of the original set for a specific finite precision. For example, normalising the model output range to the [0,1] interval and then rounding the model outputs to three digits, then to two digits and so on.[4] Rounding to two digits provides a precision of 1 in 100 (or 1:100). The minimum finite precision that produces a statistically significant difference in the performance of the model determines the precision of the model output with respect to the selected performance measure. Table 4 shows the estimated lower and upper precision bounds for the selected benchmark models using AR on our test sample. The precision of the tested models is in the range 2–10%, which agrees reasonably well with the precision of most institutions' internal scales and agency ratings. The lower precision bound indicates a performance

**Table 4. Model precision using AR**

| Model | Lower | Upper |
|---|---|---|
| ROA | 1:10 | 1:50 |
| Z-score model | 1:15 | 1:50 |
| Hazard model | 1:15 | 1:50 |
| Merton model variant | 1:20 | 1:50 |
| Non-linear model | 1:20 | 1:50 |

reduction of at least one deviation of the AR value. Refinement above the upper bound shows no difference in the value of the performance measure.

## Conclusions

We discussed an approach for validating credit risk models based on alternative model performance measures. These measures are robust and easy to implement and can be added to the standard tools used to validate models.

In particular, we introduced two types of performance measures: (a) accounting accuracy metrics, which measure the cumulative accuracy to predict defaults, and (b) information content metrics, which measure the level of uncertainty in the risk scores produced by the tested models. Both types of measures can be used to evaluate model performance over the entire range of credit quality, or can be reduced to a single summary statistic that can be used to rank order competing models.

When models appear to be performing equally well, it is important to know whether they are both producing the same information, or different information of equal value. In the former case, either model will do, while in the latter case using both models simultaneously may increase predictive power even if one model is outperforming the other. MIE and the CIER provide measures that can distinguish between cases where different models are contributing additional information, or are redundant.

The techniques described in this chapter are both powerful and flexible under the appropriate conditions. Importantly, all of these techniques produce measures that are specific to the data set on which they are based. Thus, inter-model comparisons should always be based on identical or nearly identical samples and samples representative of the general population of obligors. When large and broadly representative testing data is available, these techniques can help determine which model is likely to have the best out-of-sample predictive power.

1 *Here we used the 1968 version of the Z-score model for illustration purposes.*

2 *This resolution can allow an easy comparison with agency ratings whose precision is 1/21 ≈ 5%.*

3 *For the standard definition of mutual entropy, see Prichard and Theiler (1995).*

4 *Models whose outputs increase exponentially (such as probabilities of default) need to be transformed to a linear scale using a logarithmic transformation.*

**BIBLIOGRAPHY**

**Caouette, J., E. Altman and P. Narayanan,** 1998, *Managing Credit Risk* (John Wiley & Sons).

**Herrity, J., S. Keenan, J. Sobehart, L. Carty and E. Falkenstein,** 1999, *Measuring Private Firm Default Risk*, Moody's Investors Service Special Comment, June.

**Jaynes, E.,** 1957, "Information Theory and Statistical Mechanics", *Physical Review*, 106(4), pp. 620–30.

**Kealhofer, S., S. Kwok and W. Weng,** 1998, "Uses and Abuses of Bond Default Rates", *CreditMetrics Monitor*, first quarter, pp. 37–55.

**Keenan, S., I. Shtogrin and J. Sobehart,** 1999, *Historical Default Rates of Corporate Bond Issuers*, 1920–1998, Moody's Investors Service Special Comment, January.

**McQuown, J.,** 1993, *A Comment on Market vs. Accounting Based Measures of Default Risk*, KMV Corporation.

**Merton, R.,** 1974, "On the Pricing of Corporate Debt: The Risk Structure of Interest Rates", *Journal of Finance*, 29, pp. 449–70.

**Pierce, J.,** 1970, *Symbols, Signals and Noise: The Nature and Process of Communication* (Harper & Brothers).

**Prichard, D., and J. Theiler,** 1995, "Generalized Redundancies for Time Series Analysis", *Physica D*, 84, pp. 476–93.

**Shannon, C., and W. Weaver,** 1949, *The Mathematical Theory of Communication* (University of Illinois Press).

**Shumway, T.,** 1998, *Forecasting Bankruptcy More Accurately: A Simple Hazard Model*, Working Paper, University of Michigan Business School.

**Sobehart, J., R. Stein, V. Mikitkyanskaya and L. Li,** 2000, *Moody's Public Firm Risk Model: A Hybrid Approach to Modeling Default Risk*, Moody's Investors Service Special Comment, February.

11

# The Need for Hybrid Models

**Jorge Sobehart and Sean Keenan**

Citigroup

*Jorge Sobehart and Sean Keenan have been among the fiercest critics of KMV's default prediction methodology, arguing in favour of hybrid models that combine firm-value approaches with other default indicators. Here, they respond in turn to the rebuttals of their previous paper, reiterating their claims that pure firm-value approaches to default prediction are fundamentally flawed.*

Business, legal and regulatory pressures have created a demand for more sophisticated credit risk models that can detect the broadest spectrum of stressful conditions leading to default and provide the widest market coverage. These models are crucial to performing the valuation and monitoring functions required for active portfolio risk management, and determining capital requirements.

For a long time, there were two main approaches to default risk modelling: the statistical approach pioneered by Altman (1968), and the contingent claims analysis (CCA) approach of Merton (1974) and others. The former determines the relationship between the default event and market information and accounting variables using econometric techniques. The latter is an option theoretic view of the firm's equity based on stock prices and a few key parameters taken from the balance sheet. Merton showed that a firm's equity could be viewed as an option on the firm with strike price equal to the face value of its debt. Later, alternative "reduced-form" models have been proposed based on a simplified interpretation of credit spreads as driven only by the likelihood of default and recovery expectations of market participants. The relationship between all these models has been reviewed extensively in the academic literature (see Duffie and Singleton (1999), Kao (2000) and references therein). More recently, hybrid models, which enhance the definition of default event by combining CCA structural models with additional financial information, have been introduced as a viable alternative for practical applications.

Thanks to the steadily growing body of research by academics and practitioners, there is no shortage of models to choose from. Unfortunately, credit risk models are far less tractable than market risk models and designing appropriate tests for benchmarking and validating them is a difficult task.

In a recent study, Kealhofer and Kurbat (2001) compared the performance of several default risk models including agency ratings. Their main results are reported in Kealhofer and Kurbat (2002). Their study focuses on the performance of default risk models based on the Merton CCA approach, and discusses hybrid models that combine market information, accounting variables and credit opinions, such as agency ratings. They do not compare any version of the Merton model to a hybrid model, but compare their own Merton model with accounting ratios, Moody's ratings and an alternative Merton formulation reported in the literature. The authors concluded that agency ratings and additional financial information do not enhance the performance of options pricing-based models for predicting defaults. The study also includes a section intended as a rebuttal to the theoretical arguments presented in Sobehart and Keenan (1999).

*The authors would like to thank two anonymous referees for helpful comments. The views, analysis and conclusions in this article are those of the authors. Citigroup is not responsible for any statement or conclusion herein, and the opinions, theories and techniques presented herein do not necessarily reflect the position of the institution.*

These arguments related to the potential for bias in the pure Merton-type options pricing models for measuring credit risk. In this chapter, we review their study and find that their own tests do not support their analysis and conclusions. This is the result of:

- an incorrect interpretation of the theoretical underpinnings of hybrid models of default risk, and
- an incorrect specification of the hypothesis to be tested.

We also show how their criticisms of hybrid models rest on a misunderstanding of the theoretical underpinnings of such models. Specifically, hybrid options pricing-based models do not contradict the efficient market hypothesis because additional accounting variables and rating information are not used to forecast equity prices but to enhance the definition of default event in the structural model itself. After reviewing their testing methodology and conclusions and presenting alternative test results, we discuss some of the theoretical underpinnings of hybrid models to provide some explanation for our results and conclusions.

## Performance tests for default prediction models

Recently, a hybrid model of default risk that blends equity market information with financial ratios and agency ratings was introduced as a viable alternative for business applications. The hybrid model described in Sobehart *et al.* (2000) was constructed to overcome some of the limitations of idealised CCA options pricing models of credit risk reported in Fridson and Jonsson (1997), Sobehart and Keenan (1999) and others. While this alternative approach also seeks to make optimal use of high-frequency market-generated information, its underlying methodology is more consistent with traditional credit analysis than pure CCA models. That is, it provides a credit assessment that combines market information and additional relevant information such as profitability, liquidity and the capital structure of the firm. This contrasts with some commercial models based on a limited view of market information and its relation to credit quality. The limitations of these pure options pricing-based models are clearly shown in the poor predictability of credit spreads and bond prices, and limited ability to discriminate between changes in credit quality during periods of volatile markets (providing too many sell signals, or false positive signals).[1]

The alternative hybrid model has drawn the attention of financial institutions and, not surprisingly, of commercial vendors, some of whom have actively criticised the hybrid nature of the model. In Kealhofer and Kurbat (2002), the authors confirm their own earlier results, concluding that agency ratings and additional financial information do not add any power to options pricing-based models and also concluding that their Merton model (KMV implementation) outperforms any alternative model. Note, however, that they do not actually compare their model with a hybrid model. Their empirical tests are confined mainly to comparisons of financial ratios and agency ratings (Moody's) with their Merton model. Their results are at odds with those reported in Sobehart *et al.* (2000), who found that additional information could improve the predictive power of a Merton-type model.

To elucidate this issue, we compare Kealhofer and Kurbat's version of the Merton model (KMV's implementation) with the hybrid model described in Sobehart *et al.* (Moody's implementation) that combines a Merton model with financial ratios and ratings. Both models produce estimated default probabilities over a one-year time horizon, known as expected default frequency (EDF) and expected default probability (EDP), respectively. The data set used in this study contains more than 27,000 firm-year pairs of annual observations for both models for the period December 1995–December 1999. Each pair of observations measures the obligors' credit quality at the beginning of the following year. The data set represents a population of US non-financial firms including both rated and non-rated obligors. The data set also contains 349 default events occurring during the period January 1996–December 2000. The numbers of firm-year observations and defaults in each specific year are listed in Table 1. We ordered the observations by model output from riskier to safer, and

**Table 1. Number of firms and defaults in the sample**

| Year | Firm years | Defaults |
|---|---|---|
| 1996 | 5,099 | 41 |
| 1997 | 5,361 | 50 |
| 1998 | 5,713 | 95 |
| 1999 | 5,755 | 101 |
| 2000 | 5,487 | 62 |
| All data | 27,415 | 349 |

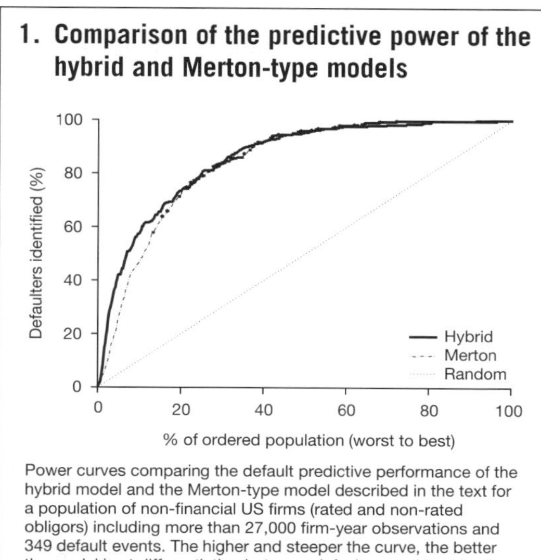


Power curves comparing the default predictive performance of the hybrid model and the Merton-type model described in the text for a population of non-financial US firms (rated and non-rated obligors) including more than 27,000 firm-year observations and 349 default events. The higher and steeper the curve, the better the model is at differentiating between defaulters and healthy firms.

**Table 2. Model accuracy ratio (AR), Spearman rank correlation (RC) and error bands for the tested models**

| Year | AR Merton | AR Hybrid | RC |
|---|---|---|---|
| 1996 | 0.690 (0.014) | 0.702 (0.022) | 0.761 (0.004) |
| 1997 | 0.658 (0.018) | 0.730 (0.015) | 0.741 (0.004) |
| 1998 | 0.676 (0.013) | 0.717 (0.010) | 0.734 (0.004) |
| 1999 | 0.700 (0.011) | 0.718 (0.015) | 0.754 (0.004) |
| 2000 | 0.711 (0.010) | 0.780 (0.012) | 0.697 (0.004) |
| All data | 0.690 (0.005) | 0.727 (0.006) | 0.742 (0.002) |

A higher AR indicates a better model.

counted the number of defaults that occurred within the following 12 months of each annual observation.

Figure 1 shows the cumulative fraction of defaults as a function of the ordered population of obligors. Interpretation of this plot is straightforward: the higher and steeper the curve, the better the model is at differentiating between defaulters and healthy firms. Figure 2 shows similar accuracy curves for individual years, indicating that the hybrid model outperforms the equity-based model consistently. Table 2 shows the accuracy ratio (AR) for each model and its characteristic error band. The AR is a summary statistic of model performance calculated as the area under the performance curve above the random line over the maximum area of an ideal model also above the random line. A higher AR indicates a better model, with a perfect model producing an AR of one and a naive model (random assignment of risk scores) producing an AR of zero. The AR error band is obtained by rejecting at random 15% of the records and recalculating the AR figure. The process is repeated 500 times to reduce the impact of outliers.

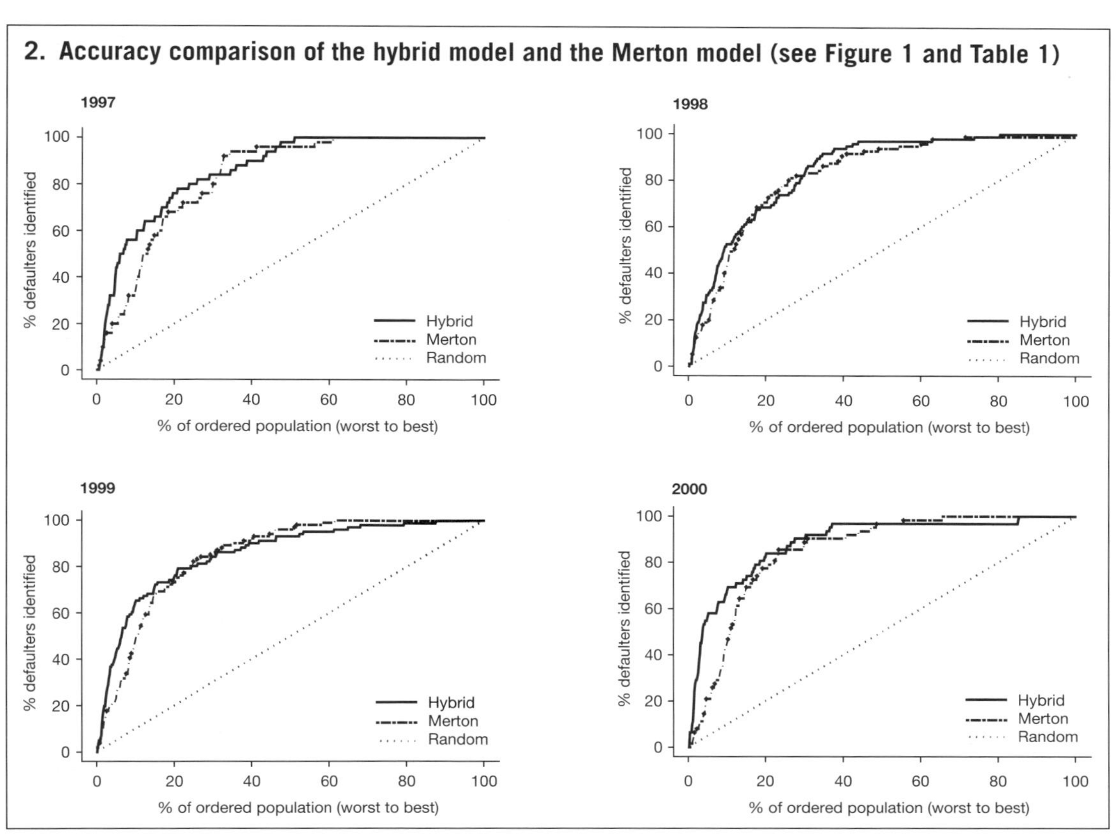

Table 2 also shows the Spearman rank correlation (RC) between the models and its error band (95% confidence level). The high AR combined with relatively low RC figures suggest that these models are complementary because they use market information in different ways. Finally, Figures 1 and 2 and Table 2 suggest that, on a stand-alone basis, hybrid models improve over state-of-the-art commercial applications of options pricing models, reducing the number of false positive signals (or sell signals). These empirical results clearly contradict the claims in Kealhofer and Kurbat (2002) against the use of hybrid models.

To understand the source of the discrepancy in the results reported in Kealhofer and Kurbat, we reviewed their empirical tests and found that their methodology does not fully support their conclusion as a result of several factors.

1. Misspecification of the hypothesis to be tested. Their main conclusion about model performance is derived from a set of tests that check to see if the number of defaults within a given period ordered by the scores of a selected model (eg, agency ratings) is uniform if conditioned on the scores of a benchmark model (eg, EDFs). An appropriate test that includes the correct distribution of false positive signals would examine the proportion of defaults in each rating category or model score (distribution of default rates).
2. The authors changed the definition of at least one of the variables in Sobehart *et al.* (2000) – (ROA) – inferring incorrect conclusions on its predictive power.
3. The authors used the recent claims and results in Boral and Falkenstein (2001) to draw incorrect conclusions about the hybrid model and Merton implementation described in Sobehart *et al.* (2000). Although Boral and Falkenstein used a similar terminology, their model, claims and conclusions are neither related to nor supported by the previous studies on hybrid models, nor was its performance ever tested against the Merton model included in the hybrid model reported previously. Therefore, making indirect inference from the performance of an unrelated model with respect to other models muddles their discussion.
4. Apparent problems arising from unreliable or sparse data. For example, the power curves in Figure 2 of Kealhofer and Kurbat's study indicate that several investment-grade firms rated by Moody's defaulted during the period used in the study. The shape of their curve seems inconsistent with the default statistics and rating distribution reported by the rating agency for the same period.

We begin by discussing the implications of Factor 1 in more detail. Kealhofer and Kurbat tested the null hypothesis that ratings provide no additional information over their model by testing the uniformity of the number of defaults within a given period by obligors ordered by ratings, after first being ordered by the scores of their model. Because the underlying distribution of ratings (or scores) is different for different models, testing the distribution of default counts alone cannot support conclusions on the performance of the models over an arbitrary population. Kealhofer and Kurbat's study purports to have avoided the aforementioned problem by converting the scores of the model on which the first grouping is based into quantiles, producing groups with roughly equal numbers of obligors.[2] Creating a uniform distribution of obligors in this way would mean that the distribution of default counts and the fraction of defaults by data bucket (default rates) would be identical, making our above criticism misplaced. In the first place, Moody's ratings are published on both a nine-category and a refined 21-category scale. The "percentile" ranks plot, which shows data grouped by Moody's percentiles (Figure 1 in Kealhofer and Kurbat) contains only 10 bars. Moreover, the distribution of ratings for Moody's-rated obligors is strongly bimodal, so that even if a 21-bar histogram were presented, we would know that the underlying uniformity of Moody's-rated obligors had not been achieved, invalidating the results. Ultimately, to achieve a uniform distribution of Moody's-rated obligors, one would either need to construct groups with overlapping ratings (mixing in the same quantile firms with different default probabilities) or use an arbitrary approach for selecting data buckets, either one of which would invalidate the tests and claims. The same criticism described for rating groupings applies to the grouping into percentiles by EDF.

To illustrate the problem with the performance test described above, let us discuss a hypothetical case. We emphasise that the hypothetical example discussed below focuses on the validity of the test used in Kealhofer and Kurbat and not on their underlying data. Assume we have two arbitrary models, 1 and 2. Let the scores of model 1 be labelled with rating symbols AAA, AA, A, BBB, … , C, and let the scores of model 2 be numbers such as 0.02, … , 20, increasing in risk. To make our discussion easier to follow, we focus on two hypothetical cohorts: C(BB) and C(0.2–2). Cohort C(BB) contains all the firms rated BB by model 1. Cohort C(0.2–2) contains firms with scores in the range (0.2, 2) from model 2. For completeness, a similar analysis would be required for all the scores in models 1 and 2. Figure 3 shows the hypothetical distribution of model 1's scores for cohort C(0.2–2) (a), the distribution of defaults within a given period by quantiles (b) and the fraction of default by score (or default rates) (c). Figure 4 shows similar distributions for cohort C(BB) as function of the scores of model 2. The distributions have been exaggerated for illustration purposes.

Following the procedure described in Kealhofer and Kurbat, if we compare the hypothetical distribution of defaults by quantile only (Figures 3(b) and 4(b)), model 2 outperforms model 1 because defaults are nearly uniform over model 1 scores but they show a positive slope for model 2. However, the results are completely misleading because quantile buckets are not rating buckets. Therefore, a test that checks the uniformity of the population of defaults as a function of the population of model scores (quantiles) does not support conclusions on the distribution of defaults as a function of the scores themselves. A more appropriate approach that removes the dependence on the distribution of scores would be to test if the default rates (fraction of defaults for each score) in cohort C(BB) are uniform as a function of the scores of model 2, and if the default rates in cohort C(0.2–2) are uniform as a function of the scores of model 1. In this example, because model 2 produces many more false positive signals than model 1 (in Figure 4c the default rate for the worst score of model 2 is below 40% compared with 50% for model 1 in Figure 3c), the opposite conclusion to the one obtained above can be reached where model 1 outperforms model 2. Of course, another set of performance issues relate to the steepness and monotonicity of default rates by model score, but we are confining our remarks mainly to those issues raised in Kealhofer and Kurbat.

## On the foundation of hybrid models

Vasicek (2000) and Kealhofer and Kurbat (2001, 2002) also criticise the theoretical underpinnings of hybrid models through a rebuttal of the arguments introduced in Sobehart and Keenan (1999), which describes the limitations of CCA models and the need for an alternative approach that can meet the requirements for practical

**3. Model 1 scores**

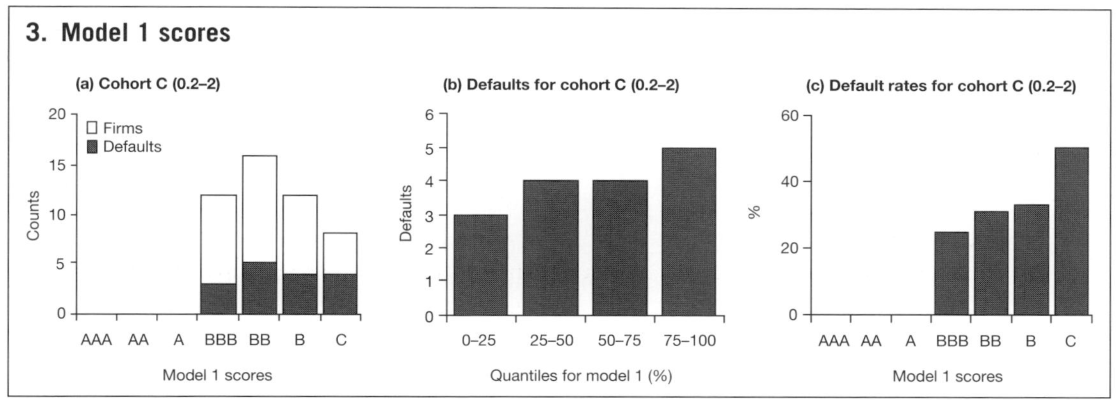


**4. Model 2 scores**

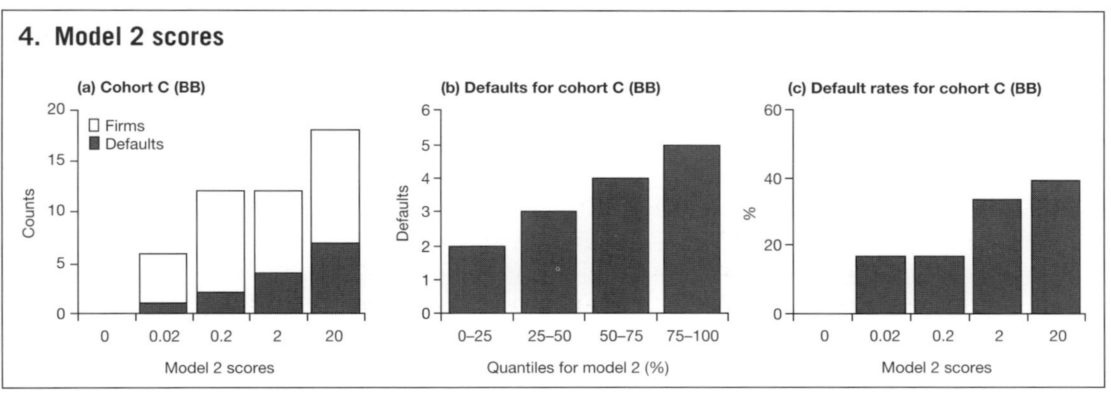

applications. More precisely, the authors criticise our arguments about the role of trading noise and modelling uncertainty in pricing, and the questionable use of no-arbitrage conditions to value non-tradable or illiquid instruments, asserting that they contradict academic views on the efficiency of markets and idealised risk-neutral pricing. Such a dogmatic stance on the efficiency of markets and the impossibility of arbitrage across asset classes would appear to conflict with the underlying reason that their Merton model based on equity prices adds value in the pricing of risky debt obligations, ie, the assumption that equity markets are better informed than the credit markets. Recently, King (2001) reported empirical evidence that counters many of the claims made on the predictive power of equity-based models and supports our arguments on the impact of trading noise, uncertainty and liquidity on model misspecification and the determination of credit risk. Their stance is also in conflict with published evidence on the limits of arbitrage and market efficiency.[3]

Another related problem with idealised models based on market equity stems from the fact that even fully informed equity prices are marginal prices and, therefore, primarily reflect marginal reallocative supply and demand conditions rather than the value of the aggregate capital stock of the firm required by these models. Differing views on the optimal deployment of the firm's assets can create a "control premium" and a steep supply curve for equity shares. The huge price swings that accompany takeover bids clearly prove this point. Tightly controlled firms with inefficiently deployed assets may trade at a discount. The opposite situation, where equity trades at a hefty premium, can also occur as a result of speculative valuation such as in the dotcom and telecom frenzies. The extent to which these supply and demand effects may be affecting market prices is unknown and is, therefore, a potential source of additional uncertainty for equity and debt valuation. This issue is fundamental in the credit risk context because equity-based models of default risk estimate the implied market value of the firm's assets and volatility from stock prices, which are then used to estimate probabilities of default.

In the real world of lending, modelling uncertainty, pricing distortions and arbitrage situations are rampant. Some corporate loans are underpriced to maintain relationships with important clients, while others may be overpriced to customers unlikely to shop for credit. More generally, most institutions' assets and liabilities do not possess the same idealised characteristics as the marketable securities for which many of these models were first developed. Another key issue is model misspecification caused by simplifying assumptions such as lognormal changes in the firm's assets, constant interest rates and volatility and simple debt structures. Thus, default risk models based on strict assumptions about market efficiency, perfect liquidity and lack of arbitrage opportunities and simplifying assumptions made for analytical convenience lose ground once the realities of real-world pricing begin to be modelled seriously.

Ideally, a purely quantitative credit risk analysis would depend only on reliable financial and market data, and on universally accepted relationships between the data and the event of default. However, no model is perfect and, in practice, data is often sparse, unreliable or non-existent. Therefore, credit risk models depend on significant subjectivity and uncertainty both in determining relevant financial input variables and determining the relationships between those variables. In contrast, supporters of pure CCA-based models assume not only that equity prices and price movements (volatility) provide an "idealised" comprehensive view of a firm's credit quality, but they also assume that their particular model implementation is the only way of interpreting market equity information. Any other interpretation using additional variables is written off as contrary to the efficient market hypothesis (Kealhofer and Kurbat, 2002): "Extremely intensive testing of equity prices over the past 30 years overwhelmingly rejects that variables such as those proposed by Moody's can be used to systematically make money in equities."

However, common sense indicates that even if equity market prices contain all the relevant information about the firm's credit quality and default likelihood, there is no guarantee that any particular structural model will reflect that information precisely. In addition, hybrid models do not contradict the efficient market hypothesis because the additional accounting variables and rating information are not used to forecast equity prices but to enhance the definition of default event in the structural model itself. More precisely, in the Merton framework, the default point is usually assumed to be a function of the liabilities of the firm only. However, there have been cases in which an otherwise solvent firm has sought the protection of the bankruptcy court for previously unanticipated future legal liabilities. There are also cases where firms that are solvent according to the Merton framework default on their obligations due to severe liquidity problems or inadequate management. In addition, ideal asset-based models cannot easily incorporate financial restructuring such as refinancing, renegotiating of debt contracts or the distressed exchange of securities, although very insightful models that address these issues have been recently reported in the academic literature (see Anderson, Sundaresan and Tychon, 1996). This is an important point because, as the credit quality of the firm deteriorates, its capacity for borrowing or refinancing can affect the likelihood of default and any strategy for hedging its debt.

Finally, the limitations of pure CCA models of credit risk are clearly summarised in Fridson and Jonsson (1997, page 38): "... while [contingent claim analysis] is fine as far as it goes, it does not go far enough in elucidating the complex relationship between the various parts of a company's capital structure".

## Conclusions

Although pure options pricing structural models provide a powerful insight into the valuation of risky debt, they often depend on significant subjective expertise and judgement of analysts and modellers who may introduce unrealistic assumptions to make the problem analytically tractable. By adding accounting information and credit opinions, hybrid models are able to include valuable information widely used by credit analysts and loan officers, and expert judgement that is not only a market standard but is backed up by decades of publicly available historical performance. Because these models are designed to assist institutions in the assessment of credit quality and the determination of capital requirements, additional independent studies comparing the performance of multiple models will greatly help institutions to understand their potential and limitations.

1 *See, for example, Wei and Guo (1997), Anderson and Sundaresan (1998) and King (2001).*

2 *In this case, obligor years since they have aggregated across time.*

3 *See, for example, the Financial Analyst Journal special issue on behavioural finance, 55(6) (1999).*

**BIBLIOGRAPHY**

**Altman, E.,** 1968, "Financial Ratios, Discriminant Analysis and the Prediction of Corporate Bankruptcy", *Journal of Finance*, September, pp. 589–609.

**Anderson, R., and S. Sundaresan,** 1998, *A Comparison Study of Structural Models of Corporate Bond Yields*, Proceedings of the Conference: Issues in Credit Risk, Capital and Defaultible Debt Valuation Center For Economic Policy Research, September.

**Anderson, R., S. Sundaresan and P. Tychon,** 1996, "Strategic Analysis of Contingent Claims", *European Economic Review*, 40, pp. 871–81.

**Boral, A., and E. Falkenstein,** 2001, "Revisiting Mr Merton", *Risk Professional*, 3, pp. 22–4.

**Duffie, D., and K. Singleton,** 1999, *Credit Risk for Financial Institutions: Management and Pricing*, Graduate School of Business, Stanford University.

**Fridson, M., and J. Jonsson,** 1997, "Contingent Claims Analysis", *Journal of Portfolio Management*, Winter, pp. 31–43.

**Kao, D.,** 2000, "Estimating and Pricing Credit Risk: An Overview", *Financial Analysts Journal*, 56(4), pp. 50–66.

**Kealhofer, S., and M. Kurbat,** 2001, *The Default Prediction Power of the Merton Approach, Relative to Debt Ratings and Accounting Variables*, KMV Corporation.

**Kealhofer, S., and M. Kurbat,** 2002, "The Power of Merton", *Risk* February.

**King, M.,** 2001, *Using Equity to Price Credit*, Credit strategy report, JP Morgan Securities, London, September.

**Merton, R.,** 1974, "On the Pricing of Corporate Debt: The Risk Structure of Interest Rates", *Journal of Finance*, 29, pp. 449–70.

**Sobehart, J., and S. Keenan,** 1999, *Equity Market Value and its Importance for Credit Analysis: Facts and Fiction*, Working Paper.

**Sobehart, J., R. Stein, V. Mikityanskaya and L. Li,** 2000, *Moody's Public Firm Risk Model: A Hybrid Approach to Modelling Short Term Default Risk*, Moody's Investor Service, rating methodology.

**Vasicek, O.,** 2000, *Comments on "Equity Market Value and its Importance for Credit Analysis: Facts and Fiction"*, KMV Corporation.

**Wei, D., and D. Guo,** 1997, "Pricing Risky Debt: An Empirical Comparison of the Longstaff and Schwartz and Merton Models", *Journal of Fixed Income*, September, pp. 8–28.

III

# DEPENDENCE IN DEFAULTS AND RECOVERIES

12

# Devil in the Parameters

**H. Ugur Koyluoglu, Anil Bangia and Thomas Garside**

Oliver, Wyman & Company; JP Morgan Chase; Oliver, Wyman & Company

*H. Ugur Koyluoglu, Anil Bangia and Thomas Garside investigate the effects of parameter inconsistencies on the results of different credit risk portfolio models on sample portfolios.*

Parameter inconsistency is a fact of life. As a result, credit portfolio modelling techniques produce significantly different aggregate and contributory results for identical portfolios. This can lead to divergent recommendations for credit risk management, risk-based pricing and portfolio optimisation.

Potential sources of inconsistency range from different estimates of default and recovery rates to incompatible correlation structures. In addition to parameter inconsistencies, modelling details may differ, especially in the tail of the portfolio loss distribution.

Current credit portfolio modelling techniques encompass microeconomic Merton-based models, such as RiskMetrics' CreditManager and KMV's PortfolioManager; econometric models like McKinsey's CreditPortfolioView; and actuarial models such as CreditRisk+ from Credit Suisse Financial Products. Koyluoglu and Hickman (1998) showed that all these techniques share the same underlying intuition and would yield very similar results if their input parameter estimates were harmonised.

This chapter studies the effect of parameter inconsistencies on the results of sample portfolios. Our approach employs parameter estimates for CreditMetrics, PortfolioManager and CreditRisk+. These are generated from the natural data sets of CreditMetrics and PortfolioManager, and from historical default rate volatility for CreditRisk+. Two single factor/single parameter models are also included for comparison.

*The authors would like to thank John Drzik, Christopher Finger, Andrew Hickman and Curtis Tange for their comments and discussions and Li Yang for help with portfolio runs. The opinions expressed are those of the authors and do not necessarily reflect the opinions of Oliver, Wyman & Company.*

We examine only the default component of portfolio credit risk and concentrate on the distribution of potential credit losses, not potential changes in market value. Therefore, all the value/credit migration-related features of the models were disabled.

Credit portfolio models require two key parameter sets as inputs:

- stand-alone risk characteristics for each asset; and
- correlation/joint default behaviour.

Clearly if the stand-alone risk characteristics for each transaction are inconsistent between modelling techniques, different results will be produced. However obtaining consistent estimates of stand-alone risk – as described by the expected default frequency (EDF) – is far from trivial. There are many different techniques to estimate EDF and it is possible to generate substantial inconsistencies before a credit portfolio model has even been run. Indeed, the results of a credit portfolio model are much more sensitive to mis-specification of EDF than to any other parameter. The goal of this chapter is not to discuss methods for estimating EDF, but to focus on the second key set of parameters that defines correlation behaviour.

There are two distinct sources of correlation parameter inconsistency between commercial models of the same modelling technique: numerical estimation procedure and granularity of parameter specification. For example, equity correlation estimates, which are used in Merton-based models to estimate asset correlations, vary according to the length or duration of the equity time series and the time step size used. Although statistical theory indicates that using more data is better as long as

**1. Granularity in parameter specification**

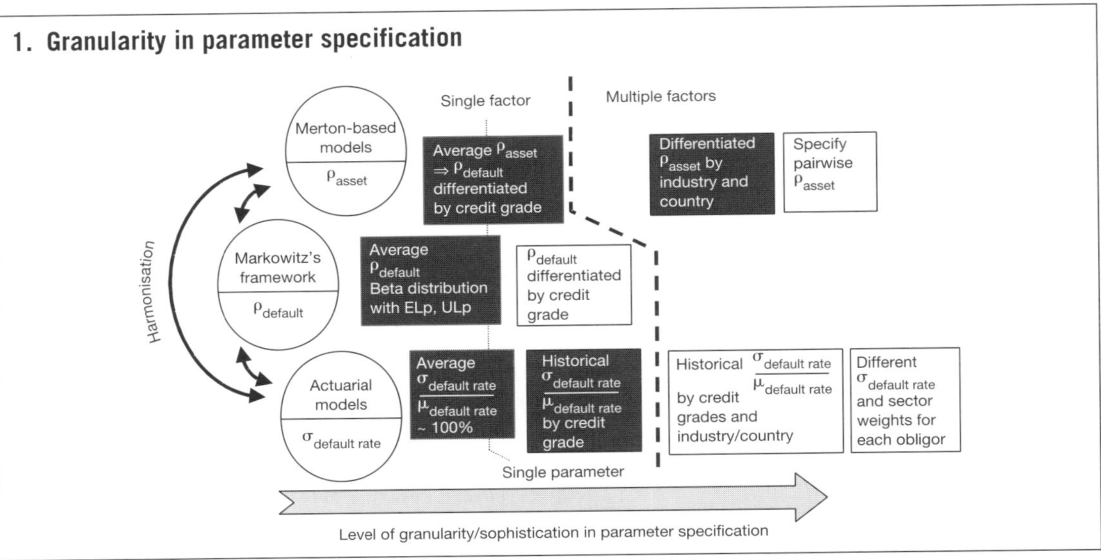


the data is clean and relevant, there is no rule for the selection of the exact time step. Asset correlations vary from time to time, increasing significantly during a crisis. Clearly, asset correlation estimates used in commercial software such as CreditMetrics and PortfolioManager vary as a result of differences in correlation estimation procedures.

The other important source of inconsistency arises as a result of differences in the granularity of parameter specification. Figure 1 shows several possible parameterisations of the models, highlighting their differences in sophistication or granularity of input variables. The shading in Figure 1 represents the modelling techniques studied.

In the case of Merton-based models, the asset correlations can be set equal to an average correlation for all assets in a single factor/single parameter approach. By construction, this yields default correlations differentiated by EDF or credit grade. Asset correlations can be further differentiated by industry and country, and even further refined to the obligor level. Both CreditManager and PortfolioManager use this increased level of granularity. However, asset correlations for obligors/segments still differ between these two models, due to differences in the parameter estimation procedure, as discussed above, and industry or country segmentation.

Figure 1 also illustrates the spectrum of choices in the modelling of default rate volatility at different granularities, as would be employed by actuarial models. Under this framework, joint default behaviour is described by using default rate volatilities and sector weights. The volatilities of default rates exhibit a strong relationship to the unconditional default rates. Therefore, the ratio of default rate volatility to the unconditional default rate (the coefficient of variation) is usually estimated, rather than the volatility itself. In the simplest case, a uniform coefficient of variation is taken for the default rate. For better accuracy, the default rate volatility can be differentiated by credit grades. Additional granularity can be obtained by differentiating the default data by country and/or industry, or assigning differentiated volatilities even at the obligor level. However, parameter estimation becomes more difficult with any increase in granularity, due to lack of data.

Although different modelling techniques propose different parameters to quantify the likelihood of joint default, they should carry the same joint default information. For example, asset correlations in the Merton-based technique, and default rate volatility estimates in the actuarial technique, should correspond.

The harmonisation framework introduced by Koyluoglu and Hickman (1998) allows us to derive implied input parameters for any given credit portfolio modelling approach from the directly observed parameters of another. For example, it is possible to estimate implied asset correlations from the directly estimated default rate volatilities.

However, in practice, when directly estimated parameters of one approach are compared with the implied parameters obtained from another, they are usually different. Such inconsistencies are hardly surprising, as very different data sets have been used for parameter estimation. For example, equity/index time series are used to estimate asset correlations, while default rate time series are used to estimate default rate volatility.

Clearly if the direct estimates are similar to the implied ones, it is possible to be more confident in the quality of the input parameters. In the case of significant differences, the smallest standard error in the estimates could be used, in addition to experience-based judgement, as a criterion for parameter selection (see Stuart and Ord, 1994). We view such analysis as an essential cross-check to confirm the validity of input parameters for credit portfolio models.

## Sample portfolio

We have run sample portfolios using five models: CreditManager; PortfolioManager; CreditRisk+; a simplified Merton-based model with a homogenous asset correlation structure; and a simple Markowitz approach with a homogenous default correlation structure. For simplicity, both the Merton model and the Markowitz approach assume the portfolio loss distribution follows a beta distribution. This study is designed only to illustrate the issues identified above, not to make general statements about the models. The direction and magnitude of differences in the risk results across models should not be assumed true for all portfolios.

We constructed two sample portfolios – a high quality portfolio and a low quality portfolio. The first is made up of 180 names and represents a large corporate loan portfolio of high credit quality (mean EDF = 20 basis points, as measured by KMV's Credit Monitor). US-based obligors make up 46% of the portfolio, Japanese 13%, UK 12% and Canadian 11%.

The second portfolio consists of lower-grade obligors selected from KMV's database (mean EDF = 240 bp). The obligors in this portfolio are from six different industry segments and eight countries. A combined portfolio was also formed with 360 obligors (mean EDF = 128 bp). The portfolio mix, in terms of grades from Moody's Investors Service, is given in Table 1. Severity was set to a constant value of 40% of exposure and all exposures were taken equally.

For CreditManager we used the asset correlations specified in version 1.0, and for PortfolioManager, version 4.32a. For simplicity, CreditRisk+ runs are based on a single systemic factor for all obligors.

We used three base assumptions for default rate volatility.

1. Using default rate volatility equal to the default rate (default $\sigma$ = default $\mu$).
2. Using differentiated coefficient of variation of the default rate by credit grade, based on historical default rates published in Carty and Lieberman (1996), and extrapolations for the better credit grades (see Table 2). Gordy (2000) suggests calibrating CreditRisk+ roughly in line with Table 2.
3. Setting the coefficient of variation of the default rate ($\sigma/\mu$) equal to a forced constant k, such that the unexpected loss of the portfolio calculated by CreditRisk+ matches the average unexpected loss calculated by the average of CreditManager and PortfolioManager.[1] These three variations of the CreditRisk+ framework are referred to as CreditRisk+, CreditRisk+h, and CreditRisk+f respectively.

We also analysed the portfolio using the simplified Markowitz and simplified Merton models. We chose parameters based on Oliver, Wyman & Company experience that would approximately match results at the unexpected loss level with the commercially available models. The average default correlation for the combined portfolio is assumed to be 3% in the Markowitz model. The default correlation is increased to 4% for the low credit quality portfolio and decreased to 1% for the high credit quality portfolio, when these are

**Table 1. Portfolio mix in terms of credit grade**

| Moody's grade | High-quality portfolio | Low-quality portfolio | Combined portfolio |
|---|---|---|---|
| Aaa | 15 | 0 | 15 |
| Aa | 46 | 0 | 46 |
| A | 66 | 0 | 66 |
| Baa | 30 | 41 | 71 |
| Ba | 17 | 98 | 115 |
| B | 6 | 41 | 47 |
| Total | 180 | 180 | 360 |

**Table 2. Coefficient of variation default rate by credit grade**

| Moody's grade | $\sigma/\mu$ (%) |
|---|---|
| Aaa-Baa1 | 300 |
| Baa2 | 240 |
| Baa3 | 170 |
| Ba1 | 130 |
| Ba2 | 100 |
| Ba3 | 80 |
| B1 | 73 |
| B2 | 63 |
| B3 | 55 |

run as independent sub-portfolios. Asset correlation is set to 20% in all the Merton model runs.

In the base case runs, we used the same EDF calibration system, therefore all models give the same expected loss and differences in risk results are caused only by correlation parameter differences and different tail specifications. In the other sets of runs, we studied variations in EDF calibrations and exposure. Only selected highlights for the base runs are described in this chapter. (The full report can be obtained from the authors.)

## Results

To compare results at the aggregate portfolio level we look at the unexpected loss and economic capital at 99.9% confidence intervals. This confidence interval is chosen to examine the behaviour of the models in the tails of the distributions. Results are normalised with respect to portfolio exposure (see Table 3).

In general, unexpected loss statistics calculated by the five different models are matched more closely than economic capital values. The higher portfolio unexpected loss estimates from CreditManager and PortfolioManager, in comparison with the Merton model, indicate that these two employ asset correlations higher than 20% on average for the combined portfolio.

The almost identical unexpected loss in the simplified Markowitz and simplified Merton models means the default correlation parameters match on the average. It is notable, however, that the actuarial approach, when parameterised using either the recommended or historically derived inputs (CreditRisk+ and CreditRisk+h), gives low estimates of unexpected loss and economic capital compared with the other models. This is due to parameter inconsistencies and indicates that both the implied asset and default correlation are lower in this case. In our experience, this effect could be caused by the fact that top-down, historically-based volatility estimates usually understate true volatility due to the skewed nature of default data to lower credits.

In addition to parameter inconsistencies, differences in modelling details cause great variations in economic capital. For example, the beta assumption used in the simplified Markowitz and simplified Merton models creates differences in economic capital estimates that are much larger than the variations in unexpected loss.

Even for CreditRisk+f, where the unexpected loss is forced to match the average of CreditManager and PortfolioManager, the economic capital estimate differs from that produced by Merton-based approaches. Here, the disparity in tail estimation is caused by model specification differences arising from the return assumption of the Merton model and the gamma distribution assumption for default rates in the actuarial model.

The unexpected loss and economic capital obtained from the different models for the high and low quality portfolios are given in Table 4.

The unexpected loss of CreditManager and PortfolioManager are similar for high and low credit quality portfolios. At the economic capital level, there is less difference between the high credit quality portfolios than the low credit quality portfolios. This suggests that CreditManager and PortfolioManager assign different asset correlations for the riskier – and generally smaller – companies in our sample.

The unexpected losses calculated by CreditManager, PortfolioManager and the simplified

**Table 3. Unexpected loss and economic capital for combined portfolio**

| | Model type | Combined portfolio with 360 obligors | |
|---|---|---|---|
| | | Unexpected loss (%) | Economic capital (99.9%) (%) |
| Merton | CreditManager | 0.73 | 6.5 |
| | PortfolioManager | 0.70 | 5.3 |
| | Simplified Merton model | 0.63 | 4.1 |
| Actuarial | CreditRisk+ | 0.56 | 3.4 |
| | CreditRisk+h | 0.52 | 2.9 |
| | CreditRisk+f (k = 1.3) | 0.71 | 4.7 |
| Markowitz | Simplified Markowitz model | 0.62 | 3.9 |

**Table 4. Unexpected loss and economic capital for high and low credit quality portfolios**

| Model type | | High credit quality portfolio | | Low credit quality portfolio | |
|---|---|---|---|---|---|
| | | Unexpected loss (%) | Economic capital (99.9%) (%) | Unexpected loss (%) | Economic capital (99.9%) (%) |
| Merton | CreditManager | 0.32 | 3.7 | 1.32 | 11.3 |
| | PortfolioManager | 0.28 | 3.3 | 1.20 | 8.7 |
| | Simplified Merton model | 0.20 | 1.77 | 1.13 | 7.1 |
| Actuarial | CreditRisk+ | 0.16 | 1.0 | 1.05 | 6.2 |
| | CreditRisk+h | 0.19 | 1.5 | 0.92 | 5.1 |
| | CreditRisk+f | 0.30 (k = 3.3) | 3.0 | 1.26 (k = 1.25) | 8.4 |
| Markowitz | Simplified Markowitz model | 0.19 | 1.75 | 1.13 | 7.1 |

Merton and simplified Markowitz models for the low credit quality portfolio are very close. This implies that for these obligors, CreditManager and PortfolioManager employ average asset correlations close to 20%, with an implied average default correlation of about 4%. The relatively close match in economic capital estimates also suggests that the beta assumption for the portfolio loss distribution is reasonable in this case. Large variations for the high credit quality portfolio are attributed to inconsistencies in asset correlation parameters.

The results obtained from three different applications of CreditRisk+ differ significantly from other approaches for the high credit quality portfolio, but are much more similar for the low credit quality portfolio. This shows that the extrapolations used for the volatility parameter of the high credit quality do not match the Merton-based correlation parameters.

## Contributory risk results

There are different definitions of the risk contribution of an asset to the aggregate risk of the portfolio:

DISCRETE MARGINAL CONTRIBUTION

This is defined as the change in the portfolio standard deviation as a result of the addition of the asset to the portfolio. One attraction of this approach is that it gives a more intuitive insight into the effects of buy/sell decisions on the portfolio standard deviation. CreditManager uses this approach to calculate risk contributions.

CONTINUOUS MARGINAL CONTRIBUTION

This is defined as the change in the portfolio standard deviation caused by a small percentage change in the size of the asset, multiplied by its size. One attraction of this approach is that it provides a mathematical decomposition of contributory standard deviation in such a way that the contributions sum up total portfolio standard deviation. PortfolioManager and CreditRisk+ use this approach to calculate risk contributions. We also used this approach in the Markowitz and Merton model runs.

In our analysis, we compared continuous marginal risk contributions, referred to as unexpected loss contributions. To do this, discrete risk contributions obtained from CreditManager runs are adjusted using a closed form formula.

Figure 2 compares the unexpected loss contributions of CreditManager and PortfolioManager. Although there is broad directional agreement, a closer examination of the results shows there

**2. Unexpected loss contributions scatter plot, CreditManager vs PortfolioManager**

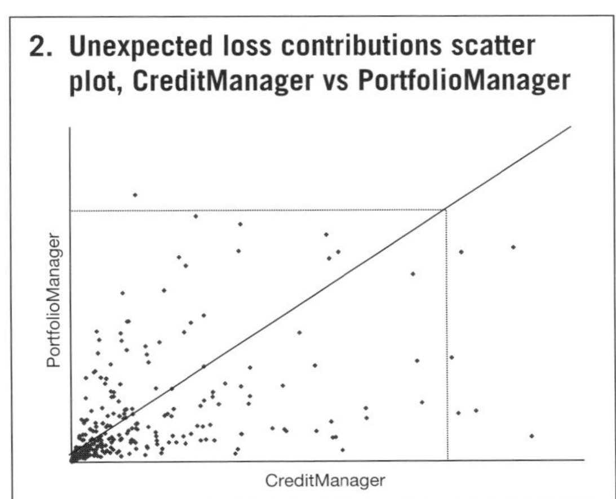

are substantial differences in unexpected loss contributions for a subset of the high-risk exposures. For these exposures, differences in unexpected loss contributions of up to 35 times were observed, and it is these exposures that appear to drive the differences in aggregate results between CreditManager and PortfolioManager described earlier.

To quantify the impact of the different models' conflicting views on contributory risk, we defined a concentration indicator:

$$Ci_i = \text{Sign}\left\{\left(\frac{\frac{ULC_i}{UL_i}}{\frac{UL_p}{\sum UL_k}}\right) - 1\right\}$$

A positive concentration indicator indicates that the asset increases concentration in the portfolio, normalised for its stand-alone risk, and vice versa. The practical interpretation of this measure is whether two models would assess an asset in the portfolio as a sell-sell (CI +ve) or a buy-buy (CI –ve) with respect to managing portfolio diversification. When the concentration indicator does not match, the models in question give conflicting results as to which assets concentrate, and which assets diversify, the portfolio. The match of concentration indicators between different models for the combined portfolio is shown in Table 5.

Table 5 shows that in over 70% of cases the different models agree which assets are relatively concentrating and which are relatively diversifying the portfolio. Agreement is higher between similar techniques, that is between Merton models (eg, CreditManager vs PortfolioManager), than between different techniques (eg, CreditRisk+ vs CreditManager).

**Table 5. Matching frequency in concentration indicator**

| | Credit-Manager (%) | Portfolio-Manager (%) | Credit-Risk+ (%) | Credit-Risk+h (%) |
|---|---|---|---|---|
| PortfolioManager | 86 | – | – | – |
| CreditRisk+ | 72 | 81 | – | – |
| CreditRisk+h | 71 | 79 | 95 | – |
| CreditRisk+f | 72 | 79 | 97 | 98 |

This is not driven by differences in modelling technique, but by the parameterisation used in this study. CreditManager and PortfolioManager construct default correlations using a similar breakdown of country and industry risk factors. In our implementation, CreditRisk+ has a simple default correlation structure. In principle, it would be possible to introduce multiple factors in CreditRisk+ in order to mimic the correlation structure of CreditManager or PortfolioManager (see Koyluoglu and Hickman, 1998 and Gordy, 2000).

However, it should be noted that, although the models agree to an encouraging extent on which assets are concentrating or diversifying the portfolio, they still differ considerably in their estimates of the degree to which this occurs. Therefore different models will give different indications of the price at which assets should be added or removed from the portfolio. These disparities are driven by parameter inconsistencies.

## Conclusions

Different credit risk models yield significantly different portfolio and contributory-level risk results for identical portfolios, if the parameter estimates used in the models correspond to their natural data set. Clearly, such differences imply different recommendations for credit risk management, risk-based pricing and portfolio optimisation.

Parameter estimation methods should be carefully analysed before portfolio optimisation is attempted. The quality of estimates available from different techniques should be compared across various sub-portfolios. For example, Merton-based asset correlations derived from equity price relationships might be most accurate for publicly traded companies, while default rate volatilities derived from historical experience might be most relevant for consumer portfolios.

Moreover, alternative Merton-based correlation estimation techniques should be compared rigorously as there is a wide disparity of results even when the same framework is used (CreditManager vs PortfolioManager). Given the wide variation in these estimates in the available models and the challenge of determining which is better, users should employ sensitivity analysis to stress test significant portfolio pricing and optimisation decisions across a range of potential parameter estimates.

1 *This is not done to correct the risk results produced by CreditRisk+, but to show that a forced match in unexpected loss of the portfolio does not necessarily mean an exact match in the tail of the distribution. The flexibility of CreditRisk+ in parameter specification is the main reason for applying such an adjustment to CreditRisk+ rather than CreditManager or PortfolioManager.*

**BIBLIOGRAPHY**

**Carty, L., and D. Lieberman,** 1996, *Corporate Bond Defaults and Default Rates 1938–1995*, Moody's Investors Service Global Credit Research, January.

**Gordy, M.,** 2000, "A Comparative Anatomy of Credit Risk Models", *Journal of Banking & Finance*, January.

**Koyluoglu, H. U., and A. Hickman,** 1998, "Reconcilable Differences", *Risk*, October, pp. 56–62.

**Stuart, A., and K. Ord,** 1994, *Kendall's Advanced Theory of Statistics, Volume 1: Distribution Theory*, Sixth Edition (New York: John Wiley & Sons).

13

# Modelling Default Correlation

**Krishan Nagpal and Reza Bahar**

HypoVereinsbank; HVB Risk Management Products, Inc.

*In the May 2001 edition of Risk, Krishan Nagpal and Reza Bahar presented an empirical study of historical default correlation. Using these results, they now show how to obtain the portfolio credit loss distribution, within a CreditMetrics-style framework.*

Modelling default correlation is hard because of the complexity involved in developing realistic models that capture its dependence on credit quality, region, industry and time horizon. Two publicly available approaches to credit risk analysis that allow one to include the effect of default correlation are detailed in the publications by Gupton, Finger and Bhatia (1997) and Credit Suisse Financial Products (1997).

CreditMetrics is a simulation-based approach where credit changes for each asset are modelled using a standard normal random variable. CreditRisk+ provides an approach to analytically obtain the loss distribution where the effect of default correlation is incorporated by assuming that the default rates are stochastically driven by independent background variables.

Recently, Nagpal and Bahar (1999) developed an approach that allows one to analytically obtain the loss distribution for a portfolio under a reasonably general class of default correlations. Here, no assumptions are made on the sources of default correlation - default rates and all pair-wise correlations are assumed to be exogenously given. Their main result shows that the loss distribution for any portfolio comprising the given assets can be obtained by suitably combining the loss distribution of the same portfolio under multiple scenarios with independent defaults. Our main objective is to extend the results presented there to the proposed structure of default correlation. The results show that portfolio credit risk analysis can be reduced to a simpler computational problem of obtaining the loss distribution under the assumption of independence. We also provide a parameterisation of solutions that can be used to obtain such a family of loss distributions, which are all consistent with the given default rates and correlations.

## The model for default correlation

In Nagpal and Bahar (2001), a model for correlation was proposed that assumed that default correlations are attributable to either the impact of economic conditions caused by being in the same region or to the effects of industry-specific events. Under the proposed model, if X and Y are two non-defaulted assets, then:

$$\begin{aligned}\Pr\{&\text{Default of X before time T} \mid \text{Y defaults before time T}\}\\ &= (1 + REG_{XY}(T) + IND_{XY}(T))\\ &\quad \times \Pr\{\text{Default of X before time T}\} \end{aligned} \tag{1}$$

where:

$$REG_{XY}(T) := \begin{cases} reg_j(T) & \text{if X and Y are both in the same region j} \\ 0 & \text{if X and Y are not in the same region} \end{cases} \tag{2}$$

$$IND_{XY}(T) := \begin{cases} ind_k(T) & \text{if X and Y are both in the same industry k} \\ 0 & \text{if X and Y are not in the same industry} \end{cases} \tag{3}$$

The above model can equivalently be viewed as describing the ratio of pair-wise default probability to the same under the assumption of independence of default events:

$$\frac{\Pr\begin{Bmatrix}\text{Joint default of X}\\ \text{and Y before time T}\end{Bmatrix}}{\Pr\begin{Bmatrix}\text{Default of X}\\ \text{before time T}\end{Bmatrix}\times\Pr\begin{Bmatrix}\text{Default of Y}\\ \text{before time T}\end{Bmatrix}} = (1+\text{REG}_{XY}(T)+\text{IND}_{XY}(T)) \quad (4)$$

In the above model, $\text{REG}_{XY}$ and $\text{IND}_{XY}$ capture the default correlation contributions that arise from being in the same region and the same industry, respectively, and are assumed to be only functions of the time horizon T and not the ratings (default probabilities) of X and Y. Even though they do not depend on the credit quality of X and Y, the proposed model is consistent with the observation that the default correlations are higher for weaker credits and almost zero for very strong credits when the coefficients REG and IND are positive (see Nagpal and Bahar, 2001).

It is shown in Nagpal and Bahar (2001) that the above model fits the observed correlations well. Correlation parameter estimates for different industry sectors in US are also described in that article.

The framework described here can also be generalised to time-varying (but known) exposures and varying maturity profiles of different obligors. If the maturity of asset X is $T_1$ and maturity of asset Y is $T_2$, then under some assumptions Equation 4 can be described as:

$$\frac{\Pr\begin{Bmatrix}\text{X defaults before } T_1 \text{ and}\\ \text{Y defaults before } T_2\end{Bmatrix}}{\Pr\begin{Bmatrix}\text{X defaults}\\ \text{before } T_1\end{Bmatrix}\times\Pr\begin{Bmatrix}\text{Y defaults}\\ \text{before } T_2\end{Bmatrix}} = (1+\text{REG}_{XY}+\text{IND}_{XY})$$

where $\text{REG}_{XY}$ and $\text{IND}_{XY}$ are independent of $T_1$ and $T_2$. The results presented here can be directly extended to time-varying exposures and different maturity profiles under the above correlation assumption by applying the approach outlined here to marginal default probabilities of each obligor (for details, see Nagpal and Bahar, 2000).

The proposed framework is conceptually similar to the CreditMetrics approach in Gupton, Finger and Bhatia (1997). Consider two companies in which the correlation is caused by one systematic risk factor. The credit changes for the two companies can be modelled using normal random variables $r_1$ and $r_2$ where:

$$r_1 = w_{1sys}r_{sys} + w_{1id}\hat{r}_1; \quad r_2 = w_{2sys}r_{sys} + w_{2id}\hat{r}_2$$

where $r_{sys}$, $\hat{r}_1$ and $\hat{r}_2$ are independent random variables that represent the contribution of systematic risk and the idiosyncratic components of the two companies. For normalisation convenience, all random variables are chosen so that they have variance one, which imposes constraints on the weights:

$$w_{1sys}^2 + w_{1id}^2 = w_{2sys}^2 + w_{2id}^2 = 1$$

In the CreditMetrics framework, company one (and, respectively, two) defaults if $r_1 \le r_1^*$ (respectively, $r_2 \le r_2^*$) where the threshold levels $r_1^*$ and $r_2^*$ are chosen to match their respective default probabilities. The weights $w_{1sys}$ and $w_{2sys}$ are chosen to match the desired correlation.

The proposed approach is equivalent to the CreditMetrics framework if one assumes: (i) the random variables $r_{sys}$, $\hat{r}_1$ and $\hat{r}_2$ are from a uniform distribution instead of normal distribution and (ii) the systematic risk weights ($w_{1sys}$ and $w_{2sys}$ above) are proportional to the default probabilities. The latter assumption includes the further assumption that the systematic risks have a greater impact on the poorer credits. To illustrate this, let us assume that the default probabilities of the two assets are $p_1$ and $p_2$ while the random variables $r_{sys}$, $\hat{r}_1$ and $\hat{r}_2$ are uniformly distributed between zero and one. Then if $w_{1sys}, w_{1id} > p_1$ and $w_{2sys}, w_{2id} > p_2$:

$$\Pr\{r_1 < p_1\} = p_1, \Pr\{r_2 < p_2\} = p_2$$
$$\Rightarrow 2w_{1sys}w_{1id} = p_1,\ 2w_{2sys}w_{2id} = p_2$$

If one additionally assumes that the weights linked to systematic risks are proportional to the default probability, ie:

$$\frac{w_{1sys}}{p_1} = \frac{w_{2sys}}{p_2} = K$$

then, using the above relationships, one can show that:

$$\text{Probability of joint default} = \Pr\{r_1 < p_1 \text{ and } r_2 < p_2\} = \frac{4K}{3}p_1 p_2$$

Thus, in this framework, the pair-wise default probabilities are proportional to what they would be if defaults were independent ($p_1p_2$). The constant K can be chosen to reflect the correlation impact of the systematic risk.

## Background and the main idea

First, we briefly review how one obtains the loss distribution in a portfolio where all the default events are independent. Let $e_i$ and $p_i$ denote the exposure amount and probability of default of the ith exposure. For simplicity, let us assume that the recovery has already been factored in determining the exposure amount so that in the case of a default of ith counterparty, the amount $e_i$ is lost. It is convenient to work in units so that all exposure amounts $e_i$ are positive integers. For a portfolio of N exposures, define the probability generating function in terms of an auxiliary variable z as:

$$F(z) := \prod_{i=1}^{i=N}\left(1 - p_i + p_i z^{e_i}\right)$$
$$= a_0 + a_1 z^{m_1} \cdots + a_k z^{m_k}$$

Then, for the given portfolio, under the assumption of independence of default events, the probability of losing zero is $a_0$ and the probability of losing $m_i$ is $a_i$ for $i = 1$ to k. The above, stated as a polynomial multiplication problem, is a standard convolution problem and provides explicit closed-form expression for the loss distribution of a portfolio of exposures provided all default events are independent.

To illustrate the idea of the approach presented here, which is based on the approach developed in Nagpal and Bahar (1999), consider a portfolio of assets rated BB, in one region but two industries. Let us assume that all the assets have a default probability of 10%. Let the regional and industry correlation factors defined in Equations 2 and 3 be $reg = 1/3$, $ind_1 = ind_2 = 1/3$. This implies that the probability of joint default if the two assets are in the same region but not in the same industry is 0.0133. Similarly, the probability of joint default for two assets in the same region and industry is 0.0167. If defaults had been independent, the joint default probability would have been 0.01.

Now consider three mutually exclusive scenarios that occur with probability 0.33 each. The defaults under each scenario are independent and the default probability of the assets under the different scenarios are as shown in Table 1. Then, for an asset in any of the two industries, its default probability is:

$$\Pr\{\text{Default}\} = \sum_{\substack{\text{Scenario}\\ 1 \text{ to } 3}} \Pr\{\text{Scenario i}\} \times \Pr\{\text{Default in Scenario i}\}$$
$$= \frac{1}{3}(0 + 0.2 + 0.1) = 0.1$$

**Table 1. The scenario probabilities and the default probabilities in different scenarios**

| Scenario | Probability | Default probabilities | |
|---|---|---|---|
| | | Industry 1 | Industry 2 |
| 1 | 0.33 | 0.0 | 0.1 |
| 2 | 0.33 | 0.2 | 0.2 |
| 3 | 0.33 | 0.1 | 0.0 |

Similarly, for any two assets that are in different industries:

$$\Pr\{\text{Joint Default}\} = \sum_{\substack{\text{Scenario}\\ 1 \text{ to } 3}} \Pr\{\text{Scenario i}\} \times \Pr\{\text{Joint Default in Scenario i}\}$$
$$= \frac{1}{3}(0 \times 0.1 + 0.2 \times 0.2 + 0.1 \times 0)$$
$$= 0.0133$$

where in the last equation one has assumed that default events are independent under each scenario. For any two assets in the same industry:

$$\Pr\{\text{Joint Default}\} = \sum_{\substack{\text{Scenario}\\ 1 \text{ to } 3}} \Pr\{\text{Scenario i}\} \times \Pr\{\text{Joint Default in Scenario i}\}$$
$$= \frac{1}{3}(0 \times 0 + 0.2 \times 0.2 + 0.1 \times 0.1)$$
$$= 0.0167$$

Thus, the three scenarios viewed as mutually exclusive outcomes produce precisely the given probability of defaults and probability of pair-wise defaults. Now, for any given portfolio of assets with these default characteristics, one can proceed to obtain the loss distribution under the three scenarios assuming independence from which the actual loss distribution can be obtained as follows:

$$\Pr\{\text{Loss} = x\} = \sum_{\substack{\text{Scenario}\\ 1 \text{ to } 3}} \Pr\{\text{Scenario i}\} \times \Pr\{\text{Loss} = x \text{ in Scenario i}\}$$

Nagpal and Bahar (1999) generalise this idea to portfolios with several types of assets. Their results show that if a portfolio is composed of L asset types, then the loss distribution under correlated defaults can be obtained by combining loss distribution of at most 2L scenarios, where under each scenario the loss distribution is obtained under the assumption of independence.

## Main results

Before describing the main results, we first give the precise problem formulation. The following list provides the data that is assumed to be known regarding the portfolio and is the notation used for the rest of the chapter:

- N is the number of different ratings in the portfolio (the default probabilities under each rating are assumed to be distinct).
- $p_i$ for $i = 1,\ldots, N$. $p_i$ is the default probability of asset with ith rating.
- J is the number of geographical regions.
- $reg_j$ for $j = 1,\ldots, J$. $reg_j$ is the regional correlation factor as defined in Equations 1 and 2 for region j.
- K is the number of industry classifications.
- $ind_k$ for $k = 1,\ldots, K$. $ind_k$ is the industry correlation factor as defined in Equations 1 and 3 for industry k.

The overall objective is to obtain loss distribution for the portfolio based on the data described above, ie, to obtain the probability associated with every possible loss amount.

*Assumption 1*

$reg_j \geq 0$ for all $j = 1,\ldots, J$ and $ind_k \geq 0$ for all $k = 1,\ldots, K$.

The above assumption implies that all correlations due to regional or industry effects must be non-negative. This assumption usually holds in credit risk due to the similar impact of economic conditions or sector-specific events on the performance of companies.

*Assumption 2*

Let $p_{max} := \max_{1 \leq i \leq N} p_i$. Then the following holds:

$$\sum_{j=1}^{J} reg_j + \sum_{k=1}^{K} ind_k \leq \frac{1-p_{max}}{p_{max}} \tag{5}$$

The above condition, loosely speaking, restricts the number and levels of region and industry-related correlations. The left-hand side increases as the default correlations increase or the number of regions or sectors increase while the right-hand side increases if the maximum default probability decreases. It is a technical condition that holds in most cases – in the US the correlation factors $reg_j$ and $ind_k$ are in the range of 0 to 0.5 (see Nagpal and Bahar, 2001). For example, if the average of $reg_j$ and $ind_k$ is 0.3 and there is a total of 10 regions and sectors, the above assumption holds if the default probability of all assets is less than 25%. Though we feel that under the proposed framework the above condition can be relaxed, we have so far been unable to obtain a reasonably general solution that works under weaker conditions.

Note that the above assumption is equivalent to:

$$\frac{p_{max}}{1-p_{max}}\left[\sum_{j=1}^{J} reg_j + \sum_{k=1}^{K} ind_k\right] \leq 1$$

which in turn implies the existence of $\gamma_1,\ldots,\gamma_{J+K}$ such that the following two conditions hold:

$$\begin{aligned} \gamma_j &\geq \frac{p_{max}}{1-p_{max}} reg_j \quad \text{for } j = 1,\ldots,J \\ \text{and } \gamma_{J+k} &\geq \frac{p_{max}}{1-p_{max}} ind_k \quad \text{for } k = 1,\ldots,K \end{aligned} \tag{6}$$

$$\sum_{q=1}^{J+K} \gamma_q = 1 \tag{7}$$

With $\gamma_S$ chosen as above, let $\alpha_S$ be chosen to be in the interval defined as follows:

$$\begin{aligned} \alpha_j &\in \left[\frac{p_{max}\sqrt{reg_j}}{(1-p_{max})\gamma_j}, \frac{1}{\sqrt{reg_j}}\right] \quad \text{for } j = 1,\ldots,J \\ \alpha_{J+k} &\in \left[\frac{p_{max}\sqrt{ind_k}}{(1-p_{max})\gamma_{J+k}}, \frac{1}{\sqrt{ind_k}}\right] \quad \text{for } k = 1,\ldots,K \end{aligned} \tag{8}$$

The fact that the above intervals are non-empty follows from Equation 6. If the correlation factors are zero ($reg_j = 0$ or $ind_k = 0$), the corresponding a can be chosen to be any positive number.

Our main result will describe default properties for each asset type in multiple scenarios. Here, the following notation would be adopted:

$$P_m(i, j, k) := \text{Default prob in mth scenario of an asset rated i that is in the jth region and kth industry} \tag{9}$$

*Theorem*

Let assumptions 1 and 2 hold and $\gamma_1,\ldots, \gamma_{J+K}, \alpha_1,\ldots, \alpha_{J+K}$ be chosen to satisfy Equations 6–8. Let $\kappa_i \in (0, 1)$ be defined as below:

$$\kappa_i = \frac{1}{1+\gamma_i \alpha_i^2} \quad \text{for } i = 1,\ldots,J+K \tag{10}$$

Define scenarios 1 to 2 (J + K) as follows:

- Defaults in each scenario are independent.
- Probability of scenario i is $\lambda_i$ where:

$$\lambda_i = \begin{cases} \gamma_s\kappa_s & (\text{if } i = 2s-1 \text{ where } s = 1,\ldots,J+K) \\ \gamma_s(1-\kappa_s) & (\text{if } i = 2s \text{ where } s = 1,\ldots,J+K) \end{cases}$$

- In scenario m, where $m = 1,\ldots, 2(J + K)$, the default probability of all assets in different regions and industries are:

$$P_m(i,j,k) = \begin{cases} \left(1-\alpha_j\sqrt{reg_j}\right) p_i & \text{if } m = 2j-1 \\ \left(1+\frac{\sqrt{reg_j}}{\alpha_j\gamma_j}\right) p_i & \text{if } m = 2j \\ \left(1-\alpha_{J+k}\sqrt{ind_k}\right) p_i & \text{if } m = 2(J+k)-1 \\ \left(1+\frac{\sqrt{ind_k}}{\alpha_{J+k}\gamma_{J+k}}\right) p_i & \text{if } m = 2(J+k) \\ p_i & \text{otherwise} \end{cases}$$

If $reg_j = 0$ (respectively, $ind_k = 0$), $P_m(i,j,k) = p_i$ for $m = \{2j-1, 2j\}$ (respectively, $P_m(i,j,k) = p_i$ for $m = \{2(J+k)-1, 2(J+k)\}$).

For the $2(J + K)$ scenarios defined above, the following holds:

- ❑ $P_m(i,j,k) \in [0,1]$ for all $i = 1,\ldots,N$; $j = 1,\ldots,J$ and $k = 1,\ldots,K$.
- ❑ When viewed together as mutually exclusive outcomes, the $2(J + K)$ scenarios with independent defaults are consistent with the given default data, or equivalently the following hold:

$$\sum_{m=1}^{2(J+K)} \lambda_m = 1 \tag{11}$$

$$\sum_{m=1}^{2(J+K)} \lambda_m P_m(i,j,k) = p_i \tag{12}$$
$$\text{for all } i = 1,\ldots,N;\ j = 1,\ldots,J \text{ and } k = 1,\ldots,K$$

$$\sum_{m=1}^{2(J+K)} \lambda_m P_m(i_1,j_1,k_1)\, P_m(i_2,j_2,k_2) = \begin{cases} p_{i_1}p_{i_2} & \text{if } j_1 \neq j_2 \text{ and } k_1 \neq k_2 \\ (1+reg_{j_1})p_{i_1}p_{i_2} & \text{if } j_1 = j_2 \text{ and } k_1 \neq k_2 \\ (1+ind_{k_1})p_{i_1}p_{i_2} & \text{if } j_1 \neq j_2 \text{ and } k_1 = k_2 \\ (1+reg_{j_1}+ind_{k_1})p_{i_1}p_{i_2} & \text{if } j_1 = j_2 \text{ and } k_1 = k_2 \end{cases} \tag{13}$$

for all $i_1$, $i_2 = 1,\ldots,N$; $j_1$, $j_2 = 1,\ldots,J$ and $k_1$, $k_2 = 1,\ldots,K$.
- ❑ The loss distribution for the given portfolio is obtained as follows:

$$\left[\text{Prob(loss} = x)\right] = \sum_{m=1}^{2(J+K)} \lambda_m \times \begin{bmatrix}\text{Prob(loss} = x) \\ \text{in scenario } m\end{bmatrix} \tag{14}$$

The above result gives a simple algorithm to obtain the loss distribution: obtain the loss distribution for the given portfolio for each of the $2(J + K)$ scenarios under the assumption of independence of default events where the default probabilities for each asset under any given scenario are as in the third part of the theorem; and obtain the overall loss distribution from Equation 14, where the scenario probabilities are as in the second part of the theorem.

Note that since $\gamma_i$ and $\alpha_i$ can be any positive real numbers that satisfy Equations 6–8, the above result also provides a parameterisation of admissible scenarios that are consistent with the given default data.

*Proof of the theorem*

Here we have to show that for the $2(J + K)$ scenarios defined in the above steps, the following items hold. For convenience, the proof for each item is shown separately.

*To show* $P_m(i,j,k) \in [0,1]$ *for all* m, i, j *and* k. From Equation 8:

$$\alpha_j \le \frac{1}{\sqrt{reg_j}} \quad \text{for } j \le J$$

Thus:

$$\left(1-\alpha_j\sqrt{reg_j}\right) p_i \ge 0$$

for all $j = 1,\ldots,J$. Similarly, from Equation 8:

$$\alpha_{J+k} \le \frac{1}{\sqrt{ind_k}} \quad \text{for } k \le K$$

Thus:

$$\left(1-\alpha_{J+k}\sqrt{ind_k}\right) p_i \ge 0$$

for all $k = 1,\ldots,K$.

From the third part of the theorem, one thus notes that $P_m(i,j,k) \ge 0$ for all m, i, j and k. From Equation 8, one concludes that:

$$\frac{\sqrt{reg_j}}{\alpha_j\gamma_j} \le \frac{1-p_{max}}{p_{max}}$$

and:

$$\frac{\sqrt{ind_k}}{\alpha_{J+k}\gamma_{J+k}} \le \frac{1-p_{max}}{p_{max}}$$

for all $j = 1,\ldots,J$ and $k = 1,\ldots,K$. Noting that $p_i \le p_{max}$ for all i, the above implies that:

$$\left(1+\frac{\sqrt{reg_j}}{\alpha_j\gamma_j}\right) p_i \le 1$$

for all $j = 1,\ldots,J$ and:

$$\left(1+\frac{\sqrt{ind_k}}{\alpha_{J+k}\gamma_{J+k}}\right) p_i \le 1$$

for all $k = 1,\ldots,K$. From the definitions of $P_m(i,j,k)$ in the third part of the theorem, one thus notes that $1 \ge P_m(i,j,k) \ge 0$ for all m, i, j and k.

*To show Equations 11-13.* Equation 11 is easily observed using Equation 7 and the definition of $\lambda_i$ in the second part of the theorem. Using the definition of $\kappa_S$ in Equation 10 one notes that:

$$\begin{aligned} \alpha_S^2 &= \frac{1-\kappa_S}{\kappa_S\gamma_S} \\ \Rightarrow \gamma_S\kappa_S\alpha_S &= \frac{1-\kappa_S}{\alpha_S} \quad \text{for all } S = 1,\ldots,J+K \end{aligned} \tag{15}$$

Let i, j and k represent rating, region and industry, respectively. Then, from the second and third parts of the theorem and Equation 15 it follows that:

$$\begin{aligned} &\sum_{m=1}^{2(J+K)} \lambda_m P_m(i,j,k) \\ &= \sum_{m=1}^{2(J+K)} \lambda_m p_i - p_i\left[\gamma_j\kappa_j\alpha_j\sqrt{reg_j} - \gamma_j(1-\kappa_j)\frac{\sqrt{reg_j}}{\alpha_j\gamma_j}\right] \\ &- p_i\left[\gamma_{J+k}\kappa_{J+k}\alpha_{J+k}\sqrt{ind_k} - \gamma_{J+k}(1-\kappa_{J+k})\frac{\sqrt{ind_k}}{\alpha_{J+k}\gamma_{J+k}}\right] \\ &= \sum_{m=1}^{2(J+K)} \lambda_m p_i = p_i \end{aligned}$$

(using Equation 15) and thus Equation 12 holds.

From the definition of $\kappa_S$ in Equation 10 one can also show the following identity:

$$\gamma_s\kappa_s\alpha_s^2 + \frac{1-\kappa_s}{\alpha_s^2\gamma_s} = 1 \quad \text{for all } s = 1,\ldots,2(J+K) \tag{16}$$

Consider a pair of assets where they have ratings $i_1$ and $i_2$ and are in regions $j_1$ and $j_2$ and industries $k_1$ and $k_2$, respectively. We will now consider the four cases of Equation 13 separately. Let $j_1 \neq j_2$ and $k_1 \neq k_2$. Then from the second and third parts of the theorem and Equation 15:

$$\begin{aligned} &\sum_{m=1}^{2(J+K)} \lambda_m P_m(i_1, j_1, k_1)P_m(i_2, j_2, k_2) \\ &= \sum_{m=1}^{2(J+K)} \lambda_m p_{i_1}p_{i_2} - p_{i_1}p_{i_2} \\ &\times \sum_{j=\{j_1, j_2\}} \left[\gamma_j\kappa_j\alpha_j\sqrt{reg_j} - \gamma_j(1-\kappa_j)\frac{\sqrt{reg_j}}{\alpha_j\gamma_j}\right] \\ &- p_{i_1}p_{i_2} \sum_{k=\{k_1,k_2\}} \left[\gamma_{J+k}\kappa_{J+k}\alpha_{J+k}\sqrt{ind_k} - \gamma_{J+k}(1-\kappa_{J+k})\frac{\sqrt{ind_k}}{\alpha_{J+k}\gamma_{J+k}}\right] \\ &= \sum_{m=1}^{2(J+K)} \lambda_m p_{i_1}p_{i_2} = p_{i_1} p_{i_2} \end{aligned}$$

If $j_1 = j_2 = j$, but $k_1 \neq k_2$:

$$\begin{aligned} &\sum_{m=1}^{2(J+K)} \lambda_m P_m(i_1, j_1, k_1)P_m(i_2, j_2, k_2) \\ &= \sum_{m=1, m\neq\{2j-1,2j\}}^{2(J+K)} \lambda_m p_{i_1}p_{i_2} \\ &+ \gamma_j p_{i_1}p_{i_2}\left[\kappa_j\left(1-\alpha_j\sqrt{reg_j}\right)^2 + (1-\kappa_j)\left(1+\frac{\sqrt{reg_j}}{\alpha_j\gamma_j}\right)^2\right] \\ &- p_{i_1}p_{i_2} \sum_{k=\{k_1,k_2\}} \left[\gamma_{J+k}\kappa_{J+k}\alpha_{J+k}\sqrt{ind_k} - \gamma_{J+k}(1-\kappa_{J+k})\frac{\sqrt{ind_k}}{\alpha_{J+k}\gamma_{J+k}}\right] \\ &= \sum_{m=1, m\neq\{2j-1,2j\}}^{2(J+K)} \lambda_m p_{i_1}p_{i_2} + \gamma_j p_{i_1}p_{i_2} + reg_j p_{i_1}p_{i_2} \\ &= (1 + reg_j)p_{i_1}p_{i_2} \end{aligned}$$

(from Equations 15 and 16).

The case of $k_1 = k_2$ but $j_1 \neq j_2$ is shown similarly. If $k_1 = k_2 = k$ and $j_1 = j_2 = j$, then:

$$\begin{aligned} &\sum_{m=1}^{2(J+K)} \lambda_m P_m(i_1, j_1, k_1)P_m(i_2, j_2, k_2) \\ &= \sum_{m=1, m\neq\{2j-1,2j,2k-1,2k\}}^{2(J+K)} \lambda_m p_{i_1}p_{i_2} \\ &+ \gamma_j p_{i_1}p_{i_2}\left[\kappa_j\left(1-\alpha_j\sqrt{reg_j}\right)^2 + (1-\kappa_j)\left(1+\frac{\sqrt{reg_j}}{\alpha_j\gamma_j}\right)^2\right] \\ &+ \gamma_{J+k} p_{i_1}p_{i_2}\left[\kappa_{J+k}\left(1-\alpha_{J+k}\sqrt{ind_k}\right)^2 + (1-\kappa_{J+k})\left(1+\frac{\sqrt{ind_k}}{\alpha_{J+k}\gamma_{J+k}}\right)^2\right] \\ &= \sum_{m=1, m\neq\{2j-1,2j,2k-1,2k\}}^{2(J+K)} \lambda_m p_{i_1}p_{i_2} + \gamma_j p_{i_1}p_{i_2} \\ &+ reg_j p_{i_1}p_{i_2} + \gamma_{J+k} p_{i_1}p_{i_2} + ind_k p_{i_1}p_{i_2} \\ &= (1 + reg_j + ind_k)p_{i_1}p_{i_2} \end{aligned}$$

*To show Equation 14.* Since the probability of scenario m is $\lambda_m$, Equation 11 guarantees that the $2(J+K)$ scenarios cover all possible outcomes if they are mutually exclusive. Equation 12 ensures that the probability of default of any asset matches its *a priori* given value,

**Table 2. The scenario probabilities and the default probabilities in different scenarios**

| | | Region 1 | | | | Region 2 | | | |
|---|---|---|---|---|---|---|---|---|---|
| | | Industry 1 | | Industry 2 | | Industry 1 | | Industry 2 | |
| Scenario | Probability | BBB | BB | BBB | BB | BBB | BB | BBB | BB |
| 1 | 0.200 | 0.009 | 0.045 | 0.009 | 0.045 | 0.020 | 0.100 | 0.020 | 0.100 |
| 2 | 0.050 | 0.064 | 0.319 | 0.064 | 0.319 | 0.020 | 0.100 | 0.020 | 0.100 |
| 3 | 0.200 | 0.020 | 0.100 | 0.020 | 0.100 | 0.011 | 0.055 | 0.011 | 0.055 |
| 4 | 0.050 | 0.020 | 0.100 | 0.020 | 0.100 | 0.056 | 0.279 | 0.056 | 0.279 |
| 5 | 0.200 | 0.006 | 0.029 | 0.020 | 0.100 | 0.006 | 0.0029 | 0.020 | 0.100 |
| 6 | 0.050 | 0.077 | 0.383 | 0.020 | 0.100 | 0.077 | 0.383 | 0.020 | 0.100 |
| 7 | 0.200 | 0.020 | 0.100 | 0.007 | 0.037 | 0.020 | 0.100 | 0.007 | 0.037 |
| 8 | 0.050 | 0.020 | 0.100 | 0.071 | 0.353 | 0.020 | 0.100 | 0.071 | 0.353 |

while Equation 13 ensures that the pair-wise default probabilities of any two assets match their given value under the correlation structure of Equation 1 provided default events under any given scenario are independent. Finally, Equation 14 follows from the observation that all scenarios are mutually exclusive and the probability of scenario m is $\lambda_m$.

## Example

Consider a portfolio of 36 BBB and 28 BB assets where the exposure amount net of recovery for any BBB asset is US$2 while that for a BB asset is US$1. Let the portfolios be in two regions and two industries with nine BBBs and seven BBs in each industry of each region. Let us assume that over the relevant horizon, the default probabilities are:

$$p_{BBB} = 0.02, p_{BB} = 0.1$$

Let the correlation factors be $reg_1 = 0.3$, $reg_2 = 0.2$, $ind_1 = 0.5$ and $ind_2 = 0.4$. With $p_{max} = 0.1$, it is easily verified that assumptions 1 and 2 hold. Next, one notices that $\gamma_i = 0.25$ and $\alpha_i = 1$ for $i = 1,...,4$ satisfy the constraints imposed by Equations 6–8. Here, we could have chosen any $\gamma_i$ and $\alpha_i$ subject to the stated constraints. Applying the second and third parts of the theorem, one obtains the scenario and default probabilities for the eight scenarios described in Table 2. One can now obtain the loss distribution for the given portfolio under all the eight scenarios assuming independence of default events and then combine them as in Equation 14 to obtain the loss distribution under the given correlation structure. Let us define this solution as "Solution 1". It can be verified that $\gamma_1 = \gamma_2 = 0.1$ and $\gamma_3 = \gamma_4 = 0.4$ with $\alpha_i = 1$ for $i = 1,...,4$ also satisfy the constraints described in Equations 6–8. Applying the steps of the theorem, one can obtain another set of scenarios that match the given default probabilities and correlations. Let us describe the loss distribution obtained under these assumptions as "Solution 2". Figure 1 shows the resulting loss distribution under the two decompositions together with the loss distribution obtained under the assumption of independence of defaults. The plot suggests low sensitivity of loss distribution to the choice of free variables for this portfolio. In most cases where there are at least three sectors and regions, we have observed sensitivity of the loss distribution to the choice of variables $\gamma_i$ and $\alpha_i$ to be low as long as they satisfy the required constraints.

**1. Loss distribution**

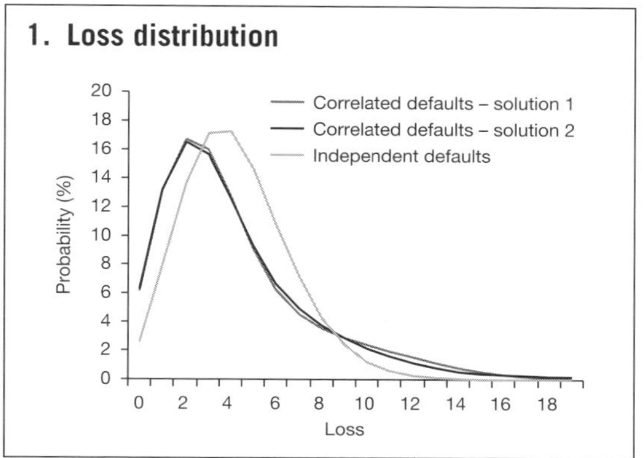


## Summary

In the first part of this chapter, we proposed a simple and compact model for default correlation that captured the correlation both regionally as well as within an industry. We have also developed an analytical approach for obtaining portfolio credit loss distribution under the proposed structure of the correlations. The approach is computationally simple and comparable to obtaining loss distribution for the independent default case. It is shown that if the portfolio assets are in J regions and K industries, then the portfolio loss distribution under the proposed correlation structure can be obtained by combining loss distribution under 2(J + K) scenarios with independent defaults.

**BIBLIOGRAPHY**

**Credit Suisse Financial Products,** 1997, *CreditRisk+, A Credit Risk Management Framework, Technical Document.*

**Gupton, G., C. Finger, and M. Bhatia,** 1997, *CreditMetrics Technical Document,* Morgan Guaranty Trust Company, New York.

**Nagpal, K., and R. Bahar,** 1999, "An Analytical Approach for Credit Risk Analysis Under Correlated Defaults", *CreditMetrics Monitor*, April.

**Nagpal, K., and R. Bahar,** 2000, *Credit Risk Modeling in Presence of Correlations, Part 2: An Analytic Approach*, Standard & Poor's.

**Nagpal, K., and R. Bahar,** 2001, "Credit Risk Modeling in Presence of Correlations, Part 1: Historical Data for US Corporates", *Risk*, March 2001, pp. 129–32.

14

# How Dependent are Defaults?

**Richard Martin, Kevin Thompson and Christopher Browne**
BNP Paribas; DrKW

*Richard Martin, Kevin Thompson and Christopher Browne discuss default rate volatility models in a conditional independence framework. They show that discretisation of the latent variable facilitates comparison of models and makes it clear what is being assumed about the frequency and severity of clusters of default events.*

Recent advances in credit risk modelling have led to the development of various credit portfolio risk models, including KMV's PortfolioManager, JP Morgan's CreditMetrics, McKinsey's CreditPortfolioView and Credit Suisse Financial Products' CreditRisk+ (for reviews, see Crouhy, Galai and Mark, 2000 and Gordy, 2000). These models have received much attention from practitioners and generated much academic study. Koyluoglu and Hickman (1998) have shown that the existing default correlation models are very similar and can be put in a conditional-independence framework in which default events are independent conditionally on an underlying or latent variable. In this chapter, we show that discretisation of the latent variable does not significantly alter the results that the models produce, and has the benefit of making clear what is being assumed about the probability and severity of clusters of default events. We also show how to calibrate a discrete latent variable model from historical data. In a companion paper (Martin, Thompson and Browne, 2001), we have shown that the saddlepoint method, a fast analytical approximation scheme that is particularly effective in the tail of the loss distribution, can easily be applied to the discrete latent variable model of dependence. This allows real portfolios to be analysed without Monte Carlo simulation, and also allows the analytical derivation of risk contributions. Finally, we discuss different ways of measuring correlation, and in particular what it means to impose constant correlation across rating classes, and show that there are profound differences between using default correlations and using the asset return correlations of the Merton model.

## Default rate modelling

DEFAULT RATE AND DEFAULT RATE VOLATILITY

We consider volatility of the underlying default rate $R$, which is the probability of default over a short time period (eg, one year). To calibrate this parameter, we may wish to examine the volatility of the observed default rate $R_{obs}$, which is the proportion of defaults in a homogeneous portfolio over a short time period. Both these quantities are related, but note that the observed default rate can vary even if the underlying default rate is constant, owing to statistical noise. In fact:

$$E[R_{obs}] = E[R]$$
$$V[R_{obs}] = \underbrace{V[R]}_{\text{"genuine"}} + \underbrace{E[R - R^2]/n}_{\text{"spurious"}}$$

in which $E$ and $V$ denote expectation and variance, and $n$ is the portfolio size. The spurious variability in the observed default rate is purely a result of statistical noise, and it vanishes as the portfolio becomes infinitely large.

Default rate modelling is predicated on conditional independence of defaults. Conditional on the underlying default rate being known, losses are independent, and the distribution of the number of losses in a homogeneous portfolio is binomial. The underlying default rate cannot be observed; only its distribution is known (or supposed). Default events are no longer independent, because when one counterparty defaults, the (posterior) distribution of the underlying default rate alters – the rate is more likely to be high – so it is more likely that there will be further defaults. Notice that the dependence between default events is indirect: default rate modelling cannot of itself account for a direct dependence between counterparty defaults, such as one counterparty being a creditor or subsidiary of another.

It is convenient to specify R via an additional layer of abstraction. Doing this allows one to take an econometric or structural viewpoint or to study portfolios consisting of different ratings. We have said that the underlying default rate is not observable. Let us suppose that R is a deterministic function of a more fundamental latent variable V, also unobservable, with density $\psi$. Then:

$$\mathbf{E}[R] = \int_{-\infty}^{\infty} R(v)\,\psi(v)\,dv,$$

$$\mathbf{E}[R^2] = \int_{-\infty}^{\infty} R^2(v)\,\psi(v)\,dv, \qquad \text{etc.}$$

By the default rate volatility, we mean the standard deviation of the underlying default rate, ie, $\mathbf{V}[R]^{1/2}$. When credit default models are compared, one is in essence comparing the different distributions of R. We can write down an expression for default correlation in terms of the mean and variance of R. The probability (conditional on R) that one particular asset defaults is simply R, and for a particular pair of assets defaulting it is $R^2$. These become $\mathbf{E}[R]$ and $\mathbf{E}[R^2]$ when the conditioning is removed. So the default correlation is:

$$\rho_D = \frac{\mathbf{E}[R^2] - \mathbf{E}[R]^2}{\mathbf{E}[R] - \mathbf{E}[R]^2}$$

Notice that the numerator of this expression is the square of the default rate volatility. We can also write down the probability of r defaults in a portfolio of size n, which is:

$$\binom{n}{r}\mathbf{E}\left[R^r(1-R)^{n-r}\right]$$

This is a binomial mixture. We can think of the uncertainty in R mixing together binomial distributions of different default rates.

## EXISTING MODELS

Under simplifying assumptions, the existing popular models can be fitted into the framework we have described. The models differ in their interpretation of the latent variable V, and in their choice of distribution of V and default rate function R(V).

### *Merton-based: KMV/CreditMetrics*

The Merton model supposes that default occurs when the level of the obligor's assets falls below the level of its debts. It is assumed that, after logarithmic and scaling transformations, the joint distribution of asset returns is multivariate standard normal. In general, the Merton model cannot be reduced to the form that we are discussing, but in an important special case it can (considered in the KMV and CreditMetrics documentation). Assume that the (transformed) asset returns $Z_i$ can be written as a correlated part V plus an uncorrelated part $U_i$, all of which are independent identically distributed standard normal:

$$Z_i = \sqrt{\rho}V + \sqrt{1-\rho}U_i$$

with $\rho$ denoting the common correlation between asset returns. Then conditional on V, the default rate for an asset of mean default rate $\bar{p}$ is:

$$R(V) = \mathbf{P}\left(Z_i < \Phi^{-1}(\bar{p}) \middle| V\right) = \Phi\left(\frac{\Phi^{-1}(\bar{p}) - \sqrt{\rho}V}{\sqrt{1-\rho}}\right)$$

and the density of V is:[1]

$$\psi(v) = \exp\left(-\frac{1}{2}v^2\right)\Big/\sqrt{2\pi}$$

The default rate volatility can be expressed in terms of the bivariate normal integral, using:

$$\mathbf{E}[R^2] = \Phi_2(\Phi^{-1}(\bar{p}), \Phi^{-1}(\bar{p}); \rho)$$

### *Econometric: CreditPortfolioView*

Here V is a macroeconomic variable, assumed normally distributed. The default rate is given as a function of V by the logit function:

$$R(V) = 1/(1 + e^{a+bV})$$

where a and b are the model parameters and the density of V is:

$$\psi(v) = \exp\left(-\frac{1}{2}v^2\right)\Big/\sqrt{2\pi}$$

Had the cumulative normal function been used instead of the logit function for R(V), the results would have been the same as those of the Merton model.

### *Actuarial: CreditRisk+*

In the simplest form of the model, V is a univariate "risk factor" with a gamma distribution of shape parameter $\alpha$ and mean one, and R is obtained by scaling it:

$$R(V) = \bar{p}\,V, \quad \psi(v) = \alpha^\alpha v^{\alpha-1} e^{-\alpha v} / \Gamma(\alpha)$$

It is possible to have more than one risk factor. The loss distribution conditional on R is approximated as a Poisson, and this combined with the choice of distribution for R allows the full loss distribution to be obtained analytically.

A slight modification of this idea is to give R a Beta(a, b) distribution instead, so its density is $v^{a-1}(1-v)^{b-1}/B(a,b)$. The mean default rate is $a(a+b)^{-1}$ and the default rate volatility is $(ab)^{1/2}(a+b)^{-1}(a+b+1)^{-1/2}$. Also, the probability of r defaults out of n is easily seen to be:

$$\binom{n}{r} B(a+r, b+n-r)/B(a,b)$$

For low default probabilities, this gives very similar results to CreditRisk+; for very low-rated assets there will be a greater discrepancy because in CreditRisk+ an asset can default more than once.

DISCRETISATION OF THE LATENT VARIABLE

In each of the above examples, the latent variable has a continuous distribution, ie, it has a continuum of states. However, it would be convenient to replace the continuous distribution with a discrete one, thereby simplifying the model so that there are a finite number of "scenarios". This has the immediate benefit of making the default rate distributions easy to compare and it is fairly straightforward to understand what each model has to say about the probability and severity of clusters of defaults.

Any quantity that is not conditional on the latent variable V is an expectation, and hence can be written as an integral:

$$E[f] = \int f(v)\,\psi(v)dv$$

For example, the mean and mean square default rate use this construction, with $f(v) = R(v)$, $R^2(v)$, respectively. What we therefore want to do is to approximate integrals, and this leads us to a well-known problem in numerical analysis. Given a distribution $\psi$, find the "best" method of approximating the integral (or expectation) $\int f(v)\psi(v)dv$ as a weighted sum of values of f plus an error term:

$$\int f(v)\,\psi(v)dv = \sum_{k=1}^{m} h_k f(v_k) + \varepsilon_m[f]$$

We can think of this as replacing the continuously distributed latent variable V having distribution $\psi$ with a discretely distributed variable W for which $P(W = v_k) = h_k$ $(1 \le k \le m)$. This can be done in many ways, and an attractive choice is Gaussian quadrature. The Gaussian quadrature formula of order m allows polynomials of degree <2m to be integrated exactly (ie, $\varepsilon_m[f] = 0$ if the 2mth derivative of f vanishes). This means that W has the same first $2m-1$ moments as V has. If f is a smooth function, this method works very well indeed and remarkably good accuracy can be achieved with only a small number of terms. There are well-known methods of obtaining the Gaussian quadrature coefficients $h_k$, $v_k$ for the cases in which $\psi$ is a normal, gamma or beta density, which are precisely the cases we have been talking about. There are also procedures for calculating the coefficients for other distributions. For further details, consult Press *et al.* (1992) or a numerical analysis text, eg, Kopal (1955).

HISTORICAL CALIBRATION OF DISCRETE LATENT VARIABLE MODELS

As we pointed out earlier, observed default rates in a finite portfolio would be volatile even if the underlying default rate were constant. In analysing historical default rates, we therefore have to be careful in distinguishing real from spurious volatility. We assume that we have annual default data over a period of M years (eg, the Moody's Investors Service data given in summarised form by Carty and Lieberman, 1998, page 327) and that in year i there are $n_i$ defaults out of a possible $N_i$.

We can frame M hypotheses $H_c$, $1 \le c \le M$, where $H_c$ is defined so that the M years can be partitioned into c clusters and that within the kth cluster the unconditional default rate is a constant, $\alpha_k$. The $(H_c)$ are nested, in the sense that $H_c$ is a special case of $H_{c+1}$. Hypothesis $H_1$ says that all the observed default rate variability is spurious (or, that the underlying default rate is the same each year). By contrast, hypothesis $H_M$ says that all the observed variability is genuine (or, that the underlying and observed default rates are equal). We introduce the notation that year i belongs to cluster $\kappa(i)$ for each i. For the hypothesis $H_c$, the log-likelihood function is:

$$L_c = \sum_{k=1}^{c} \sum_{i|\kappa(i)=k} \ln\left[\binom{N_i}{n_i} \alpha_k^{n_i} (1-\alpha_k)^{N_i - n_i}\right]$$

and we must estimate $(\alpha_k)_{k=1}^{c}$ and $(\kappa(i))_{i=1}^{M}$. This is best done by maximising $L_c$, for which the following method is ideal.[2] First, select the κs at random (between 1 and c), which just means randomly assigning years to clusters. Then maximise $L_c$ with respect to the αs keeping the κs fixed, by putting:

$$\alpha_k = \sum_{i|\kappa(i)=k} n_i \Big/ \sum_{i|\kappa(i)=k} N_i$$

**1. Results of the historical calibration and discretisations of the models**

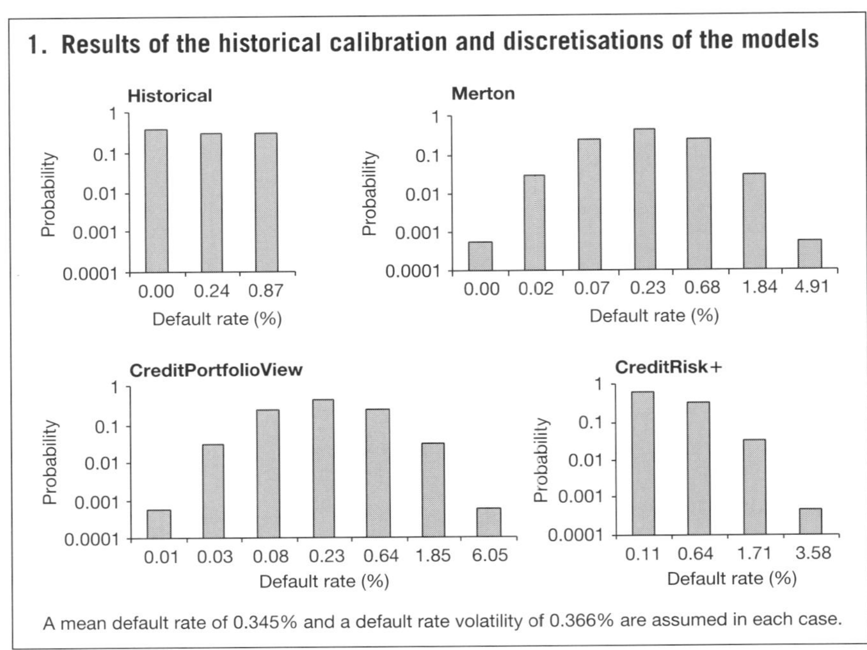


A mean default rate of 0.345% and a default rate volatility of 0.366% are assumed in each case.

Next, fix the newly obtained αs and maximise $L_c$ with respect to the κs, by putting κ(i) equal to the value of k that maximises:

$$\alpha_k^{n_i}(1-\alpha_k)^{N_i-n_i}$$

Then go back and re-estimate the αs, then re-estimate the κs and carry on until a stable state is achieved. At each stage $L_c$ must increase, and as there are only a finite number of ways of selecting the κs, it follows that convergence occurs in a finite number of steps (in practice, two or three often suffice). It is a good idea to go back and repeat the whole procedure from different starting points, to be sure of finding the global maximum.

For each hypothesis, the likelihood-ratio test statistic of $H_c$ against $H_M$ is $2(L_M - L_c)$, which roughly follows a chi-squared distribution with $M - c$ degrees of freedom.[3] As the hypotheses are nested, we must have $2(L_M - L_1) \geq 2(L_M - L_2) \geq \ldots \geq 0$. Taking in turn $H_1$, then $H_2$, $H_3$ and so on, we will find an $H_c$ that is accepted at the level of significance we desire, and with it the calibrated model.

We applied this method to 29 years of Moody's yearly default data, considering ratings Baa1, Baa2, Baa3, Ba1 and Ba2, and lumping them together. (If one considers only one rating, there is insufficient data to achieve a meaningful result. This is a real problem with the high-grade bonds, on which there have been hardly any defaults in the past 30 years.) $H_1$ was rejected, so the data shows evidence of variability in the underlying default rate. $H_2$ was accepted even at a significance level of 20%; going to three clusters improved the fit a little more and thereafter there was negligible improvement in fit. The first graph in Figure 1 shows the state probabilities (ie, cluster sizes divided by M) and default rates $\alpha_k$ for the three-cluster model. Note that the worst-case default rate is not particularly severe, probably because the last 30 years have been reasonably benign and there have not been any catastrophic years. The mean default rate is 0.345% and the standard deviation is 0.366%. In the conditional independence framework, we can think of V as a macroeconomic variable taking three states, "good", "medium" and "bad".

## Comparisons and portfolio analysis

What is of direct interest to a portfoliomanager is not the distribution of the underlying default rate but its effect on the risk of a portfolio. There are different ways of assessing risk. The simplest is the mean–variance framework. It is apparent that in this framework the only information needed about default rates is their mean and variance. In a portfolio of assets of equal rating and exposures ($a_j$), the mean loss is $E[R]A_1$ and the variance is $E[R](1 - E[R])A_2 + V[R](A_1^2 - A_2)$, where $A_1 = \Sigma a_j$ and $A_2 = \Sigma a_j^2$. A similar result holds if the ratings are different: only default rates and (second-order) correlations matter.

The main problem with mean–variance is that real loss distributions are not normal, and it pays insufficient attention to extreme risks. This is why the value-at-risk is often preferred. Here, we shall use 99.97% confidence, the level an AA-rated institution would need. We shall see that, even when calibrated to agree on the mean and variance of the underlying default rate, the three models described above and the historical calibration give very different answers.

COMPARISON BY MODEL DISCRETISATION

We calibrate the three models described above so that the mean default rate is 0.345% and the default rate volatility is 0.366% (see Table 1). These will then agree with the historical calibration. As we are interested in 99.97% confidence, we consider a quadrature formula that is of reasonably high order (to get good accuracy), but not so high that the "worst case" occurs with probability <0.03%. We can reasonably expect the 99.97% VAR to be sensitive to the severity of the worst cases. It is apparent from Figure 1 that the four models have different things to say about these: in order of decreasing severity we have CreditPortfolioView, Merton, CreditRisk+ and Historical.

COMPARISON BY MONTE CARLO SIMULATION

It is easy to simulate from a latent-variable model, because of the conditional independence: simulate the underlying default rate, then simulate independent loss events using that rate, and repeat many times. As a test, we consider a portfolio of 200 assets under the different models of correlation. The exposures are fixed and unequal, being obtained by sampling from a gamma distribution with mean of one and standard deviation of one-half; the recovery rate is zero. In Figure 2a, the three continuous-variable models described above are being simulated, along with the historical calibration (which is discrete); the fifth curve shows the effect of no correlation. In Figure 2b, the continuous-variable models have been discretised as in Figure 1, and the last two curves have been transcribed directly. These two sets of results agree closely. Further, when arranged in decreasing order of VAR, the models appear in the same order as given in the previous paragraph.

COMPARISON BY ASYMPTOTIC ANALYSIS

A further attraction of discrete latent variable models is that the moment generating function (MGF) of the loss distribution may be calculated easily. The tail of the loss distribution can then be approximated by the saddlepoint method, which is known to work well for this type of problem (Martin, Thompson and Browne, 2001). This avoids the use of simulation and, as we will show in forthcoming articles, allows analytical computation of risk contributions and the efficient frontier in the mean-VAR (as opposed to mean-variance) framework. Conditional on the latent variable, the MGF of the total loss is the product of the MGFs of the individual losses. The unconditional MGF is obtained by integrating-out the latent variable. For a discrete variable, this integration reduces to a weighted sum, which is much easier to evaluate. The agreement between the saddlepoint method and Monte Carlo is very good.[4]

**Table 1. Summary of model comparison results**

| Model | Parameters | Quadrature rule |
|---|---|---|
| Merton | $\bar{p} = 0.345\%, \rho = 9.0\%$ | Gauss–Hermite |
| CreditPortfolioView | $a = 6.08, b = 0.89$ | Gauss–Hermite |
| CreditRisk+ | $\bar{p} = 0.345\%, \alpha = 0.889$ | Gauss–Laguerre |

All models agree on the default rate mean (0.345%) and standard deviation (0.366%).

**2. Loss exceedance curves for the various correlation models on a test portfolio**

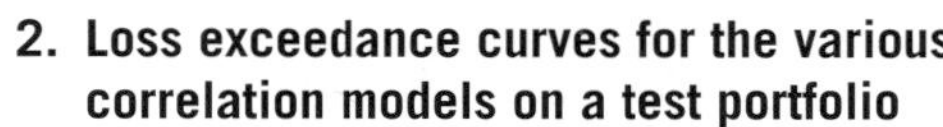

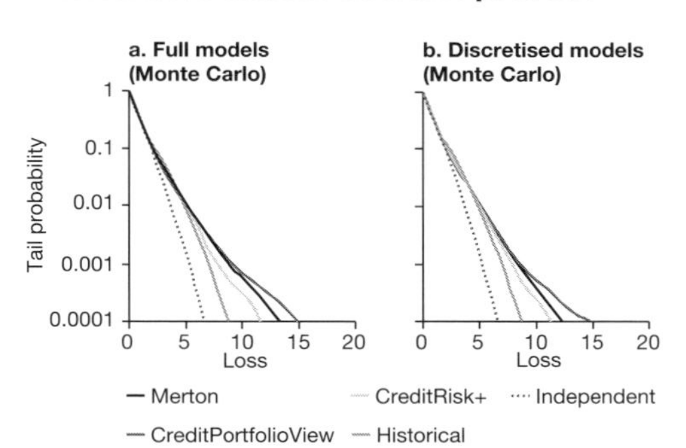


In (a), we have the three models given in the article ("Existing models"), the historical calibration and a fifth curve for independent loss events. In (b), the three models have been discretised (see Table 1 and Figure 1).

## The Merton model, and defining correlation

In this section we shall consider two questions:

1. In the Merton model, the default correlations arise from asset return correlation. If we use stock market returns, do we get a "sensible" default rate volatility?
2. What does it mean to impose "constant" correlation across ratings?

The second question pertains to the "right" definition of correlation. There are two possibilities: we can employ the Merton model and use the asset return correlation r, or we can use default correlation or default rate volatility. Let us define the relative default rate volatility to be:

$$\sigma^* = \sqrt{\mathbf{V}[R]}/\mathbf{E}[R]$$

and introduce a quantity $q = \mathbf{E}[R^2]/\mathbf{E}[R]^2$, which we shall call the q-multiplier. This is related to $\sigma^*$ by $q = \sigma^{*2} + 1$, and has the interpretation:

$$q = \frac{\text{Default probability of asset A, given that asset B has defaulted}}{\text{Default probability of asset A}}$$

for two different equally rated assets A and B. It is the factor by which we should multiply A's default rate when we learn that B has defaulted. For no correlation, $q = 1$. In our tests presented earlier, q was 2.13. Note that although q is related to the (Pearson) correlation coefficient between the default events ($\rho_{def} = p(q - 1)/(1 - p)$), the latter is "typically" very low for high-grade assets. For example, when $q = 2.13$ and $p = 0.345\%$ (as earlier) we have $\rho_{def} = 0.39\%$, which is superficially a negligible amount of correlation (considering that a correlation coefficient is normalised to lie between minus one and one), but it had a significant effect on the loss distribution, as Figure 2 shows. The problem with $\rho_{def}$ is that normalising the covariance with respect to the product of the standard deviations is fine for normal distributions, but produces rather strange results for the binomial (1, p) distribution, as the standard deviation is proportional to $p^{1/2}$, not p, for small p. Therefore, we regard the q-multiplier as more meaningful.

First, let us choose to make q constant across ratings. A value of two corresponds to the default rate volatility equalling the average default rate. As we have seen, this is fairly consistent with historical observation and this sort of level of relative volatility is regarded as appropriate by CreditRisk+. In Figure 3a, we show as a function of average default rate the implied asset return correlation and a measure of the extreme default rate. For the purposes of this discussion, we are defining this as the 99.97% point of the default rate distribution. (Although this alone does not determine the 99.97% VAR of a portfolio, it is a useful indicator.) Notice that the implied asset correlations are low, particularly for higher ratings where the implied asset correlation is only 5–10% (recall also that in the previous section, the Merton model was calibrated with $\rho = 9\%$).

Alternatively, we can make $\rho$ constant. One could reasonably argue that a value of one-third is a "moderate" correlation, which we might expect to see in the stock market (indeed correlations between stocks are often higher; see Figure 3b). Now, for an asset of mean default rate 0.04%, the 99.97% point of the default rate distribution is 4.65% (as opposed to 0.44% in Figure 3a). This is very high. Further, the q-multiplier is 29. By believing this, we would imply that, for a portfolio of two such assets, a default of one asset would cause the default probability of the other to jump from 0.04% (rating A2/A3) to 1.16% (rating Ba2, six ratings lower). Again, this does seem rather extreme. Accordingly, if we put stock market correlations into the Merton model we are likely to end up with very large clusters of defaults. It can be argued that a significant component of stock market returns comes from the general mood of participants – as seen in the recent rise and fall of technology stocks – and this needs stripping out to get at the correlation between the true asset levels. But while the true asset level can be obtained once a year from the balance sheet, it is difficult to see how it can be calculated daily,

**3. What is the meaning of equal correlation, across ratings?**

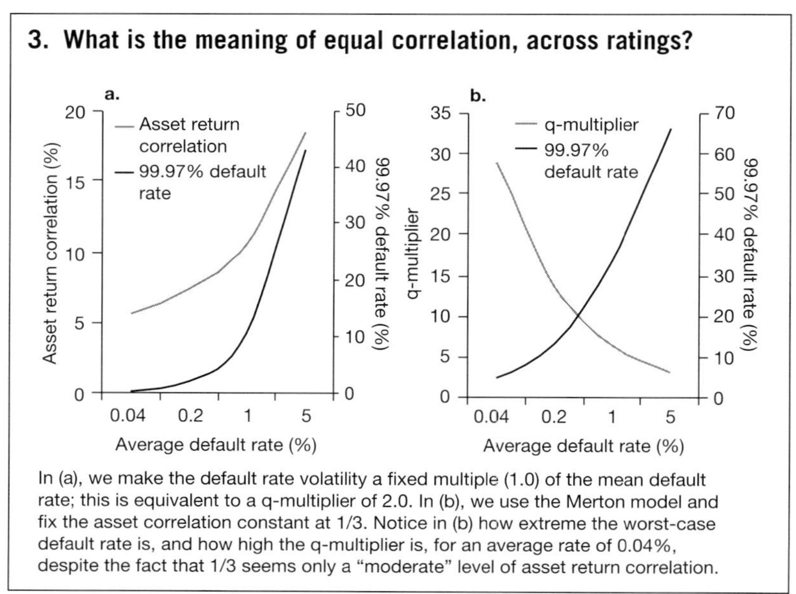


In (a), we make the default rate volatility a fixed multiple (1.0) of the mean default rate; this is equivalent to a q-multiplier of 2.0. In (b), we use the Merton model and fix the asset correlation constant at 1/3. Notice in (b) how extreme the worst-case default rate is, and how high the q-multiplier is, for an average rate of 0.04%, despite the fact that 1/3 seems only a "moderate" level of asset return correlation.

and so the use of stock market data to impute default correlation must be regarded with caution.

## Conclusion

We have demonstrated the use of the discrete latent variable correlation model, which can replace the continuous latent variable model with negligible loss of precision and can be used in conjunction with the saddlepoint method.

One problem with the notion of correlation is that so many people think only of pair-wise correlations (and even pair-wise correlation may be defined in many ways). But this is not the whole picture: those wishing to look at the VAR a long way into the tail need to recollect that it depends not on pairs of events but on large clusters. A good correlation model, which must lie at the heart of effective portfolio and capital management, ought to provide explicit information about this.

Despite the claims and counter-claims of the various practitioners, all default rate models end up guessing the probability and severity of extreme default rates (some may not even realise that they are guessing). Note that with the historical calibration it is not possible to talk about a state of the latent variable that occurs with probability 0.03%, when there are only a few decades of default data available. This is why in Figure 1 there is no extreme, rare state in the historical calibration. Accordingly, it is not very sensible to talk either about accuracy of the extremities of the default rate distribution or about accuracy of the ensuing VAR calculations. We have not expressed a preference for one model over another, as it is more important to know what each model is saying about frequency and severity of clusters of defaults. Indeed, the rating agencies should be aware of this: when a counterparty is rated, a set of default probabilities describing its robustness in different states of the underlying economy is more useful than a single default probability reflecting an average over the economic cycle.

1 *We make the distinction between the random variable* (V) *and the value that it takes* (v).

2 *See the discussion in Bishop (1997) on the expectation maximisation algorithm.*

3 *The chi-squared approximation is unreliable when there is little data, or where the cell populations are highly unbalanced, and it is better to use Monte Carlo simulation to find the distribution of the test statistic.*

4 *This is demonstrated in the longer version of this chapter.*

**BIBLIOGRAPHY**

**Bishop, C.,** 1997, *Neural Networks for Pattern Recognition* (Oxford University Press).

**Carty, L., and D. Lieberman,** 1998, "Historical Default Rates of Corporate Bond Issuers, 1920–1996 and Moody's Rating Migration and Credit Quality Correlation", in S. Das (ed), *Credit Derivatives*, Chapters 9 and 10 (New York: John Wiley & Sons).

**Credit Suisse Financial Products,** 1997, *CreditRisk+: A CreditRisk Management Framework*, London, www.csfb.com/creditrisk.

**Crouhy, M., D. Galai and R. Mark,** 2000, "A Comparative Analysis of Current Credit Risk Models", *Journal of Banking and Finance*, 24, pp. 59–117.

**Gordy, M.,** 2000, "A Comparative Anatomy of Current Credit Risk Models", *Journal of Banking and Finance*, 24, pp. 119–49.

**Kopal, Z.,** 1955, *Numerical Analysis* (Chapman & Hall).

**Koyluoglu, H., and A. Hickman,** 1998, "Reconcilable Differences", *Risk*, October, pp. 56–62.

**Martin, R., K. Thompson and C. Browne,** 2001, "Taking to the Saddle", *Risk*, June, pp. 91–4.

**Press, P., S. Teukolsky, W. Vetterling and B. Flannery,** 1992, *Numerical Recipes in C: The Art of Scientific Computing*, Second Edition (Cambridge University Press).

# 15

# Copulas and Credit Models

**Rüdiger Frey, Alexander McNeil and Mark Nyfeler**
University of Leipzig; ETH Zurich;
UBS Warburg

*Latent variable models of default are used extensively in both internal credit rating methodologies and the pricing of exotic credit derivatives. But, as Rüdiger Frey, Alexander McNeil and Mark Nyfeler demonstrate using the copula formalism, such models are badly specified using default correlation and, worse still, can expose users to considerable model risk.*

In this chapter, we focus on the latent variable approach to modelling credit portfolio losses. This methodology underlies all models that descend from Merton's firm-value model (Merton, 1974). In particular, it underlies the most important industry models, such as those proposed by KMV Corporation and CreditMetrics.

In these models, default of an obligor occurs if a latent variable, often interpreted as the value of the obligor's assets, falls below some threshold, often interpreted as the value of the obligor's liabilities. Dependence between default events is caused by dependence between the latent variables. The correlation matrix of the latent variables is often calibrated by developing factor models that relate changes in asset value to changes in a small number of economic factors. For further reading, see papers by Koyluoglu and Hickman (1998), Gordy (2000) and Crouhy, Galai and Mark (2000).

A core assumption of the KMV and CreditMetrics models is the multivariate normality of the latent variables. However, there is no compelling reason for choosing a multivariate normal (Gaussian) distribution for asset values. The aim of this chapter is to show that the aggregate portfolio loss distribution is often very sensitive to the exact nature of the multivariate distribution of the latent variables.

This is not simply a question of asset correlation. Even when individual default probabilities of obligors and the matrix of latent variable correlations are held fixed, it is still possible to develop alternative models that lead to much heavier-tailed loss distributions. A useful source of alternative models is the family of multivariate normal mixture distributions, which includes Student's t distribution and the generalised hyperbolic distribution. In most cases, it is as easy to base latent variable models on these mixture distributions as it is to base them on the multivariate normal distribution.

An elegant way of understanding how a multivariate latent variable distribution determines the distribution of the number of defaults in a portfolio is to use the concept of copulas. In this chapter, we show that it is the copula (or dependence structure) of the latent variables that determines the higher-order joint default probabilities for groups of obligors, and thus determines the extreme risk that there are many defaults in the portfolio.

If we choose alternative latent variable distributions in the normal mixture family then we implicitly work with alternative copulas that often differ markedly from the copula of a Gaussian distribution. Some of these copulas, such as the t copula, possess tail dependence and, in contrast to the multivariate normal, have a much greater tendency to generate simultaneous extreme values (Embrechts, McNeil and Straumann, 1999 and 2001). This effect is highly important in latent variable models, since simultaneous low asset values will lead to many joint defaults, and past experience shows that realistic credit risk models need to be able to give sufficient weight to scenarios where many joint defaults occur.

This chapter may be understood as a model risk study in the context of latent variable models. Individual default probabilities and asset correlations are insufficient to determine the portfolio loss distribution, since they do not fix the copula of the latent variables. For large portfolios of tens of thousands of counterparties, there remains considerable model risk. Risk managers who employ the latent variable methodology should be aware of this.

## Latent variable models

Consider a portfolio of $m$ obligors and fix some time horizon $T$, typically one year. For $1 \le i \le m$, let the random variable $Y_i$ be the default indicator for obligor $i$ at time $T$, taking values in $\{0, 1\}$. We interpret the value one as default and zero as non-default. At time $t = 0$, all obligors are assumed to be in a non-default state.

Let $X = (X_1,..,X_m)'$ be an $m$-dimensional random vector with continuous marginal distributions representing the latent variables at time $T$ and let $(D_1,..,D_m)$ be a vector of deterministic cut-off levels. We call $(X_i, D_i)_{1 \le i \le m}$ a latent variable model for the binary random vector $Y = (Y_1,..,Y_m)'$ if the following relationship holds:

$$Y_i = 1 \Leftrightarrow X_i \le D_i \qquad (1)$$

In the KMV model, the latent variables $X_i$ are assumed to be multivariate Gaussian and are interpreted as relative changes in the firm's asset value (so-called asset returns). To determine the thresholds $D_i$, an option pricing technique based on historical firm value data, is used. The asset return correlations are calibrated by assuming that asset returns follow a factor model, where the underlying factors are interpreted as a set of macroeconomic variables.

CreditMetrics is usually presented as a multistate latent variable model. The $X_i$ are again assumed to be multivariate Gaussian, and their range is partitioned to represent a series of rating classes of decreasing creditworthiness, culminating in default. The cut-off levels that define these classes are chosen so that default and rating state transition probabilities agree with historical data. Latent variable correlations are again determined by assuming a factor model structure.

The differences between KMV and CreditMetrics are really differences of presentation rather than differences of substance. The terms defining the model $(X_i, D_i)_{1 \le i \le m}$ may be interpreted and calibrated in slightly different ways, but in assuming multivariate Gaussian-ity of the latent variables, the models turn out to be structurally equivalent. To understand this assertion, we review the concept of copulas and state a simple proposition that is the basis for comparing existing models, and defining new and structurally different models.

## Copulas

Copulas are simply the joint distribution functions of random vectors with standard uniform marginal distributions. Their value in statistics is that they provide a way of understanding how marginal distributions of single risks are coupled together to form joint distributions of groups of risks, ie, they provide a way of understanding the idea of statistical dependence.

There are two main ways of using the copula idea. We can extract copulas from well-known multivariate distribution functions. We can also create new multivariate distribution functions by joining arbitrary marginal distributions together with copulas. These ideas are summarised in the following proposition, known as Sklar's theorem; see Nelsen (1999) for proof.

*Proposition 1*

Let $F$ be a joint distribution function with continuous margins $F_1,..,F_m$. Then there exists a unique copula $C\colon [0, 1]^m \to [0, 1]$, such that:

$$F(x_1,\ldots,x_m) = C(F_1(x_1),\ldots,F_m(x_m)) \qquad (2)$$

holds. Conversely, if $C$ is a copula and $F_1,..,F_m$ are distribution functions, then the function $F$ given by Equation 2 is a joint distribution function with margins $F_1,..,F_m$.

We extract a unique copula $C$ from a multivariate distribution function $F$ with continuous margins $F_1,..,F_m$ by calculating:

$$C(u_1,\ldots,u_m) = F\left(F_1^{-1}(u_1),\ldots,F_m^{-1}(u_m)\right)$$

where $F_1^{-1},..,F_m^{-1}$ are (generalised) inverses of $F_1,..,F_m$. We call $C$ the copula of $F$, or of any random vector with distribution function $F$. The copula of a random vector remains invariant under strictly increasing component-wise transformations of the vector – an appealing property that is not shared by the correlation matrix.

Returning to the credit application, if we assume that the latent variables $X$ have a multivariate Gaussian distribution with correlation matrix $R$ then the copula of $X$ may be represented by:

$$C_R^{Ga}(u_1,\ldots,u_m) = \Phi_R\left(\Phi^{-1}(u_1),\ldots,\Phi^{-1}(u_m)\right)$$

where $\Phi_R$ denotes the joint distribution function of a standard $d$-dimensional normal random vector with correlation matrix $R$, and $\Phi$ is the distribution function of univariate standard normal. $C_R^{Ga}$ is known as the Gaussian copula, and this is the latent variable dependence structure that implicitly underlies all standard industry models.

Below (see "Alternative latent variable copulas"), we will consider building latent variable models with copulas other than the Gaussian. We conclude this section by noting that it is possible to build latent variable models with the Gaussian copula, but with marginal distributions other than univariate normal. An alternative latent variable model proposed by Li (2000) uses this idea. In this model, $X_1, \ldots, X_m$ are interpreted as times to default for each of the obligors and the thresholds $D_1, \ldots, D_m$ are all set to take the value T, the time horizon. Each $X_i$ is assumed to have an exponential distribution with parameter $\lambda_i$ and the multivariate distribution function F of **X** is constructed by using the converse of Sklar's theorem to join the exponential margins together with a Gaussian copula. This yields the distribution function:

$$F(x_1, \ldots, x_m) = C_R^{Ga}\left(1 - \exp(-\lambda_1 x_1), \ldots, 1 - \exp(-\lambda_m x_m)\right)$$

## The role of copulas in latent variable models

To understand that the use of the Gaussian copula leads to models that are structurally equivalent, we introduce a formal definition of equivalence for latent variable models and present a simple new result.

*Definition 1*

Let $(X_i, D_i)_{1 \le i \le m}$ and $(\tilde{X}_i, \tilde{D}_i)_{1 \le i \le m}$ be two latent variable models generating default indicator vectors **Y** and $\tilde{\mathbf{Y}}$. The models are called equivalent if $\mathbf{Y} \stackrel{d}{=} \tilde{\mathbf{Y}}$.

Thus two models are equivalent if they give rise to exactly the same default indicator distribution, which means of course that the distribution of the number of defaults in the portfolio will be the same.

A sufficient condition for two latent variable models to be equivalent is that individual default probabilities are the same in both models and the copulas of the latent variables are the same. Formally, we have the following, which is proved in Frey and McNeil (2001).

*Proposition 2*

Consider two latent variable models $(X_i, D_i)_{1 \le i \le m}$ and $(\tilde{X}_i, \tilde{D}_i)_{1 \le i \le m}$ with default indicator vectors **Y** and $\tilde{\mathbf{Y}}$. The models are equivalent if:

- ❑ $P(X_i \le D_i) = P(\tilde{X}_i \le \tilde{D}_i)$, $i \in \{1, \ldots, m\}$.
- ❑ **X** and $\tilde{\mathbf{X}}$ have the same copula.

Thus, KMV, CreditMetrics and the approach of Li (2000) can all be thought of as essentially equivalent approaches. If they are calibrated in consistent ways, they will lead to very similar results.

We underline the importance of latent variable copulas in credit risk models by noting that higher-order joint default probabilities can be written in terms of copulas and individual obligor default probabilities. Consider an arbitrary subset of k obligors $\{i_1, \ldots, i_k\} \subset \{1, \ldots, m\}$, with individual default probabilities $p_{i_1}, \ldots, p_{i_k}$. Then the joint default probability of all k obligors is given by:

$$\begin{aligned} P\left(Y_{i_1} = 1, \ldots, Y_{i_k} = 1\right) &= P\left(X_{i_1} \le D_{i_1}, \ldots, X_{i_k} \le D_{i_k}\right) \\ &= C_{i_1, \ldots, i_k}\left(p_{i_1}, \ldots, p_{i_k}\right) \end{aligned}$$

where $C_{i_1, \ldots, i_k}$ is a k-dimensional marginal distribution of the copula C of **X** (and thus is itself a copula). If we are looking for alternative copulas that lead to higher extreme risk of many joint defaults than the Gaussian, then we should look for copulas that tend to give large values of $P(Y_{i_1} = 1, \ldots, Y_{i_k} = 1)$ for small values of $p_{i_1}, \ldots, p_{i_k}$.

## Alternative latent variable copulas

There are many alternative copulas to the Gaussian. We choose to work with the copulas that are implicit in the kinds of multivariate distributions that might be considered natural alternative models for asset values and asset returns. It would also be possible to work with families of simple closed-form parametric copulas such as the Archimedean family (Nelsen, 1999).

A popular family of distributions for modelling financial market returns is the family of multivariate normal mixture models. When relaxing the assumption of multivariate normality for asset returns, it seems natural to look at this family, which contains such distributions as the multivariate t and the hyperbolic.

A member of the m-dimensional family of variance mixtures of normal distributions is equal in distribution to the product of a scalar random variable S and a normal random vector $\mathbf{Z} = (Z_1, \ldots, Z_m)$. That is:

$$\mathbf{X} \stackrel{d}{=} S\mathbf{Z} \qquad (3)$$

where **Z** is multivariate normal with mean vector zero and covariance matrix $\Sigma$, and S is positive, independent of **Z** and has a finite second moment. Normal variance mixture distributions inherit the correlation matrix of the multivariate normal distribution of Z:

$$\text{Corr}(X_i, X_j) = \text{Corr}(Z_i, Z_j) \tag{4}$$

which means essentially that the correlation matrices of these models can be calibrated in the same way as that of the Gaussian model.

For a concrete example, we consider the t distribution. X is said to have an m-dimensional Student t distribution with $\nu$ degrees of freedom (written $X \sim t_m(\nu, 0, \Sigma)$) if:

$$S = \sqrt{\frac{\nu}{W}} \tag{5}$$

where W has a chi-squared distribution with $\nu$ degrees of freedom.

We choose the t distribution for our analysis for two reasons. First, it converges to the Gaussian distribution as the degree of freedom parameter $\nu \to \infty$. This enables us to start with an approximately normal model and move away from this gradually by choosing progressively smaller values of $\nu$. Second, the copula that is implicit in the multivariate t is very different from the Gaussian copula. It has the property of tail dependence, so it tends to generate simultaneous extreme events with higher probabilities than the Gaussian copula. This is important in our context, as this leads to higher probabilities of joint defaults.

**1. Gaussian dependence vs t dependence**

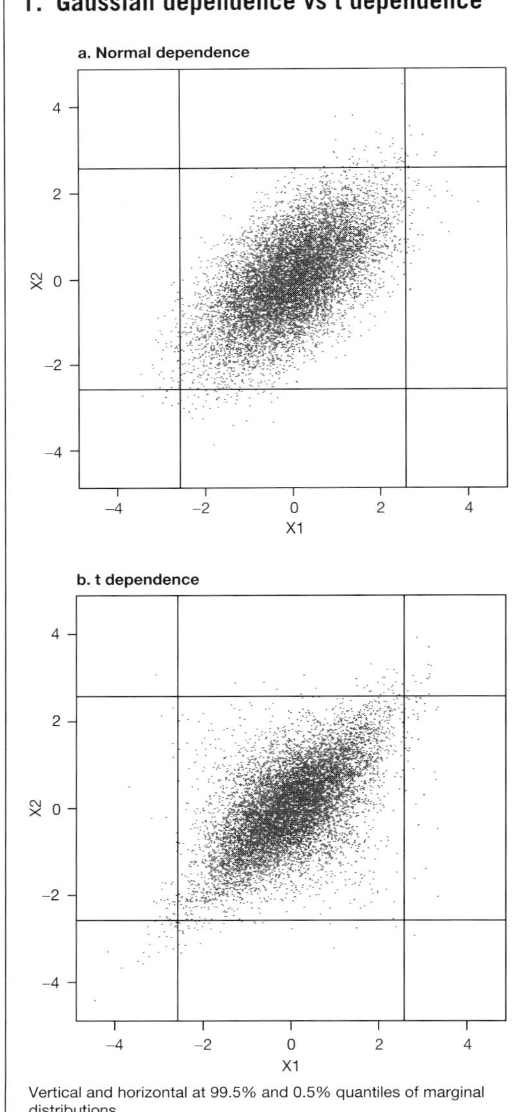


Vertical and horizontal at 99.5% and 0.5% quantiles of marginal distributions.

Figure 1 contrasts the lack of tail dependence of the Gaussian copula with the strong tail dependence of the copula of a t distribution with $\nu = 3$ degrees of freedom. The top plot shows 5,000 points from a standard bivariate normal distribution; the bottom plot shows 5,000 points from a composite distribution with a t copula and standard normal margins. The linear correlation in both plots is 0.7. Clearly, in the lower left and upper right quadrants, the t dependence structure produces more joint extreme values close to the diagonal.

## Comparison of the models

For simplicity, we compare the normal and the t copulas in the framework of homogeneous portfolios, where all default probabilities are identical and where the asset correlation of any two counterparties equals a given constant $\rho > 0$. The models are:

- Gaussian latent variables, $X \sim N_m(0, R)$.
- Student t latent variables, $X \sim t_m(\nu, 0, R)$.

where R is an equicorrelation matrix with off-diagonal element $\rho$.

In both cases, we choose cut-off levels so that $P(Y_i = 1) = \pi$, $1 \le i \le m$, for some fixed default probability parameter $\pi$. Comparison of the models is performed by a simulation study where we vary the portfolio size m, the individual default probabilities $\pi$, the correlation of the latent variables $\rho$ and the degrees of freedom parameter $\nu$ of the t latent variables.

We define three groups of decreasing credit quality, which we label A, B and C. The groups are characterised by the parameter settings in Table 1. The $\pi$-values do not correspond exactly to the A, B and C rating categories used by any of the well-known rating agencies, but they are nonetheless realistic values for Gaussian latent variable models for real obligors and were chosen after discussions with UBS Switzerland.

**Table 1. Values of $\pi$ (default probability) and $\rho$ (asset correlation) for the three groups in the simulation study**

| Group | $\pi$ (%) | $\rho$ (%) |
|---|---|---|
| A | 0.01 | 2.58 |
| B | 0.50 | 3.80 |
| C | 7.50 | 9.21 |

**2. Ratio of quantiles of loss distributions**

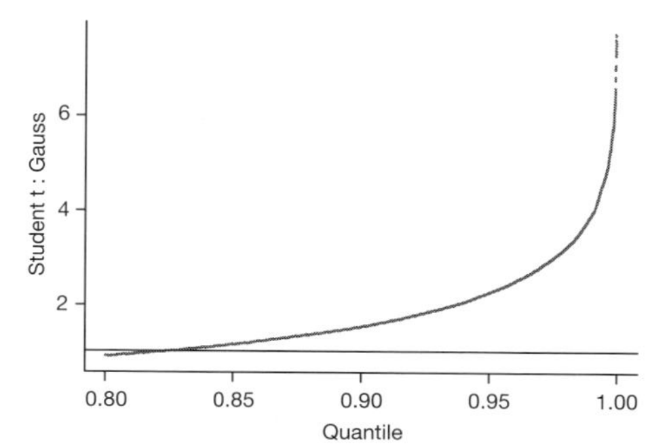


Ratio of estimated quantiles of distribution of M for Student t model with 10 degrees of freedom and Gaussian model in case of Group B with 10,000 obligors.

In all simulations, we generate 100,000 realisations of $M = \sum_{i=1}^{m} Y_i$, the total number of defaulting obligors. Of course, $E(M) = m\pi$ in all cases, and it is easily confirmed that the empirical average number of defaults is always very close to $m\pi$. Of greater interest are high quantiles of the distribution of M, which give a better indication of the extreme risk in the model and are consistent with the value-at-risk approach to measuring risk. We denote the empirically estimated 95% and 99% quantiles of the distribution of the number of defaults M by $m_{0.95}$ and $m_{0.99}$ respectively and tabulate them in Table 2. In Figure 2, we plot the ratio of estimated quantiles for a Student t model with 10 degrees of freedom, and a Gaussian model in the case of group B and a portfolio of size 10,000.

Clearly, $\nu$ has a massive influence on these risk measures, particularly for groups of poorer credit quality (B and C). If we only specify the latent variable correlation $\rho$ and do not fix the degrees of freedom $\nu$, then our inference concerning extreme risk is subject to huge model risk. For example, for the 10,000 obligors in group B, Figure 2 can be interpreted as saying that when we move from a Gaussian model to a t model with 10 degrees of freedom, our 95% VAR is inflated by a factor of 2.2, 99% VAR by 4.0, 99.5% VAR by 4.8 and 99.9% VAR by 6.1.

## Extensions and conclusions

It is clear that the impact of different latent variable copulas on the tail of the distribution of M, the number of defaults, will carry over to the tail of the total loss distribution. Suppose we denote the credit exposure of obligor i to the lender by $e_i$ and the loss-given default by the random variable $L_i$ with distribution on $[0, 1]$. The total loss will be given by:

$$\text{Loss} = \sum_{i=1}^{m} Y_i L_i e_i$$

The loss given defaults are usually taken to be independent of each other and independent of the default indicators $Y_i$. In a model of this kind, Nyfeler (2000) has confirmed that the distribution of the latent variables has the anticipated effect on the tail of the total loss distribution.

Moreover, the phenomenon we have demonstrated in a homogeneous portfolio may also be

**Table 2. Results of simulation study**

| m | Group | $m_{0.95}$ | | | | $m_{0.99}$ | | | |
|---|---|---|---|---|---|---|---|---|---|
| | | $\nu=\infty$ | $\nu=50$ | $\nu=10$ | $\nu=4$ | $\nu=\infty$ | $\nu=50$ | $\nu=10$ | $\nu=4$ |
| 1,000 | A | 2 | 3 | 3 | 0 | 3 | 6 | 13 | 12 |
| 1,000 | B | 12 | 16 | 24 | 25 | 17 | 28 | 61 | 110 |
| 1,000 | C | 163 | 173 | 209 | 261 | 222 | 241 | 306 | 396 |
| 10,000 | A | 14 | 23 | 24 | 3 | 21 | 49 | 118 | 126 |
| 10,000 | B | 109 | 153 | 239 | 250 | 157 | 261 | 589 | 1,074 |
| 10,000 | C | 1,618 | 1,723 | 2,085 | 2,587 | 2,206 | 2,400 | 3,067 | 3,916 |

Estimated 95th and 99th percentiles of the distribution of M, the number of defaulting obligors, in an exchangeable model. See Table 1 for the values of $\pi$ and $\rho$ corresponding to the three groups A, B and C.

observed in more heterogeneous portfolios comprising counterparties with widely differing default probabilities and more complex asset correlation matrices. This has been confirmed by simulation studies at UBS Switzerland.

The basic message is that asset correlations are not enough to describe dependence between defaults. Asset correlations do not fully specify the copula of the latent variables and much model risk remains. The assumption of a Gaussian copula may not adequately model the potential extreme risk in the portfolio. Models allowing tail dependence of latent variables (such as the multivariate t copula) show that much more worrying scenarios are possible. Clearly, this finding is also very important for the pricing of basket credit derivatives.

**BIBLIOGRAPHY**

**Crouhy, M., D. Galai and R. Mark,** 2000, "A Comparative Analysis of Current Credit Risk Models", *Journal of Banking and Finance*, 24, pp. 59–117.

**Embrechts, P., A. McNeil and D. Straumann,** 1999, "Correlation: Pitfalls and Alternatives", *Risk*, May, pp. 93–113.

**Embrechts, P., A. McNeil and D. Straumann,** 2001, "Correlation and Dependency in Risk Management: Properties and Pitfalls", in M. Dempster, and H. Moffatt (eds), *Risk Management: Value at Risk and Beyond*, Forthcoming (Cambridge University Press). Preprint available from http://www.math.ethz.ch/~mcneil.

**Frey, R., and A. McNeil,** 2001, *Modelling Dependent Defaults*, Preprint, ETH Zurich, available from http://www.math.ethz.ch/~mcneil.

**Gordy, M.,** 2000, "A Comparative Anatomy of Credit Risk Models", *Journal of Banking and Finance*, 24, pp. 119–49.

**Koyluoglu, U., and A. Hickman,** 1998, "Reconcilable Differences", *Risk*, October, pp. 56–62.

**Li, D.,** 2000, "On Default Correlation: A Copula Function Approach", *Journal of Fixed Income*, 9(4), March, pp. 43–54.

**Merton, R.,** 1974, "On the Pricing of Corporate Debt: The Risk Structure of Interest Rates", *Journal of Finance*, 29, pp. 449–70.

**Nelsen, R.,** 1999, *An Introduction to Copulas* (New York: Springer).

**Nyfeler, M.,** 2000, *Modelling Dependencies in Credit Risk Management*, Diploma thesis, ETH Zurich, available from http://www.Risklab.ch/Papers.html.

16

# Collateral Damage

**Jon Frye**

Federal Reserve Bank of Chicago

*Most credit risk models focus on default probability, while making simple recovery assumptions for collateralised loans. As Jon Frye shows here, this is a mistake, because the same factors that increase default rates can also decrease the value of loan collateral.*

If a borrower defaults on a loan, a bank's recovery may depend on the value of the loan collateral. The value of collateral, like the value of other assets, fluctuates with economic conditions. If the economy experiences a downturn, a bank can experience a double misfortune: many obligors default, and the value of collateral is damaged.

Conventional credit models overlook the effect of economic conditions on collateral. They allow default to vary from year to year, but they hold fixed the average value of collateral and the average level of recovery.

The distinctive feature of the credit model presented here is that an economic downturn causes damage to the value of collateral. When systematic collateral damage enters the credit model, the capital allocated to a highly collateralised loan can double or triple.[1]

Taking collateral damage into account complicates a credit capital model. However, the results of the model can be well approximated by a function of expected loss alone. Expected loss can therefore be used as the basis of a credit capital estimate. This estimate is simpler, and can be more accurate than using the results of a conventional credit model that ignores the role of collateral damage.

*The views expressed are those of the author and do not necessarily reflect those of the Federal Reserve Bank of Chicago. He would like to thank many readers for helpful comments on earlier versions, especially Lisa Ashley, Robert Bliss, Richard Cahill, Paul Calem, Matthew Foss, Michael Gordy, David Jones, Catherine Lemieux, Michael Lesiak, Carol Lobbes, Laura McGrew, Perry Mehta, James Nelson, Edmund Waggoner and participants at the 1999 FRB-Chicago Capital Markets Conference.*

## Credit capital model

The credit capital model uses the conditional approach suggested by Finger (1999) and Gordy (2000). The variables in the model depend on a systematic risk factor, a random variable representing the good years and bad years of the economy. The co-variation between two variables stems from their mutual dependence on the systematic factor. Two variables that relate strongly to the systematic factor relate strongly to each other and therefore have a strong correlation.

Exposure of US$1 is assumed to each obligor j. At the end of a one-year analysis horizon, the value of collateral is a random number characterised by three positive parameters: its amount, $\mu_j$; its volatility, $\sigma_j$; and its sensitivity to X, the systematic risk factor, also known as its "loading", $q_j$:

$$\text{Collateral}_j = \mu_j(1 + \sigma_j C_j) \quad \text{and} \tag{1}$$

$$C_j = q_j X + \sqrt{1 - q_j^2}\, Z_j \tag{2}$$

where X and $Z_j$ have independent standard normal distributions.

Equation 2 implies that $C_j$ has a standard normal distribution. When the systematic factor exceeds zero, both $C_j$ and $\text{Collateral}_j$ tend to be greater than average, but that also depends on an idiosyncratic risk factor, $Z_j$, which affects only the collateral of obligor j. Equation 1 shows each unit of collateral value has a normal distribution with mean equal to 1.00 and standard deviation equal to $\sigma_j$.

The overall financial condition of the obligor, $A_j$, also depends on the systematic risk factor via a positive loading, $p_j$:

$$A_j = p_j X + \sqrt{1 - p_j^2}\, X_j \tag{3}$$

where $X_j$ have standard normal distributions independent of each other, X and $Z_j$.

When X exceeds zero, obligor j tends to prosper. $A_j$ also depends on the idiosyncratic variable $X_j$, which affects the fortunes of obligor j and nothing else. $A_j$ may take on a wide range of values, having a standard normal distribution. This specification ignores the influences that may exist between $X_j$ and collateral, and/or between $Z_j$ and $A_j$. These non-systematic influences have a relatively minor effect on credit capital.

The correlation between two obligors depends on their loadings on the systematic risk factor X:

$$\begin{aligned} \mathrm{Corr}[A_j, A_k] &= \mathrm{Cov}\left[p_j X + \sqrt{1-p_j^2}X_j, p_k X + \sqrt{1-p_k^2}X_k\right] \\ &= p_j p_k \end{aligned} \quad (4)$$

An obligor defaults if its financial condition falls below a threshold. Let $D_j$ represent the default event:

$$D_j = 1 \text{ if } A_j < \Phi^{-1}(PD_j);\ D_j = 0 \text{ otherwise} \quad (5)$$

where $PD_j$ represents the probability of default for obligor j, and $\Phi^{-1}$ is the inverse cumulative standard normal distribution. Equation 5 thus ensures obligor j defaults with probability $PD_j$: $\text{Prob}\ [D_j = 1] = E\ [D_j] = PD_j$.

If default occurs, the bank can recover, properly discounted and net of foreclosure expenses, no more than the loan amount:

$$\begin{aligned} &\text{Recovery}_j = \text{Min}[1, \text{Collateral}_j], \text{ that is,} \\ &LGD_j = \text{Max}[0, 1 - \text{Collateral}_j] \end{aligned} \quad (6)$$

If default occurs and collateral value exceeds exposure, the bank has no loss. If default occurs and collateral value is less than zero, the bank may lose more than US$1. Taking the average of loss given default (LGD) over all possible outcomes produces the expected loss given default (ELGD). Solving backward, the ELGD of a loan implies the level of $\mu_j$.

For simplicity, the model includes losses due only to default and not due to downgrade or changes in pricing spreads. The amount lost to obligor j is then the product of the default event and the loss given default:

$$\text{Loss}_j = D_j LGD_j \quad (7)$$

Taking the sum over all j equals the total credit loss. Monte Carlo simulation or other means can then determine the distribution for random realisations of the systematic factor X and of the idiosyncratic factors $X_j$ and $Z_j$.

Capital models are used by some banks to target the credit ratings they receive from rating agencies. A bank that targets an investment-grade rating might wish to hold enough credit capital to absorb the loss that arises in 99.9% of Monte Carlo simulation runs. We may speak of a target solvency of 99.9% or of a target insolvency of 0.1%. The latter equals $\alpha$, the final parameter of the credit capital model.

In Equation 7, $D_j$ depends on X and $X_j$, and $LGD_j$ depends on X and $Z_j$. Conditional on a realisation X = x, these factors are independent:

$$E\left[\text{Loss}_j \mid X = x\right] = E\left[D_j \mid X = x\right] \times E\left[LGD_j \mid X = x\right] \quad (8)$$

Thus, given a state of the economy as represented by X = x, the conditional expected loss for a loan equals the product of its conditional PD and its conditional ELGD.[2] An increase in x causes both conditional PD and conditional ELGD to decrease. Therefore, when X is at percentile $\alpha$, conditional EL is at percentile $(1 - \alpha)$.

We want to find the increase in target capital when a particular loan is added to the credit portfolio. Marginal capital depends on the portfolio to which the loan is added. We assume that the portfolio is large enough to be fully diversified. Then the marginal capital of a loan can be treated as equal to the mathematical expectation of loss conditional on $X = \alpha$. Therefore, a bank that has an insolvency target of 0.1% can substitute the 0.1 percentile of the standard normal, $x = -3.09$, in Equation 8 to obtain credit capital for a loan characterised by the five parameters $\sigma_j$, $p_j$, $q_j$, $PD_j$ and $\mu_j$.

The novel feature of the model is that LGD depends on the state of the economy. This feature is not present in conventional credit models. For example, CreditMetrics first determines obligor default and then independently determines LGD. Any risk in recovery is purely idiosyncratic, equivalent to forcing q = 0. CreditRisk+ assumes LGD is a known amount. The variance of recovery is zero, equivalent to forcing $\sigma = 0$. The capital model presented here can mimic these models. If q is set to zero (or if $\sigma$ is set to zero), conditional ELGD does not respond to the state of the economy, but becomes, instead, a constant.

## Quantifying collateral damage

Next we find representative values of the parameters $\sigma$, p and q. We then demonstrate the importance of collateral damage for an example loan. Finally, repeat the analysis for loans having a range of ELGD.

The parameter $\sigma$ might apply to a number of assets pledged as collateral: inventory, receivables, negotiable instruments, title documents, intangibles, etc. In addition, other assets with uncertain values may be awarded to the bank as a general creditor. For this mixture of assets, no single estimate of $\sigma$ can be entirely satisfactory. To obtain a representative estimate, Moody's Investors Service provides summary data for 98 senior secured bank loans. On these, average recovery equals 70.26%, with standard deviation equal to 21.33%. The implied estimate of $\sigma$ equals $21.33/70.26 = 30\%$. However, the recovery achieved on a loan is apt to be closer to the recovery expected on the same loan than to the overall average recovery. Therefore, the raw estimate is apt to overstate $\sigma$. We take $\sigma = 20\%$ as the representative value, with robustness checks using $\sigma = 15\%$ and $\sigma = 25\%$.

We take 0.5 as the representative value of p. Equation 4 then implies that any pair of obligors has a correlation of $(0.5)^2 = 25\%$. This accords with the average level of asset correlation suggested by the CreditMetrics Technical Document (1997). Checks of robustness are performed at $p = 0.4$ and $p = 0.6$.

No studies known to the author provide an estimate of q, the loading of collateral on the systematic factor. It appears, however, that the representative value of q is greater than or equal to p. First, all assets tend to decline with the systematic factor, whether or not they may become the source of recovery on a bank loan. If this overall systematic effect were the only channel of influence, one would suppose that $q = p$.

Two additional channels of influence increase the effect of X on collateral in an economic slump. A low value of X leads to financial distress for many obligors, and for some banks. An obligor in financial distress might devote fewer resources to resolving customer complaints, maintaining equipment and safeguarding its fixed investments. The affected assets – accounts receivable, vehicles and real estate – serve as collateral. Thus, the assets a bank obtains may already have been degraded by previous attempts to extract value. A bank must also anticipate the effects of its own distress. In the circumstances envisioned by the capital model, a bank has nearly exhausted its capital cushion. It then faces unusual pressure to liquidate assets even if it cannot obtain the best price. The value a bank actually realises from collateral may therefore be even more depressed than the values of other assets. Two channels of influence – the actions of distressed obligors before they default, and the actions of the distressed bank itself after it receives collateral – make collateral values unusually sensitive to an economic slump. It is difficult to see an opposing influence that would selectively protect collateral from systematic risk.[3] We assume that representative q is equal to p, with robustness checks of $q = p + 0.10$ and $q = p + 0.20$.

**1. Effect of X on a loan: PD = 5%, ELGD = 10%**

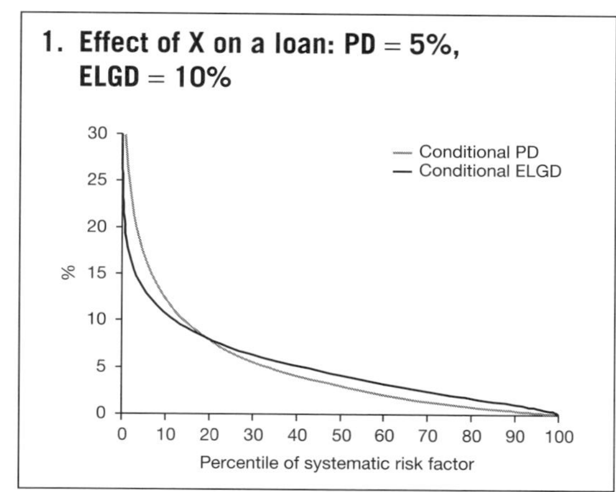


Using the representative values of the parameters $\sigma$, p and q, we take the example of a relatively low-rated obligor that has provided a high level of collateral. Specifically, Figure 1 analyses a loan having PD = 5% and ELGD = 10%. The horizontal axis is calibrated to the percentiles of X. The two lines represent the two factors on the right-hand side of Equation 8. The average of conditional PD equals the unconditional PD of 5%. The PD-weighted average of conditional ELGD equals the unconditional ELGD of 10%.

Thus, Figure 1 shows how the overall levels of PD and ELGD distribute conditionally across states of the economy. For most states, one sees relatively benign levels of both variables. But in a severe economic slump, both conditional PD and conditional ELGD rise with a vengeance. To prepare for this adverse circumstance, banks hold capital.

Suppose a bank targets its own insolvency at $\alpha = 0.10\%$. In Figure 1, this point appears 0.1% of the distance along the axis, almost at the extreme left. The corresponding levels of conditional PD and conditional ELGD are 45.4% and 26.1%, respectively. According to Equation 8, the product of these two equals credit capital: $45.4\% \times 26.1\% = 11.8\%$.

If the bank uses a conventional credit model to allocate capital for this loan, it makes a significant error. It ignores the increase in LGD that comes about in the economic slump. Specifically, it assigns capital equal to $45.4\% \times 10\% = 4.5\%$. The accurate target is 2.61 times this allocation, because the effect of collateral damage is to increase ELGD from its overall value of 10% to its value in an economic slump, 26.1%. Statistical data on the performance of bank loans would be preferable to such a prediction by a model. But data do not exist regarding LGD in an economic slump of this severity. Until we have such data, it would be risky to assume an economic slump has no effect on LGD.

## Capital and expected loss

This section compares the loan of Figure 1 with a second loan having equal expected loss. The equality of expected loss implies a near-equality of capital. The comparison is extended to loans with a range of combinations characteristics, and the same conclusion is found. The conclusion is then checked, both for a range of values of the model parameters σ, p, q and α, and for a fundamental change in the specification of the model.

The loan in the previous example has PD = 5% and ELGD = 10%. Table 1 compares that loan with a second loan having the same EL, but having ELGD = 50%. The middle of the table shows the first loan is more affected by collateral damage. The lower the ELGD of a loan, the greater potential it has to rise in an economic slump. An economic slump affects the ELGD of each loan, but it has a greater proportional effect on the first one, having a lower ELGD.

The two loans also differ in PD. The second loan has lower PD. In an economic slump, the PD of the second loan rises about 18-fold, while the PD of the first loan rises only about nine-fold. The lower the PD of an obligor, the greater potential it has to rise in an economic slump. An economic slump affects the PD of each loan, but it has a greater proportional effect on the second one, having a lower PD.

The economic slump raises both ELGDs and both PDs. Of the two ELGDs, the proportional effect is greater for the first loan. Of the two PDs, the proportional effect is greater for the second loan. The product of the two effects is nearly the same, and so the two loans require nearly the same capital. In fact, by a narrow margin the first loan requires greater capital (11.8%) than the second loan (11.0%). This is contrary to the verdict of a conventional model. As shown at the bottom of Table 1, the conventional model reverses the ranking and presents an alarmingly rosy view of the low-ELGD loan.

The two loans in Table 1 have the same EL and require nearly the same capital. (That the two loans divide EL differently between PD and ELGD has relatively little importance.) The relationship between EL and capital generalises readily, as shown in the context of a stylised bank internal rating system.

**Table 1. Expected performance of two loans**

| Overall expectation | | | | | |
|---|---|---|---|---|---|
| | PD (%) | × | ELGD (%) | = | EL (%) |
| First loan | 5.0 | | 10.0 | | 0.5 |
| Second loan | 1.0 | | 50.0 | | 0.5 |
| **Expectation in an economic slump; target α = 0.1%** | | | | | |
| | PD (%) | × | ELGD (%) | = | Capital (%) |
| First loan | 45.4 | | 26.1 | | 11.8 |
| Second loan | 18.4 | | 60.2 | | 11.1 |
| **Economic slump in a conventional credit model** | | | | | |
| | PD (%) | × | ELGD (%) | = | Capital (%) |
| First loan | 45.4 | | 10.0 | | 4.5 |
| Second loan | 18.4 | | 50.0 | | 9.2 |

Many banks use one-dimensional internal risk rating systems. These systems initially assign a risk rating based on the characteristics of the obligor. The rating might be upgraded based on the amount of collateral securing a particular loan. A collateralised loan to a poorer-rated obligor then has the same rating as an uncollateralised loan to a better-rated obligor. This resembles the relationship of the two loans in Table 1. The first loan has relatively lower ELGD, and the second loan has relatively lower PD. The product of ELGD and PD can therefore be nearly equal for the two loans. When this is so throughout every rating grade, the rating system can be characterised as an EL system, even if it is not intentionally based on expected loss.

EL rating systems appear to be the norm. After a thorough study, Treacy and Carey (1998) of the Federal Reserve characterise the rating systems of nearly all large US banks as measuring EL. (They characterise some as measuring PD as well, separately.) We therefore assume the interplay between PD and ELGD results in uniform EL within a rating grade.

We establish grades for EL = 0.025%, 0.05%, 0.1%, 0.2%, 0.4%, 0.8% and 1.6%. This range includes most bankable assets. Within any rating grade, a conventional model allocates less capital to loans having lower ELGD, as shown in Figure 2. (The target is low investment grade, α = 0.5%.) The five lines depict capital for five levels of

ELGD. The top line depicts ELGD = 100%, and the bottom line depicts ELGD = 6.25%. In the rating grade where EL = 0.1%, these correspond to PD = 0.1% and PD = 1.6%, respectively.

Within any EL grade, the conventional model allocates more capital to loans with higher ELGD and lower PD. That is because the conventional model splits EL into PD and ELGD – and then looks only at the systematic risk in the PD fraction. In an economic slump, the greatest proportional increase in default occurs in obligors with the lowest PD. Therefore, within an EL rating grade, the conventional model concludes that more capital is required for loans where the probability of default is low.

The difference between Figures 2 and 3 is the effect of collateral damage. The lower the ELGD, the more collateral and the more systematic risk is held by the bank. Therefore, the lines with the lowest ELGD rise the most in the transition from Figure 2 to Figure 3. Not only do they rise, they rise to approximately the same level. The result is that credit capital is approximately a function of expected loss alone.

Examination of Figures 2 and 3 leads to three conclusions. First, the effect of collateral damage increases capital for all loans (except for ELGD = 100%) and markedly increases capital for low-ELGD loans. Second, the low-ELGD lines in Figure 3 are much closer to the line representing ELGD = 100% than they are to their own representations in Figure 2. It appears more accurate to adjust the inputs for a low-ELGD loan – to adjust ELGD to 100% and to adjust PD downward, maintaining the same level of EL – than it is to simply accept the results of the conventional model using the unadjusted input. Third, a function of expected loss provides an estimate of credit capital that is more accurate than using both PD and ELGD in a conventional credit model.

These conclusions are tested for robustness. Thirty-six combinations of parameter values are used to recreate Figures 2 and 3. Three levels of $\sigma$ (15%, 20% and 25%) are combined with six combinations of values for p and q ({0.4, 0.4}, {0.4, 0.5}, {0.4, 0.6}, {0.5, 0.5}, {0.5, 0.6} and {0.6, 0.6}) and examined at two settings of $\alpha$ (0.1% and 0.5%). Each of the 36 pairs of charts supports all three of the conclusions stated above.[4]

These conclusions are not only robust for a range of parameter values, but also for a change in the mathematical specification of the model. In this specification there is no explicit role for collateral. Instead, recovery is modelled directly as a beta distribution, as is done in CreditMetrics. The model allows collateral damage to enter by conditioning recovery on the value of $C_j$. Specifically, replacing Equation 1 we have:

$$\text{Recovery}_j = \text{BetaInv}[\Phi(C_j), \text{mean} = \mu, \text{s.d.} = \sigma] \quad (9)$$

Figure 4 shows the results of the conditional beta recovery model. It resembles the normal model of Figure 3, except that the beta recovery model allocates slightly more capital to low-ELGD loans. Robustness checks of the beta recovery model also resemble the robustness checks of their normal model counterparts.[5] The conclusion – that capital depends principally on expected loss – is therefore robust with

**2. Capital in a conventional credit model**

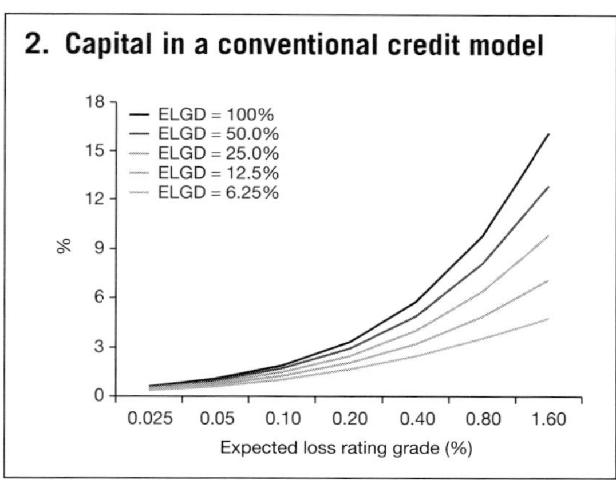


**3. Capital including collateral damage**

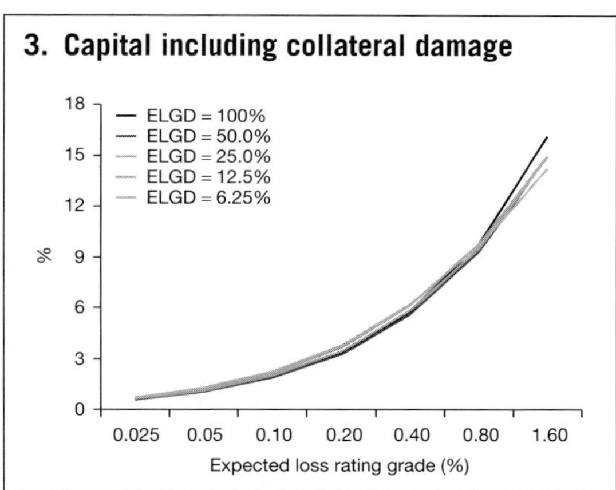


**4. Robustness with conditional beta recovery**

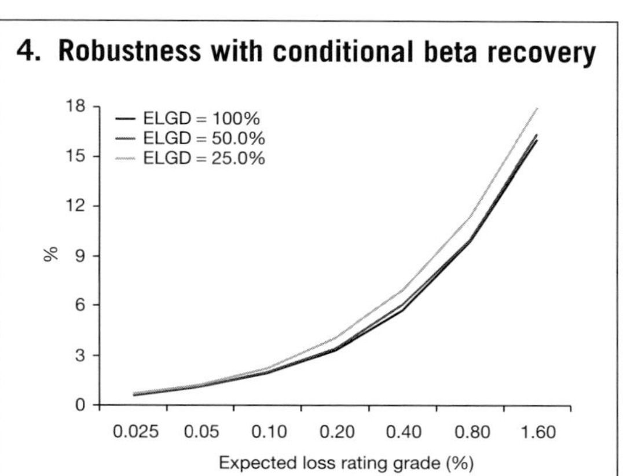

respect both to changes in parameter values and to a change in the model specification.

To account for the effects of collateral damage in a credit portfolio, the best solution would be to correctly model the effects of PD, ELGD, $\sigma$, p and q along the lines suggested in this chapter or in some other way. Most banks would find that they have neither the data nor the systems to adopt this approach in the near term. A second-best solution is to estimate capital as a function of expected loss, stratifying the portfolio by uniform $\sigma$, p and q as in the above.

For current users of a conventional credit model, a second-best solution appears to be an appropriate adjustment of the inputs. The suggestion is to adjust PD downward and to adjust ELGD to unity, keeping the product equal to the EL of the original loan.[6] The adjusted loan should contribute approximately the risk of the original loan including the risk of collateral damage. This adjustment is available to users of both CreditMetrics and CreditRisk+.

## Conclusion

The credit capital model presented in this chapter takes note of an effect well known to bankers: the credit cycle can produce a double misfortune involving greater-than-average default frequency and poorer-than-average recoveries. Of the two misfortunes, conventional credit models analyse the first and ignore the second. They can therefore assign alarmingly little capital to well-collateralised loans.

The effect of economic conditions on loan recoveries complicates the capital model. However, the results of the full model are well approximated by a function of expected loss. This conclusion holds for an alternative model specification and for a robust range of parameter values.

These results contain several messages. To bank lending and credit policy officers, the results repeat a message most often heard following large credit losses: collateral should not lead to complacency, because collateral value can decline at exactly the moment that a bank gains ownership. To bank portfolio credit analysts who use models to estimate portfolio risk, the results warn that all sources of systematic risk must be included. Lacking that, the inputs to existing models should be adjusted for more accurate results. To bank supervisors attempting to assess credit risk, the results suggest that a simple estimate of credit capital can be expedient and accurate.

Naturally, bank credit models should be expanded to cover as many sources of risk as possible. An estimate based on expected loss would not be completely accurate or ideal. However, the expected loss approach may provide a better estimate than some current credit models. Until models evolve to incorporate the systematic risk of both default and recovery, a credit capital estimate based on expected loss may be the best solution.

1 *We give broad meanings to two terms. "Collateral" here includes all the assets a bank obtains as a consequence of default, including, but not limited to, the assets pledged as collateral in a loan document. "Capital" refers to equity capital and to accumulated loan loss reserves, both of which help banks weather stressful periods.*

2 *Conditional EL, conditional PD and conditional ELGD refer to the expectation conditional on the realisation of* X. *Given* X, *the expectation is taken across all* j. *When conditioning is clear from context, the modifier may be suppressed. Otherwise, when the variables are not designated as "conditional", they have the usual meaning of an all-inclusive expectation.*

3 *Some specific collateral, such as cash or Treasury securities, has a low value of* q, *but these cases are far from the norm.*

4 *An Excel workbook with these results is available from the author at Jon.Frye@chi.frb.org.*

5 *Robustness checks with lower* q *and/or lower* $\sigma$ *can include lower levels of ELGD. They reach the same conclusions about the relationship of EL to credit capital.*

6 *Many CreditRisk+ users adjust model inputs now. They adjust exposure (rather than PD) downward as they adjust ELGD to unity, keeping the product equal to that of the original loan. This affects ELGD but not PD, so the EL of the proxy loan differs from the EL of the original. The difference in EL leads to the understatement of capital seen in Figure 2. Mechanically, the understatement comes about because the downward adjustment of exposure dominates the upward adjustment of ELGD.*

**BIBLIOGRAPHY**

**Credit Suisse Financial Products,** 1997, *CreditRisk+: A Credit Risk Management Framework.*

**Finger, C.,** 1999, "Conditional Approaches for CreditMetrics Portfolio Distributions", *CreditMetrics Monitor*, April.

**Gordy, M.,** 2000, "A Comparative Anatomy of Credit Risk Models", *Journal of Banking & Finance*, January, pp. 119–49.

**Gupton, G., C. Finger and M. Bhatia,** 1997, *CreditMetrics Technical Document*, JP Morgan.

**Moody's Investors Service,** 1999, *Global Credit Research*, Historical Default Rates of Corporate Bond Issuers, 1920–98.

**Treacy, W., and M. Carey,** 1998, "Credit Risk Rating at Large US Banks", *Federal Reserve Bulletin*, November, pp. 897–921.

17

# Depressing Recoveries

**Jon Frye**

Federal Reserve Bank of Chicago

*In Frye (2000) Jon Frye suggested that well-known credit portfolio models were deficient because they assumed that recovery rates were independent of default rates. Here, using historical default data, he finds evidence in support of his earlier work.*

The current US expansion is the longest and strongest in economic history. It has been a boon for US banking institutions, which have enjoyed a long period of relatively low default rates. And perhaps the economic good times will roll on forever. But an eventual reversal – an economic downturn – seems more likely. If the downturn is severe, the misfortune for banks may be twofold: a higher rate of default among their borrowers, and a lower rate of recovery on defaulted loans.

Defending against economic downturns is the main reason banks hold capital. Increasingly, banks manage their capital with guidance from new portfolio credit models such as CreditManager or CreditRisk+. But when these models look to the next economic downturn, they allow for only one misfortune, an increase in the default rate. The other misfortune, a possible simultaneous decrease in average recovery, evades analysis. If banks depend upon such models, they might enter a severe downturn holding too little capital.

The degree of potential shortfall is easy to grasp. Suppose one of the first-generation credit models accurately projects that in a severe downturn a bank will experience a 10% default rate. Overall credit loss is approximately equal to the default rate times the flip side of loan recovery, loss given default (LGD). But in the first-generation models, LGD does not depend on default. If long-term average LGD is 25%, these models will project that LGD will equal 25% on average in any year, and that capital of 2.5% will withstand the downturn.

However, the same economic conditions that cause default to rise to 10% might also cause LGD to rise above its long-term average. If, in the downturn, LGD rises to 50%, the need for capital to withstand the downturn would equal 5% rather than 2.5%. If credit models overlook the possible doubling of LGD in a severe downturn, they understate capital by half.

This study examines data on US corporate bonds and finds significant synchrony between default and recovery. It then fits the model presented in Frye (2000) to this data. Extrapolating the model to the conditions that produce a 10% default rate, recovery falls by 25% in absolute terms from its normal-year average. If that decline pertains to recoveries on bank loans as well as on bonds, the LGD at banks could double from the normal-year average.

## The data

Because the focus of this study is on banks and the credit risk at banks, the ideal data set would be a long history of bank loans, loan defaults and eventual loan recovery amounts. Though efforts are under way to collect such data, this data set does not exist at present. Fortunately, rating agencies collect equivalent data for rated bonds.

This study uses the Moody's Default Risk Service database, which contains extensive information about debt issues rated by Moody's since 1970. It includes information about bank loans, corporate bonds and sovereign bonds; it includes information about entities domiciled in many different countries; and it includes information about bonds that are guaranteed by second entities as well as about unbacked bonds.

*The author thanks Sarah Mangi for superb research assistance. The views expressed are the author's and do not necessarily represent the views of the management of the Federal Reserve Bank of Chicago or the views of the Federal Reserve System.*

**1. Annual default rates**

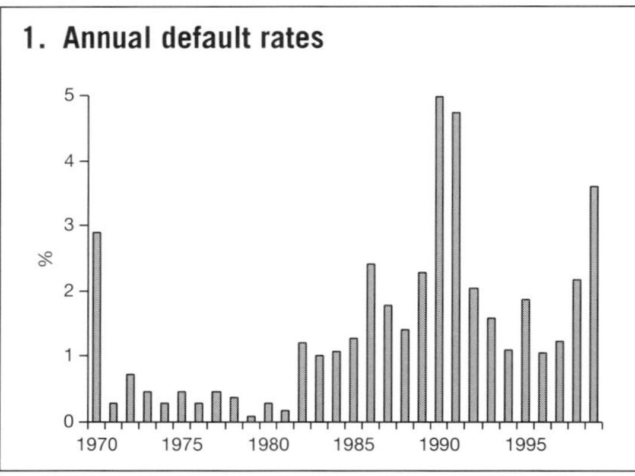


**2. Recovery in high- and low-default years**

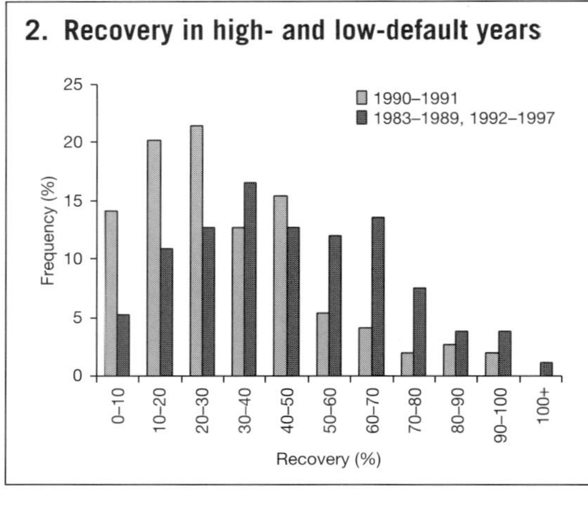


Some selection criteria help make sense of the data. The first selection criterion limits the sample to entities domiciled in the US. This restriction is desirable because economic conditions in different countries are not perfectly synchronised and it would require a multi-factor credit model to capture the difference in timing between countries. The credit model employed here, by contrast, is driven by a single factor.

Moody's supplies a "broad industry group" and a "specific industry group" for each rated issuer. The second selection criterion eliminates certain broad groups (banking, finance, insurance, other non-bank, real estate finance, securities, sovereign, structured finance and thrifts), and, within what remains, it eliminates certain narrow groups such as finance conduit. What are left are the non-financial issuers within the broad groups of industrial, public utility and transportation. Like the first selection criterion, the second criterion is meant to produce issuers that respond to a similar risk factor, while keeping the number of issuers as large as possible. The result of this selection is the default universe of this study.

Figure 1 shows the annual default rate in the default universe. The default rate calculation is the same as that used by Moody's and equals the ratio of two numbers. The numerator is the number of defaults that occur among issuers that had a Moody's rating on the first day of the year. The denominator is the number of issuers that had a Moody's rating at the beginning of the year, less half the number that had their rating withdrawn in the course of the year.[1]

The recovery universe is further limited by three additional selection criteria. First, the database contains rated loans as well as rated bonds. To keep this study narrowly focused, the first recovery criterion eliminates loans. Second, some bonds are guaranteed by a second entity. If those bonds default, recovery is markedly greater than on unbacked bonds. Therefore, the second recovery criterion eliminates bonds backed by a second entity. Third, there must be a recovery amount available; the third recovery criterion eliminates defaulted bonds for which Moody's does not have a "default price".

Moody's observes the default price one month after the first occurrence of a default event (this is usually a missed payment or bankruptcy). The default price therefore represents the market valuation of the probability distribution of possible future recovery. This market valuation differs from the eventual recovery itself. Nonetheless, most bond recovery studies rely on market valuations, and the present study assumes that the market valuations are accurate on average in a given year.

Having defined the default universe and the recovery universe, Figure 2 gets to the heart of things. It contrasts the distribution of recovery in the high-default years of 1990 and 1991 to the distribution of recovery in other years. The low-recovery bars on the left of the diagram are dominated by defaults that occur in the high-default years, and the high-recovery bars on the right of the diagram tend to reflect defaults in other years. This suggests that the distribution of recovery is different in a high-default year from a low-default year. The suggestion is confirmed by a simple chi-square test: the difference between the histograms is highly significant.[2] The credit model described next puts a shape on this difference, so that we can develop an idea of expected recovery in a severe economic downturn.

## The model

This study uses a model that is nearly identical to the model presented in Frye (2000). But while that article implies recovery from an equation that determines collateral, this study models recovery directly. The reason is simply that the Moody's database observes recovery, not collateral.

The model presented here, like that in Frye (2000), draws heavily from models suggested by Gordy (2000) and Finger (1999). These models are driven by a single systematic risk factor rather than by a multitude of correlation parameters. This simplification, of course, lacks a great deal of detail, but is appropriate for studying general influences such as an economic downturn. The present model departs from Gordy and Finger by allowing recovery, as well as default, to depend on the state of the systematic risk factor.

The systematic risk factor, X, is the central player. It affects the fortunes of every firm and the amount of every recovery. If X takes a low value, there is a greater than average expected rate of default and a lower than average expected rate of recovery. These effects move the expected rates of default and recovery, but they affect individual events only as tendencies. Thus with high levels of X there can be some defaults and some unfavourable recoveries.

From the standpoint of a given firm j in the model, two factors affect it. First is the level of X, which has a simultaneous effect on every other firm. Second is the level of an independent factor $X_j$ that affects only firm j. These two - the systematic risk factor X and the idiosyncratic risk factor $X_j$ - combine to determine the level of firm j's asset value index, $A_j$:

$$A_j = pX + \sqrt{1-p^2}X_j \qquad (1)$$

The two risk factors, X and $X_j$, are assumed to have independent standard normal distributions, which implies that $A_j$ has a standard normal distribution. One can imagine a mapping from the asset value index to the dollar value of the assets of firm j, but the "work" in the model is done by the index, $A_j$.

The parameter p plays an important role in the asset Equation 1. It controls how much the systematic factor affects the set of issuers. If an economy has a low value of p (near zero), issuers have little connection to the state of the economy. In such an economy, each issuer finds its independent, idiosyncratic factor to be far more important than the common factor. Therefore the prosperity (or default) of one firm has little connection to the prosperity (or default) of other firms. In such an economy, the default rate is relatively constant from year to year. On the other hand, if an economy has a high value of p, each issuer is strongly tied to the general economy. An economy with a high level of p is a highly cyclical economy, and any year that X takes a low value will be a bad year for many issuers. Thus, an economy having a large value of p will have a severe credit cycle.

In the model, a firm defaults when its asset value index falls below a threshold. The level of the threshold is chosen to produce the long-term probability of default of the firm in question. Letting $D_j$ symbolise the default event of firm j:

$$D_j = 1 \quad \text{if } A_j < \Phi^{-1}(PD_j); \quad D_j = 0 \quad \text{otherwise} \qquad (2)$$

where $PD_j$ is the probability of default of firm j.

Like Gordy's and Finger's models, this model assumes that the portfolio is large and fully diversified. The law of large numbers then implies that, conditional on a level of X, the observed default frequency approximates its conditionally expected rate:

$$\begin{aligned} DF_j &= P[A_j < \Phi^{-1}(PD_j)\ |X = x] \\ &= P\left[px + \sqrt{1-p^2}X_j < \Phi^{-1}(PD_j)\right] \\ &= P\left[X_j < \frac{\Phi^{-1}(PD_j) - px}{\sqrt{1-p^2}}\right] = \Phi\left[\frac{\Phi^{-1}(PD_j) - px}{\sqrt{1-p^2}}\right] \qquad (3) \end{aligned}$$

Turning to the recovery side, the recovery equation is similar to asset Equation 1. Recovery in default j depends on the systematic factor X and also on an idiosyncratic factor, $Z_j$, which affects only the recovery in default j:

$$R_j = \mu_j + \sigma qX + \sigma\sqrt{1-q^2}Z_j \qquad (4)$$

$Z_j$ is assumed to have a standard normal distribution independent of X. Therefore, $R_j$ has a normal distribution with mean $\mu$ and variance $\sigma^2$.[3] The parameters $\mu$, $\sigma$ and q may be interpreted as the quantity, quality and sensitivity of recovery. The sensitivity parameter, q, controls the strength of the effect of the systematic factor on recovery. This role is parallel to the role of p in the asset equation; note that $\text{Corr}(A_j, X) = p$ and $\text{Corr}(R_j, X) = q$.

## Fitting the model to data

The need to fit Equation 3 to data leads to the final criterion defining the data sample. Equation 3 requires a probability of default for every issuer. That probability is estimated by the long-term average one-year default rate of issuers holding the same Moody's rating. However, there are several ratings for which long-term history is simply not available. In 1982, Moody's abandoned the grades of A and B. It reclassified the substantial number of firms having those ratings into the new "alphanumeric" grades of A1, A2, A3, and so forth.

Similarly, in 1997, Moody's began to abandon the Caa grade and began to reclassify Caa-rated obligors into new classes Caa1, Caa2 and Caa3. To avoid the very short histories of certain rating grades, the model is fit to the 15-year sample period 1983–1997, the longest historical period for which the Moody's scale is uniform.

The estimation is by conditional maximum likelihood. An overview of the conditional approach is as follows. First, the default data alone is used to estimate $p$ by maximum likelihood. Given $p$, the portfolio generalisation of Equation 3 implies the level of $X$ each year. These implied levels of $X$ are combined with the recovery data to estimate the other parameters by a second maximisation. This approach departs from the ideal because it uses only default data to estimate the levels of $X$, rather than making use of the information about $X$ that might be contained in the recovery data. On the other hand, it is intuitively appealing that default data is used to estimate $p$ (which governs the severity of the default cycle), and recovery data is used to estimate the other parameters (which govern the quantity, quality and sensitivity of recovery).

A more detailed discussion of the estimation approach requires restating Equations 3 and 4 with detailed subscripts. The subscript $t$ counts the $T = 15$ years of the data sample. The subscript $r$ counts the $R = 19$ rating grades (Aaa, Aa1, Aa2, Aa3, A1, A2, A3, Baa1, Baa2, Baa3, Ba1, Ba2, Ba3, B1, B2, B3, Caa, Ca and C). Then, in year $t$, the conditional default rate of a firm rated $r$ equals:

$$DF_{t,r} = \Phi\left[\frac{\Phi^{-1}(PD_r) - pX_t}{\sqrt{1-p^2}}\right] \qquad (5)$$

where $PD_r$ equals the long-term average default rate of firms rated $r$.

Let $h_{t,r}$ represent the fraction of the default universe rated $r$ in year $t$. Then the conditional default rate of the default universe equals:

$$DF_t = \sum_{r=1}^{R} h_{t,r} DF_{t,r} = g_p(X_t) \qquad (6)$$

The function $g$ is monotonic, so it can be inverted numerically with respect to $X_t$. Given that $X_t$ has a standard normal distribution, the change-of-variable technique produces the density of $DF_t$.

Assuming independence from year to year, the joint density of the 15 years of default rate data is a function of the default rate data $\{DF_t\}$, the portfolio proportions $\{h_{t,r}\}$, the long-term default rates $\{PD_r\}$ and the unknown parameter $p$. Maximising the density with respect to $p$ provides the estimate $p = 0.23$. Given $p$, Equation 6 says that the default rate in any year depends only on the level of $X_t$. Therefore, we can imply $X_t$ for each year.

The estimated levels of $X_t$ are put to use in the recovery equation. The subscript $j$ now counts the $J = 4$ seniority classes (senior secured, senior unsecured, senior subordinated and subordinated). Moody's assigns these classifications at the time of issuance. Though subjective and unchanging, these classifications provide some information about the amount of recovery in the event of default. Therefore, a distinct level of $\mu$ is estimated for each seniority class.

Sometimes a defaulting firm will have several outstanding bonds classified, for example, as senior subordinated. The model has nothing to say about the difference in recovery among these bonds. Therefore, the symbol $R_{t,j,i}$ denotes the dollar-weighted average recovery in year $t$ of bonds of the $j$th seniority class issued by the $i$th defaulting issuer:

$$R_{t,j,i} = \mu_j + \sigma q X_t + \sigma\sqrt{1-q^2}\,Z_{t,j,i} \qquad (7)$$

The symbol $N_{t,j}$ is the number of recoveries in year $t$ and seniority class $j$. Then average recovery in year $t$ equals:

$$R_t = \frac{\sum_{j=1}^{J}\sum_{i=1}^{N_{t,j}} R_{t,j,i}}{\sum_{j=1}^{J} N_{t,j}} \qquad (8)$$

where $R_t$ has a normal distribution. Again, assuming independence from year to year we can maximise the density of the data with respect to $\{\mu_j\}$, $\sigma$ and $q$, and obtain the parameter estimates shown in Table 1.

**Table 1. Model parameters and estimates**

| Parameter | Estimate |
|---|---|
| $p$ | 0.23 |
| $q$ | 0.17 |
| $\sigma$ | 0.32 |
| $\mu$ (senior secured) | 0.47 |
| $\mu$ (senior unsecured) | 0.70 |
| $\mu$ (senior subordinated) | 0.12 |
| $\mu$ (subordinated) | 0.41 |

## Sizing up the fit

This section discusses the estimates of the parameter values, the agreement between the model and the data, and the implication of the model for bond recovery in an economic downturn.

The estimate of $\sigma$ implies great uncertainty in any particular recovery event. The difference between zero recovery and 96% recovery is only three standard deviations. Despite this uncertainty, recovery depends on systematic risk: the estimate of q is nearly as great as the estimate of p.

The near-equality of p and q was foreseen in Frye (2000) as follows. The two parameters measure the sensitivity to X of two kinds of asset values. These asset values are, of course, the asset values of firms and the amounts recovered on debt instruments. Taken at a very high level of abstraction, assets are assets and there is little reason to suspect a major difference in their sensitivities. Further, since recovery value derives from the asset value of a firm, there is reason to suspect that the two parameters are similar.

The near-equality of p and q supports the "expected loss (EL) equivalent" substitution rule discussed in Frye (2000). This rule says that two debts having the same EL (but having possibly a different division of EL into probability of default and expected LGD) will require nearly the same amount of capital. A prominent credit model, CreditMetrics' CreditManager, does not observe the EL-substitution rule, and within an EL grade it allocates less capital – too little capital, according to the present model – to debts having a low expected LGD. Therefore, the present model suggests that CreditManager may estimate too little capital overall and that it may misallocate capital between debts.

The pattern of estimates of $\{\mu_j\}$ would be expected to decline from the strongest seniority class (senior secured) to the weakest (subordinated). Instead, there are breaks in the pattern, for example, the relatively low estimate of 0.12 for the senior-subordinated class. The breaks arise primarily because of the distribution of recoveries across years. As a class, senior-subordinated debt gained acceptance rather late in the sample period. Most of the senior-subordinated defaults occur in 1995 or later, when the systematic factor X took large positive values. This results in a boost for senior-subordinated recoveries. To compensate, the optimisation routine attributes a low value to $\mu_{(\text{senior-subordinated})}$. In fact, none of the seniority classes are distributed as expected across the years. A contributing reason to this is the low number of observations. There are only 405 cases in the recovery universe and 30 cases in the senior-subordinated class.

**3. Data and model**

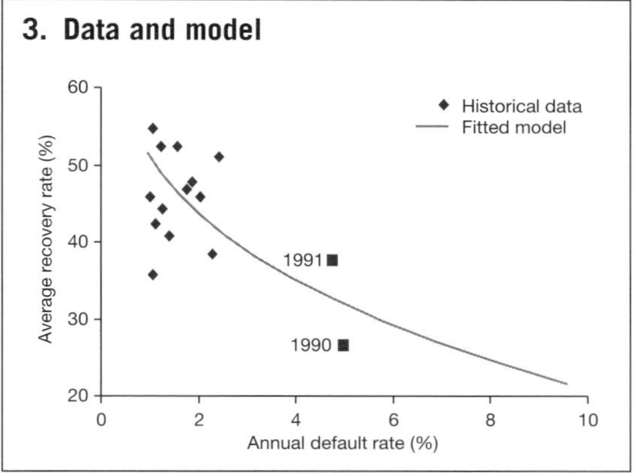


Figure 3 compares the data – the annual default rate in the default universe and the average recovery rate in the recovery universe – to the fitted model. The line for the fitted model is constructed by substituting a range of values of X into Equations 6 and 8. These calculations assume the average distribution of the portfolio across rating grades and the average distribution of defaults across seniority classes. Because Figure 3 compares historical data (which depends on the actual distribution across rating grades and across seniority classes) to a projection that uses the long-term average portfolio, the true fit of the model is better than the impression given in Figure 3.

The most interesting part of Figure 3 is on the right, which extrapolates the estimated model beyond historical experience. According to the model, if the systematic risk factor pushes the default rate to a level of 10%, average recovery might fall to about 20%. This contrasts to the normal-year average of 45% or so. Thus, in a severe economic downturn, recovery on defaulted bonds might fall by about 25 percentage points from the norm.

## Loan recovery in a downturn

Ideally, one could fit the same model to data on loans. However, the first loan recovery in the Moody's database occurs in late 1996, and there are recoveries from only fifteen defaults in total.[4] Clearly, this data is not sufficient to fit the present model.

Instead, we attempt to adjust the model parameters to better reflect loans. The critical assumption is that the p and q relevant to loans are equal to the values estimated for bonds. It appears that the level of $\sigma$ may be lower for loans than for bonds. The standard deviation of the 14 senior-secured loan recoveries is 26%, compared with a

**Table 2. Estimated LGD of bonds and loans in an economic downturn**

| | | (1) | (2) | (3) | (4) | (5) |
|---|---|---|---|---|---|---|
| Parameter values | p | 0.23 | 0.23 | 0.23 | 0.23 | 0.23 |
| | q | 0.17 | 0.17 | 0.17 | 0.17 | 0.17 |
| | $\sigma$ | 0.32 | 0.32 | 0.32 | 0.25 | 0.25 |
| | PD (%) | 1.99 | 2.00 | 0.20 | 2.00 | 0.20 |
| | ELGD (%) | 59.1 | 30.7 | 30.7 | 30.7 | 30.7 |
| Normal state, X = 0 | Default (%) | 1.8 | 1.7 | 0.2 | 1.7 | 0.2 |
| | LGD (%) | 55 | 28 | 27 | 28 | 28 |
| Depressed state, X = –4.5 | Default (%) | 10.4 | 14.8 | 2.9 | 14.8 | 2.9 |
| | LGD (%) | 80 | 52 | 51 | 47 | 47 |
| Increase in LGD | % | 45 | 89 | 92 | 68 | 69 |

(1) Estimated parameters; Moody's average PD and average ELGD
(2) Estimated parameters, low-quality loans
(3) Estimated parameters, high-quality loans
(4) Reduced value of $\sigma$, low-quality loans
(5) Reduced value of $\sigma$, high-quality loans

value of 31% for senior-secured bonds in the same historical period. Therefore, we adopt two representative values for $\sigma$: 0.32 as estimated above, and 0.25. It also appears that loan recovery exceeds bond recovery. The average of the 14 senior-secured loan recoveries is 69.3%, compared with a value of 47.8% for senior-secured bonds in the same historical period. We adopt the representative value of 30.7% for the expected LGD of loans.

Table 2 shows the implications. The first column reflects the average Moody's portfolio. In this column, the "normal" state and the "depressed" state identify two points along the locus of Figure 3. LGD is 80% in the depressed state, a 45% increase from the normal state. The other columns reflect parameters more appropriate for loans. Columns 2 and 3 employ $\sigma = 0.32$, which implies that in the depressed state LGD nearly doubles. The difference between Columns 2 and 3 shows that the level of PD has very little influence on systematic recovery risk. Columns 4 and 5 use the estimate $\sigma = 25\%$. This implies that in the depressed state LGD increases about 70%.

The message of Table 2 repeats the message that began this chapter. In a period of high default, it is intuitive that debt recovery would run low. This intuition is confirmed by data on US corporate bonds. Using that data to estimate an appropriate credit model, we can extrapolate that in a severe economic downturn bond recoveries might decline by 20–25 percentage points from the normal-year average. Loan recoveries may decline by a similar amount, but from a higher level. This could cause loss given default to increase by nearly 100% and to have a proportionate effect on economic capital. Such systematic recovery risk is absent from first-generation credit models. Therefore, these models may significantly understate the capital required at banking institutions.

1 *Moody's justifies this procedure as follows. The withdrawal of a rating is not generally associated with a loss for the investor – the bonds mature or they are called or defeased. After the withdrawal, an issuer default does not appear in the database. Therefore, from the perspective of the database, a firm with a withdrawn rating is subject to default for only the fraction of the year prior to withdrawal. On average, this fraction is one-half, which accounts for the adjustment to the denominator.*

2 *The chi-square statistic of the count data equals 40.7 with eight degrees of freedom, significant at a level of 0.000003. This test combines the recoveries greater than 80 in order to keep expected cell frequencies greater than five. Both this test and Figure 3 use the dollar-weighted averaging and the 1983–1997 sample period that are introduced later. In several years within the 1970–1981 period, the average default price was low despite favourable default rate experience. This anomaly might be explained by low liquidity in the defaulted-bond market in those years.*

3 *Thus the distribution of the assets that govern recovery* ($R_j$) *is similar to the distribution of the assets that govern default* ($A_j$)*. An alternative specification of recovery might be bounded on* [0,1]*, eg, recovery might have a beta distribution. However, Moody's default prices are not bounded at 100%, as shown in Figure 3.*

4 *This is according to the set of loan codes provided by Moody's.*

**BIBLIOGRAPHY**

**Finger, C.,** 1999, "Conditional Approaches for CreditMetrics Portfolio Distributions", *CreditMetrics Monitor*, April.

**Frye, J.,** 2000, "Collateral Damage", *Risk*, April, pp. 91–4.

**Gordy, M.,** 2000, "A Comparative Anatomy of Credit Risk Models", *Journal of Banking and Finance*, January, pp. 119–49.

**Moody's Investors Service,** 2000, *Default Risk Service Database.*

IV

# VALUE-AT-RISK FOR CREDIT PORTFOLIOS

18

# Integrating Correlations

**Peter Bürgisser, Alexandre Kurth, Armin Wagner and Michael Wolf**
Paderborn University, Germany; UBS

*How can a credit portfolio be diversified? Although popular for its tractability, CreditRisk+ fails to answer this vital question. By modelling the default correlation between industry sectors, Peter Bürgisser, Alexandre Kurth, Armin Wagner and Michael Wolf attempt to provide a solution.*

In the past few years, the quantitative modelling of credit risk has received much attention within the financial industry. Several models have been released to the public, notably CreditRisk+, CreditMetrics and CreditPortfolioView, from Credit Suisse Financial Products, JP Morgan and McKinsey & Company, respectively. Although different approaches to credit risk are used, studies have shown that the models yield similar results if the parameters are set in a consistent way (see, for example, Koyluoglu and Hickman, 1998). CreditRisk+ in particular is ideal for practical implementation and has some useful features, namely: (a) few assumptions have to be made; (b) the methodology is transparent and based on concepts already used in the insurance business; and (c) the loss distribution can be calculated analytically in an efficient way using an iterative procedure.

One of the shortcomings of the CreditRisk+ model is the assumption of independent sectors. The sectors represent, for example, different regions or industries within the economy and individual obligors can be assigned to particular sectors (henceforth, we shall use sector and industry interchangeably). To perform a sector analysis, the authors of CreditRisk+ propose apportioning an obligor's systematic credit risk across a mixture of independent sectors. However, such an approach is difficult to realise in practice.

In this chapter, we present a framework for extending the CreditRisk+ model by examining correlations between industries, and derive a formula for the unexpected loss and risk contributions. The correct modelling of correlations of default risk between sectors is very important for examining the effects of diversification on active portfolio management. Note that only the loss from defaults of counterparties is modelled.

The chapter is organised as follows: we first derive the probability generating function of the loss distribution for one industry sector following the CreditRisk+ approach. This is then generalised to several sectors to obtain the first two moments of the loss distribution, as well as a loss distribution consistent with the observed correlations between sectors.

## Loss distribution for one industry sector

We will express the loss distribution of a loan portfolio by its probability generating function, which is defined as a power series of the form:

$$G(z) = \sum_{n\geq 0} p(n)z^n \qquad (1)$$

where $p(n)$ is the probability of losing the amount $n$ and $z$ is a formal variable. Generating functions possess some useful features (see Appendix) and are preferred to probability distributions in this chapter, although both are just different representations of the same thing. In the following, we express all losses and exposures as integer multiples of some fixed chosen unit. Let $p_A$ be the default probability of obligor A and $\nu_A$ be its exposure net of recovery. The recovery rates are assumed to be constant. The loss distribution for a single obligor A, having two possible states with $n = 0$ (no default) and $n = \nu_A$ (default), can be

*Opinions expressed herein are the authors' and do not necessarily reflect the opinions of UBS. The authors wish to thank a referee for valuable remarks.*

expressed by the following probability generating function:

$$G_A(z) = (1 - p_A)z^0 + p_A z^{\nu_A} = 1 + p_A(z^{\nu_A} - 1) \quad (2)$$

Assuming independence of default events between obligors – an assumption that is relaxed in Equation 4 – we obtain the generating function for the portfolio loss distribution (see Appendix):

$$\begin{aligned} G(z) &= \prod_A G_A(z) = \exp\left[\sum_A \log(1 + p_A(z^{\nu_A} - 1))\right] \\ &\approx \exp\left[\sum_A p_A(z^{\nu_A} - 1)\right] =: \exp[P(z) - P(1)] \quad (3) \end{aligned}$$

where we use the approximation $\log(1 + h) \approx h$, which is valid for small default probabilities – a good assumption for most loan portfolios. We call $P(z) = \Sigma_A p_A z^{\nu_A}$ the portfolio polynomial. This polynomial contains all the relevant information about the portfolio for our purpose, ie, the expected number of defaults per exposure. The distribution described by the generating function in Equation 3 is compound Poisson (see Bühlmann, 1970). In the special case of identical exposures $\nu_A = 1$, we have $P(z) = \mu z$, where $\mu = \Sigma_A p_A$ is the expected number of defaults in the portfolio. The resulting distribution is Poisson. In fact, this is the distribution of the number of defaults.

In the next step, the model is refined to include the systematic risk of correlated changes in the default rates, thereby dropping the assumption of the independence of default events in Equation 3. This is achieved by introducing a random scaling factor $\gamma$ that models changes in the economy. The variable $\gamma$ describes the relative number of default events in the economy normalised to the mean equal to one. Let $g(\gamma)$ be the corresponding probability density function with variance $\sigma^2$, which we call the relative default variance. Note that this quantity is independent of the portfolio.

To obtain the generating function F(z) of the unconditional loss distribution, we average the conditional generating function $G^{(\gamma)}(z)$ over the possible states of the economy, characterised by $\gamma$:

$$F(z) = \int_0^\infty G^{(\gamma)}(z) g(\gamma) d\gamma = \int_0^\infty \exp[\gamma(P(z) - P(1))] g(\gamma) d\gamma \quad (4)$$

Here, it is assumed that the generating function of the loss distribution conditioned on the state of the economy $\gamma$ is $G^{(\gamma)}(z) = \exp[\gamma(P(z) - P(1))]$. This means that the systematic default risk affects all obligors in the same way (see box, "Remark 1").

The expectation (expected loss: EL) and the standard deviation (unexpected loss: UL) of the loss distribution can be expressed as follows:

$$\begin{aligned} EL &= P'(1) = \sum_A p_A \nu_A \\ UL^2 &= P'(1)^2 \sigma^2 + P''(1) + P'(1) \end{aligned} \quad (5)$$

The expressions $P'(1)$ and $P''(1)$ are the first and second derivatives of the portfolio polynomial P(z) at $z = 1$. It is important to note that the expected loss and variance of the losses depend only on the portfolio polynomial P(z) and the relative default variance $\sigma^2$. The shape of the default distribution $g(\gamma)$ is thus irrelevant for calculating EL and UL. From Equation 5, we obtain the variance as in CreditRisk+, relating the volatility in the losses UL to the relative default variance $\sigma^2$, and the portfolio structure:

$$UL^2 = \sigma^2 EL^2 + \sum_A p_A \nu_A^2 \quad (6)$$

The first expression represents the risk due to systematic changes in the economy, reflected by the relative default variance. The second term is the risk contribution due to the statistical nature of default events, which is only important for either small portfolios or for cases with low systematic risk. For large and homogeneous

## PANEL 1. REMARK 1

If we assume $g(\gamma)$ follows a gamma distribution, then F(z) can be expressed analytically, and the explicit form of the loss distribution is amenable to efficient calculation (see Credit Suisse Financial Products, 1997). When counting the number of defaults (ie, formally putting $\nu_A = 1$ and, consequently, $P(z) = \mu z$), the corresponding distribution is negative binomial (see Bühlmann, 1970).

Moreover, the distribution of losses allows the following mathematical description: suppose that $X_1, X_2, X_3, \ldots$ are independent identically distributed, having as generating function the polynomial $P(z)/\mu$, and let M be negative binomially distributed, independent of the $X_i$. Then the distribution of losses is given by $\Sigma_{i=1}^M X_i$.

portfolios and values $\sigma$ of the order of one, the credit risk is only driven by the EL, scaled with the systematic risk factor $\sigma$. The detailed structure of the portfolio does not affect the loss distribution. From Equation 6, we also derive that the variance of the number of defaults in the portfolio equals $\sigma^2\mu^2 + \mu$ (put $\nu_A = 1$). For large portfolios and $\sigma \neq 0$ this is roughly the variance of the number of defaults $\sigma^2\mu^2$ observed in the economy.

## ...and for several industry sectors

For simplicity, we first restrict ourselves to two correlated industries. We now have a portfolio polynomial for each industry, $P_1(z)$ and $P_2(w)$ defined as before, by assigning each obligor to one industry. The probability generating function in the conditional case is given by the product of the individual generating functions, having a form as in Equation 3:

$$G(z,w) = \exp[P_1(z) - P_1(1)]\exp[P_2(w) - P_2(1)] \quad (7)$$

To derive the generating function for the unconditional case, we average over all possible states of the economy. These states are now modelled by the joint distribution of two scaling factors $\gamma_1$, $\gamma_2$ with density $g(\gamma_1, \gamma_2)$, describing the relative number of default events in the two industry sectors, each normalised to mean one. We thus incorporate the default correlations between the two industries. The loss distribution is now given by the following probability generating function:

$$F(z,w) = \int_0^\infty\int_0^\infty G^{(\gamma_1,\gamma_2)}(z,w)g(\gamma_1,\gamma_2)d\gamma_1 d\gamma_2 \quad (8)$$

where

$$G^{(\gamma_1,\gamma_2)}(z,w) = \exp[\gamma_1(P_1(z) - P_1(1))] \times \exp[\gamma_2(P_2(w) - P_2(1))]$$

is the generating function of the losses conditioned on the state $(\gamma_1, \gamma_2)$.

At this point, it would be natural to take some suitable two-dimensional generalisation of the gamma distribution for $g(\gamma_1, \gamma_2)$, which would allow the explicit calculation of the full loss distribution. However, as already seen in the case of one industry sector, the standard deviation of the loss does not depend on the specific form of the density function. The specification of g is thus only relevant for the overall loss distribution and the calculation of the risk capital. In addition, there are few data to support the exact shape of a multi-dimensional distribution for default events. That is why we proceed in a different way: we first calculate the UL of the overall portfolio and then use the single-sector approach to calculate the full loss distribution.

We proceed directly to calculate the expected loss EL and the unexpected loss UL. The expected loss by industry sector is:

$$EL_1 = P_1'(1) \qquad EL_2 = P_2'(1) \quad (9)$$

The variances of the losses per industry and the covariance of the losses between the two industries are given by (for further details, see Appendix):

$$\begin{aligned} UL_1^2 &= P_1'(1)^2\sigma_1^2 + P_1''(1) + P_1'(1) \\ UL_2^2 &= P_2'(1)^2\sigma_2^2 + P_2''(1) + P_2'(1) \\ Cov_{1,2} &= P_1'(1)P_2'(1)Cov(\gamma_1,\gamma_2) \end{aligned} \quad (10)$$

It is now easy to derive the desired formula for the unexpected loss UL of the overall portfolio using the relationship $UL^2 = UL_1^2 + UL_2^2 + 2Cov_{1,2}$, where we express the covariance by the corresponding correlation and the variances:

$$UL^2 = \sigma_1^2 EL_1^2 + \sigma_2^2 EL_2^2 + 2Cor(\gamma_1,\gamma_2)\sigma_1\sigma_2 EL_1 EL_2 + \sum_A p_A\nu_A^2 \quad (11)$$

In the general situation of N industry sectors, $k = 1,\ldots, N$, we obtain in analogy:

$$UL^2 = \sum_k \sigma_k^2 EL_k^2 + \sum_{\substack{k,\ell \\ k\neq\ell}} Cor(\gamma_k,\gamma_\ell)\sigma_k\sigma_\ell EL_k EL_\ell + \sum_A p_A\nu_A^2 \quad (12)$$

Again, as in the single-sector case, the first two sums represent the risk due to systematic changes in the industries, reflected by the relative default variances, and the correlations between them. The third sum is the risk contribution due to the statistical nature of default events, which – as in the single-sector case – is only important for small portfolios or for cases with low systematic risk. The correlation between sectors – if positive, as is usually observed in the economy – increases the systematic risk contribution and becomes very important when working with many sectors (see box, "Remark 2").

Equation 12 allows one to calculate the UL of the portfolio loss distribution in a manner consistent with the observed sector covariance matrix. It also lays the foundation to calculate UL risk contributions at the level of individual obligors, as shown below.

To calculate the full loss distribution, we match the UL from the CreditRisk+ single-sector approach

## PANEL 2. REMARK 2

To estimate the risk parameters – the relative default variance and the correlation of default events between industries – one can choose between three approaches: (1) using industry-specific time series of historically observed default events; (2) using asset values of firms to derive pair-wise asset correlations, which are then linked to the relevant default correlations using the Merton model (1974); and (3) using a factor model that relates the relative number of default events to macroeconomic drivers.

The method to be applied depends on the type of portfolio: while time series of defaults are suited for middle-market portfolios with mostly non-quoted firms, the asset value approach is best for portfolios with large corporates. A limiting factor for both methods is the time period over which data exists. Here, a factor model has some advantage because time series of the drivers of default are available far back in time.

(Equation 6) to the UL from Equation 12:

$$\sigma^2 EL^2 = \sum_k \sigma_k^2 EL_k^2 + \sum_{\substack{k,\ell \\ k \neq \ell}} Cor(\gamma_k, \gamma_\ell)\sigma_k \sigma_\ell EL_k EL_\ell \quad (13)$$

The relative default variance $\sigma^2$ is determined by Equation 13. The parameter $\sigma$ is now used for the gamma distribution in CreditRisk+ to calculate the portfolio loss distribution and the overall economic capital.

### An illustrative example

To illustrate the correct application of the formulas, we provide a very simple example, in Swiss francs. We choose two industry sectors, each with 1,000 obligors with identical exposures (net of recovery) and identical default probabilities per sector. The relative default variance is assumed to be $\sigma_k^2 = 0.75^2$ for both sectors. The detailed figures are shown in Table 1. Note that the major driver for the UL is the risk due to the systematic variation of the number of defaults, which contributes $0.75 \times EL = 30$ to the sector ULs.

If we consider the overall portfolio, we have to take the correlation of default events between the two industry sectors into account, which is assumed to be 50%. We get the results shown in Table 2.

**Table 1. Parameters for the two sectors of the sample portfolio**

| | Sector 1 | Sector 2 |
|---|---|---|
| Number of obligors | 1,000 | 1,000 |
| Exposure per obligor | 1 | 2 |
| Default probability $p_A$ (%) | 4 | 2 |
| Relative default variance | $0.75^2$ | $0.75^2$ |
| EL | 40 | 40 |
| $UL^2$ (see Equation 6) | 940 | 980 |
| UL | 30.7 | 31.3 |

**Table 2. Overall portfolio parameters**

| | Overall portfolio (sector 1 and 2) |
|---|---|
| Sector correlation (%) | 50 |
| Number of obligors | 2,000 |
| Relative default variance | $0.65^2$ |
| EL | 80 |
| $UL^2$ (see Equation 11) | 2,820 |
| UL | 53.1 |

If we neglect the correlation between the two sectors, the UL will be only 43.8 – about 20% smaller than with a correlation of 50%. Notice that a correlation of 50% between sectors is not unusually high, since it does not correspond to individual default events, but to the correlation on an aggregated level.

Given the UL of the overall portfolio, we obtain from Equation 13 the relative default variance of the combined portfolio $\sigma^2 = 0.65^2$. This compares with a relative default variance of $0.53^2$, if we assume independence of the two sectors, thus underestimating the risk in the overall portfolio. Using the calculated value for $\sigma$, we can now derive the complete loss distribution assuming a gamma-distributed number of default events in the economy, as done in CreditRisk+ (see Figure 1).

### Calculating risk contributions

Most banks are changing their approach to their loan business, moving from a buy-and-hold strategy towards active portfolio management. The credit risk of complete sectors is sold to investors or credit risk is taken over from other banks with

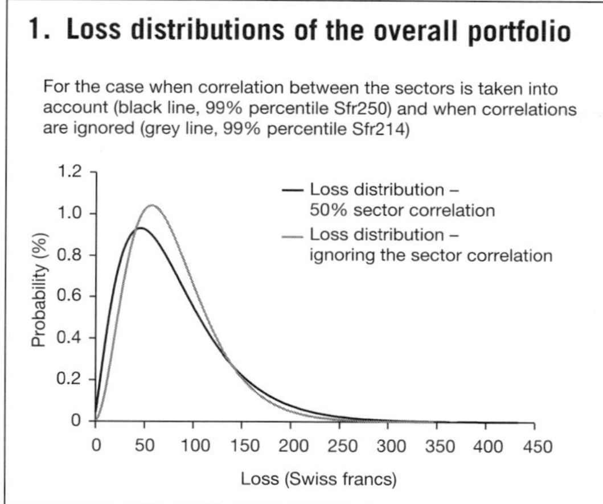


**1. Loss distributions of the overall portfolio**

For the case when correlation between the sectors is taken into account (black line, 99% percentile Sfr250) and when correlations are ignored (grey line, 99% percentile Sfr214)

the goal of diversifying existing portfolios. These transactions can only be valued correctly if their relationship to the existing portfolio is taken into account. The sector approach is an efficient and practical way of doing this - we need to know only the risk inherent in the sector to be transferred (stand-alone) and its correlation to the rest of the portfolio. Given this information, we can calculate the risk contributions of the sector to the overall portfolio risk, using the approach presented above. Therefore, the ability to take sector correlations into account when calculating risk contributions is a prerequisite for active portfolio management.

In general, the risk contribution of a single obligor A can be defined as follows:

$$RC_A = \nu_A \frac{\partial UL}{\partial \nu_A} = \frac{\nu_A}{2UL}\frac{\partial UL^2}{\partial \nu_A} \tag{14}$$

To clarify, $RC_A$ is the sensitivity of the portfolio UL with respect to changes of the exposure $\nu_A$ of obligor A times its exposure. The risk contributions of all obligors add up to the UL of the portfolio. Using the UL formula (Equation 11) developed above, by a straightforward calculation we obtain the following expression for the risk contribution of an obligor A in sector k:

$$RC_A = \frac{p_A \nu_A}{UL}\left[\sigma_k^2 EL_k + \sum_{\ell:\ell\neq k} Cor(\gamma_k,\gamma_\ell)\sigma_k\sigma_\ell EL_\ell + \nu_A\right] \tag{15}$$

Again, the first two terms in the bracket represent the systematic risk, incorporating sector default correlations, whereas the last term is due to the statistical nature of default. The risk contribution of a complete sector is obtained by adding up the risk contributions of all obligors in the sector.

## Summary

For active portfolio management, sector analysis is an important ingredient if one is to benefit from diversification.

The standard CreditRisk+ approach is based on independent industry sectors. To perform a sector analysis, the authors of CreditRisk+ propose apportioning the default probability per obligor to different independent industries. However, such an approach is difficult to realise in practice.

We have extended the sector approach to a framework that takes the correlations between sectors directly into account. The procedure is easy to implement, and allows one to calculate the unexpected loss, individual risk contributions and the loss distribution of the full portfolio.

## Appendix

Throughout our chapter, rather than dealing with probability distributions directly, we use probability generating functions instead. The reason is that generating functions are a compact way of representing discrete probability distributions, which also have some useful properties, namely (see, for example, Lindgren, 1968):

- the generating function of the sum of two independent random variables is the product of the generating functions of the individual variables; and
- the moments of the probability distribution can be expressed by the derivatives of the generating function.

As an illustration, we derive the covariance formula (Equation 10) in the two-industry case. In general, the probability generating function F(z, w) of a two-dimensional discrete distribution has the form:

$$F(z,w) = \sum_{m,n} p(m,n) z^m w^n$$

where p(m, n) denotes the probability of the state (m, n). It is easy to check that the covariance can be expressed by:

$$Cov_{1,2} = \left(\frac{\partial^2 F}{\partial z \partial w} - \frac{\partial F}{\partial z}\frac{\partial F}{\partial w}\right)(1,1)$$

We now calculate the mixed derivative for our specific generating function F(z, w) from Equation 8. This implies:

$$\begin{aligned}\frac{\partial^2 F}{\partial z \partial w}(1,1) &= \int_0^\infty\int_0^\infty \frac{\partial^2 G^{(\gamma_1,\gamma_2)}}{\partial z \partial w}(1,1) g(\gamma_1,\gamma_2) d\gamma_1 d\gamma_2 \\ &= P_1'(1) P_2'(1) E(\gamma_1,\gamma_2)\end{aligned}$$

where we have used:

$$\frac{\partial^2 G^{(\gamma_1,\gamma_2)}}{\partial z \partial w}(z,w) = \gamma_1 P_1'(z)\gamma_2 P_2'(w) G^{(\gamma_1,\gamma_2)}(z,w)$$

In a similar way, one can show that:

$$\frac{\partial F}{\partial z}(1,1) = P_1'(1)E(\gamma_1)$$

and:

$$\frac{\partial F}{\partial w}(1,1) = P_2'(1)E(\gamma_2)$$

Altogether, we obtain:

$$\begin{aligned}\mathrm{Cov}_{1,2} &= P_1'(1)P_2'(1)(E(\gamma_1,\gamma_2) - E(\gamma_1)E(\gamma_2)) \\ &= P_1'(1)P_2'(1)\mathrm{Cov}(\gamma_1,\gamma_2)\end{aligned}$$

**BIBLIOGRAPHY**

**Bühlmann, H.,** 1970, *Mathematical Methods in Risk Theory* (Springer Verlag).

**Credit Suisse Financial Products,** 1997, *CreditRisk+, A Credit Risk Management Framework*.

**Gupton, G., C. Finger and M. Bhatia,** 1997, *CreditMetrics Technical Document*, Morgan Guaranty Trust Company.

**Koyluoglu, H., and A. Hickman,** 1998, "Reconcilable Differences", *Risk*, October, pp. 56–62.

**Lindgren, B.,** 1968, *Statistical Theory* (New York: The Macmillan Company).

**McKinsey & Company,** 1998, *Credit Portfolio View*.

**Merton, R.,** 1974, "On the Pricing of Corporate Debt: The Risk Structure of Interest Rates", *Journal of Finance*, 29, pp. 449–70.

19

# Taking to the Saddle

**Richard Martin, Kevin Thompson and Christopher Browne**

BNP Paribas; DrKW

*Portfolio modelling and management usually rely on simulation techniques. In the first of a series of chapters, Richard Martin, Kevin Thompson and Christopher Browne take portfolio modelling a step further, proposing an analytical technique to construct the loss distribution of correlated events and exploring the insights that it brings.*

The rapid and accurate construction of the loss distribution, and with it the calculation of value-at-risk, is at the heart of modern portfolio and capital management. In a previous article (Arvanitis *et al.*, 1998), two of the authors of this chapter introduced the saddlepoint method for constructing a fast and accurate analytical approximation to the tail of the loss distribution for a portfolio of assets that have credit default risk. Other applications of the technique have been suggested in catastrophe, operational and insurance risk. Some rather restrictive assumptions were made in that chapter, the most restrictive of which was that default events were assumed to be independent. In this chapter, we describe the technique in more depth and show how to extend it using a general procedure for modelling dependent events. The saddlepoint method is based on the construction of the moment generating function (MGF), which is an ideal tool for analysing the distribution of sums of individual losses, and the way we model correlation allows the MGF to be calculated easily.

In later chapters, we will show how to obtain the risk contributions in a portfolio and how to optimise return-on-VAR without recourse to Monte Carlo simulation. We will also consider the analysis of counterparty risk in derivatives deals where, because of market risk, the exposures are stochastic.

It is worth briefly comparing this method with another method for analysing the tails of distributions – extreme value theory (EVT). EVT is primarily concerned with the distributions of sample maxima (or other order statistics) and also finds application in fitting the tail of a distribution to observed data. On the other hand, the problem we are considering here is primarily one of sums of random variables, for which MGF-based methods are more appropriate. The theory that we shall develop gives considerably stronger results than EVT and allows one to go from a model to a loss distribution (and subsequent analysis) without the need for simulation, thereby removing a layer of uncertainty from the process.

*A longer version of this chapter is available on request.*

## MGFs and the saddlepoint method

MOMENT GENERATING FUNCTIONS

When constructing a portfolio loss distribution, one wants to evaluate the probability density function (PDF) of a sum of random variables. The PDF of a sum of independent random variables is equal to the convolution of the respective PDFs of the individual asset loss distributions. The evaluation of this convolution is a difficult problem analytically, is computationally very intensive and in full generality is impractical for any realistically sized portfolio. We shall describe some machinery that allows the distribution to be approximated with considerably less effort using MGFs.

The MGF of a random variable $X$ with density $f_X$ is an analytic function of the complex variable $s$, given by:

$$M_X(s) = \mathbf{E}[e^{sX}] = \int e^{st} f_X(t)dt \qquad (1)$$

provided that the integral exists. If the density of $X$ decays sufficiently rapidly in the tails (eg, if $X$ is normal or bounded, though neither condition is necessary), then $M_X(s)$ is defined for all $s$.

The relationship shown in Equation 1 can be inverted:

$$f_X(t) = \frac{1}{2\pi i}\int_{-i\infty}^{+i\infty} e^{-st} M_X(s)\,ds \tag{2}$$

in which the path of integration is up the imaginary axis.

The MGF of a sum of independent random variables ($Y = \Sigma_j a_j X_j$) is simply the product of the MGFs of the respective random variables:

$$M_Y(s) = \prod_j M_{X_j}(a_j s) \tag{3}$$

As an example, a portfolio that consists of $n$ assets, with default probabilities $p_j$ and losses-given-default $a_j$, can be modelled as a sum of $n$ binary variables. The MGF of the portfolio loss $Y$ is then given by:

$$M_Y(s) = \prod_{j=1}^{n} (1 - p_j + p_j \exp(a_j s)) \tag{4}$$

We can include the effect of uncertain recovery rates by making the jth loss follow a Gaussian distribution of mean $a_j$ and variance $\sigma_j^2$, by replacing $\exp(a_j s)$ with $\exp(a_j s + \frac{1}{2}\sigma_j^2 s^2)$. Note also that the default probabilities or exposures need not be identical.[1] We now wish to use the inversion formula in Equation 2 to find the PDF of $Y$, ie, the PDF of the portfolio loss. In principle, we could discretise and truncate Equation 2, which is a Fourier integral, and use the fast Fourier transform algorithm. One does have to be very careful about truncation and discretisation of Fourier integrals, however, as it is easy to introduce artefacts (see Press *et al.*, 1992, for a fuller discussion). Alternatively, we can approximate the integral using the saddlepoint method. We introduce the method next and discuss its accuracy later on.

## SADDLEPOINT METHOD

It is convenient to define the cumulant generating function $K_Y(s) = \log M_Y(s)$, so that Equation 2 becomes:

$$f_Y(t) = \frac{1}{2\pi i}\int_{-i\infty}^{+i\infty} \exp(K_Y(s) - st)\,ds \tag{5}$$

The saddlepoint approximation (see, eg, Daniels, 1987 and Jensen, 1995) consists of finding the saddlepoint(s) – points at which the term in the exponential is stationary – and then Taylor-expanding as far as a quadratic and doing the resulting Gaussian integral. The saddlepoint is $s = \hat{t}$, obeying:

$$K_Y'(\hat{t}) = t \tag{6}$$

in which the prime denotes differentiation with respect to $s$. Since $K_Y$ is convex, there is a unique saddlepoint $\hat{t}$ on the real axis, for each point $t$ "in" the distribution of $Y$.[2] When $t = \mathbf{E}[Y]$, the saddlepoint is at the origin ($\hat{t} = 0$). If $Y$ is bounded, then as $t \to \min(Y)$, $\hat{t} \to -\infty$, and as $t \to \max(Y)$, $\hat{t} \to +\infty$. The correspondence see in Equation 6 is extremely important because it enables us to relate a quantile $t$ of the distribution (or a part of the distribution near it) to $K_Y$ evaluated at $\hat{t}$ (or a part of the complex plane near it). We show that it is this correspondence that, among other things, gives the analytical expression for the portfolio VAR. In a later chapter, we will show that the sensitivity of the VAR to asset allocation can also be obtained.

To obtain the saddlepoint approximation to the portfolio PDF, we perform a Taylor expansion on $K_Y(s) - st$, as far as the quadratic term, and calculate the resulting Gaussian integral:

$$f_Y(t) \approx \frac{\exp(K_Y(\hat{t}) - t\hat{t})}{2\pi i}\int_{-i\infty}^{+i\infty} \exp\left(\tfrac{1}{2}(s-\hat{t})^2 K_Y''(\hat{t})\right) ds = \frac{\exp(K_Y(\hat{t}) - t\hat{t})}{\sqrt{2\pi K_Y''(\hat{t})}} \tag{7}$$

The tail probability can also be written as a contour integral involving the MGF:

$$\begin{aligned} P(Y > t) &= \frac{1}{2\pi i}\int_{-i\infty,(0+)}^{+i\infty} \frac{\exp(K_Y(s) - st)}{s}\,ds \\ &\approx \frac{\exp(K_Y(\hat{t}) - t\hat{t})}{2\pi i}\int_{-i\infty,(0+)}^{+i\infty} \frac{\exp\left(\frac{1}{2}(s-t)^2 K_Y''(\hat{t})\right)}{s}\,ds \\ &= \begin{cases} \exp\left(K_Y(\hat{t}) - t\hat{t} + \frac{1}{2}\hat{t}^2 K_Y''(\hat{t})\right)\Phi\left(-\sqrt{\hat{t}^2 K_Y''(\hat{t})}\right) & (t > \mathbf{E}[Y]) \\ \frac{1}{2} & (t = \mathbf{E}[Y]) \\ 1 - \exp\left(K_Y(\hat{t}) - t\hat{t} + \frac{1}{2}\hat{t}^2 K_Y''(\hat{t})\right)\Phi\left(-\sqrt{\hat{t}^2 K_Y''(\hat{t})}\right) & (t < \mathbf{E}[Y]) \end{cases} \\ &\equiv \tilde{\mathbf{P}}(Y > t) \text{ say} \end{aligned} \tag{8}$$

with $\Phi$ denoting the cumulative normal distribution function. The notation $(0+)$ indicates that the contour runs to the right of the origin in order to avoid the pole there. These are the lowest-order expressions; higher-order approximations can be derived (Daniels, 1987). In Equation 8, we have distinguished the cases $t > \mathbf{E}[Y]$ and $t < \mathbf{E}[Y]$, because in the latter the saddlepoint is on the left of the origin and the contour has to be pulled over the pole at the origin (giving rise to a change of sign and a contribution of one to the result). Other quantities such as the expected shortfall can be dealt with similarly.

Provided that one can calculate $K_Y(s)$, $K_Y'(s)$, $K_Y''(s)$ for any value of $s$, it is quite easy to use the saddlepoint method in practice. For example, to calculate the saddlepoint VAR, ie, the value $t$ such that $\tilde{\mathbf{P}}(Y > t) = p$, for a given probability $p$, we use

Equation 8 with t replaced by $K'_Y(\hat{t})$ (as per Equation 6) and adjust $\hat{t}$ until the right-hand side of Equation 8 becomes equal to p. This is a straightforward root-finding problem. Later, when we introduce correlation, we shall choose a model structure that allows rapid calculation of $K_Y(s)$, $K'_Y(s)$, $K''_Y(s)$.

There may or may not be other saddlepoints off the real axis. The reason that the contribution from the principal saddlepoint, on the real axis, is the most important is that it gives the "envelope" of the distribution. When the true distribution is discrete, the saddlepoint approximation gives a smoothed-out version that, far from being inconvenient, is generally helpful in VAR calculations.

### EXAMPLE 1: SADDLEPOINT METHOD FOR INDEPENDENT EVENTS

Figure 1a shows the loss exceedance curve (VAR against tail probability) for portfolios of 20 and 2,000 assets each of unit exposure, zero recovery rate and default probability 0.36%, which (for a one-year horizon) roughly corresponds to Moody's Investors Service's Baa3 rating. Default events are assumed to be independent. In this example, the true loss distributions, taken to be Poisson distributed with means 0.072, 7.2 respectively, are compared with the saddlepoint approximation and normal approximation for each portfolio. For the larger portfolio, the saddlepoint approximation is uniformly valid; it is known that for large numbers of independent random variables that the saddlepoint approximation is a uniform asymptotic approximator (Daniels, 1987), which (loosely) means that the whole distribution is approximated well. For the smaller portfolio, the main source of error arises from trying to approximate a discrete distribution with a continuous one. The saddlepoint approximation does, however, make a reasonable attempt to smooth out the "steps". In practice, of course, such steps would not occur. Even if all the exposures were identical, the presence of stochastic recovery rates would smooth the loss distribution in much the same way that the saddlepoint approximation has done. The resulting distribution would look very similar to the saddlepoint approximation shown in Figure 1a, except for small losses (the density has a delta-function at the origin, and this would not be smoothed). The "stepping" effect also diminishes when the exposures are made unequal, because different combinations of defaulting counterparties then produce different losses. Figure 1b shows the results for the same portfolios, but with fixed unequal exposures, selected randomly from a gamma distribution with mean one and standard deviation 0.5. In this case, the true distribution cannot be found by another analytical technique, so Monte Carlo simulation was used to assess the accuracy of the saddlepoint approximation. A million simulations were taken. Again, the approximation is excellent for the large portfolio. For the smaller one, it works very well for a tail probability of ~0.03 or less. As a final point, note how bad the normal approximation is, particularly on the small portfolios.

### ACCURACY OF THE SADDLEPOINT METHOD

We have seen that the saddlepoint method works well. In this section, we want to give some indication of why this is. We can start by observing that the saddlepoint method is exact if the true distribution is normal, because in that case $K_Y(s) = E[Y]s + \frac{1}{2}V[Y]s^2$ and nothing is lost in the quadratic approximation inherent in the saddlepoint method. But the saddlepoint technique also performs well when the loss distribution diverges significantly from the normal distribution.

To demonstrate this, we presented (in Arvanitis *et al.*, 1998) results for the analytical approximation for a very skewed loss distribution, generated by a portfolio of 50 independent loans with unit exposure and a default probability of 1%. The saddlepoint approximation gave accurate VAR

**1. Independent default events: true v. saddlepoint approximation**

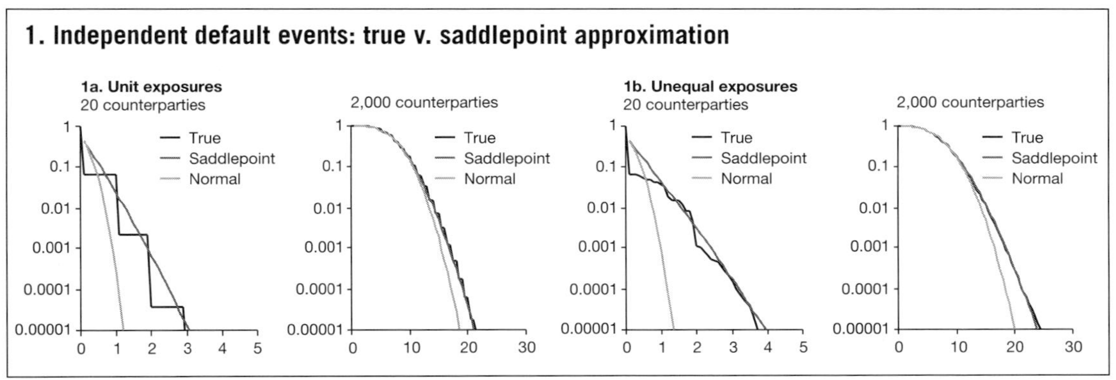

estimates (only a few per cent out). The Edgeworth correction to the central limit theorem was also considered, but it performed poorly, giving a negative PDF in places and not approximating the tail very well, mainly because the normal approximation is so far out to start with. Daniels (1987) gives a fuller discussion of the Edgeworth expansion.

Here is another view of the accuracy of the saddlepoint technique. A sum of independent losses of equal, small probability and unit size has a Poisson distribution: the probability of the loss being $t$ is $e^{-\mu}\mu^t/t!$ where $\mu$ is the mean. The MGF of the total loss $Y$ is $M_Y(s) = \exp(\mu(e^s - 1))$. Performing saddlepoint approximation, we find $\hat{t} = \ln(t/\mu)$ and obtain:

$$p_Y(t) \approx \frac{e^{-\mu}\mu^t}{\sqrt{2\pi t}\,(t/e)^t} \tag{9}$$

The denominator of this expression is Stirling's approximation to $t!$, which is asymptotic for large $t$ and remarkably good even for small $t$ (it gives 0.92, 1.92, 5.84, 23.5 for 1!, 2!, 3!, 4!). As $t$ becomes large, we move into the tail of the distribution, and the accuracy is even better. Jensen (1995) discusses this and gives other examples of what he calls the "marvellous" accuracy of saddlepoint approximations.

These theoretical arguments, and the practical effectiveness of the saddlepoint method, justify its use as a "black box" instead of (or alongside) Monte Carlo simulation in problems where the exposures and/or default probabilities are unequal and where independence is no longer assumed – for such portfolios the loss distribution is not a simple binomial or Poisson and the exact calculation is very difficult.

## Extension to correlated variables

When dependent random variables are added, it is no longer correct to multiply together their MGFs. However, certain correlation models allow the MGF of the sum of dependent variables to be calculated reasonably easily and others do not. Two major approaches to modelling correlation have emerged. These are the structural (Merton, 1974) model, used in the KMV and CreditMetrics systems, and the reduced-form model, to which the following approach is more closely related. Crouhy, Galai and Mark (2000) give a good overview of the current models. But before discussing these approaches we will mention the model that we are going to treat in this chapter.

DISCRETE LATENT VARIABLE MODEL

We assume that default events are independent conditionally on a latent or explanatory variable $W$, say, that has a discrete distribution.[3] The values that $W$ takes are not important and so they may as well be numbered 1, 2, .... As a simple example, we might have the model given in Table 1.

The variable $W$ cannot be observed. Default events become independent because when one asset defaults it is more likely that $W = 3, 4$ (high default rates) and less likely that $W = 1, 2$ (low default rates), and so other assets are more likely to default. One attractive aspect of this type of model is that it is clear what is being assumed about the probability and severity of clusters of default events. In particular, from Table 1 we see (by considering $W = 4$) that, one year in 10, on average, a portfolio of 100 Baa3 counterparties will suffer, on average, two defaults. Another attractive aspect is that the existing popular credit risk models can be approximated in this framework. Crouhy, Galai and Mark (2000) discuss their underlying similarity and we push the discussion further in a companion paper (Martin, Thompson and Browne, 2001). But most important from the point of view of this chapter is the fact that the MGF of the portfolio loss can be calculated in closed form, as we now show.

Let $Y = \Sigma_j a_j X_j$ in which $(X_j)$ are independent conditionally on a discretely distributed latent variable $W$. If $W$ takes value $k$ with probability $h_k$, and we write $M_Y(s|k)$ for $E[e^{sY}|W = k]$, then:

$$\begin{aligned} M_Y(s) &= \sum_k h_k M_Y(s|k) = \sum_k h_k \prod_j M_{X_j}(a_j s|k) \\ &= \sum_k h_k \prod_j (1 - p_{jk} + p_{jk}\exp(a_j s)) \end{aligned} \tag{10}$$

where $p_{jk}$ is the probability of the $j$th obligor defaulting, given that $W = k$. (Note that if $W$ had a continuous distribution then the $k$-summation would be an integral.) So the MGF is a weighted average of products of the individual MGFs. This and its first two derivatives are easily calculated in

**Table 1. Simple conditional independence model of default rates**

| W | 1 (%) | 2 (%) | 3 (%) | 4 (%) |
|---|---|---|---|---|
| State probability | 20 | 40 | 30 | 10 |
| Baa3 default rate | 0.0 | 0.1 | 0.4 | 2.0 |

The mean default rate is 0.36%, and the standard deviation 0.57%.

**2. Conditional independence tree**

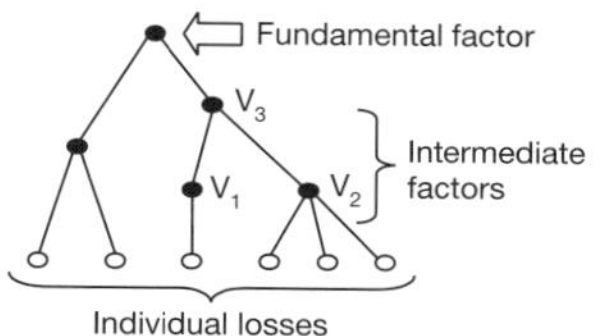


White circles represent individual loss variables, black circles are explanatory variables. $V_1$ and $V_2$ are conditionally independent given $V_3$. The MGF of the total loss can be calculated recursively.

closed form, so $K_Y(s) = \log M_Y(s)$ and its first two derivatives can be calculated too. This is all we need.

This correlation model can be extended to more complex networks, such as the one shown in Figure 2 in which the variables are represented as nodes connected by edges. Two variables $V_1$ and $V_2$ are independent conditionally on a third variable, $V_3$, if cutting all edges that join $V_3$ removes all paths between $V_1$ and $V_2$. This is the basis of graphical modelling (Edwards, 1995). An important special case, which we treat here, is when the network is a tree (which means that there is at most one path between any two nodes), the extremities correspond to individual losses and one wishes to find the distribution of the total loss. Monte Carlo simulation is very straightforward. Starting at the top of the figure, we choose at random the state of that variable, and conditional on it we choose at random the state of each variable to which it is connected (their distributions will depend on the state of the first variable). This is continued recursively until we end up at the extremities of the tree, which are the individual loss variables, whereupon the losses are added up. The procedure is then repeated many times. Also, we can calculate the MGF of the total loss. By conditioning on the variable at the top of the figure, we split the figure into two components that are statistically independent (so their MGFs are multiplied). To calculate the unconditional MGF, we calculate the conditional MGFs and take a weighted average. This can all be done recursively and at high speed.[4]

BRIEF DISCUSSION OF OTHER MODELS[5]

The well-known Merton (1974) model assumes default to be generated by the asset returns of a company falling below its liabilities (for further details, refer to CreditMetrics Monitor). By assuming that, after logarithmic and scaling transformations, the joint distribution of asset returns $(Z_j)_{j=1}^n$ is multivariate standard normal (and hence uniquely determined by its correlation matrix $\Gamma$), one arrives at a joint distribution of default events $(X_j)_{j=1}^n$ that is uniquely determined by the marginal default probabilities and $\Gamma$. The MGF of the total loss $Y = \Sigma_j a_j X_j$ is

$$M_Y(s) = \int \ldots \int \exp\left(\sum_{j=1}^{n} 1\left[\Phi(z_j) < p_j\right] a_j s\right) \frac{\exp\left(-\frac{1}{2} z^T \Gamma^{-1} z\right)}{\sqrt{(2\pi)^n \det \Gamma}} dz_1 \ldots dz_n \tag{11}$$

in which 1[] denotes the indicator function. In general, this requires a multidimensional integral to be evaluated – a hopeless task on a large portfolio. However, if the correlation matrix is such that the correlation can be explained by a single factor, and each asset return $Z_i$ written as the sum of a correlated part $V$ and an uncorrelated part, then Equation 11 can be reduced to a single integral over $V$. This integral can then be discretised by Gaussian quadrature, and we end up with the discrete latent variable model.

Reduced-form models treat default events themselves as a stochastic process and seek to model its statistical properties. In McKinsey's CreditPortfolioView, it is supposed that there exist normally distributed econometric risk factors and that the default rate is obtained from a weighted sum of these by a simple transformation. By discretising the distribution of the risk factors, we obtain the discrete latent variable model. In Credit Suisse Financial Products' CreditRisk+, the risk factors are assumed, for reasons of analytical tractability, to follow independent gamma distributions, and the portfolio loss distribution conditional on these is approximated as a Poisson. This is seen to be a rather similar approach to CreditPortfolioView, the main differences being the calculation, which does not require Monte Carlo simulation, and the fact that no econometric interpretation need be given for the risk factors. Again, discretisation of the risk factors gives us the discrete latent variable model. Finally, we can also examine observed instances of default over a period of some years and cluster them into regimes of low, medium and high default rate (we can have as many regimes as are necessary to give an acceptable fit to the data). By doing so, we are in essence saying that the default rate is a latent random variable with a discrete distribution.

EXAMPLE 2: SADDLEPOINT METHOD FOR DEPENDENT EVENTS

We revisit the two portfolios considered in Example 1, this time introducing correlation using the model of Table 1. Note that the average default rate remains at 0.36%, so the introduction of correlation has no effect on the expected loss. Figures 3a and 3b show the results for portfolios

**3. Dependent default events: true v. saddlepoint approximation**

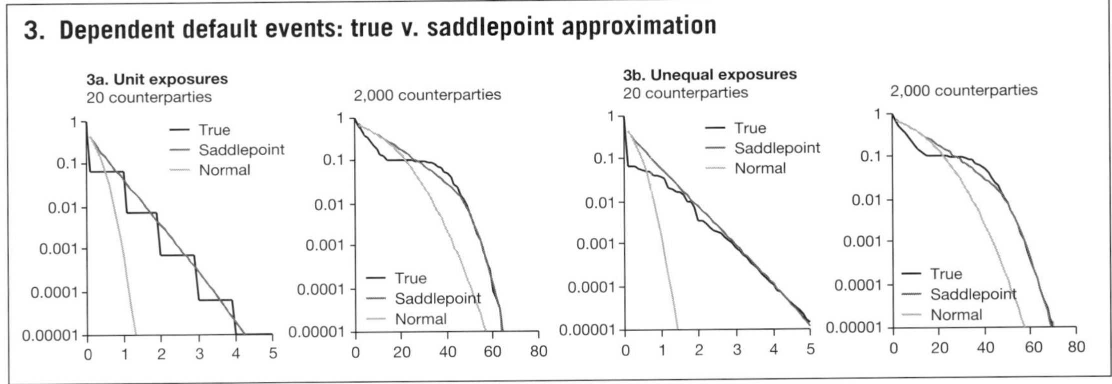


of size 20 and 2,000, and of equal and unequal exposures. Again, the saddlepoint approximation performs well in the tail, and most of the remarks that we made for Example 1 apply here. The only new matter is that for the large portfolio of correlated events, the saddlepoint approximation works well in the tail but not near the origin (whereas for the independent case it worked well everywhere). This is because the convergence property of the saddlepoint method, which gives uniform asymptotic approximation in the limit of large portfolio size, no longer holds if we relax the assumption of independence. In fact, the limiting distribution is a Gaussian mixture model rather than a simple Gaussian.

It is interesting to examine the effect of correlation on the VAR at, for example, 99.97% confidence. Consider the portfolios of unequal exposures (Figures 1b and 3b) with and without correlation. When correlation is introduced, the VAR of the 20-asset portfolio increases by 25% from 2.8 to 3.5, whereas the VAR of the 2,000-asset portfolio increases by a factor of three, from 20 to 61. This is expected: a large or well-diversified portfolio will be more sensitive to an overall increase in correlation than a small or poorly diversified one. Finally, notice that the normal approximation is even worse than it was for independent loss events.

## Conclusions

The saddlepoint method allows us to go from a model of loss events to a portfolio loss distribution without the need for Monte Carlo simulation. In our test examples, we have shown that it accurately approximates the tail, but note that on very badly diversified portfolios, when one exposure greatly exceeds the others, the accuracy is not as good. In later chapters, the saddlepoint method will bring further analytical insights into portfolio management, allowing risk contributions and the efficient frontier to be calculated analytically.

1 *We do not need to work on Equation 4 to make it tidier. It is interesting to compare this with the CreditRisk+ methodology: at this stage we diverge because we work with Equation 4 directly, whereas CreditRisk+ makes a Poisson approximation and "buckets" the exposures to keep the distribution discrete, performing the convolution directly.*

2 *See the discussion on the Legendre-Fenchel transform in Jensen (1995), and related discussion on large deviation theory.*

3 *This approach has been considered in the CreditMetrics literature (Nagpal and Bahar, 1999), but the full benefits of it do not seem to have been appreciated.*

4 *For our example, a fast PC can run 1 million simulations on a portfolio of 20 assets in about five seconds. A portfolio of 2,000 assets takes about 10 minutes. Note that the operation count is directly proportional to portfolio size. This compares extremely favourably with other proprietary and commercial models. Of course, the saddlepoint approximation is computed in a fraction of a second.*

5 *The issues in this section are discussed more fully in the cited companion paper.*

**BIBLIOGRAPHY**

**Arvanitis, A., C. Browne, J. Gregory and R. Martin,** 1998, "A Credit Risk Toolbox", *Risk*, December, pp. 50–5.

**Crouhy, M., D. Galai and R. Mark,** 2000, "A Comparative Analysis of Current Credit Risk Models", *Journal of Banking and Finance*, 24, pp. 59–117.

**Daniels, H.,** 1987, "Tail Probability Approximations", *International Statistical Review*, 55, pp. 37–48.

**Edwards, D.,** 1995, *Introduction to Graphical Modelling* (Springer).

**Jensen, J.**, 1995, *Saddlepoint Approximations* (Oxford University Press).

**Martin, R., K. Thompson and C. Browne,** 2001, "How Dependent are Defaults?", *Risk*, July, pp. 87–90.

**Merton, R.,** 1974, "On the Pricing of Corporate Debt: The Risk Structure of Interest Rates", *Journal of Finance*, 29, pp. 449–70.

**Nagpal, K., and R. Bahar,** 1999, "An Analytical Approach for Credit Risk Analysis Under Correlated Defaults", *CreditMetrics Monitor*, April, pp. 51–74.

**Press, W., S. Teukolsky, W. Vetterling and B. Flannery,** 1992, *Numerical Recipes in C: The Art of Scientific Computing*, Second Edition (Cambridge University Press).

20

# Calculating Portfolio Loss

**Sandro Merino and Mark Nyfeler**

UBS

*For credit portfolios, analytical methods work best for tail risk, while Monte Carlo is used to model expected loss. However, products such as CDOs require a model for the entire distribution. Sandro Merino and Mark Nyfeler meet the challenge by combining fast Fourier transforms and Monte Carlo within the conditional independence framework.*

The credit risk models developed by KMV (PortfolioManager), JP Morgan (CreditMetrics), McKinsey (CreditPortfolioView) and Credit Suisse Financial Products (CreditRisk+) are widely considered as industry benchmarks. Hickman and Koyluoglu (1998) and Gordy (2000) have shown that these models are mathematically very similar and share a so-called conditional-independence framework.

For general portfolios, the saddlepoint approximation has been shown to provide an extremely efficient and accurate approach to determine the tail of loss distributions (Martin, Thompson and Browne, 2001) within the conditional-independence framework. However, if information on both the body and the tail matters (as is the case in the application to collateralised debt obligations (CDOs)), then the saddlepoint approximation cannot be applied since in general it fails to produce accurate results for the distribution's body (see Table 3).

The algorithm we describe in this chapter combines techniques from numerical mathematics and actuarial science. We have implemented the algorithm in a mathematical software package and are able to compute the loss distribution of credit portfolios containing 500,000 counterparties within four hours with adequate accuracy (on a standard personal computer). We find that it is not necessary to either simplify the credit risk model or the portfolio structure to calculate the body and the tail of the portfolio loss distribution. The algorithm turns out to be particularly useful for analysing and designing CDO structures.

*The authors thank Daniel Lehner, Michael März, Andrea Schaerli, Jean-Marc Schneider, Banu Simmons-Sueer and Frithjof Weber for their valuable contributions during the conception and implementation of the technique presented here. They would also like to thank two anonymous referees for their suggestions and professor Hans Rudolf Künsch at ETH Zurich for a helpful discussion.*

## Modelling default rates

For a portfolio of m counterparties, we consider for any obligor i the volatility of the corresponding, underlying default rate (probability) $Q_i$, which stands for the probability of default over a short period of time (eg, one year). The most common approach for modelling default rates is to assume that these rates are influenced by a (typically) small set of latent variables $(W_1,\ldots, W_p)$ that are common to all obligors. These latent variables represent systematic risk factors. We write:

$$Q_i = f_i(\mathbf{W}), \quad \mathbf{W} = (W_1,\ldots,W_p) \sim F \qquad (1)$$

for some functions $f_i$ and some distribution function F. Large loan portfolios are typically segmented into groups of obligors that are assumed to respond equally to the latent variables (ie, they share the same function $f_i$).

*Example 1*

The default rate volatility model of CreditRisk+ is given by:

$$Q_i = \bar{q}_i \sum_{j=1}^{p} a_{ij} W_j \qquad (2)$$

where $(W_j)_j$ are independent Gamma$(1, \sigma_j^2)$ distributed, $\sum_{j=1}^{p} a_{ij} = 1$, $a_{ij} \geq 0$ for all i, j. Here $\bar{q}_i$ denotes the expected default frequency of obligor i.

In applications and examples, we will always assume that the expected default frequency $\bar{q}_i$ is known for all counterparties, eg, inferred from a rating process.

*Example 2*
Credit risk models based on the Merton approach (such as KMV or CreditMetrics) model the asset-returns $(X_i)_i$ of companies by a (standard) multivariate normal distribution. Default occurs if the corresponding return falls below a certain threshold. Parameter estimation is done by calibrating a factor model:

$$X_i = \sum_{j=1}^{p} a_{ij} W_j + \sigma_i \varepsilon_i \quad (3)$$

Here $\mathbf{W}$ is assumed to be multivariate (standard) normal and $(\varepsilon_i)_i$ represents independent, firm-specific normally distributed risk. Since $\bar{q}_i$ is assumed to be known, the asset-return factor model can be written as a default rate volatility model:

$$Q_i = \Phi\left(\frac{\Phi^{-1}(\bar{q}_i) - \sum_{j=1}^{p} a_{ij} W_j}{\sigma_i}\right) \quad (4)$$

where $\Phi$ denotes the standard normal cumulative distribution function.

## Modelling credit risk

When analysing the credit risk of a bond or loan portfolio, the total losses over a fixed time period are often modelled as a random variable:

$$L := \sum_{i=1}^{m} Y_i S_i l_i \quad (5)$$

where $Y_i$ stands for the default indicator, $S_i$ for the loss severity and $l_i$ for the exposure to the ith counterparty. The variable $Y_i$ takes the value one with probability $\bar{q}_i$ and the value zero with probability $1 - \bar{q}_i$. We will always assume the exposures $l_i$ to be constant, and we set all severities equal to one to keep the notation simple. Furthermore, all exposures are assumed to be integer, which amounts to expressing exposures in terms of integer multiples of a predefined base unit of loss (eg, US$1 million).

The conditional-independence framework assumes that, given the state of the latent variables $\mathbf{W}$ (representing systematic risk), the indicator variables $Y_i$ are independent, ie, $(Y_i|\mathbf{W})_i$ independent. This means that the remaining risk, given the systematic part, is considered as purely idiosyncratic (obligor-specific). Consequently, we can define a credit model based on a conditional-independence framework as:

$$Q_i = f_i(\mathbf{W}), \quad \mathbf{W} \sim F \quad (6)$$

$$\left(Y_i|W\right)_i \sim \text{Bernoulli}(Q_i), \text{independent} \quad (7)$$

$$L = \sum_{i=1}^{m} Y_i l_i (\in \mathbb{N}_0) \quad (8)$$

We will now turn to the task of deriving the probability density $\mathbf{p}^L$ of the loss variable L, given in terms of $p_n^L = P[L = n]$ for $n = 0, 1, \ldots$, up to the level $n = N$.

## A general representation of the portfolio loss distribution

The unconditional probability $P[L = n]$ can be obtained from the conditional probabilities by integration with respect to the distribution of $\mathbf{W}$:[1]

$$P[L = n] = \int_{\mathbb{R}^p} P\left[L = n \middle| \mathbf{W} = \mathbf{w}\right] dF(\mathbf{w}) \quad (9)$$

Furthermore, the conditional-independence property of the default indicators $(Y_i)_i$ allows for a closed-form solution for the integrand. By definition of the model, we have $L|\mathbf{W} = \Sigma_{i=1}^{m}(Y_i l_i|\mathbf{W})$, a sum of independent random variables. By elementary probability theory, it follows that the distribution of $(L|\mathbf{W} = \mathbf{w})$ is equal to the convolution of the distributions of $(Y_i l_i|\mathbf{W} = \mathbf{w})_i$. Or in mathematical terms:

$$\mathbf{p}^{L|\mathbf{W}=\mathbf{w}} = \left(\bigotimes_{i=1}^{m} \mathbf{p}^{Y_i l_i|\mathbf{W}=\mathbf{w}}\right) \quad (10)$$

where $\mathbf{x} \otimes \mathbf{y}$ denotes the convolution of two discrete densities $\mathbf{x}$, $\mathbf{y}$.[2] Rewriting Equation 9 in vector notation yields:

$$\mathbf{p}^L = \int_{\mathbb{R}^p} \left(\bigotimes_{i=1}^{m} \mathbf{p}^{Y_i l_i|\mathbf{W}=\mathbf{w}}\right) dF(\mathbf{w}) \quad (11)$$

As a consequence, deriving the portfolio loss density reduces to:

- ❑ Analytical derivation of the integrand (given in Equation 10).
- ❑ Numerical integration of the integrand in p-dimensions (as in Equation 11).

To reduce the computational burden for the convolutions and the p-dimensional integration, the application of the following techniques from numerical and actuarial mathematics is essential: Poisson approximation; fast Fourier transform; and numerical integration using quasi-Monte Carlo methods.

## Numerical computation of the portfolio loss distribution

We will explain how the above-mentioned techniques can be applied to obtain an efficient numerical algorithm for evaluating the general formula seen in Equation 11.

### EVALUATING THE INTEGRAND $p^{L|W=w}$

A solution for fast and efficient evaluation of the integrand in Equation 10 is obtained by making use of the Poisson approximation. That is, we assume the indicators $(Y_i|\mathbf{W})_i$ to be Poisson distributed with parameter $f_i(\mathbf{W})$ rather than Bernoulli distributed. This is a standard technique in actuarial science and provides a very accurate approximation for small probabilities, as is indeed the case for default probabilities in typical loan portfolios.

As a consequence of the Poisson approximation, it becomes convenient to group counterparties with equal exposures into exposure buckets. Obligors in the same exposure bucket are identified by the indexes $B_j := \{i \mid l_i = \bar{l}_j\}$ for some $\bar{l}_j$, $j = 1,\ldots, v$. We denote by $L_j$ the loss variable of the sub-portfolio generated by bucket $B_j$. Then we can rewrite the conditional portfolio loss variable as a sum of the v exposure buckets:

$$L|\mathbf{W} = \sum_{j=1}^{v}\left(\bar{l}_j \sum_{i\in B_j}\left(Y_i|\mathbf{W}\right)\right) = \sum_{j=1}^{v}\left(L_j|\mathbf{W}\right) \qquad (12)$$

Note that the conditional loss variables $(L_j|\mathbf{W})_j$ are independent. Since the sum of independent Poisson random variables is still Poisson distributed it follows immediately that:

$$\sum_{i\in B_j}\left(Y_i|\mathbf{W}=\mathbf{w}\right) \sim \text{Poisson}(\lambda_j(\mathbf{w})), \quad \lambda_j(\mathbf{w}) := \sum_{i\in B_j} f_i(\mathbf{w}) \quad (13)$$

Consequently, the conditional probability density of a sub-portfolio $B_j$ is easily calculated by:

$$P\left[L_j = k|\mathbf{W}=\mathbf{w}\right] = \begin{cases} \dfrac{\lambda_j(\mathbf{w})^n}{n!}\exp(-\lambda_j(\mathbf{w})) & \text{if } k = n\bar{l}_j, n\in\mathbb{N}_0 \\ 0 & \text{else} \end{cases} \qquad (14)$$

for $k = 0, 1,\ldots, N$. The number of distributions involved in the convolution problem has now reduced from m (number of obligors) to v (number of exposure buckets) since the conditional-independence framework allows to write:

$$p^{L|\mathbf{W}=\mathbf{w}} = \left(\bigotimes_{j=1}^{v} p^{L_j|\mathbf{W}=\mathbf{w}}\right) \qquad (15)$$

Note that large loan portfolios containing 500,000 counterparties can usually be grouped into 10–200 exposure buckets.

For efficient evaluation of Equation 15, we use the discrete Fourier transformation, denoted by $\mathcal{F}$.[3] The Fourier transform can be applied for computing convolutions, since for the vectors $\mathbf{x}$, $\mathbf{y}$ we have:

$$\mathbf{x}\otimes\mathbf{y} = \mathcal{F}^{-1}(\mathcal{F}(\mathbf{x})\odot\mathcal{F}(\mathbf{y})) \qquad (16)$$

where $\odot$ denotes the component-wise multiplication $(\mathbf{x}\odot\mathbf{y})_k := x_k y_k$ of two vectors with equal length. More precisely, Equation 16 only holds if the vectors $\mathbf{x}$, $\mathbf{y}$ on the right-hand side of the above equation are extended by N zeros (so-called "zero-pads"). By slight abuse of notation, we use the same symbol for vectors and their zero-padded extension. We will discuss this issue below, along with the choice of vector length N.

Numerically, Equation 16 is best processed by the fast Fourier transform (FFT) algorithm. This algorithm reduces the number of multiplications required to determine $\mathcal{F}(\mathbf{x})$ to $\frac{1}{2}N\log_2(N)$ if $\log_2(N) \in\mathbb{N}$, whereas the standard convolution algorithm for computing $\mathbf{x}\otimes\mathbf{y}$ requires $\frac{1}{2}N(N-1)$ multiplications.[4]

### REMARKS ON THE PANJER RECURSION

An alternative to the proposed method is that the portfolio conditional loss distribution can be generated directly with the so-called Panjer recursion as applied in the classical CreditRisk+ model. For v exposure buckets, the Panjer recursion just requires $v\times N$ multiplications to determine a conditional loss distribution $p^L|\mathbf{W}=\mathbf{w}$ compared with $\frac{v}{2}N\log_2(N)$ for FFT. In practical applications, N is usually smaller than 10,000, ie, $\frac{1}{2}\log_2(N)$ is smaller than seven. This factor seven advantage is usually lost for the following reasons:

- The Panjer algorithm can run into an underflow problem since the first point of the iteration starts at $P[L = 0|\mathbf{W} = \mathbf{w}] = \exp(-\mu(\mathbf{w}))$, where $\mu(\mathbf{w})$ is the sum of the conditional expected default frequencies of all counterparties. If this number is larger than 750, then double precision arithmetic rounds it to zero and the recursion is stuck at zero. It is nevertheless possible, yet tedious, to avoid this underflow problem by repeatedly rescaling units but the initial factor seven advantage is certainly lost.

- With the Fourier transform, vector operations can be used whereas the Panjer recursion requires "while" or "for" loops in the iteration. Thus, even if no underflow occurs, the factor seven can easily be lost in the computer code. This is especially true for environments such as Matlab or SPlus, which heavily rely on vector operations for speed.[5]

NUMERICAL INTEGRATION IN p-DIMENSIONS

For numerically integrating Equation 9, we apply the strong law of large numbers, which yields:

$$\int_{R^p} P\left[L = n \middle| \mathbf{W} = \mathbf{w}\right] dF(\mathbf{w}) = \lim_{K\to\infty} \frac{1}{K}\sum_{k=1}^{K} P\left[L = n \middle| \mathbf{W} = \mathbf{w}^k\right] \qquad (17)$$

where $(\mathbf{w}^k)_k$ is a sequence of independent draws from the distribution $F$ of $\mathbf{W}$. Hence, for sufficiently large $K$ the loss probabilities are approximated by:

$$P\left[L = n\right] \approx \frac{1}{K}\sum_{k=1}^{K} P\left[L = n \middle| \mathbf{W} = \mathbf{w}^k\right], \quad n = 0, 1, \ldots \qquad (18)$$

The number of latent variables $p$ in credit portfolio models is typically in the range of 1–10. To increase the rate of convergence of the Monte Carlo estimates when simulating in several dimensions ($p > 1$) quasi-random (or low-discrepancy) numbers outperform standard pseudo-random numbers. Quasi-random numbers are more evenly scattered in the $[0, 1]^p$-cube. Since in applications the integrand is a smooth function of $\mathbf{W}$, the rate of convergence increases substantially.

By the linearity of the Fourier transform, we can rewrite Equation 18 as follows:

$$\mathbf{p}^L \overset{(18)}{\approx} \frac{1}{K}\sum_{k=1}^{K} \mathbf{p}^{L|\mathbf{W}=\mathbf{w}^k} \qquad (19)$$

$$\overset{(15),(16)}{=} \frac{1}{K}\sum_{k=1}^{K}\left(\mathcal{F}^{-1}\left(\bigodot_{j=1}^{v}\mathcal{F}\left(\mathbf{p}^{L_j|\mathbf{W}=\mathbf{w}^k}\right)\right)\right) \qquad (20)$$

$$= \mathcal{F}^{-1}\left(\frac{1}{K}\sum_{k=1}^{K}\left(\bigodot_{j=1}^{v}\mathcal{F}\left(\mathbf{p}^{L_j|\mathbf{W}=\mathbf{w}^k}\right)\right)\right) \qquad (21)$$

Hence, the inverse FT needs to be carried out only once rather than in every simulation step, providing a simple but effective reduction of computational time. Therefore, as shown by Equation 21, the numerical integration is carried out in the Fourier space.

THE ALGORITHM IN A NUTSHELL

To provide a concise illustration of the algorithm, we consider a simple case of a portfolio consisting of just four obligors with an exposure distribution of {1, 2, 4, 8}. Consequently, we have four exposure buckets $B_j$, $j = 1,\ldots,4$, each containing one obligor. We assume a default rate volatility model with a single binary latent variable $W$ ($p = 1$). Here, $W$ describes the state of the economy with two possible outcomes, good or bad.

By the Poisson approximation, the number of defaults in each sub-portfolio, conditional on the state of the economy, is Poisson distributed (see Equation 13). The remaining task, namely processing Equation 21 from right to left, is represented in Figure 1. For either of the two given states of the economy, the conditional loss distributions of each exposure bucket are (fast) Fourier transformed and component-wise multiplied. As a result, we retrieve the two conditional Fourier-transformed portfolio loss densities for each state of the economy. By performing a weighted average of the two sequences, each weighting reflecting the relative frequency of the corresponding state of the economy, we arrive at the unconditional Fourier-transformed loss distribution. Finally, we apply the inverse (fast) Fourier transform to obtain the (unconditional) portfolio loss distribution.

## Accuracy of the method

Since the exposure bands can be chosen in a fine-grained way and the number of draws from the distribution of systematic risk factors can be increased, the quality of the method relies heavily on the accuracy of the Poisson approximation, applied in Equation 13. Since this particular approximation is used to obtain the conditional portfolio loss distribution, we investigate the error for each simulation step, conditional on the systematic risk factors. Averaging the error encountered in each simulation step gives the error for the unconditional loss distribution.

THE POISSON APPROXIMATION

Rigorous error estimates for the approximation can be found in Barbour (2001). The error is assessed by the measure of total variation:

$$d_{TV}(G,H) := \sup_{A\subset\mathbb{Z}^+}[G(A) - H(A)] \qquad (22)$$

Conditional on a state of the latent variable $\mathbf{W} = \mathbf{w}$, let $G$ and $H$ denote the probability measures induced by the number of defaults in exposure bucket $B_j$ and its Poisson approximation

**1. Graphical representation of the algorithm for deriving the portfolio loss distribution**

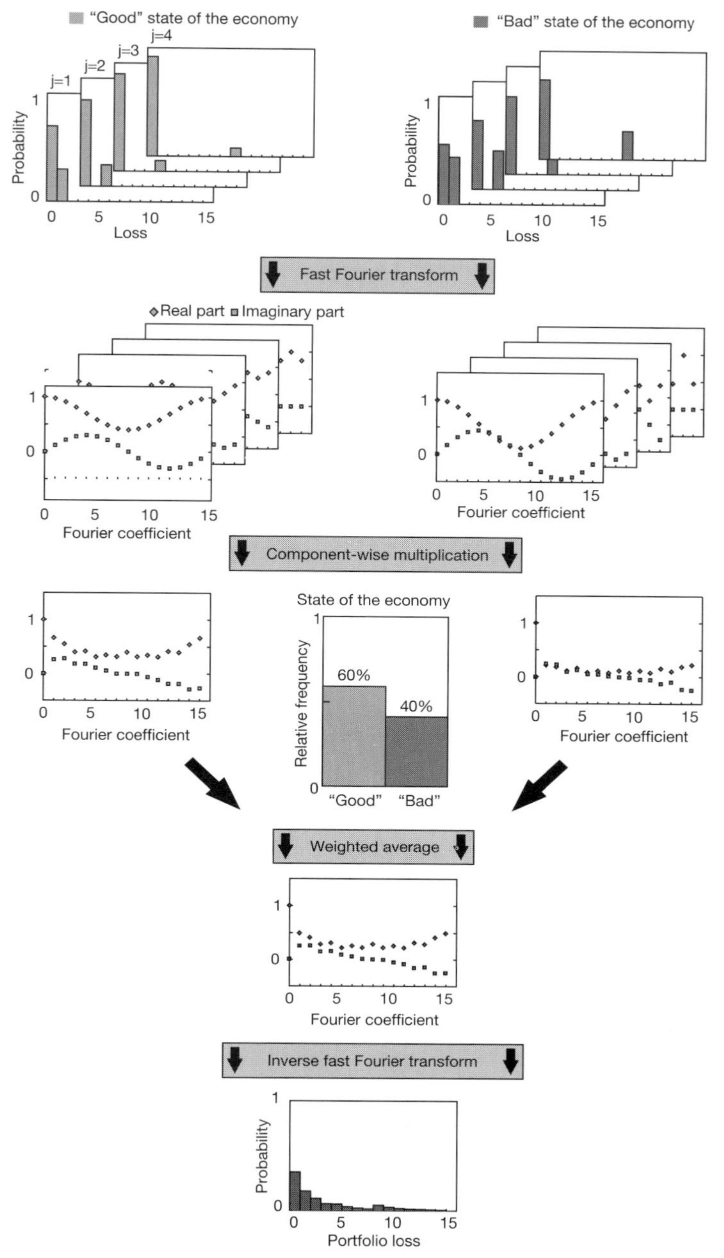

respectively:

$$\mathbf{W} = \mathbf{w} : \sum_{i\in B_j} \tilde{Y}_i \sim G, \quad (\tilde{Y}_i)_{i\in B_j} \sim \text{indep. Bernoulli}(Q_i) \quad (23)$$

$$\mathbf{W} = \mathbf{w} : \sum_{i\in B_j} Y_i \sim H, \quad (Y_i)_{i\in B_j} \sim \text{indep. Poisson}(Q_i) \quad (24)$$

In this setting the optimal upper error bound (EB) is given by:

$$d_{TV}(G,H) \le EB := \left(1 - e^{-\sum_{i\in B_j} Q_i}\right) \frac{\sum_{i\in B_j} Q_i^2}{\sum_{i\in B_j} Q_i} \quad (25)$$

Table 1 provides error bounds for exposure buckets of different size N and for uniform obligor quality distributions, ie, $(Q_i)_i$ independent identically distributed uniformly on an interval of type $[0, \varepsilon]$.

Two observations are important: the error is uniformly bounded with respect to the number of counterparties N and the approximation error decreases with smaller counterparty default probabilities $(Q_i)_i$.

It turns out that the error actually found in applications is often much lower than the rigorous upper bounds suggest. To see this, we investigate the effective approximation error encountered

**Table 1. Error bounds for the Poisson approximation**

| N | $Q_i$ uniform on | EB (%) |
|---|---|---|
| 2,000 | [0, 1%] | 0.66 |
| 2,000 | [0, 3%] | 1.98 |
| 2,000 | [0, 10%] | 6.60 |
| 20 | [0, 3%] | 0.56 |
| 200 | [0, 3%] | 1.97 |
| 2,000 | [0, 3%] | 1.98 |

**Table 2. Numerical method (NM) vs full Monte Carlo simulation (fMC): statistics of the loss distribution**

| | NM | fMC | Δ (%) |
|---|---|---|---|
| Mean | 2,932 | 2,923 | 0.31 |
| Std dev | 2,351 | 2,359 | –0.34 |
| Skewness | 1.589 | 1.607 | –1.12 |
| $VAR_{80\%}$ | 4,540 | 4,518 | 0.49 |
| $VAR_{90\%}$ | 6,050 | 6,067 | –0.28 |
| $VAR_{95\%}$ | 7,530 | 7,544 | –0.19 |

**2. Numerical method vs full Monte Carlo simulation (100,000 and 1m respectively)**

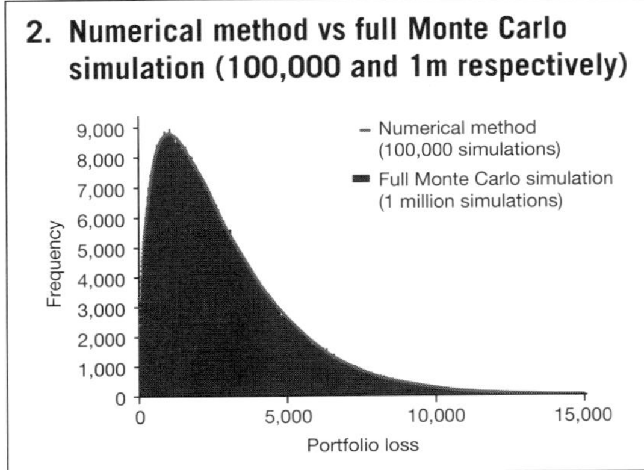


**3. Poisson approximation vs saddlepoint method in the tail**

$(Q_i)_i$ iid uniformly on [0, 3%], 2,000 counterparties. The logarithmic scale highlights the very high accuracy of both methods.

for a credit portfolio containing 15,000 obligors with the following underlying default rate volatility model:

$$Q_i = \bar{q}_i W, \quad W \sim \text{gamma}(1, 0.8) \qquad (26)$$[6]

Counterparty exposures $(l_i)_i$ for this particular portfolio are generated by stretching variates by a factor of 100 drawn from a Beta(1.2, 5) distribution. Additionally, we allocate all obligors in the portfolio evenly among three rating classes, ie, each rating bucket contains 5,000 entities. According to a counterparty's rating, it is assumed to have one of the following expected default frequencies: 0.5%, 1% or 1.5%. The portfolio loss distribution is provided in Figure 2.

The match of the two distributions is almost perfect! To underline the accuracy, we provide some statistics of the two distributions in Table 2.

An efficient yet very accurate approximation method for determining the tail of credit loss distributions is the saddlepoint method. Therefore, we will benchmark the results obtained with our method to both the saddlepoint method and the true loss distribution. We will only present the results at the level of the conditional loss distribution in order to allow for a direct comparison with the results for the saddlepoint method obtained by Martin, Thompson and Browne (2001). Since the method we propose makes use of the Poisson approximation in each exposure bucket, we assume all counterparties in the next test portfolio to have equal exposure.

An appropriate graphical representation of tail probabilities is given by the logarithmic plot in Figure 3, the so-called loss exceedance curve (VAR against tail probability).

In Table 3, it is shown that, in contrast to the Poisson approximation, the saddlepoint method fails to produce accurate values for the body of the loss distribution.

## THE FOURIER TRANSFORM AND THE MAXIMAL LOSS LEVEL N

As we have already mentioned, Equation 16 only holds if the vectors are extended by zero-pads. More precisely, the convolution of two vectors

**Table 3. Poisson approximation vs saddlepoint method for the body of the distribution**

| t | $P(L \le t)$ | | | $\Delta$ | |
|---|---|---|---|---|---|
| | True (%) | Saddle (%) | Poisson (%) | Saddle (%) | Poisson (%) |
| 20 | 4.12 | 3.19 | 4.27 | 22.42 | 3.59 |
| 24 | 17.73 | 14.83 | 17.99 | 16.37 | 1.45 |
| 28 | 43.80 | 39.03 | 43.91 | 10.91 | 0.25 |
| 32 | 71.88 | 67.84 | 71.72 | 5.62 | 0.22 |
| 36 | 90.07 | 88.12 | 89.85 | 2.16 | 0.24 |
| 40 | 97.54 | 96.93 | 97.42 | 0.63 | 0.12 |

$(Q_i)_i$ iid uniformly on [0, 3%], 2,000 counterparties

$\mathbf{u}, \mathbf{v} \in \mathbb{C}^{n+1}$ is given by:

$$\mathbf{u} \otimes \mathbf{v} = \mathcal{F}_{2n+1}^{-1}\left(\mathcal{F}_{2n+1}\left(u_0,\ldots,u_n,\underbrace{0,\ldots,0}_{n}\right)\right.$$
$$\left.\odot \mathcal{F}_{2n+1}\left(v_0,\ldots,v_n,\underbrace{0,\ldots,0}_{n}\right)\right) \qquad (27)^7$$

From Equation 14 we know that the probabilities in the tail of the conditional loss vectors $(p^{L_i|W=w})_j$ decay exponentially towards zero. Hence, if we choose N to be large enough, we can ensure that these conditional loss vectors are already padded with numbers that are extremely close to zero.[8] In other words, the vectors are already zero-padded and we can work with a constant vector length throughout the algorithm.

Since the maximum loss level N, expressed as a multiple of the base unit of loss $\hat{u}$, defines the length of the vectors in the algorithm it needs to be fixed when the numerical method is initialised. Hence, we need criteria for choosing N: recall that for a given portfolio both the choice of base unit and N jointly determine the computational cost of the numerical method. To achieve the highest possible efficiency when using the FFT, N should always be chosen such that $\log_2(N + 1) \in \mathbb{N}$. Furthermore, the choice of N depends on the structure of the underlying portfolio:

- For small, poorly diversified portfolios (containing fewer than 1,000 counterparties), choose N as large as the total portfolio exposure, ie, $N(\hat{u}) \ge \Sigma_i l_i(\hat{u})$.
- For well-diversified portfolios, N can be chosen considerably lower (the diversification effect). Our experience showed that the Chebyshev inequality with a confidence level of 1% provides a good rule of thumb. That is, choose N such that:

$$P[L > N] \le \frac{1}{N^2}(E[L]^2 + \sigma^2(L)) \approx 1\% \qquad (28)$$

Expectation and variance of the portfolio loss can be derived analytically or simply be estimated conservatively.

Since we were not able to derive rigorous error estimates in terms of N, it is commendable to back-test the accuracy in the tail obtained for a certain choice of N against the saddlepoint method (as illustrated in Figure 3). However, with the above choice of N, we have never observed any relevant deviations from results obtained with the saddlepoint method.[9]

## Applications

Here, we present two important applications of the numerical method described above.

### RISK ANALYSIS OF CDO STRUCTURES

We will describe how the conditional-independence framework can be applied to quantify the risk transfer involved in CDO structures. In a simple CDO structure, a bank buys credit protection on a specified sub-portfolio of its total credit portfolio. Usually a self-retention is involved (equity tranche) and losses exceeding the self-retention up to a specified maximum are covered by the protection provider on a quota share basis (quota share on the transferred tranche). One key question for the buyer of the credit protection is: how does the hedge on the sub-portfolio change the overall credit loss distribution? The advantage of the following treatment of this question is that the approach is fully consistent with the bank's internal credit risk model (as long as a conditional independence framework is chosen), and no

**4. Risk transfer function R**

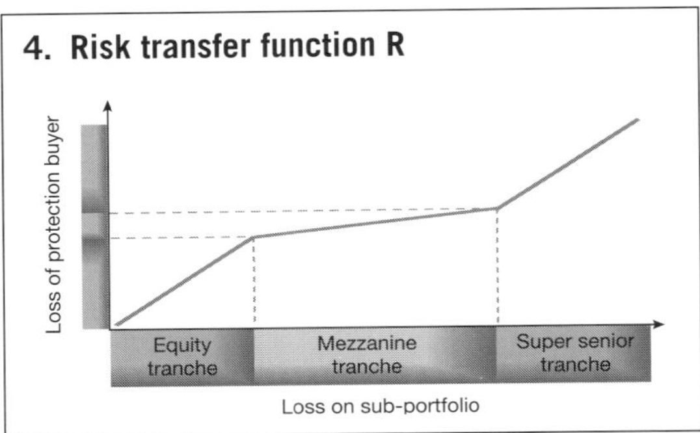


**5. Applying the risk transfer function to the conditional loss distribution of the sub-portfolio**

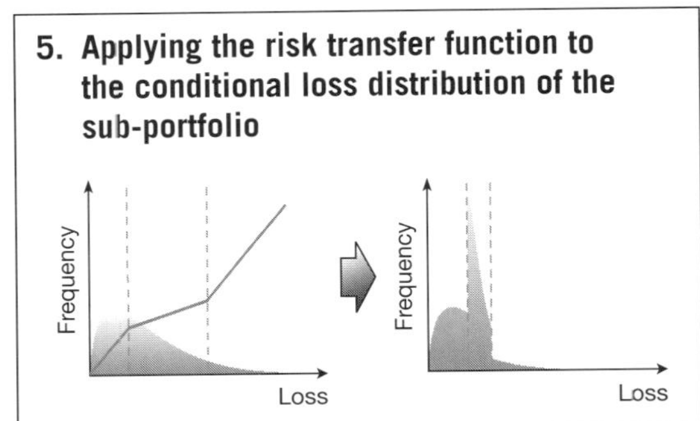


separate and potentially inconsistent model for the risk analysis of CDO structures needs to be introduced *ad hoc*.

- ❑ Applying the risk transfer function to a sub-portfolio. The effect of the credit protection on the sub-portfolio can be determined by applying a risk transfer function that contains the specific features of the credit protection agreement (attachment points, quota share). A typical risk transfer function R is shown in Figure 4. The impact of the risk transfer function on the sub-portfolio can easily be determined for any given state of the latent variable $W = w$. In fact, if $p^{L_S}| W = w$ is the conditional loss distribution of the sub-portfolio then the distribution of the transformed random variable $R(L_S^{W=w})$ is the conditional loss distribution of the sub-portfolio incorporating the hedging effect of the credit protection. Since R is usually a piece-wise linear and increasing function, it is not necessary to resort to a Monte Carlo simulation to determine the density of $R(L_S^{W=w})$ since it can easily be derived from the conditional loss distribution of the sub-portfolio $p^{L_S}|W = w$.
- ❑ Assessing the impact of the CDO on the bank's total credit risk. Note that for each given state of the latent variable the transformed loss distribution of the sub-portfolio and the loss distribution of the rest of the bank's credit portfolio can be simply aggregated by convolution since they are (conditionally) independent.[10]

By repeating the above aggregation step for each state of the latent variable, we can determine the unconditional loss distribution of the whole portfolio taking into account the credit protection on the sub-portfolio. The process of applying the risk transfer function R is illustrated in Figure 5. This is just a simple modification of the general algorithm illustrated in Figure 1.

APPLICATION TO STRESS LOSS ANALYSIS

The fact that we do not impose any restrictions on the dependence structure among the latent variables allows us to study the impact of so-called stress dependence structures (stress copulas, see Nyfeler, 2000).

As mentioned above, Merton-type models assume asset returns $(X_i)_i$ to be (standard) multivariate normally distributed. More generally, a mixture of normal distribution can be considered. This model is defined as:

$$X_i = SZ_i \quad \mathbf{Z} \sim \text{Normal}(0, \Sigma), S > 0 \tag{29}$$

$$S, \mathbf{Z} \text{ independent} \tag{30}$$

So a more general set-up causes the $(X_i)_i$ to be "extremal dependent", a property relating to extreme value theory, thereby preserving asset correlations since $\text{Corr}(X_i, X_j) = \text{Corr}(Z_i, Z_j)$.

An often considered member of the mixture of normal family is the t-distribution with a "degrees of freedom" parameter $v$, which arises for $S = \sqrt{\frac{v}{U}}$ and $U$ is chi-squared distributed with $v$ degrees of freedom.

We note that the higher degree of sophistication of the dependency model does not lead to higher computational costs using our method.

1 *See Ash and Doléans-Dade (2000) for details.*

2 *If* $x$ *and* $y$ *have length* $j$ *and* $k$*, respectively, then their convolution* $x \otimes y$ *has length* $j + k - 1$.

3 *The* $n$*-dimensional discrete Fourier transform* $\mathcal{F}_n$ *is a linear isomorphism from* $\mathbb{C}^n$ *to* $\mathbb{C}^n$*. When no confusion seems likely, we will not show the dimension* $n$ *in our notation and write* $\mathcal{F}$ *for* $\mathcal{F}_n$.

4 *We note that the Fourier transform of the Poisson distribution has a simple closed-form solution. If* $\bar{l}_j = 1$*, this could be used to determine* $\mathcal{F}(\mathbf{p}^{L_j}|W = w)$ *but even in this simplest situation the FFT turns out to be faster than the evaluation of the explicit formula.*

5 *Programming is an art and a science.*

6 *Corresponds to the one-factor CreditRisk+ default rate volatility model, volatility = 80%.*

7 *The minimal length of the zero-pads is* n, *but they may be chosen longer.*

8 $\mathcal{F}$ *and* $\mathcal{F}^{-1}$ *are continuous linear maps. Therefore, small input errors can be controlled.*

9 *A simple way to crosscheck for accuracy is to compare the expected loss and variance of the numerically determined distribution with the analytically derived exact values.*

10 *We need to assume that each counterparty is either a member of the sub-portfolio or not.*

**BIBLIOGRAPHY**

**Ash, R., and C. Doléans-Dade,** 2000, *Probability and Measure Theory* (San Diego: Academic Press).

**Barbour, A.,** 2001, "Topics in Poisson Approximation", in D. Shanbhag and D. Rao (eds), *Stochastic Processes: Theory and Methods, Handbook of Statistics*, pp. 79–115 (Elsevier Science).

**Credit Suisse First Boston,** 1997, *CreditRisk+: A Credit Risk Management Framework*, Technical Document, available at www.csfb.com/creditrisk.

**Gordy, M.,** 2000, "A Comparative Anatomy of Credit Risk Models", *Journal of Banking & Finance*, 24, pp. 119–49.

**Hickman, A., and H. Koyluoglu,** 1998, "Reconcilable Differences", *Risk*, October, pp. 56–62.

**Martin, R., K. Thompson and C. Browne,** 2001, "Taking to the Saddle", *Risk*, June, pp. 91–94.

**Nyfeler, M.,** 2000, *Modelling Dependencies in Credit Risk Management*, Diploma thesis, ETH Zurich, available at www.risklab.ch/Papers.html.

# V

# BASEL II

21

# IRB Approach Explained

**Tom Wilde**

Credit Suisse First Boston

*Tom Wilde sheds light on the assumptions and parameters underlying the internal ratings-based approach.*

Beyond the contentious multipliers and add-ons present in the internal ratings-based approach (IRB, Basel, 2001), lie equations that have generally been welcomed. The Basel Committee on Banking Supervision has been applauded for bringing bank capital more into line with credit risk modelling theory. However, the IRB calculations do lack some transparency. Here, I show how the base risk weights of the IRB approach are determined and discuss the granularity adjustment, which fits into the same framework. The interested reader should also refer to Gordy (2000b), which reports the actual modelling work on which the IRB approach is based.

## A brief history of credit risk modelling

The context of the IRB approach is the theory of credit risk modelling. In recent years, commercial or publicly available models of credit risk have appeared, notably KMV's CreditMonitor, JP Morgan's[1] CreditMetrics, Credit Suisse First Boston's CreditRisk+ and McKinsey's CreditPortfolioView. The ideas behind these models are due in part to earlier authors, notably Merton (see, for example, Merton, 1974; Vasicek, 1987).

Hickman and Koyluoglu (1998) pointed out that the models all derive from a common framework in which part of each model deals with systematic risk, and a "second stage" assesses the additional unsystematic component. Systematic risk has the same meaning as in the capital asset pricing model, being the sensitivity of the overall condition of the portfolio to the economy, which cannot be diversified away. Hickman and Koyluoglu also showed that the different choices made in the publicly available models can broadly be compensated for by appropriate parameterisation (see also Gordy, 2000a, which contains an in-depth analysis of CreditMetrics and CreditRisk+).

Risk managers, regulators, consultants and academics have all now contributed to this theory, so there is now an accepted general framework for measuring credit risk (Finger, 1999; Belkin, Suchower and Forest, 1998; Lucas *et al.*, 1999 are some further important contributions to the theory.)

## The common framework

We summarise the common framework from Hickman and Koyluoglu (1998). Suppose there are systematic factors, or drivers of default, represented mathematically by random variables $X_1,\ldots,X_n$, such that the probability of default of any obligor A in the portfolio is given by some specified function:[2]

$$\text{Probability of default} = P_A(X_1,\ldots,X_n)$$

The variables $X_1,\ldots,X_n$ "represent" systematic factors that affect default rates, and which can be real (such as interest rates, share price indexes or macroeconomic data) or formal (such as factors derived from principal component analysis). For a given model, the functional dependence $P_A(X_1,\ldots,X_n)$ typically has a fixed functional form, with additional parameters specified for each obligor reflecting their intrinsic credit quality and sensitivity to the variables. The specification of this function and of the variables $X_1,\ldots,X_n$ is the source of most of the differences between the commercially available credit risk models.

*The first half of this chapter is based on an unpublished document presented by the International Swaps and Derivatives Association to US regulators in September 1999. The second half, on the new Accord's granularity adjustment, is new.*

Default probabilities therefore depend on factors that can also affect other obligors, and in this way systematic risk is modelled. Normally, this is the main risk inherent in the portfolio. However, the systematic factors only affect the probability that an obligor will default; there is still an element of chance about the actual number of defaults or the amount of loss. This element of pure luck is the source of unsystematic risk. Unlike systematic risk, it will only be important for a portfolio that is small or has large exposures.

If $n = 1$, the model is called a one-factor model. Only one random variable models the systematic element of uncertainty in the portfolio. The one-factor models are the simplified relatives of the commercial models, and are the models used to set the IRB risk weights. Specifically, the simplified form of CreditMetrics is used to calculate base risk weights, and CreditRisk+ assists in the calculation of the granularity adjustment.

By using one-factor models, there is no need to use a commercial model directly, and the parameterisation issues for the more detailed models are avoided as much as possible. However, there is a less obvious additional advantage: one-factor models give rise to additive capital requirements. This property is important because it is the reason why the risk weights in the IRB approach do not have to be calibrated with reference to any particular test portfolio; subject to the modelling assumptions, they are reasonably valid for all portfolios.

Before using a credit risk model, the Basel Committee has needed to set parameters whose values must be determined by other considerations than modelling alone.[3] Thus capital for credit risk will be calculated at 99.5% confidence over a one-year time horizon, and including expected loss. The concepts presented below do not depend in any way on these particular parameters but we will find it convenient to use them to avoid cumbersome "over-general" notation.

A risk or capital weight is a factor to be applied to, say, loans, so that the total across all loans adds up to the capital required for the whole portfolio, ie:

$$\text{Capital requirement} = \sum(\text{Exposure} \times \text{capital weight}) \tag{1}$$

or, equivalently, in the language of risk weights (which are capital requirements scaled up by 12.5):

$$\text{Capital requirement} = \sum(\text{Exposure} \times \text{risk weight}) \times 8\% \tag{2}$$

The problem is that capital was not defined as a sum of weights, but as the result of a portfolio calculation. Can total capital, in fact, be expressed as suggested by Equation 1? The weights used would have to be valid across a wide range of portfolios.[4] In short, the Committee must reconcile the following two objectives:

1. capital requirements should add up, to a reasonable approximation, to 99.5% percentile loss; and
2. capital weights must depend only on properties of the individual transaction, as in Equations 1 and 2.

However, these objectives are not contradictory if a one-factor model is used. This is the key advantage of one-factor models.

But to take advantage of the additive behaviour of one-factor models, capital must be calculated by looking only at systematic risk. The unsystematic component, which is normally much smaller, is not tractable in the same way. The granularity adjustment deals with this component.

### Systematic risk and its contributions

Normally, in finance, systematic risk is measured via covariance ("betas" in the classic portfolio theory), but the framework described above makes available a whole statistical distribution analogous to the loss distribution, but measuring only systematic risk.

Assume we are modelling the loss distribution from a portfolio $\Pi$, using the common framework and the notation above. Let $E_A$ be the average loss given default (for simplicity, we take exposure to mean loss amount given default, so that average recovery is already factored in) and $\sigma(E_A)$ be its proportional standard deviation (the standard deviation in dollars is then $E_A\sigma(E_A)$). Now suppose we know the values of the systematic variables $X_1,\ldots,X_n$. This is like knowing the state of the economy. Then the average loss from the portfolio, and its variance,[5] are:

$$\mu = \sum_A E_A P_A(X_1,\ldots,X_n) \tag{3}$$

$$\sigma^2 = \sum_A E_A^2\left(P_A(1-P_A) + P_A\sigma^2(E_A)\right) \tag{4}$$

The actual loss is drawn from a statistical distribution with this mean and variance. Systematic risk distribution means that, if the portfolio is sufficiently fine grained, the variance conditional on $X_1,\ldots,X_n$ will be small, and so (eg, by Chebyshev's inequality) the conditional distribution of losses will just be the conditional average loss "with certainty". The uncertainty remaining then arises from the fact that we do not know the values of the variables $X_1,\ldots,X_n$. The distribution of losses is the distribution of the conditional mean loss in Equation 3. This random variable is called the systematic loss of the portfolio $\Pi$.

From the original portfolio $\Pi$ construct a portfolio $\Pi_m$ by replacing each A with m new obligors $A_1,\ldots,A_m$ each having exposure $E_A/m$ but the same default probability $P_A(X_1,\ldots,X_n)$. As m tends to infinity, the portfolios form a sequence that we think of as having a limit $\Pi_\infty$ called the systematic portfolio. $\Pi_\infty$ is what the Basel Committee calls an "infinitely fine grained" portfolio. We can check that the conditional variance (Equation 4) of $\Pi$ gets divided by m in this process, while the mean (Equation 3) is unaffected. So the notional portfolio $\Pi_\infty$ has as its total loss distribution just the systematic distribution (Equation 3), ie, the random variable $\mu$ defined by Equation 3 is the systematic loss distribution of $\Pi$.

For any statistic for the original portfolio $\Pi$, there is the corresponding equivalent systematic statistic, which is the statistic evaluated on $\Pi_\infty$, or equivalently on the systematic loss distribution (Equation 3). Of particular importance are the systematic percentiles, such as the systematic loss 99.5% percentile, which is defined as the 99.5% confidence point on the systematic loss distribution. These are the quantities used to define capital in the IRB approach.

Putting Equation 1 another way, the capital weight should be the marginal contribution made to the 99.5% point on the loss distribution by each exposure (think of Equation 1 for the original portfolio, and for the portfolio with one exposure removed). Analogously, the systematic risk contribution is the contribution made to the systematic 99.5% point. We write $RC_A$ and $SRC_A$ for these two risk contributions. The systematic loss distribution is given by Equation 3 as the distribution of $\mu$. This looks promisingly like a sum of random variables, one for each obligor. Suppose now that we are using a one-factor model, ie, $n = 1$. Then the systematic loss distribution is just:

$$\sum_A E_A P_A(X)$$

Now provided this is an increasing function of X (in practice each $P_A(X)$ will be increasing by suitable choice of X, so this condition is not serious), the 99.5th percentile of this distribution is just:

$$\sum_A E_A P_A(X_{99.5\%})$$

and therefore the difference made to this by obligor A is just:

$$SRC_A = E_A P_A(X_{99.5\%})$$

We have achieved our goal of a model in which systematic risk contributions depend only on the properties of an individual obligor.

## The IRB risk weights

We apply the theory above to the IRB risk weights. These were derived using the one-factor form of CreditMetrics. In this model, the systematic factor X is a standard normal random variable (the systematic variable has a "real" interpretation as minus the normalised systematic component of asset return for each obligor).[6] Using N() to denote the cumulative normal density function, the functional dependence is given by the well-known Vasicek formula:[7]

$$P_A = N\left(\frac{N^{-1}(p_A) + X\rho_A^{1/2}}{(1-\rho_A)^{1/2}}\right) \quad (5)$$

where $\rho_A$ is the "asset R – squared" for obligor A and $p_A$ is the unconditional default probability (the formula does not make it obvious that $p_A$ is the average of $P_A$ but this is clear from the derivation of the Vasicek formula).[8] The systematic risk contribution at 99.5% confidence is derived by setting X equal to its 99.5% value 2.576, and multiplying by the exposure. Thus:

$$SRC_A = E_A N\left(\frac{N^{-1}(p_A) + 2.576\rho_A^{1/2}}{(1-\rho_A)^{1/2}}\right) \quad (6)$$

Using the Committee's choice of $\rho_A = \rho = 20\%$ (Basel, 2001, paragraph 172), we can confirm the IRB risk weights for corporates directly. We calculate:

$$(1-\rho_A)^{-1/2} = 0.8^{-1/2} = 1.118$$

and

$$\frac{2.576\ \rho_A^{1/2}}{(1-\rho_A)^{1/2}} = 1.288$$

These are the coefficients in the middle term in Basel (2001, paragraph 171). The retail risk weights (Basel, 2001, paragraph 310) can be derived similarly with $\rho = 8\%$.

## The calibration factor

The full IRB risk weight is given as:

$$976.5 \times N(1.118N^{-1}(p_A) + 1.288) \times \text{(Maturity adjustment)}$$

(see Basel, 2001, paragraph 171). The middle term is Equation 6. The last term is an adjustment representing the additional capital required against fair-value changes based on a loan of three years' maturity. Its form is derived empirically (the Committee refer to "judgemental pooling of information") and we do not discuss it here, except to note that it becomes one for a loan of explicit one-year maturity (to see this, calculate the risk weight in Basel, 2001, paragraph 159, for an asset with maturity M = 1. The third term of the present base risk weight cancels with the maturity adjustment.)

The first term is a "calibration adjustment". This number is mostly due to conventions about the way risk weights are stated, so to see the real scaling factor we must disentangle these. What factor would give a "pure modelling" result, ie, just amount to Equation 6? For an asset with loss given default equal to 50%, the capital requirement factor free of any scaling should be just $50\% \times N(1.118N^{-1}(p_A) + 1.288)$. To achieve this effect, the base risk weight should be set at:

$$100/0.08 \times 50\% \times N(1.118N^{-1}(p_A)+1.288)$$

We have $100/0.08 \times 50\% = 625$, so the Basel Committee seems to have employed a scaling factor of $976.5/625 = 1.56$ approximately, but that is not quite right. Later, 4% of the capital calculated here is rebated against the granularity adjustment (see Basel, 2001, paragraph 432). There is no free lunch, however. This same 4% is first produced by grossing up the baseline charge (Basel, 2001, paragraph 171) by 1/0.96, ie, so that only 96% of the number calculated covers all the base risk, leaving 4% free to cover granularity risk. Thus the actual multiplier is:

$$976.5/625 \times 0.96 = 149.99\%$$

The Committee does not mention this multiplier explicitly, preferring to present the calibration in terms of the capital requirement for a specific asset (Basel, 2001, paragraph 172). This may reflect their original approach, but one can assume they have also rounded up to arrive at 1.5 exactly.

## The granularity adjustment

We have shown how the base risk weights quantify systematic risk exactly according to the credit risk modelling framework introduced above. But the question of unsystematic risk remains. Put another way, the risk weights add up to the 99.5% point of the loss distribution of $\Pi_\infty$, not $\Pi$ itself. In general, this should be expected to be close, but an underestimate of total risk, and possibly a material understatement for a small portfolio or one with large exposures. Figures 1 and 2 show actual and systematic loss distributions for a typical large and small portfolio. The distributions are similar for the large portfolio but very different for the small portfolio.

**1. Loss distribution – large portfolio**

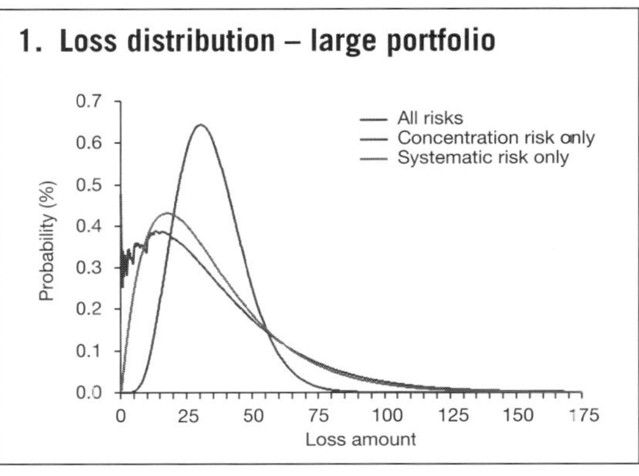


**2. Loss distribution – small portfolio**

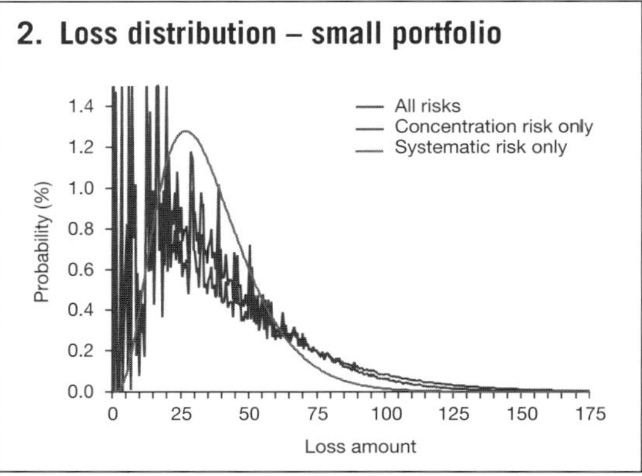


The task to be performed by the granularity adjustment (Basel, 2001, Chapter 8) is to adjust the 99.5% point on the systematic loss distribution to try to achieve the corresponding point of the actual loss distribution.

The adjustment (before rebating 4% of the base risk weight charge already surcharged within the base risk weight) is given as $GA = GSF/n^*$ where $n^*$ is the reciprocal of the "Herfindahl index". The granularity scaling factor GSF is given in Basel (2001, paragraph 457) by:

$$GSF = (0.6 + 1.8LGD_{AG})(9.5 + 13.75PD_{AG}/F_{AG})$$

and is a scaled version of the formula given in paragraph 456:

$$\beta = (0.4 + 1.2LGD_{AG})(0.76 + 1.1PD_{AG}/F_{AG}) \quad (7)$$

where the scaling factor is 18.75 (=1.5/0.08, arising from the transition to assets from capital, and the further multiplier of 1.5 consistent with the factor already applied to the base risk weights).

Unlike the base risk weights, the granularity adjustment is based on CreditRisk+ with one factor.

Here, default rates are parameterised depending on a gamma distributed random variable X, with the following relation replacing Equation 5:

$$P_A = p_A(1-\omega_A+\omega_A X)$$

Here X has mean 1 and variance $\sigma(X)$, and the parameter $\omega_A$ is called the "factor loading". It describes how X affects the default rate of A, where $0 \le \omega_A \le 1$. The systematic risk contribution for obligor A is therefore $SRC_A = E_A p_A(1 - \omega_A + \omega_A X_{99.5\%})$ in place of Equation 6.

Since two models are being used, they must be calibrated somehow. The Committee recognises that this is not a perfect situation but chooses the best place to stitch the models together, namely at the 99.5% confidence level (Basel, 2001, paragraph 446). Thus the weight $\omega_A$ is chosen so that CreditRisk+ agrees with the CreditMetrics model used for the base risk weights, ie, the systematic risk contributions from the two models coincide at 99.5%. This requirement is presented as:

$$F_A = p_A(1-\omega_A+\omega_A X_{99.5\%}) - p_A = p_A\omega_A(X_{99.5\%}-1)$$

where $F_A$ is "systematic risk sensitivity" defined in Basel (2001, paragraph 431), ie, the excess of the CreditMetrics systematic risk contribution over the default probability.

The gamma distributed X is parameterised with $\sigma(X) = 2$ (Basel, 2001, paragraph 445) and this leads to $X_{99.5\%} = 12.007$ (this is easy to check using GAMMAINV(0.995,0.25,4) in Excel). So the condition for equal percentiles is:

$$\begin{aligned} p_A\omega_A\sigma(X) &= F_A\frac{\sigma}{(X_{99.5\%}-1)} \\ &= F_A\frac{2}{(12.007-1)} = 0.182F_A \end{aligned} \quad (8)$$

as given in Basel (2001, paragraph 454).

To understand the granularity adjustment, we rephrase the Herfindahl index in terms of a more universal concept, the variance of the loss distribution. From Equation 4, the variance of the portfolio loss distribution conditional on X is:

$$\sigma^2(\Pi|X) = \sum_A E_A^2\left(P_A(X)(1-P_A(X)) + P_A(X)\,\sigma^2(E_A)\right)$$

So, the total variance of the loss distribution is:

$$\sigma^2(\Pi) = \sigma^2\left(\sum_A E_A P_A\right) + \sum_A E_A^2\left(p_A(1-p_A) - \sigma^2(P_A) + p_A\,\sigma^2(E_A)\right)$$

using $p_A$ as the average of $P_A$. The left-hand summand is the variance of the systematic loss variable $\mu$ given by Equation 3. The other summand is called the unsystematic variance:

$$\sigma^2_{Unsys} = \sum_A E_A^2\left(p_A(1-p_A) - \sigma^2(P_A) + p_A\sigma^2(E_A)\right) \quad (9)$$

In our one-factor CreditRisk+ model we have:

$$\sigma^2(P_A) = p_A^2\omega_A^2\sigma^2(X) \quad (10)$$

and so substituting into Equation 9:

$$\sigma^2_{Unsys} = \sum_A\left(E_A^2\left(p_A - p_A^2 - p_A^2\omega_A^2\sigma^2(X)\right) + E_A^2 p_A\,\sigma^2(E_A)\right) \quad (11)$$

The IRB approach chooses a specific form for recovery rate volatility, (Basel, 2001, paragraph 447), which, in our notation,[9] is:

$$\sigma^2(E_A) = \frac{LGD_A(1-LGD_A)}{4LGD_A^2} = \frac{(1-LGD_A)}{4LGD_A}$$

To make our notation comparable with Basel (2001), we write our $E_A$ as $EAD_A \times LGD_A$, where exposure before recovery is $EAD_A$. Then Equation 11, using Equation 8, becomes:

$$\sigma^2_{Unsys} = \sum_A EAD_A^2\left(LGD_A^2\left(p_A - p_A^2 - 0.033F_A^2\right) + 0.25p_A LGD_A\left(1-LGD_A\right)\right)$$

where 0.033 is the square of 0.182. This is given in Basel (2001, paragraph 452), except that our summation is directly over obligors.[10] Also, by ignoring terms of order higher than one in default probabilities, the denominator of the fraction for $A_b$ is very nearly $PD_{AG}LGD_{AG}(0.25 + 0.75LGD_{AG})$. We substitute all this in the sum in Basel (2001, paragraph 455). The easiest way to do this is to assume that each risk grade contains only one obligor, so $H_b = 1$. We obtain, very nearly:

$$H^* = \frac{1}{n^*} = \frac{4\sigma^2_{Unsys}}{\left(\sum_A EAD_A\right)(1+3LGD_{AG})\,EL} \quad (12)$$

where:

$$EL = \left(\sum_A EAD_A\right)LGD_{AG}PD_{AG} = \sum_A E_A p_A$$

is the mean loss from the portfolio. So, the Herfindahl index $H^*$ contains much the same information as the unsystematic variance of the loss distribution. An odd term $1 + 3LGD_{AG}$ seems to have been stripped out, but this exact term is reinstated as one of the brackets in the equation for $\beta$, as can be seen by examining Equation 7.

What does the IRB equation for the granularity adjustment look like in terms of unsystematic variance? Using Equations 7 and 12, we can rewrite the adjustment as:

$$\begin{aligned} GA &= \left( \sum_A EAD_A \right) \beta / n^* \\ &= 1.6 \times \left(0.76 + 1.1 PD_{AG}/F_{AG}\right) \times \sigma^2_{Unsys}/EL \end{aligned}$$

Thus the only information the granularity adjustment uses about the unsystematic risk is the unsystematic variance. This is not surprising - in general, no other reliable information about the unsystematic risk to use. A significant part of the unsystematic risk arises from the supposed recovery rate volatility, for which we used an assumption about variance, but no other information.

There is an alternative presentation of these facts. The actual adjustment is the result of the careful numerical work described in Gordy (2000b), but if one had nothing else to go on what would be one's first estimate of the granularity adjustment? Many practitioners would have scaled portfolio systematic unexpected loss by the ratio of standard deviations, ie, applied the formula:

$$\begin{aligned} GA_{estimate} &= UL \times \left( \left( \sigma^2_{Total}/\sigma^2_{Sys} \right)^{1/2} - 1 \right) \\ &\cong UL \times \sigma^2_{Unsys}/2\sigma^2_{Sys} \end{aligned}$$

In the one-factor CreditRisk+ model, we can use Equation 12 to work this out. To do this, we also need to calculate the systematic component of variance, which we obtain from Equation 10 bearing in mind that $\sigma(X) = 2$. After some manipulation, one obtains an equation similar to the actual adjustment:

$$GA_{estimate} = \left(9.47 PD_{AG}/F_{AG}\right)\left(0.4 + 1.2 LGD_{AG}\right)/n^*$$

This is a moderately successful approximation to the actual granularity adjustment and tends to overestimate, though it is close enough to provide a "reasonableness check". The crossover point where this expression agrees exactly to the actual adjustment expression is $0.76 = 8.37 PD_{AG}/F_{AG}$, which happens for a default probability of about 30 basis points. The two expressions are within 25% of each other up to about a default probability of 1.30%.

## Conclusion

The IRB risk weights and granularity adjustment are derived from a general framework of ideas that deserves to be widely understood as part of the basic language of risk management. The IRB approach is not necessarily right or the best possible, but at least rules derived from a general framework are better than a patchwork of inconsistent special cases. But this clear conceptual approach really only exists for the IRB risk weights and granularity adjustment - if the same approach had penetrated throughout the new Accord, then arguably there could have been different proposals in several areas. For example, the definition of default and discussion of "through-the-cycle" versus "point-in-time" default probabilities, the treatment of retail assets, the treatment of credit risk mitigation (the "w factor") and joint default risk, and the treatment of counterparty risk are all areas that can be considered in the light of the ideas above, at least as one valid point of view, and this approach has not been adopted as universally as it could have been.

1 *Now RiskMetrics Group.*

2 *We use* P *for the random variable representing default rates and* p *for the average of* P *over values of the variables. In most cases, the form of* P *is chosen so that its average* p *is an explicit parameter to be input.*

3 *It is valid to debate the choices they have made but that is not the purpose of this chapter.*

4 *Calculations using an "example portfolio" do not establish that certain weights are appropriate or not. What is needed is a general theory that shows certain weights will indeed hold in general.*

5 *The variance formula is obtained by directly applying the definition of variance for a single obligor* A*, with loss equal to the (uncertain) loss given default in the event of default, or zero otherwise. The portfolio variance is just the sum across obligors because they are independent conditional on the* $X_{1-n}$.

6 *Not quite lognormal assets, as apparently claimed in Basel (2001, paragraph 172), but the point is minor.*

7 *See, for example, Hickman and Koyluoglu (1998) or Finger (1999).*

8 *Thus* p *is the unconditional chance of default over the next year, including good and bad economic outcomes. This can be compared with guidance from the New Accord on default probabilities. A "long run average" (Basel, 2001, paragraph 217) roughly corresponds to observing* $p_A$ *from a time series of historic outcomes for obligors starting out in the same condition as* A *(these are realisations of* P*, not* p*), but* p *is arguably not "forward looking", as required by paragraph 218, as it depends only on the spot characteristics of* A.

9 *The division by* LGD[2] *is needed because we refer to proportional volatility of* LGD.

10 *There is no need for the intervening risk grades in Basel (2001), and, unfortunately, if the recovery rate is not constant, then, as a result of this formulation, the result can depend somewhat on the particular choice of grades. To avoid the issue, assume recovery rates are constant across grades - after all, grades may be chosen at will and need not contain more than one obligor.*

**BIBLIOGRAPHY**

**Basel Committee on Banking Supervision,** 2001, *The New Basel Capital Accord*, IRB Consultative Document, Bank for International Settlements, January.

**Belkin, B., S. Suchower and L. Forest Jr,** 1998, "The Effect of Systematic Credit Risk on Loan Portfolio Value at Risk and Loan Pricing", *CreditMetrics Monitor*, March.

**Finger, C.,** 1999, "Conditional Approaches for CreditMetrics Portfolio Distributions", *CreditMetrics Monitor*, April.

**Gordy, M.,** 2000a, "A Comparative Anatomy of Credit Risk Models", *Journal of Banking and Finance*, 24, pp. 119–49.

**Gordy, M.,** 2000b, *A Risk Factor Model Foundation for Ratings Based Capital Rules*, Working Paper, September.

**Hickman, A., and U. Koyluoglu,** 1998, "Reconcilable Differences", *Risk*, October, pp. 56–62.

**Lucas, A., P. Klaassen, P. Spreij and S. Straetmans,** 1999, *An Analytic Approach to Credit Risk of Large Corporate Bond and Loan Portfolios*, Research Memorandum, Vrije Universiteit, Amsterdam, February.

**Merton, R.,** 1974, "On The Pricing of Corporate Debt: The Risk Structure of Interest Rates", *Journal of Finance*, 29, pp. 449–70.

**Vasicek, O.,** 1987, *Probability of Loss on Loan Portfolio*, KMV Corporation.

22

# Pro-cyclicality in the New Basel Accord


**D. Wilson Ervin and Tom Wilde**

Credit Suisse First Boston



*Could Basel II worsen recessions? By backtesting the proposed capital rules to the last recession, D. Wilson Ervin and Tom Wilde argue that the increased risk sensitivity of loan portfolio regulatory capital in the new Accord could have unwelcome systemic side effects.*


The proposed new capital Accord (Basel, 2001) is designed to be more sensitive to risk in general and to credit risk in particular. Lower-rated assets will cost more in terms of capital in both the standardised and, especially, the internal ratings-based (IRB) approach. Greater risk sensitivity is seen as desirable because it should promote risk-adjusted business decisions and improve capital allocation within banks as well as improving capital allocation across banks. The new rules will require more capital to be held at riskier banks, which should reduce the risk of a bank default.

However, in a risk-sensitive regime, capital will also be more sensitive to risk changes across time, which raises serious issues. Under the new Accord, bank capital ratios will tend to rise and fall much more with the credit cycle unless mitigating actions are taken. For example, according to calculations described below, a bank capitalised at 8% in January 1990 with a broadly diversified BBB-rated loan portfolio would, without actively managing its portfolio, have finished 1990 (a recession year) with a capitalisation of 6.8% under the IRB approach. (This uses rating migration statistics published in Standard & Poor's, 2001, and assumes no active management of its portfolio.) The impact of the same scenario under the current capital regime would be a modest drop of only 0.2%, to 7.8%. The impact on capital ratios under the new regime is approximately six times the impact under the old regime in this scenario, a major increase in capital volatility. Similar effects occur for other ratings grades and for other years where adverse credit conditions were observed.

The additional volatility in capital ratios is likely to affect how banks manage their capital planning and business strategy. If banks or regulators try to maintain the stable ratios of the current system, they will have to manage credit assets much more aggressively than at present, for example, by curtailing lending or selling assets in a downturn. While active management of regulatory capital constraints has worked reasonably well for trading assets under the current market risk regime (though it is not without serious critics), it is likely to be problematic for the less liquid assets covered under the credit risk regime.[1]

The capital volatility caused by credit cycles will affect the whole banking industry, not just individual banks.[2] This could have important effects on the overall economy if banks in aggregate are forced to change their lending behaviour to maintain their capital ratios at times of economic stress. If banks respond by restricting new lending, the supply of available credit will be reduced during the adverse part of the credit cycle, which would amplify, not reduce, credit cycles and potentially exacerbate economic swings ("pro-cyclicality"). Paradoxically, this behaviour could undermine the role of banks as "critical shock absorbers for market economies", subverting one of the fundamental motivations cited as a "driving force" behind the current round of capital revisions, and one of the core public policy goals underlying bank regulation.[3]

In this chapter, we do not attempt to estimate the potential magnitude of the effect on the economy as a whole. However, we note that the impact on capital ratios is relatively large under the new proposal for lending-oriented banks. The degree of change in new lending flows required to restore the original ratio is likely to be even larger.[4]

It is important for bank management to understand how regulators will treat these swings in minimum regulatory capital requirement in advance of any implementation. The proposals are a substantial departure from the current regime, and different regulatory interpretations could have very different implications for bank behaviour. In addition, rating agencies currently put some weight on regulatory ratios, and will need to address the substantial difference between the old and the new rules. Clearly, bank management will need to understand how to adapt their strategies with respect to this audience as well.

Possible approaches to addressing the issue of capital volatility and pro-cyclicality are detailed at the end of this chapter. Many of these solutions involve difficult trade-offs, because the objective of risk sensitivity is fundamentally opposed to that of capital stability over time. Among them, we favour solutions that dampen sensitivity to economic cycles and allow risk capital ratios to fluctuate without penalty. This could be accomplished either via explicit regulatory guidance, or through various mechanical techniques (eg, the use of flexible capital buffers, or even the use of original ratings in the IRB approach). We believe that this issue is a critical one for a successful capital regime, but that it has yet to be addressed sufficiently by the Basel Committee.

## The new Accord

The new Accord gives two alternative frameworks for calculating credit risk capital:

THE STANDARDISED APPROACH

This is designed to be used by smaller or less sophisticated banks. This approach is similar to the current framework but with a reduced capital requirement for assets with high-quality external ratings and some increased requirements for poor-quality externally rated assets.

THE INTERNAL RATINGS-BASED APPROACH (IRB)

This is a more risk-sensitive approach, likely to be used by many banks. Capital requirements are determined relative to an internally assessed probability of default. Capital requirements under the IRB approach are non-linear in the rating and very sensitive to credit quality, especially for middle- to low-quality assets.[5] Figure 1 shows capital requirements by rating under the three approaches (for the IRB approach, historic default rates by

**1. Capital requirements by rating**

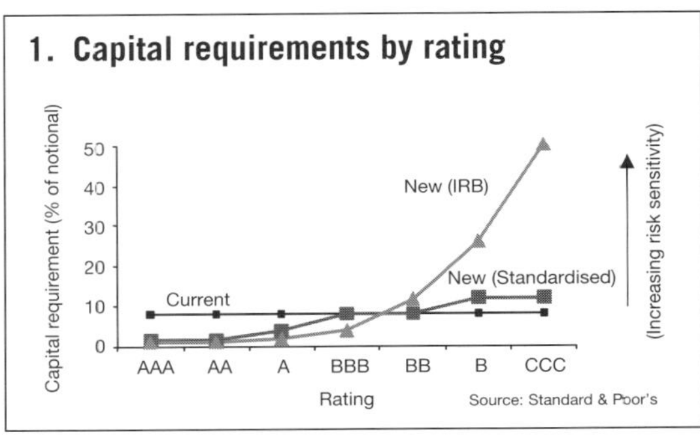


rating published by Standard and Poor's have been used).

The increased risk sensitivity of the approaches, particularly the IRB approach, has many desirable attributes, especially to encourage risk-sensitive behaviour within banks (more capital required for lower-quality loans within a bank) and across banks (more capital required for banks with lower-quality overall portfolios). However, as a natural consequence there is more risk sensitivity across time as well, increasing the danger of additional economic cycle reinforcement in the new Accord. Given that the majority of the world's larger banking institutions are expected to use some form of the IRB for regulatory capital calculation, this chapter restricts its focus to the IRB approach from here.

## Risk sensitivity and capital volatility

Risk sensitivity and capital volatility are fundamentally related. The more a capital regime differentiates by quality of asset, the more capital will fluctuate when assets improve or deteriorate in quality. The following are some observations about the relationship between these two characteristics:

- Under any capital regime, whether risk sensitive or not, erosion of capital due to actual defaults and provisioning requirements will always tend to be recognised in adverse credit environments, provided prudent accounting principles are followed.
- A certain minimum level of cycle reinforcement is thereby built in. Defaults erode capital in the banking system, restricting the supply of credit available to performing borrowers. The current Capital Adequacy Directive regime more or less represents this minimum for credit portfolios, since it does not distinguish the risk characteristics of non-defaulted assets (all are assigned 8% capital). This minimum level effect is present equally under the proposed Accord and the existing Accord.

**2. Migrations and default rates 1981–2000**

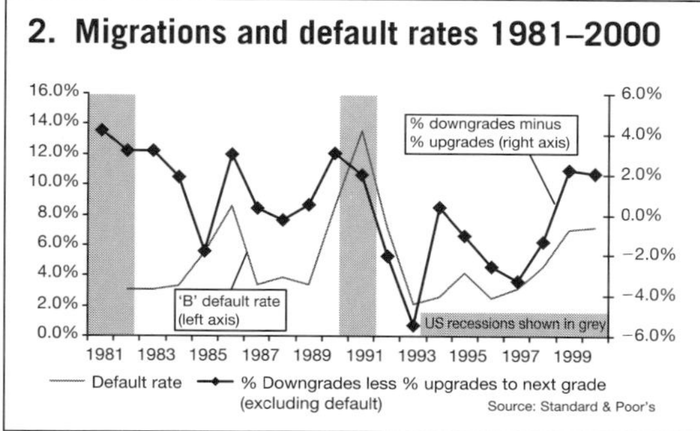

Source: Standard & Poor's

**Table 1. Credit ratings migration – 1990 transition matrix**

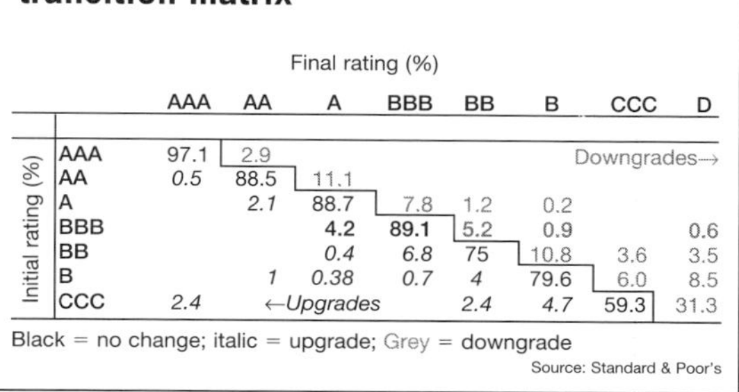

| Initial rating (%) | Final rating (%) AAA | AA | A | BBB | BB | B | CCC | D |
|---|---|---|---|---|---|---|---|---|
| AAA | 97.1 | 2.9 | | | | | Downgrades→ | |
| AA | *0.5* | 88.5 | 11.1 | | | | | |
| A | | *2.1* | 88.7 | 7.8 | 1.2 | 0.2 | | |
| BBB | | | **4.2** | **89.1** | **5.2** | **0.9** | | **0.6** |
| BB | | | *0.4* | *6.8* | 75 | 10.8 | 3.6 | 3.5 |
| B | | *1* | *0.38* | *0.7* | *4* | 79.6 | 6.0 | 8.5 |
| CCC | *2.4* | | *←Upgrades* | | *2.4* | *4.7* | 59.3 | 31.3 |

Black = no change; italic = upgrade; Grey = downgrade

Source: Standard & Poor's

- ❑ Any approach that further distinguishes riskiness of assets will be sensitive not just to erosion of capital from actual losses, but also to increased capital requirements for performing assets that have been downgraded or considered "closer" to default. The IRB approach of the new Accord increases risk capital exponentially as assets move down the ratings curve, as shown in Figure 1.
- ❑ Economic downturns are typically associated with systemically higher levels of ratings downgrades and relatively low levels of upgrades (they are also associated with higher levels of actual defaults). This effect is shown in Figure 2 (using default rates for "single B-rated" assets as a proxy for overall default rates).[6]
- ❑ During severe downturn years, the amount of net downgrades can be substantial, even for credit ratings that attempt to rate "through the economic cycle", such as those of Moody's Investors Service or S&P (rating systems that focus on "spot" risk, such as KMV, are likely to be even substantially more volatile). The impact of systemic ratings movements is considered in the next section, which discusses the impact of a high downgrade year on bank capital.

## Example: the year 1990

As an example, we consider the impact on bank capital ratios of a "1990 scenario", which was an adverse year for overall ratings migration and the start of a recession.[7] The upgrades and downgrades experienced in that year, as tabulated by Standard & Poor's, are shown in Table 1.

The capital required under the proposed rules (IRB approach) will rise significantly in a year such as 1990. Table 2 calculates the capital requirement for a bank that started the year with a portfolio of BBB-rated loans (bold numbers). Any defaults during the year are assumed to generate an effective capital charge of 50%.[8] The current and IRB capital calculations are detailed in Table 2.

In this scenario, the capital requirement for the sample portfolio rises from 4.0% at the start of the year (100% of the portfolio rated BBB) to 4.8% at the end, based on the average level of migrations as illustrated. This represents an increase of about 20% in required capital.[9]

Put another way, a bank that started 1990 with an 8% capital ratio would see its capital ratio fall to 6.8% (= 8% × 4%/4.8%) by year-end, assuming no extra capital was raised.

By comparison, the capital impact under the current Basel guidelines is small - Table 2 shows an increase of about 3% in capital requirements, corresponding to a reduction to 7.8% (= 8% × 8.0%/8.2%) in capital ratio. Capital ratios under the current regime are affected only by default losses. There is no effect from lower ratings for performing assets that are "closer to default" (higher "credit risk") under the current rules.

Change in capital is substantial under the new system even though downgrades outpaced upgrades by only 1.9%. This is caused by the exponential nature of the risk weights, where each 1% of downgrades "cost" roughly 7.6% in extra capital (ie, BBB has a 4% requirement versus BB at 11.6%), whereas the upgrades only "save" 2.2% in capital.

1990 was not an unusual or extreme event. On the same basis, 1986 was slightly worse, though both of these years may be surpassed by 2001 if current trends continue.

If a bank wanted to preserve its ratios, it could stop lending, sell assets or raise more capital. The first outcome could create a significant economic effect, while the second and third would require a price penalty under stressed conditions. This penalty could be substantial if all market participants were engaging in the same efforts at the same time, and this could cause a significant impact to the overall credit markets. The possibility that the new rules could create - indeed compel - damaging "herd behaviour" along these lines could seriously impact the reliance on

**Table 2. Current and IRB capital calculations**

| Rating | Beginning of year (%) | End of year (%) | IRB capital weight (%) | Capital requirement (%) | Rating | Beginning of year (%) | End of year (%) | IRB capital weight (%) | Capital requirement (%) |
|---|---|---|---|---|---|---|---|---|---|
| AAA | | 0.0 | × 1.1 = | 0.0 | AAA | | 0.0 | × 8.0 = | 0.0 |
| AA | | 0.0 | × 1.1 = | 0.0 | AA | | 0.0 | × 8.0 = | 0.0 |
| A | | 4.2 | × 1.8 = | 0.1 | A | | 4.2 | × 8.0 = | 0.3 |
| BBB | 100.00 | 89.1 | × 4.0 = | 4.0 3.5 | BBB | 100.00 | 89.1 | × 8.0 = | 8.0 7.1 |
| BB | | 5.2 | × 11.6 = | 0.6 | BB | | 5.2 | × 8.0 = | 0.4 |
| B | | 0.9 | × 26.0 = | 0.2 | B | | 0.9 | × 8.0 = | 0.1 |
| CCC | | 0.0 | × 50.0 = | 0.0 | CCC | | 0.0 | × 8.0 = | 0.0 |
| D | See note 7 | 0.6 | × 50.0 = | 0.3 | D | See note 7 | 0.6 | × 50.0 = | 0.3 |
| Total ending capital requirement | | | | 4.8% | Total ending capital requirement | | | | 8.2% |
| Initial capital requirement (100% BBB) | | | | 4.0% | Initial capital requirement (100% BBB) | | | | 8.0% |
| % increase in capital requirement | | | | 19.4% | % increase in capital requirement | | | | 3.0% |

market disciplines, which is otherwise a relatively strong and constructive feature of the proposed revisions. Alternatively, it could restrict new lending, which could have a significant economic impact. In the remaining sections, we discuss various approaches for addressing the capital volatility issue. What measures against pro-cyclicality are incorporated in the new Accord, and what more radical approaches are there to combat this risk?

## Assessing solutions for pro-cyclicality

Any solution to pro-cyclicality will involve some compromises to the risk sensitivity of the proposed regime. Risk sensitivity is only a desirable element, not the only or even the primary objective in formulating a capital regime. Regulatory capital is not another version of the economic capital models on which banks base internal risk decisions. What is important is that regulatory capital should produce good public policy incentives for bank behaviour.

Four key incentives of a regulatory capital framework are desirable and relevant to this discussion:

1. Risk sensitivity within an institution, which is desirable for improving risk selection.
2. Risk sensitivity across banks, which is desirable for allocating more capital to riskier institutions.
3. Risk sensitivity across time, which is desirable for ensuring capital is maintained at a sufficient level even during difficult times.
4. Capital requirements which are consistent through time and do not exacerbate economic cycles.

Goals one and two do not require compromise, while goals three and four conflict and require an intelligent balance. This gives us a way of judging the various solutions presented below: the better solutions are those that balance three and four without sacrificing one and two.

## Provisions in existing capital regimes

### TRIGGER AND TARGET RATIOS

National authorities' implementations of the current Accord in some cases already reflect an attempt to deal with capital volatility by imposing buffer capital on banks. For example, for institutions regulated by the UK Financial Services Authority, the so-called trigger ratio (set somewhere above 8%/4% of total capital or tier-one capital) gives the minimum ratio required to be held while the (even) higher target ratio acts as a "warning light".[10] Temporary planned breaches of the target ratio are tolerated provided the authority agrees that capital can be restored, and similarly unplanned breaches lead to imposition of a remedial regime. The "prompt corrective action" regimes in the US are much the same.

However, these regimes are not specifically designed to combat pro-cyclicality. Their main purpose appears to be to allow supervisors to require capital ratios that are more prudent than the basic "8%" rule, and to adjust their own capital requirements to suit individual qualitative assessments of banks' internal control environment.

Although a target-type regime can form part of the defence against pro-cyclicality (see below), the critical element is missing from the current systems, namely the explicit ability to adjust overall capital targets for market conditions. This should include adjustments to require less capital when necessitated by economic circumstances.

## Provisions in the new Accord

BUFFER CAPITAL

The new Accord expands on "buffer capital" mechanisms in place today by requiring banks to plan their forward capital requirements, including regular assessments of their capital adequacy relative to stress tests.[11] In practice, banks may need "buffer" capital well in excess of the minimum requirements. This is a key issue for the overall calibration of the approach; even if minimum requirements are unchanged, banks may need far more actual capital to carry their business through a cycle.[12] If the IRB capital weights were reduced to allow for the creation of a significant buffer, however, then the IRB approach could become more attractive and the buffer could be used to absorb fluctuations in systemic asset quality.

"FORWARD-LOOKING" RATINGS

The new Accord states that ratings or PD estimates should assess a "long-run average" risk and that the assessment should be "forward looking".[13] These guidelines can be seen as instructions to compensate for future changes in economic conditions (a "long-run average" assessment is neutral if it observes companies of the same intrinsic quality against the background of various economic conditions). On the other hand, the "forward-looking" requirement suggests that assessments should be relatively pessimistic in an economic upturn, by looking forward to a change in the cycle, and correspondingly optimistic in a downturn.

The capital volatility estimates presented in this chapter were done with reference to S&P ratings migration statistics. S&P ratings already attempt to rate "through a cycle". A rating system that is even more "through-the-cycle" and "forward looking" (ie, less cyclical) will be challenging to implement. Banks must assess where they are in a credit cycle to correct to a long-run average. If this assessment is done on a qualitative basis, it may reduce the statistical underpinnings of rating systems, putting pressure on the integrity of the bank's rating process and making continued supervisory approval more difficult. We are sceptical that the capital volatility issue can be addressed simply by further emphasis on making ratings more forward looking, or by banks maintaining large capital buffers without any assurance that these would be available for release when needed.

## What more can be done?

We discuss several further responses below. Of these, only the first one, flattening the IRB curve, is to our knowledge currently being considered by the Basel Committee.

FLATTENING THE IRB CURVE

One partial answer to capital volatility is to change the steepness of the IRB curve, or, in other words, the rate with which the IRB risk weight increases with increasing PD. The slope of the IRB risk weight function depends on the asset correlation, currently set to the value $r = 20\%$. The curve could be flattened by changing this parameter or by making it dependent on credit quality, possibly with a compensating change to the overall multiplier. Analytically, flattening the curve amounts to adopting a "blend" of IRB and the current approach. Moreover, reduced pro-cyclicality is at the expense of less incentivisation between different asset choices at the same time; this is the type of risk sensitivity we have argued it is important to preserve. This approach sacrifices all the risk sensitivity goals (goals one, two and three) to improve consistency through time. We think sacrificing goals one and two is an unnecessary loss.

USE OF ORIGINAL RATINGS, RATHER THAN CURRENT RATINGS IN THE IRB APPROACH

A more radical approach to the pro-cyclicality problem could be to use an asset's rating at the time of inception or purchase, instead of the current rating, to determine its risk weight. Thus a loan originated at "BB" would attract a fixed capital requirement related to its initially assessed default risk (apart, possibly for the maturity element), regardless of its subsequent rating, providing it remained performing. The privilege should not extend to a subsequent purchaser or protection provider – these counterparties would always have to reflect the current rating, which would therefore influence the pricing of any transaction connected with the loan.

This suggestion results in a number of challenging issues but also has some attractive properties. It uncouples the connection between a bank's capital requirement and the current quality of its assets, one of the deepest assumptions about what a risk system should look like. It could lead to capital levels for the same asset being different in different banks, which violates another important principle behind the new Accord. Moreover, there may be capital arbitrage opportunities inherent in the approach. However, it preserves, in full, the risk sensitivity of the current proposals at the point of decision, because the rating at that time determines the capital requirement. It would thereby preserve all of the benefits of goals one and two. Modifications of this approach, such as limiting the amount of difference between the original and current PD estimate or rating, would allow a balance to be struck between goals three and four. This approach thus provides flexibility to reduce capital volatility while preserving many of the Basel objectives.

EXPLICIT REGULATORY GUIDANCE

Another radical solution that moderates capital volatility would be to let the aggregate amount of capital in the system float with the "cycle". This is actually similar to what happens today, where the credit quality of bank portfolios deteriorates during a recession, but no additional capital is required (except to provide for actual defaults). However, in an IRB-regulated world, regulatory guidance would probably need to be explicit to counterbalance the capital effects calculated above. For example, an acceptable industry ratio could be estimated regularly (perhaps quarterly) based on average credit migration statistics or economic conditions during the period. Banks would then be judged relative to an overall benchmark, rather than an absolute level. This would enable the cyclical impact to be "re-indexed" to today's structure, without losing the other benefits of risk sensitivity (better capital allocation within banks and across banks).

Guidance on lending standards is currently given verbally, through announcements that tighten or relax standards. To address the issues raised above, the amount of guidance from regulatory authorities on lending standards would have to become far more explicit, quantitative and timely. For example, regulators could announce the quantitative amount of credit re-indexing to banks via a variable multiplier, reducing or increasing the capital charge for all banks by some percentage, negating when necessary the systemic effect of downgrades on capital ratios and lending activity. (Banks with bad credit experience relative to the average would still have to adjust their lending behaviour, however.)[14]

Regulators could apply this index to govern the amount of "buffer capital" held at banks, or it could be applied directly as a scalar that would be multiplied against overall credit risk capital. It could also be delegated to individual banks (for example, as a "through-the-cycle" scalar adjustment to all credit ratings). However, the delegated approach might weaken the benefit of risk sensitivity across banks if implemented differently at different banks (though that could also be monitored and controlled by supervisors).

Despite many issues (frequency of announcements, how to establish a re-indexing ratio for banks with portfolios located in different regions experiencing different cycles), this approach does offer a possible escape from simple compromises between risk sensitivity and capital stability.

## Rating agencies

To the extent that rating agencies use capital ratios to inform their ratings of banks, the capital volatility noted above could result in more volatility for bank credit ratings, unless rating agencies also make provisions for this effect.[15] Bank managers are sensitive to their public ratings, and are likely to play to this audience, which could create some pro-cyclicality regardless of the regulatory response.

## Conclusions

Risk sensitivity is regarded as a desirable characteristic because it enables better discrimination between good and bad credits. While that has important benefits for capital allocation within banks and across banks, it raises significant problems when considered across time, due to the effect of systemic ratings fluctuations from credit cycles. Capital volatility through time is increased materially under the proposed new regime, and the effects appear to be material when tested in light of past cycles. This impact will have a meaningful effect on capital planning for banks, for rating agencies and regulators, and on the relative attractiveness of the IRB approach compared with the standardised approach.

Capital volatility may also have a significant impact on the credit markets and the economy overall, depending on how regulators decide to interpret and control these fluctuations. If they decide to maintain bank capital ratios and bank credit, then banks must raise capital (which will probably be difficult in adverse markets), sell assets or restrict new lending. Given that these effects are systemic in nature, the pro-cyclical impact of such a response on the overall credit markets and the economy could be material.[16] If regulators decide instead to permit capital ratios to fall during a credit cycle, they can potentially avoid those problems, but would be explicitly deciding to let bank capital ratios and bank credits deteriorate.

This difficult choice is faced under any regulated capital regime, where all participants have to adhere to uniform rules. In an adverse credit cycle, the real risk (say, of insolvency) faced by an owner of a credit portfolio is clearly greater, whether the regime requires more capital or not. There is no alternative to either requiring asset reduction/more capital, or tolerating a higher risk of bank defaults at such times. It is this trade-off that the Basel Committee must evaluate and decide on.

The question is how to achieve an appropriate balance between these issues. For market risk, the Basel Committee decided to choose to maintain bank credit quality. Under the VAR system, trading risks are "weighted" by the amount of loss they would cause on the 99% worst period observed in a population of market data from a recent period. After a severe crisis, this historic market data will tend to exhibit more volatility, and each trading position is essentially assigned a higher risk weight. The size of positions that can be accommodated by a fixed amount of market risk capital is effectively reduced, driving banks that wish to maintain a constant amount of market risk capital to sell or hedge positions just after a crisis. This risk must be transferred into the market, potentially adding to stress at a difficult time.

While the market risk decision is certainly important, the answer for credit risk will be much more significant. Capital governed by market risk calculations typically covers only 10% to 20% of total capital for most international banks. Fluctuations in market parameters can be handled in the current system by stretching bank ratios modestly. Moreover, market risk assets tend to be relatively liquid, and have a large proportion of non-bank participants, which means that they can also be managed by market sales at a reasonable cost. Credit risk assets are less liquid and comprise a significantly larger proportion of capital. The capital volatility impact for credit risk will be more significant, more challenging and must be aggressively addressed.

In our discussion of the various solutions above, we have recognised that all involve a reduction in risk sensitivity. Some also reduce all the good incentives provided by the IRB approach while other solutions are more targeted and therefore preferable. For example, the possibility of flattening the IRB curve is relatively unappealing as it simply trades off all the benefits of risk sensitivity as a way to mitigate, but not eliminate, the problem. Simply trying to rate more "through-the-cycle" has natural limitations. Of the choices discussed above, we believe that the most promising avenues are some form of managed capital buffer or explicit regulatory guidance. We also think that the "original ratings" approach is worthy of more exploration.

The choice of how credit risk capital volatility is addressed will ultimately depend on the priorities of bank regulators – whether bank safety *per se* is the primary aim or whether the "public good" benefits of a more stable credit risk capital allocation system are more important. Banks already have significant motivation for their own safety, that of self-preservation. We would suggest that, from a regulatory perspective, the "public good" aspect should be considered the more important since it forms the underlying rationale for public bank capital regulation in the first place.

1 *Market risk capital is governed by VAR calculations, which typically use a data set of recent historical market moves to estimate a 99% worst-case loss for a portfolio. After a crisis, the data set is likely to have larger extreme moves and the VAR for a given portfolio is likely to be larger. This means that a fixed VAR or regulatory capital limit will restrict traders to smaller positions just after a crisis.*

2 *While some banks may be able to avoid downgraded assets, it is unlikely that the banking industry as a whole can do so.*

3 *Danièle Nouy (Chair, BIS Models Task force), presentation to IIF, Paris, 28 June, 2001.*

4 *In order to restore their ratios, banks would need to reduce the overall balance of loans, which would require a large cut in the supply of new loans given the longer term nature of many portfolios. For example, in the scenario cited above, the capital charge for the BBB portfolio increased by 20% in 1990. If that bank had a portfolio with a 3-year average life, it would normally make new loans equal to 33% of the balance every year (to maintain a stable portfolio). Unless capital could be saved elsewhere, the capital available for new loans would have to be cut from 33% to only 20% (=100%–67% × 1.2), implying a reduction of 40% (=(33%–20%)/33%) in new lending – even assuming that lending could be done at the same mix of credit qualities as before the scenario. Alternatively, banks could try to sell assets to maintain capital ratios, though this would likely occur at a time when credit asset values are generally depressed, and potentially aggravate financial losses at a time when bank profitability is already impaired.*

5 *The steepness of IRB risk weights against rating is a reflection of the fact that default probabilities rise dramatically as one steps down the rating grades. The comparison with current and standardised capital has to be made by rating grade, however, as only the IRB approach depends explicitly on PD.*

6 *Uses data from Standard & Poor's, 2001. Net downgrade statistic shown is the proportion of instances of downgrade to the next whole letter rating less proportion of instances of upgrade, over all ratings except "D" (ie, performing grades only – defaults excluded). Single B default rates are used as a proxy for default rates generally; the cycle observed for other grades is broadly similar.*

7 *Actual defaults peaked later, in 1991, which was also the year when US economic growth slipped below zero.*

8 *To avoid accounting issues we assume that a defaulted loan costs an amount of capital equal to an average LGD of 50%. Depending on the ultimate rules for specific provisioning, a heavier charge than this is possible.*

9 *It could be asserted that the bank was still better off in outright terms since the IRB approach still charges a lower overall amount of capital under the IRB, even after the migration event (4.8%) than the current system (8.2%). That would imply that there was a large buffer available to cushion the shock, so that perhaps this volatility would not be binding. However, other elements in the new Accord, such as additional charges for equities and operational risk, will produce a net increase in capital charges for most banks versus the current system (at least as originally proposed), and that may also add to volatility. The effect on market risk measured by VAR has also not been considered (see note 1).*

10 *The FSA system of trigger and target ratios will be discontinued in November 2001. The new system has similar aims. Trigger ratios will be replaced by Individual Capital Ratios while explicit target ratios will no longer be set, reliance being placed instead on supervision of institutions' internal capital policies. See FSA (2001) for details.*

11 *Basel (2001), Pillar II, "Four Key Principles of Supervisory Review", Principle 1. See also paragraph 297 under requirements to be eligible for the IRB approach.*

12 *It has also been pointed out that potential buffer requirements, whether imposed or held by banks voluntarily, will alter the incentives for banks to qualify for the IRB approach. See Jokivuolle and Peura (2001).*

13 *Basel (2001), paragraph 270 and IRB document, paragraph 70.*

14 *This type of policy change would be similar to how reserve or margin requirements were managed historically. These announcements could be made similar to interest rate policy; indeed they could become important policy tools in their own right. This could also remove much of the disincentive to adopt the IRB approach noted in Jokivoulle and Peura (2001).*

15 *Moreover, since many bank assets are often issued or guaranteed by other banks, banks ratings volatility could further increase the severity of migrations observed in bank portfolios above historic levels. This could create an additional adverse systemic feedback element.*

16 *The systemic impact will clearly depend on the percentage of lending assets that are governed by the IRB approach in the future. We would expect this to be significant, given that the major international banks are expected to adopt one of the IRB approaches.*

**BIBLIOGRAPHY**

**Basel Committee on Banking Supervision,** 2001, *The New Basel Capital Accord*, Bank for International Settlements, January.

**Financial Services Authority,** 2001, *Individual Capital Ratios for Banks Policy Statement*, May.

**Jokivuolle, E., and S. Peura,** 2001, "Regulatory Capital Volatility", *Risk*, May, pp. 95–8.

**Standard & Poor's,** 2001, *Ratings Performance 2000 – Default, Transition, Recovery, and Spreads*, January.

# 23

# The Maturity Effect on Credit Risk Capital

**Michael Kalkbrener and Ludger Overbeck**
Deutsche Bank

*In a mark-to-market approach to credit risk capital, ratings or spread volatility has the effect of making longer-maturity loans more capital-intensive. This is incorporated in the current Basel II proposals via a maturity adjustment factor. Arguing that regulatory capital rules should focus on extreme risks rather than migration risk, Michael Kalkbrener and Ludger Overbeck simulate the effect of various migration data on model portfolios, and conclude that the Basel II maturity factor should be set considerably lower.*

In this chapter, we analyse maturity effects on the risk capital for credit portfolios. Conceptually, we deal with the question of how the risk capital of a loan or bond with maturity $m_1$, eg, three years, differs from the risk capital of a loan with maturity $m_2$, eg, seven years. These maturity factors are important in light of the Basel II discussion (Basel Committee on Banking Supervision, 2001). Since internal credit risk models are not accepted, regulatory authorities suggest capturing maturity effects in terms of multipliers. Basel II allows measurement of the risk of a standard asset (with a maturity of three years) by internal ratings. The impact of other maturities should then be expressed in terms of fixed multipliers applied to the capital of the three-year asset. This chapter attempts to give some insight into the derivation and size of these factors. In general, our adjustments are lower than in the mark-to-market approach of the current Basel II proposal.

To be consistent with industry standards and the formal derivation of the risk weight function in the Basel II consultation paper, we assume that risk capital is based on a planning horizon of one year. Our setting for calculating risk capital is similar to the CreditMetrics/KMV approach (JP Morgan, 1997; Vasicek, 1997; Kealhofer, 1995; Overbeck and Stahl, 2001). The rating or creditworthiness of all counterparties at year one is determined by an underlying multivariate variable $\vec{A}$, which might be called the "asset-value process" or, more generally, the "ability-to-pay process". A loss distribution of the credit portfolio is calculated by revaluation based on the ability-to-pay process and the maturity structure of the portfolio. The risk capital of the portfolio corresponds to a quantile of its loss distribution. Details of this model are given below.

*The views expressed are those of the authors and do not necessarily reflect the position of Deutsche Bank.*

We present two different approaches to analyse maturity effects. The first, called the "one-particle approach", is based on a notion of contributory capital of an individual credit in a portfolio. The second approach considers how the capital of an entire portfolio changes if the maturity of all loans in the portfolio change.

In the one-particle approach, we construct a diversified portfolio of loans with different ratings and maturities. We add one loan C and calculate its contributory economic capital $E_1$. Then the maturity of the loan is changed and its contributory economic capital $E_2$ is calculated again. The quotient between $E_1$ and $E_2$ measures the maturity effect for the rating class of C. This analysis is done for all rating classes.

We use two definitions of contributory capital, namely one based on the covariance of a loan with the portfolio and one based on contributory expected shortfall, ie, the average contribution of a loan to very large portfolio losses. Both capital allocation techniques are based on Monte Carlo simulation. The covariance approach is independent of the quantile chosen for the definition of capital and is – in our opinion – not suitable for the calculation of maturity adjustments. In contrast, contributory expected shortfall is sensitive to the quantile. It turns out that with higher quantiles, ie, if capital is defined in terms of extreme risk, the influence of maturity decreases significantly.

The second approach, the "portfolio approach", focuses on portfolios that consist of loans of the same credit quality and maturity. Capital is defined as the credit-VAR of the entire portfolio. Maturity adjustments are determined by varying the maturity of the portfolio and calculating corresponding changes in portfolio capital. We use Monte Carlo simulation to calculate maturity adjustments for portfolios of different rating and size and give evidence that adjustments converge if portfolio size increases. The limits are the maturity adjustments for infinite portfolios, which we calculate by an analytic generalisation of the risk weight function BRW (benchmark risk weight) in the Basel proposal (Basel Committee on Banking Supervision, 2001). In general, maturity adjustments obtained by this homogeneous portfolio approach are similar to those based on contributory expected shortfall in the one-particle approach.

## MAIN RESULTS

Maturity effects increase with credit quality, ie, higher ratings have higher maturity adjustments than lower ratings. This qualitative result can easily be verified by each of the estimation techniques used in this chapter. It is also in line with the adjustments proposed in the Basel II consultation paper. However, the quantification of maturity effects is a more challenging task. One problem is that maturity adjustments heavily depend on estimation techniques and parameter settings. In this chapter, we experiment with the following parameters:

### *Migration matrices*

We use the one-year migration matrix presented by Standard & Poor's (S&P, 1999), the KMV matrix (Kealhofer, Kwok and Weng, 1998) and a matrix (abbreviated as GC) constructed from migration data on German corporates (see Appendix: transition matrices). In all tests, the choice of the migration matrix is critical. The KMV matrix produces the highest and the S&P matrix the lowest maturity adjustments.

### *Spreads*

The revaluation of the portfolio at the end of the one-year planning period is based on credit spreads and their corresponding multi-year default probabilities. The spreads are either market spreads or are derived from migration matrices (and therefore based on historical data). Despite the fact that a proper mark-to-market of traded credit products has to be based on market spreads, we believe that historical spreads have some advantages for the analysis of maturity effects: historical spreads are less volatile and they do not reflect liquidity risk and risk aversion (including the cost of risk capital that we intend to derive). Another argument against market spreads is the fact that most loans are not liquid assets. In our analysis, we use historical spreads as well as market spreads (see Appendix: corporate bond spreads). Results show that maturity adjustments are sensitive to the choice of spreads. In particular, the comparatively high spreads in September 2001 lead to higher adjustments.

### *Quantiles*

Expected shortfall contributions for single exposures and credit-VAR for portfolios are defined with respect to specific quantiles. We show that maturity effects rapidly decrease if higher quantiles are considered.

### *Other parameters*

We experiment with different government yield curves, recovery assumptions, one- and multifactor correlation models, and different average asset correlations. The variations in results are minor compared with matrix, spread and quantile effects.

We use different estimation techniques for maturity adjustments:

- Although the VAR/CoVAR technique has obvious disadvantages if applied to fat tail distributions, it is the standard technique for allocating credit economic capital (EC). We therefore use VAR/CoVAR allocation in the one-particle approach: this approach based on covariance produces maturity adjustments that are significantly higher than those calculated with other techniques. The results are independent of the quantile chosen for the definition of capital.
- The one-particle approach based on shortfall contributions and the homogeneous portfolio approach give consistent results. For instance,

we obtain the following factors between a one-year facility and a seven-year facility for the best rating class[1] with the GC matrix (see Tables 5 and 7): 2.68 and 2.22 respectively for the 99.9065% and 99.98% quantile with the one-particle-approach, and 2.43 and 1.97 with the portfolio approach.

Our results show that the impact of maturity decreases if the confidence level for capital is increased. This is consistent with the evidence that extreme loss events in credit risk are predominately caused by defaults (see JP Morgan, 1997). Our findings therefore give evidence that at least for regulatory purposes, which should focus on systemic extreme risk, the adjustments in the mark-to-market approach of the current Basel II consultation paper are too high. Based on the results in this chapter, our recommendation is to cap maturity adjustments between one and seven years at 2.5. In our opinion, higher adjustments would lead to a misallocation of capital, namely against the volatility of migration and not against extreme losses.

## Basic model

The calculation of maturity adjustments is based on risk capital and risk contributions, which are derived from the underlying loss variables of the portfolio and individual exposures. This section presents the basic model.

### LOSS VARIABLES

Each loan $C_i$ in the portfolio has a loss variable $L_i$, which specifies the value of the loan at the planning horizon of one year. The portfolio loss is defined by the random variable $L = \Sigma_{i=1}^{N} L_i$, where $N$ is the number of facilities in the portfolio.

### ABILITY TO PAY

Let $\vec{A}$ be an N-variate standardised[2] normally distributed random variable with correlation matrix $R$. We call the ith component of $\vec{A}$ the "ability to pay" of loan $C_i$. The general model is $L_i = L(A_i, m_i)$, ie, the value and the loss function of the loan depends solely on the ability to pay of the counterparty and the maturity $m_i$ of the loan.[3] In the KMV concept, $L$ is a continuous function of $A_i$. For simplicity, we assume in this chapter that it is a step function, ie, only a finite number of values can be obtained. In credit risk modelling, it is common to identify these finitely many states with credit ratings.

### RATINGS AND TRANSITION MATRICES

We use the S&P rating scheme consisting of the rating classes AAA, AA, A, BBB, BB, B and CCC. These ratings are identified with numbers one to seven, and the additional rating class default with eight. A one-year migration matrix $M = (p_{ij})_{i,\,j=1,\ldots,\,8}$ specifies the probabilities $p_{ij}$ that a company migrates from rating $i$ to rating $j$ in a one-year period. We use three different transition matrices for our analysis: the S&P matrix in Standard & Poor's (1999), the KMV matrix in Kealhofer, Kwok and Weng (1998) and a transition matrix GC derived from migration data on German corporates. The exact definition of these three matrices is given in "Appendix: transition matrices".

The values of the "ability-to-pay" processes $A_1, \ldots, A_N$ in one year determine the ratings of the loans: the rating migration is simulated by defining thresholds $D_{k,i}$ in the distribution of the $A_i$ such that the event "counterparty $i$ migrates to rating $k$" coincides with the event "the value of $A_i$ in one year lies between $D_{k,i}$ and $D_{k+1,i}$".

### REVALUATION TECHNIQUES AND SPREADS

We assume that each facility $C_i$ in the portfolio has the cashflow profile of a bullet bond at par. Each $C_i$ is revaluated under the assumption that it is rated $k = 1, \ldots, 8$ in one year, yielding eight different values $V_1, \ldots, V_8$ of $C_i$. The revaluation formula is based on government bond yields and multi-year default probabilities, which are derived from transition matrices[4] or corporate bond spreads (see "Appendix: corporate bond spreads" for the specification of spreads used in this chapter). The loss variable $L_i$ is defined by subtracting the vector $(V_1, \ldots, V_8)$ from the value $\overline{V}$ of $C_i$ if its current rating has not changed.

### ECONOMIC CAPITAL

The economic capital of the portfolio is either defined as a quantile of the loss variable $L$ or as a quantile minus the mean of $L$. We have used both definitions in our analysis and have not found a significant impact on maturity adjustments.

## One-particle approach

Here we construct a diversified portfolio with different ratings and maturities. We add one loan $C$ and calculate its contributory economic capital $E_1$. In the next step, the maturity of the loan is changed and its contributory economic capital $E_2$ is calculated again. The quotient between $E_1$ and $E_2$ measures the maturity effect for the rating class of $C$.

CONSTRUCTION OF A DIVERSIFIED PORTFOLIO

Let $\{0.03, 0.05, 0.1, 0.2, 1, 3.3, 15\}$ be a set of default probabilities (in per cent) and $\{1, 2, 3, 4, 5, 6, 7\}$ a set of maturities (in years). We consider a portfolio P that consists of 98 loans, each possible default probability and maturity combination appearing twice. Now we add a single loan $C_{p,m}$ to the portfolio with default probability $p \in \{0.03, 0.05, 0.1, 0.2, 1, 3.3, 15\}$ and maturity $m \in \{1, 3, 7\}$. In this way, 21 different portfolios $P_{p,m} := P \cup \{C_{p,m}\}$ are obtained. It is assumed that all loans have the same notional. In the initial test scenario, the recovery rate of each loan is 50% and the correlation structure is specified by a one-factor model with all asset correlations equal to 35%.

CONTRIBUTORY EC BASED ON VAR/CoVAR

The VAR/CoVAR contribution technique is the standard approach developed in the capital asset pricing model. Risk contributions are proportional to covariances of loss variables of individual loans and portfolios. Since we are not interested in absolute contributory EC numbers but only in ratios of contributory economic capital, we proceed as follows. For each $p \in \{0.03, 0.05, 0.1, 0.2, 1, 3.3, 15\}$ and $m \in \{1, 3, 7\}$ the loss variables of loan $C_{p,m}$ and portfolio $P_{p,m}$ are simulated[5] and the covariance $cov_{p,m}$ is calculated. In accordance with the definition of maturity adjustments in the Basel proposal, risk contributions are normalised at three years, ie, we calculate $cov_{p,m}/cov_{p,3}$. Note that the results are independent of the quantile chosen for the capital definition.

*Test: GC matrix*

We derive migration probabilities and multi-year default probabilities from the GC matrix and obtain the results shown in Table 1. This table is structured as follows: the rows correspond to the different default probabilities 0.03%, 0.05%, 0.1%, 0.2%, 1%, 3.3% and 15% and the columns correspond to the considered maturities one, three and seven years. Since the table is normalised to the three-year capital, all entries in the second column are one. As an example, the first entry, "0.42", in the first row means that the capital for a one-year deal with a default probability of 0.03 is 42% of the capital for a three-year deal with the same default probability.

Note that, since not all of the default probabilities 0.03%, 0.05%, 0.1%, 0.2%, 1%, 3.3% and 15% correspond to GC ratings, the transition probabilities of some loans are calculated by interpolation in the GC matrix. For instance, the transition probabilities for a loan with PD = 0.1 are obtained by linear interpolation between the transition probabilities of the rating class 1 (PD = 0.07) and rating class 2 (PD = 0.2).

**Table 1. VAR/CoVAR: GC matrix**

| | 1 | 3 | 7 |
|---|---|---|---|
| 0.03 | 0.42 | 1 | 1.77 |
| 0.05 | 0.45 | 1 | 1.73 |
| 0.10 | 0.57 | 1 | 1.58 |
| 0.20 | 0.74 | 1 | 1.37 |
| 1.00 | 0.75 | 1 | 1.23 |
| 3.30 | 0.83 | 1 | 1.13 |
| 15.00 | 0.97 | 1 | 1.03 |

Table 1 shows that maturity effects increase with credit quality. This qualitative result has been verified with each of the estimation techniques used in this chapter. In the following we will therefore focus on adjustments for the senior rating class (PD = 0.03). Full results for all rating classes are presented in an extended version of this chapter (Kalkbrener and Overbeck, 2001).

*Tests: S&P and KMV matrix*

We repeat the above test with the same portfolio but use the S&P and KMV matrix instead of the German corporates. Table 2 shows the maturity adjustments for the senior rating class obtained with each of the three matrices.

The differences are significant. The factors between one and seven years are 4.21 for the GC matrix, 2.93 for the S&P matrix and 9.66 for the KMV matrix. There are two main reasons for these differences:

1. migration volatility, which can be read off the diagonal of the migration matrix. KMV postulates a very high migration probability. For instance, only 66% remain in the best rating class compared with 91% in the S&P matrix. Higher migration probabilities induce higher capital requirements; and

**Table 2. VAR/CoVAR: different matrices**

| GC | | | S&P | | | KMV | | |
|---|---|---|---|---|---|---|---|---|
| 1 | 3 | 7 | 1 | 3 | 7 | 1 | 3 | 7 |
| 0.42 | 1 | 1.77 | 0.57 | 1 | 1.67 | 0.29 | 1 | 2.80 |

**Table 3. VAR/CoVAR: different spreads**

| Spreads 97 | | | Spreads 01 | | |
|---|---|---|---|---|---|
| 1 | 3 | 7 | 1 | 3 | 7 |
| 0.55 | 1 | 1.92 | 0.34 | 1 | 2.59 |

2. revaluation, which is driven by the last column of the migration matrix. The impact of migration varies since the differences in the default probabilities of different ratings are important. The steepest gradient can be found in the S&P matrix. The default probabilities range from 0.01–20%, whereas KMV only covers 0.02–10.13%. The GC matrix shows the most stable repricing, the range being from 0.07–6%.

Obviously, the high maturity adjustments obtained with the KMV matrix are caused by its high migration volatility, which is not fully compensated by its less volatile repricing (compared with S&P).

*Tests: S&P with market spreads*

In the previous tests, revaluation was based on multi-year default probabilities obtained from historical transition matrices. Here, multi-year default probabilities are derived from the corporate bond spreads in "Appendix: corporate bond spreads". Since these bond spreads are based on the S&P rating system, we use the S&P transition matrix for the specification of the one-year migration probabilities (results are shown in Table 3). Note that the comparatively high spreads on September 25, 2001 lead to higher adjustments.

*Additional tests*

We did additional tests with the GC matrix by: using different government yield curves; changing the recovery rate to 70%; varying average asset correlations between 20% and 50%; replacing the one-factor model by a 10-factor model;[6] and using randomly generated portfolios.[7] Our results show that these changes have little effect compared with differences caused by using different transition matrices and spreads.

## CONTRIBUTORY EC BASED ON EXPECTED SHORTFALL

*Alternative economic capital definition*

From a risk management point of view, holding the economic capital based on a quantile, say the 99.5% quantile, as a cushion against the portfolio means that on average in 199 out of 200 years the capital would cover all losses. The disadvantage of this definition is that it does not take the size of the losses in the extreme 0.5% tail into account. Hence, this approach towards economic capital resembles an "all or nothing" rule. In particular, in a "bad" year (one out of 200) the capital does not cushion the losses. An alternative to EC based on quantiles is the following capital definition, which focuses on large portfolio losses. Consider those losses that exceed a given amount K and let economic capital (based on shortfall) be defined by:

$$EC_K(S) := E\left[L \middle| L > K\right]$$

Hence, economic capital based on shortfall covers the average "bad" loss. This approach also motivates the following definition of contributory capital based on coherent risk measures.

Coherency is analysed in detail by Artzner *et al.* (1999) and Delbaen (2001). They show that for continuous distributions, $EC_K(S)$ is coherent if K is a quantile of L. Coherency requires a risk measure to satisfy a set of axioms or first principles that a reasonable risk measure should obey. These axioms include sublinearity. It is also shown that the risk measures defined in terms of quantiles are not coherent in general.

*Risk contributions*

An important advantage of $EC_K(S)$ is the simple allocation of risk capital to a single transaction (see Overbeck, 2000). The contribution to shortfall risk, CSR, or shortfall contribution is defined by:

$$CSR_i = E\left[L_i \middle| L > K\right]$$

that is, the capital for a single loan is its average loss in bad years. Hence, a capital quota of more than 100% is impossible, in contrast to the classical VAR/CoVAR approach.

*Tests with different matrices and spreads*

We calculate the shortfall contributions of the loans $C_{p,m}$ in the portfolios $P_{p,m}$. The threshold K is defined by $E[L | L > K] = \alpha\text{-quantile}$, where $\alpha = 99.9065\%$. Table 4 shows the results obtained with all three matrices and two sets of market spreads.

These maturity adjustments are considerably smaller than those implied by the standard allocation technique based on covariances. For instance, the KMV factor between one and seven years for the senior rating decreased from 9.66 to 3.2. This result is not surprising from an economic point of view. Migration increases volatility, but

**Table 4. Expected shortfall**

| GC | | | S&P | | | KMV | | | Spreads 97 | | | Spreads 01 | | |
|---|---|---|---|---|---|---|---|---|---|---|---|---|---|---|
| 1 | 3 | 7 | 1 | 3 | 7 | 1 | 3 | 7 | 1 | 3 | 7 | 1 | 3 | 7 |
| 0.56 | 1 | 1.50 | 0.69 | 1 | 1.39 | 0.54 | 1 | 1.73 | 0.67 | 1 | 1.75 | 0.61 | 1 | 1.87 |

**Table 5. Expected shortfall: different quantiles**

| | GC | S&P | KMV | S'97 | S'01 |
|---|---|---|---|---|---|
| VAR/CoVAR | 4.21 | 2.93 | 9.66 | 3.49 | 7.62 |
| 99.50% | 2.94 | 2.16 | 4.35 | 2.92 | 5.40 |
| 99.91% | 2.68 | 2.01 | 3.20 | 2.61 | 3.07 |
| 99.98% | 2.22 | 1.74 | 2.60 | 1.74 | 2.36 |

not necessarily "extreme" or "tail" risk, which is the basis for expected shortfall and also the main concern of regulators. This becomes particularly obvious for the KMV matrix, which has high migration volatility.

To analyse the quantile effect, calculations are repeated for the 99.5% and 99.98% quantiles. Table 5 compares factors between one and seven years for the senior rating.

The structure of results is consistent across transition matrices and spreads. The highest factors are obtained in the VAR/CoVAR approach. Factors significantly decrease if higher quantiles are considered (between 1.74 and 2.6 for the 99.98% quantile).

## Portfolio approach

### CONSTRUCTION OF HOMOGENEOUS PORTFOLIOS

Here, we consider portfolios that are not diversified in terms of maturities, ie, all loans in the portfolio have the same maturity. Furthermore, we make the additional assumption that all loans in a portfolio have the same rating. Of course, this is not a realistic assumption but is similar to the one used in the Basel proposal. In this proposal, the regulatory capital charge of a single loan with default probability $p$ equals the quantile of a percentage loss distribution of an infinitely large homogeneous portfolio with default probability $p$ and asset correlation 20%. This is consistent with a one-factor model for an infinite granular portfolio. Since the one-factor model is portfolio invariant, there is no differentiation between different portfolios. In particular, it is not sensitive to diversification efforts.

We consider 21 homogeneous portfolios $P_{p,m}$, $p \in \{0.03, 0.05, 0.1, 0.2, 1, 3.3, 15\}$ and $m \in \{1, 3, 7\}$, each consisting of 100 loans with default probability $p$ and maturity $m$. It is assumed that the correlation structure is specified by a one-factor model with all asset correlations equal to $\rho$. Capital is defined as the credit-VAR of the entire portfolio. The maturity effect is determined by varying the maturity of the portfolio and calculating corresponding changes in portfolio capital.[8]

### TESTS WITH PORTFOLIOS OF DIFFERENT SIZE

The first three numbers, 0.64, 1, 1.37, in Table 6 are the ratios:

$$\text{q-quantile}(P_{p,m})/\text{q-quantile}(P_{p,3}) \qquad m = 1, 3, 7$$

for $q = 99.9065\%$ and the senior rating $p = 0.03$. The asset correlation $\rho = 35\%$ is used. Rating migration and multi-year default probabilities are specified by the GC matrix. The calculations are repeated for portfolios consisting of 400 loans. The last three numbers correspond to portfolios with an infinite number of loans. For these infinite portfolios, the portfolio loss variable equals (see Finger, 1999; Lucas *et al.*, 2001; Kalkbrener and Overbeck, 2001):

$$L_i(1) + \sum_{j=1}^{7} (L_i(j+1) - L_i(j)) N\left((c_j - \sqrt{\rho} Y)/\sqrt{1-\rho}\right) \quad (1)$$

where $L_i(1), \ldots, L_i(8)$ and $p_i(1), \ldots, p_i(8)$ respectively specify the loss function and the one-year migration probabilities of the individual loans $C_i$,[9] $Y$ is a standard normally distributed variable, $N$ denotes the standard normal distribution function and:

$$c_j := N^{-1}\left(\sum_{l=1+j}^{8} p_i(l)\right) \quad (2)$$

**Table 6. Convergence**

| 100 loans | | | 400 loans | | | ∞ loans | | |
|---|---|---|---|---|---|---|---|---|
| 1 | 3 | 7 | 1 | 3 | 7 | 1 | 3 | 7 |
| 0.64 | 1 | 1.37 | 0.61 | 1 | 1.44 | 0.60 | 1 | 1.46 |

**Table 7. Infinite granular portfolio**

| | GC | S&P | KMV | S'97 | S'01 |
|---|---|---|---|---|---|
| 99.50% | 3.46 | 2.57 | 6.10 | 2.46 | 5.41 |
| 99.91% | 2.43 | 2.09 | 3.73 | 1.95 | 3.54 |
| 99.98% | 1.97 | 1.82 | 2.72 | 1.69 | 2.69 |

Since the correlation structure is specified by a one-factor model, the credit-VAR can be calculated analytically. In contrast, the results for the finite portfolios have been obtained by 400,000 Monte Carlo simulations.

As expected, maturity adjustments converge to the limit specified by the infinite portfolio. Note that the results are similar to those obtained by shortfall contribution. This similarity can also be observed for the other matrices, spreads and quantiles. Table 7 displays factors between one and seven years for the senior rating calculated with analytic formula (1). Note that these adjustments have the same magnitude as the maturity adjustments based on contributory expected shortfall in the "one-particle approach" (see Table 5).

## Conclusion

For regulatory purposes, the required capital is formally based on a 99.9065% quantile. Taking all add-ons into account, actual capital requirements correspond to a much higher quantile. The results in this chapter support the view that on this extreme security level, migration and therefore maturity are of minor importance. Maturity adjustments calculated with methods sensitive to quantiles are significantly lower than adjustments obtained with the classical VAR/CoVAR contribution technique. Our results show that if capital requirements are based on high quantiles a maturity adjustment factor of 2.5 between one year and seven years is a conservative setting even for the best rating classes.

## Appendix

CORPORATE BOND SPREADS

We use the following corporate bond spreads under normal and distressed market conditions:

| | Spreads 97 | | | | |
|---|---|---|---|---|---|
| | 1y | 2y | 3y | 5y | 7y |
| AAA | 0.16 | 0.18 | 0.22 | 0.25 | 0.31 |
| AA | 0.20 | 0.22 | 0.26 | 0.30 | 0.35 |
| A | 0.27 | 0.30 | 0.32 | 0.37 | 0.42 |
| BBB | 0.44 | 0.46 | 0.50 | 0.52 | 0.56 |
| BB | 0.89 | 1.06 | 1.20 | 1.41 | 1.59 |
| B | 1.50 | 1.63 | 1.83 | 2.11 | 2.37 |
| CCC | 2.55 | 3.00 | 4.00 | 5.00 | 6.00 |
| | Spreads 01 | | | | |
| | 1y | 2y | 3y | 5y | 7y |
| AAA | 0.40 | 0.45 | 0.50 | 0.60 | 0.74 |
| AA | 0.53 | 0.60 | 0.65 | 0.76 | 0.90 |
| A | 0.80 | 0.90 | 1.01 | 1.18 | 1.36 |
| BBB | 1.21 | 1.30 | 1.41 | 1.59 | 1.79 |
| BB | 2.58 | 2.91 | 3.16 | 3.50 | 3.73 |
| B | 4.41 | 4.83 | 5.41 | 6.25 | 6.98 |
| CCC | 6.00 | 6.50 | 8.00 | 9.00 | 10.25 |

Spreads 97 are the spreads of US industrial bonds over government yields on July 11, 1997 and Spreads 01 are the same on September 25, 2001. The rating system is S&P. The data source is file SPRDCRV.TXT from CreditMetrics. Spreads 97 have also been used in Gordy and Heitfield (2001).

TRANSITION MATRICES

We use three different transition matrices for our analysis. The following transition matrix is based on Standard & Poor's (1999):

| | AAA | AA | A | BBB | BB | B | CCC | Def |
|---|---|---|---|---|---|---|---|---|
| AAA | 91.39 | 7.91 | 0.52 | 0.08 | 0.04 | 0.03 | 0.02 | 0.01 |
| AA | 0.72 | 91.62 | 6.77 | 0.64 | 0.07 | 0.12 | 0.03 | 0.03 |
| A | 0.08 | 2.40 | 91.05 | 5.45 | 0.66 | 0.28 | 0.01 | 0.07 |
| BBB | 0.05 | 0.30 | 6.03 | 86.66 | 5.36 | 1.22 | 0.18 | 0.20 |
| BB | 0.02 | 0.13 | 0.66 | 7.49 | 80.78 | 8.86 | 1.04 | 1.02 |
| B | 0.00 | 0.08 | 0.35 | 0.50 | 6.67 | 83.56 | 3.68 | 5.16 |
| CCC | 0.13 | 0.00 | 0.34 | 0.69 | 1.71 | 12.50 | 64.63 | 20.00 |
| Def | 0.00 | 0.00 | 0.00 | 0.00 | 0.00 | 0.00 | 0.00 | 100.00 |

Kealhofer, Kwok and Weng (1998) question that rating changes are a good indicator for credit quality changes. In particular, they claim that rating agencies are too slow in changing ratings and therefore the probability of staying in a grade overstates the true probability of keeping approximately the same credit quality. Therefore, the following approach based on KMV's expected default frequencies (EDFs) is proposed. Firms are classified based upon non-overlapping ranges of default probabilities. Each of these ranges corresponds to a rating class, ie, firms with default rates less than or equal to 0.02% are in AAA, 0.03% to 0.06% corresponds to AA, etc. The historical frequencies of changes from one range to another are calculated from the history of changes in default rates as measured by EDFs. This gives the following KMV one-year transition matrix:

| | AAA | AA | A | BBB | BB | B | CCC | Def |
|---|---|---|---|---|---|---|---|---|
| AAA | 66.26 | 22.22 | 7.37 | 2.45 | 0.86 | 0.67 | 0.15 | 0.02 |
| AA | 21.66 | 43.04 | 25.83 | 6.56 | 1.99 | 0.68 | 0.20 | 0.04 |
| A | 2.76 | 20.34 | 44.19 | 22.94 | 7.42 | 1.97 | 0.28 | 0.10 |
| BBB | 0.30 | 2.80 | 22.63 | 42.54 | 23.52 | 6.95 | 1.00 | 0.26 |
| BB | 0.08 | 0.24 | 3.69 | 22.93 | 44.41 | 24.53 | 3.41 | 0.71 |
| B | 0.01 | 0.05 | 0.39 | 3.48 | 20.47 | 53.01 | 20.58 | 2.01 |
| CCC | 0.00 | 0.01 | 0.09 | 0.26 | 1.79 | 17.77 | 69.95 | 10.13 |
| Def | 0.00 | 0.00 | 0.00 | 0.00 | 0.00 | 0.00 | 0.00 | 100.00 |

The third transition matrix, abbreviated as the GC matrix, is derived from migration data on German corporates (see also Machauer and Weber, 1998):

| | AAA | AA | A | BBB | BB | B | CCC | Def |
|---|---|---|---|---|---|---|---|---|
| AAA | 71.55 | 19.86 | 5.43 | 1.90 | 0.24 | 0.37 | 0.58 | 0.07 |
| AA | 2.18 | 71.06 | 21.14 | 4.14 | 0.70 | 0.29 | 0.29 | 0.20 |
| A | 0.18 | 6.43 | 69.72 | 19.47 | 2.54 | 0.80 | 0.51 | 0.35 |
| BBB | 0.06 | 1.10 | 16.43 | 64.74 | 11.26 | 3.84 | 1.77 | 0.80 |
| BB | 0.07 | 0.64 | 5.39 | 27.86 | 43.23 | 14.34 | 6.87 | 1.60 |
| B | 0.02 | 0.42 | 3.12 | 12.95 | 16.48 | 45.46 | 18.55 | 3.00 |
| CCC | 0.16 | 0.61 | 2.36 | 3.75 | 4.26 | 8.67 | 74.19 | 6.00 |
| Def | 0.00 | 0.00 | 0.00 | 0.00 | 0.00 | 0.00 | 0.00 | 100.00 |

1 *The best rating class has a one-year default probability of 3bp.*

2 *This means that all standard deviations are one.*

3 *We assume that all loans have the same valuation function, ie, have the same product specification but only different maturities.*

4 *Note that the last column of each transition matrix* M *specifies the one-year default probabilities for all rating classes. Under the assumption that the rating process is a time-homogeneous Markov process, the* t*-year default probabilities can be obtained from the last column of the* t*-th power of* M.

5 *Our results are based on 400,000 Monte Carlo simulations.*

6 *Factor loadings are randomly generated such that average correlation is close to 35%.*

7 *Portfolios consist of 98 loans. Possible PDs are 0.03, 0.05, 0.1, 0.2, 1, 3.3 and 15% and maturities are from one to seven years. Exposure size varies between 10 and 100. Exposures and maturities are uniformly distributed in each rating class.*

8 *Note that in this model the contributory capital of each loan equals the total risk capital divided by the number of loans regardless of the capital allocation technique used.*

9 *As defined in "Basic model", the seven non-default rating classes correspond to 1,..., 7 and default corresponds to 8.*

**BIBLIOGRAPHY**

**Artzner, P., F. Delbaen, J-M. Eber and D. Heath,** 1999, "Coherent Measures of Risk", *Mathematical Finance*, 9, pp. 203–28.

**Basel Committee on Banking Supervision,** 2001, *The Internal Ratings-Based Approach*, Consultative document.

**Delbaen, F.,** 2001, *Coherent Risk Measures*, Lecture notes, Scuola Normale Superiore di Pisa.

**Finger, C.,** 1999, "Conditional Approaches for CreditMetrics Portfolio Distribution", *Credit Monitor*, 1, April, pp. 14–33.

**Gordy, M., and E. Heitfield,** 2001, *Maturity Effects in a Class of Multi-period Default Mode Models*, Board of Governors of the Federal Reserve System, Washington DC.

**JP Morgan,** 1997, *CreditMetrics Technical Document.*

**Kalkbrener, M., and L. Overbeck,** 2001, *Maturity as a Factor for Credit Risk Capital*, Technical document, CIB/CRM/ RAI Risk Research & Development, Deutsche Bank, Frankfurt.

**Kealhofer, S.,** 1995, "Managing Default Risk in Derivative Portfolios", in *Derivative Credit Risk: Advances in Measurement and Management* (Renaissance Risk Publications).

**Kealhofer, S., S. Kwok and W. Weng,** 1998, *Uses and Abuses of Bond Default Rates*, KMV Corporation, San Francisco.

**Lucas, A., P. Klaassen, P. Spreij and S. Straetmans,** 2001, "An Analytic Approach to Credit Risk of Large Corporate Bond and Loan Portfolios", *Journal of Banking and Finance,* 25(9), pp. 1635–64.

**Machauer, A., and M. Weber,** 1998, *Bank Behavior Based on Internal Credit Ratings of Borrowers*, Working Paper 98/08, Center for Financial Studies, Frankfurt.

**Overbeck, L.,** 2000, *Allocation of Economic Capital in Loan Portfolios*, proceedings "Measuring Risk in Complex Stochastic Systems", Berlin, 1999, in Stahl and Härdle (eds), *Lecture Notes in Statistics* (Springer).

**Overbeck, L., and G. Stahl,** 2001, "Stochastic Models in Risk Managing a Credit Portfolio", Forthcoming, *Kredit und Kapital.*

**Standard & Poor's,** 1999, *Standard & Poor's Rating Performance 1998*, New York.

**Vasicek, O.,** 1997, "Credit Valuation", *Net Exposure*, 1, October.

VI

# ASYMPTOTIC METHODS IN VAR

# 24

# Loan Portfolio Value

**Oldrich Vasicek**

Moody's KMV

*Using a conditional independence framework, Oldrich Vasicek derives a useful limiting form for the portfolio loss distribution with a single systematic factor. He then derives a risk-neutral distribution suitable for traded portfolios, and shows how credit migration and granularity can be incorporated into this model too.*

The amount of capital needed to support a portfolio of debt securities depends on the probability distribution of the portfolio loss. Consider a portfolio of loans, each of which is subject to default resulting in a loss to the lender. Suppose the portfolio is financed partly by equity capital and partly by borrowed funds. The credit quality of the lender's notes will depend on the probability that the loss on the portfolio exceeds the equity capital. To achieve a certain credit rating of its notes (say Aa on a rating agency scale), the lender needs to keep the probability of default on the notes at the level corresponding to that rating (about 0.001 for the Aa quality). It means that the equity capital allocated to the portfolio must be equal to the percentile of the distribution of the portfolio loss that corresponds to the desired probability.

In addition to determining the capital needed to support a loan portfolio, the probability distribution of portfolio losses has a number of other applications. It can be used in regulatory reporting, measuring portfolio risk, calculation of value-at-risk, portfolio optimisation, and structuring and pricing debt portfolio derivatives such as collateralised debt obligations (CDOs).

In this chapter, we derive the distribution of the portfolio loss under certain assumptions. It is shown that this distribution converges with increasing portfolio size to a limiting type, whose analytical form is given here. The results of the first two sections of this chapter are contained in the author's technical notes, Vasicek (1987, 1991). For a review of recent literature on the subject, see, for instance, Pykhtin and Dev (2002).

*The author would like to thank Yim Lee for the computer simulations used for this chapter.*

## The limiting distribution of portfolio losses

Assume that a loan defaults if the value of the borrower's assets at the loan maturity T falls below the contractual value B of its obligations payable. Let $A_i$ be the value of the ith borrower's assets, described by the process:

$$dA_i = \mu_i A_i dt + \sigma_i A_i dx_i$$

The asset value at T can be represented as:

$$\log A_i(T) = \log A_i + \mu_i T - \frac{1}{2}\sigma_i^2 T + \sigma_i \sqrt{T} X_i \qquad (1)$$

where $X_i$ is a standard normal variable. The probability of default of the ith loan is then:

$$p_i = P\left[A_i(T) < B_i\right] = P\left[X_i < c_i\right] = N(c_i)$$

where:

$$c_i = \frac{\log B_i - \log A_i - \mu_i T + \frac{1}{2}\sigma_i^2 T}{\sigma_i \sqrt{T}}$$

and N is the cumulative normal distribution function.

Consider a portfolio consisting of n loans in equal dollar amounts. Let the probability of default on any one loan be p, and assume that the asset values of the borrowing companies are correlated with a coefficient ρ for any two companies.

We will further assume that all loans have the same term T.

Let $L_i$ be the gross loss (before recoveries) on the ith loan, so that $L_i = 1$ if the ith borrower defaults and $L_i = 0$ otherwise. Let L be the portfolio percentage gross loss:

$$L = \frac{1}{n}\sum_{i=1}^{n} L_i$$

If the events of default on the loans in the portfolio were independent of each other, the portfolio loss distribution would converge, by the central limit theorem, to a normal distribution as the portfolio size increases. Because the defaults are not independent, however, the conditions of the central limit theorem are not satisfied and L is not asymptotically normal. It turns out, however, that the distribution of the portfolio loss does converge to a limiting form, which we will now proceed to derive.

The variables $X_i$ in Equation 1 are jointly standard normal with equal pair-wise correlations ρ, and can therefore be represented as:

$$X_i = Y\sqrt{\rho} + Z_i\sqrt{1-\rho} \tag{2}$$

where $Y, Z_1, Z_2, \ldots, Z_n$ are mutually independent standard normal variables. (This is not an assumption, but a property of the equicorrelated normal distribution.) The variable Y can be interpreted as a portfolio common factor, such as an economic index, over the interval (0, T). Then the term $Y\sqrt{\rho}$ is the company's exposure to the common factor and the term $Z_i\sqrt{(1-\rho)}$ represents the company's specific risk.

We will evaluate the probability of the portfolio loss as the expectation over the common factor Y of the conditional probability given Y. This can be interpreted as assuming various scenarios for the economy, determining the probability of a given portfolio loss under each scenario and then weighting each scenario by its likelihood.

When the common factor is fixed, the conditional probability of loss on any one loan is:

$$p(Y) = P\left[L_i = 1 \middle| Y\right] = N\left(\frac{N^{-1}(p) - Y\sqrt{\rho}}{\sqrt{1-\rho}}\right) \tag{3}$$

The quantity p(Y) provides the loan default probability under the given scenario. The unconditional default probability p is the average of the conditional probabilities over the scenarios.

Conditional on the value of Y, the variables $L_i$ are independent equally distributed variables with a finite variance. The portfolio loss conditional on Y converges, by the law of large numbers, to its expectation p(Y) as $n \to \infty$. Then:

$$P[L \le x] = P\left[p(Y) \le x\right] = P\left[Y \ge p^{-1}(x)\right] = N\left(-p^{-1}(x)\right)$$

and on substitution, the cumulative distribution function of loan losses on a very large portfolio is in the limit:

$$P[L \le x] = N\left(\frac{\sqrt{1-\rho}\,N^{-1}(x) - N^{-1}(p)}{\sqrt{\rho}}\right) \tag{4}$$

This result is given in Vasicek (1991).

The convergence of the portfolio loss distribution to the limiting form above actually holds even for portfolios with unequal weights. Let the portfolio weights be $w_1, w_2, \ldots, w_n$ with $\Sigma w_i = 1$. The portfolio loss:

$$L = \sum_{i=1}^{n} w_i L_i$$

conditional on Y converges to its expectation p(Y) whenever (and this is a necessary and sufficient condition):

$$\sum_{i=1}^{n} w_i^2 \to 0$$

In other words, if the portfolio contains a sufficiently large number of loans without it being dominated by a few loans much larger than the rest, the limiting distribution provides a good approximation for the portfolio loss.

## Properties of the loss distribution

The portfolio loss distribution given by the cumulative distribution function:

$$F(x; p, \rho) = N\left(\frac{\sqrt{1-\rho}\,N^{-1}(x) - N^{-1}(p)}{\sqrt{\rho}}\right) \tag{5}$$

is a continuous distribution concentrated on the interval $0 \le x \le 1$. It forms a two-parameter family with the parameters $0 < p, \rho < 1$. When $\rho \to 0$, it converges to a one-point distribution concentrated at $L = p$. When $\rho \to 1$, it converges to a zero-one distribution with probabilities p and $1 - p$, respectively. When $p \to 0$ or $p \to 1$, the distribution becomes concentrated at $L = 0$ or $L = 1$, respectively. The distribution possesses a symmetry property:

$$F(x; p; \rho) = 1 - F(1 - x; 1 - p, \rho)$$

**1. Portfolio loss distribution ($p = 0.02$, $\rho = 0.1$)**

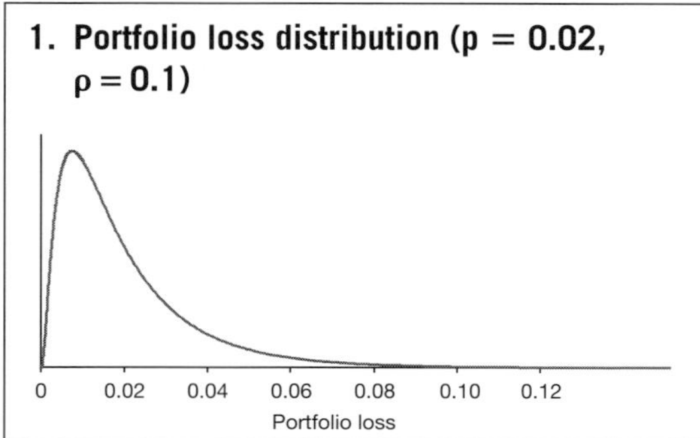


The loss distribution has the density:

$$f(x;p,\rho) = \sqrt{\frac{1-\rho}{\rho}} \exp\left(-\frac{1}{2\rho}\left(\sqrt{1-\rho}N^{-1}(x) - N^{-1}(p)\right)^2 + \frac{1}{2}\left(N^{-1}(x)\right)^2\right)$$

which is unimodal with the mode at:

$$L_{mode} = N\left(\frac{\sqrt{1-\rho}}{1-2\rho}N^{-1}(p)\right)$$

when $\rho < 0.5$, monotone when $\rho = 0.5$ and U-shaped when $\rho > 0.5$. This density is shown in Figure 1 for $p = 0.02$, $\rho = 0.1$. The mean of the distribution is $E(L) = p$ and the variance is:

$$s^2 = \text{Var}\, L = N_2\left(N^{-1}(p), N^{-1}(p), \rho\right) - p^2$$

where $N_2$ is the bivariate cumulative normal distribution function. The inverse of this distribution, that is, the $\alpha$-percentile value of $L$, is given by:

$$L_\alpha = F(\alpha; 1-p, 1-\rho)$$

The portfolio loss distribution is highly skewed and leptokurtic. Table 1 lists the values of the $\alpha$-percentile $L_\alpha$ expressed as the number of standard deviations from the mean, for several values of the parameters. The $\alpha$-percentiles of the standard normal distribution are shown for comparison.

**Table 1. Values of $(L_\alpha - p)/s$ for the portfolio loss distribution**

| p | ρ | α = 0.9 | α = 0.99 | α = 0.999 | α = 0.9999 |
|---|---|---|---|---|---|
| 0.01 | 0.1 | 1.19 | 3.8 | 7.0 | 10.7 |
| 0.01 | 0.4 | 0.55 | 4.5 | 11.0 | 18.2 |
| 0.001 | 0.1 | 0.98 | 4.1 | 8.8 | 15.4 |
| 0.001 | 0.4 | 0.12 | 3.2 | 13.2 | 31.8 |
| Normal | | 1.28 | 2.3 | 3.1 | 3.7 |

These values manifest the extreme non-normality of the loss distribution. Suppose a lender holds a large portfolio of loans to firms whose pair-wise asset correlation is $\rho = 0.4$ and whose probability of default is $p = 0.01$. The portfolio expected loss is $E(L) = 0.01$ and the standard deviation is $s = 0.0277$. If the lender wishes to hold the probability of default on his notes at $1 - \alpha = 0.001$, he will need enough capital to cover 11.0 times the portfolio standard deviation. If the loss distribution were normal, 3.1 times the standard deviation would suffice.

## The risk-neutral distribution

The portfolio loss distribution given by Equation 4 is the actual probability distribution. This is the distribution from which to calculate the probability of a loss of a certain magnitude for the purposes of determining the necessary capital or of calculating VAR. This is also the distribution to be used in structuring CDOs, that is, in calculating the probability of loss and the expected loss for a given tranche. For the purposes of pricing the tranches, however, it is necessary to use the risk-neutral probability distribution. The risk-neutral distribution is calculated in the same way as above, except that the default probabilities are evaluated under the risk-neutral measure $P^*$:

$$p^* = P^*\left[A(T) < B\right] = N\left(\frac{\log B - \log A - rT + \frac{1}{2}\sigma^2 T}{\sigma\sqrt{T}}\right)$$

where $r$ is the risk-free rate. The risk-neutral probability is related to the actual probability of default by the equation:

$$p^* = N\left(N^{-1}(p) + \lambda\rho_M\sqrt{T}\right) \quad (6)$$

where $\rho_M$ is the correlation of the firm asset value with the market and $\lambda = (\mu_M - r)/\sigma_M$ is the market price of risk. The risk-neutral portfolio loss distribution is then given by:

$$P^*\left[L \le x\right] = N\left(\frac{\sqrt{1-\rho}N^{-1}(x) - N^{-1}(p^*)}{\sqrt{\rho}}\right) \quad (7)$$

Thus, a derivative security (such as a CDO tranche written against the portfolio) that pays at time $T$ an amount $C(L)$ contingent on the portfolio loss is valued at:

$$V = e^{-rT}E^*\left[C(L)\right]$$

where the expectation is taken with respect to Equation 7. For instance, a default protection for losses in excess of $L_0$ is priced at:

$$V = e^{-rT}E^*[(L - L_0)_+] = e^{-rT}\left(p^* - N_2\left(N^{-1}(p^*), N^{-1}(L_0), \sqrt{1-\rho}\right)\right)$$

## The portfolio market value

So far, we have discussed the loss due to loan defaults. Now suppose that the maturity date T of the loan is past the date H for which the portfolio value is considered (the horizon date). If the credit quality of a borrower deteriorates, the value of the loan will decline, resulting in a loss (this is often referred to as the loss due to "credit migration"). We will investigate the distribution of the loss resulting from changes in the marked-to-market portfolio value.

The value of the debt at time 0 is the expected present value of the loan payments under the risk-neutral measure:

$$D = e^{-rT}(1 - Gp^*)$$

where G is the loss-given default and $p^*$ is the risk-neutral probability of default. At time H, the value of the loan is:

$$D(H) = e^{-r(T-H)}\left(1 - GN\left(\frac{\log B - \log A(H) - r(T-H) + \frac{1}{2}\sigma^2(T-H)}{\sigma\sqrt{T-H}}\right)\right)$$

Define the loan loss $L_i$ at time H as the difference between the risk-free value and the market value of the loan at H:

$$L_i = e^{-r(T-H)} - D(H)$$

This definition of loss is chosen purely for convenience. If the loss is defined in a different way (for instance, as the difference between the accrued value and the market value), it will only result in a shift of the portfolio loss distribution by a location parameter.

The loss on the ith loan can be written as:

$$L_i = aN\left(b\sqrt{\frac{T}{T-H}} - X_i\sqrt{\frac{H}{T-H}}\right)$$

where:

$$a = Ge^{-r(T-H)},\ b = N^{-1}(p) + \lambda\rho_M\frac{T-H}{\sqrt{T}}$$

and the standard normal variables $X_i$ defined over the horizon H by:

$$\log A_i(H) = \log A_i + \mu_i H - \frac{1}{2}\sigma_i^2 H + \sigma_i\sqrt{H}X_i$$

are subject to Equation 2.

Let L be the market value loss at time H of a loan portfolio with weights $w_i$. The conditional mean of $L_i$ given Y can be calculated as:

$$\mu(Y) = E\left[L_i|Y\right] = aN\left(b\sqrt{\frac{T}{T-\rho H}} - Y\sqrt{\frac{\rho H}{T-\rho H}}\right)$$

The losses conditional on the factor Y are independent, and therefore the portfolio loss L conditional on Y converges to its mean value $E[L|Y] = \mu(Y)$ as $\Sigma w_i^2 \to \infty$. The limiting distribution of L is then:

$$P[L \le x] = P\left[\mu(Y) \le x\right] = F\left(\frac{x}{a}; N(b), \frac{\rho H}{T}\right) \quad (8)$$

We see that the limiting distribution of the portfolio loss is of the same type as Equation 5 whether the loss is defined as the decline in the market value or the realised loss at maturity. In fact, the results of the section on the distribution of loss due to default are just a special case of this section for T = H.

The risk-neutral distribution for the loss due to market value change is given by:

$$p^*[L \le x] = F\left(\frac{x}{a}; p^*, \frac{\rho H}{T}\right) \quad (9)$$

## Adjustment for granularity

Equation 8 relies on the convergence of the portfolio loss L given Y to its mean value $\mu(Y)$, which means that the conditional variance $Var(L|Y) \to 0$. When the portfolio is not sufficiently large for the law of large numbers to take hold, we need to take into account the non-zero value of $Var(L|Y)$. Consider a portfolio of uniform credits with weights $w_1, w_2, \ldots, w_n$ and put:

$$\delta = \sum_{i=1}^{n} w_i^2$$

The conditional variance of the portfolio loss L given Y is:

$$Var\left(L|Y\right) = \delta a^2\left(N_2\left(U, U, \frac{(1-\rho)H}{T-\rho H}\right) - N^2(U)\right)$$

where:

$$U = b\sqrt{\frac{T}{T-\rho H}} - Y\sqrt{\frac{\rho H}{T-\rho H}}$$

The unconditional mean and variance of the portfolio loss are $E(L) = aN(b)$ and:

$$\begin{aligned} \operatorname{Var} L &= E\left[\operatorname{Var}\left(L|Y\right)\right] + \operatorname{Var}\left[E\left(L|Y\right)\right] \\ &= \delta a^2 N_2\left(b, b, \frac{H}{T}\right) + (1-\delta) a^2 N_2\left(b, b, \frac{\rho H}{T}\right) - a^2 N^2(b) \end{aligned} \quad (10)$$

Taking the first two terms in the tetrachoric expansion of the bivariate normal distribution function $N_2(x, x, \rho) = N^2(x) + \rho n^2(x)$, where $n$ is the normal density function, we have approximately:

$$\begin{aligned} \operatorname{Var}(L) &= \delta a^2 n^2(b)\frac{H}{T} + (1-\delta) a^2 n^2(b)\frac{\rho H}{T} \\ &= a^2 N_2\left(b, b, \left(\rho + \delta(1-\rho)\right)\frac{H}{T}\right) - a^2 N^2(b) \end{aligned}$$

Approximating the loan loss distribution by the distribution seen in Equation 5 with the same mean and variance, we get:

$$P[L \le x] = F\left(\frac{x}{a}; N(b), \left(\rho + \delta(1-\rho)\right)\frac{H}{T}\right) \quad (11)$$

This expression is in fact exact for both extremes $n \to \infty$, $\delta = 0$ and $n = 1$, $\delta = 1$.

Equation (11) provides an adjustment for the "granularity" of the portfolio. In particular, the finite portfolio adjustment to the distribution of the gross loss at the maturity date is obtained by putting $H = T$, $a = 1$ to yield:

$$P[L \le x] = F\left(x; p, \rho + \delta(1-\rho)\right) \quad (12)$$

## Summary

We have shown that the distribution of the loan portfolio loss converges, with increasing portfolio size, to the limiting type given by Equation 5.

**2. Simulated loss distribution for an actual portfolio**

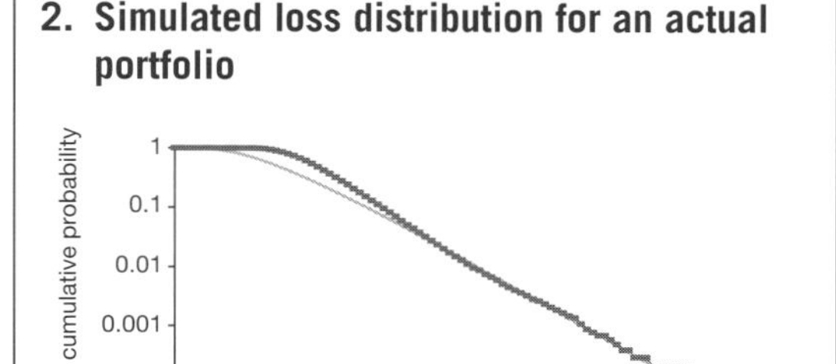


It means that this distribution can be used to represent the loan loss behaviour of large portfolios. The loan loss can be a realised loss on loans maturing before the horizon date, or a market value deficiency on loans whose term is longer than the horizon period.

The limiting probability distribution of portfolio losses has been derived under the assumption that all loans in the portfolio have the same maturity, the same probability of default and the same pair-wise correlation of the borrower assets. Curiously, however, computer simulations show that the family shown in Equation 5 appears to provide a reasonably good fit to the tail of the loss distribution for more general portfolios. To illustrate this point, Figure 2 gives the results of Monte Carlo simulations of an actual bank portfolio. The portfolio consisted of 479 loans in amounts ranging from 0.0002% to 8.7%, with $\delta = 0.039$. The maturities ranged from six months to six years and the default probabilities from 0.0002 to 0.064. The loss-given default averaged 0.54. The asset returns were generated with 14 common factors. The plot shows the simulated cumulative distribution function of the loss in one year (dots) and the fitted limiting distribution function (solid line).

**BIBLIOGRAPHY**

**Pykhtin, M., and A. Dev,** 2002, "Credit Risk in Asset Securitisations: an Analytical Model", *Risk*, May, pp. S16–S20.

**Vasicek, O.,** 1987, *Probability of Loss on Loan Portfolio*, KMV Corporation, available at www.kmv.com.

**Vasicek, O.,** 1991, *Limiting Loan Loss Probability Distribution*, KMV Corporation, available at www.kmv.com.

25

# Probing Granularity

**Tom Wilde**

Credit Suisse First Boston

*The granularity adjustment, which adjusts risk weightings for credit portfolio diversification, is one of Basel II's key modelling assumptions. Here, Tom Wilde uncovers a weakness in this assumption arising from the differences in the underlying credit portfolio models incorporated within the internal ratings-based approach.*

In June 2001, nearly a month after the consultation period for Basel II ended, the Basel Committee on Banking Supervision relented on its implementation schedule. Basel II will now not be implemented until 2005, with an additional round of consultation in 2002. It seems that the committee has listened to the debate that has raged over all aspects of the proposal, from the operational risk charge to the "w" charge for credit derivatives.

Here, we return to another contentious issue: the granularity adjustment within Basel II's internal ratings-based (IRB) approach. In an earlier article (Wilde, 2001), we attempted to explain the IRB approach to assessing capital for credit risk from the Basel Committee (Basel, 2001). We showed that the granularity adjustment seemed reasonable by comparing it with the result of scaling by standard deviations. In this chapter, we reconsider the granularity adjustment more critically: it seems roughly right, but how accurate is it, and are the assumptions made in deriving it justified?

The work behind the granularity adjustment is explained in Gordy (2001). There is a weak link in the application of this analysis to Basel II:[1] the Vasicek approach used to calibrate the base risk weights (see Wilde, 2001, and the references there) is replaced by a version of CreditRisk+, the credit risk model introduced by Credit Suisse First Boston in 1997. This is justified (Basel, 2001, paragraph 444) only by the statement that the two models have tails that align closely. In fact, as we show below, the granularity adjustment depends subtly on tail shape aspects that are not preserved by the switch of model. Avoiding switching models gives a different adjustment given by Equation 3 below.

## The granularity adjustment

The granularity adjustment is given in Basel II, by the following Equation:

$$\beta_{\text{Actual}} = (0.4 + 1.2\text{LGD})\left(0.76 + 1.1\frac{\text{PD}}{\text{F}}\right) \quad (1)$$

The precise meaning of $\beta$ is introduced in paragraph 442 of Basel (2001). In this equation, PD is the default probability and $\text{F} = \text{N}(1.118\text{N}^{-1}(\text{PD}) + 1.288) - \text{PD}$ is the systematic risk sensitivity (Basel, 2001, paragraph 431).[2] Equation 1 is then scaled by a factor of $1.5 \times 1/0.08 = 18.75$, where the factor of one-and-a-half is the same arbitrary scaling factor currently applied to the base risk weights, to give the granularity scaling factor actually used for the calculation (Basel, 2001, paragraph 457). We will work directly with Equation 1.

We present a theoretical general formula for the granularity adjustment. Calculating this formula for the CreditRisk+ model used in Basel II gives the following "theoretical granularity adjustment":

$$\beta^{\text{CreditRisk+}}_{\text{Theoretical}} = (0.4 + 1.2\text{LGD})\left(0.762 + 1.075\frac{\text{PD}}{\text{F}}\right) \quad (2)$$

in striking agreement with Basel II's numerically derived granularity adjustment seen in Equation 1.

Having verified the formula in the case of the CreditRisk+ model, we naturally ask what result it

*The author thanks Michael Gordy for corrections and improvements on earlier versions of this chapter, and for stimulating this work through Gordy (2001) and the relevant parts of Basel II.*

gives for the Vasicek distribution. By a similar calculation to Equation 2, we get:

$$\beta^{\text{Vasicek}}_{\text{Theoretical}} = (0.4 + 1.2\text{LGD})\left(0.32 + 4.19\frac{\text{PD}}{\text{F}}\right) \quad (3)$$

We concluded before that, based on standard deviations, the granularity adjustment seems reasonable (Wilde, 2001). That conclusion is consistent with these results. Surprisingly, Equations 1 and 3 are quite similar for most portfolios because the fraction PD/F is quite insensitive to PD, so the coefficients in Equations 1–3 have only a mild effect on the results. Equations 1 and 3 coincide for PD = 2% approximately and are within about 10% of one another for PD in the range 1.1% to 3.5%. Equation 3 gives a higher adjustment for default rates above 2%, otherwise a lower one. Equation 3 can claim to be more correct than Equations 1 or 2 because its derivation does not involve a switch of model, so that, unlike Basel II's Equation 1, it is fully consistent with the rest of the IRB approach. Unfortunately, that does not really mean Equation 3 is "right". One could argue that the IRB approach could have been built on a CreditRisk+ framework, in which case Equation 1 would have been the correct choice instead. This difference between the models cannot be made to go away since all available parameters have been used to calibrate the models at their 99.5% percentiles. So, the adjustment is intrinsically model-dependent. This conclusion is, of course, mitigated by the fact that the results of Equations 1–3 are comparable over a wide range of default probabilities.

Numerical work is presented at the end of this chapter to check that Equation 3 actually does coincide with the slope of the adjustment when the Vasicek distribution is used. This is an appropriate check as the theoretical result (Equation 4 below) is a "first-order approximation". Agreement with numerical results is good. The agreement between Equations 1 and 2 can be viewed as a numerical check on the formula in the CreditRisk+ case.

## Theoretical formula

Basel II is built on the idea of a one-factor credit risk model, where the base risk weights measure the systematic risk present. To state the formula providing a theoretical value for the granularity adjustment, we need to set up some notation. We have tried to be consistent with Wilde (2001). Thus, suppose that Y is a loss distribution with X as the systematic factor, and with conditional mean and variance given by:

$$\mu(x) = \mu\left(Y \middle| X = x\right) \quad \text{and} \quad \sigma^2(x) = \sigma^2\left(Y \middle| X = x\right)$$

The distribution of $\mu(X)$ is the systematic loss distribution. We use P to denote the default probability of an obligor as a function of X and p to denote its average value, ie, the unconditional default probability of A. Let the probability density function of X be $f_X(x)$. Let $X_q$ be the percentile of X corresponding to confidence level $1 - q$ (eg, in the case of the gamma distribution used in Basel II, $q = 0.5\%$, ie, $1 - q = 99.5\%$, and $X_q = 12.007$ is the corresponding value of X). The corresponding systematic percentile of Y is $L = \mu(X_q)$. Let $L + \Delta L$ be the actual percentile $Y_q$ of Y. Then $\Delta L$ is the "granularity adjustment". Then the following formula gives a theoretical first-order approximation to the granularity adjustment, with the understanding that the right-hand side is to be evaluated at $x = X_q$:

$$\Delta L \cong -\frac{1}{2f_X}\frac{d}{dx}\left(\frac{f_X\sigma^2}{d\mu/dx}\right) \quad (4)$$

To be more precise, we are saying that Equation 4 gives the granularity adjustment to "first order in the unsystematic variance". Unfortunately, it is tricky to formulate exactly what this means because for any actual portfolio the adjustment is not a function of the unsystematic variance only, but clearly depends on the detailed composition of the portfolio. One way of avoiding this difficulty is to use the systematic risk process described in Wilde (2001). We start with a portfolio $\Pi = \Pi_1$ with conditional mean and variance $\mu(x)$ and $\sigma^2(x)$ and construct a sequence of portfolios $\Pi_m$ by replacing each obligor $A \in \Pi$ with m new obligors $A_1, \ldots, A_m$, each having exposure $E_A/m$ but the same default probability and proportional recovery rate volatility as A. As m tends to infinity, the loss distributions of $\Pi_m$ tend to the systematic loss distribution $\mu(X)$ and we can notionally associate this with a "systematic portfolio" $\Pi_\infty$. Then for every value of X the conditional unsystematic variance of $\Pi_m$ satisfies $\sigma_m^2(x) = \sigma^2(x)/m$. Moreover, since we specified the starting portfolio $\Pi = \Pi_1$ everything is just a function of m. This allows us to write Equation 4 in the following more precise form, where $L^{(m)}$ is the percentile of $\Pi_m$ and $L = L^{(\infty)}$ is the systematic percentile:

$$L^{(m)} - L^{(\infty)} = -\frac{1}{2mf_X}\frac{d}{dx}\left(\frac{f_X\sigma^2}{d\mu/dx}\right)\Bigg|_{x=X_q} + O\left(\frac{1}{m^2}\right) \quad (5)$$

If $\Pi = \Pi_1$ is a single obligor with unit exposure then $\Pi_m$ is just a homogeneous portfolio with m obligors each having exposure 1/m, ie, with total exposure of one unit. From the definition of the slope β, which is the subject of Equation 1 (Basel, 2001, paragraph 443), we see that Equation 5 is exactly equivalent to the following statement:

$$\beta = -\frac{1}{2f_X}\frac{d}{dx}\left(\frac{f_X\sigma^2}{d\mu/dx}\right)\Bigg|_{x=X_q} \tag{6}$$

In other words, we are giving a formula for the slope of the lines on chart 7 of Basel II at the origin.[3] Here, μ and $\sigma^2$ are for $\Pi_1$, which is a single obligor with unit exposure. This sounds odd but note that the term in brackets does not depend on the number m of obligors since μ and $\sigma^2$ scale by m, so their ratio is the same for all $\Pi_m$ in the sequence.

We start the derivation of Equation 4. First, we can assume that $\mu(X) = X$. In this case, Equation 4 is just Equation 7:

$$\Delta L \cong -\frac{1}{2f_\mu}\frac{d(f_\mu\sigma^2)}{d\mu} \tag{7}$$

This is sufficient because it Equation 4 as follows. For any monotonically increasing $\mu = \mu(X)$, we have the probability densities $f\mu = f_X dx/d\mu$. Substituting this into Equation 7, we get:

$$\Delta L \cong -\frac{1}{2f_X dx/d\mu}\frac{d(f_X\sigma^2 dx/d\mu)}{d\mu} = -\frac{1}{2f_X}\frac{d}{dx}\left(\frac{f_X\sigma^2}{d\mu/dx}\right)$$

which is Equation 4. As a further simplification, instead of looking at percentiles we look instead at the amount of "extra probability" at the percentile. In fact, let $q + \Delta q$ be the probability that the actual loss will exceed L. (By definition, the systematic loss variable has probability q of exceeding L.) Then:

$$\Delta q \cong -\frac{1}{2}\frac{d(f_\mu\sigma^2)}{d\mu} \tag{8}$$

Intuitively, ΔL is the amount by which we have to shift the percentile to the right to compensate for the extra probability Δq, so we expect $\Delta q = f(L)\Delta L$ to first order in ΔL from which Equation 4 clearly follows from Equation 8. The correct equation, bearing in mind that f is the density of X not Y, is actually $\Delta q = 0.5(f(L) + f(L - \Delta L))\Delta L$, but this can be shown to be the same as $\Delta q = f(L)\Delta L$ to first order. Now we focus on Equation 8. To give insight into Equation 8, rewrite it as:

**1. Impact of unsystematic risk**

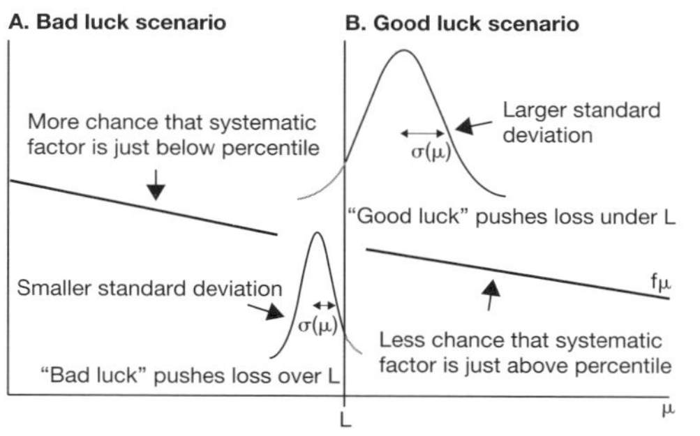

$$\Delta q \cong -\frac{1}{2}\left(\sigma^2\frac{df_\mu}{d\mu} + f_\mu\frac{d\sigma^2}{d\mu}\right) \tag{9}$$

There are two terms. Since we are looking at the tail of the density function $f_\mu$, one would expect the first term in brackets to be negative (the density slopes downwards in the tail). On the other hand, from the usual formula for variance we know it is normally increasing as a function of the default probabilities, meaning that the second summand should be increasing. The two summands represent offsetting effects that can easily be described with the aid of Figure 1.

To experience a loss over L, if there is not too much unsystematic risk present, the systematic factor must be close to L. Poor economic conditions are all but required to get a 99.5% loss; in all but the smallest portfolios, the chance of such a loss by sheer bad luck is negligible. If the systematic factor is slightly below L, losses might be "pushed above" L by a small amount of bad luck (ie, accidental defaults and poor recovery rates). Conversely, there is a chance of being saved by good luck when the factor is slightly above L. These offset as follows (see Figure 1):

- There is slightly more chance of the factor being just below than just above L, so the bad luck scenario A is more likely. The imbalance contributes a positive term $-1/2\sigma^2 df_\mu/d\mu$.
- But the good luck scenario B is more powerful, because volatility (including the benefit of a lower than expected loss outcome) is greater when default rates are higher. This contributes the negative offsetting term $-1/2f_\mu d\sigma^2/d\mu$.

The above should be motivation for the following demonstration of Equation 8. We have been able to assume $\mu(x) = x$. In particular, L is the $(1 - q)$-percentile of X. We write $x = L + t$ to centre the integration around L, and have the following formula from general probability theory:

$$q+\Delta q=\int_{t=-\infty}^{\infty} P\left(\text{Loss} \geq L \mid x=L+t\right) f_X(L+t)dt$$

where P in the integrand stands for probability. Since q is the probability that x > L, we also have:

$$\Delta q=\int_{t=-\infty}^{0} P\left(\text{Loss} \geq L \mid \mu=L+t\right) f_X(L+t)dt + \int_{t=0}^{\infty} \left(P\left(\text{Loss} \geq L \mid x=L+t\right)-1\right) f_X(L+t)dt$$

We now make three approximations, all justified by closeness to L. First, consider the limit process described before Equation 5. Passing from $\Pi=\Pi_1$ to $\Pi_m$ replaces each obligor with m independent obligors, having m identical independent loss outcomes. The conditional distribution of losses is therefore asymptotically normal for every value of μ and so it is plausible to approximate the conditional probabilities in the integrands by cumulative normal densities. Since the conditional average $\mu(x) = x$ we have, using the symmetry of the normal distribution:

$$P\left(\text{Loss} \geq L \mid x=L+t\right) = 1-N\left(\frac{-t}{\sigma(L+t)}\right)=N\left(\frac{t}{\sigma(L+t)}\right)$$

where N is the cumulative normal function. Next, if the unsystematic risk is small (ie, m is large in Equation 5), then the problem is "local" in that the systematic variable μ has to be close to L to give any significant probability of crossing over L. We therefore should be able to make linear approximations within the integrand that are valid near L. First, we can approximate the density f, and write:

$$\Delta q=\int_{-\infty}^{\infty} (f(L)+t f'(L)) G\left(\frac{t}{\sigma(L+t)}\right)dt$$

where we have introduced G defined by:

$$G(y)=\begin{cases} N(y)-1 & y>0 \\ N(y) & y \leq 0 \end{cases}$$

Similarly, we can write:

$$\frac{t}{\sigma(L+t)}=\frac{t}{\sigma(L)}\left(1-\frac{t}{\sigma(L)}\frac{d\sigma}{dt}(t=0)\right)$$

In what follows $\sigma'(L)$ refers to the derivative $d\sigma/dt(0) = d\sigma/d\mu(L)$. Hence:

$$\Delta q=\int_{-\infty}^{\infty} (f(L)+tf'(L)) G\left(\frac{t}{\sigma(L)}\left(1-\frac{t}{\sigma(L)}\sigma'(L)\right)\right)dt$$

Next, by splitting the integral into positive and negative t and substituting –t for t in the positive half, we get the equivalent formula $\Delta q = \Delta q_1 - \Delta q_2$, where:

$$\Delta q_{1,2}=\int_{-\infty}^{0} (f(L) \pm tf'(L)) N\left(\frac{t}{\sigma(L)}\left(1 \mp \frac{t}{\sigma(L)}\sigma'(L)\right)\right)dt$$

As a further first-order approximation, write:[4]

$$N\left(\frac{t}{\sigma(L)}\left(1 \mp \frac{t}{\sigma(L)}\sigma'(L)\right)\right)=N\left(\frac{t}{\sigma(L)}\right) \mp \frac{t^2}{\sigma^2(L)}\sigma'(L) n\left(\frac{t}{\sigma(L)}\right)$$

where $n(x) = dN/dx$ is the normal density function. We obtain:

$$\Delta q_{1,2}=\int_{-\infty}^{0} (f(L) \pm t f'(L)) N\left(\frac{t}{\sigma(L)}\right)dt \mp \sigma'(L)\int_{-\infty}^{0} (f(L) \pm t f'(L))\frac{t^2}{\sigma^2(L)} n\left(\frac{t}{\sigma(L)}\right)dt$$

The terms without a plus or minus sign in front cancel out in the sum $\Delta q = \Delta q_1 - \Delta q_2$, leaving:

$$\Delta q = 2f'(L)\int_{-\infty}^{0} tN\left(\frac{t}{\sigma(L)}\right)dt - 2\sigma'(L)\frac{f(L)}{\sigma^2(L)}\int_{-\infty}^{0} t^2 n\left(\frac{t}{\sigma(L)}\right)dt$$

We can now change variables and get:

$$\Delta q = 2f'(L)\,\sigma^2(L)\int_{-\infty}^{0} yN(y)\,dy - 2\sigma(L)\,\sigma'(L) f(L)\int_{-\infty}^{0} y^2 n(y)dy$$

The two integrals have the (exact) values respectively (integrate by parts):

$$\int_{-\infty}^{0} yN(y)dy = -\frac{1}{4} \quad \text{and} \quad \int_{-\infty}^{0} y^2 n(y)dy = +\frac{1}{2}$$

So, at last, remembering that $x = \mu = L + t$, we obtain:

$$\Delta q = -\frac{1}{2}\frac{df}{d\mu}(L)\,\sigma^2(L) - \frac{1}{2}\frac{d\sigma^2}{d\mu}(L)f(L)$$

which is Equation 9.

Let us now calculate Equation 4 for the CreditRisk+ model used to derive the granularity adjustment in Basel II. We will only show the result for a homogeneous portfolio with m obligors, using Equation 6, because this is what is comparable with the work in Basel II. Basel II has default probabilities $P_A(x) = p_A(1 - \omega_A + \omega_A X)$, where X is gamma with mean one and standard deviation $\sigma = 2$, or equivalently parameters

$\alpha = 0.25$, $\beta = 4$ (Basel, 2001, paragraph 445). $\omega_A$ is the "factor loading" (Basel, 2001, paragraph 446). The 99.5% percentile of X has the value 12.007. To apply Equation 6, we only need to consider a single obligor with exposure one and we have:[5]

$$\begin{aligned} \mu(x) &= \mathrm{LGD}\,p(1-\omega+\omega x) \quad \text{and} \\ \sigma^2(x) &= (\mathrm{LGD}^2+\mathrm{VLGD}^2)\,p(1-\omega+\omega x) \end{aligned} \tag{10}$$

In the IRB approach, the volatility of loss given default VLGD is defined as a proportion of exposure at default (Basel, 2001, paragraph 447) as:

$$\mathrm{VLGD} = 0.5\sqrt{\mathrm{LGD}(1-\mathrm{LGD})}$$

Substituting into $\sigma^2(x)$, we get:

$$\sigma^2(x) = \mathrm{LGD}(0.25+0.75\mathrm{LGD})\,p(1-\omega+\omega x)$$

On differentiating:

$$\begin{aligned} \frac{d\mu}{dx} &= \mathrm{LGD}\,p\,\omega \quad \text{and} \\ \frac{d\sigma^2}{dx} &= \mathrm{LGD}(0.25+0.75\mathrm{LGD})\,p\,\omega \end{aligned}$$

Also, we need the logarithmic derivative of the density function of the gamma distribution at the 99.5% point 12.007. Since $f(x) \propto x^{\alpha-1}e^{-x/\beta}$ and given that $\alpha = 0.25$ and $\beta = 4$ we have:

$$\frac{f'}{f} = \frac{\alpha-1}{x} - \frac{1}{\beta} = \frac{-0.75}{12.007} - 0.25 \cong -0.3125$$

So, using Equation 6 we get:

$$\beta = -\frac{1}{2\mathrm{LGD}p\omega}\left(-0.3125\sigma^2 + \frac{d\sigma^2}{dx}\right)$$

which is:

$$\begin{aligned} \beta = {} & -1/(2\omega)(0.25+0.75\mathrm{LGD}) \\ & \times(-0.3125(1+11.007\,\omega)+\omega) \end{aligned}$$

After some simplification and scaling the first bracket to look the same as Basel II, this is:

$$\beta = (0.4+1.2\mathrm{LGD})(0.762+0.098/\omega)$$

We now replace the factor loading parameter $\omega$. Basel II shows that $F/PD = (X_{99.5\%} - 1)\omega = 11.007\omega$ is the equation required to calibrate the CreditRisk+ and Vasicek models together. Using this, we calculate:

$$\begin{aligned} \beta &= (0.4+1.2\mathrm{LGD})\left(0.762+0.098\times 11.007\frac{PD}{F}\right) \\ &= (0.4+1.2\mathrm{LGD})\left(0.762+1.075\frac{PD}{F}\right) \end{aligned}$$

which is Equation 2.

Basel II extends its approach to inhomogeneous portfolios by replacing them with a "hypothetical" homogeneous portfolio with the same amount of unsystematic risk (Basel, 2001, paragraph 452). However, since Equations 4–6 are also valid for inhomogeneous portfolios (having different exposure sizes and/or PDs), one can follow the analysis above to calculate the theoretical inhomogeneous adjustment directly, without this extra step. The formulas obtained are not equivalent to the method chosen by Basel. Numerical work is needed to determine which formulas are more accurate.

Next we sketch the derivation in the case of the Vasicek model used for the base risk weights. In the Vasicek model, and in the derivation of the base risk weights (Basel, 2001, paragraph 172), the specific dependence on the factor X is:

$$P_A(X) = N\left(\frac{N^{-1}(p_A)+\rho_A^{1/2}X}{(1-\rho_A)^{1/2}}\right) \tag{11}$$

where X is now standard normally distributed, ie, $f_X(x) = n(x)$. In Basel II, the parameters are $\rho = 20\%$ and $X = 2.57$, its 99.5% value. As before, we use Equation 6, namely:

$$\begin{aligned} \beta &= -\frac{1}{2f_X}\frac{d}{dx}\left(\frac{f_X\sigma^2}{d\mu/dx}\right) \\ &= \frac{-1}{2f_X}\left(\frac{d(f_X\sigma^2)/dx}{d\mu/dx} - \frac{f_X\sigma^2 d^2\mu/dx^2}{(d\mu/dx)^2}\right) \end{aligned}$$

As $d(\log f_X(x))/dx = -x$, this is:

$$\beta = -\frac{1}{2}\left(\frac{-x\sigma^2}{d\mu/dx} + \frac{d\sigma^2/dx}{d\mu/dx} - \frac{\sigma^2 d^2\mu/dx^2}{(d\mu/dx)^2}\right)$$

As in the CreditRisk+ calculation above, we can put a portfolio consisting of a single obligor into the equation. In place of Equation 10, we have:

$$\begin{aligned} \mu(x) &= \mathrm{LGD}P_A(x) \quad \text{and} \\ \sigma^2(x) &= (\mathrm{LGD}^2+\mathrm{VLGD}^2)\,P_A(x) \end{aligned}$$

Rearranging, we get:

$$\beta = -\frac{(\mathrm{LGD}^2+\mathrm{VLGD}^2)}{2\mathrm{LGD}}\left(1 - \frac{P_A}{dP_A/dx}\left(x + \frac{d^2P_A/dx^2}{dP_A/dx}\right)\right)$$

Differentiating Equation 11, we get:

$$\frac{dP_A}{dx} = \frac{\rho_A^{1/2}}{(1-\rho_A)^{1/2}}\,n\left(\frac{N^{-1}(p_A)+\rho_A^{1/2}x}{(1-\rho_A)^{1/2}}\right)$$

and:

$$\frac{d^2P_A}{dx^2} = -\frac{\rho_A\left(N^{-1}(p_A)+\rho_A^{1/2}x\right)}{(1-\rho_A)^{3/2}}\, n\left(\frac{N^{-1}(p_A)+\rho_A^{1/2}x}{(1-\rho_A)^{1/2}}\right)$$

We therefore obtain:

$$\beta = \frac{-(LGD^2+VLGD^2)}{2LGD}\left(1 - N\left(\frac{N^{-1}(p)+\rho^{1/2}x}{(1-\rho)^{1/2}}\right)\right.$$
$$\left.\times \frac{x(1-2\rho)-\rho^{1/2}\,N^{1}(p)}{\rho^{1/2}(1-\rho)^{1/2} n\left((N^{-1}(p)+\rho^{1/2}x)/(1-\rho)^{1/2}\right)}\right)$$

We now substitute the Basel assumptions:

$$VLGD = 0.5\sqrt{LGD(1-LGD)}$$

as we did in the CreditRisk+ case above and the Basel parameters $\rho = 20\%$ (Basel, 2001, paragraph 172) and $X = 2.57$, its 99.5% value. After scaling the first factor to look like Basel's $0.4 + 1.2LGD$, we get:

$$\beta = (0.4+1.2LGD) \times \left(-0.3125 + \frac{N\left(1.118N^{-1}(p)+1.288\right)\left(1.2074-0.3494N^{-1}(p)\right)}{n\left(1.118N^{-1}(p)+1.288\right)}\right) \qquad (12)$$

The second factor in Equation 12 is very different in form from the corresponding equation for CreditRisk+, but we may do a linear fit to PD/F where, as above, F is the systematic risk sensitivity. The function is very linear in the range $0.03\% < PD < 10.00\%$ and linear regression in that interval gives the coefficients:

$$\beta^{Vasicek}_{Theoretical} = (0.4+1.2LGD)\left(0.32+4.19\frac{PD}{F}\right)$$

with R-squared = 99.95%. This is Equation 3.

It is prudent to use numerical work to verify that Equation 3 is indeed a better estimate of the granularity adjustment for a Vasicek modelled portfolio. In Table 1, we show the granularity

**Table 1. Granularity adjustment**

| N = 200 Default probability (%) | Granularity adjustment (%) | | | |
|---|---|---|---|---|
| | Basel, ie, CreditRisk+ | | Vasicek | |
| | Eqn 1 | Numerical | Eqn 3 | Numerical |
| 0.10 | 0.42 | 0.38 | 0.30 | 0.30 |
| 1.00 | 0.45 | 0.44 | 0.40 | 0.42 |
| 2.50 | 0.47 | 0.46 | 0.48 | 0.51 |
| 6.00 | 0.50 | 0.50 | 0.63 | 0.65 |
| 15.00 | 0.59 | 0.56 | 0.95 | 0.94 |

adjustment, calculated both using Equations 1 and 3 and numerically. We have chosen the portfolio with 200 obligors corresponding to chart 5 in Basel II.

The CreditRisk+ adjustments are those presented in Basel II. (The actual figures are not given, but they can easily be read off from chart 5, where they are the right-hand-most points.)[6] As can be seen from the above chart, the numerical results for CreditRisk+ do indeed agree closely with the results obtained using Equation 1. The Vasicek results above, obtained using Equation 3, also show good agreement with the corresponding numerical results. This serves to numerically verify Equation 3.

But, as predicted, the Vasicek results and Basel II's CreditRisk+ results are rather different, with the Vasicek results showing a stronger dependence on the default probability. In this sense, then, the granularity adjustment as presented in Basel II is inaccurate and the belief expressed in its derivation, that the change to CreditRisk+ from the Vasicek model used to calibrate the base risk weights will not affect the results, is unjustified. If any coefficients have the right to stand in paragraph 456 of Basel II, they are 0.32 and 4.19, not 0.76 and 1.1.

1 *It is to be stressed that this weakness is in the application of the methods of Gordy (2001), not in the methods themselves, some of which the results of this chapter serve to verify.*

2 *In the application in Basel II,* PD, LGD *and* F *are actually averages (in the theoretical work they are not). The averaging process in Basel II reduces to the case of a homogeneous portfolio. In contrast, our formulas should give accurate answers for all portfolios. Some comments on inhomogeneous portfolios are made in the text but there is not room to discuss this issue in full.*

3 *Except that our formula is valid whether the starting portfolio is homogeneous or not.*

4 *To justify all these approximations, one should review their behaviour in the limit process to an infinitely granular portfolio. This can be done, essentially making rigorous the intuition that the problem is "local to* L*". This leads to a rigorous demonstration of Equation 5, but we rely on intuition here.*

5 *These are first order in the default probabilities* p. *The exact formulas are well known but are given for example in Wilde (2001, Equations 3 and 4). When trying to replicate numerical results obtained using CreditRisk+, one should keep the first-order assumption because it is intrinsically used by that model.*

6 *It is worth noting that both the Basel (Equation 1) and Vasicek (Equation 3) granularity adjustments are accurate (relative, of course, to simulations using the CreditRisk+ and Vasicek models respectively) for values of* N *down to as low as 10–20, well off to the right of chart 5 in Basel (2001).*

**BIBLIOGRAPHY**

**Basel Committee on Banking Supervision,** 2001, *The New Basel Capital Accord*, IRB Consultative Document, Bank for International Settlements, January.

**Gordy, M.,** 2001, *A Risk Factor Model Foundation for Ratings Based Capital Rules*, Working Paper, February.

**Wilde, T.,** 2001, "IRB Approach Explained", *Risk*, May, pp. 87–90.

26

# Analytical Approach to Credit Risk Modelling

**Michael Pykhtin and Ashish Dev**

Keycorp

*The increasing popularity of VAR-based credit portfolio risk models has led to a growing recognition that Monte Carlo techniques are inadequate for economic capital calculations. Here, Michael Pykhtin and Ashish Dev present a new analytical alternative to Monte Carlo that builds on recent research.*

There have been significant advances recently in understanding credit risk. Several advanced credit risk models, such as CreditMetrics and CreditRisk+, have been developed (see Crouhy, Galai and Mark, 2000, for a comprehensive review and Gordy, 2000, for a comparative analysis). The most important output of these models, the economic capital, is calculated from the distribution of portfolio credit losses over certain time horizon in the value-at-risk framework. It is defined as the difference between the $q$-percentile of the distribution of the portfolio losses and the expected portfolio loss, where $q$ is the level of confidence chosen to maintain a certain credit rating.

More and more commercial banks and other financial institutions are starting to utilise the VAR approach to credit risk management. Regardless of the particular flavour of the VAR-based credit model they use, the vast majority of these institutions perform Monte Carlo simulations to generate the distribution of credit portfolio losses. However, any result based on Monte Carlo methods has an inherent noise, whose magnitude decreases very slowly, at the rate of $1/\sqrt{N}$, as the number of runs, $N$, increases. Thus, the computation time required to reduce this noise to acceptable levels is typically very large, particularly for large portfolios.

In this chapter, we explore analytical alternatives to Monte Carlo simulations that allow us to reduce the computation time tremendously. We chose Jon Frye's model (Frye, 2000a and 2000b) for this study because it is closely related to CreditMetrics, capable of capturing the effect of collateral damage and explicitly based on only one systematic risk factor (see Gordy, 2001, or Wilde, 2001a, for a comprehensive discussion on systematic risk factors). The one-factor model used in the Basel II accord (Basel, 2001) is a simplified version of Frye's model.

In the context of Frye's model, we have applied ideas from Gordy (2001) and have derived an analytical formula for the capital under the assumption that each exposure in the portfolio is an arbitrarily small fraction of the total exposure. We will use the term "asymptotic capital" for the capital calculated by this formula, and the term "asymptotic formula" to refer to the formula. The asymptotic formula can be used instead of Monte Carlo simulations in the case of large enough portfolios. It is also possible to avoid Monte Carlo simulations for non-asymptotic cases of a portfolio of arbitrary (large or small) size if one assumes that the portfolio is homogeneous (ie, same principal, same probabilities of default and same correlations for all obligors). Under this assumption, we have derived the distribution of losses for Frye's model analytically. With the ability to calculate the distribution of losses directly, it is not difficult to calculate the percentile that determines the capital.

Being able to compute capital fast and accurately under assumptions of both infinite and finite portfolios exactly, we have surveyed recent analytical approximations to the difference

*The authors would like to thank anonymous referees for their thoughtful comments, which helped improve the chapter in many respects.*

between the two quantities, generally known as "granularity adjustment". We also present our own analytical formula for the granularity adjustment, which is more accurate than the ones proposed in the literature.

## Description of the model

Frye's model includes losses only due to defaults (default mode) and not due to downgrades.[1] We consider a portfolio of M loans, jth loan having the principal $A_j$ over a certain time horizon (eg, one year). The weight of a loan in the portfolio is defined as a ratio of its principal to the total principal of the portfolio: $w_j = A_j/\Sigma_{i=1}^{M} A_i$. Obligor j has probability of default $p_j$ over the horizon. For each obligor j we define a binary random variable $D_j$ which takes on value one with probability $p_j$ (jth obligor defaults), and value zero with probability $(1 - p_j)$ (jth obligor does not default). Random variable describing the total number of defaults is defined as $D = \Sigma_{j=1}^{M} D_j$.

Following Frye (2000a and 2000b), we introduce a set of continuous random variables $\{X_j\}_{j=1}^{M}$ that describe financial well-being of a given obligor over the time horizon. They can also be viewed as the standardised returns on the obligors' assets at the horizon. These variables have standard normal distribution and trigger defaults whenever $X_j < X_j^D \equiv N^{-1}(p_j)$. They can be written as

$$X_j = a_j Y + \sqrt{1 - a_j^2} Z_j \tag{1}$$

where random variables Y and $Z_j$ are all independent and have standard normal distribution, and the correlation between financial well-beings (or asset returns) of obligors i and j is given by $\rho_{ij}^X = a_i a_j$. Y is the only systematic risk factor in the model, while $Z_j$ is an idiosyncratic variable describing individual fortunes of obligor j. With positive factor loadings $a_j$, the risk factor can be interpreted as the state variable showing the overall condition of the economy. Higher values of Y mean a stronger economy, better-off obligors and fewer defaults within the horizon.

If obligor j defaults, the bank loses a fraction $Q_j$ of the face value $A_j$ of one loan. We model them as identically distributed random variables with expectation $\mu^Q$ and standard deviation $\sigma^Q$:

$$Q_j = \mu^Q + \sigma^Q W_j \tag{2}$$

We assume that random variables $W_j$ are normally distributed.[2] Variables $Q_j$ are very similar to conventional loss given default (LGD), but there is a subtle but important difference. Variables $Q_j$ are functions of the corresponding collateral values and are well defined regardless of the event of default. Traditionally, LGD is defined only in the event of default. To avoid confusion between these two alternative definitions, we will call variables $Q_j$ "potential LGD" (or PLGD), since they determine what would be the loss if default happened. The effect of this subtle distinction is that, generally, expected LGD is not equal to $\mu^Q$ (see below).

Most credit risk models assume that LGD variables are independent from default variables. By doing this they overlook the effect of "collateral damage" captured by Frye's model. LGD is mostly determined by the value of the collateral, which, like any other asset, depends on the economy. The value of the collateral tends to be lower when the economy is weak and higher when the economy is strong. Thus, not only does economic recession bring more defaults, but it also reduces the value of the collateral, which, in turn, leads to increasing LGD. This conceptual argument is supported empirically in Moody's (2000) and was also mentioned in Wilde (2000).

This effect of collateral damage can be captured by assuming that variables $W_j$ linearly depend upon the economy Y:

$$W_j = -b_j Y + \sqrt{1 - b_j^2} \zeta_j \tag{3}$$

where $\zeta_j$ are independent and have standard normal distribution, and the minus sign (with positive $b_j$) insures the correct qualitative effect.

The correlation between PLGDs of obligors i and j is given by $\rho_{ij}^Q = b_i b_j$, while the correlation between well-being of obligor i and PLGD of obligor j is $\rho_{ij}^{XQ} = a_i b_j$. The total percentage portfolio loss, L, is given then by:

$$L = \sum_{j=1}^{M} w_j Q_j D_j = \sum_{j=1}^{M} w_j \left[\mu^Q + \sigma^Q W_j\right] 1_{\{X_j < X_j^D\}} \tag{4}$$

where $1\{\cdot\}$ is the indicator function.

## Analytical solutions of the model

The cornerstone of our analytical approach is to condition loss given by Equation 4 on the only risk factor in Frye's model – the economy random variable Y. We will rewrite the loss given by Equation 4 as a function of the economy:

$$\begin{aligned} L(Y) &= \sum_{j=1}^{M} w_j Q_j(Y) D_j(Y) \\ &= \sum_{j=1}^{M} w_j \left[\hat{\mu}_j^Q(Y) + \sigma^Q \sqrt{1 - b_j^2} \zeta_j\right] 1_{\{Z_j < \hat{X}_j^D(Y)\}} \end{aligned} \tag{5}$$

where:

$$\hat{\mu}_j^Q(Y) = \mu^Q - \sigma^Q b_j Y \quad (6)$$

is the jth obligor's expected PLGD conditional on the economy, and $\hat{X}_j^D(Y)$ is the jth obligor's default threshold conditional on the economy and given by:

$$\hat{X}_j^D(Y) = \left(X_j^D - a_j Y\right) \Big/ \sqrt{1 - a_j^2} \quad (7)$$

The conditional binary default variable, $D_j(Y)$, is defined similar to the unconditional one: it takes on value one when jth obligor defaults given that the economy is in state Y (ie, $Z_j < \hat{X}_j^D(Y)$) and value zero otherwise. The conditional probability of default, $\hat{p}_j(Y)$ is given by:

$$\hat{p}_j(Y) = N\left(\hat{X}_j^D(Y)\right) \quad (8)$$

where $N(\cdot)$ is the cumulative standard normal distribution function. The total number of defaults conditional on the economy can be defined as $D(Y) = \Sigma_{j=1}^M D_j(Y)$. All our analysis in this section will be based on Equation 5.

## Expected portfolio loss

If we try to calculate expected portfolio loss directly from Equation 4, we obtain:

$$E[L] = \sum_{j=1}^M w_j E[Q_j D_j] = \sum_{j=1}^M w_j [\mu^Q p_j + \mathrm{cov}(Q_j, D_j)]$$

The covariance term appears due to common dependence of PLGD and default variables upon the economy. However, conditionally on the state of economy, these variables are independent, and we can obtain the conditional expected loss, $E[L|Y]$, directly from Equation 5:

$$E\left[L \middle| Y\right] = \sum_{j=1}^M w_j \hat{\mu}_j^Q(Y) \hat{p}_j(Y) \quad (9)$$

where $\hat{\mu}_j^Q(Y)$ is the jth obligor's conditional expected PLGD given by Equation 6 and $\hat{p}_j(Y)$ is the jth obligor's conditional probability of default given by Equation 8. Then, taking full expectation, we obtain the unconditional expected loss:

$$\begin{aligned} E[L] &= E\left[E\left[L \middle| Y\right]\right] = \int_{-\infty}^{\infty} dy\, n(y) \sum_{j=1}^M w_j \hat{p}_j(y) \hat{\mu}_j^Q(y) \\ &= \sum_{j=1}^M w_j \int_{-\infty}^{\infty} dy\, n(y) \hat{p}_j(y) (\mu^Q - \sigma^Q b_j y) \\ &= \sum_{j=1}^M w_j \left[\mu^Q \int_{-\infty}^{\infty} dy\, n(y) \hat{p}_j(y) - \sigma^Q b_j \int_{-\infty}^{\infty} dy\, n(y) \hat{p}_j(y) y\right] \\ &= \sum_{j=1}^M w_j \left[\mu^Q p_j + \sigma^Q a_j b_j\, n\left(X_j^D\right)\right] \end{aligned} \quad (10)$$

where $n(\cdot)$ is the density of the standard normal distribution.

For homogeneous portfolios (same probability of default p and factor loadings a and b), it is easy to relate expected conventional LGD, $\tilde{\mu}$ to expected potential LGD, $\mu^Q$. With the conventional definition of LGD, expected loss for a loan equals to the product of $\tilde{\mu}$ and p, so that from Equation 10 we obtain:

$$\tilde{\mu} = \mu^Q + \sigma^Q \frac{ab}{p} n(X^D)$$

## Asymptotic properties of portfolio loss

In the limit of infinitely large size, all the idiosyncratic risk in the portfolio is completely diversified. It means that the only risk left in the portfolio is the uncertainty of the systematic risk factors. It has been proven in Gordy (2001) that loss of such a portfolio, $L^\infty$, is just the expected loss conditional on the risk factors. The only risk factor in Frye's model is the state of the economy Y, and the asymptotic loss, $L^\infty = E[L|Y]$, is given by Equation 9.

Both the conditional probability of default $\hat{p}_j(Y)$ given by Equation 8 and the conditional expected PLGD $\hat{\mu}_j^Q(Y)$ given by Equation 6 are decreasing functions of Y. Thus, the asymptotic loss itself is a decreasing function of Y, and the q-percentile of the loss distribution, $l_q^\infty$, is determined by $(1 - q)$-percentile of the economy, $y_{1-q}$:

$$l_q^\infty = \sum_{j=1}^M w_j \hat{\mu}_j^Q(y_{1-q}) \hat{p}_j(y_{1-q}) \quad (11)$$

The asymptotic capital, $K^\infty$, can be defined as the difference between the q-percentile of the asymptotic loss distribution and the expected loss:[3]

$$\begin{aligned} K^\infty = \sum_{j=1}^M w_j \Big[ & \mu^Q(\hat{p}_j(y_{1-q}) - p_j) \\ & + \sigma^Q b_j (y_q \hat{p}_j(y_{1-q}) - a_j n(X_j^D)) \Big] \end{aligned} \quad (12)$$

where in the second term we have taken into account the relation $y_{1-q} = -y_q$ (to make the formula for the capital more intuitive we use positive percentile $y_q$).

The remarkable property of Equation 12 apart from its simplicity is the asymptotic capital additivity: the total capital for a large portfolio of loans is the weighted sum of the marginal capitals for individual loans. In other words, the capital required to add a loan to a large portfolio depends only on the properties of that loan and of that obligor and does not depend on the properties of the portfolio or of other obligors:

$$K_j^{\infty} = \mu^Q(\hat{p}_j(y_{1-q}) - p_j) + \sigma^Q b_j\left(y_q\hat{p}_j(y_{1-q}) - a_j n(X_j^D)\right) \quad (13)$$

Such additivity of the capital is a very desirable property of a credit risk model from the point of view of loan pricing.

Gordy (2001) has shown that, generally, two conditions are necessary for capital additivity. One of them is that the portfolio is large and no obligor accounts for a significant fraction of the portfolio, ie, that the maximum of the weights $w_j$ is small. The other condition is that there is only a single systematic risk factor driving all the correlations in the model.

All of the results of this subsection are strictly true only in the limit $M \to \infty$. But how relevant are the asymptotic results to a real portfolio of a finite size? And do there exist exact analytical methods for finite portfolios? In what follows we address these questions. Below, we derive the exact loss distribution for a homogeneous portfolio of arbitrary size. then we analyse the difference between the exact and asymptotic capitals for a homogeneous portfolio.

## Loss distribution for a homogeneous portfolio

To derive the cumulative loss distribution in a tractable form for a portfolio of arbitrary size we have to assume that the portfolio is homogeneous. More precisely, we assume that all the loans in the portfolio have the same weight $w = 1/M$, that all obligors have the same probability of default $p$, and the same factor loadings $a$ and $b$. Asset return correlation $\rho^X = a^2$, PLGD correlation $\rho^Q = b^2$, and asset-PLGD correlation $\rho^{XQ} = ab$ are all uniform across the portfolio.

Our derivation again will be based on the portfolio loss given by Equation 5. The cumulative loss distribution, $F_L(l)$, is the probability that $L < l$ for any possible value of $l$. The key idea of our derivation is to express the unconditional probability that $L < l$ via the probability of the same event conditional on the state of the economy $y$:

$$F_L(l) \equiv \Pr[L < l] = \int_{-\infty}^{\infty} dy\, n(y) \Pr\left[L < l \middle| Y = y\right] = \int_{-\infty}^{\infty} dy\, n(y) \Pr[L(y) < l] \quad (14)$$

where conditional loss $L(y)$ is the loss given by Equation 5 with random value $Y$ being replaced by one of its states $y$.

Since the portfolio is homogeneous, its total loss will depend only on the total number of defaults and it will not depend on what particular loans defaulted. Thus, the next logical step is to condition portfolio loss further on total number of defaults $m$:

$$\Pr[L(y) < l] = \sum_{m=0}^{M} \Pr\left[L(y) < l \middle| D(y) = m\right] \Pr[D(y) = m] \quad (15)$$

where the conditional number of defaults $D(y)$ is defined above (random variable $Y$ is again replaced by its value $y$). Conditional default variables $D_j(y)$ have one major advantage over the unconditional ones: they are independent. It means that the total number of defaults $D(y)$ has binomial distribution:

$$\Pr[D(y) = m] = \binom{M}{m} [\hat{p}(y)]^m [1 - \hat{p}(y)]^{M-m} \quad (16)$$

From Equation 5, it follows that the portfolio loss conditional on the state of the economy, $Y = y$, and the total number of defaults given that state of the economy, $D(y) = m$, is $(1/M)\Sigma_{i=0}^{m} Q_i(y)$, and, since the conditional PLGD random variables $Q_i(y)$ are independent and have normal distribution, the conditional probability of $L(y) < l$ is

$$\Pr\left[L(y) < l \middle| D(y) = m\right] = N\left(\frac{(lM/m) - \hat{\mu}^Q(y)}{\left(\sigma^Q/\sqrt{m}\right)\sqrt{1-b^2}}\right) \quad (17)$$

Now, having determined all the components entering Equation 15, we can finally include them into the unconditional cumulative distribution of losses given by Equation 14:

$$F_L(l) = \int_{-\infty}^{\infty} dy\, n(y) \sum_{m=0}^{M} \binom{M}{m} [\hat{p}(y)]^m [1 - \hat{p}(y)]^{M-m} \times N\left(\frac{(lM/m) - \hat{\mu}^Q(y)}{\left(\sigma^Q/\sqrt{m}\right)\sqrt{1-b^2}}\right) \quad (18)$$

The probability density of losses, $f_L(l)$, is given by the first derivative of $F_L(l)$:

$$f_L(l) = \int_{-\infty}^{\infty} dy\, n(y) \sum_{m=0}^{M} \frac{M}{m} \frac{\binom{M}{m} [\hat{p}(y)]^m [1 - \hat{p}(y)]^{M-m}}{\left(\sigma^Q/\sqrt{m}\right)\sqrt{1-b^2}} \times n\left(\frac{(lM/m) - \hat{\mu}^Q(y)}{\left(\sigma^Q/\sqrt{m}\right)\sqrt{1-b^2}}\right) \quad (19)$$

The right-hand side of Equations 18 and 19 can be easily evaluated numerically for any loss value one. Since the standard normal density $n(y)$ goes to zero very fast, the infinite limits in the integrals can be safely replaced by the finite ones.[4] After replacing the integrals by a discrete sum,[5] the calculation of both the cumulative distribution and the probability density of losses is just an evaluation of a double sum that can be quickly performed even on a mid-level PC.

The capital is defined as the difference between the q-percentile of the loss distribution, $l_q$, and the expected loss, $\mu_L$, given by Equation 10. To find the q-percentile of the loss distribution, one must solve the equation:

$$F_L(l_q) = q \tag{20}$$

We solve Equation 20 iteratively, using the bisection method for the first several iterations, and then switching to Newton's method to accelerate convergence.[6]

This method has a tremendous advantage over Monte Carlo simulations in both speed and accuracy. Its only real disadvantage is that it is applicable directly only to homogeneous portfolios. It is possible, however, to overcome this disadvantage. One may divide the portfolio into homogeneous sub-portfolios and calculate capital for each sub-portfolio separately. The sum of the sub-portfolio capitals will clearly overestimate the true capital for the heterogeneous portfolio. We think it is appropriate to scale this sum down by the ratio of standard deviations. One can calculate the standard deviation of loss both for the heterogeneous portfolio and for each of the homogeneous sub-portfolios. Then, the ratio of the standard deviation of loss for the heterogeneous portfolio to the sum of standard deviations of the sub-portfolios can be used as the scale-down factor. The computation of standard deviations is possible even in the case of a multi-factor model.

## Granularity adjustment

The asymptotic capital formula given by Equation 12 has been derived under the assumption that all the idiosyncratic risk is completely diversified away. It means that the asymptotic capital formula is strictly valid only for a portfolio such that the weight of its largest exposure is infinitesimally small. All real-world portfolios violate this assumption and, therefore, one might question the relevance of the asymptotic formula. Indeed, since any finite-size portfolio carries some undiversified idiosyncratic risk, the asymptotic formula must underestimate the "true" capital. The difference between the "true" capital and the asymptotic capital (ie, the capital computed with Equation 12 regardless of the portfolio size) is known as granularity adjustment. We will denote it as G.

**1. Different models of granularity adjustment**

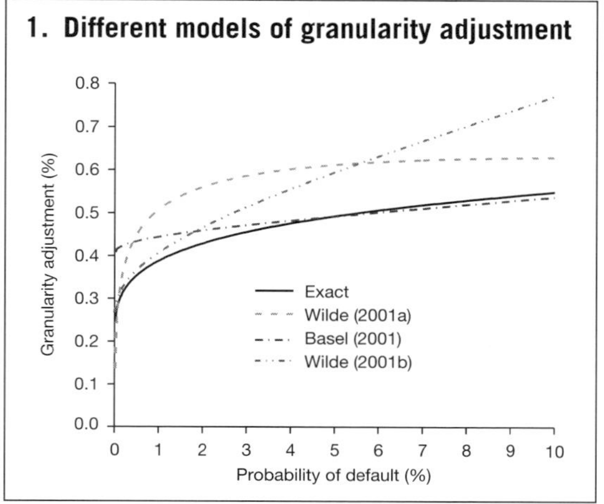


For homogeneous portfolios, we can calculate capital by using either Equation 12 or Equations 18, 19 and 20. Thus, staying within the framework of Frye's model, we can calculate the granularity adjustment exactly and are in position to analyse various analytical approximations to it developed earlier. Since all of these approximations were made for the case of idiosyncratic LGDs (in this case the distributions of LGD and PLGD are identical, and there is no reason to make a distinction between them), we set $b = 0$[7] in Equation 12, which now simplifies to:

$$K^{\infty} = \mu^Q(\hat{p}(y_{1-q}) - p) \tag{21}$$

This reduced form of Frye's model is essentially Vasicek's model (Vasicek, 1987), which is an ingredient of the Basel II proposal (Basel, 2001). As a basis for comparison, we have shown by the solid line in Figure 1 the granularity adjustment for a portfolio of 200 loans, calculated according to our method, as a function of the probability of default. We chose the parameters to match chart 5 in Basel II: the confidence level q is 99.5%, asset correlation $\rho^X$ is 20%, expected LGD $\mu^Q$ is set to 50%, while the standard deviation of LGD is:

$$\sigma^Q = \frac{1}{2}\sqrt{\mu^Q(1-\mu^Q)} \tag{22}$$

We are aware of three recent approaches to granularity adjustment, as follows.

SCALING BY STANDARD DEVIATIONS

This approach has been discussed in Wilde (2001a). The granularity adjustment in this approach is defined as:

$$G \equiv K^M - K^{\infty} = K^{\infty}\left(\sigma_L^M - \sigma_L^{\infty}\right)/\sigma_L^{\infty} \tag{23}$$

where $\sigma_L^M$ and $\sigma_L^\infty$ are standard deviations of the percentage loss for portfolios of finite (M loans) and infinite sizes, respectively, and it is shown by the dashed line in Figure 1. It is clear that this approach tends to overestimate the granularity adjustment by roughly 20%. We have found that this behaviour is very persistent for a wide range of $\mu^Q$ and $\sigma^Q$, which suggests that scaling G down by 20% will work reasonably well. The function itself, however, is more concave than the exact result, and will never provide a close fit.

BASEL'S APPROACH

Basel II suggests (paragraph 456 of Basel, 2001) the following formula for the granularity adjustment[8] with the assumptions of $q = 99.5\%$ and $\rho^X = 20\%$:

$$G = (0.4 + 1.2\mu^Q)\left(0.76 + 1.10\frac{p}{F}\right)\frac{1}{M} \qquad (24)$$

where we have used Basel's notation $F \equiv N(1.118N^{-1}(p) + 1.288) - p$. Equation 24 is based on the excellent work by Gordy (2001). Gordy has shown that the leading term in G is inversely proportional to the portfolio size M. For a given portfolio size, he also analysed the behaviour of the granularity adjustment as a function of probability of default and expected LGD, and Equation 24 is the output of his analysis. The Basel's granularity adjustment is shown in Figure 1 by the dash-dotted line. We can see from the plot that the Basel's formula does not provide a good fit to the exact result, particularly at low default probabilities. As Wilde (2001b) has pointed out, this discrepancy is due to the fact that Gordy used Vasicek's model to estimate the asymptotic capital, and a version of CreditRisk+ to estimate the capital for a finite portfolio.

WILDE'S APPROACH

Wilde (2001b) has made a brilliant effort of deriving the leading 1/M term for the granularity adjustment analytically. For the case of Frye's model, his result is:[9]

$$G = -\frac{1}{2Mn(y_{1-q})}\frac{d}{dy}\left[\frac{n(-y)\hat\sigma_1^2(y)}{d\hat\mu_1(y)/dy}\right]_{y=y_{1-q}} + O\left(\frac{1}{M^2}\right) \qquad (25)$$

where $\hat\mu_1(y)$ and $\hat\sigma_1^2(y)$ are the mean and the variance of the loss of the portfolio of one loan conditional on the state of the economy y. Assuming the setup of Vasicek's model with:

$$\hat\mu_1(y) = \mu^Q\hat p(y) \quad \text{and} \quad \sigma_1^2(y) = [(\mu^Q)^2 + (\sigma^Q)^2]\hat p(y) \qquad (26)$$

Wilde arrived at:[10]

$$G = \frac{(\mu^Q)^2 + (\sigma^Q)^2}{2\mu^Q} \times \left(\frac{\hat p(y_{1-q})}{n\left(\hat X^D(y_{1-q})\right)}\,\frac{y_q(1-2\rho^X) - X^D\sqrt{\rho^X}}{\sqrt{\rho^X}\sqrt{1-\rho^X}} - 1\right)\frac{1}{M} + O\left(\frac{1}{M^2}\right) \qquad (27)$$

Using Basel's standard deviation assumption given by Equation 22 along with the Basel's values of $q = 99.5\%$ and $\rho^X = 20\%$, he arrived at the excellent fit to Equation (27):[11]

$$G = (0.4 + 1.2\mu^Q)\left(0.32 + 4.19\frac{p}{F}\right)\frac{1}{M} \qquad (28)$$

The plot of the granularity adjustment given by Equation 28 is shown by the dash-double-dotted line in Figure 1. From the plot it is clear that Equation 28 adequately describes the reality only for small default probabilities, but is much worse than Gordy's granularity adjustment (Equation 24) for large but reasonable default probabilities. Moreover, Wilde compares his approximate analytical result with numerical one in his Figure A, and they seem to agree. Therefore, his numerical result does not match our exact result, which is also puzzling.

Thus, all the three granularity adjustments, ie, Equations 23, 24 and 28, are not very good for all ranges of default probabilities. It is somewhat unexpected that none of the three granularity adjustments dominates another and it is difficult to justify one over the others. The most promising of the three approaches is given by Equation 28; but it has something missing in its recipe.

## Correct formulation

The fact that Wilde's correction given by Equation 28 works well for small default probabilities provides a hint that somewhere in his derivation Wilde may have made an inappropriate assumption of small default probabilities. Indeed, such an assumption was made by him when he linearised conditional variance as a function of conditional default probability in Equation 26 above.[12] The correct expression is:

$$\sigma_1^2(y) = [(\mu^Q)^2 + (\sigma^Q)^2]\hat p(y) - (\mu^Q)^2\hat p^2(y) \qquad (29)$$

and the linearisation is not appropriate here because conditional default probability will be estimated at a fractional percentile of the economy, $y_{1-q}$, which makes this conditional probability large even for relatively small unconditional default probabilities (eg, for unconditional probability $p = 20\%$, the conditional probability will be $\hat{p}(y_{0.5\%}) = 29\%$ with Basel's $\rho^X = 20\%$, $q \geqslant 99.5\%$).

Thus, it is not difficult to amend Wilde's formulas for Vasicek's model by using the complete expression for the conditional variance (Equation 29) with his main result (Equation 25). As the result of this procedure, Equation 27 acquires an extra term:

$$G = \frac{(\mu^Q)^2 + (\sigma^Q)^2}{2\mu^Q} \times \left( \frac{\hat{p}(y_{1-q})}{n(\hat{X}^D(y_{1-q}))} \frac{y_q(1-2\rho^X) - X^D\sqrt{\rho^X}}{\sqrt{\rho^X}\sqrt{1-\rho^X}} - 1 \right) \frac{1}{M} - \frac{\mu^Q \hat{p}(y_{1-q})}{2} \times \left( \frac{\hat{p}(y_{1-q})}{n(\hat{X}^D(y_{1-q}))} \frac{y_q(1-2\rho^X) - X^D\sqrt{\rho^X}}{\sqrt{\rho^X}\sqrt{1-\rho^X}} - 2 \right) \frac{1}{M} + O\left(\frac{1}{M^2}\right) \quad (30)$$

Comparing the terms in Equations 27, 28 and 30, it is not difficult to write the correct version of Equation 28 without even making a fit:

$$G = (0.4 + 1.2\mu^Q)\left(0.32 + 4.19\frac{p}{F}\right)\frac{1}{M} - 1.6\mu^Q(F+p)\left(0.0075 + 4.19\frac{p}{F}\right)\frac{1}{M} \quad (31)$$

For Basel II parameters, Equation 31 indeed provides a superb fit to Equation 30. In Figure 2, we have plotted the granularity adjustment given by Equation 31 (the dashed line) along with our exact result for Vasicek's model (the solid line) for the same values of the parameters as in Figure 1. We see that the difference between our exact and corrected Wilde's granularity adjustments is negligible. Moreover, comparing the two results for larger portfolios, we have concluded that this difference is entirely due to $O(1/M^2)$ terms. As for Wilde's numerical result, it does not match our exact result because Wilde used the same linearised expression for conditional variance (Equation 26) in his numerical calculations as in his analytical approximation.

**2. Proposed granularity adjustment (Equation 31)**

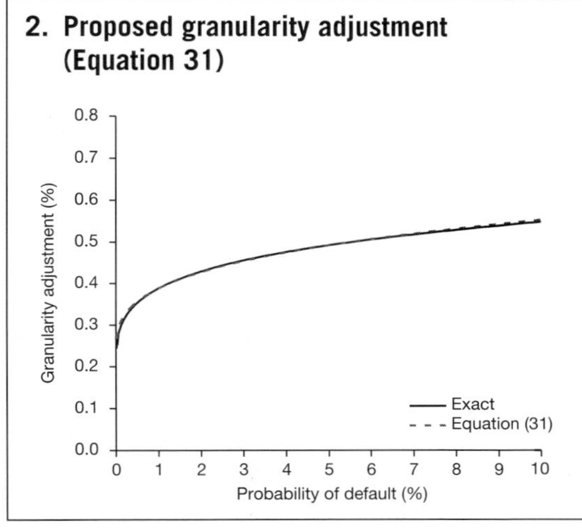


## Conclusion

The vast majority of financial institutions that use advanced credit risk models for capital allocation purposes rely on time-consuming and inaccurate Monte Carlo simulations. In this chapter, we have applied analytical methods to a fairly general default-mode one-factor credit risk model. For the case of asymptotically large portfolio, we have obtained an analytical formula for the economic capital (Equation 12). The formula can be easily implemented.

The application of the asymptotic formula to any real finite size portfolio, however, leads to an underestimation of the economic capital due to undiversified portion of idiosyncratic risk. We have derived the distribution of losses for a homogeneous portfolio of arbitrarily small or large size analytically (Equation 18). The capital can be easily calculated from the distribution with the help of Newton's method. Although these calculations have to be done numerically and cannot be implemented in Excel, they have a tremendous advantage over Monte Carlo simulations in terms of speed and accuracy.

Finally, using our ability to calculate capital exactly for both infinite and finite homogeneous portfolios, we have analysed existing approaches to the problem of granularity adjustment. We have shown that Wilde's general result indeed gives the dominant 1/M term to the granularity adjustment. We have also shown that, in applying Wilde's general result, it is inappropriate to linearise conditional standard deviation in conditional probability of default. Using the exact expression for the conditional standard deviation along with Wilde's general result, we have derived a granularity adjustment (Equation 31) that dominates other granularity adjustments proposed in the literature. The Basel Committee may or may not retain the granularity adjustment explicitly in the next version of Basel II. But the usefulness of the concept will not diminish. Availability of an analytical formula which accurately accounts for a finite portfolio size will help banks assess the underlying credit risk better.

1 *The extension of the model to the mark-to-market (MTM) framework is straightforward. In the MTM mode, the asymptotic capital can still be calculated by an analytical formula. The distribution of losses for a homogeneous portfolio can also be derived. Its computation time, however, grows too steeply (as* $M^n$*, where* n *is the number of credit ratings) with the size of the portfolio* M *to be useful in practice.*

2 *Here we follow Frye (2000b). To achieve analytical tractability, we do not restrict* $Q_j$ *variables to lie in the* [0, 1] *interval. This assumption may not be intuitively appealing, but it allows for analytical tractability and its effect on the output of the model is negligible for realistic values of the model parameters.*

3 *In deriving Equation 12, we assume that the portfolio is asymptotically large* ($M \to \infty$) *and its loss is given by* $L^\infty$*. Further in the chapter, we will apply Equation 12 and the term asymptotic capital to finite portfolios.*

4 *Integrating from –6 to 6 is enough for most practical purposes.*

5 *We have found that it is enough to divide each unit interval of* y *into 20 subintervals of equal size. Thus, the total number of terms in the discretised version of the integrals from –6 to 6 is 240.*

6 *Newton's method requires a good initial guess. The bisection method is used to provide such a guess.*

7 *We have also analysed the granularity adjustment for a range of non-zero* b*. Even though the capital depends strongly on* b*, we have found that the granularity adjustment's dependence upon* b *is much weaker. We varied* b *from 0 to 0.45 (roughly corresponding to 20% correlation between individual LGDs) and found that the corresponding change in the granularity adjustment was always under 10% of its* $b = 0$ *value.*

8 *It is possible that Basel Committee may remove the granularity adjustment part from the next version of Basel II. Nevertheless, granularity adjustment will remain an important concept in capital allocation (particularly for banks relying on asymptotic results).*

9 *Equation 25 is a version of Equation 5 in Wilde (2001b) for a normally distributed risk factor. Our risk factor* Y *is related to Wilde's risk factor* X *as* $Y = -X$.

10 *In the published version of Wilde (2001b), Equations 27 and 28 are incorrect. We present these equations in the correct form, as they appear in the corrected version of Wilde (2001b), available from* Risk.

11 *This is exactly Equation 3 from the corrected version of Wilde (2001b).*

12 *It is given by an unnumbered equation on page 106 in Wilde (2001b). Wilde explicitly mentions the linearisation in footnote 5 on page 105.*


**BIBLIOGRAPHY**

**Basel Committee on Banking Supervision,** 2001, *The Internal Ratings-Based Approach*, Supporting document to the New Basel Capital Accord, January.

**Crouhy, M., D. Galai, and R. Mark,** 2000, "A Comparative Analysis of Current Credit Risk Models", *Journal of Banking and Finance*, 24, pp. 59–117.

**Frye, J.,** 2000a, "Collateral Damage", *Risk*, April, pp. 91–4.

**Frye, J.,** 2000b, "Depressing Recoveries", *Risk*, November, pp. 108–11.

**Gordy, M.,** 2000, "A Comparative Anatomy of Credit Risk Models", *Journal of Banking and Finance*, 24, pp. 119–49.

**Gordy, M.,** 2001, "*A Risk-Factor Model Foundation for Ratings-Based Bank Capital Rules*", Working Paper, February.

**Moody's Investors Service,** 2000, "Historical Default Rates of Corporate Bond Issuers, 1920–1999", *Global Credit Research*, January.

**Vasicek, O.,** 1987, *Probability of Loss on Loan Portfolio*, KMV Corporation.

**Wilde, T.,** 2000, "CreditRisk+", in S. Das (ed.), *Credit Derivatives and Credit Linked Notes*, Second Edition, pp. 589–619.

**Wilde, T.,** 2001a, "IRB Approach Explained", *Risk*, May, pp. 87–90.

**Wilde, T.,** 2001b, "Probing Granularity", *Risk*, August, pp. 103–6.

# 27

# Unsystematic Credit Risk

**Richard Martin and Tom Wilde**

BNP Paribas; Credit Suisse First Boston

*Although Basel has shifted its treatment of unsystematic credit risk from the first, capital rules pillar (where it was called the "granularity adjustment") to the second, supervisory pillar of the forthcoming Accord, this issue is of great practical importance. Here, Richard Martin and Tom Wilde present new analytical results regarding the unsystematic risk component of credit portfolios, providing formulas for the sensitivity of credit portfolio value-at-risk to risk concentrations.*

This chapter sets out to compare some new approaches to credit risk modelling, particularly the granularity adjustment invented by Michael Gordy (2001) and derived theoretically by Wilde (2001b), a risk contribution formula from saddlepoint approximation (Martin, Thompson and Browne, 2001a), and earlier work of Gourieroux, Laurent and Scaillet (2000) on contributions to value-at-risk.

These approaches all assess the amount by which percentiles change when a new risk is added to a portfolio. In the papers of Martin, Thompson and Browne and Gourieroux, Laurent and Scaillet, the risk is associated with a new asset, while in the granularity adjustment, which has its recent origins in the Basel II reforms of regulatory capital, the risk is all the concentration risk in a portfolio of loans. We shall see that the underlying method is the same, whatever the origin of the new risk. This is an important observation: these methods can be used for building up VAR or economic capital from the different risks present, not just for assessing the marginal impact of a new asset. The methods require further development and we do not present finished tools for risk management, but there is considerable promise in these approaches, particularly for assessing portfolio credit risk.[1]

*The comments expressed here are those of the authors and do not necessarily represent the views of Credit Suisse Group, Credit Suisse First Boston or BNP Paribas.*

THE GRANULARITY ADJUSTMENT

This was conceived as part of the Basel II proposals for reforming the calculation of regulatory capital for credit risk (Basel Committee on Banking Supervision, 2001). The approach and the phrase "granularity adjustment" were created by Gordy (2001).

The granularity adjustment proved unpopular with banks commenting on the Basel II proposals in 2001, many of whom considered it too complex for a regulatory capital setting, and it seems likely to be dropped from the final Basel rules. But the technique is useful and merits further investigation outside the regulatory capital debate.

To understand the granularity adjustment method, suppose for example that we wish to calculate the distribution of losses from a portfolio of loans – a task for which one would use a credit risk portfolio model. The granularity adjustment works as follows.

First, assess economic or systematic risk. This can be defined as the risk the portfolio would have if all its loans were subdivided into "infinitely many" infinitesimal loans. Such a hypothetical portfolio is called "infinitely granular". Within most models of credit risk, the economic risk of the portfolio is technically easier to calculate than the total risk. In particular, in a one-factor model, systematic risk can be calculated as a sum of stand-alone contributions, each dependent only on the characteristics of that facility, and in fact this is the basis on which the Basel "IRB risk weights" were constructed (see, eg, Gordy, 2001, or Wilde, 2001a).

Then, adjust for concentration risk, that is, the granularity adjustment. The actual portfolio typically has more risk than the hypothetical "infinitely granular" portfolio, due to the presence of loans of finite size. It turns out that the marginal impact of this extra risk on the percentiles of the loss distribution can be assessed analytically with good accuracy. It is this circumstance that makes the granularity adjustment method successful.

THE WORK OF GOURIEROUX, LAURENT AND SCAILLET

Gordy's approach to granularity was empirical, but a theoretical result was published afterwards by Wilde (2001b).[2] However, essential priority belongs to Gourieroux, Laurent and Scaillet (2000) for a closely related result from which the theoretical granularity adjustment can be derived, as we will demonstrate below.

These three authors worked in the context of market risk VAR and addressed the problem of calculating marginal impact for an added position. Despite the different setting, the mathematics is similar. In the VAR context, the role of the systematic portfolio is played by the existing portfolio, and the marginal impact is that of all the risk of a single position, instead of the concentration risk of all assets.

THE SADDLEPOINT METHOD

The saddlepoint method is a powerful technique for approximating integrals used in the physical sciences, engineering and statistics. Martin, Thompson and Browne (2001a–c) developed and published the application of this method to portfolio credit risk. See also Gordy (2002) for an application of related ideas to CreditRisk+.

The saddlepoint method is based on the moment-generating function and Laplace transform, and has no direct resemblance to the granularity adjustment. But, Martin, Thompson and Browne (2001a, Equation 8) also gave a formula, based on the saddlepoint technique, for calculating the marginal impact of a new exposure in a portfolio. Like Gourieroux, Laurent and Scaillet's result, their formula also gives the marginal impact of any new risk, whether due to a new position or due to the inclusion of concentration risk on all positions. The saddlepoint risk contribution gives a "rival" granularity adjustment. The comparison of these adjustments is interesting, as we shall see below.

In this chapter, we attempt to explain, relate and compare these techniques, as follows. We begin with the known formulas for the first and second derivatives of VAR (Gourieroux, Laurent and Scaillet, 2000). We offer a proof based on a general result for derivatives of the cumulative density function and a second proof using the heat equation. We then derive Wilde's granularity adjustment formula (Wilde, 2001b, Equation 7). In the second half of the chapter, we compare the formulas resulting from the granularity adjustment and saddlepoint techniques. These have an interesting formal similarity. We give a case where they agree exactly and conjecture that it is, in a sense, unique. We illustrate the complementary nature of these methods with an example that also illustrates some of the convergence issues.

## Derivatives of VAR

If I add a small extra risk to a portfolio, what is the effect on VAR? This simple question can be abstractly formulated as follows. Let $X$ and $U$ be any random variables (not required to be independent), and form the family of random variables $Y_\varepsilon = X + \varepsilon U$ indexed by a parameter $\varepsilon$. Then $Y_\varepsilon$ is the "perturbation" of $X = Y_0$, formed by adding an amount $\varepsilon$ of new risk represented by $U$. As we mentioned, the new risk could be from a new exposure or from including a new risk, such as concentration risk, within the scope of the modelling.

Denote by $t_p(Y_\varepsilon)$ the quantile of $Y_\varepsilon$ at "confidence level" $1 - p$, that is, $P(Y_\varepsilon \le t_p(Y_\varepsilon)) = 1 - p$. We use this notation uniformly for all random variables. If $p = 1\%$, then the percentile is often called VAR $t_p(X)$, alternatively $t_p(Y_0)$, is the "unperturbed" or "base" VAR, and we can think of $t_p(Y_\varepsilon)$ as "perturbed" VAR. We seek formulas for the "derivatives of VAR":

$$\frac{d^n}{d\varepsilon^n} t_p(y_\varepsilon)$$

at $\varepsilon = 0$. These formulas are useful. For example, in the context of market risk VAR, the "risk contribution" of a new position represented by the random variable $U$ is simply $dt_p/d\varepsilon$. The same expression in the context of credit risk reduces to the so-called systematic risk contribution underlying the Basel II approach.

*Theorem A (first derivative of VAR)*

This is from Gourieroux, Laurent and Scaillet (2000), Tasche (2000) and Lemus-Rodriguez (1999)[3]:

$$\left.\frac{d}{d\varepsilon} t_p(y_\varepsilon)\right|_{\varepsilon=0} = \mathbb{E}\left(U \middle| X = t_p(X)\right)$$

where the vertical bar inside the expectation denotes conditioning on $X = t_p(X)$. Thus a small amount of added risk $\varepsilon U$ adds its expected value to the percentile, conditional on X being at the percentile in the first place.

Suppose U is deterministic, taking the value u, say, with certainty. In that case $\mathbb{E}(U|X) = u$, regardless of the value of X, so $dt_p(Y_\varepsilon)/d\varepsilon = u$. In fact, adding U to X just results in each percentile of X being shifted by u, so the result of theorem A is exact.

A more interesting special case is where the conditional expectation of U is zero: $\mathbb{E}(U|X) = 0$. Theorem A then says $dt_p(Y_\varepsilon)/d\varepsilon = 0$, so to first order in $\varepsilon$ the addition of U does not move the percentile. The effect of U is at second order. In particular, for the granularity adjustment the variable U represents concentration risk, and satisfies $\mathbb{E}(U|X) = 0$ everywhere. The granularity adjustment is therefore a second-order effect for which we need theorem B.

*Theorem B (second derivative of VAR)*

This is from Gourieroux, Laurent and Scaillet (2000). Retaining the notation above, let now $f_X$ be the density function of X. Then:

$$\left.\frac{d^2}{d\varepsilon^2} t_p(Y_\varepsilon)\right|_{\varepsilon=0} = \left. -\frac{d}{dx}V(x) - \frac{d(\ln(f_x))}{dx}V(x)\right|_{x=t_p(X)}$$

Or, written more neatly:

$$\left.\frac{d^2}{d\varepsilon^2} t_p(Y_\varepsilon)\right|_{\varepsilon=0} = \left. -\frac{1}{f_X}\frac{d(V(x)f_X)}{dx}\right|_{x=t_p(x)}$$

where $V(x) = V(U|X = x)$ is the variance of the conditional random variable $U|X = x$.

Theorem B was published in Gourieroux, Laurent and Scaillet (2000) and Theorem A by several authors in 1999 (see Tasche, 2000, for references). We derive both these results from a general result for all derivatives of the cumulative density function.

*Theorem C*

Let $F_{Y_\varepsilon}(x) = P(Y_\varepsilon \le x)$ be the cumulative density function of $Y_\varepsilon$. Then for $m > 0$:

$$\left.\frac{\partial^m F_{Y_\varepsilon}}{\partial \varepsilon^m}\right|_{\varepsilon=0} = (-1)^m \frac{d^{m-1}}{dx^{m-1}}(\mu_m(x) f_X(x))$$

where $\mu_m(x) = \mathbb{E}(U^m|X = x)$ is the mth non-central moment of U, conditional on $X = x$. It is later convenient to refer to $\mu_m(x)$ as plain $\mu_m$ but note that this always refers to the conditional moment – the unconditional moments of U do not enter into our discussion. As an aside, Theorem C can be viewed as a generalisation of the Gram–Charlier type A series (see Stuart and Ord, 1993, Equation 6.33). The Gram–Charlier series is essentially the special case where X and U are independent.

We demonstrate Theorem C using the moment-generating function, as we will need this later for our comparison with the saddlepoint approximation.[4] By definition of the moment-generating function:

$$M_{Y_\varepsilon}(s) = \mathbb{E}(e^{sX+s\varepsilon U})$$

Differentiating m times and setting $\varepsilon = 0$ gives:

$$\left.\frac{\partial^m M_{Y_\varepsilon}}{\partial \varepsilon^m}\right|_{\varepsilon=0} = s^m \mathbb{E}(U^m e^{sX}) \tag{1}$$

The inversion theorem recovers the density function of $Y_\varepsilon$ from its moment-generating function by the Laplace transform:

$$f_{Y_\varepsilon}(x) = \frac{1}{2\pi i}\int_{-i\infty}^{i\infty} M_{Y_\varepsilon}(s)e^{-sx}ds$$

Differentiating m times and setting $\varepsilon = 0$, then substituting Equation 1 gives:

$$\begin{aligned}\left.\frac{\partial^m}{\partial \varepsilon^m} f_{Y_\varepsilon}(x)\right|_{\varepsilon=0} &= \frac{1}{2\pi i}\mathbb{E}\left(\int_{-i\infty}^{i\infty} s^m U^m e^{s(X-x)}ds\right) \\ &= \frac{1}{2\pi i}(-1)^m \frac{d^m}{dx^m}\mathbb{E}\left(U^m \int_{-i\infty}^{i\infty} e^{s(X-x)}ds\right)\end{aligned}$$

But:

$$(2\pi i)^{-1}\int_{-i\infty}^{i\infty} e^{s(X-x)}ds = \delta_{X=x}$$

the delta function. Further, $\mathbb{E}(U^m \delta_{X=x}) = \mu_m(x) f(x)$. Hence:

$$\begin{aligned}\left.\frac{\partial^m}{\partial \varepsilon^m} f_{Y_\varepsilon}(x)\right|_{\varepsilon=0} &= (-1)^m \frac{d^m}{dx^m}\mathbb{E}(U^m \delta_{X-x}) \\ &= (-1)^m \frac{d^m}{dx^m}(\mu_m f)\end{aligned} \tag{2}$$

Theorem C follows after integrating Equation 2 once to get the cumulative density function (we need a mild assumption about the tail densities of X and U to ensure the boundary term vanishes).

DERIVATION OF THEOREMS A AND B

Theorem C in the cases $m = 1$ and 2 has the same statistical content as Theorems A and B, and to obtain A and B we only need to "invert" C to express its results in terms of percentiles. This is merely calculus.[5] It is convenient to simplify the notation slightly before we begin. We write $t(\varepsilon)$ instead of

$t_p(Y_\varepsilon)$, suppressing p, which is fixed. Then:

$$F_{Y_\varepsilon}(t(\varepsilon)) = 1 - p = \text{constant}$$

and we want to view this as an implicit relationship satisfied by the explicit function $t = t(\varepsilon)$. Write $F(\varepsilon, t) = F_{Y_\varepsilon}(t(\varepsilon))$ to display the joint dependence on t and ε. For a small change dε and accompanying change dt we have, by the chain rule $F_\varepsilon d\varepsilon + F_t dt = 0$, where the subscripts denote partial derivatives. Hence (this is a standard result of calculus):

$$\frac{dt}{d\varepsilon} = -\frac{F_\varepsilon}{F_t} \tag{3}$$

Taking the total derivative with respect to ε gives the second derivative, also a standard result:

$$\frac{d^2t}{d\varepsilon^2} = \frac{-F_t^2F_{\varepsilon\varepsilon} + 2F_\varepsilon F_t F_{\varepsilon t} - F_\varepsilon^2 F_{tt}}{F_t^3} \tag{4}$$

Set m = 1 in theorem C, giving:

$$\left.\frac{\partial F_{Y_\varepsilon}}{\partial \varepsilon}\right|_{\varepsilon=0} = -\mu_1 f$$

Then, using Equation 3, noting that $F_t = f$:

$$\left.\frac{\partial}{\partial \varepsilon} t_p(Y_\varepsilon)\right|_{\varepsilon=0} = -\frac{F_\varepsilon}{F_t} = \frac{\mu_1 f}{f} = \mu_1$$

which is just Theorem A. Theorem B is similar, beginning with Theorem C for m = 2:

$$F_{\varepsilon\varepsilon} = \left.\frac{\partial^2 F_{Y_\varepsilon}}{\partial \varepsilon^2}\right|_{\varepsilon=0} = \frac{d}{dx}(\mu_2 f)$$

and using Equation 4 to obtain:

$$\frac{d^2t}{d\varepsilon^2} = \frac{-1}{f^3}\left(f^2\frac{d}{dx}(\mu_2 f) - 2\mu_1 f^2 \frac{d}{dx}(\mu_1 f) + (\mu_1 f)^2\frac{df}{dx}\right)$$

which, after some algebra, simplifies to:

$$\frac{d^2t}{d\varepsilon^2} = -\frac{1}{f}\frac{d}{dx}(\mu_2 f - \mu_1^2 f)$$

This is Theorem B, because $\mu_2(x) - \mu_1^2(x) = V(x)$, the variance of the conditional distribution.

## THE GRANULARITY ADJUSTMENT

We mentioned in the introduction that the granularity adjustment is a formula for the effect of concentration risk in a portfolio. The original granularity adjustment was the empirical adjustment presented by Gordy (2001), for which he used CreditRisk+. Wilde then gave a formula for the adjustment in any one-factor credit model (Wilde, 2001b, Equation 7, reproduced as Equation 8 below). There is a manifest similarity with Theorem B, and indeed Wilde's formula follows from Theorems A and B, as we will now show.

For background on one-factor credit risk models, see Wilde (2001a and 2001b). Briefly, in a one-factor model, correlation or systematic risk is modelled by a single random variable X, on which all default probabilities depend, and with the stipulation that conditional on X, the credit behaviour of different assets is independent. In this context, Wilde (2001b) defined a systematic limit process: let $\Pi = \Pi_1$ be a portfolio of loans with exposures $E_A$ and default probabilities $P_A(X)$, displaying the dependence on X. We construct a portfolio $\Pi_n$ by dividing each $E_A$ into n exposures $E_A/n$, assigning the same default behaviour specified by $P_A(X)$ to each new loan. Let $Y_n$ be the loss distribution of $\Pi_n$.[6] For large n, $Y_n$ tends to the systematic loss distribution, which is the distribution defined of the random variable $\Sigma_A E_A P_A(X)$. At this stage X is an abstract "systematic risk factor", but Wilde (2001b) mentions we may identify X with the systematic loss variable $\Sigma_A E_A P_A(X)$, compensating by modifying the functions $P_A(X)$. Then $Y_n$ tends to X as n tends to infinity, and the difference (in terms of percentiles) is the granularity adjustment.

To apply Theorems A and B to the granularity adjustment, write $Y_n = X + U$, where $U_n = Y_n - X$ is the "perturbation" due to concentration risk. The one-factor modelling assumptions imply that, conditional on X = x, we have:

$$\mathbb{E}\left(U_n \middle| X = x\right) \equiv 0 \tag{5}$$

$$V\left(U_n \middle| X = x\right) = n\sum_A (E_A/n)^2 P_A(1 - P_A) = V(x)/n \tag{6}$$

where $V(x) = V(Y|X = x)$ is the conditional variance. Equation 5 follows from the fact that the conditional expected loss is independent of n, hence letting $n \to \infty$, equal to $\mathbb{E}(X - X|X = x) = 0$.

It is convenient to introduce u where $u = 1/n$. Also write $\varepsilon = \sqrt{u}$ and:

$$\sigma(x) = \sqrt{V(x)}$$

for the conditional standard deviation. Then Equations 5 and 6 imply:

$$Y_u = X + \sqrt{u}\sigma(x)Z_u$$

where $Z_u$ has mean zero and unit variance. If $Z_u$ were independent of u, then we could immediately apply Theorems A and B. But the third and higher cumulants of U depend on u; they all tend to zero as u tends to zero (it can be seen after the fashion of Equation 6 that $\kappa_m(U_n) = n^{1-m}\kappa_m(U)$).

Theorem B does not deal with this situation, but it is really a technicality; intuition suggests that, since the higher moments of U do not appear in Theorem B, they should not matter even if they vary with u provided they behave well (and in this case they tend to zero).

To deal explicitly with the difficulty, introduce a second variable v such that:

$$Y_{u,v} = X + \sqrt{u}\sigma(x)Z_v$$

and let $t = t(u, v)$ be the p-percentile regarded temporarily as a function of both u and v. Then we want the diagonal derivative $dt/du = dt(u, u)/du = \partial t/\partial u + \partial t/\partial v$ by the chain rule.[7] At $u = 0$ we have $Y_{0,v} = X$ for all v; hence $\partial t/\partial v = 0$. Therefore at $u = v = 0$:

$$dt(u, u)/du = \partial t(u, 0)/\partial u$$

Setting $v = 0$, we have:

$$Y_u = X + \sqrt{u}\sigma(x)Z = X + \varepsilon\sigma(x)Z \tag{7}$$

where $Z = Z_0$ is a random variable with mean zero and unit variance. (Z is actually unit-normal because its cumulants other than the second are zero by the argument above. Note that we do not need this fact to apply Theorem B, but we will use it for our second proof and for work on the granularity adjustment below.)

Theorem A now gives $dt_p/d\varepsilon = \sigma(x)\mathbb{E}(Z) = 0$ for all x, so the first derivative with respect to ε is zero. In fact the "non-bias" condition discussed above, holds. Now Theorem B gives:

$$\left.\frac{d^2t_p}{d\varepsilon^2}\right|_{\varepsilon=0} = -\frac{1}{f_X}\frac{d}{dx}\left(f_x V\left(U|X\right)\right)$$

By l'Hopital's rule:

$$\frac{dt_p}{du}(0) = \lim_{\varepsilon\to 0}\frac{dt_p/d\varepsilon}{2\varepsilon} = \frac{1}{2}\frac{d^2t_p}{d\varepsilon^2}$$

Hence, we arrive at:

$$\left.\frac{dt_p}{du}\right|_{u=0} = -\frac{1}{2f_X}\frac{d}{dx}\left(f_x V(x)\right)\Big|_{x=t_p} \tag{8}$$

which is Wilde's granularity formula. Note the slightly complicated way that Equation 8 is related to Theorems A and B. Although Equation 8 is a first derivative, it is taken with respect to $u = \varepsilon^2$ and so is related to the second derivative with respect to ε, while the first derivative with respect to ε vanishes everywhere.

## ANOTHER PROOF USING THE HEAT EQUATION

In going from Theorem B to Equation 8, we met a technicality. The systematic limit process gives rise to a family of random variables:

$$Y_u = X + \sqrt{u}\sigma(x)Z_u$$

in which the perturbation changes shape as well as scales, becoming normal in the limit $u \to 0$. We showed that (provided one accepts a differentiability assumption) we could replace $Z_u$ with $Z_0$, which is a fixed random variable. But we noted that $Z_0$ is in fact unit-normal. Hence, a weaker form of Theorem B, in which the perturbation U is assumed normal, is all that is needed for Wilde's formula shown in Equation 8.

In view of this, we thought it worth including the following direct elegant proof of the granularity adjustment formula, which avoids the use of transforms but does assume normality. This proof is interesting because it is very similar to work by Avellaneda and Zhu (2001, Equation 10) in a different context - in fact these authors also write down an equation equivalent to Equation 8. First, recall that the heat kernel:

$$g(v, w) = \frac{1}{\sqrt{2\pi v}}e^{-\frac{1}{2}(w^2/v)}$$

satisfies the heat equation $g_v = 1/2g_{ww}$ with initial condition $g(0, w) = \delta(w)$, where δ is the delta function. The cumulative density function of Equation 7:

$$Y_u = X + \sqrt{u}\sigma(x)Z$$

can be written out directly when Z is assumed to be standard normal:

$$1 - p = P(Y \le y) = \int_{x=-\infty}^{y}\int_{w=-\infty}^{+\infty} f_X(w)g\left(uV(w), x - w\right)dwdx$$

For fixed y, differentiating this expression and using the heat equation we obtain:

$$\frac{\partial}{\partial u}P(Y \le y) = \int_{x=-\infty}^{y}\int_{w=-\infty}^{+\infty} f_X(w)V(w)\frac{1}{2}g_{ww}\left(uV(w), x - w\right)dwdx$$

We can integrate the inner integral by parts (twice) – the boundary terms disappear each time:

$$\frac{\partial}{\partial u}P(Y \le y) = \frac{1}{2}\int_{x=-\infty}^{y}\int_{w=-\infty}^{+\infty}\frac{d^2\left(f_X V(x)\right)}{dw^2}g\left(uV(x), x - w\right)dwdx$$

Finally, letting $u \to 0$ and using the initial condition, this is:

$$\frac{\partial}{\partial u} P(Y \le y)\bigg|_{u=0} = \frac{1}{2}\frac{d(f_X V(x))}{dx}\bigg|_y \qquad (9)$$

This formula appears in Avellaneda and Zhu (2001, Equation 10). We now let $y = t_p(Y_u)$ vary with $u$, keeping $P(Y \le t_p(Y_u)) = 1 - p$ constant. By Equation 3 again:

$$\frac{dt_p}{du} = -\frac{\partial P / \partial u}{\partial P / \partial y}$$

At $u = 0$, by definition $\partial P/\partial y = f_X(y)$, while $\partial P/\partial u$ is given by Equation 9. Substituting we get:

$$\frac{dt_p}{du} = -\frac{1}{2f_X}\frac{\partial}{\partial x}(f_X V)$$

which is the granularity adjustment seen in Equation 8 again.

## Saddlepoint methods

In this section, we introduce the saddlepoint version of the granularity adjustment, and ask when the two agree.

### SADDLEPOINT RISK CONTRIBUTION

We consider:

$$Y_u = X + \sqrt{u}\sigma(x)Z$$

as in Equation 7. The exact first derivative of the percentiles $t_p(Y_u)$ is given by the granularity adjustment in Equation 8. The saddlepoint equivalent of Equation 8 is due to Martin, Thompson and Browne (2001a, Equation 8). In our current notation, their formula reads:

$$\frac{\partial t_p(Y_u)}{\partial u}\bigg|_{u=0} = \frac{1}{\hat{t}}\frac{\partial}{\partial u}(\ln M_{Y_u}(s))\bigg|_{u=0,s=\hat{t}} \qquad (10)$$

where the saddlepoint $\hat{t}$ is the solution of:

$$\frac{\partial M_X(s)}{\partial s}\bigg|_{\hat{t}} = t_p M_X(\hat{t})$$

Martin, Thompson and Browne gave this result in terms of sensitivity to the allocation of a new asset to a portfolio, but the result and its demonstration remain valid for any parameter on which the distribution depends. Here, we choose the parameter $u$ representing the amount of concentration risk present. To evaluate Equation 10, we calculate the moment-generating function of $Y_u$. We have:

$$M_{Y_u}(s) = E(e^{sY}) = \int_{-\infty}^{+\infty} \left(e^{sY_u} \middle| x\right) f(x)dx = \int_{-\infty}^{+\infty} e^{sx+\frac{1}{2}uV(x)s^2} f(x)dx$$

where we have made use of the fact that $Z$ is standard normal. Therefore:

$$\frac{\partial M_{Y_u}(s)}{\partial u}\bigg|_{u=0,s=t} = \frac{1}{2}\hat{t}^2 \int_{-\infty}^{+\infty} V(x)e^{tx}f(x)dx \qquad (11)$$

Therefore, substituting in Equation 10:

$$\frac{\partial t_p}{\partial u}\bigg|_{u=0} = \frac{1}{\hat{t}M_X(\hat{t})}\frac{\partial M_{Y_u}(s)}{\partial u}\bigg|_{u=0,s=\hat{t}} = \frac{\hat{t}}{2M_X(\hat{t})}\int_{-\infty}^{+\infty} V(x)e^{\hat{t}x}f(x)dx \qquad (12)$$

Equation 12 is the saddlepoint equivalent of the granularity adjustment formula in Equation 8. We may write it in the form:

$$\frac{dt_p}{du}\bigg|_{u=0} = \frac{\hat{t}L(fV)}{2Lf} = \frac{1}{2Lf}L\left(\frac{d}{dx}(fV)\right) \qquad (12a)$$

where $L$ denotes the Laplace transform and the right-hand side is evaluated at the saddlepoint (the second equality is a general property of Laplace transforms).

Despite their somewhat similar appearance, Equations 12 and 8 usually give different results, as we shall see. Since Equation 8 is the exact derivative of percentiles, it follows that Equation 12 is usually "wrong" in the limit of small added risk. However, in practice Equation 12 may be more useful; our focus in practice is not usually the value of the derivative itself but approximate risk for a portfolio with non-zero granularity, and we may well care about a range of percentiles. As we shall see by an example, Equation 12 can give a better overall approximation to the shape of the distribution. The situation is similar to approximating a function over an interval using either a power series expansion, which will be very exact near the origin but less so further away, or a Fourier series, which will have the wrong slope at the origin but be a better uniform fit.

### AGREEMENT BETWEEN THE SADDLEPOINT AND GRANULARITY ADJUSTMENTS

The two adjustments actually do agree in at least one important case, essentially CreditRisk+ with one sector.[8] Specifically, using the notation for one-factor models from our discussion above Equation 5, suppose a model satisfies the following two conditions:

- ❑ The conditional variance $V(Y|X = x)$ is proportional to the systematic variable $X$.[9]
- ❑ The systematic loss distribution $X$ is gamma distributed.

In CreditRisk+ with one sector the first condition holds because CreditRisk+ makes each default probability proportional to X, where X, the systematic loss distribution, is gamma distributed with mean equal to the portfolio mean loss $\mu = \alpha\beta$, and with variance $\alpha\beta^2$. Default probabilities are proportional to X. We write this in terms of the scaled variable $X/\mu$, which has mean one:

$$P_A(x) = p_A X/\mu \text{ and } V(X) = (\Sigma_A E_A^2 p_A)X/\mu = \sigma_{US}^2 X/\mu$$

where $\sigma_{US}^2 = \Sigma_A E_A^2 p_A$ is the "unsystematic component of variance". The formula for V(X) is exact for CreditRisk+ since that model neglects squares of default probabilities. With these relations, Equation 12 gives:

$$\left.\frac{dt_p}{du}\right|_{u=0} = \frac{\hat{t}\sigma_{US}^2/\mu}{2M_X(\hat{t})}\int_{-\infty}^{+\infty} xe^{\hat{t}x}f(x)dx = \frac{\hat{t}t_p\sigma_{US}^2}{2\mu} \quad (13)$$

We assumed X is gamma distributed, that is, $f(x) \propto x^{\alpha-1}e^{-x/\beta}$, and it is easily checked that:

$$\frac{\partial M_X(s)}{\partial s} = \frac{-\alpha}{s-1/\beta}M_X(s)$$

so the saddlepoint is given by the relationships:

$$\frac{-\alpha}{\hat{t}-1/\beta} = t_p \quad \text{or} \quad \hat{t} = \frac{1}{\beta} - \frac{\alpha}{t_p} \quad (14)$$

Therefore, combining Equations 13 and 14 and using $\alpha\beta = \mu$ we have:

$$\left.\frac{\partial t_p}{\partial u}\right|_{u=0} = \frac{\hat{t}t_p\sigma_{US}^2}{2\mu} = \frac{t_p\sigma_{US}^2}{2\mu}\left(\frac{1}{\beta} - \frac{\alpha}{t_p}\right) = \frac{\sigma_{US}^2(t_p-\mu)}{2\mu\beta} \quad (15)$$

This is the saddlepoint granularity adjustment.

On the other hand, the result of using Equation 8 is:

$$\left.\frac{dt_p}{du}\right|_{u=0} = -\frac{\sigma_{US}^2}{2\mu f_X}\left.\frac{d(xf_X)}{dx}\right|_{x=t_p}$$

$$= -\frac{\sigma_{US}^2}{2\mu}x^{1-\alpha}e^{x/\beta}\left.\frac{d(x^\alpha e^{-x/\beta})}{dx}\right|_{x=t_p} = \frac{\sigma_{US}^2(t_p-\mu)}{2\mu\beta} \quad (16)$$

Equations 15 and 16 are the same - the two methods lead to the same result in the case of CreditRisk+ with one sector.

The agreement is nice, but further examples suggest similarity between the risk contributions ends there - we see a simple example below. We conjecture that (for models with conditional variance proportional to the systematic factor), the saddlepoint and the granularity adjustment are the same only if X has the gamma distribution. This has no practical implication, but seems to present a genuine mathematical challenge.[10]

**1. Density functions: perturbed exponential distribution and approximants**

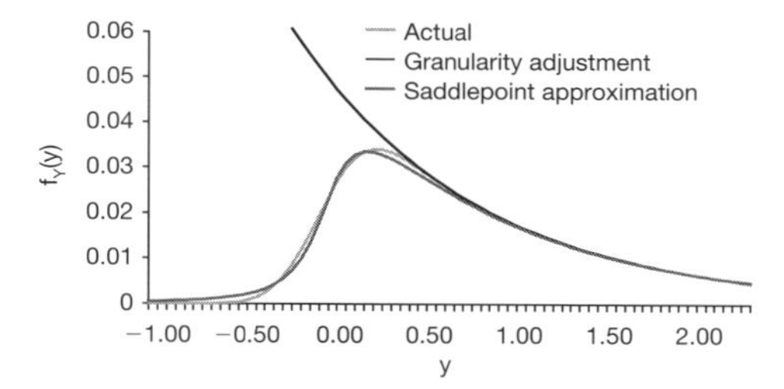

AN ILLUSTRATIVE CASE OF DISAGREEMENT

We turn to an example where the two methods do not agree, and consider perhaps the simplest case where we "perturb" an exponential distribution adding independent normally distributed risk:

$$Y = X + \varepsilon Z; \quad F_X(x) = 1 - e^{-x}; \quad Z \sim N(0,1)$$

The exact cumulative density function of Y is:

$$F_Y(y) = N\left(\frac{y}{\varepsilon}\right) - N\left(\frac{y}{\varepsilon} - \varepsilon\right)e^{\varepsilon^2/2-y}$$

Figure 1 shows the marginal density $f_Y(y)$ with its granularity adjustment and saddlepoint approximations for $\varepsilon = 1$. The approximations display different behaviour. The saddlepoint is uniformly good, while the granularity adjustment is very good in the right tail but diverges at the left-hand end of the distribution. Before discussing this behaviour, we show our calculations of the two approximations.

*Granularity adjustment*

Theorem A gives $dt_p/d\varepsilon = 0$ at $\varepsilon = 0$ (the non-bias condition holds) and Theorem B gives $d^2t_p/d\varepsilon^2 = 1$ at $\varepsilon = 0$. Note these are exact; they are not approximations. In this special case, however, it can also be shown that the derivatives $d^m t_p/d\varepsilon^m$, vanish for $m \geq 3$. Therefore, the Taylor series for $t_p(\varepsilon)$ is exactly:

$$t_p(\varepsilon) = t_p(0) + \varepsilon^2/2 = -\ln p + \varepsilon^2/2$$

It is important to note there is no approximation here; this is the Taylor series expansion for $t_p(\varepsilon)$. Theorems A and B are exact results, not approximations. The reason the granularity adjustment is not exact is that $t_p(\varepsilon)$ is not the sum of its (convergent) Taylor series. The Taylor series can easily be rearranged in terms of a cumulative density function having the percentiles $t_p(\varepsilon) = -\ln p + \varepsilon^2/2$; this is:

$$F_Y(y) = P(Y \leq y) = 1 - e^{\varepsilon^2/2-y}$$

Hence, this is the best "granularity adjustment" approximation that can be obtained for Y, even taking all derivatives into account. It clearly is not equal to Y, although it is an excellent approximation in the tail where x is large. The associated density function $f_Y(y) = e^{\varepsilon^2/2-y}$ is the granularity adjustment line on Figure 1 (with $\varepsilon = 1$).[11]

This failure could have been foreseen. The formulas given by Theorems A and B depend only on the density of X and its derivatives at the point t. There is no way of knowing when, as in this case, $f_X$ is not determined globally by those derivatives. Thus, the exponential density agrees with $e^{-x}$ for $x \geq 0$ but is zero for $x < 0$. This problem is apt to occur for any distribution used in the modelling of credit risk, since positive-valued distributions are typically required.

However, as in this case, the approximation is a good fit in the tail of the distribution. This is because in the tail we are far from the region $x < 0$, so that in the convolution integral for $f_Y$ one can approximate $f_X$ by $e^{-x}$ for $x < 0$ without significant error.

*Saddlepoint approximation*

Repeating the procedure with the saddlepoint approximation formula in Equation 12 gives instead:

$$F_Y(y) = 1 - e^{\left(\varepsilon^2/2 - y - \sqrt{(\varepsilon^2/2-y)^2+\varepsilon^2}\right)/2}$$

The saddlepoint method is a much better overall fit, as Figure 1 shows, while the granularity adjustment is uneven, being a somewhat better fit in the tail (in this case) but diverging from the real distribution on the left-hand side.

## Conclusion

We have compared two approaches to calculating the effect on percentiles of adding a small amount of extra risk to a portfolio. The first of these is the "granularity adjustment" method conceived by Gordy (2001) in the context of Basel II. The second is a saddlepoint formula for risk contributions given by Martin, Thompson and Browne (2001a).

Wilde's theoretical adjustment should be seen as a consequence of earlier work by Gourieroux, Laurent and Scaillet (2000). The particular hallmark of their work is the appearance of conditional moments of the added risk (these do not appear, for example, in the Cornish–Fisher expansion), and the fact that the derivatives of VAR (Theorems A and B) are exact.

We showed with CreditRisk+ that it is easy to calculate the granularity adjustment in a one-factor credit risk model, and used this example to show that the granularity adjustment and the saddlepoint method give the same result in this case. Another example illustrated that the granularity adjustment and saddlepoint are normally different. The saddlepoint method gives a good overall approximation, while the granularity adjustment has variable performance but is very good in the tail of the distribution.

This example also illustrates some more profound difficulties with the granularity adjustment, particularly that percentiles sought may not be the sums of their Taylor series. This is a subtle difficulty, but may not be a serious drawback in practice where a good approximation to percentiles, not perfection, is sought. This is demonstrated by Gordy's original granularity adjustment, which is a surprisingly accurate measure of concentration risk. Although the methods presented here are not ready for general use, we hope by writing this chapter to have stimulated interest in their properties, and are sure that wider applications will be found.

1 *Since this chapter is not an overview, we do not present the various alternatives for assessing portfolio credit risk, but many techniques now exist in addition to Monte Carlo, once thought to be the natural approach. Any one of these may be more suitable in a given case then the techniques discussed here, and it is not our intention to make a practical comparison in this chapter.*

2 *See Pykhtin and Dev (2002), for interesting further work connected with Basel II.*

3 *Gourieroux, Laurent and Scaillet (2000) state Theorems A and B for general* $\varepsilon$. *We have stated Theorems A and B in the case* $\varepsilon = 0$ *to suit our point of view of* U *as a perturbation, but for each theorem the general case is essentially equivalent, after replacing the base distribution* X *with* $X + \varepsilon U$.

4 *This makes it difficult to give precise conditions for Theorems A–C to be valid. However, although we use the moment-generating function, our calculations do not require existence of real moments, because integration is always limited to the imaginary axis – we could have used the characteristic function. (The saddlepoint methods presented do require a real moment-generating function.) On the other hand, for Theorem C to make sense, clearly the specified derivatives of* f *and* $\mu_m$ *must exist. See Tasche (2000), Haaf and Tasche (2001) and Gourieroux, Laurent and Scaillet (2000) for information about rigorous conditions for the first two derivatives.*

5 *Since Theorem C is valid for all* m, *the only difficulty in generalising Theorems A and B to higher derivatives is in performing the "inversion". This can be done – the authors hope to publish a general formula in a sequel.*

6 *There is a conflict of notation as the subscript* n *used here is not the same as the subscript* ε *used earlier, but the meaning of the subscript should be clear from the context.*

7 *This expression will be valid provided* $t = t(u,v)$ *is differentiable as a function of* u *and* v, *which we assume.*

8 *See the CreditRisk+ technical document (Credit Suisse First Boston, 1997).*

9 *For portfolios with all exposures the same size, conditional variance is automatically proportional to the systematic variable provided squares of default probabilities are neglected, for taking all exposures to be unit size, the conditional distribution is a Poisson distribution, in which the variance and the mean are automatically equal. Hence, for these portfolios, the first bulletpoint is redundant.*

10 *The question of exact saddlepoint approximation (see Jensen, 1995, for discussion) suggests itself as related, particularly as the gamma distribution also occurs, but we have not been able to make a connection.*

11 *Genuinely small values of* ε *give the same qualitative behaviour as shown in Figure 1 – the power series involved here all have infinite radii of convergence so there is no natural scale.*

**BIBLIOGRAPHY**

**Avellaneda, M., and J. Zhu,** 2001, "Distance to Default", *Risk*, December, pp. 125-9.

**Basel Committee on Banking Supervision,** 2001, *The New Basel Capital Accord*, IRB Consultative Document, Bank for International Settlements, January.

**Credit Suisse First Boston,** 1997, *CreditRisk+ – A Credit Risk Management Framework*, Available from www.csfb.com/creditrisk.

**Gordy, M.,** 2001, *A Risk Factor Model Foundation For Ratings Based Capital Rules,* Working Paper, Federal Reserve Board, Washington, February.

**Gordy, M.,** 2002, "Saddlepoint Approximation of CreditRisk+", *Journal of Banking and Finance*, 26(7), August, pp. 1337-55.

**Gourieroux, C., J-P. Laurent and O. Scaillet,** 2000, "Sensitivity Analysis of Values at Risk", *Journal of Empirical Finance*, 7, pp. 225-45.

**Haaf, H., and D. Tasche,** 2001, "Calculating Value-at-risk Contributions in CreditRisk+", *ETH Zurich*, November, updated February 2002.

**Jensen, J.,** 1995, *Saddle-point Approximations* (Oxford University Press).

**Lemus-Rodriguez, G.,** 1999, *Portfolio Optimization with Qquantile-based Risk Measures*, PhD thesis, Massachusetts Institute of Technology.

**Martin, R., K. Thompson and C. Browne,** 2001a, "VAR: Who Contributes and How Much", *Risk* August, pp. 99-102.

**Martin, R., K. Thompson and C. Browne,** 2001b, "How Dependent are Defaults?", *Risk*, June, pp. 87-90.

**Martin, R., K. Thompson and C. Browne,** 2001c, "Taking to the Saddle", *Risk*, July, pp. 91-4.

**Pykhtin, M., and A. Dev,** 2002, "Analytical Approach to Credit Risk Modelling", *Risk*, March, pp. S26-S32.

**Stuart, A., and K. Ord,** 1993, *Kendall's Advanced Theory of Statistics. Volume 1: Distribution Theory*, Sixth Edition (Arnold).

**Tasche, D.,** 2000, "Conditional Expectation as Quantile Derivative", *Zentrum Mathematik*, Technische Universität München, November.

**Wilde, T.,** 2001a, "The IRB Approach Explained", *Risk*, May, pp. 87-90.

**Wilde, T.,** 2001b, "Probing Granularity", *Risk*, August, pp. 103-6.

# VII

# PRICING MULTI-NAME DEFAULT RISK

# 28

# Copula Vulnerability

**Umberto Cherubini and Elisa Luciano**
University of Bologna & Polyhedron Computational Finance;
University of Turin

*Arguing that previous research into derivatives counterparty credit risk has failed to properly capture links between market value and dealer default probability, Umberto Cherubini and Elisa Luciano model this co-dependence using a copula approach, and show how to hedge default-prone derivatives positions.*

The bankruptcy and default of Enron, the energy trading company involved in power derivatives, has concentrated attention on the question of counterparty risk in derivatives transactions, and the issue of correlation between derivatives exposure and the main business of the counterparty. Is it wise to buy options on some underlying asset from counterparties that have large exposures to it? They would certainly know the business and the market better than other counterparties, but their exposure to the underlying market may cause them to default on their derivatives obligation. For instance, buying a put option on a power derivative from a counterparty whose production may be severely hampered by a decrease in electricity prices leaves the long end of the contract exposed to the default of the counterparty. In fact, the long end loses in the event against which the protection was sought in the first place, that is, a decrease in electricity prices. Similarly, buying protection against default by an Argentinian obligor from an Argentinian bank may not be most effective way to reduce credit risk.

The pricing of vulnerable derivatives, that is, derivatives exposed to default of the counterparty, has been the object of much study. All this literature has focused on specific pricing approaches. The typical model is a Black–Scholes setting for the underlying asset and a structural or reduced-form model for the default probability of the counterparty.

*The authors wish to thank two anonymous referees for helpful suggestions.*

As for the modelling of the underlying asset, it is well known that current option pricing techniques go far beyond the standard Black–Scholes formulas, and try to account for the smile and term structure effects of the volatility surface, as well as for market liquidity. The latter problem is particularly relevant in over-the-counter transactions, which are typically based on non-standardised products, and it is for these transactions that counterparty risk is also relevant. For credit risk, the models used in banks are far more involved than the stylised structural and reduced-form approaches available in the literature.

The vulnerable derivatives pricing models are typically based on streamlined assumptions, and the prices cannot be directly compared with those of similar default-free derivatives written on the same asset. The bottom line is that one would like to price vulnerable derivatives in a general setting, able to integrate the sophisticated pricing models used for default-free derivatives with the credit risk model used by the bank as a whole.

Here, we show that a model based on copula functions is able to accomplish this. The model uses copulas to couple asset pricing and credit risk models. Pricing vulnerable derivatives is intrinsically a bivariate problem, involving the option ending up in-the-money and the writer of the option having survived by the exercise time. What is relevant for pricing is the joint probability of these two events, and it is well known that copula functions may provide a very flexible way of representing this joint distribution. Based on this idea, we will show how to derive a vulnerable pricing kernel, which could be used to price vulnerable derivatives just like the default-free ones. The model presented here is derived in a complete market setting, while Cherubini and Luciano (2001, 2002) present the same results in a more general incomplete market model.

## What are copula functions?

A copula is simply a way to represent joint probabilities, namely joint distribution functions, via their marginal distributions. Given two random variables X and Y, let us denote as $F(x, y)$ their joint distribution function, $F(x, y) = \Pr(X \leq x, Y \leq y)$, and as $1 - Q(x)$ and $1 - G(y)$ their marginal ones. There exists a copula function $\tilde{C}(1 - Q, 1 - G)$ such that, equivalently to $F(x, y)$, one can write $\tilde{C}(1 - Q(x), 1 - G(y))$.

Analogously, if one wants the joint survival function, $\bar{F}(x, y) = \Pr(X > x, Y > y)$, there is a copula C that allows it to be written in terms of the marginal survival functions $\bar{F}(x, y) = C(Q(x), G(y))$ (for a proof, and for a discussion of basic copula properties, see Nelsen, 1998). In contrast with the joint survival function $\bar{F}$, the copula C represents dependence only, since the marginal behaviour is completely described by the univariate functions Q and G. Copula functions are always required to stay between the bounds $C^- = \max(Q + G - 1, 0)$ and $C^+ = \min(Q, G)$, which are known as the Fréchet bounds and correspond to perfect (nonlinear) negative and positive dependence respectively. In addition, X and Y are independent if their copula is the so-called product one, $C^\perp = QG$.

We also recall some very simple properties that will be used below, for option pricing. Say $C_{HH}(Q, G) = C(Q, G)$ is a copula function, representing – for $Q = Q(x)$ and $G = G(y)$ – the survival probability that X and Y exceed x and y respectively. Then the functions $C_{HL}(Q, 1 - G) = Q - C_{HH}(Q, G)$, $C_{LH}(1 - Q, G) = G - C_{HH}(Q, G)$ and $C_{LL}(1 - Q, 1 - G) = 1 - Q - G + C_{HH}(Q, G)$ are also copula functions. They respectively represent the probabilities that $X > x$, $Y \leq y$, that $X \leq x$, $Y > y$, and that both X and Y are below the thresholds x and y. We may anticipate the way in which we will use this result: if $C_{HH}(Q, G)$ denotes the probability that an option ends up in-the-money and the counterparty survives, then $C_{HL}(Q, 1 - G) = Q - C_{HH}(Q, G)$ denotes the probability that the option ends in-the-money and the counterparty defaults.

## Vulnerable digital options

Using the results reported above, we may recover the vulnerable pricing kernel in a simple way. We know that in a default-free world the pricing kernel is represented by a digital option, whose financial meaning is the limit of a vertical spread. A vertical call spread in the limit converges to a digital call option paying a fixed amount – normalised here to one – if the underlying is above a given strike at expiry. Similarly, a vertical put spread converges to a digital put option paying one unit if the underlying is below or at the strike. Following Breeden and Litzenberg (1978), once one knows the value of digital options, the value of a vanilla call option can be calculated by simply integrating the digital call option from the strike to infinity; similarly, the vanilla put option is recovered by integrating the digital put option from zero to the strike.

The same idea can be applied to vulnerable derivatives, once we devise a way to recover the defaultable pricing kernel. Therefore, we focus the analysis on the case of vulnerable digital options. Such options pay one in case of exercise and survival of the counterparty, the writer's recovery rate in case of exercise of the option and default of the counterparty, and zero otherwise.

Assume a vulnerable digital call option, which we denote as $VD_H$, written on some underlying S for a given maturity T and strike K. Denote as $Q(K)$ the risk-neutral probability that the option will end up in-the-money, that is, that $S(T) > K$, and as G the probability that the counterparty will survive beyond time T. Let us also assume, for the sake of simplicity, that both the recovery rate in case of default, R, and the risk-free discount factor, B, are known. Under the standard no-arbitrage setting, there exists a risk-neutral measure under which the value of the vulnerable digital call option is:

$$VD_H = B[C_{HH}(Q, G) + RC_{HL}(Q, 1 - G)]$$

where $C_{HH}(Q, G)$ denotes the probability that an option ends up in-the-money and the counterparty survives, while $C_{HL}(Q, 1 - G)$ is the probability that the option ends in-the-money and the counterparty defaults. The extensions of the model to relax the assumptions concerning the recovery rate and the risk-free discount factor deserve some discussion. To account for a stochastic recovery rate, the natural extension is to condition on any given recovery rate, and to obtain the price by integration over the probability density function of the recovery rate itself. As for the case of stochastic interest rates, the extension of the model is immediate if we work under the relevant forward martingale measure, which enables us to factorise the discount factor and the expected payout exactly as in the equation above.

If we substitute the result recalled above, $C_{HH}(Q, G) = Q - C_{HL}(Q, 1 - G)$, we may rewrite the price as:

$$VD_H = BQ - B(1 - R)C_{HL}(Q, 1 - G)$$

Notice that BQ(K) is the price of the option if it were default-free. The vulnerable digital option is then equal to a default-free digital option minus a term representing counterparty risk. The latter is the discounted value of the loss-given default figure (1 – R) weighted by the joint probability of the events of exercise of the option and default of the counterparty.

Using the same technique, we can recover the price of the corresponding vulnerable digital put option, that is, the option paying one unit if the price of the underlying asset is lower than or equal to K at time T. If we denote as $VD_L$ the digital put option, we have:

$$VD_L = B(1 - Q) - B(1 - R)C_{LL}(1 - Q, 1 - G)$$

We may use the results at the end of the "What are copula functions?" section to recover a precise relationship between vulnerable digital call and put options:

$$\begin{aligned} VD_L &= B(1 - Q) - B(1 - R)[(1 - G) - C_{HL}(Q, 1 - G)] \\ &= B - VD_H - B(1 - R)(1 - G) \end{aligned}$$

This relationship ensures that the prices of the two options rule out arbitrage opportunities. To check this, assume we buy a vulnerable digital call and put option with the same strike and exercise from the same counterparty. Say that we also buy, for a price $P_D$, a defaultable zero-coupon bond issued by the same counterparty for the same maturity T. Its price can be written as $P_D = B - B(1 - R)(1 - G)$. It is easy to check that:

$$VD_H + VD_L = B - B(1 - R)(1 - G) = P_D$$

and buying the two options is the same as purchasing a defaultable zero-coupon bond. Notice that, from a technical point of view, the no-arbitrage requirement is guaranteed by the relationship between copulas derived from distribution functions and those generated by the corresponding survival probabilities, which we introduced at the end of the previous section.

Using the language of credit risk, we may define the discounted expected loss on the zero-coupon bond issued by the counterparty as:

$$Del = B - P_D = B(1 - R)(1 - G) = B \times Lgd \times Dp$$

where Lgd = 1 – R is the loss-given default figure and Dp = 1 – G is the default probability. Using the same language, we may also rewrite the pricing formulas above. For example, the vulnerable digital put option may be written as:

$$VD_L = B(1 - Q) - Del + B \times Lgd \times C_{HL}(Q, Dp)$$

**1. Counterparty risk of digital call options**

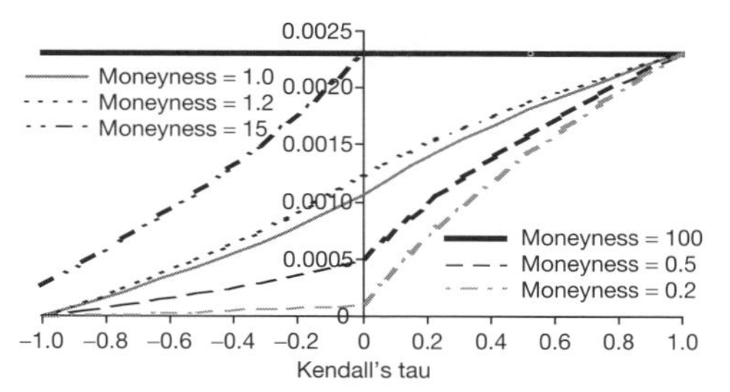


This shows that our approach is fully general and is able to host any specification for the default-free pricing kernel, as well as for the default probability and the loss-given default figures provided by the credit risk model used in the institution. Once a specific copula function $C_{HL}(. , .)$ is chosen, the model can be fully calibrated relying on "in-house" option pricing and credit risk models.

The pricing kernel $VD_H$ is that of the default-free economy, $D_H$, minus a term that accounts for counterparty risk and is specified using copula functions. As an example, Figure 1 represents the behaviour of such a term, for a specific choice of copula function, the mixture copula. This copula is simply a linear combination of the perfect positive (negative) dependence case with independence one and allows us to calibrate any value of positive (negative) imperfect dependence. The value of counterparty risk is reported as a function of the dependence between exercise events and default of the counterparty, measured by Kendall $\tau$ statistics. The underlying asset is lognormal with 20% volatility and the time to exercise is one year. The lognormal choice is obviously done for the sake of simplicity, but any other choice would fit. For simplicity, the risk-free rate is set to zero. The counterparty is assumed to be rated Baa3. Using Moody's data, we set the expected loss figure (Lgd × Dp) at 0.231% and the recovery rate at 55%. The relationship is reported for several degrees of moneyness of the option.

As expected, risk is increasing not only with dependence of exercise and default, but also with moneyness: far out-of-the-money options have zero risk, while deep in-the-money options have risk equal to the discounted expected loss of the counterparty, for every level of dependency. However, the level of moneyness needed to get the latter result is very high.

## Call and put options

We now use the idea in Breeden and Litzenberger (1978) to recover vulnerable call and put option prices from the defaultable pricing kernel.[1] We recall that the price of a default-free European-style call option can be written as:

$$O_c = \int_K^\infty D_H(u)du = B\int_K^\infty Q(u)du$$

where $D_H(u)$ is the default-free digital call option with strike u and the same maturity as $O_c$, which we observed to be equal to $BQ(u)$. By applying the same principle to the vulnerable digital call option, we may likewise obtain:

$$VO_C = \int_K^\infty VD_H(u)du = O_c - B \times Lgd\int_K^\infty C_{HL}(Q(u), D_p)du$$

Since the call price is obtained by integrating the digital option above the strike, K, the integral of digital counterparty risk, represented by copula functions, shows up. As for digital options, the difference between the vulnerable call price, $VO_c$, and the default-free one, $O_c$, measures counterparty risk.

Along the same lines, the value of vulnerable put options, $VO_p$, can be calculated by integrating the vulnerable digital put options from zero to the strike, that is:

$$VO_p = \int_0^K VD_L(u)du = O_p - K \times Del + B \times Lgd\int_0^K C_{HL}(Q(u), Dp)du$$

where $O_p$ denotes the default-free put option. Using the no-arbitrage relationship between digital call and put options, it is easy to recover a version of the vulnerable put-call parity relation that holds in full generality. The latter is:

$$VO_p + S = VO_c + KP_D + B \times Lgd\int_0^\infty C_{HL}(Q(u), Dp)du$$

where S is the underlying. With respect to the put-call parity relation between default-free put and call options, it is worth noting that the strike is discounted using the defaultable bond price $P_D$ instead of the risk-free factor B and that an integral term shows up, accounting for counterparty risk.

We prove that there are three important cases in which the price of the vulnerable option may be recovered in closed form.

The first has to do with independence between the exercise events of the option and default of the counterparty. In this case, the probability of the two events can be factorised and, as we recalled above, $C_{HL}(Q, Dp) = C^{\perp}(Q, D_p) = Q \times Dp$. Let us therefore denote the corresponding vulnerable option prices as $VO_c^{\perp}$ and $VO_p^{\perp}$. One can easily verify that $VO_c^{\perp} = O_c - O_c \times Dp \times Lgd$ and $VO_p^{\perp} = O_p - O_p \times Dp \times Lgd$.

The second case has to do with perfect positive dependence, where we know that $C_{HL}(Q, Dp) = C^{+}(Q, Dp) = \min(Q, Dp)$. Even in this case the solution may be calculated in closed form. For the call option, we have:

$$VO_c^{+} = O_c - [Del \times \max(K^* - K, 0) + Lgd \times O_c(S, t; \max(K^*, K), T)]$$

where $O_c(S, \max(K^*, K), T)$ is the price of a call with underlying S and maturity T, as for the vulnerable, but with strike $\max(K^*, K)$. The strike $K^*$ is such that $Q(K^*) = Dp$. In other words, it is a strike price such that the exercise probability of the default-free call is equal to the default probability of the counterparty. Similarly, the perfect dependence case of a put option can be recovered as:

$$VO_p^{+} = O_p - [Del \times \max(K - K^{**}, 0) + Lgd \times O_p(S, t; \min(K^{**}, K), T)]$$

where $K^{**}$ is such that $Q(K^{**}) = 1 - Dp$. Then, $K^{**}$ is a strike price such that the exercise probability of a call option is equal to the survival probability of the counterparty.

Notice that in both cases the evaluation of the vulnerable derivative only requires knowledge of the pricing formulas for the corresponding default-free products. More precisely, in the case of perfect dependence, counterparty risk is represented by a short position in the spread $B - P_D = Del$, which can be traded in the market using a credit derivatives contract, that is, a credit default swap, and a short position in a default-free option. This suggests a very straightforward super-hedging strategy for vulnerable options. To be more explicit, in the worst-case scenario of perfect dependence, counterparty risk of a call option can be hedged by buying protection using a default swap for an amount equal to $\max(K^* - K, 0)$ and by buying Lgd call options with strike $\max(K, K^*)$. Similarly, the super-hedging strategy for put options involves buying protection in $\max(K - K^{**}, 0)$ default swaps and in Lgd put options with strike $\min(K, K^{**})$.

Furthermore, for all practical purposes both the call option evaluated at strike $K^*$ and the put option at $K^{**}$ are far out-of-the-money. If we add that the two options are multiplied times the loss-given default, we may approximate the prices as:

$$VO_c^{+} \cong O_c - Del \times \max(K^* - K, 0)$$
$$VO_p^{+} \cong O_p - Del \times \max(K - K^{**}, 0)$$

and the super-hedging strategy can be effectively implemented by using the credit derivative only.

It may be proved that we can also recover closed-form solutions for the case of perfect negative dependence between exercise of the option and default of the counterparty. We know that in this case $C_{HL}(Q, Dp) = C^-(Q, Dp) = \max(Q + Dp - 1, 0)$. We can calculate analytically $VO_c^-$ as:

$$(1 - Lgd) \times O_c + Lgd \times O_c(S, t; \max(K^{**}, K), T) - \max(K^{**} - K, 0)[B \times Lgd - Del]$$

for the call option and $VO_p^-$ as:

$$(1 - Lgd) \times O_p + Lgd \times O_p(S, t; \min(K^*, K), T) - \max(K - K^*, 0)[B \times Lgd - Del]$$

for the put option. Since, as noticed above, at $K^*$ ($K^{**}$) the call (put) option is far out-of-the-money, for a broad range of strikes $K^* \geq K \geq K^{**}$ we get zero counterparty risk:

$$VO_c^- = O_c \qquad VO_p^- = O_p$$

## The Fréchet family of copulas

The above results are particularly relevant not only because they provide extreme reference values, in closed form, for vulnerable options, but also because they can provide closed-form evaluation for the imperfect dependence case, under a particular class of copula functions. A very simple way to generate a copula function is to define a linear combination of the minimum, maximum and product copulas. In practice, define:

$$C_{HL} = \beta \max(Q + Dp - 1, 0) + (1 - \alpha - \beta) Q \times Dp + \alpha \min(Q, Dp)$$

with $0 \leq \alpha, \beta \leq 1$ and $\alpha + \beta \leq 1$. By construction, copula functions in this family, known as the Fréchet family, cover all extreme dependence cases, a property technically known as comprehensiveness. It is clear that for all these copulas we get a closed-form solution for call and put options. More explicitly, we have:

$$VO_c = \beta VO_c^- + (1 - \alpha - \beta) VO_c^{\perp} + \alpha VO_c^+$$
$$VO_p = \beta VO_p^- + (1 - \alpha - \beta) VO_p^{\perp} + \alpha VO_p^+$$

Any couple of values of the parameters $\alpha$ and $\beta$ determines a particular level of dependence, which may be measured using non-parametric indexes such as Spearman's $\rho$ and Kendall's $\tau$. In particular, we have:

$$\rho = \alpha - \beta \qquad \tau = \frac{(\beta - \alpha)(2 + \beta + \alpha)}{3}$$

A particular case of the Fréchet family of copulas is represented by the so-called mixture copula, used in Li (2000). In this case, we use a mixture of the perfect positive dependence and independence ($1 \geq \alpha \geq 0$ and $\beta = 0$) to represent positive dependence, and a mixture of perfect negative dependence and independence ($1 \geq \beta \geq 0$ and $\alpha = 0$) to represent negative dependence. Namely, we have:

$$C_{HL} = \begin{cases} (1 + \alpha) C^{\perp} - \alpha C^- & \alpha \leq 0 \\ \alpha C^+ + (1 - \alpha) C^{\perp} & \alpha \geq 0 \end{cases}$$

**2. Counterparty risk of vulnerable call options**

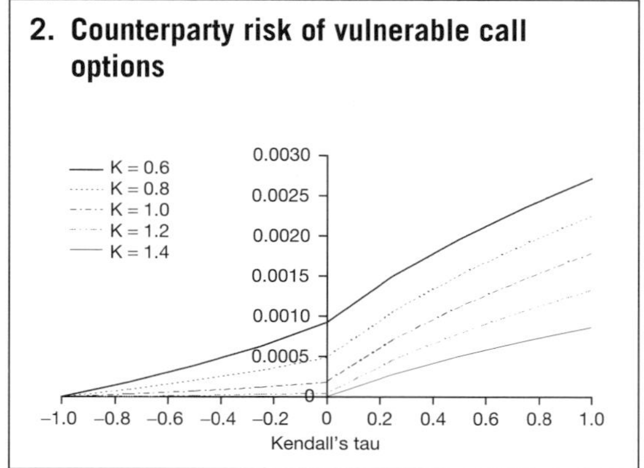


Using mixture copulas and the Black–Scholes setting, we can calculate counterparty risk for different values of the dependence statistics, for example the Kendall $\tau$. The relationship between counterparty risk and dependence for a call option is shown in Figure 2, for different moneyness levels. The counterparty is again assumed to be rated Baa3.

Finally, to show the effect of dependence for different rating classes of the counterparty, we show in Table 1 the value of counterparty risk as a percentage of the value of the corresponding default-free call option. The option is assumed to be at-the-money, with one year to the exercise date and a volatility parameter of 20%.

## Calibration to market data

We now discuss a simple strategy to calibrate the model to market data. The advantage of using a copula function approach is obviously to separate the specification of the marginal distributions and the dependence structure.

As with the specification of marginal distributions, the literature is wide. The probability of exercise of the option is recovered by calculation of the derivative of the price of the option with respect to the strike. The probability of default of the counterparty can be recovered from information on equity prices, as suggested in structural models, and/or from credit spread curves or default swaps, as indicated in reduced-form models. In the application at hand, it is particularly relevant to use firm-specific

**Table 1. Counterparty risk as a percentage of the value of the default-free option (at-the-money call, %)**

| Kendall $\tau$ | AAA | Aaa3 | A3 | Baa3 | Ba3 | B3 | Caa3 |
|---|---|---|---|---|---|---|---|
| 1.00 | 0.00117 | 0.02700 | 0.27620 | 2.24963 | 10.88450 | 30.93574 | 59.66535 |
| 0.75 | 0.00094 | 0.02200 | 0.22594 | 1.85151 | 9.04262 | 26.09492 | 53.42897 |
| 0.50 | 0.00069 | 0.01639 | 0.16946 | 1.40410 | 6.97275 | 20.65490 | 46.42065 |
| 0.25 | 0.00040 | 0.00984 | 0.10365 | 0.88277 | 4.56084 | 14.31590 | 38.25417 |
| 0.00 | 0.00003 | 0.00166 | 0.02137 | 0.23100 | 1.54550 | 6.39100 | 28.04461 |
| −0.25 | 0.00002 | 0.00112 | 0.01447 | 0.15642 | 1.04650 | 4.32750 | 18.98969 |
| −0.50 | 0.00001 | 0.00070 | 0.00895 | 0.09676 | 0.64735 | 2.67694 | 11.74680 |
| −0.75 | 0.00001 | 0.00033 | 0.00421 | 0.04556 | 0.30481 | 1.26046 | 5.53108 |
| −1.00 | 0.00000 | 0.00000 | 0.00000 | 0.00000 | 0.00000 | 0.00000 | 0.00000 |

information on the default risk of the counterparty, beyond the information contained in the rating. In fact, a different counterparty with the same rating may well show different dependence with respect to a given underlying asset.

As for dependence, the time-series of exercise probability of the option, derived from option market data, and default probability of the counterparty, recovered mainly from equity prices and default swaps, can be used to calibrate the copula function. The calibration procedure can be particularly easy for copula functions indexed by a single parameter. In this case, the historical information on marginal probabilities can be used to estimate their dependence structure, by calculating rank correlation or Kendall's $\tau$ figures. The relevant parameter of the copula function is then recovered in such a way as to fit the same non-parametric dependence figure.

An obvious criticism of this very simple approach is that time-series information enables us to specify the dependence structure under the objective probability measure, which may in principle differ from that of the risk-neutral measure. Unfortunately, in an incomplete market pricing problem such as this, relying on historical information is often necessary. However, Rosenberg (2001) gives conditions under which the objective probability dependence structure is preserved under the risk-neutral one.

Using this mixed implied and historical approach also enables us to address the issue of choice of a specific copula function. For example, Frees and Valdez (1998) propose a very easy QQ plot approach to select the right copula in the Archimedean class (see also Durrleman, Nikeghbali and Roncalli, 2000, for a more general review of the topic).

## Conclusions and future research

We have shown that copula functions, which have long been used in statistics to turn marginal distributions into joint distributions, may be a useful tool for coupling pricing models in finance. In our particular application, coupling an option pricing model with a credit risk one yields a flexible way to price vulnerable options, that is, options with counterparty risk. Of course, many developments are conceivable along this path. In the first place, the same modelling strategy that we followed for the vulnerable option may be extended and applied to other pricing problems, providing flexible solutions for complex issues. Along these lines, the natural development of our work is to extend the approach to more complex products. As an example, one could consider the extension to American-style or Bermudan products, in which the pricing problem is made more complicated by the probability of early exercise, or to barrier options, which involve a joint probability of ending up in-the-money and hitting the barrier.

From an empirical point of view, the main open problem is to devise tools to select a specific copula function for any pricing problem. The class of mixture copulas that we used is probably too limited to provide a good fit to the data. So, for a better fit one should trade the closed-form solution that is available for this class for more complex functions, at the cost of resorting to numerical integration. Choices such as Frank, Clayton or Plackett copulas are often used in financial applications but, as can be seen from the rich classification presented in even an introductory book such as Nelsen (1998), the set from which to choose may be extremely large.

1 *An anonymous referee suggested the equivalent approach of specifying the vulnerable payout using indicator functions. In the European-style call option case, for example, we would have* $\max[S(T) - K, 0][1 - (1 - R)\mathbf{1}(\tau \leq T)]$ *where* $\mathbf{1}$ *is the indicator function of the event of default by the time of exercise of the option. In this case, the valuation of the option involves the calculation of the integral:*

$$\iint \max[S(T) - K, 0][1 - (1 - R)\mathbf{1}(\tau \leq T)]C_{12}(Q, G)dQdG$$

*where* $C_{12}$ *denotes the cross-derivative of the copula function. In general, the calculation has to be carried out numerically.*

**BIBLIOGRAPHY**

**Breeden, D., and R. Litzenberger,** 1978, "Prices of State Contingent Claims Implicit in Option Prices", *Journal of Business*, 51, pp. 621–51.

**Cherubini, U., and E. Luciano,** 2001, *Pricing Vulnerable Options with Copulas*, Available at www.papers.ssrn.com.

**Cherubini, U., and E. Luciano,** 2002, "Bivariate Option Pricing with Copulas", *Applied Mathematical Finance*, 9, pp. 69–85.

**Durrleman, V., A. Nikeghbali and T. Roncalli,** 2000, *Which Copula is the Right One?*, Working Paper, Crédit Lyonnais.

**Frees, E., and E. Valdez,** 1998, "Understanding Relationships using Copulas", *North American Actuarial Journal*, 2, pp. 1–25.

**Li, D.,** 2000, "On Default Correlation: A Copula Function Approach", *Journal of Fixed Income*, March, pp. 43–54.

**Nelsen, R.,** 1998, *Introduction to Copulas* (Berlin: Springer Verlag).

**Rosenberg, Y.,** 2001, *Nonparametric Pricing of Multivariate Contingent Claims*, Working Paper, New York University Stern School of Business.

29

# Pricing Default Baskets

**Wolfgang Schmidt and Ian Ward**

Frankfurt Business School for Banking and Finance; Deutsche Bank

The credit derivatives business has grown dramatically in recent years. Credit default swaps are the main plain-vanilla credit derivative product, and also serve as a building block for credit-linked notes and other synthetic credit investments. A credit default swap offers protection against default of a certain underlying entity over a specified time horizon. A premium (spread) $s$ is paid on a regular basis and on a certain notional amount $N$ as an insurance fee against the losses from default of a risky position of notional $N$, eg, a bond. The payment of the premium $s$ stops at maturity or at default of the underlying credit, whichever comes first. At the time of default before maturity of the trade, the protection buyer receives the payment $N(1 - R)$, where $R$ is the recovery rate of the underlying credit risky instrument.

More sophisticated credit derivative products are linked to several underlying credits. They include synthetic collateralised debt obligations, default swaps on certain tranches of losses from a portfolio or basket default swaps. What these products have in common is that they offer access to tailor-made profiles of credit risk that is appealing to both credit investors and hedgers seeking to redistribute their credit risk or to release regulatory capital.

In this chapter, we will illustrate the modelling difficulties involved with multi-credit derivative products. We will use a basket default swap as an example. A basket default swap is like an insurance contract that offers protection against the event of the $k$th default on a basket of $n(n \geq k)$ underlying names. It is similar to a plain default swap but the credit event to insure against is the event of the $k$th default. Again, a premium (spread) $s$ is paid as an insurance fee until maturity or the event of the $k$th default in return for a compensation for the loss. We denote by $s^{kth}$ the fair spread in a $k$th-to-default swap, ie, the spread making the value of this swap today equal to zero.

Most popular are first-to-default swaps, ie, $k = 1$. As we will see below, a first-to-default swap offers highly attractive spreads to a credit investor (protection seller).

If the $n$ underlying credits in the basket default swap are independent, the fair spread $s^{first}$ is expected to be close to the sum of the fair default swap spreads $s_i$ over all underlyings $i = 1,\ldots, n$. If the underlying credits are in some sense "totally" dependent, the first default will be the one with the worst spread, therefore $s^{first} = \max(s_1,\ldots, s_n)$. We will provide some intuitive explanation for these two facts later.

So how can we describe dependencies between the underlying credits in our model? Traditionally, dependencies are measured by correlation, which can be problematic because it only quantifies the linear dependence (see Embrechts, McNeil and Straumann, 1999). Also, it is not quite clear which correlation, ie, the correlation between which variables, should be modelled.

Once we have chosen a model for the dependencies between defaults, the most important problem - besides pricing the derivative - is the impact of the dependencies on the hedging strategies. The main focus of this chapter is to show that if there are dependencies between default times then at the time of default of one credit the spreads of the remaining face a certain spread change (spread widening).

*This chapter was a Masterclass paper with Deustsche Bank in* Risk *Magazine, introduced by Wolfgang Schmidt and Ian Ward. The authors would like to thank two anonymous referees for valuable comments.*

## Modelling dependence via copulas

To our knowledge, the concept of copulas applied to the problem of dependent defaults first appeared in Li (2000). Here, we give just an outline of this approach.

We denote by $\tau_1, \ldots, \tau_n$ the random default times for credits $i = 1, \ldots, n$. Write $(B(t))_{t \geq 0}$ for the curve of risk-free discount factors (zero bond prices) and $(P_i(t))_{t \geq 0}$ for the curve of cumulative (risk-neutral) default probabilities for credit $i$:

$$P_i(t) = P(\tau_i < t)$$

Let $s_i(T_m)$ denote the fair default swap spread on credit $i$ and maturity $T_m$ as quoted in the market. Then, assuming a deterministic recovery rate $R_i$ for credit $i$ we have by definition:[1]

$$\begin{aligned} 0 = s_i(T_m)\sum_{k=1}^{m} \Delta_k B(T_k)(1 - P_i(T_k)) \\ -(1 - R_i)\int_0^{T_m} B(u)\, P_i(du) \end{aligned} \qquad (1)$$

where $\Delta_k$ is the day-count fraction for the period $k$. The first term in the equation above is the present value of the payments of the spread $s_i(T_m)$, which is paid at each $T_k$ provided there has been no default – so the payment is valued using the risk-free discount factor $B(T_k)$ multiplied by the survival probability $(1 - P_i(T_k))$.[2] The integral describes the present value of the payment of $(1 - R_i)$ at the time of default. For a default "at" time $u$, we have to discount with $B(u)$ and multiply with the probability $P_i(du)$ that default happens "around" $u$.

From these equations, one can extract the market implied (risk-neutral) default curve $P_i(t)$ for each credit $i$ from quoted market spreads $s_i(T_m)$.

Now we come to the problem of modelling the dependence between defaults. The default curve $P_i(t)$ gives us the market implied (risk-neutral) distribution of the random default time $\tau_i$. The cashflows in a basket default swap are functions of the whole random vector $(\tau_1, \ldots, \tau_n)$. To evaluate a basket default swap today following the principles of no-arbitrage pricing, all we need is today's (risk-neutral) joint distribution of the $\tau_i$'s:

$$P(\tau_1 < t_1, \ldots, \tau_n < t_n)$$

So we have to link the given marginal distributions $P_i$ to a joint distribution and this is exactly what a so-called copula is supposed to achieve (see Frees and Valdez, 1998, and Nelsen, 1999).

Remember that the transformed default time $U_i = P_i(\tau_i)$ admits a uniform distribution on the interval [0, 1]. Therefore:

$$C(u_1, \ldots, u_n) := P(U_1 < u_1, \ldots, U_n < u_n) \qquad (2)$$

defines a joint distribution with uniform marginals. The function $C(u_1, \ldots, u_n)$ is called a copula and the joint distribution of $(\tau_1, \ldots, \tau_n)$ can be written as:

$$P(\tau_1 < t_1, \ldots, \tau_n < t_n) = C(P_1(t_1), \ldots, P_n(t_n)) \qquad (3)$$

So we see that the copula links the marginal distributions into a joint distribution, thereby separating the dependence structure $C$ from the marginal distributions.

To build a model for dependent defaults, we start with some dependent uniform random variables $(U_1, \ldots, U_n)$ omitting the copula $C$ and then we define our default times by:[3]

$$\tau_i = P_i^{(-1)}(U_i)$$

Observe that a famous theorem (see Nelsen, 1999) on copulas states that any joint distribution can be reduced to a copula and the marginal distributions. Thus, any model for dependent defaults has an equivalent copula representation, although it may be difficult to write down the copula explicitly.

One of the most elementary copulas is the normal copula, which appears as follows. Assume $(Y_1, \ldots, Y_n)$ follows an n-dimensional standard normal distribution with correlation matrix $(\rho_{ij})$. Then $U_i = N(Y_i)$ is uniform on [0, 1] and their joint distribution is:[4]

$$C(u_1, \ldots, u_n) = N(N^{(-1)}(u_1), \ldots, N^{(-1)}(u_n), (\rho_{ij}))$$

So for a normal copula our default times would be modelled as $\tau_i = P_i^{(-1)}(N(Y_i))$.

There are various different copulas generating all kinds of dependencies. As shown in Frey, McNeil and Nyfeler (2001), the choice of the copula entails a significant amount of model risk. The advantage of the normal copula, however, is that it is related to the latent variable approach to model defaults following the famous Merton firm-value approach (1974). Assume the default event of entity $i$ up to time $T$ is driven by a single random variable $A_i$ (ability to pay variable, eg, the asset value) being below a certain trigger level $c_i(T)$:[5]

$$\tau_i < T \Leftrightarrow A_i < c_i(T)$$

If $A_i$ admits a standard normal distribution,[6] then to be consistent with our given default curve, we set $c_i(T) = N^{(-1)}(P_i(T))$. Now, if we calculate pairwise joint default probabilities in that approach, we get:

$$P(\tau_i < T, \tau_j < T) = P(A_i < c_i(T), A_j < c_j(T)) \\ = N\left(N^{(-1)}(P_i(T)), N^{(-1)}(P_j(T)), \rho_{ij}^A\right)$$

To make these probabilities coincide with those from the normal copula approach, we see that the asset correlation $\rho_{ij}^A$ above and the correlation $\rho_{ij}$ in the normal copula have to be the same.[7] This makes this approach particularly appealing in practice since those correlations can in principle be estimated from data (if available) or one can use correlations as provided, eg, by KMV (*www.kmv.com*).

## Pricing basket default swaps

To price a basket default swap, we need the distribution of the time $\tau^{kth}$ of the kth default. In particular, $\tau^{first} = \min(\tau_1, \ldots, \tau_n)$ and its distribution is just:

$$P(\tau^{first} < t) = 1 - P(\tau_1 \geq t, \ldots, \tau_n \geq t) \qquad (4)$$

where the right-hand side can be calculated from the copula and the marginal distributions. A corresponding but more involved formula can be written down for the distribution of $\tau^{kth}$.

The fair spread $s^{kth}$ for maturity $T_m$ is then defined by the relation:

$$0 = s^{kth} \sum_{\iota=1}^{m} \Delta_\iota B(T_\iota) P(\tau^{kth} > T_\iota) \\ - \sum_{i=1}^{n} (1 - R_i) \int_0^{T_m} B(u) P(\tau^{kth} \in du, \tau^{kth} = \tau_i)$$

The intuition behind this equation is similar to our discussion of Equation 1. The first part is the present value of the spread payments, which stop at time $\tau^{kth}$ of the kth default and are therefore valued with the respective probabilities. The second term is the value of the payment at the time of the kth default. Since the recovery may be different for the underlying names, we have to sum over all underlying names $i = 1, \ldots, n$. For all times $0 < u \leq T_m$ the respective payment $(1 - R_i)$ has to be discounted with $B(u)$ and weighted with the probabilities that the kth default happens around u and that the kth name defaulting is just i.[8]

As a simple example, consider a basket of $n = 3$ credits with fair spreads $s_1 = 1.10\%$, $s_2 = 1.00\%$ and $s_3 = 0.90\%$, respectively, for all maturities and assuming a recovery rate of $R_i = 20\%$ throughout.[9] We model the default dependence via a normal copula with flat (asset) correlations $\rho_{ij} = 50\%$. Table 1 shows the fair kth-to-default swap spread for maturities from one to five years.

**Table 1. Fair kth-to-default swap spread for maturities from one to five years**

| Maturity | $s^{first}$ (%) | $s^{2nd}$ (%) | $s^{3rd}$ (%) |
|---|---|---|---|
| 1y | 2.63 | 0.34 | 0.04 |
| 2y | 2.56 | 0.42 | 0.06 |
| 3y | 2.51 | 0.47 | 0.08 |
| 4y | 2.47 | 0.51 | 0.09 |
| 5y | 2.44 | 0.55 | 0.10 |

**1. Fair kth-to-default spread vs correlation**

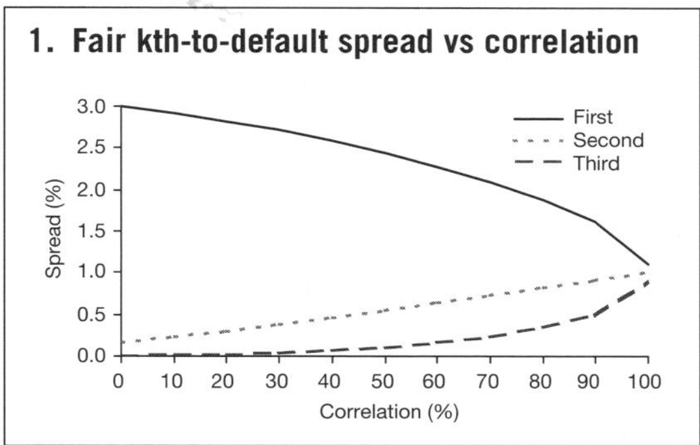


Figure 1 shows how the fair kth-to-default swap spread varies if we change our correlation in the normal copula from 0% to 100%. The figure as well as the numbers in Table 1 show a somewhat surprising result: the sum over all kth-to-default swap spreads is greater than the sum of the individual default swap spreads:

$$\sum_{k=1}^{n} s^{kth} > \sum_{i=1}^{n} s_i$$

Since all kth-to-default swaps on one side and all plain default swaps on the other side insure exactly the same risks (namely, all defaults), one would expect that the spreads add up to the same amount. However, this is not true since there is a windfall effect in the first-to-default swap: at the time of first default we stop paying the huge spread $s^{first}$ on one side but on the plain-vanilla side we stop paying just the spread $s_i$ of the first defaulting credit i. Of course, the sum of the present values of the plain default swap spread payments and the sum of the present values of all basket default swap spread payments are equal.

Also Figure 1 shows a fact mentioned earlier. Namely, in the extreme case of $\rho_{ij} = 1$ for all $i$, $j$ the first to default spread is the worst of all underlyings. The reason is obvious: in the case of perfect correlation all state variables $Y_i$ in the normal copula are identical and since the distribution function $P(t)$ of the name with the worst spread dominates all others, this credit defaults first.[10]

The other extreme case is that all default times are independent, which means $\rho_{ij} = 0$ for all $i$, $j$ in the normal copula model. In this case, the fair spread on the first default is very close to (but usually not exactly) the sum of the individual spreads. How can we explain this? An intuitive no-arbitrage argument is the following. Let us assume that the term structure of credit spreads $s_i$ is flat for each name $i$ in our basket. Our first strategy is to buy protection on the first default. Here we have to pay the fair first-to-default spread $s^{first}$ until the time of first default or maturity. The other strategy is to buy protection on all individual names $i = 1,\dots, n$, via plain default swaps. This requires us to pay all spreads $s_i$ up to the time of default of credit $i$ or maturity. In particular, we have to pay $\Sigma_{i=1}^{n} s_i$ until the time of first default. We also agree that, if there is a default (before maturity), we then unwind our plain default swaps on all the remaining names. Clearly, both strategies protect exactly the same default risks. Since there is independence and the term structure of credit spreads is flat, there is no impact from the realised default on the fair spreads of the remaining names and there will be no costs for unwinding. This proves that the fair first-to-default spread must be the sum of the individual ones.

This brings us to our main topic, namely, how do dependencies between defaults affect hedging strategies? In particular, how do defaults affect spreads in the model?

## Hedging the risks

When we have to hedge a position in a basket default swap, we face two main types of risk. The first is spread risk, which is the risk arising from the fact that the spreads $s_i$ for the underlying names, which we have used to back out the default curve $P_i(t)$, will not be stationary. This is the risk arising from the changing credit quality of the individual names. The second is event risk. In the case of an event occurring in which a payment on the basket default swap is triggered, we have to make an event payment, for which we need an appropriate offsetting hedge position.

Although difficult in practice, to hedge these two sources of risk simultaneously we need in principle at least two default-sensitive instruments per credit to hedge with. However, in our discussion of hedging below, we will focus on the event risk.[11]

Assume we have bought protection on the first to default. As a hedge, we will sell protection via plain-vanilla default swaps on each of the underlying names. To hedge the spread risk, we calculate the sensitivities of the basket with regard to changes in the individual default curves $P_i(t)$. A spread hedge position is then created by offsetting these risks by appropriate positions in plain-vanilla default swaps.

The event risk is trickier. Assume that our dynamic hedge at time $t$ in the underlying names $i = 1,\dots, n$ consists of sold protection for percentage notional amounts $N_1(t),\dots, N_n(t)$ and fair spreads $s_1(t),\dots, s_n(t)$. If there is a default at time $t$ and assuming that credit $i$ is the first to default, we receive from the first-to-default swap the event premium $(1 - R_i)$ whereas in our hedge position we have to pay $(1 - R_i)N_i(t)$ in the plain default swap on credit $i$. The remaining positions in credits $j \neq i$ now have to be unwound in the market at the prevailing market conditions. But, because the underlying names are dependent, the spreads in these underlyings will face a spread widening as a consequence of the default of credit $i$.[12]

## Spread widenings implied from the copula

Denote by $\Delta_i^j(t)$ the spread widening on credit $j$ in case of credit $i$ defaulting first and at time $t$. It is interesting to see how the implied spread widening is reflected in our copula model approach. If there is nothing known about defaults until time $t$, the default curve for credit $j$ as implied from our approach will be basically the forward default curve:

$$1-\frac{1-P_i(s)}{1-P_i(t)}, \quad s \geq t$$

However, at the time of the first default $\tau_{min} = \min(\tau_1,\dots, \tau_n)$, to get the default curves for the surviving names we have to look at the conditional distribution of $\tau_j$ given $\tau_{min} = t$. Since the default times are dependent via the copula $C$, this distribution will be different from the forward default curve, thereby implying some spread widening. Observe that at time $t$, assuming that there has been no default until $t$, the conditional default curves for each credit will also be different from the forward curve. Assuming a "positive" dependence, the no-default conditional default curve will, in general, be below the forward curve.

Consider the simplest example of $n = 2$ names linked by a normal copula:

$$\tau_i = P_i^{(-1)}(N(Y_i)), \quad i = 1, 2$$

with standard normal random variables $Y_1$, $Y_2$ with correlation $\rho$. The default probability for credit 2 given that credit 1 defaulted at time t is:

$$P\left(\tau_2 < s \middle| \tau_1 = t\right) = P\left(Y_2 < N^{(-1)}(P_2(s)) \middle| Y_1 = N^{(-1)}(P_1(t))\right)$$

Now the distribution of $Y_2$ given $Y_1 = x$ is again normal but with mean $\rho x$ and variance $1 - \rho^2$:

$$Y_2 \middle| Y_1 = x \sim N(\rho x, 1 - \rho^2)$$

Consequently:

$$P\left(\tau_2 < s \middle| \tau_1 = t\right) = N\left(\frac{N^{(-1)}(P_2(s)) - \rho N^{(-1)}(P_1(t))}{\sqrt{1-\rho^2}}\right)$$

and we obtain for $s > t$:[13]

$$P\left(\tau_2 < s \middle| \tau_{min} = \tau_1 = t\right) = 1 - P\left(\tau_2 \geq s \middle| \tau_2 > t, \tau_1 = t\right)$$

$$= 1 - \frac{N\left(\dfrac{-N^{(-1)}(P_2(s)) + \rho N^{(-1)}(P_1(t))}{\sqrt{1-\rho^2}}\right)}{N\left(\dfrac{-N^{(-1)}(P_2(t)) + \rho N^{(-1)}(P_1(t))}{\sqrt{1-\rho^2}}\right)}$$

Now let us investigate the general case. Let the joint distribution of the default times $(\tau_1,\ldots,\tau_n)$ be given by Equation 3, ie, $\tau_i = P_i^{(-1)}(U_i)$ with uniforms $(U_1,\ldots,U_n)$ and the copula 2. Denote by $\hat{C}$ the copula corresponding to the uniforms $(1 - U_1,\ldots, 1 - U_n)$:

$$\hat{C}(x_1,\ldots,x_n) = P(1 - U_1 < x_1,\ldots,1 - U_n < x_n)$$

Using $\hat{C}$, the joint survival probability can be written as:

$$P(\tau_1 > t_1,\ldots,\tau_n > t_n) = \hat{C}(1 - P_1(t_1),\ldots,1 - P_n(t_n))$$

Now the default curve for credit j at the time of first default $\tau_{min} = \tau_i = t$ is given by:[14]

$$P\left(\tau_j < s \middle| \tau_{min} = \tau_i = t\right) = 1 - \frac{\left.\dfrac{\partial}{\partial x_i}\hat{C}(x_1,\ldots,x_n)\right|_{x_j = 1 - P_j(s), x_k = 1 - P_k(t), k \neq j}}{\left.\dfrac{\partial}{\partial x_i}\hat{C}(x_1,\ldots,x_n)\right|_{x_j = 1 - P_j(t), j = 1,\ldots,n}}, \quad s > t \qquad (5)$$

To illustrate the impact of the default of credit i at time t on credit j we translate the default curve for credit j into the corresponding default intensity (hazard rate):

$$\lambda_j^{\tau_{min} = \tau_i = t}(s), \quad s > t$$

which is defined by the relationship:

$$P\left(\tau_j < s \middle| \tau_{min} = \tau_i = t\right) = 1 - \exp\left(-\int_t^s \lambda_j^{\tau_{min} = \tau_i = t}(u)du\right)$$

Intuitively, the hazard rate is the continuously compounded spread for the case of no recovery.

For the example considered above, ie, $n = 3$ credits with fair spreads $s_1 = 1.10\%$, $s_2 = 1.00\%$ and $s_3 = 0.90\%$ and recoveries $R_i = 20\%$, we obtain Figure 2 for the default intensity for credit $j = 3$ if the first default is $\tau_{min} = \tau_1 = t$ and assuming a correlation of 30%. For five-year maturity default swaps, Table 2 shows how this translates into a spread widening $\Delta_i^j(t)$ for credit j at the time t of the first default, which is assumed to be credit i.

Given a flat correlation structure, we see that the size of the spread widenings depends on the quality of the credit first defaulting. If the first

**2. Intensity of credit 3 after first default (credit 1)**

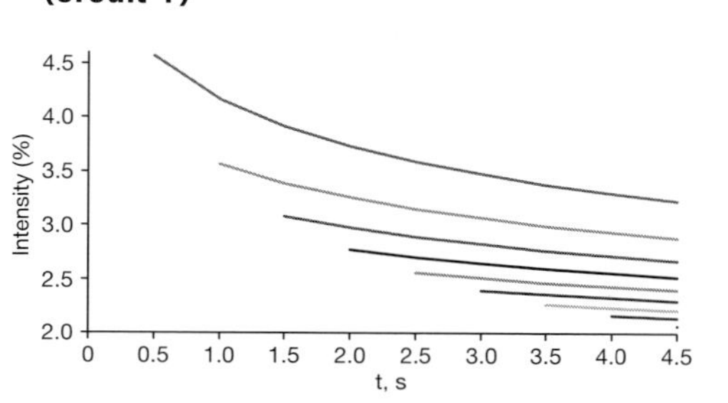


**Table 2. Implied spread widenings**

| $\tau_{min} = t$ | $\Delta_1^2(t)$ (%) | $\Delta_1^3(t)$ (%) | $\Delta_2^1(t)$ (%) | $\Delta_2^3(t)$ (%) | $\Delta_3^1(t)$ (%) | $\Delta_3^2(t)$ (%) |
|---|---|---|---|---|---|---|
| 0.5 | 2.26 | 2.08 | 2.47 | 2.12 | 2.52 | 2.35 |
| 1.0 | 1.78 | 1.63 | 1.96 | 1.67 | 2.00 | 1.86 |
| 1.5 | 1.51 | 1.38 | 1.67 | 1.41 | 1.71 | 1.58 |
| 2.0 | 1.32 | 1.21 | 1.47 | 1.24 | 1.50 | 1.39 |
| 2.5 | 1.18 | 1.08 | 1.32 | 1.11 | 1.35 | 1.25 |
| 3.0 | 1.07 | 0.98 | 1.20 | 1.01 | 1.23 | 1.14 |
| 3.5 | 0.98 | 0.90 | 1.10 | 0.92 | 1.13 | 1.04 |
| 4.0 | 0.91 | 0.82 | 1.02 | 0.85 | 1.05 | 0.96 |
| 4.5 | 0.84 | 0.76 | 0.95 | 0.79 | 0.98 | 0.90 |

name defaulting is less risky, then its impact is higher, eg, $\Delta_3^2 > \Delta_1^2$. Also the implied spread widening admits a pronounced term structure. The earlier the first default, the higher the impact on the remaining spreads.

## Conclusion

We discussed the problem of modelling dependent defaults, which is particularly important for pricing credit derivatives on baskets of underlying names. Using an approach based on copulas, we investigated the impact of dependencies on pricing and hedging basket default swaps. We quantified the default implied spread widenings in the case of a normal copula. The normal copula is particularly appealing since the correlations needed are basically asset correlations.

There are various other approaches to the problem of dependent defaults based on other types of copulas, structural models, etc. When deciding on a modelling approach one has to be careful concerning the appropriateness of the hedging implications.

## Appendix

OUTLINE OF THE PROOF OF EQUATION 5

The proof of Equation 5 requires only elementary probability calculus. To simplify the notation, consider the particular case of $j = n$ and $i = 1$ in Equation 5. First, it is easy to see that for $s > t$:

$$P\left(\tau_n > s \middle| \tau_{min} = \tau_1 = t\right) = \frac{P\left(\tau_n > s, \tau_k > t, k \neq 1 \middle| \tau_1 = t\right)}{P\left(\tau_k > t, k \neq 1 \middle| \tau_1 = t\right)}$$

If $f(x_1, \ldots, x_n)$ denotes the joint density of the random vector $(\tau_1, \ldots, \tau_n)$ and $f_1(x)$ is the marginal density of $\tau_1$, then the conditional density for $(\tau_k, k \neq 1)|\tau_1 = t$ is known to be:

$$\frac{f(t, x_2, \ldots, x_n)}{f_1(t)}$$

This implies:

$$P\left(\tau_n > s \middle| \tau_{min} = \tau_1 = t\right) = \frac{\int_t^\infty \ldots \int_t^\infty \int_s^\infty f(t, x_2, \ldots, x_n) dx_2 \ldots dx_n}{\int_t^\infty \ldots \int_t^\infty f(t, x_2, \ldots, x_n) dx_2 \ldots dx_n}$$

The integrals above are related to the joint survival function $F(x_1, \ldots, x_n)$, which is defined as:

$$\begin{aligned} F(t_1, \ldots, t_n) &= P(\tau_1 > t_1, \ldots, \tau_n > t_n) \\ &= \hat{C}(1 - P_1(t_1), \ldots, 1 - P_n(t_n)) \end{aligned}$$

by the relation:

$$\int_t^\infty \ldots \int_t^\infty \int_s^\infty f(t, x_2, \ldots, x_n)\, dx_2 \ldots dx_n = (-1)\frac{\partial}{\partial x_1} F(t, t, \ldots, t, s)$$

1 *Here, we ignore the fact that at default one usually has to pay the accrued premium.*

2 *We assume here that risk-free rates and defaults are independent.*

3 $P_i^{(-1)}$ *is the inverse of the distribution function* $P_i$, *which was assumed to be strictly increasing.*

4 N *denotes the standard normal distribution function and* $N^{(-1)}$ *its inverse. The* n*-dimensional normal distribution function with correlation* $(\rho_{ij})$ *is* $N(\ldots, (\rho_{ij}))$.

5 *Observe that in the Merton approach default of risky debt is only triggered at its maturity* T *when the asset value at this time turns out to be below the face value of debt.*

6 *This is not a critical assumption, since, for example, a lognormal state variable can be easily transformed into a normal one, transforming the trigger level in the same way.*

7 *However, since the asset value approach above can only model defaults up to a single time horizon, the calibration between the two models can be done only for one fixed horizon* T.

8 *We assume that there are no joint defaults at exactly the same time.*

9 *In practice, it is common to consider baskets comprising of names with quite similar credit quality. If one name in the baskets admits a substantial higher spread compared with the others, this name would dominate the basket and the resulting pick-up for the risk of the first default would not be as interesting.*

10 *Of course, we have to assume that the recoveries are the same across all credits.*

11 *The copula model makes no explicit assumptions about the dynamics of the spreads, which is why in the copula framework spread risk is basically a model risk.*

12 *Assuming a kind of "positive" dependence.*

13 *Observe that in the extreme case of* $P_1(t) >> P_2(s)$ *even if* $\rho > 0$ *this conditional default probability is not always higher than the forward default probability. However, in practice this is just an academic situation.*

14 *Of course, we have to impose some technical smoothness conditions on* $\hat{C}$.

## BIBLIOGRAPHY

**Embrechts, P., A. McNeil and D. Straumann,** 1999, "Correlation: Pitfalls and Alternatives", *Risk*, May, pp. 93–113.

**Frees, E., and E. Valdez,** 1998, "Understanding Relationships Using Copulas", *North American Actuarial Journal*, 2(1), pp. 1–25.

**Frey, R., A. McNeil and M. Nyfeler,** 2001, "Copulas and Credit Models", *Risk*, October, pp. 111–13.

**Li, D.,** 2000, "On Default Correlation: A Copula Function Approach", *Journal of Fixed Income*, March, pp. 43–54.

**Merton, R.,** 1974, "On the Pricing of Corporate Debt: The Risk Structure of Interest Rates", *Journal of Finance*, 29, pp. 449–70.

**Nelsen, R.,** 1999, *An Introduction to Copulas* (Springer).

30

# Long or Short in CDOs

**Hans Boscher and Ian Ward**

Deutsche Bank

*Hans Boscher and Ian Ward focus on larger reference portfolios of 100 credits. Arguing that calibration issues favour the use of the normal copula as a pricing method, they investigate the sensitivity of tranched CDO pricing to correlation and recovery rate assumptions.*

Although the majority of credit-linked products are still related to a single credit, the demand for multi-credit products, such as collateralised debt obligations (CDOs), has increased significantly in recent years. The valuation of these securities is highly sensitive to model parameters such as the correlation between different credits or the individual credit recovery rates. These model parameters can be difficult to infer from market observables. In this chapter, we investigate the impact of the correlation and the recovery rate, which we assume to be deterministic, on the loss distribution of CDOs and its consequences with respect to pricing.

The models used in this study are the normal copula model and Moody's binomial expansion technique (BET). The qualitative properties of these models were found to be very similar, so we discuss primarily the results from a normal copula model. Since only continuous distributions are involved in this model, the results tend to be smoother than the result from the BET. However, because of its "discrete nature" the BET often gives more comprehensible explanations.

First, the normal copula model and the BET are introduced. Then we outline the design of the study and investigate the impact of correlation and actual recovery rate on the loss distribution of the different tranches of a CDO. The consequences with respect to pricing are also discussed. This is followed by an analysis of the so-called windfall profits that arise from early defaults.

*This chapter was a Masterclass paper with Deutsche Bank in* Risk *Magazine, introduced by Hans Boscher and Ian Ward. The authors wish to thank Wolfgang Schmidt and Baudouin Miroux for valuable comments.*

## General notation

We consider a portfolio of positions of $n$ credits with random default times $\tau_1,\ldots,\tau_n$. The distribution of $\tau_i$ is given by:

$$\mathbf{P}(\tau_i \leq t) = F_i(t), \quad t \geq 0 \tag{1}$$

Here, $F_i(t)$ denotes the cumulative probability function of credit $i$, which is assumed to be known. Those probabilities can be derived from market quotes on risky bonds or default swaps (see Khuong-Huu, 1999).

The probability of joint default of credits $i$ and $j$ until time $T$ is given by:

$$\mathbf{P}(\tau_i \leq T, \tau_j \leq T) = F_i(T)F_j(T) + \rho^e_{i,j}(T)\sqrt{F_i(T)(1-F_i(T))F_j(T)(1-F_j(T))} \tag{2}$$

where:

$$\rho^e_{i,j}(T) = \operatorname{cor}\left(\mathbf{1}_{\{t_i \leq T\}}, \mathbf{1}_{\{t_j \leq T\}}\right) \tag{3}$$

denotes the so-called default event correlation between credit $i$ and credit $j$ at the time horizon $T$.

Furthermore, let $N_i$ and $R_i$ denote the notional amount of the position in credit $i$ and its recovery rate, respectively. We assume that the recovery rate is deterministic. Then the loss $L_i(T)$ for the position in credit $i$ is given by:

$$L_i(T) = (1 - R_i)N_i\mathbf{1}_{\{t_i \leq T\}} \tag{4}$$

and the portfolio loss $L(T)$ up to time $T$ is just $L(T) = \Sigma_i L_i(T)$. Note that the loss and the portfolio loss are stochastic and their distribution is often intractable.

MOODY'S BET

We provide a short outline of the BET model and refer to Cifuentes *et al.* (1998) and Gluck and Remeza (2000) for a more detailed description of the original BET.

The main idea of the BET model can be summarised as follows. We replace the pool of n correlated credits by a pool of $m < n$ uncorrelated credits each with a notional amount $\tilde{N} = \Sigma_i N_i/m$ such that the first two moments of the loss distribution match those of the original pool. The quantity m is called the diversity score. The advantage of this approach is that the loss distribution of uncorrelated credits is a binomial distribution, a tractable distribution for loss. For the expected loss and the variance of the loss of the original portfolio we get with $p_i := F_i(T)$:

$$\mathbb{E}L(T) = \sum_i (1 - R_i)N_i p_i \quad (5)$$

$$\mathbb{V}L_i(T) = (1 - R_i)^2 N_i^2 p_i(1 - p_i) \quad (6)$$

$$\mathbb{V}L(T) = \sum_i \mathbb{V}L_i(T) + \sum_{i,j,i \neq j} \rho_{i,j}^e(T)\sqrt{\mathbb{V}L_i(T)\mathbb{V}L_j(T)} \quad (7)$$

It is easy to see that the variance of the loss increases with increasing correlation. Note that this version of Moody's BET takes into account the recovery rate with respect to the calculation of the moments of the loss distribution. The square root of the variance of the losses, $\sqrt{\mathbb{V}L(T)}$, is also called unexpected loss.

Now we consider a pool consisting of m independent and identically distributed credits with notional amounts $\tilde{N}$, recovery rate $\tilde{R} = \Sigma_i^n N_i R_i/(\tilde{N}m)$ and default probability $\tilde{p}$. We want to choose m and $\tilde{p}$ such that the expected and unexpected loss of both pools match. The expected loss of the pool and its variance is given by:

$$\mathbb{E}\tilde{L}(T) = (1 - \tilde{R})\tilde{N}m\tilde{p} \quad (8)$$

$$\mathbb{V}\tilde{L}(T) = (1 - \tilde{R})^2\tilde{N}^2 m\tilde{p}(1 - \tilde{p}) \quad (9)$$

To approximate the original pool of dependent credits by a pool of independent credits we have to determine m and the default probability $\tilde{p}$ such that (5) and (7) match (8) and (9), respectively. The solution of this system of equations is given by:

$$\tilde{p} = \frac{\sum_i (1 - R_i)N_i p_i}{(1 - \tilde{R})\tilde{N}m} \quad (10)$$

$$m = \frac{\mathbb{E}L(T)\left[(1 - \tilde{R})\tilde{N} - \mathbb{E}L(T)\right]}{\mathbb{V}L(T)} \quad (11)$$

In general the quantity m will not be an integer but will be rounded to an integer for use in the model.

It is easy to see that the diversity score will decrease with increasing correlation whereas the default probability p is determined only by the notional amount and the recovery rates.

THE NORMAL COPULA MODEL

For completeness, we provide a brief outline of the normal copula model below. For a more detailed description, see Li (2000).

Suppose we are looking for a model that provides us with a random default time given its distribution function $F(t) = \mathbf{P}(\tau \le t)$. In a Monte Carlo model, samples of uniform random variables U are generated and realisations of $\tau$ are obtained via $\tau = F^{-1}(U)$. This concept can be extended to the case of multiple possible dependent random default times. Because:

$$\begin{aligned}&\mathbf{P}(\tau_1 \le t_1, \ldots, \tau_n \le t_n) \\ &\quad = \mathbf{P}(U_1 \le F_1(t_1), \ldots, \tau_n \le F_n(t_n))\end{aligned} \quad (12)$$

we obtain $\tau_1 = F_1^{-1}(U_1), \ldots, \tau_n = F_n^{-1}(U_n)$ where $U_1, \ldots, U_n$ are dependent uniforms. However, the generation of dependent uniforms turns out to be a difficult job.

A copula is defined as the joint distribution function of possibly dependent uniforms, ie:

$$\mathbf{P}(U_1 \le x_1, \ldots, U_n \le x_n) =: C(x_1, \ldots, x_n) \quad (13)$$

For a given copula $C(x_1, \ldots, x_n)$ and given marginal distribution $F_i$, the joint distribution of $t_1, \ldots, t_n$ is given by:

$$\mathbf{P}(\tau_1 \le x_1, \ldots, \tau_n \le x_n) =: C(F_1(x_1), \ldots, F_n(x_n)) \quad (14)$$

The copula separates the dependence between random variables and the marginal distributions $F_i$.

One of the simplest and widely used copulas is the normal copula. Let the distribution function of $(Y_1, \ldots, Y_n)$ be given by the distribution function of the n-dimensional normal distribution, $N(x_1, \ldots, x_n, \Sigma)$, then for $(U_1, \ldots, U_n)$ with $U_i = N(Y_i)$, $i = 1, \ldots, n$:

$$\begin{aligned}&\mathbf{P}(U_1 \le x_1, \ldots, U_n \le x_n) \\ &\quad = N\left(N^{-1}(x_1), \ldots, N_n^{-1}(x_n)\right) : C(x_1, \ldots, x_n)\end{aligned} \quad (15)$$

and the random default times can be obtained by:

$$\tau_i = F_i^{-1}(N(Y_i)), \quad i = 1,\ldots,n \qquad (16)$$

Here $\Sigma = (\rho_{i,j})$, $i = 1,\ldots,n$, $j = 1,\ldots,n$ denotes the matrix of (asset) correlations between credits $i$ and $j$.

The popularity of the normal copula is due to its relation to the well-known Merton firm model (Merton, 1974). As shown in Li (2000) and Schmidt and Ward (2002), to make the joint default probabilities of the Merton model coincide with those of the normal copula the asset correlations $(\rho^A_{i,j})$ of the Merton model have to match the correlations $(\rho_{i,j})$ of the normal copula. Asset correlations can be estimated from historical data or can be obtained from KMV (see *www.kmv.com*).

Many market participants prefer the normal copula over, eg, a t-copula because a t-copula is even harder to calibrate. Given that we observe only default swap spreads, it is very difficult to estimate the number of degrees of freedom of a t-copula, a parameter that is also linked to the default correlation. Furthermore, in case of an early default the higher tail dependence of the t-copula results in a bigger spread widening. This makes a model based on a copula with joint extremes, such as the t-copula, more time inhomogeneous and thus less realistic. The relatively easy implementation also contributes to the popularity of the normal copula.

As pointed out in Frey, McNeil and Nyfeler (2001), the copula has an impact on the loss distribution and hence the fair spread of individual portfolio tranches. However, for the purpose of this study we consider the choice of the copula to be less important. We are primarily interested in the change of moments of the loss distribution and fair spreads of individual tranches with respect to changes of recovery rate and correlation rather than in the absolute levels of these quantities. Since the qualitative results are the same in the BET model as in the normal copula model, we do not expect the major findings of this investigation to be affected significantly by the choice of the copula.

## Study design

We investigate the effect of correlation and recovery rate on the pricing of CDOs. First, we give a short introduction to portfolio default swaps before we describe the design of the study.

### PORTFOLIO DEFAULT SWAPS

A portfolio default swap is a credit derivatives instrument that allows the transfer of exposure to specific losses in a collateral pool due to default.

In a typical portfolio default swap, there are two parties, which we will refer to as the buyer and seller of protection. The buyer of protection pays a spread on the remaining notional of a tranche at regular intervals and in return the seller of protection compensates the buyer for any loss in that tranche at the time defaults in the portfolio occur.

The buyer of protection will view the swap as insurance against loss, and the seller of protection will view the swap as an investment with leveraged return for accepting the default risk of the tranche.

Consider a portfolio default swap on a tranche with size $N_T$ above a first loss tranche of size $N_L$. The fair portfolio default swap spread $s_T$ for maturity $T_m$ is defined by the relation:

$$0 = s_T \sum_{l=1}^{m} \Delta_l B(T_l)(N_T - L_T(T_l)) - \int_0^{T_m} B(u) L_T(du) \qquad (17)$$

where $L_T(t)$ denotes the random variable for loss in the tranche at time $t$, $B(t)$ the risk-free discounting function and $\Delta_l$ the day count fraction for period $l$. If $L(t)$ is the total loss in the portfolio at time $t$ then $L_T(t)$ can be written as $L_T(t) = \min(\max(L(t) - N_L, 0), N_T)$.

Equation 17 comprises two terms: the present value of the protection premium or spread payments and the present value of losses in the tranche discounted from the time of default.

### THE DESIGN

To focus on the relevant parameters - correlation and recovery rate - we choose a somewhat artificial design. The pool consists of $n = 100$ credits with identical characteristics. Each underlying has a notional amount of 100 and trades at a default swap spread of 100 basis points. Also we admit the same recovery rate for every credit. This ensures that the probability of default, $F_i(T) = p_i =: p$, is identical for all underlyings. Furthermore, it is assumed that each pair of credits $(i, j)$ is correlated with the same asset correlation $\rho_{(i,j)} =: \rho$. We then defined five different tranches (see Table 1). This means that the equity tranche E is hit by the first 1.5% of the losses followed by a mezzanine tranche D that takes the next 1.5% of the losses thereafter.

Clearly, such a homogeneous design is not found in practice. Real CDOs are much more heterogeneous, especially with respect to spreads, recovery rates or correlations. However, choosing the same values for these model parameters allows us to focus on the effect of changing correlation and recovery within a simplified framework where

**Table 1. Tranches and losses**

| Tranche | Losses (%) |
|---|---|
| E | 0.00–1.50 |
| D | 1.50–3.00 |
| C | 3.00–5.00 |
| B | 5.00–8.00 |
| A | 8.00–100.00 |

**1. Loss vs correlation**

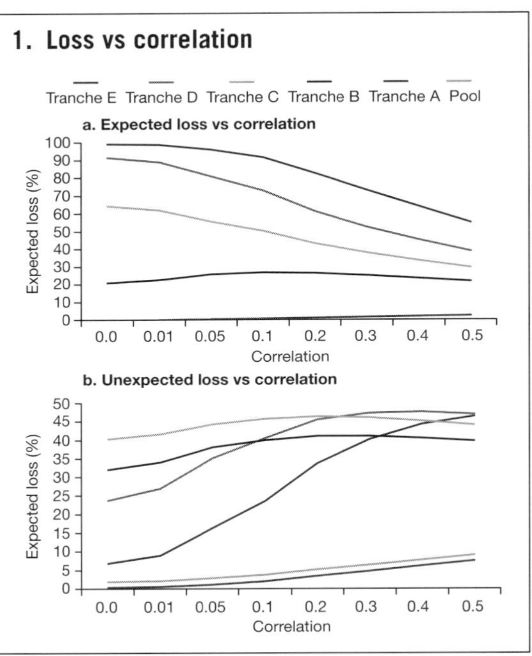


the interaction between notionals, recovery rates and single name spreads does not complicate the analysis of the results.

For each tranche, we calculated the first two moments of the loss distribution and the fair spread for protection on losses in this tranche. To investigate the effect of correlation and recovery rate, we performed these calculations for various values of recovery rates and correlation. Also, we looked at the loss distribution for the whole pool.

## Results

### TRANCHE RISK VERSUS CORRELATION

We first investigate the expected loss of each individual tranche and the expected loss of the whole pool. We assume a maturity of five years, ie, $T = 5$, and a recovery rate $R = 20\%$. The correlation $\rho$ varies between zero and 0.5. Figure 1a shows the percentage expected loss per tranche for different values of $\rho$.

The main findings are:

- The expected loss in the lower tranches, E, D and C, decreases when correlation increases.
- The expected loss in the senior tranche, A, increases when correlation increases.
- With increasing correlation, the expected loss in tranche B first increases up to a certain level. Afterwards, it goes down if correlation increases further.

Apparently the investor in an equity tranche is long correlation whereas an investor in the senior tranche benefits from lower correlation. The reason for this can be motivated very well in the BET model.

Let:

$$b(k;m,\tilde{p}) = \binom{m}{k}\tilde{p}^k(1-\tilde{p})^{m-k} \qquad (18)$$

denote the probability function of a binomial distributed random variable with parameters $m$ and $\tilde{p}$. We consider the case of zero correlation and a recovery rate $R = 20\%$. The diversity score $m$ in this case is just the number of credits, ie, $m = n = 100$. The percentage expected loss of the equity tranche E can easily be calculated as:

$$\mathbb{E}L_E(T) = b(1;100,\tilde{p})\frac{100-20}{150} + \sum_{k=2}^{100} b(k;100,\tilde{p}) \qquad (19)$$

$$= \tilde{p}(1-\tilde{p})^{99}\frac{80}{150} + \sum_{k=2}^{100}\binom{100}{k}\tilde{p}^k(1-\tilde{p})^{100-k} \qquad (20)$$

More generally, the percentage expected loss of the equity tranche that takes the first losses up to a fraction of $q$ of the pool notional $N$ is given by:

$$\mathbb{E}L_E(T) = \sum_{k=0}^{m} b(k;m,\tilde{p})\min\left(\frac{k(1-\tilde{R})}{qm},1\right) \qquad (21)$$

$$= 1 - \sum_{k=0}^{\left[\frac{qm}{1-R}\right]} b(k;m,\tilde{p})\left(1-\frac{k(1-\tilde{R})}{qm}\right) \qquad (22)$$

where $[x]$ denotes the largest integer smaller than $x$. Now, with increasing correlation the diversity score $m$ will decrease since the portfolio becomes less diversified. A smaller diversity score implies that the notional $\tilde{N}$ for each of the $m$ credits increases, ie, it needs less default events to wipe out the equity tranche completely. Moreover, since for $k < (m + 1)\tilde{p}$, $b(k; m, \tilde{p})$ increases if $m$ decreases, it is more likely that a sufficient number of defaults will happen in the case of a high correlation than in the case of a low correlation.

The same argument explains the increase of the expected loss in the most senior tranches. With increasing correlation, the variance of the

**Table 2. Default probability and expected loss (%)**

| Recovery | Default probability | Expected loss |
|---|---|---|
| 0 | 4.85 | 4.85 |
| 10 | 5.38 | 4.84 |
| 20 | 6.03 | 4.82 |
| 30 | 6.86 | 4.80 |
| 40 | 7.95 | 4.77 |
| 50 | 9.45 | 4.73 |
| 60 | 11.66 | 4.66 |
| 70 | 15.20 | 4.56 |
| 80 | 21.84 | 4.37 |

**2. Loss vs recovery rate**

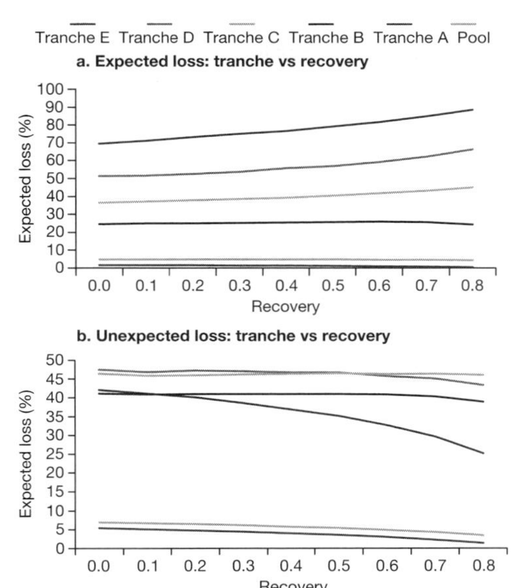


loss in the pool increases, thus increasing the probability that some of the losses affect the senior tranches.

The unexpected loss, which is defined as the standard deviation of the loss for the entire portfolio and for each tranche in the pool, is illustrated in Figure 1b. From Equation 7, it is clear that with increasing correlation the unexpected loss of the portfolio as well as the unexpected loss of the outer tranches A and E increases.

TRANCHE RISK VERSUS RECOVERY RATE

To investigate the impact of the recovery rate, we fix the correlation at $\rho = 0.3$. For different values of the recovery rate R between 0% and 80%, we keep the default swap spread constant at 100bp and repeat the bootstrap for the implied default probabilities. Table 2 shows the cumulative default probability and the expected loss of the pool for time $T = 5$ and for various values of R.

Figure 2a shows the expected loss of each tranche and of the pool for different values of the recovery rate R. The main results can be summarised as follows:

- The expected loss of the equity tranche, E, and the mezzanine tranche, D, increases with increasing recovery rate.
- The expected loss of the senior tranche, A, decreases with increasing recovery rate.
- The lower tranches, C, D and E, are more sensitive to the recovery rate than the upper tranches, A and B.

The reason for this can be seen in Figure 2b, which shows the unexpected loss for each tranche.

For every tranche as well as for the pool, the unexpected loss is a monotonically decreasing function of the recovery rate. As pointed out above, this decrease in unexpected loss is the reason for the increase of expected loss in subordinated tranches and the decrease in senior tranches, respectively. A higher unexpected loss shifts the loss distribution from its centre further out to its tails, thus increasing the probability for losses in the senior tranches but reducing the probability of losses in the equity tranche.

However, as can be seen from Table 2, the expected loss of the whole pool is slightly decreasing with the increasing recovery rate. This leads to an increase in the expected loss of the equity tranche. Hence, the increase in unexpected loss alone does not explain the results of Figure 2a. However, the decrease in expected loss is so small that it cannot offset the effect from the increase in unexpected loss.

The BET model again helps us understand why the unexpected loss decreases with the increasing recovery rate. If we assume that risk-free interest rates are zero, it holds that:

$$p_R = 1 - e^{-\frac{s}{1-R}T}$$

where s denotes the default swap spread. Using Equation 6 we get:

$$\frac{\partial}{\partial R}\mathbb{V}L_i(T) = N(1-R)(1-p_R)\left[-2p_R + \frac{sT}{1-R}(1-2p_R)\right] \quad (23)$$

The term in square brackets is less than zero for positive s. This can be easily verified by calculating its derivative with respect to $s/(1-R)$.

FAIR SPREADS VERSUS CORRELATION AND RECOVERY

The results above provide a basic understanding of how recovery rates and correlation influence the loss distributions. However, from a trader's perspective it is more important to see how these results transfer into market prices, ie, how correlation and the recovery rate affect the fair spreads for each tranche.

Figure 3 shows how the fair portfolio default swap spreads for each tranche vary for different correlations and recovery rates. It is clear that for the senior tranche the spread increases with an increase in correlation and decrease in recovery rates. The converse is true for the equity tranche.

**3. Fair default swap spreads**

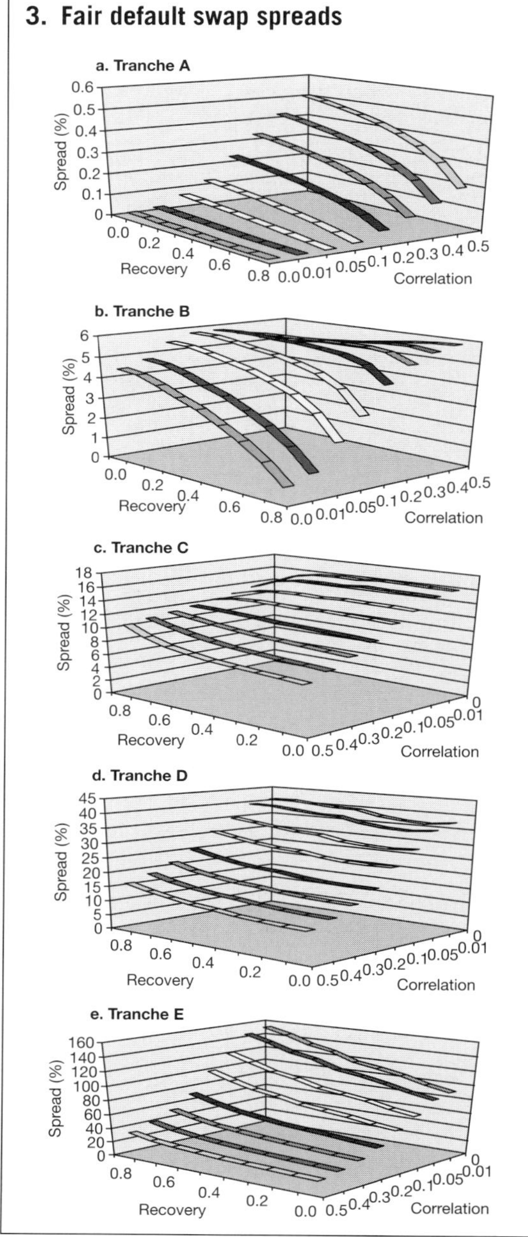


This behaviour of spreads can be explained simply by the fact that spreads and expected loss move in the same direction, as we would expect. Therefore, we need only look at the effect of correlation and recovery on the expected loss in a tranche to predict how the spread of the fair portfolio default swap will change.

Spreads for mezzanine tranches appear to behave in a similar way to the senior tranche for certain ranges of correlation and recovery and the equity tranche in other ranges. As a consequence, the mezzanine tranches demonstrate some reduced sensitivity to correlation and recovery rate, eg, tranche B and C spreads change very little as recovery changes when correlation is between 5% and 20%, and tranche B spreads change a relatively small amount for recovery below 20%. This suggests it may be possible to find a tranche within a collateral pool with low correlation and recovery risk by varying the size of the tranche and the size of the first-loss tranche below it.

It is also noticeable that changing recovery with fixed correlation results in significant changes to the fair portfolio default swap spreads, particularly in the first-loss tranches. For example, in tranche E the spreads have a relative increase of more than 20% for a change in the recovery from 20% to 60%. Our assumption of recovery rates within the portfolio may have a significant effect on valuation and this suggests that we should consider recovery rates in the portfolio to be stochastic.

It should be emphasised that the exact behaviour of each tranche depends on its location within the pool relative to the expected loss and unexpected loss of the pool.

THE WINDFALL EFFECT AND THE TIMING OF DEFAULTS

Let us consider the situation where we buy protection on all tranches within the portfolio using portfolio default swaps and hedge the risk of default in the portfolio by selling protection using single-name default swaps. In the event of a credit default, the compensation of loss received from the portfolio default swaps exactly matches and offsets the loss compensation paid on the hedges. However, the average spread paid on the portfolio default swaps is much greater than the average spread of 100 bp received on the default swap hedges, ie, this position has high negative carry for the portfolio default swap protection buyer.

A similar observation was made in Schmidt and Ward (2002), where the sum of the fair spreads for the first-, second- and third-to-default basket

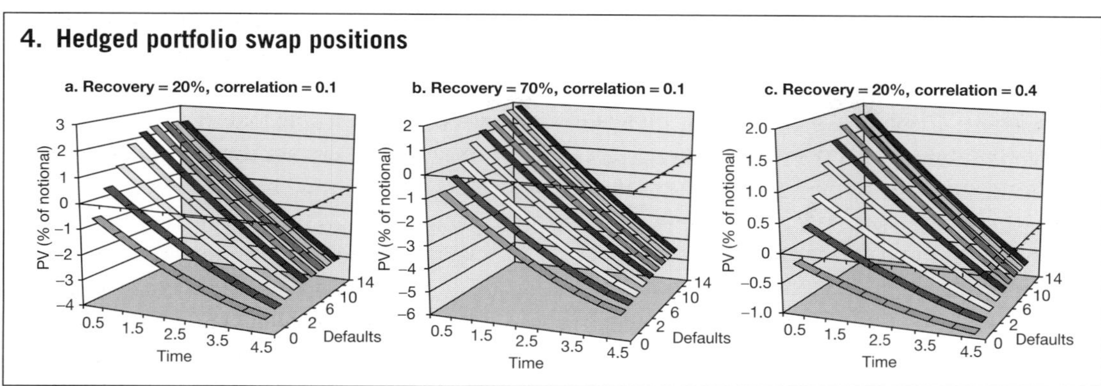


**4. Hedged portfolio swap positions**

default swaps in a basket of three credits was always greater than the sum of the fair spreads for the single-name default swaps. The reason for both of these situations is the same. The average life of derivatives contingent on the lower tranches of the portfolio is much shorter than those contingent on the senior tranches. The present value of all the spread payments on the hedges and on the portfolio default swaps are the same but we do not expect to pay the higher spreads on the riskier tranches for as long as we expect to pay the lower spreads on the less risky tranches.

A consequence of this is that we may benefit from an unexpected high number of early defaults that consume the lower tranches of the portfolio (where we pay high spreads) leaving the senior tranche portfolio swap (where we pay low spreads) while still receiving the spreads from the default swap hedges on the remaining credits. This potential benefit due to defaults is referred to as "windfall gain". The converse is also possible and in the worst-case scenario, no defaults occur before the maturity of the portfolio and we will pay far more for protection against loss through the portfolio default swaps than we receive for providing protection through the default swap hedges.

We now present an analysis of the effect of the number and timing of defaults on our hedged portfolio default swap position.

Under each scenario, the cashflows on the portfolio default swap and default swap hedges prior to the default date are considered risk-free and discounted to today using a risk-free discount factor curve. The remaining portfolio default swap and default swap hedges are adjusted for the defaults in the scenario, valued to the future default date using the normal copula model with today's default curves decayed to the forward spreads and then valued to today using a risk-free discount factor curve.

Figure 4 shows the present value of a hedged portfolio default swap position from the point of view of the portfolio default swap protection buyer (the buyer), expressed as a percentage of the total pool notional, for scenarios of number and time of defaults. In each scenario it is assumed that all the defaults occur at the same time, that no defaults occur before and that any number of further defaults may occur after. Though this is unlikely, it simplifies our calculations, and is the most conservative calculation of windfall gain for the portfolio default protection buyer.

The results show that if no credits default before the maturity of the portfolio, the buyer can be sure of losing money. If one credit defaults in the first six months or two credits default in the first year, then the buyer will make money because the payments on the equity tranche have been reduced sooner than expected. As the number of defaults increases, the time at which these defaults must occur for a positive present value becomes greater. However, there is a time horizon of two-and-a-half years where if no credits default before this time, the buyer will have losses, regardless of how many credits default after this time. If the number of credit defaults is large enough to reduce the notional of all of the tranches below the senior tranche to zero, any further defaults will go against the buyer because the reduction of the spread received from the default swap hedges will be greater than the reduction in the payments on the senior tranche. For a recovery rate of 20% (see Figure 4a), this can be seen when more than 10 credits default; the lower the recovery in the portfolio, the smaller credit defaults required.

If the recovery rate in the portfolio increases from 20% to 70% (see Figure 4b) the time horizon T, where the buyer will face losses if no credit defaults before T, has moved closer to today.

The explanation for this is if recovery rates increase, the lower tranches of the pool have higher expected loss and higher portfolio default swap spreads. It follows then that the defaults must happen sooner for the buyer to have a positive present value. If the recovery rate is fixed at 20% but correlation increases from 10% to 40% (see Figure 4c), the time horizon for defaults moves away from today. Similarly, this is due to the fair portfolio default swap spreads for the lower tranches decreasing with an increase in correlation.

**BIBLIOGRAPHY**

**Cifuentes, A., I. Efrat, J. Gluck, and E. Murphy,** 1998, "Buying and Selling Credit Risk: A Perspective on Credit Link Obligations", in *Credit Derivatives: Applications for Risk Management, Investment and Portfolio Optimisation,* (Risk Books).

**Frey, R., A. McNeil and M. Nyfeler,** 2001, "Copulas and Credit Models", *Risk*, October, pp. 111–13.

**Gluck, J., and H. Remeza,** 2000, "Moody's Approach to Rating Multisector CDOs", *Moody's Investor Service*, September, pp. 1–20.

**Khuong-Huu, P.,** 1999, "The Price of Credit", *Risk*, December, pp. 68–71.

**Li, D.,** 2000, "On Default Correlation: A Copula Function Approach", *Journal of Fixed Income*, March, pp. 115–18.

**Merton, R.,** 1974, "On the Pricing of Corporate Debt: The Risk Structure of Interest Rates", *Journal of Finance*, 29, pp. 449–70.

**Schmidt, W., and I. Ward,** 2002, "Pricing a Basket", *Risk*, January, pp. 115–18.

# 31

# Extreme Events and Default Baskets

**Roy Mashal and Marco Naldi**
Lehman Brothers

*As the markets in synthetic CDOs and basket credit default swaps grow in size, copula methods, which relate reference portfolio loss distributions to underlying asset correlations, are emerging as the favoured pricing approach within the Merton framework. However, a lively debate continues over the choice of copula to be used. In the first of two themed articles, Roy Mashal and Marco Naldi argue that for pricing small baskets,* t *copulas are essential to properly account for extreme event risk.*

Specifying an appropriate model for dependent defaults is the core problem in valuing multi-name credit derivatives. Different dependence structures produce different default distributions, which in turn affect the valuation of products such as collateralised debt obligation tranches and basket default swaps.

Several credit models rely on Merton's (1974) idea that a firm defaults when its asset value drops below its liabilities. A straightforward extension of this framework to the multivariate case suggests that the dependence structure of defaults is determined by the underlying joint distribution of asset returns. Many existing portfolio models implicitly assume multivariate normality for the joint distribution of asset returns, even if this is incompatible with the extreme joint realisations that we observe in the data. Extreme joint movements do happen more often than the Gaussian distribution would predict.

This chapter builds upon ideas introduced by Li (2000) and Frey, McNeil and Nyfeler (2001), and presents a simulation-based pricing model that accounts for extreme events. After describing the properties of its simulation engine, we discuss how to make the model operational, with particular reference to the estimation of the parameters that determine the likelihood of extreme events.

While several recent articles have pointed out the inappropriateness of the Gaussian assumption, little has been said about the impact of a more realistic distribution on the valuation of multi-name credit derivatives. In this chapter, we quantify the pricing consequences of taking extreme events into consideration. For this purpose, we focus our attention on basket default swaps, since the valuation of these contracts is particularly sensitive to the dependence structure of defaults.

In an nth-to-default basket swap, two counterparties agree on a maturity and a set of reference assets, and enter into a contract whereby the protection seller periodically receives a premium (also called "basket spread") from the protection buyer. In exchange, the protection seller stands ready to pay the protection buyer par minus recovery of the nth referenced defaulter in the event that the nth default occurs before the agreed-upon maturity (see Figure 1). First- and second-to-default swaps are the most popular orders of protection.

## Default correlation and the distribution of asset returns

Default correlation measures the tendency of two credits to default jointly within a specified horizon. Formally, it is defined as the correlation between two binary random variables that indicate

*The authors would like to thank Arthur Berd, Mark Broadie, Paul Glasserman, Hua He, Prafulla Nabar, Dominic O'Kane, Lutz Schloegl and two anonymous referees for comments and suggestions.*

**1. nth-to-default basket swap**

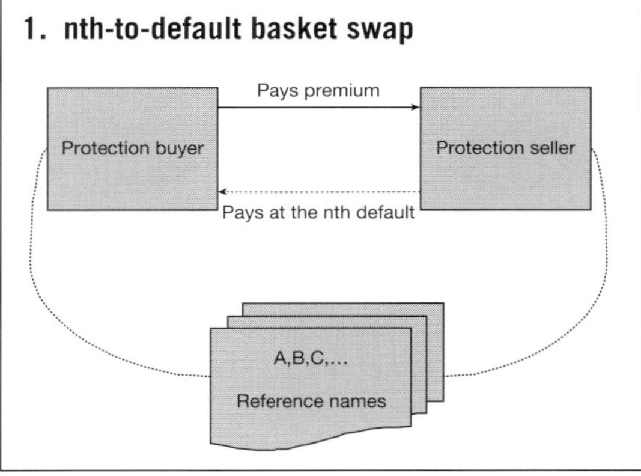


defaults, ie:

$$\rho_D = \frac{p_{AB} - p_A p_B}{\sqrt{p_A(1-p_A)}\sqrt{p_B(1-p_B)}} \tag{1}$$

where $p_A$ and $p_B$ are the marginal default probabilities for credits A and B, and $p_{AB}$ is the joint default probability. Of course, $p_A$, $p_B$ and $p_{AB}$ all refer to a specific horizon. Notice that default correlation increases linearly with the joint probability of default and is equal to zero if the two default events are independent.

Default correlations are the fundamental drivers in the valuation of multi-name credit derivatives. Unfortunately, the scarcity of default data makes joint default probabilities, and thus default correlations, very hard to estimate directly. As a result, researchers have developed alternative methods to calibrate the frequency of joint defaults within their valuation models.

One way to simulate correlated defaults relies on the use of copula functions. Generally speaking, copulas are used to link marginal and joint distribution functions. In an influential article, Li (2000) employs a Gaussian copula to obtain the joint distribution of default times, and shows how to use it as the probability law underlying an efficient time-to-default simulation. This procedure is extremely useful for valuing multi-issuer credit derivatives, since one can extract (risk-neutral) marginal default probabilities from liquid single-name products, and then value multi-name contracts by simulating correlated default times.

To illustrate Li's model, consider a simple scenario with two credits A and B, whose default times $T_A$ and $T_B$ have marginal distribution functions $F_A$ and $F_B$. A joint distribution that correlates $T_A$ and $T_B$ while respecting their marginals can be obtained by means of a bivariate normal copula:

$$F_N(x,y) = P(T_A < x, T_B < y) = \Phi_{2,r}\left(\Phi^{-1}(F_A(x)), \Phi^{-1}(F_B(y))\right) \tag{2}$$

where $\Phi_{2,r}$ denotes a bivariate standard normal distribution with correlation r, and $\Phi$ is a univariate standard normal distribution. Taking limits, it is straightforward to verify that this joint distribution is perfectly legitimate in that it respects the marginals that we started with.

Note that if we restrict our attention to the diagonal $x = y$, the distribution function in Equation 2 can be reinterpreted in the context of a structural model where:

- default of credit A is caused by the firm's normally distributed asset return falling below the threshold $\Phi^{-1}(F_A(\cdot))$ (and similarly for credit B); and
- the parameter r represents the correlation between the jointly normal asset returns of the obligors.

In other words, the choice of a copula function for survival times can be viewed as a particular distributional assumption for asset returns. As a consequence, reasonable proxies for the copula parameters (such as r in Equation 2) can be calculated from observable equity return series.

Nyfeler (2000) and Frey and McNeil (2001) show that some of the most popular credit models in the market are in fact equivalent to the one characterised by the distribution function in Equation 2.[1] The assumption of normality of asset returns, however, is certainly not innocuous, since a multivariate normal distribution does not allow for extreme joint events to happen with the frequency that the data suggests.

Figure 2 shows a bivariate scatterplot of standardised equity returns using seven years of monthly data (August 1994–July 2001). To the extent that equity returns proxy for asset returns, this figure highlights the major problem with the Gaussian assumption. According to the normal distribution, the most extreme joint realisations in this plot have a likelihood of happening of about

**2. Standardised monthly returns**

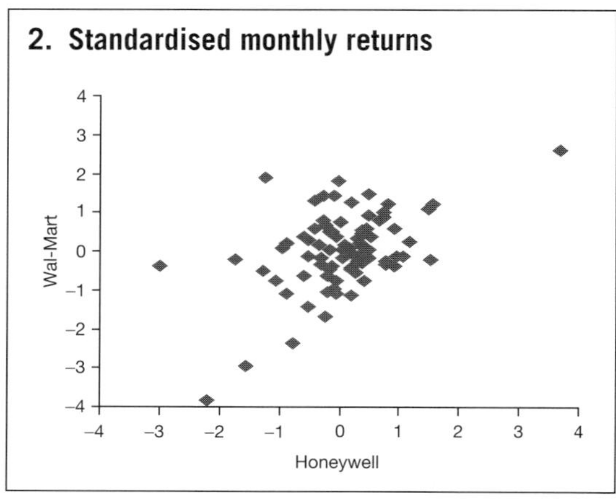

one in 100,000. Yet we observe them in a sample of 84 points.

The ability of a multivariate distribution to accommodate joint extreme events can be related to the concept of "tail dependence". Formally, for two random variables X and Y with marginal distributions $F_X$ and $F_Y$, a measure of (lower) tail dependence can be defined as:

$$\lambda := \lim_{u \to 0^+} P\left(Y < F_Y^{-1}(u) \middle| X < F_X^{-1}(u)\right) \quad (3)$$

In words, $\lambda$ measures the probability that Y will have a realisation in the tail of its distribution given that X has had a realisation in the tail of its own. The problem with the multivariate normal distribution is that $\lambda$ is equal to zero for all $r < 1$. Another manifestation of the same problem can be seen in the thinness of the tails of a multivariate normal density, which implies that there is very little probability mass on extreme joint events.

To evaluate the pricing impact of tail dependence, we employ a generalisation of the model described by Equation 2. More specifically, we link the marginal distributions of default times through a t copula. Continuing with our bivariate example, we simulate default times $T_A$ and $T_B$ using the joint distribution:

$$F_t(x, y) = P(T_A < x, T_B < y) = t_{2,\nu,r}\left(t_\nu^{-1}(F_A(x)), t_\nu^{-1}(F_B(y))\right) \quad (4)$$

where $t_{2,\nu,r}$ is a bivariate standard t distribution with $\nu$ degrees of freedom and correlation r, and $t_\nu$ is a univariate standard t distribution with $\nu$ degrees of freedom. The choice of a t copula for default times is consistent with the assumption that asset returns follow a multivariate t distribution.[2] Since two jointly $t_{2,\nu}$ variables are marginally $t_\nu$ distributed, we can interpret $t_\nu^{-1}(F_A(\cdot))$ and $t_\nu^{-1}(F_B(\cdot))$ as default thresholds, and $t_{2,\nu,r}$ as the joint distribution of asset returns.[3] In the next section, we exploit this interpretation to estimate the copula parameters.

Lindskog (2000), Frey and McNeil (2001) and Schonbucher and Schubert (2001), among others, study alternative forms of dependence such as Clayton and Gumbel copulas. These are legitimate ways to join the marginal distributions of default times and introduce tail dependencies. In this chapter, we employ the model in Equation 4 for three main reasons.

First, a t distribution seems like a reasonable model for asset returns, largely because of its ability to accommodate heavy tails. In a seminal study, Blattberg and Gonedes (1974) find that a t distribution with a low number of degrees of freedom (10 or fewer) offers an adequate representation for the univariate behaviour of most Dow Jones Industrial Average stocks returns. Second, using a t copula allows for a very efficient simulation of survival times. Third, the t distribution is a straightforward generalisation of the normal distribution, in the sense that a multivariate normal is nested in a multivariate t as a limiting case. In the next section, we take advantage of this relation and let the data choose the most appropriate element of a parameterised family of distributions.

Compared with a standard normal, a standard t distribution has an additional parameter, the number of degrees of freedom. As this number goes to infinity, the t distribution tends to the normal distribution, ie, it displays no tail-dependence. But for a finite number of degrees of freedom, the t distribution allows for extreme joint realisations. To illustrate this point, consider a bivariate standard t with correlation r and $\nu$ degrees of freedom. The value of $\lambda$ for this distribution can be shown to be equal to:

$$\lambda = 2t_{\nu+1}\left(-\frac{\sqrt{\nu+1}\sqrt{1-r}}{\sqrt{1+r}}\right) > 0, \quad |r| < 1 \quad (5)$$

where $t_\nu$ stands for a univariate t with $\nu$ degrees of freedom.

Table 1 shows the values of $\lambda$ for a bivariate standard t as a function of the correlation coefficient r and the degrees of freedom $\nu$. The last row refers to the normal case ($\nu = \infty$). To understand the meaning of these numbers, consider the case where the distribution is characterised by 10 degrees of freedom and 30% correlation. In this scenario, knowing that the return of the first name has had an extremely negative realisation leaves us with a 3.31% probability that the return of the second name will also have an extremely negative realisation. This is very different from the prediction of a jointly normal distribution. In the

**Table 1. Tail dependence ($\lambda$)**

| $\nu$ \ r | –0.5 | 0 | 0.3 | 0.5 | 0.9 | 1 |
|---|---|---|---|---|---|---|
| 3 | 0.0257 | 0.1161 | 0.2161 | 0.3125 | 0.6701 | 1 |
| 10 | 0.0001 | 0.0068 | **0.0331** | 0.0819 | 0.4627 | 1 |
| 15 | 0.0000 | 0.0010 | 0.0097 | 0.0346 | 0.3724 | 1 |
| 20 | 0.0000 | 0.0002 | 0.0029 | 0.0151 | 0.3051 | 1 |
| $\infty$ | 0 | 0 | 0 | 0 | 0 | 1 |

**3. Asset correlation versus default correlation**

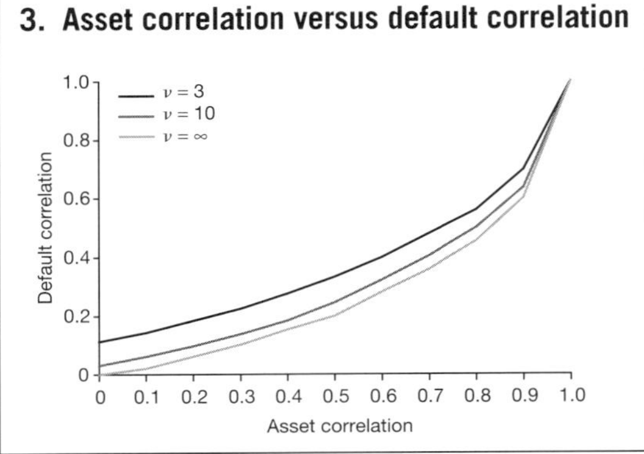


last section of this chapter, we quantify the pricing impact of this difference.

The relation between the tail dependence of asset returns and the dependence of default events is shown in Figure 3. Using a five-year horizon and two credits whose default times are exponentially distributed with yearly hazard rates of 1%, this graph compares a normal copula and a t-copula with three and 10 degrees of freedom. Tail dependence increases default correlation for any value of asset correlation. In particular, notice that even when asset returns are uncorrelated (ie, linearly independent), tail dependence can produce a significant amount of default correlation.

## Estimation and testing

To simulate default times from the joint distribution specified in Equation 4, we need to estimate its parameters. Using time series of equity returns to proxy for asset returns, we can estimate these parameters by maximum likelihood. Moreover, since a multivariate t distribution tends to a normal distribution as the number of degrees of freedom increases (ie, $F_t \rightarrow F_N$ as $\nu \rightarrow \infty$), the normality assumption is actually nested in our framework as a special case. Therefore, we can carry out likelihood ratio tests for the null hypothesis that returns are jointly normal. For the analysis in this section and the next, we consider the baskets described in Table 2.

Using seven years of monthly equity returns from August 1994–July 2001 ($R = (R_1, R_2, \ldots, R_T)$, $R_i \in \mathbb{R}^m$, and $T = 84$), we construct the likelihood of the sample as:

$$L(\nu, \Sigma; R) = \sum_{t=1}^{T} \log(t_{m,\nu,\Sigma}(R_t)) \qquad (6)$$

where m is the number of reference credits, and $t_{m,\nu,\Sigma}$ is the density of an m-dimensional t with $\nu$ degrees of freedom and correlation $\Sigma$.[4] We then estimate our parameters as:

$$(\nu, \Sigma)_{ML} = \underset{\nu,\Sigma}{\arg\max}\ L(\nu, \Sigma; R) \qquad (7)$$

and test the null hypothesis of normality using the likelihood ratio:

$$-2\ln\left(\frac{L(\nu = \infty)}{L(\nu_{ML})}\right) \sim \mathrm{Chi}^2(1) \qquad (8)$$

where $\mathrm{Chi}^2(1)$ indicates a chi-square distribution with one degree of freedom.[5]

Figures 4–6 plot the likelihood for our three baskets as a function of the degrees of freedom. The maximum likelihood estimates are shown to be nine, seven and nine, respectively, detecting the presence of a significant amount of tail dependence in the data. To confirm the inadequacy of the normal distribution, the same

**Table 2. Basket examples**

| Basket | Reference names |
|---|---|
| 1 | Fleet Boston, AT&T, IBM, Eastman Kodak |
| 2 | Honeywell, BellSouth, Wal-Mart, First Data |
| 3 | Union of the names in baskets 1 and 2 |

**4. Basket 1 log-likelihood function**

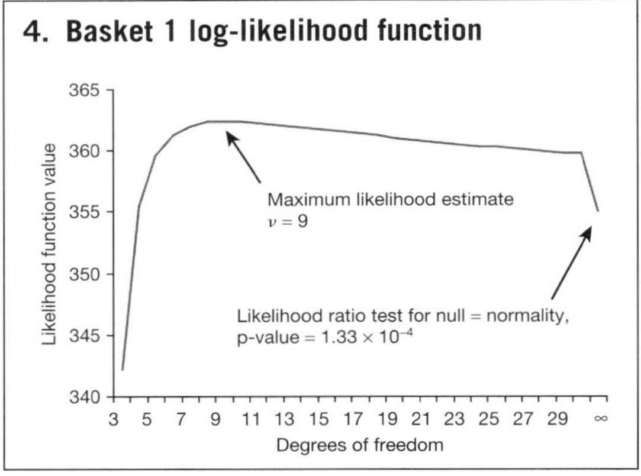


**5. Basket 2 log-likelihood function**

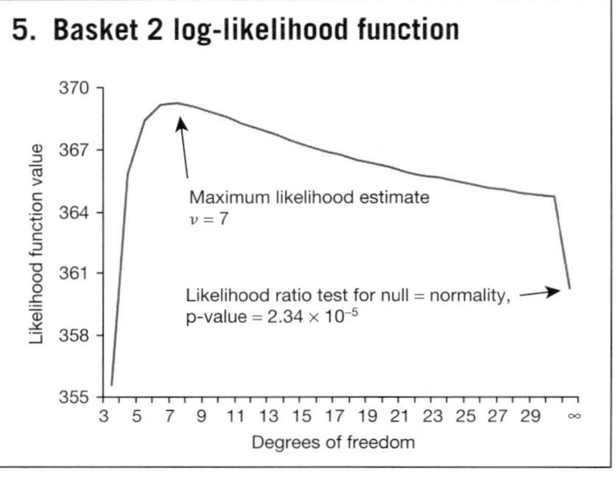

**6. Basket 3 log-likelihood function**

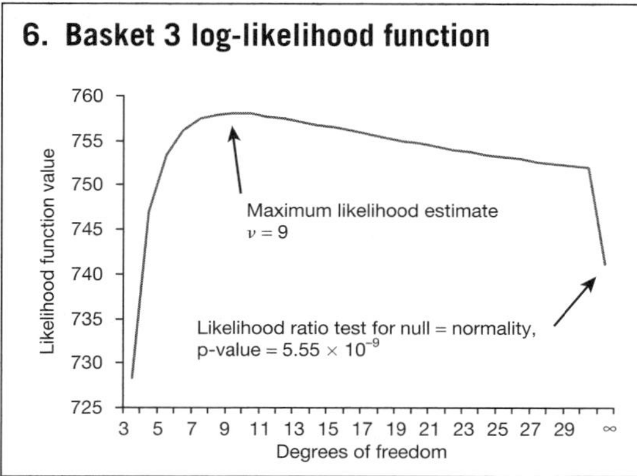


figures also report the p-values of the likelihood ratio tests for the null hypothesis of normality. They suggest that we can reject normality with an infinitesimal probability of making a mistake. This result is by no means specific to the chosen examples. We have obtained analogous results with dozens of different portfolios.

## The impact of tail dependence on the valuation of default baskets

Taking extreme events into account has significant consequences for the valuation of basket default swaps. Other things being equal, simulating defaults by means of a fat-tailed copula increases the probability of joint defaults and therefore default correlations as defined in Equation 1. The sign of the relation between basket premiums and default correlations, however, depends on the order of the basket.

The value of first-to-default protection is always monotonically decreasing in default correlations. Therefore, when we allow for joint extreme events, first-to-default protection becomes unambiguously cheaper.

The value of second-to-default protection is not necessarily monotonic in default correlations. Rather, it generally increases up to a maximum, then decreases. The location of the turning point depends on all other parameters and, in particular, on the number of names in the basket. With a low number of names, second-to-default protection is generally increasing in default correlations over most of the domain. Intuitively, with only a handful of names in the portfolio, the event that at least two of them default becomes more likely as we increase their tendency to default together.

These qualitative relations are consistent with the results reported in Table 3, where we compare the valuation of first- and second-to-default swaps using a normal copula and a t copula for default times. The reference names for the baskets are reported in Table 2. The marginal distributions of default times are assumed to have deterministic, piecewise-flat hazard rates, calibrated to the single-name default swap market. All deals have a maturity equal to three years and have been priced using information (Libor curve, market-implied hazard rates, estimated parameters of t copula) available as of the end of July 2001. Premiums are in basis points and standard errors of the Monte Carlo estimators (as a percentage of the premiums) are reported in brackets.

**Table 3. Valuation of three-year default baskets (as of July 2001): normal versus t**

| Basket | | Premium (standard error) | |
|---|---|---|---|
| | | First-to-default | Second-to-default |
| 1 | N dbn | 236 (0.28%) | 29 (0.75%) |
| | t dbn | 224 (0.26%) | 36 (0.67%) |
| | Diff | –5% | 24% |
| 2 | N dbn | 140 (0.34%) | 12 (1.15%) |
| | t dbn | 129 (0.35%) | 19 (0.92%) |
| | Diff | –8% | 58% |
| 3 | N dbn | 350 (0.29%) | 64 (0.71%) |
| | t dbn | 316 (0.31%) | 76 (0.66%) |
| | Diff | –10% | 19% |

## Conclusion

The pricing differences shown above suggest that abandoning the popular assumption of Gaussian dependence has a significant impact on the valuation of default baskets. As basket swaps and other multi-name credit instruments become more liquid, differences of this magnitude will have to be taken into consideration by any active market player, and the choice among alternative valuation methods will have to be carefully considered.

The framework used in this chapter has two important advantages. First, by generalising the Gaussian dependence structure in a parametric fashion, and employing maximum likelihood estimation, we let the available data choose the most appropriate amount of tail dependence to be used in the simulation of correlated defaults. Second, the benefits of a more realistic dependence structure come at a relatively low cost. From a computational point of view, both the maximum likelihood estimation and the time-to-default simulation are only moderately more expensive when we employ a t rather than a normal copula.

1 *Two multi-name credit models are said to be equivalent if the associated default indicators are equal in distribution. This implies that their default distributions are the same.*

2 *Notice, however, that infinitely many other joint distributions possess a* t-*copula (see Mashal and Naldi, 2002, for more details).*

3 *An* m-*dimensional standard* t *distribution with* $\nu$ *degrees of freedom and correlation matrix* $\Sigma$ *has density given by:*

$$t_{m,\nu,\Sigma} = \frac{\Gamma\left(\frac{m+\nu}{2}\right)(\det(\Sigma))^{-\frac{1}{2}}}{\Gamma\left(\frac{\nu}{2}\right)(\nu\pi)^{\frac{m}{2}}}\left(1+\frac{x'\Sigma^{-1}x}{\nu}\right)^{-\left(\frac{m+\nu}{2}\right)}, \quad x \in \Re^m$$

*where* $\Gamma$ *indicates the gamma function.*

4 *Notice that the factorisation in Equation 6 implicitly assumes that the return vector is serially independent and identically distributed. One could in principle use a conditional factorisation and model a time-varying dependence structure, but that would lead to a significantly more complicated implementation.*

5 *See Johnson and Kotz (1972) for more details on the multivariate* t *distribution. A simple algorithm to calculate the maximum likelihood estimate of* $\Sigma$ *for a given value of* $\nu$ *can be found in Bouye* et al. *(2000). The likelihood ratio test is implemented using the approximate null* n = 10,000.

**BIBLIOGRAPHY**

**Blattberg, R., and N. Gonedes,** 1974, "A Comparison of the Stable and Student Distributions as Statistical Models for Stock Prices", *Journal of Business*, 47, pp. 244–80.

**Bouye, E., V. Durrleman, A. Nikeghbali, G. Riboulet and T. Roncalli,** 2000, *Copulas for Finance*, Working Paper, Groupe de Recerche Operationnelle, Credit Lyonnais, Paris.

**Frey, R., and A. McNeil,** 2001, *Modelling Dependent Defaults*, Working Paper, Swiss Federal Institute of Technology.

**Frey, R., A. McNeil and M. Nyfeler,** 2001, "Copulas and Credit Models", *Risk*, October, pp. 111–14.

**Johnson, N., and S. Kotz,** 1972, *Continuous Multivariate Distributions*, (New York: Wiley).

**Li, D.,** 2000, "On Default Correlation: A Copula Function Approach", *Journal of Fixed Income*, 9, March, pp. 43–54.

**Lindskog, F.,** 2000, *Modelling Dependence with Copulas and Applications to Risk Management*, Master thesis, Swiss Federal Institute of Technology.

**Mashal, R., and M. Naldi,** 2002, *Pricing Multi-name Credit Derivatives: A Heavy-tailed Hybrid Approach*, Working Paper, Graduate School of Business, Columbia University.

**Merton, R.,** 1974, "On the Pricing of Corporate Debt: The Risk Structure of Interest Rates", *Journal of Finance*, 29, May, pp. 449–70.

**Nyfeler, M.,** 2000, *Modelling Dependencies in Credit Risk Management*, Diploma Thesis, Swiss Federal Institute of Technology.

**Schonbucher, P., and D. Schubert,** 2001, *Copula-dependent Default Risk in Intensity Models*, Working Paper, Department of Statistics, Bonn University.

VIII

# VALUE-AT-RISK FOR ASSET SECURITISATIONS

# 32

# Credit Risk in Asset Securitisations: An Analytical Model

**Michael Pykhtin and Ashish Dev**
Keycorp

*How much capital should banks reserve against investments in portfolio securitisations? Asserting that recent proposals on this subject by Basel are inconsistent, Michael Pykhtin and Ashish Dev propose a new analytical model suitable for tranches of large portfolios.*

The Basel Committee on Banking Supervision is continuing its work on Basel II, which is scheduled to replace the original Basel Accord of 1988. The purpose of the new Accord is to make the regulatory capital better reflect the underlying risks. One of its most recent efforts is "Working Paper on the Treatment of Asset Securitisations" (Basel, 2001b), where it explores ways of assessing risk of securitisation tranches. Depending upon whether a tranche is rated, two different methods for regulatory capital calculation are suggested in Basel II for banks qualified for the internal-ratings based (IRB) approach. The method proposed for rated tranches is based on scaling the capital calculated with foundation IRB formula for a corporate loan of the same rating and with 50% loss given default (LGD). The scaling factors proposed for this ABS (asset-backed securities) scaling factors method are equal to one for highly rated tranches (Moody's ratings Aaa, Aa and A), and exceed one for lower-rated tranches. Tranches with Moody's ratings below Ba3 get 100% capital. For unrated tranches, regulatory capital calculation is based on the IRB capital, $K_{IRB}$, computed for the underlying portfolio. Tranches with both bounds below $K_{IRB}$ require 100% capital, while for tranches above $K_{IRB}$, a supervisory formula is suggested for computing the capital.

There is a major shortcoming in Basel's proposed approach to securitisations in comparison with its approach to commercial and consumer loans, described in Basel (2001a). For the latter, the regulatory capital allocation rules are based on a simple analytical model (the asymptotic case of default-mode one-factor CreditMetrics model, also known as Vasicek's model), which correctly captures the most essential part of the underlying risk. No such model is apparent in the case of capital for securitisation tranches in Basel (2001b).

In this chapter, we are trying to amend this disadvantage of Basel's approach to securitisation. We present an analytical model, which adequately describes the risk of a securitisation tranche for the case of asymptotically fine-grained underlying portfolio and allocates capital accordingly. In this chapter, we define capital to be the $q$-percentile of the loss distribution associated with an instrument, where $q$ is the confidence level chosen to maintain a certain credit rating. Basel II very reasonably suggests $q = 99.5\%$. To facilitate comparisons with Basel (2001b) further, we use Basel's notations whenever possible.

*The authors would like to thank John Mingo for valuable discussions. They also thank anonymous referees for their helpful comments.*

## Stand-alone tranche and Basel's supervisory formula

We will assume that securitisation is based on an underlying portfolio of loans, whose loss, $L$, is distributed according to some probability density function $f(\cdot)$. We will denote the probability that the portfolio loss will exceed level $l$ by $G(l)$. There is an obvious relation between these two functions: $f = -dG/dl$. The capital for the underlying portfolio, $K_{IRB}$, is defined as a q-percentile of this distribution and, therefore, must satisfy the relation $G(K_{IRB}) = 1 - q$.

Let us consider a stand-alone tranche with the lower bound $T_1$ and the upper bound $T_2$. This specification means that an investor who owns this tranche will experience no losses if $L \le T_1$ but will experience loss of $L - T_1$ if $T_1 < L \le T_2$ and $T_1 - T_2$ if $L > T_2$. Thus, the distribution of percentage loss of this stand-alone tranche, U, will be given by the distribution of loss of the underlying portfolio, $f(\cdot)$, between $T_1(U = 0\%)$ and $T_2(U = 100\%)$. In addition, there will be Dirac delta-function spikes at 0% with the weight $1 - G(T_1)$ and at 100% with the weight $G(T_2)$. The capital factor for a stand-alone tranche, $K_{s-a}$ will be, therefore, 0% if $K_{IRB} \le T_1$, 100% if $K_{IRB} > T_2$ and $(K_{IRB} - T_1)/(T_2 - T_1)$ otherwise.[1] Formally, this can be written as an integral:

$$K_{s-a} = \frac{1}{T_2 - T_1} \int_{T_1}^{T_2} dl\, h_{s-a}(l, K_{IRB}) \quad (1)$$

where:

$$h_{s-a}(l, K_{IRB}) = 1_{\{l<K_{IRB}\}} \quad (2)$$

is the marginal capital charge (s–a denotes stand-alone tranche) ie, the capital charged for an infinitesimally thin tranche (ITT), and $1_{\{\cdot\}}$ denotes the indicator function. Thus, the capital applied to a tranche is the average of the marginal capital charge between the tranche bounds. For a stand-alone ITT, it takes value 100% for portfolio loss below $K_{IRB}$ and value 0% for portfolio loss above $K_{IRB}$. It is shown in Figure 1 by the dashed line.

Equation 1 has one major disadvantage. For any tranche with $T_1 > K_{IRB}$ it assigns zero capital. This situation is particularly unacceptable for regulators. The supervisory formula proposed in Basel (2001b) takes the form of Equation 2 with a different marginal capital charge proposed:

$$h_{Basel}(l, K_{IRB}) = 1_{\{l<K_{IRB}\}} + 1_{\{l>K_{IRB}\}} \exp\left[-\delta(l - K_{IRB})\right] \quad (3)$$

Equation 3 differs from the marginal capital charge for stand-alone tranche given by Equation 2 by the exponential tail for losses exceeding $K_{IRB}$. This tail assures that capital charge is strictly positive for any tranche. The total of capital charges

**1. Marginal capital suggested in Basel (2001b)**

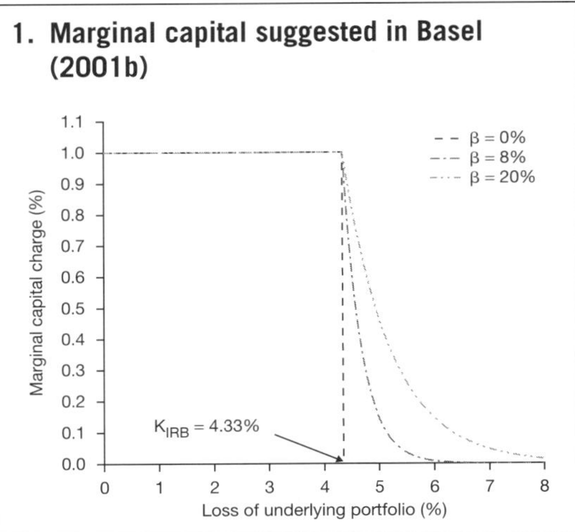


is equal to $K_{IRB}$ for tranches below $K_{IRB}$, and to $\beta K_{IRB}$ for tranches above $K_{IRB}$, where $\beta$ is some premium uniquely related to parameter $\delta$. In Figure 1, we have shown Basel's marginal capital charge given by Equation 3 for three different levels of premium $\beta$.

Basel's supervisory formula retains the form of Equation 1, while assigning finite capital to senior tranches. Its major disadvantage, however, is in the arbitrariness of the second term in its right-hand side of Equation 3. Moreover, we do not see how one can justify economically why the total capital across all tranches should exceed $K_{IRB}$. If one considers a stand-alone tranche, the total capital must be equal to $K_{IRB}$. If, alternatively, the tranche is considered as a part of a large portfolio, we would expect the total capital to be somewhat below $K_{IRB}$ due to extra diversification.

## Model

In this section, we present an analytical model for deriving the risk of a securitisation tranche in portfolio context and to calculate capital accordingly. Before we start making further assumptions, we will compute expected loss associated with a tranche. Rating agencies use expected loss as the basis for their ratings of tranches (Moody's, 2000). Therefore, it is important to be able to estimate it effectively. Expected loss of a tranche by definition is:

$$E[U] = \int_{T_1}^{T_2} dl\, f(l) \frac{l - T_1}{T_2 - T_1} + \int_{T_2}^{1} dl\, f(l) \quad (4)$$

By applying integration by parts to the first term in the right-hand side of Equation 4 we obtain:

$$E[U] = \frac{1}{T_2 - T_1} \int_{T_1}^{T_2} dl\, G(l) \quad (5)$$

Thus, expected loss of a tranche can be computed as the average of the complementary cumulative distribution of loss of the underlying portfolio between the tranche bounds – the result remarkably similar to the one given by Equation 1.

Equation 5 has a very appealing interpretation. Let us imagine an ITT centred at underlying portfolio loss level $l$. We can think of it as of a loan with probability of default $G(l)$ and deterministic LGD of 100%. The expected loss of this tranche is $G(l)$, being the product of default probability and expected LGD. Therefore, expected loss of a finite tranche is just the average of expected losses of all ITTs located between the finite tranche boundaries. This result is very intuitive if one thinks of a finite tranche as an infinite portfolio of ITTs.

Under certain assumptions, we can explore the similarity between ITTs and loans further. For the underlying portfolio of loans, we assume that individual obligors default with probability $p$ if their asset values fall below their liabilities. The average correlation between the individual normally distributed asset returns, $\rho_A$, describes their common dependence upon one normally distributed systematic risk factor $Y$ (see Gordy, 2001 or Wilde, 2001 for a comprehensive discussion on systematic risk factors). We assume stochastic, independent, identically distributed LGDs with expected value of $\mu$. Let us also assume that the underlying portfolio is large enough to be considered asymptotically fine-grained. This is the setup of Vasicek's model, whose asymptotic complementary loss distribution is well-known (Vasicek, 1991):

$$G(l) = \begin{cases} N\left(\dfrac{N^{-1}(p) - \sqrt{1-\rho_A}\, N^{-1}(l/\mu)}{\sqrt{\rho_A}}\right) & \text{if } l < \mu \\ 0 & \text{otherwise} \end{cases} \qquad (6)$$

$K_{IRB}$ then directly follows from Equation 6:

$$K_{IRB} = \mu N\left(\frac{N^{-1}(p) + \sqrt{\rho_A}\, N^{-1}(q)}{\sqrt{1-\rho_A}}\right) \qquad (7)$$

An ITT centred at loss level $l$ has a natural property of a Merton-style model that it defaults whenever a continuous variable (loss of the underlying portfolio) crosses a threshold (loss level $l$). Since the underlying portfolio is asymptotically fine-grained, its loss is a deterministic monotonic function of the risk factor $Y$. Therefore, default happens with probability $G(l)$ when a normally distributed variable (ie, $Y$) crosses a threshold, which suggests the use of Vasicek's model for the ITT capital calculation.

Some care should be taken in this use of Vasicek's model. We assume that a tranche (and, therefore, an ITT) is kept by a financial institution as a part of a large, diversified portfolio of assets. We will call this portfolio super-portfolio to avoid confusion with the underlying portfolio of loans. We also assume that losses of this super-portfolio are driven by another standardised normally distributed single risk factor, $Z$. To take advantage of Vasicek's model, we further assume that the super-portfolio is asymptotically fine-grained and that financial institution's exposure to the tranche is small compared to the total exposure in the super-portfolio.[2] When we treat an ITT as a part of the super-portfolio, the systematic risk factor of the underlying portfolio, $Y$, will play the role of the standardised individual asset return in this setup. We will assume linear dependence between $Y$ and $Z$ given by:

$$Y = \sqrt{\rho_Y}\, Z + \sqrt{1-\rho_Y}\, \varepsilon \qquad (8)$$

where the correlation between risk factor $Y$ and risk factor $Z$ is given by $\sqrt{\rho_Y}$, and $\varepsilon$ is independent of $Z$. Parameter $\rho_Y$ itself is analogous to the asset return correlation in conventional Vasicek's model. But in contrast to obligor asset return, which has a lot of idiosyncratic risk, the variable that triggers default of a single ITT represents an already diversified portfolio. Therefore, this analog of asset return correlation must be much higher than in a conventional application of Vasicek's model.

Taking into account these considerations, we can state that the capital for an ITT centred at level $l$, equals its probability of default conditional upon the risk factor $Z$ being equal to its $(1 - q)$-percentile. Therefore, we can use Vasicek's formula with $G(l)$ as the default probability and write the capital for this ITT as

$$h_{s-p}(l, \rho_Y) = N\left(\frac{N^{-1}[G(l)] + \sqrt{\rho_Y}\, N^{-1}(q)}{\sqrt{1-\rho_Y}}\right) \qquad (9)$$

where $s - p$ stands for super-portfolio, $N(\cdot)$ denotes the cumulative normal distribution, and $N^{-1}(\cdot)$ denotes its inverse. The conditional default probability is nothing but the complementary loss distribution of the underlying portfolio conditional on the risk factor $Z$ being equal to its $(1 - q)$-percentile, $N^{-1}(1 - q)$.[3]

Now, having established the capital for an ITT, we will use it to determine the capital for a tranche with arbitrary bounds $T_1$ and $T_2$. We can divide the interval between $T_1$ and $T_2$ into an infinitely large set of infinitesimally thin sub-intervals and think of the finite tranche as an infinitely large set of ITTs defined on these sub-intervals. Since the super-portfolio is asymptotically fine-grained and it is driven by only one systematic risk factor (risk factor Y, which drives the losses in the underlying pool, is just another normalised asset return for the super-portfolio), the capital for any of its parts equals the weighted sum of capitals for individual assets forming this part (Gordy, 2001). Applied to a finite tranche, this statement is equivalent to

$$K_{s-p} = \frac{1}{T_2 - T_1} \int_{T_1}^{T_2} dl\, h_{s-p}(l, \rho_Y) \quad (10)$$

Thus, the capital for a finite tranche in the context of large super-portfolio, $K_{s-p}$, can be computed by applying Vasicek's model to a portfolio of equally weighted loans with the same deterministic 100% LGD, but different default probabilities $G(l)$. The assumed "asset return" correlation should be much higher (90% is a reasonable value) than in a typical application of Vasicek's model to a portfolio of corporate loans (20% used in Basel, 2001a). The capital given by Equation 10 has the appealing form of Equation 1. Moreover, the stand-alone case described by Equation 1 is just a special case of Equation 10 with $\rho_Y = 100\%$.

The integral in Equation 10 can be evaluated analytically. The result is

$$K_{s-p} = \frac{H(T_2) - H(T_1)}{T_2 - T_1} \quad (11)$$

with

$$H(T) = \begin{cases} \mu N_2\left(N^{-1}\left(\frac{T}{\mu}\right), \frac{N^{-1}(p) + \sqrt{\rho_A \rho_Y}\, N^{-1}(q)}{\sqrt{1-\rho_A\rho_Y}}, \sqrt{\frac{1-\rho_A}{1-\rho_A\rho_Y}}\right) & \text{if } T < \mu \\ \mu N\left(\frac{N^{-1}(p) + \sqrt{\rho_A\rho_Y}\, N^{-1}(q)}{\sqrt{1-\rho_A\rho_Y}}\right) & \text{otherwise} \end{cases} \quad (12)$$

where $N_2(\cdot,\cdot,\cdot)$ is the bivariate cumulative normal distribution function. Its numerical evaluation is discussed in great detail in Vasicek (1998).

The proposed model results in a simple analytical expression for the securitisation tranche capital. But since this expression has been derived under certain assumptions, one might wonder about the applicability of the model. Let us summarise these assumptions. We have assumed that:

a. the portfolio of loans underlying the securitisation tranche is asymptotically fine-grained;
b. this portfolio of loans is driven by a single systematic risk factor Y;
c. the super-portfolio where the tranche is held is asymptotically fine-grained;
d. the super-portfolio is driven by another single systematic risk factor Z; and
e. investor's exposure to the tranche is small compared to total exposure in the super-portfolio.

Is there any justification for these assumptions and how restrictive are they?

Assumption (a) certainly holds for any underlying pool of consumer loans (which constitute the vast majority of securitisations). For corporate underlying portfolios, the applicability of assumption (a) depends on the portfolio size and the average grade (probability of default) of loans in the portfolio. A good indicator of applicability of assumption (a) will be the ratio of the granularity adjustment (can be found in Pykhtin and Dev, 2002) to $K_{IRB}$. If this ratio does not exceed a few per cent, assumption (a) is reasonable. As a rule of thumb, the minimum portfolio size will be a few hundred loans for non-investment grades, and a few thousand loans for investment grades.

Strictly speaking, assumption (b) never holds, because there is definitely more than one geographically and industry-defined systematic risk factors. Replacing them by only one risk factor is certainly an approximation. However, this approximation is extensively used because it is extremely difficult to come up with a reliable correlation matrix for the risk factors due to lack of data, while an estimate of an average single correlation can be obtained (eg, in Gordy 2000). Besides, assumption (b) allows for an analytical solution for the capital. Coupled with assumption (a), it gains another property: the marginal capital for a loan becomes independent of the composition of the portfolio. Since regulatory rules must be portfolio-invariant, this property is particularly valuable for regulators (Vasicek's model is used in Basel, 2001a).

Assumption (c) holds for large, well-diversified banks. Here we assume that a tranche is held by an investor in a large diversified portfolio of loans and other tranches (super-portfolio, assumption (c)). Losses of the underlying pool are strongly (but not perfectly) correlated with the losses in the super-portfolio. To account for this correlation, it is enough assume that losses of the super-portfolio are driven by another single risk factor, Z. In reality, of course, there are more than one risk factors driving losses in the super-portfolio. But assumption (d) can be motivated by repeating the motivation for assumption (b) above.

Assumption (e) is necessary for treating a tranche as another asset in the super-portfolio in one-factor framework. With assumption (e), the super-portfolio remains fine-grained even with the tranche included, and application of one-factor Vasicek's model is valid. Since investor's exposure to the tranche typically does not exceed a few per cent of its total exposure, assumption (e) is reasonable for most cases.

In the next section, we compare model predictions with Basel (2001b). The comparisons are true under the above assumptions, in particular, that of asymptotically fine-grained underlying portfolio.

## Comparison of model results with Basel

In all examples that follow, we will consider the underlying portfolio with the parameters $p = 1.2\%$, $\mu = 40\%$, and $\rho_A = 20\%$.[4] To facilitate comparisons with Basel, we assume the same confidence level $q = 99.5\%$ for all tranches as well as for the underlying portfolio. Equation 7 yields $K_{IRB} = 4.33\%$ for this portfolio. The solid line in Figure 2 shows the complementary loss distribution of the underlying portfolio, $G(l)$, computed according to Equation 6. According to Equation 5, $G(l)$ also serves as the marginal expected loss for tranches. In Figure 2, we also show marginal capital charge given by Equation 9 for three different values of $\rho_Y$. The dashed curve represents the stand-alone case ($\rho_Y = 100\%$), the dash-dotted curve corresponds to $\rho_Y = 98\%$, the dash-double-dotted curve corresponds to $\rho_Y = 90\%$. The total capital allocated for all tranches will be different for different correlation assumptions, being always equal to $K_{IRB}$ for the case of $\rho_Y = 100\%$ and less than $K_{IRB}$ for all other values of $\rho_Y$. The lower the value of $\rho_Y$, the higher the benefit of extra diversification and the lower the total capital. We can think of this diversification benefit in terms of Basel's relative premiums $\beta$ being negative.[5]

In Table 1, we show how our model allocates capital for three different securitisation schemes: a single tranche, which takes all losses, two tranches separated by $K_{IRB}$, and three tranches with boundaries at 3% (below $K_{IRB}$) and 6% (above $K_{IRB}$). For comparison, we also show how Basel's supervisory formula would allocate capital for these tranches for two values of assumed premium $\beta$. The case of a single tranche shows the total allocation of capital, which is simply $(1 + \beta)K_{IRB}$. In our model, values of $\beta$ are implied by assumed values of $\rho_Y$ and are shown in Table 1 (eg, $\rho_Y = 90\%$ implies $\beta = -8.34\%$). The two-tranche securitisation scheme shows what part of the total capital is allocated for tranches below and above $K_{IRB}$. Basel's supervisory formula always allocates $K_{IRB}$ to the first-loss position, and $\beta K_{IRB}$ to the senior tranche.[6] In our model, the total capital allocated for both tranches is always less than $K_{IRB}$, but nevertheless, non-zero capital is always allocated for the senior tranche.

**2. Marginal capital and expected loss**

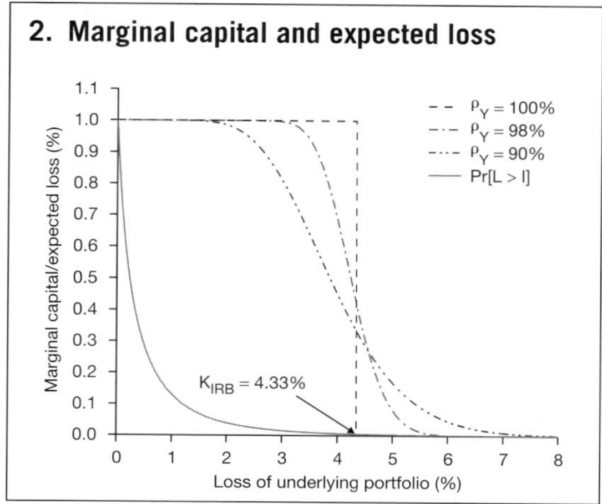


The three-tranche securitisation scheme presents a more realistic case with $K_{IRB}$ being in the middle of the mezzanine tranche. To make a meaningful comparison with Basel's supervisory formula, we need some rule of choosing correlation $\rho_Y$ to match any given Basel's premium $\beta$. We think that it is appropriate to choose $\rho_Y$ in such a way that the capital for all tranches above $K_{IRB}$, allocated by our model, would be the same as the one allocated by the supervisory formula. From the two-tranche part of Table 1, we can see that this rule approximately holds for $\rho_Y = 90\%$ (0.31% capital) and $\beta = 8\%$ (0.36% capital), and we can compare these cases for the three-tranche setup. This comparison leads to a conclusion that, under the assumptions listed in the preceding sections, Basel's supervisory formula overestimates the risk of mezzanine tranches and underestimates the risk of senior tranches.[7] This conclusion holds true for any asymptotically fine-grained underlying portfolio (and not just for this example), as long as the total capital above $K_{IRB}$ is the same under our model and the supervisory formula.[8]

In Basel's ABS scaling factors' approach, capital is assigned to tranches on the basis of their external rating. This is done by scaling the 50% LGD capital assigned to corporate loans by the foundation

IRB formula (see Basel, 2001a). For the case of Moody's ratings, the scaling factors are given in Table 1 on page 7 of Basel (2001b). To make our comparison with Basel (2001b) unambiguous, we will consider only Moody's ratings in this chapter. Moody's assigns ratings based on its opinion on the unconditional expected loss associated with a given tranche (Moody's, 2000).[9] For each tranche in Table 1, we have computed expected loss according to Equation 5, and then assigned a Moody's rating by finding the nearest one-year expected loss from Table 2 in Moody's (2000). Having assigned the rating, we listed the capital implied by this rating in Basel's ABS scaling factors approach (Table 1 in Basel, 2001b). Comparing these capital factors with the ones generated by our model, one can conclude that they fail to adequately reflect the risk of mezzanine and senior tranches. Generally, Basel's ABS scaling factors approach severely overestimates the risk of senior tranches (as in both the two- and three-tranche schemes in Table 1). For mezzanine tranches, the ABS scaling factors approach tends to underestimate the risk for lower ratings (as in the three-tranche scheme in Table 1) and overestimate it for higher ratings, as we will soon see in Table 2. Moreover, the two Basel approaches are not internally consistent between themselves.

A legitimate question to ask is whether it is generally possible to obtain a one-to-one relation between expected loss of a tranche (ie, its rating) and the capital. For an ITT centred at some loss level $l$, such a relation does exist: the capital $h_{s-p}(l, \rho_Y)$ is indeed a unique function of expected loss $G(l)$ according to Equation 9. Moreover, from Equation 9 it is clear that this relation is invariant with respect to the parameters of the underlying portfolio. For a tranche of a finite size, the capital will be portfolio dependent. This dependence increases with the tranche size, and is quite strong for senior tranches. For a given underlying portfolio, the expected loss of a tranche with one of the bounds fixed (ie, first-loss positions with $T_1 = 0\%$ or senior tranches with $T_2 = 100\%$), uniquely determines the capital. The capital for a mezzanine tranche, whose bounds can be changed without affecting expected loss, may additionally depend on the tranche size. Formally, it is not difficult to show that the capital for a mezzanine tranche is a unique function of expected loss if and only if the marginal capital $h_{s-p}(l, \rho_Y)$ is a linear function of marginal expected loss $G(l)$. Looking at Equation 9, we can clearly see that this is not the case.

The lack of uniqueness between the expected loss and the capital for mezzanine tranches can be easily shown. One can imagine an ITT at some loss

**Table 1. Comparison of capital allocation between proposed model and Basel**

| Tranche limits (%) | Expected loss (%) | Moody's rating | Capital (%) | | | | | |
|---|---|---|---|---|---|---|---|---|
| | | | Proposed model | | Stand-alone | Basel: supervisory formula | | Basel: ABS scaling factors |
| | | | $\rho = 90.0\%$ $\beta = -8.34\%$ | $\rho = 98.0\%$ $\beta = -1.68\%$ | $\beta = 0\%$ | $\beta = 8\%$ | $\beta = 20\%$ | |
| 0–100 | 0.48 | Ba1 | 3.97 | 4.26 | 4.33 | 4.68 | 5.20 | 16.00 |
| 0–4.33 | 10.92 | Caa | 84.91 | 94.31 | 100.00 | 100.00 | 100.00 | 100.00 |
| 4.33–100 | 0.0073 | A2 | 0.31 | 0.18 | 0.00 | 0.36 | 0.91 | 1.52 |
| Total | 0.48 | – | 3.97 | 4.26 | 4.33 | 4.68 | 5.20 | 5.78 |
| 0–3 | 15.37 | Caa | 97.16 | 99.99 | 100.00 | 100.00 | 100.00 | 100.00 |
| 3–6 | 0.56 | Ba1 | 34.18 | 41.98 | 44.40 | 55.85 | 69.07 | 16.00 |
| 6–100 | 0.0024 | Aa3 | 0.0321 | 0.0003 | 0.0000 | 0.0030 | 0.1344 | 1.1200 |
| Total | 0.48 | – | 3.97 | 4.26 | 4.33 | 4.68 | 5.20 | 4.53 |

**Table 2. Dependence of capital for a rated mezzanine tranche upon its size**

| Location of 0%-thick tranche (%) | Expected loss (%) | Moody's rating | Model capital (%), given tranche size | | | | | Basel capital: ABS SF (%) |
|---|---|---|---|---|---|---|---|---|
| | | | 0% | 1% | 2% | 3% | 4% | |
| 3.00 | 1.51 | Ba3 | 80.8 | 78.7 | 73.0 | 65.3 | 57.7 | 41.8 |
| 6.50 | 0.104 | Baa2 | 2.23 | 2.33 | 2.58 | 2.96 | 3.38 | 5.84 |

level $l_0$ with the expected loss $G(l_0)$. The capital for this ITT will be given by $h_{s-p}(l,\rho_Y)$. Then, we can always choose the bounds $T_1 < l_0$ and $T_2 > l_0$ in such a way that the expected loss will be the same, ie, $G(l_0)$. The capital will be given by Equation 10 and will not be equal to $h_{s-p}(l_0,\rho_Y)$ generally: it may increase or decrease depending on where $l_0$ is located with respect to $K_{IRB}$. For values of $l_0$ significantly below $K_{IRB}$, the capital decreases as a function of the tranche size, while for values significantly above $K_{IRB}$ it increases. In Table 2, we show how the capital for a mezzanine tranche changes with the tranche size for two values of $l_0$: 3% (below $K_{IRB}$) and 6.5% (above $K_{IRB}$) assuming $\rho_Y = 90\%$.[10] The expected loss for these two cases very closely corresponds to Moody's Ba3 and Baa2 ratings, respectively, according to Table 2 in Moody's (2000). We used these ratings to show the capital implied by them in Basel's ABS scaling factors approach (Table 1 in Basel, 2001b).

## Conclusion

In its continuing efforts to prepare Basel II, the Basel Committee on Banking Supervision presented a working paper on capital allocation rules for securitisation tranches (Basel, 2001b). Neither of Basel's proposed approaches to securitisation, however, seem to be derived from such a general and conceptually sound framework as their approach to corporate and consumer loans (Basel, 2001a).

In this chapter we have presented a capital allocation model for securitisation tranches that might serve as the basis for such a framework. The model is purely analytical and does not require any simulations. Effectively, we use Vasicek's model (the same as the asymptotic version of default-mode one-factor CreditMetrics model), which is the core of Basel (2001a), at two levels. First, we use it in a conventional manner to obtain the loss distribution of the underlying portfolio of loans. Then, we have observed that any securitisation tranche can be viewed as an infinite portfolio of all ITTs located between its bounds. We have shown that ITTs behave the same way as loans with deterministic 100% LGD. We have assumed that all the ITTs are parts of a large super-portfolio of assets, and have applied the Vasicek model again. Since the underlying portfolio is already highly diversified, much higher "asset correlation" (at the level of 90%) is necessary to obtain the capital for a tranche. We would like to emphasise that it is not appropriate to apply Vasicek's model to a tranche of a finite size, assuming any single "probability of default" (such as the probability of the tranche being hit by the underlying losses). Instead, Vasicek's model should be applied to individual ITTs composing the tranche and each having its own "probability of default."

For typical securitisation examples, we compared capital factors calculated with the help of the proposed model, with the ones implied by the two Basel approaches. We have shown that for asymptotically fine-grained underlying portfolio, Basel's supervisory formula overestimates the risk of mezzanine tranches and underestimates the risk of senior tranches. We have also shown that for asymptotically fine-grained underlying portfolio, Basel's ABS scaling factors approach, overestimates the risk of senior tranches and for mezzanine tranches, the ABS scaling factors approach tends to underestimate the risk for lower ratings and overestimate it for higher ratings.

1 *It assumed that capital for any tranche is computed at the same confidence level as* $K_{IRB}$.

2 *Specifically, we assume that (a) the systematic factor* $\varepsilon$ *has no material influence on the performance of the super-portfolio other than through its influence on the ABS tranche, and (b) that the size of the tranche is small relative to the super-portfolio. These assumptions are necessary for the super-portfolio to remain fine-grained and to be driven by a single systematic risk factor, after including the tranche. It effectively reduces our original two-factor set-up to the one-factor framework of Vasicek's model.*

3 *In Equation 9, we used the relation* $N^{-1}(1 - q) = -N^{-1}(q)$, *which comes from the symmetry of normal distribution.*

4 *Default probability for loans in the underlying pool corresponds to Ba Moody's rating on average. By requiring that the granularity adjustment must be under 3% of* $K_{IRB}$, *we find that the model is applicable to portfolios larger than 500 loans.*

5 *For the sake of exposition, we assume that everybody who owns tranches in the underlying pool holds them in similar super-portfolios of assets (ie, we assume the same* $\rho_Y$ *for all tranches). In reality, super-portfolios of different investors may have different correlations with the underlying portfolio. Particularly, for originators (who usually hold the first-loss position), appropriate* $\rho_Y$ *may be 100%, as it is assumed in Basel (2001b).*

6 *Table 1 shows capital as a fraction of the tranche size. Therefore, the capital allocated by Basel supervisory formula below* $K_{IRB}$ *is listed in Table 1 as 100% and the capital above* $K_{IRB}$ *as* $\beta K_{IRB}/(1 - K_{IRB})$.

7 *Perhaps this is the reason Basel's supervisory formula has a floor for the level of capital for every tranche.*

8 *The supervisory formula can be significantly improved just by dividing it by 2.5. Then, the exponential tail will start with the value of 0.4 at* $K_{IRB}$ *instead of 1, and parameter* $d$ *will be approximately 2.5 times as small for the same premium* $b$.

*Smaller* d *means "heavier" tail, so that more capital will be allocated for senior tranches.*

9 *Other rating agencies use tranche's "probability of default,"* $G(T_1)$, *as the basis for their ratings. However, we believe that* $G(T_1)$ *does not represent a tranche's risk adequately. For example, this approach would give the same rating to a mezzanine and a senior tranche with the same lower bound. Clearly, the mezzanine tranche has higher potential for loss, and therefore is riskier. Thus the method of rating, based on tranche "probability of default," is inadequate to capture the true risk and therefore, capital should not be assigned on the basis of such ratings.*

10 *The dependence is stronger for higher correlation values.*


## BIBLIOGRAPHY

**Basel Committee on Banking Supervision,** 2001a, *The Internal Ratings-Based Approach*, Supporting Document to the New Basel Capital Accord, January.

**Basel Committee on Banking Supervision,** 2001b, *Working Paper on the Treatment of Asset Securitisations*, Working Paper, October.

**Gordy, M.,** 2000, "A Comparative Anatomy of Credit Risk Models", *Journal of Banking and Finance*, 24, pp. 119–49.

**Gordy, M.,** 2001, *A Risk-Factor Model Foundation for Ratings-Based Bank Capital Rules*, Working Paper, February.

**Moody's Investors Service,** 2000, *The Lognormal Method Applied to ABS Analysis*, Special Report, International Structured Finance, July.

**Pykhtin, M., and A. Dev,** 2002, "Analytical Approach to Credit Risk Modeling", *Risk*, March, pp. S26–S32.

**Vasicek, O.,** 1991, *Limiting Loan Loss Probability Distribution*, KMV Corporation.

**Vasicek, O.,** 1998, "A Series Expansion for the Bivariate Normal Integral", *Journal of Computational Finance*, 1(4), Summer.

**Wilde, T.,** 2001, "IRB Approach Explained", *Risk*, May, pp. 87–90.

33

# Coarse-grained CDOs

**Michael Pykhtin and Ashish Dev**

Keycorp

*While analytical models of credit portfolio risk using conditional independence have been one of the most promising areas of recent research, they often involve granularity assumptions that are violated in CDO reference portfolios. Here, Michael Pykhtin and Ashish Dev lift the usual fine-grained portfolio restriction to calculate CDO loss distributions for coarse-grained reference portfolios. Interestingly, they show that senior tranches are particularly sensitive to the level of granularity.*

In a recent article (Pykhtin and Dev, 2002b), we presented an analytical model that described the credit risk of a securitisation tranche kept by an investor in a portfolio and allocated capital accordingly. The model is based on several key assumptions:

a. the portfolio of loans underlying the securitisation tranche is asymptotically fine-grained;
b. this portfolio of loans is driven by a single systematic risk factor;
c. the investor's portfolio where the tranche is held is asymptotically fine-grained;
d. the investor's portfolio is driven by another single systematic risk factor; and
e. the investor's exposure to the tranche is small compared with the total exposure in its portfolio.

However, while assumptions (b) to (e) are reasonable for most cases, assumption (a) may not hold, depending on the properties of the underlying portfolio. The underlying portfolio in a typical consumer loan securitisation has such a large number of loans (with no significant individual exposures) that it can be safely regarded as asymptotically fine-grained. Therefore, the model is appropriate for consumer asset-backed securities (ABSs). On the other hand, when the underlying portfolio is composed of large corporate loans, it may contain only tens or hundreds of such loans. This is certainly not enough for an investment-grade portfolio to be considered fine-grained (see Gordy, 2001, for details). It is desirable to have a model whose applicability would not be restricted by assumption (a) and can therefore be used for credit risk in tranches of collateralised debt obligations (CDOs).

In this chapter, we present a new version of our model that does not rely on the underlying portfolio being fine-grained. There is, however, a price to pay for this generalisation: we have to assume that the underlying portfolio is homogeneous (that is, all the loans in the portfolio are characterised by the same set of parameters).

The chapter is organised as follows. In the next section, we briefly outline the set-up of our model along with those general results that are not tied to the fine-granularity of the underlying portfolio. After that, we derive new results for a homogeneous portfolio with an arbitrary number of loans. These new results converge to their fine-granularity versions from Pykhtin and Dev (2002b) as the number of loans in the underlying portfolio increases. We then demonstrate model predictions on investment-grade and non-investment-grade homogeneous portfolios with different numbers of loans.

## Model: general specification

We assume that securitisation is based on an underlying portfolio of loans, whose loss rate (due to loan defaults) at a time horizon, $L$, is distributed according to some probability distribution. We will denote the probability that the portfolio loss rate will exceed level $l$ by $G(l)$. The default-mode capital rate for the underlying portfolio on a stand-alone basis, $K_{s-a}$, is defined as a $q$-percentile of this distribution and, therefore, must satisfy the relation $G(K_{s-a}) = 1 - q$.

We assume that a securitisation tranche with the lower bound $T_1$ and upper bound $T_2$ is defined on this portfolio. The expected loss rate for this tranche, $U(T_1, T_2)$, is given by:

$$U(T_1, T_2) = \frac{1}{T_2 - T_1} \int_{T_1}^{T_2} dl\, G(l) \tag{1}$$

Equation 1 can be interpreted as the expected loss rate of an infinite portfolio of infinitesimally thin tranches (ITTs) centred at underlying portfolio loss levels $l$. An ITT is much easier to handle than a tranche of a finite size because we can think of it as a loan with probability of default $G(l)$ and deterministic loss-given default (LGD) of 100% (and, therefore, with an expected loss rate of $G(l)$).

For the underlying portfolio, we assume that it consists of $M$ identical loans, each having probability of default $p$.[1] Following Vasicek (1987), we introduce a set of continuous random variables $\{X_i\}_{i=1}^{M}$ that describe the financial well-being of a given borrower at the time horizon. These variables have standard normal distribution and trigger defaults whenever $X_i < N^{-1}(p)$ (where $N^{-1}(\cdot)$ is the function inverse to cumulative standard normal distribution). They can be interpreted as standardised returns on a borrower's assets and written as:

$$X_i = \sqrt{\rho_A}\, Y + \sqrt{1-\rho_A}\, \xi_i \tag{2}$$

where $Y$ is a standardised normally distributed systematic risk factor that drives losses in the underlying portfolio, $\xi_i$ are independent standardised normally distributed random variables that describe the individual fortunes of borrowers, and $\rho_A$ is the asset correlation coefficient. We assume that the LGDs are independent (both between themselves and from asset returns) normally distributed random variables with mean $\mu$ and standard deviation $\sigma$.[2]

Next, we assume that the tranche is held by an investor in a large, diversified portfolio of assets. We will call this portfolio the "super-portfolio" to avoid confusion with the underlying portfolio of loans and will assume that the super-portfolio is asymptotically fine-grained (that is, any single exposure in the super-portfolio is negligible compared with the total exposure). We also assume that the losses of this super-portfolio are driven by a single standardised (that is, with mean zero and variance one) normally distributed risk factor $Z$. To find capital for the tranche, we need to specify the relationship between the risk factors $Y$ (driving losses in the underlying portfolio) and $Z$ (driving losses in the super-portfolio). As in Pykhtin and Dev (2002b), we assume a linear form for this relation:

$$Y = \sqrt{\rho_Y}\, Z + \sqrt{1-\rho_Y}\, \varepsilon \tag{3}$$

where $G(l|z_{1-q})$ is a standard normal variable independent of $Z$. Correlation between the risk factors $Y$ (driving losses in the underlying portfolio) and $Z$ (driving losses in the super-portfolio) is given by $\sqrt{\rho_Y}$, as can be seen immediately from Equation 3.

We further assume that the investor's exposure to the tranche is small compared with its total exposure in the super-portfolio.[3] This assumption allows us to treat the tranche as just another asset in the fine-grained super-portfolio (that is, the super-portfolio remains fine-grained after inclusion of the tranche) driven by risk factor $Z$. It has been shown by Gordy (2001) and others in the context of a one-factor model that capital for a fine-grained portfolio asymptotically converges to systematic risk capital. Systematic risk capital for the super-portfolio is given by its expected loss conditional on risk factor $Z$ being equal to its $(1 - q)$-percentile $z_{1-q} = -N^{-1}(q)$. Since expectations are additive, the tranche contribution to the total systematic capital does not depend on the composition of the super-portfolio and is given by the tranche expected loss conditional on $Z = z_{1-q}$:

$$K_{TR}(T_1, T_2) = \frac{1}{T_2 - T_1} \int_{T_1}^{T_2} dl\, G\left(l \middle| z_{1-q}\right) \tag{4}$$

where $G(l|z_{1-q})$ denotes the probability that, conditionally on $Z = z_{1-q}$, the loss rate in the underlying portfolio will exceed level $l$. As with the expected loss rate in Equation 1, Equation 4 can be interpreted as the capital rate of an infinite portfolio of ITTs centred at underlying portfolio loss levels $l$. The analogy between ITTs and loans is working again: the capital rate for an ITT is given by the product of its LGD of 100% and conditional "probability of default", $G(l|z_{1-q})$.

In Pykhtin and Dev (2002b), we made an extra assumption that the underlying portfolio is asymptotically fine-grained, and showed that it is appropriate to use Vasicek's formula (with $\rho_Y$ as asset correlation) for the ITT's conditional "probability of default" in Equation 4. While this assumption is appropriate for many cases (such as securitisations of consumer portfolios), there are securitisations based on a small number of loans (such as CDOs) when the underlying portfolio is far from being fine-grained. In the next section, we present a model extension for underlying portfolios with an arbitrary number of loans.[4]

## Model: granular case

In Pykhtin and Dev (2002a), we showed that the complementary loss distribution for a homogeneous portfolio is given by:

$$G(l) = 1 - \int_{-\infty}^{\infty} dy\, n(y) \sum_{m=0}^{M} \binom{M}{m} [\hat{p}(y)]^m [1-\hat{p}(y)]^{M-m} N[x_m(l)] \tag{5}$$

where $n(\cdot)$ is the probability density of the standard normal distribution, $N(\cdot)$ is the cumulative standard normal distribution function, $m$ denotes number of defaults in the portfolio, $\hat{p}(Y)$ is the probability of default conditional on risk factor $Y$ and given by:

$$\hat{p}(Y) = N\left(\frac{N^{-1}(p) - \sqrt{\rho_A}\,Y}{\sqrt{1-\rho_A}}\right) \tag{6}$$

and:

$$x_m(l) = \frac{(lM/m) - \mu}{\left(\sigma/\sqrt{m}\right)} \tag{7}$$

The capital rate for the underlying portfolio on the stand-alone basis, $K^M_{s-a}$, will depend on the number of loans in the portfolio $M$. This capital can be found directly from Equation 5 by solving numerically $G(K^M_{s-a}) = 1 - q$. The capital rate for a portfolio with a finite number of loans $M$ can also be viewed as the sum of the capital rate for the infinite portfolio, $K^{\infty}_{s-a}$, given by:

$$K^{\infty}_{s-a} = \mu N\left[\frac{N^{-1}(p) + \sqrt{\rho_A}\,N^{-1}(q)}{\sqrt{1-\rho_A}}\right] \tag{8}$$

and the granularity adjustment,[5] which is inversely proportional to $M$ (see Gordy, 2001, for details). An elegant method of estimating the granularity adjustment analytically is reported in Wilde (2001), and a very accurate closed-form approximation based on this method is available in Pykhtin and Dev (2002a).

The expected loss rate for the tranche can be found by substituting Equation 5 into Equation 1. Integration over loss level $l$ can be performed analytically:[6]

$$U(T_1,T_2) = 1 - \int_{-\infty}^{\infty} dy\, n(y) \sum_{m=0}^{M} \binom{M}{m} [\hat{p}(y)]^m [1-\hat{p}(y)]^{M-m} \frac{h_m(T_2) - h_m(T_1)}{T_2 - T_1} \tag{9}$$

with $h_m(T)$ defined as:

$$h_m(T) = \frac{m}{M}\frac{\sigma}{\sqrt{m}}\left(x_m(T)N[x_m(T)] + n[x_m(T)]\right) \tag{10}$$

The right-hand side of Equation 9 (as well as of Equation 5) can easily be evaluated numerically. Since the standard normal density $n(\varepsilon)$ goes to zero very fast, infinite limits in the integral can be safely replaced by finite ones.[7] After approximating the integral by a discrete sum, the calculation reduces to the evaluation of a double sum, which can be quickly performed even on a mid-level PC.[8] The problem of large binomial coefficients for large $M$ can easily be avoided by computing binomial probabilities $P^M_m(p)$ recursively according to:

$$P^M_m(p) = \frac{M-m+1}{m}\frac{p}{1-p}P^M_{m-1}(p)$$

This is computationally costless since a sum over $m$ is computed anyway.

Since the capital rate for a tranche is just the conditional expected loss rate, its calculation can be done similarly. The ITT conditional "probability of default" can be written as:

$$G\left(l \middle| z_{1-q}\right) = \Pr\left[L > l \middle| z_{1-q}\right] = E\left(\Pr\left[L > l \middle| z_{1-q}; \varepsilon\right] \middle| z_{1-q}\right) \tag{11}$$

The probability inside the expectation in Equation 11 is conditional on both $Z$ and $\varepsilon$. This conditioning makes defaults in the underlying portfolio independent, with the probability of default $\tilde{p}(z_{1-q}, \varepsilon)$ given by:

$$\tilde{p}(z_{1-q},\varepsilon) = N\left(\frac{N^{-1}[\hat{p}(z_{1-q})] - \sqrt{\rho_\varepsilon}\,\varepsilon}{\sqrt{1-\rho_\varepsilon}}\right) \tag{12}$$

where:

$$\rho_\varepsilon = \frac{\rho_A(1-\rho_Y)}{1-\rho_A\rho_Y} \tag{13}$$

and $\hat{p}(Z)$ is probability of default conditional on $Z$:

$$\hat{p}(Z) = N\left(\frac{N^{-1}(p) - \sqrt{\rho_A\rho_Y}\,Z}{\sqrt{1-\rho_A\rho_Y}}\right) \tag{14}$$

Taking this conditional independence into account, one can easily find that the cumulative probability distribution of losses in the underlying portfolio, conditional on both Z and $\varepsilon$, will be given by the integrand of Equation 5, with $\hat{p}(y)$ being replaced by $\tilde{p}(z_{1-q}, \varepsilon)$ as the conditional default probability in the binomial distribution:[9]

$$\Pr\left[L > l \middle| z_{1-q}; \varepsilon\right] = 1 - \sum_{m=0}^{M} \binom{M}{m} \left[\tilde{p}(z_{1-q}, \varepsilon)\right]^{m} \left[1 - \tilde{p}(z_{1-q}, \varepsilon)\right]^{M-m} N\left[x_m(l)\right] \tag{15}$$

Substituting Equation 15 into Equation 11 and spelling out the conditional expectation, we obtain:

$$G\left(l \middle| z_{1-q}\right) = 1 - \int_{-\infty}^{\infty} d\varepsilon\, n(\varepsilon) \sum_{m=0}^{M} \binom{M}{m} [\tilde{p}(z_{1-q}, \varepsilon)]^{m} [1 - \tilde{p}(z_{1-q}, \varepsilon)]^{M-m} N[x_m(l)] \tag{16}$$

Substitution of Equation 16 into Equation 4 yields:

$$K_{TR}(T_1, T_2) = 1 - \int_{-\infty}^{\infty} d\varepsilon\, n(\varepsilon) \sum_{m=0}^{M} \binom{M}{m} [\tilde{p}(z_{1-q}, \varepsilon)]^{m} [1 - \tilde{p}(z_{1-q}, \varepsilon)]^{M-m} \times \frac{h_m(T_2) - h_m(T_1)}{T_2 - T_1} \tag{17}$$

where $h_m(T)$ is defined by Equation 10. Numerical calculation of the tranche capital rate can be done similarly to the calculation of tranche expected loss rate discussed above.

The capital rate for all the tranches of a securitisation scheme (assuming the same confidence level q) is given by $K_{TR}(0, 1)$. Since keeping all the tranches of a securitisation is the same as keeping the underlying portfolio, $K_{TR}(0, 1)$ should be equal to the capital rate for the underlying portfolio considered as a part of the super-portfolio. To distinguish this capital from $K_{s-a}^{M}$ (which is the capital for the underlying portfolio considered stand-alone), we will denote it as $K_{DIV}$ (where DIV stands for diversification, referring to the extra diversification the underlying portfolio receives from being part of the super-portfolio). Since the super-portfolio is asymptotically fine-grained, with the underlying portfolio being its small fraction, $K_{DIV}$ does not depend on M and is given by the expected loss rate of the underlying portfolio conditional on $Z = z_{1-q}$:

$$K_{DIV} = \mu N\left(\frac{N^{-1}(p) + \sqrt{\rho_A \rho_Y} N^{-1}(q)}{\sqrt{1 - \rho_A \rho_Y}}\right) \tag{18}$$

From examining Equation 17, one can see that $K_{TR}(0, 1)$ is exactly equal to $K_{DIV}$ only in the limit $\sigma \to 0$. The difference between $K_{TR}(0, 1)$ and $K_{DIV}$ for cases of finite $\sigma$ results from our assumption that individual LGD random variables are not bounded above or below, which technically may lead to portfolio loss rates outside the [0, 1] interval. However, such events are highly unlikely, and this difference is negligible for practically important cases.

## Examples

In the examples shown in this section, we assume the same confidence level, $q = 99.5\%$, for all tranches as well as for the underlying portfolio. The "asset correlation" parameter for securitisation tranches, $\rho_Y$, will be set at 90%.[10] The standard deviation of the LGD will be determined from the expected LGD by the formula suggested in Gordy (2001):

$$\sigma = \frac{1}{2}\sqrt{\mu(1 - \mu)}$$

We show the results for two distinct underlying portfolios, both having expected LGD $\mu = 40\%$ and asset correlation $\rho_A = 20\%$. One portfolio is investment grade, with the probability of default being $p = 0.15\%$ (we will call it portfolio A), the other is non-investment grade, with $p = 1.2\%$ (we will call it portfolio B; this is exactly the same portfolio as the one considered in Pykhtin and Dev, 2002b). In Figure 1 (for portfolio A) and 2 (for portfolio B), we show tranche marginal capital, $G(l|z_{1-q})$, as a function of loss level l, calculated according to Equation 16 for five different values of M: infinite number of loans,[11] 500 loans, 100 loans, 50 loans and 30 loans. From Figures 1 and 2, it is clear that tranche marginal capital for investment-grade portfolio A is much more sensitive to the variation of the number of underlying loans than that for non-investment-grade portfolio B. This is what

**1. Tranche marginal capital for different values of M: portfolio A (p = 0.15%)**

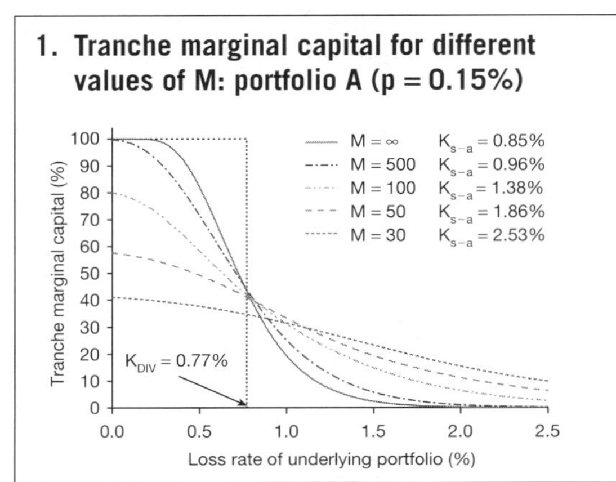

**2. Tranche marginal capital for different values of M: portfolio B (p = 1.2%)**

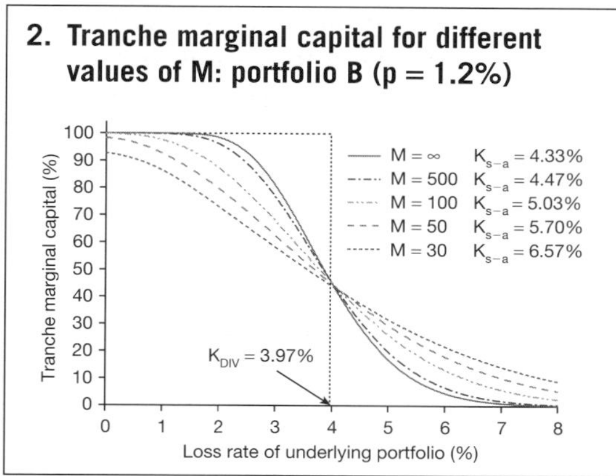


one would expect, because, at the same number of loans, the granularity risk represents a higher fraction of the total risk for portfolios with lower probability of default.

The main observation apparent from Figures 1 and 2 is that as one moves, keeping the other parameters the same, from the asymptotic case ($M = \infty$) to smaller and smaller number of loans (that is, move from one curve to another), marginal capital associated with more senior ITTs increases, while marginal capital associated with more junior ITTs decreases. This behaviour is very intuitive: lack of diversification in any portfolio leads to an increasing risk of very high losses. The crossover region, where marginal capital changes its behaviour from increasing to decreasing with the number of loans, is very localised and surprisingly well-defined. For a wide range of model parameters (not only for the two cases shown in Figures 1 and 2), the transition occurs in the vicinity of $K_{DIV}$, with marginal capital being between 40% and 50%.[12] This approximate rule breaks down only for extremely non-granular cases (such as the $M = 30$ case of portfolio A in Figure 1), when the conditional (on risk factor Z being equal to its $(1 - q)$-percentile) probability of exactly zero losses, ie, $1 - G(0|z_{1-q})$, exceeds 50%.

Since the total area under the curves in Figures 1 and 2 does not depend on the number of loans M (it is equal to $K_{DIV}$), it is clear that generally, as M is getting smaller, senior tranches ($T_2 = 1$) become riskier, while first-loss positions ($T_1 = 0$) become less risky. For mezzanine tranches, the capital associated with them can either increase or decrease depending on the location of the tranche. In most practical applications, the centre of a mezzanine tranche will be significantly above $K_{DIV}$, and the risk of such a tranche will increase with reduction of M. If the tranche centre is below $K_{DIV}$, the risk will decrease with reduction of M.

To show quantitatively how portfolio granularity will affect the risk of securitisation tranches, we define a sample securitisation scheme on portfolio A. The first-loss piece will take all the losses below $K_{DIV}$. Immediately above the first-loss piece, there will be two mezzanine tranches, each being 0.25% thick. The senior tranche will take all the losses above $K_{DIV} + 0.5\%$. In Table 1, we show the capital for the underlying portfolio and for these tranches (as a fraction of their size) at different values of M. It is clear from Table 1 that the higher the credit quality of a mezzanine tranche, the greater is its sensitivity to M. The senior tranche is the most sensitive to the portfolio granularity, and this is what one would expect, since higher loss levels are more affected by the lack of diversification than lower ones.

## Conclusion

In Pykhtin and Dev (2002b), we presented a model of credit risk in tranches of securitisations with underlying portfolios that are asymptotically fine-grained. This situation prevails in the case of typical consumer ABSs. In contrast, the underlying portfolios in CDOs consist of a relatively small number of loans. In this chapter, we present a model of credit risk in securitisation tranches with

**Table 1. Capital rates for sample securitisation tranches defined on portfolio A**

| Portfolio or tranche | Capital rate as function of number of loans (%) | | | | | |
|---|---|---|---|---|---|---|
| | ∞ | 500 | 200 | 100 | 50 | 30 |
| Portfolio A (stand-alone) | 0.85 | 0.96 | 1.12 | 1.38 | 1.86 | 2.53 |
| 0–100% | 0.77 | 0.77 | 0.77 | 0.77 | 0.77 | 0.77 |
| 0–0.77% | 84.80 | 78.60 | 72.00 | 63.80 | 51.00 | 38.40 |
| 0.77–1.02% | 29.50 | 33.10 | 35.10 | 35.80 | 36.70 | 32.90 |
| 1.02–1.27% | 11.40 | 17.10 | 21.80 | 25.50 | 28.60 | 29.10 |
| 1.27–100% | 0.01 | 0.04 | 0.07 | 0.13 | 0.22 | 0.33 |

homogeneous underlying portfolios containing an arbitrary number of loans. The model is analytical in the sense that it does not require any simulations. It does, however, require a numerical calculation of a one-dimensional integral.

By applying the model to different underlying portfolios, we have shown that granularity of the underlying portfolio has a very strong effect on the credit risk of securitisation tranches (particularly for investment-grade underlying portfolios). The less granular the portfolio, the greater is the credit risk for most mezzanine and all senior tranches. This effect increases with the seniority of a tranche.

1 *The results of this section are quite general and can be extended to non-homogeneous underlying portfolios as well.*

2 *We do not restrict LGD variables to lie in the* [0, 1] *interval. This assumption may not be intuitively appealing, but it allows for analytical tractability, while its effect on the output of the model is negligible for realistic values of the model parameters.*

3 *Strictly speaking, we are assuming that tranche exposure is negligible compared with the total exposure in the super-portfolio. Practically, the results based on this assumption are accurate if the tranche represents no more than a few per cent of the total exposure in the super-portfolio.*

4 *The results of the next section are valid only for homogeneous portfolios.*

5 *Granularity adjustment is a measure of the idiosyncratic credit risk left in a portfolio. It is defined as the difference between the* q*-percentiles of loss distribution of a real portfolio and those of a corresponding asymptotically fine-grained portfolio.*

6 *The relation* $\int dtN(t) = tN(t) + n(t)$ *has been used in the integration.*

7 *Integrating from −6 to 6 is enough for most practical purposes.*

8 *For a portfolio of 1,000 loans, typical computation time on a Pentium-III 733 MHz PC is just a few hundredths of a second.*

9 *This derivation is identical to the derivation of Equation 5, which can be found in Pykhtin and Dev (2002a).*

10 *We varied this parameter in Pykhtin and Dev (2002b), but will keep it fixed for this study.*

11 *For the infinite portfolio, we used the asymptotic result of Pykhtin and Dev (2002b).*

12 *This allows for a simplified closed-form approximation to the model, similar in form to the supervisory formula in the Basel October 2001 working paper (Basel, 2001). For loss levels above* $K_{DIV}$*, the ITT marginal capital can be crudely approximated by an exponential tail. Therefore, the approximation will take the form* $K_{ITT}(l) \approx 0.45 \exp[-\gamma(l - K_{DIV})/\mu]$*, where parameter* $\gamma$ *depends mostly on the number of loans,* M*, and probability of default,* p.

**BIBLIOGRAPHY**

**Basel Committee on Banking Supervision,** 2001, *Working Paper on the Treatment of Asset Securitisations*, Working Paper, October.

**Gordy, M.,** 2001, *A Risk-Factor Model Foundation for Ratings-Based Bank Capital Rules*, Working Paper, February.

**Pykhtin, M., and A. Dev**, 2002a, "Analytical Approach to Credit Risk Modelling", *Risk*, March, pp. S26–S32.

**Pykhtin, M., and A. Dev,** 2002b, "Credit Risk in Asset Securitisations: Analytical Model", *Risk*, May, pp. S16–S20.

**Vasicek, O.,** 1987, *Probability of Loss on Loan Portfolio*, KMV Corporation.

**Wilde, T.,** 2001, "Probing Granularity", *Risk*, August, pp. 103–6.

# 34

# Random Tranches

**Michael B. Gordy and David Jones**
US Federal Reserve Board

*How should economic or regulatory capital be allocated to tranches of securitisations? The standard Basel conditional dependence calculations are complicated in this case by non-linearity effects and complex deal dependence. Here, Michael Gordy and David Jones present an uncertainty in loss provision approach that simplifies these problems, and leads to a single economic capital formula suitable for regulatory purposes.*

This chapter sets out a simple method for estimating the credit risk economic capital associated with securitisation exposures, which are defined as credit exposures created by repackaging the cashflows from a pool of assets into various tranches or asset-backed securities. Our approach is motivated by the need for an effective and easily implemented regulatory capital rule for securitisation exposures. Consequently, it is designed to be fully compatible with the model underpinning the Basel Committee on Banking Supervision's (2001) proposed internal ratings-based (IRB) approach to regulatory capital requirements against whole loans and other bank assets. Cost-effective application to a wide variety of securitisations and participating institutions dictates that our approach be parsimonious, in the sense of using minimal information on the contents of the securitised pool and on the contractual design of the securitisation, as well as computationally tractable.

The role played by securitisations in unravelling the 1988 Capital Accord demonstrates the need for a regulatory capital regime that is based on an internally consistent approach to quantifying portfolio credit risk. Since 1988, securitisations have become a major funding vehicle and portfolio risk management tool for banks. Concurrently, however, banks have also learned to exploit inconsistencies within the current Accord, under which credit risks assumed through securitisation transactions often entail much lower regulatory capital charges than similar risks assumed through traditional loan portfolios (see Jones, 2000). Curtailing such regulatory arbitrage, while at the same time encouraging the effective hedging of credit risks through securitisation and other techniques, are primary objectives behind the Basel Committee's efforts to revamp the Accord.

The model foundation for the IRB approach is a special case of the class of credit value-at-risk models exemplified by CreditMetrics (Gupton, Finger and Bhatia, 1997) and KMV PortfolioManager (Kealhofer and Bohn, 2001). Economic capital is set to cover total mark-to-market credit losses over a one-year horizon with probability $q$.[1] It is assumed that the credit portfolio is infinitely fine-grained in the sense that any single obligor represents a negligible share of the portfolio's total exposure, and that a single, common systematic risk factor drives all dependence across credit losses in the portfolio. An important implication of this asymptotic single risk factor (ASRF) framework is that the economic capital requirement for the portfolio equals the portfolio's expected loss conditional on the systematic risk factor taking a value equal to the $q$th percentile of its probability distribution. Given the linearity of the expectation operator, this result implies that economic capital for each instrument in the portfolio (whether that instrument is a whole loan or a tranche of a securitisation) is its own expected loss conditional on the $q$th percentile of the systematic risk factor, and thus is independent

*The authors thank Erik Heitfield and William Perraudin for helpful comments. The opinions expressed here are those of the authors, and do not reflect the views of the Federal Reserve's Board of Governors or its staff.*

of the composition of the rest of its portfolio.[2] When applied to securitisations, the ASRF framework – and the model developed herein – implies "capital neutrality" in the sense that the sum of the economic capital charges for the individual tranches of a securitisation equals the economic capital for the underlying collateral pool (denoted $\mathcal{K}_{irb}$).

Importantly, our approach does not require that the securitised asset pool itself be infinitely fine-grained. Rather, a sufficient condition is that the bank's total exposure to each securitised pool (that is, through the tranches held by the bank) be small relative to the bank's overall portfolio. Thus, our model can be applied to securitisations of pools ranging from a single loan to infinitely many loans.

This chapter's main innovation is adapting the ASRF framework to permit the economic capital for an individual securitisation tranche to be estimated using a relatively simple closed-form expression and parsimonious set of inputs. Computational ease and informational parsimony are especially important practical considerations when attempting to develop a cost-effective regulatory capital treatment for securitisations. The distribution of payouts to participants in a securitisation (often termed the cashflow "waterfall") can be quite complex and deal-specific, depending, for example, on the time profiles of the pool's defaults, recoveries, and principal and interest payments on the underlying loans. For regulatory capital purposes, it is not practical to attempt to account for the myriad possible deal-specific attributes of the waterfall.

Pykhtin and Dev (2002, 2003) propose cutting through these complexities by assuming that, for a particular tranche, the waterfall can be summarised in terms of the tranche's par value or thickness $\mathsf{T}$ and its credit enhancement level $\zeta$, defined as the sum of the par values of all more-junior tranches. In practice, such information is readily available to market participants. Pykhtin and Dev also assume that economic losses experienced by the pool over the model horizon are allocated deterministically according to a strict loss prioritisation (SLP) rule, that is, the tranche absorbs pool losses only in excess of $\zeta$, up to a maximum of $\mathsf{T}$. However, when embedded in the ASRF framework, these assumptions imply an unsatisfactory knife-edge property: for an infinitely fine-grained pool, a tranche's economic capital requirement is dollar-for-dollar (100%) if $\zeta + \mathsf{T}$ is less than or equal to $\mathcal{K}_{irb}$, and zero if $\zeta$ exceeds $\mathcal{K}_{irb}$. Pykhtin and Dev circumvent this problem by assuming pool losses are driven by a systematic risk factor that is correlated imperfectly with the dominant risk factor driving losses on the remainder of the bank's portfolio.

In contrast, our model retains the basic ASRF setup for characterising the pool's loss distribution, while assuming that the pool's economic losses over the horizon are distributed among tranches according to a generalised version of SLP that is subject to random errors (referred to as the uncertainty in loss prioritisation (ULP) model). A divergence from the strict prioritisation of economic credit losses over the analysis horizon can arise from at least two sources. First, few securitisations actually call for strict prioritisation of all cashflows, as subordinated tranches typically are entitled to some cash payouts prior to more-senior investors being paid out in full. Second, even with strict prioritisation of cashflows over the life of a securitisation, the credit enhancement level $\zeta$ generally understates the ability of more-junior tranches to absorb economic losses to the extent their contractual yield is higher than the rate of interest on the underlying loans in the pool.[3]

It should be emphasised that we are *not* suggesting that there is operational or legal risk in the execution of securitisation contracts. The new source of uncertainty introduced in this chapter instead reflects the potential gap between the accounting representation of the tranche (that is, its position and thickness relative to other holders of principal) and its vulnerability to economic loss. We draw our intuition from the long vein of econometrics literature on models with hidden parameters.[4] The details of the contractual cashflow waterfall are material but unobservable parameters in the "true" model of the securitisation. From the perspective of the econometrician (in our case, the regulator), such parameters act as sources of random error that must be "integrated out" rather than ignored. Were one to have unimpeded access to all details of the securitisation contract, a "full information" model such as that of Duffie and Garleanu (2001) would naturally be preferred.

For a homogeneous pool of one-year loans (equivalent to the simple default-mode structure used by Pykhtin and Dev), the ULP model implies that a tranche's economic capital is closely approximated by a function of seven inputs: the economic capital for the pool as a whole ($\mathcal{K}_{irb}$); the number of loans in the pool ($\mathsf{n}$); the expected loss rate given default for these loans (LGD); the tranche's nominal credit enhancement level ($\zeta$) and thickness (T); and model parameters $\tau$ and $\gamma$ that control the magnitude of uncertainty in loss prioritisation and in loss given default, respectively. For regulatory capital purposes, the first five parameters would be supplied by a bank, while the $\tau$ and $\gamma$ parameters would be set by supervisors. In addition to its regulatory capital applications, the model might also be used by banks for internal economic capital assessment in situations where an institution's aggregate securitisation exposures represent a relatively small fraction of its overall credit portfolio and it would not be cost-effective to develop highly customised models to handle the specific details of each transactions.

We first develop the ULP model under very general assumptions, similar to those in Gordy (2002). A general methodology for simplifying computation of capital charges is then expounded. The model specification is completed in the following section, where we impose the specific functional forms and distributional assumptions to which the IRB approach is calibrated. This ensures full consistency between the IRB approach and our proposed treatment of securitisation exposures. We also test the robustness of our simplified computational method, and find it highly accurate across a very broad range of possible pool characteristics. We then conclude with a discussion of maturity effects and other aspects of application in practice.

## ULP model

As with the treatment of whole loans, we seek to have capital sufficient to cover credit loss up to some percentile q of the loss distribution. We assume that both the loan originator and tranche investor have asymptotically fine-grained portfolios even when exposure to the borrowers in the collateral pool is excluded. The pool itself need not be assumed to be asymptotically fine-grained, but we do require that the tranches held by originator and investor represent trivial shares of their respective total portfolios. We also assume a single systematic risk factor X. Let L be book-value (or "default-mode") losses incurred within the pool as a share of total pool exposure, and let $H_q(\cdot)$ be the cumulative distribution function (cdf) of L conditional on $X = x_q$, where $x_q$ denotes the qth percentile of the distribution of X. We need make only very weak restrictions on the underlying model of portfolio risk. For example, it could make any of a wide variety of distributional assumptions on X and on recovery risk. The technical requirements are those set out in Gordy (2002).

The collateral pool is securitised into a set of prioritised tranches 1,..., m, where tranche one is most junior, tranche two is next most junior, and so on. Let $\vec{S} = (S_1,\ldots, S_m)$ denote the ownership shares of the tranches (so summing to one), and let $\vec{Z} = (Z_1,\ldots, Z_m)$ be the cumulative shares defined by $Z_j = \Sigma_{i\le j} S_i$. Assume for the moment that losses are allocated deterministically in accordance with SLP, and let $K_{slp}(z)$ be the cumulative capital charge (as a share of total pool exposure) on the junior-most share z of the structure. Under the ASRF assumptions, this is given by:

$$\begin{aligned} K_{slp}(z) &= E\left[\min\{z,L\}\middle|X = x_q\right] \\ &= \int_0^1 \min\{z,l\}dH_q(l) \\ &= z - \int_0^z H_q(l)dl \qquad (1) \end{aligned}$$

where the last equality follows from integration-by-parts. Capital is then allocated as $K_{slp}(Z_1)$ for the junior-most tranche, $K_{slp}(Z_2) - K_{slp}(Z_1)$ for the next tranche, and so on.

We now generalise this basic result to allow for uncertainty in loss prioritisation. To recognise that securitisation structures are highly complex and that economic notions of exposure share and priority may not fully align with the legal notions, we treat $\vec{S}$ as a random vector. A natural choice of distribution is the Dirichlet distribution, which is a multivariate generalisation of the beta distribution (see Johnson and Kotz, 1972, section 40.5). Let $\omega_1,\ldots, \omega_m$ be the notional stakes of the tranches. We assume that the share vector $\vec{S}$ is distributed Dirichlet with parameters $(\tau\omega_1,\ldots, \tau\omega_m)$, where $\tau > 0$ is a chosen precision parameter, which implies that the expected value of share $S_j$ is simply $\omega_j$. By making the Dirichlet assumption, we permit the realised share vector to "wiggle" around the expected value $(\omega_1,\ldots, \omega_m)$ and yet still always add up to one. As $\tau \to \infty$, the wiggle room disappears, and the distribution of $\vec{S}$ becomes degenerate at $(\omega_1,\ldots, \omega_m)$.

When $\vec{S}$ is independent of all other risks in the portfolio, the ASRF assumptions imply (as usual) that the appropriate capital charge for a tranche is its conditional expected loss.[5] The capital charge allocated to tranche j is thus:

$$E\left[\min\{Z_j,L\} - \min\{Z_{j-1},L\}\middle|X = x_q\right]$$

per dollar of pool collateral. The linear nature of the expectation operator is extremely convenient here, because it implies that we need only worry about the marginal distributions of the $Z_j$ and not the entire joint distribution. The marginal distribution of $Z_j$ is beta with parameters $\tau\zeta_j, \tau(1 - \zeta_j)$, where $\zeta_j$ is the cumulative expected share defined by $\zeta_j = \Sigma_{i \le j}\omega_i$. We then have:

$$\begin{aligned}
E\left[\min\{Z_j, L\} \middle| X = x_q\right] &= E[Z_j] - E\left[\int_0^{Z_j} H_q(l)dl\right] \\
&= \zeta_j - \int_0^1 \frac{z^{\tau\zeta_j - 1}(1-z)^{\tau(1-\zeta_j)-1}}{B(\tau\zeta_j, \tau(1-\zeta_j))} \int_0^z H_q(l)dl\,dz \\
&= \zeta_j - \int_0^1 (1 - B(z; \tau\zeta_j, \tau(1-\zeta_j)))H_q(z)dz
\end{aligned}$$

where the function $B(y; a, b)$ is the beta$(a, b)$ cdf evaluated at $y$.[6] As this expression does not depend on any tranche division point other than $\zeta_j$, we can write the cumulative capital function as a smooth function of the cumulative nominal share $\zeta$:

$$\begin{aligned}
K(\zeta) &\equiv E\left[\min\{Z_\zeta, L\} \middle| X = x_q\right] \\
&= \zeta - \int_0^1 (1 - B(z; \tau\zeta, \tau(1-\zeta)))H_q(z)dz \qquad (2)
\end{aligned}$$

where $Z_\zeta$ represents the random cumulative "effective" ownership share assigned to the cumulative nominal share $\zeta$, and is distributed beta$(\tau\zeta, \tau(1 - \zeta))$. Capital assigned to tranche $j$ is then simply $K(\zeta_j) - K(\zeta_{j-1})$.

By construction, the sum of capital charges across all tranches is $K(1)$. As $\zeta \to 1$, the beta cdf $B(z; \tau\zeta, \tau(1 - \zeta))$ goes to zero for all $z < 1$, so:

$$K(1) = 1 - \int_0^1 H_q(z)dz = E\left[L \middle| x_q\right] = \mathcal{K}_{irb}$$

Thus, as under the SLP case, the ULP model requires the same total capital on the collateral pool whether the pool is securitised or retained on balance sheet.

Intuitively, the ULP model smoothes the SLP model over all possible realisations of ownership shares $\vec{S}$. Equation 2 embeds the SLP rule of Equation 1 as a limiting case. As $\tau \to \infty$, uncertainty in the division of risk vanishes, and the beta cdf for $Z_\zeta$ converges to $\mathbf{1}_{\{z \ge \zeta\}}$. Thus:

$$\begin{aligned}
\lim_{\tau\to\infty} K(\zeta) &= \zeta - \int_0^1 (1 - \mathbf{1}_{\{z\ge\zeta\}})H_q(z)dz \\
&= \zeta - \int_0^\zeta H_q(z)dz = K_{slp}(\zeta)
\end{aligned}$$

As $\tau \to 0$, the contractual exposure shares become less and less informative about the actual division of risk. The limiting distribution for $Z_\zeta$ is Bernoulli such that $Z_\zeta = 1$ with probability $\zeta$ and $Z_\zeta = 0$ with probability $1 - \zeta$. Thus:

$$\lim_{\tau\to 0} B(z; \tau\zeta, \tau(1-\zeta)) = 1 - \zeta \quad \forall z \in (0,1)$$

Substitute this result in Equation 2 to obtain:

$$\lim_{\tau\to 0} K(\zeta) = \zeta - \int_0^1 \zeta H_q(z)dz = \zeta E\left[L \middle| x_q\right]$$

which implies a proportional sharing of $\mathcal{K}_{irb}$ across the tranches (that is, the tranches are treated as *pari passu*). Intermediate values of $\tau$ correspond to greater or lesser degrees of smoothing between these extremes.

If the collateral pool is itself asymptotically fine-grained, as is a reasonable characterisation of most retail securitisations, then Equation 2 has a simple analytic solution. In the asymptotic case, $H_q(z) = \mathbf{1}_{\{z \ge E[L|x_q]\}}$, so:

$$\int_0^\zeta H_q(z)dz = \max\left\{0, \zeta - E\left[L \middle| x_q\right]\right\}$$

Integrating over the distribution of $Z_\zeta$, we find:

$$\begin{aligned}
K(\zeta) = \zeta B\left(E\left[L \middle| x_q\right]; \tau\zeta + 1, \tau(1-\zeta)\right) \\
+ E\left[L \middle| x_q\right]\left(1 - B\left(E\left[L \middle| x_q\right]; \tau\zeta, \tau(1-\zeta)\right)\right) \qquad (3)
\end{aligned}$$

In the SLP case, any tranche of a securitisation of an asymptotically fine-grained pool that is senior to the $\mathcal{K}_{irb}$ threshold requires zero capital, and any tranche of such a securitisation that is strictly junior to the $\mathcal{K}_{irb}$ threshold requires dollar-for-dollar capital. In our generalised model, such senior tranches always require some capital because of the possibility that the "realised" exposure of the senior tranches exceeds $1 - \mathcal{K}_{irb}$, and such junior tranches require less than dollar-for-dollar capital because of the possibility that their realised exposure is less than $\mathcal{K}_{irb}$. Thus, the extended model unambiguously increases capital for tranches senior to $\mathcal{K}_{irb}$, and unambiguously reduces capital for tranches junior to $\mathcal{K}_{irb}$. For tranches that straddle this breakpoint, the effect is ambiguous but typically small.

For less fine-grained pools, uncertainty in loss prioritisation has a smaller effect. Figure 1 shows the effect of $\tau$ and $n$ using the model specification set out below. The case of $n = \infty$ is shown in the right-hand panels. When $\tau = \infty$, marginal capital is dollar-for-dollar up to $\mathcal{K}_{irb}$ and zero thereafter. Setting $\tau = 1{,}000$ provides a modest degree of smoothing, and much lower values of $\tau$ a much greater degree of smoothing. For a portfolio of

**1. Effect of $\tau$ on capital and marginal capital**

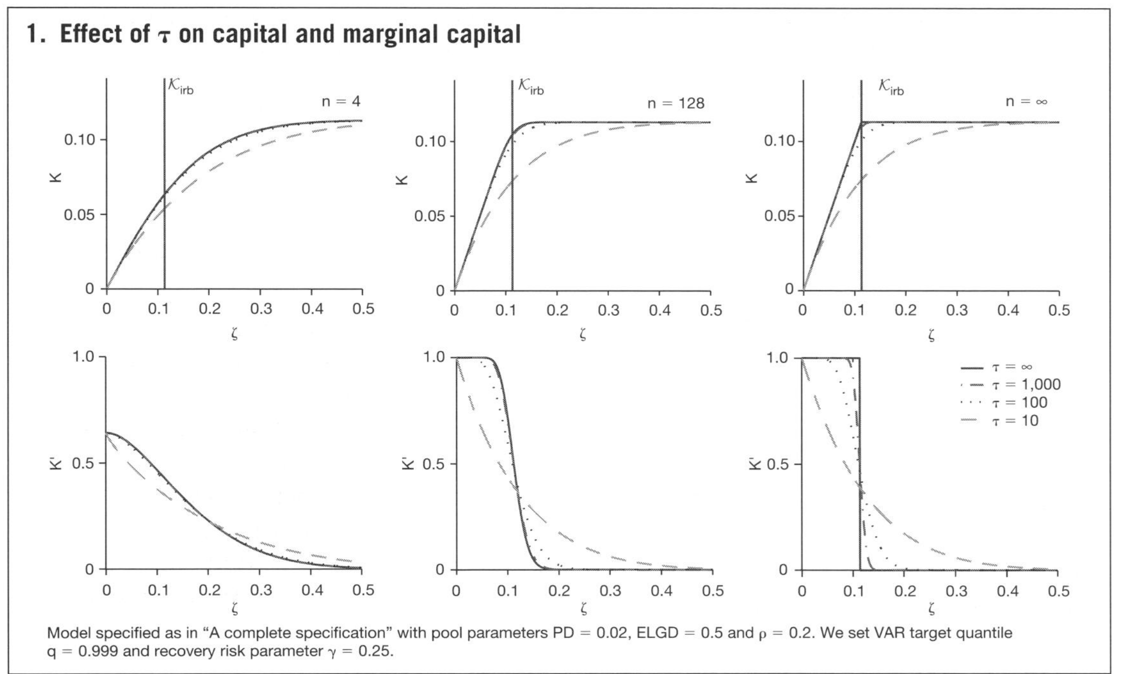


Model specified as in "A complete specification" with pool parameters PD = 0.02, ELGD = 0.5 and ρ = 0.2. We set VAR target quantile q = 0.999 and recovery risk parameter γ = 0.25.

n = 128 (middle column of panels), which might be representative of the most fine-grained collateralised debt obligation collateral pools, undiversified idiosyncratic risk is sufficient to smooth away the cliff effect at $\mathcal{K}_{irb}$.[7] In this case, the capital and marginal capital curves for $\tau = 1{,}000$ are indistinguishable from those of $\tau = \infty$. Uncertainty in loss prioritisation has no material effect on capital unless $\tau$ is below, say, 100. When n = 4 (left-hand column of panels), idiosyncratic risk within the pool has a dominant effect on the distribution of losses across tranches, and $\tau$ must be extremely low (around 10) for uncertainty in $\vec{S}$ to have any additional smoothing effect.

## Fitting a simple functional form to $K(\zeta)$

Unless we restrict ourselves to analysis of securitisations of asymptotically fine-grained pools, the conditional loss distribution $H_q(z)$ is likely to be analytically intractable, and the solution for $K(\zeta)$ in Equation 2 requires numerical integration or simulation.[8] For regulatory purposes, a simpler and more transparent functional solution is required, even if it comes at slight expense of precision.

We define the fitting function $F(\cdot)$ by:

$$F(\zeta) = 1 - \frac{K'(\zeta)}{K'(0)} \tag{4}$$

This definition is useful because it lets us exploit three known properties of the first derivative of $K(\zeta)$: $K'(\zeta)$ is non-increasing on the unit interval, and we have $K'(1) = 0$ and $K'(0) = 1 - H_q(0)$.[9] From these properties, we see that $F(\zeta)$ is non-decreasing on the unit interval and that $F(0) = 0$ and $F(1) = 1$. Thus, F behaves like a cumulative distribution function for a random variable with support on the unit interval. Although this cdf is typically of intractable form, we might expect that it can be closely approximated by the cdf of a simple distribution such as the beta. In this section, we derive the mean $\mu$ and variance $\sigma^2$ of F.

To get the mean parameter, we rearrange Equation 4 as $K'(\zeta) = K'(0)(1 - F(\zeta))$, and integrate to get:

$$K(\zeta) = K'(0)\int_0^{\zeta}(1 - F(y))\,dy$$

At $\zeta = 1$, we can integrate by parts to get:

$$\int_0^1 F(y)\,dy = 1 - \int_0^1 y f(y)\,dy = 1 - \mu$$

which implies that:

$$\mu = \frac{K(1)}{K'(0)} = \frac{E\left[L \middle| x_q\right]}{1 - H_q(0)} \tag{5}$$

The variance of F is more challenging. By definition:

$$\sigma^2 = \int_0^1 y^2 f(y)\,dy - \mu^2 = \frac{-1}{K'(0)}\int_0^1 y^2 K''(y)\,dy - \mu^2$$

Integration by parts twice to remove the double differentiation on K, followed by use of Equation 2, gives:

$$\sigma^2 = \frac{1}{K'(0)}\left(1 - 2\int_0^1 \Xi_\tau(z)H_q(z)dz\right) - \mu^2 \qquad (6)$$

where the function $\Xi_\tau(z)$ is defined by:

$$\Xi_\tau(z) \equiv \int_0^1 B(z;\tau u, \tau(1-u))du$$

The $\Xi_\tau$ function can be understood as the unconditional cdf of a random variable Y that has conditional distribution $Y|U \sim \text{beta}(\tau U, \tau(1-U))$, where $U \sim \text{uniform}[0, 1]$.

The difficulty remains in the integration of $\Xi_\tau(z)H_q(z)$. For finite $\tau$, the $\Xi_\tau(z)$ function does not have an analytical solution. However, for reasonably large values of $\tau$, say $\tau = 100$ or larger, $\Xi_\tau(z)$ can be approximated to very high precision by:

$$\hat{\Xi}_\tau(z) = z + \frac{1}{\tau}\left(\frac{1}{2} - z\right)$$

Our approximation methodology for $\Xi_\tau(z)$ is developed in greater generality and tested in a technical note available from the authors.[10] The approximation is exact when $\tau = \infty$.

Applying integration by parts, we find:

$$\begin{aligned}2\int_0^1 \hat{\Xi}_\tau(z)H_q(z)dz &= 1 - \int_0^1\left(z^2 + \frac{1}{\tau}(z - z^2)\right)h_q(z)dz \\ &= 1 - \left(V[L|x_q] + E[L|x_q]^2\right. \\ &\quad \left. + \frac{1}{\tau}\left(E[L|x_q](1 - E[L|x_q]) - V[L|x_q]\right)\right)\end{aligned}$$

Therefore, substitution of $\hat{\Xi}_\tau(z)$ for $\Xi_\tau(z)$ in Equation 6 yields the closed-form solution:

$$\begin{aligned}\sigma^2 &= \frac{1}{K'(0)}\left(V[L|x_q] + E[L|x_q]^2\right) - \mu^2 \\ &\quad + \frac{1}{\tau}\frac{1}{K'(0)}\left(E[L|x_q](1 - E[L|x_q]) - V[L|x_q]\right) \qquad (7)\end{aligned}$$

The expression for $\sigma^2$ has been arranged to show that it naturally decomposes into two components. The first is the contribution of undiversified idiosyncratic risk in the underlying pool (that is, the impact of pool granularity), and equals the formula for $\sigma^2$ in the SLP case. The second is the contribution of uncertainty in loss prioritisation and is inversely proportional to $\tau$.

The calculations simplify further in the special case of $n = \infty$, which includes most securitisations of retail pools. When $n = \infty$, $K'(0) = 1$ and $V[L|x_q] = 0$, so we have $\mu = E[L|x_q]$ and $\sigma^2 = (1/\tau)E[L|x_q](1 - E[L|x_q])$.

## A complete specification

So far, we have not needed to specify a model for portfolio loss or to choose a cdf to assign to the fitting function. To arrive at an implementable formulation, we now complete our specification.

We assume that the securitised pool is homogeneous and that the conditional loss distribution $H_q$ comes from a single-factor default-mode model with idiosyncratic recovery risk. This implies that the number of defaults in a portfolio of n loans is distributed $\text{binomial}(p_q, n)$, where $p_q$ is the conditional probability (given $X = x_q$) of default for a single loan in the pool. If LGD for a single default has a continuous distribution, then $H_q$ is continuous on unit interval support, except that there is probability mass at $L = 0$. The probability of zero loss is the probability that every borrower performs, so $H_q(0) = (1 - p_q)^n$. If LGD has mean ELGD and standard deviation VLGD, then the mean and variance of the conditional loss distribution are given by $E[L|x_q] = \text{ELGD} \times p_q$ and:

$$V[L|x_q] = \frac{1}{n}(\text{ELGD}^2 p_q(1 - p_q) + p_q \text{VLGD}^2) \qquad (8)$$

To retain consistency with the IRB treatment of whole loans, we adopt the CreditMetrics model of obligor dependence and LGD volatility. That is, we assume that X has standard normal distribution and that the conditional probability of default is given by:

$$p_q = \Phi\left(\frac{\Phi^{-1}(PD) + \Phi^{-1}(q)\sqrt{\rho}}{\sqrt{1-\rho}}\right)$$

where $\Phi$ is the standard normal cdf, PD is the unconditional probability of default and $\rho$ is the correlation in asset returns.[11] Loss rates given default are drawn as independent beta random variables. Following the convention in CreditMetrics and KMV PortfolioManager, we assume the variance of loss given default is given by:

$$\text{VLGD}^2 = \gamma \text{ELGD}(1 - \text{ELGD})$$

where $\gamma$ is a parameter in [0, 1]. Special cases include $\gamma = 0$, which corresponds to fixed LGD rates (no recovery risk), and $\gamma = 1$, which arises when LGD is distributed Bernoulli (that is, zero recovery with probability ELGD, full recovery otherwise).

A variety of two-parameter distributions for approximating the fitting function would lead to a closed-form solution for the capital function. The beta distribution would be a natural choice given its unit interval support, and we have found that it provides an excellent fit as well under a wide range of parameter values.[12] Let $\theta$ be the precision of F defined by:

$$\theta \equiv \frac{\mu(1-\mu)}{\sigma^2} - 1$$

The parameter $\theta$ measures the precision of F in the same manner as $\tau$ measures the precision of the distribution for ownership shares $\vec{S}$.

To distinguish between the "true" fitting function, which is of intractable form, and our approximation based on the beta cdf, let $\hat{F}$ denote the approximation. Similarly, let $\hat{K}$ denote the approximation implied by $\hat{F}$ to the true K function. The solution to $\hat{K}(\zeta)$ is given by:

$$\begin{aligned}\hat{K}(\zeta) &= \int_0^{\zeta} \hat{K}'(y)\,dy = K'(0)\int_0^{\zeta}(1-\hat{F}(y))\,dy \\ &= (1-H_q(0))\big(\zeta(1-B(\zeta;\theta\mu,\theta(1-\mu))) \\ &\quad + \mu B(\zeta;\theta\mu+1,\theta(1-\mu))\big) \qquad (9)\end{aligned}$$

Note that when $n = \infty$, we have $\theta = \tau - 1$ and $\hat{K}(\zeta)$ simplifies to:

$$\begin{aligned}\hat{K}(\zeta) &= \zeta\big(1-B(\zeta;(\tau-1)\mathcal{K}_{irb},(\tau-1)(1-\mathcal{K}_{irb}))\big) \\ &\quad + \mathcal{K}_{irb}B(\zeta;(\tau-1)\mathcal{K}_{irb}+1,(\tau-1)(1-\mathcal{K}_{irb})) \qquad (10)\end{aligned}$$

We have examined the robustness of our fitted $\hat{K}(\zeta)$ to the "true" $K(\zeta)$ given by Equation 2. For each combination of parameters (n, PD, LGD, $\rho$, $\tau$), we calculate the theoretical K function by Monte Carlo and the fitted $\hat{K}$ function by Equation 9. Throughout the exercise, we fix constant the VAR target quantile q at 0.999, and set the recovery risk parameter to $\gamma = 0.25$. We then measure the relative root mean squared error (RMSE) as:

$$\text{RMSE} = \frac{1}{\mathcal{K}_{irb}}\sqrt{\int_0^1 (K(\zeta)-\hat{K}(\zeta))^2 d\zeta}$$

We performed these calculations for each combination of:

$$\begin{aligned}n &\in \{1,4,16,64,256,\infty\} \\ PD &\in \{0.1,0.2,0.5,1,2,4,6,10,15\} \\ &\quad \text{(in percentage points)} \\ LGD &\in \{0.05,0.20,0.35,0.5,0.65,0.8,0.95\} \\ \rho &\in \{0.04,0.08,0.12,0.16,0.20,0.24,0.28,0.32\} \\ &\quad \text{(asset correlation)} \\ \tau &\in \{100,200,400,600,800,1000,1600,3200\}\end{aligned}$$

In total, this exercise covered 24,192 parameter combinations. Each Monte Carlo simulation featured 200,000 trials.

We find that the fitted $\hat{K}$ function performs extremely well nearly everywhere in the parameter space. The only exception arises when the pool is comprised of a single loan to an investment-grade borrower with expected LGD of 5% and asset-correlation under 12%. In this case, relative RMSE reaches as high as 10.3% of $\mathcal{K}_{irb}$. For loans with very low PD and very low expected LGD, simulation noise is of large relative magnitude, so the high RMSE may be due in part to error in estimating K rather than in $\hat{K}$. Furthermore, $\mathcal{K}_{irb}$ is always quite small in these cases (less than 0.005), so a fitting error of 10% has a negligible impact on absolute capital requirements. Perhaps most importantly, this peculiar combination of parameters does not arise under the proposed new Basel Accord. Low PD borrowers cannot be assigned low asset correlations unless they are retail or small corporate borrowers, in which case the loans are invariably far too small to comprise an entire securitised pool.

Excluding the exceptional case, the median relative RMSE is 0.15%. That is, at the median, RMSE is less than one sixth of 1% of $\mathcal{K}_{irb}$ for the parameter combination. The maximum relative RMSE is less than 5.5% of $\mathcal{K}_{irb}$. The performance of the fitting function is shown in Figure 2 for four very different collateral pools. $\mathcal{K}_{irb}$ varies across these examples by a factor of six, and n varies from one to infinity, yet in each case the fit is excellent. Indeed, in the bottom two panels, it is impossible to distinguish the two curves. Figure 3 shows the

**2. Performance of fitted $\hat{K}(\zeta)$**

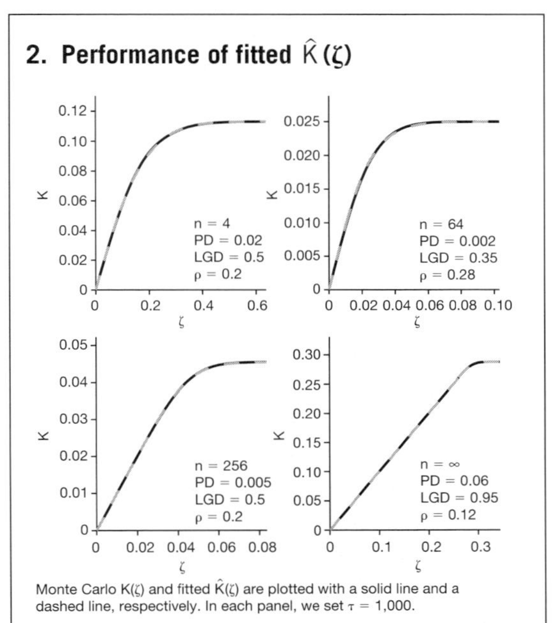


Monte Carlo $K(\zeta)$ and fitted $\hat{K}(\zeta)$ are plotted with a solid line and a dashed line, respectively. In each panel, we set $\tau$ = 1,000.

**3. Performance of fitted marginal capital**

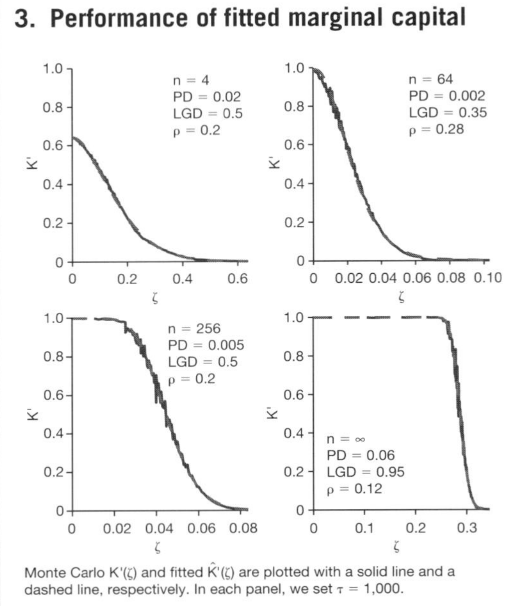


Monte Carlo $K'(\zeta)$ and fitted $\hat{K}'(\zeta)$ are plotted with a solid line and a dashed line, respectively. In each panel, we set $\tau = 1{,}000$.

Monte Carlo and fitted marginal capital curves ($K'(\zeta)$) for the same four examples. The simulations produce somewhat jagged estimates of marginal capital, so the fitted function may indeed provide the more accurate curve.

## Application to regulatory capital treatment

The ULP capital charge implied by Equation 9 on a tranche with credit enhancement level $\zeta$ and thickness $T$ is $(\hat{K}(\zeta + T) - \hat{K}(\zeta))/T$ per dollar of tranche par value. The calculations make use of a number of intermediate quantities, such as $\mathcal{K}_{irb}$, that depend ultimately on the collateral pool parameters $n$, PD, ELGD and asset correlation $\rho$, as well as on regulatory parameters $q$, $\tau$ and $\gamma$. Further simplification can be obtained by noting that PD, $\rho$ and $q$ enter the calculations only via $p_q$, and that $p_q = \mathcal{K}_{irb}/\text{ELGD}$. Thus, a sufficient set of pool parameters is $n$, $\mathcal{K}_{irb}$ and ELGD. These are the pool-level inputs to the $K$ function in Basel Committee on Banking Supervision (2002).[13]

As a practical matter, parameterisation of the ULP in terms of $\mathcal{K}_{irb}$ compensates for some of the limitations of the model's default-mode notion of credit loss.[14] Strictly speaking, the model assumes that the underlying assets are of one-year maturity. If the pool were of longer maturity, there would be no mechanism in the model for recognition of economic losses in the pool due to rating migrations short of default. Absence of arbitrage implies that economic losses in the pool must equal the sum of economic losses to the tranches.[15] Under the IRB approach, capital charges for the underlying pool incorporate maturity effects, so parameterisation in terms of $\mathcal{K}_{irb}$ may be more robust than parameterisation in terms of PD and $\rho$.

In a similar vein, the model also assumes that the pool contains only simple whole loans or bonds. In practice, it is now not uncommon for securitised pools to include, for example, tranches of other securitisations. Modelling the performance of such pool assets requires more than the simple CreditMetrics-based function of PD, ELGD and asset correlation. However, $\mathcal{K}_{irb}$ can be obtained for a wide variety of assets, so we can avoid the hazardous task of assigning PD and asset correlation parameters to complex asset types.[16] By parameterising the ULP model in terms of the $\mathcal{K}_{irb}$ of the underlying pool, we at least impose the appropriate total economic capital requirement on the securitisation as a whole. An open question, and topic of ongoing research, is whether this convenient approach to extending the applicability of the model can lead to significant misallocation of economic capital across the tranches.

1 *In this context, credit losses reflect valuation changes that result from credit quality migrations or defaults by obligors, but exclude valuation changes arising from general movements of interest rates and the market price of risk.*

2 *See Gordy (2002) for a derivation of this result under minimal restrictions on the portfolio and very general modelling assumptions.*

3 *Consider a homogeneous US\$100 pool of 8% one-year loans. Suppose the most junior tranche has an initial value of US\$20 and pays 20%, while the US\$80 senior tranche pays 5%. From the perspective of the senior tranche,* $\zeta = 20$ *and* $T = 80$. *However, suppose that 22% of the loans default, implying a total cashflow available for distribution of US\$84.24. In this case, the senior tranche would still be paid in full even though the pool's loss exceeds* $\zeta$. *Excess spread accounts, which are often seen in securitisations of credit card receivables, create a similar effect.*

4 *We also take inspiration from the literature on the potential misalignment of accounting with economic measures (for example, Fisher and McGowan, 1983).*

5 *If securitisation instruments were to account jointly for a significant share of the portfolio, and if (conditional on* $X = x_q$*) the* $\vec{S}$ *were not independent across those securitisations, then the risk in loss prioritisation would not be diversified away, and thus would demand capital of its own. Similar reasoning motivates the assumption that the investor's exposure to the obligors in the collateral pool constitutes a trivial share of the portfolio.*

6 *The final expression is obtained using integration by parts of* $v \times du$, *where the* $du$ *part is the beta density and the* $v$ *part is the integral over* $H_q$.

7 *Conversations with market participants suggest that few collateralised debt obligations contain more than 200 names.*

*When corrected for concentration in exposure sizes, as in Gordy (2002), we would expect that "effective* n*" would typically be less than 100.*

**8** *Monte Carlo simulation of* $K(\zeta)$ *is straightforward but computationally intensive. Since* $K(\zeta) = E[\min\{Z_\zeta, L\}|x_q]$, *we need only draw a sample of* $\{z_1,\ldots, z_T\}$ *for* $Z_\zeta$ *and a sample of* $\{l_1,\ldots, l_T\}$ *for* L *(from the* $H_q$ *distribution).* $K(\zeta)$ *is estimated by* $(1/T)\sum\min\{z_i, l_i\}$. *A fresh sample of the* $z_i$ *must be drawn for each value of* $\zeta$.

**9** *To obtain the derivative of* $K(\zeta)$ *at* $\zeta = 0$, *note that the expression* $(1 - B(z; \tau\zeta, \tau(1 - \zeta)))$ *in Equation 2 behaves like a step function at* $\zeta$ *in the neighbourhood of* $\zeta = 0$. *Therefore, its derivative with respect to* $\zeta$ *at* $\zeta = 0$ *is the Dirac delta function.*

**10** *Our note "On the approximation of* $\Xi_\tau(z)$ *in the ULP model" may be downloaded at mgordy.tripod.com.*

**11** *See Koyluoglu and Hickman (1998) or Gordy (2000) for a derivation of* $p_q$ *from the CreditMetrics model. This same expression appeared earlier in Vasicek's (1991) analysis of the asymptotic loss distribution in KMV PortfolioManager.*

**12** *If we ignore the upper bound on loss at* $\zeta = 1$, *the gamma and lognormal distributions are also reasonable choices and yield closed-form* $K(\zeta)$. *However, the beta provides the best fit overall. It should be noted that this application of the beta cdf has nothing to do with our use of the beta as the distribution for* $Z_\zeta$ *and the distribution for LGD.*

**13** *The proposed supervisory formula approach (SFA) specifies capital for a tranche of credit enhancement level* $\zeta$ *and thickness* T *as* $(S[\zeta + T] - S[\zeta])$ *times the notional size of the collateral pool. The function* $S|\zeta|$ *has at its baseline the ULP* $K(\zeta)$ *function of Equation 9, but imposes certain supervisory overrides on top (including dollar-for-dollar capital up to* $\mathcal{K}_{irb}$ *and a floor level of marginal capital). The SFA calibration assumes* $q = 0.999$, $\tau = 1{,}000$ *and* $\gamma = 0.25$. *The expression for* $V[L|x_q]$ *in Equation 8 can be rearranged to equal the SFA* v *parameter. Otherwise, the translation from SFA notation to our own is straightforward. See Basel Committee on Banking Supervision (2002, annex 3, paragraph 574).*

**14** *Pykhtin and Dev's (2002, 2003) model suffers from the same limitations.*

**15** *Much as a decline in the asset value of a firm will be spread among shareholders and bondholders, a decline in the value of the pool will not be allocated by strict prioritisation, but rather will be spread to some degree across all tranches.*

**16** *The problem of assigning ELGD remains, but the effect of this parameter is of secondary order when* $\mathcal{K}_{irb}$ *is held fixed and* n *is large enough that* $H_q(0) \approx 0$.

**BIBLIOGRAPHY**

**Basel Committee on Bank Supervision,** 2001, *The Internal Ratings-Based Approach: Supporting Document to the New Basel Capital Accord,* Bank for International Settlements, January.

**Basel Committee on Bank Supervision,** 2002, *Second Working Paper on Securitisation,* Bank for International Settlements, October.

**Duffie, D., and N. Garleanu,** 2001, "Risk and Valuation of Collateralized Debt Obligations", *Financial Analysts Journal,* January–February, 57(1), pp. 41–59.

**Fisher, F., and J. McGowan,** 1983, "On the Misuse of Accounting Rates of Return to Infer Monopoly Profits", *American Economic Review,* March, 73(1), pp. 82–97.

**Gordy, M.,** 2000, "A Comparative Anatomy of Credit Risk Models", *Journal of Banking and Finance,* 24(1–2), January, pp. 119–49.

**Gordy, M.,** 2002, *A Risk-Factor Model Foundation for Ratings-Based Bank Capital Rules,* FEDS 2002-55, Board of Governors of the Federal Reserve System, October.

**Gupton, G., C. Finger and M. Bhatia,** 1997, *CreditMetrics – Technical Document,* JP Morgan, April.

**Johnson, N., and S. Kotz,** 1972, *Distributions in Statistics: Continuous Multivariate Distributions* (John Wiley & Sons).

**Jones, D.,** 2000, "Emerging Problems with the Basel Capital Accord: Regulatory Capital Arbitrage and Related Issues", *Journal of Banking and Finance,* 24(1–2), January, pp. 35–58.

**Kealhofer, S., and J. Bohn,** 2001, *Portfolio Management of Default Risk,* KMV Corporation, May.

**Koyluoglu, H., and A. Hickman,** 1998, "Reconcilable Differences", *Risk,* October, pp. 56–62.

**Pykhtin, M., and A. Dev,** 2002, "Credit Risk in Asset Securitizations: An Analytical Model", *Risk,* May, pp. S16–S20.

**Pykhtin, M., and A. Dev,** 2003, "Coarse-Grained CDOs", *Risk,* January, pp. 113–16.

**Vasicek, O.,** 1991, *Limiting Loan Loss Probability Distribution,* KMV Corporation, August.

# Index

INDEX

INDEX

# Other Titles by Risk Books

**Credit: The Complete Guide to Pricing, Hedging and Risk Management**
By Angelo Arvanitis and Jon Gregory
ISBN: 1 899332 73 1

**Credit Ratings: Methodologies, Rationale and Default Risk**
Edited by Michael K. Ong
ISBN: 1 899332 69 3

**Internal Credit Risk Models: Capital Allocation and Performance Measurement**
By Michael K. Ong
ISBN: 1 899332 03 0

**Credit Risk: Models and Management**
Edited by David Shimko
ISBN: 1 899332 32 4

**Credit Derivatives: Applications for Risk Management, Investment and Portfolio Optimisation**
ISBN: 1 899332 61 8

**Derivative Credit Risk: Further Advances in Measurement and Management**
2nd Edition
ISBN: 1 899332 48 0

**Derivatives: The Tools that Changed Finance**
By Phelim P. Boyle and Feidhlim Boyle
ISBN: 1 899332 88 X

**Hedge Fund Risk Transparency: Unravelling the Complex and Controversial Debate**
By Leslie Rahl
ISBN: 1 904339 04 2

For more information on these titles, as well as the full range of books and executive reports published by Risk Books, please visit the on-line bookstore at **www.riskbooks.com**. Alternatively phone customer services in the UK on +44 (0) 879 240 8859 or fax +44 (0) 20 7484 9800 and request the latest books catalogue.